From the Bonn to the Berlin Republic

FROM THE BONN TO THE BERLIN REPUBLIC

• • • • • • • • • • • • • • •

Germany at the
Twentieth Anniversary of Unification

edited by

Jeffrey J. Anderson and Eric Langenbacher

Berghahn Books
New York • Oxford

Published in 2010 by
Berghahn Books

www.berghahnbooks.com

©2010 Berghahn Books

Library of Congress Cataloging-in-Publication Data

A C.I.P. record of this book is available from the Library of Congress

British Library Cataloguing in Publication Data

A catalogue record for this book is available from the British Library

Printed in the United States on acid-free paper

ISBN: 978-0-85745-221-4

CONTENTS

• • • • • • • • • • • • • • • •

Anniversaries are occasions for gift-giving, and so we would like to take this opportunity to express our sincere thanks to those who gave liberally of their time and creative energies in order to bring this initiative to a successful conclusion. First, we would like to thank our contributors, many of whom came together at Georgetown University in May 2009 to present works-in-progress and to share ideas about how the essays might be improved and extended. The May workshop would not have been possible without the care and attention of Katherine Carta, Stacey Hall, and Christina Ruby of Georgetown University's BMW Center for German and European Studies. We also thank Marion and Vivian Berghahn, Martha Hoffman and Ann Przyzycki for their expert advice and guidance in the various editorial and publishing phases. Finally, we would like to thank each other for establishing an editorial partnership and intellectual exchange that made this venture truly enjoyable from the start.

Jeffrey J. Anderson & Eric Langenbacher
August 2010

INTRODUCTION

●●●●●●●●●●●●●●●●

Jeffrey J. Anderson

Continuity through Change

'Tis the season of anniversaries in Germany. 2009 unfolded like a hit parade of history. March ushered in the sixtieth anniversary of the founding of the Federal Republic and May witnessed the sixtieth anniversary of the end of the Berlin Blockade. After a summer lull, the seventieth anniversary of Nazi Germany's invasion of Poland fell on 1 September and in October, the twentieth anniversary of the first Monday demonstration in Leipzig took place. Finally, the month of November offered up a major date–the twentieth anniversary of the fall of the Berlin Wall–and a lesser one, suited more for the political connoisseur: the fortieth anniversary of the Social Democratic Party's (SPD) ratification of the Godesberger Program. 2010, of course, culminates in October with the twentieth anniversary of unification.

This string of national anniversaries is intertwined with a broader fabric of European remembrance. In 2008, Germans and their neighbors celebrated the fiftieth anniversary of the signing of the Treaty of Rome, which launched the comprehensive European integration project that has culminated in the European Union. And just over a year from now, in 2011, Europe and the rest of the world will observe the twentieth anniversary of the collapse of the Soviet Union, which marked the formal beginning of the post Cold War era, a period that is still taking shape. Both of these developments–the quest for European unity and the broader East-West conflict–have been central components of the narrative of recent German political development. Taken together, this list of anniversaries reads like an out-of-sequence capsule of modern Germany history–the plunge into the abyss of world war; the slow path to redemption through democracy; the hardening of the Cold War and the division of Germany;

the embrace of a great political consensus around the social market economy; the yearning for change in the other part of Germany; the beginning of the end of division.

An anniversary can be a time of celebration, an occasion to tally up accomplishments and successes. Yet, it can also be a wistful time, laced with nostalgia and disappointment over opportunities lost and roads not taken. Whatever the dominant mood, an anniversary is a time for remembering, for searching one's personal and collective memories, and for thinking about how the past informs the present and future. Twenty years ago, Germans were in a reflective frame of mind, having just observed the fortieth anniversary of the inauguration of their postwar democracy. In the days and weeks following the breaching of the Berlin Wall, many Germans (and not a few of their neighbors) drew on memories to predict a weakening of democracy at home, and an eventual parting of ways for Germany and its European neighbors. These critics feared that unified Germany's political future would be patterned on its dismal prewar past. Their pessimism looked on four decades of peace and prosperity in West Germany–just months earlier, the Federal Republic had celebrated the fortieth anniversary of its founding–as an interlude of sorts, one whose end would see the country gravitate back toward an aggressive, unattached, and "realist" foreign policy. Germany would soon seek to hoist its western anchor, and chart its own way in Mitteleuropa; some pundits even forecasted a drive for nuclear weapons. Suffice it to say that the intervening twenty years revealed that the power of these historical memories and prognoses based on them have waned considerably.

In 1989, there were many who maintained that a more contemporary set of historical memories, drawing on the Bonn Republic's formula of stable democracy, social market economy, and membership in Western European and transatlantic networks, would have a tonic effect on a unified Germany. The strongest and most self-confident of these arguments were directed at the domestic formula for unification. Any notion of a "third way," entailing a search for a blend of the best that both Germanys had to offer, was soon swept aside in favor of a wholesale transfer of western law and institutions to the east. This process was both comprehensive and rapid, and sprang from a firm belief on the part of West German elites and mass public that their system had proven itself over the past four decades and was capable of quickly stabilizing the east

When it came to foreign policy, however, the self-confidence of the west still shone through, but it took on more nuanced ones. The older prewar memories still mattered, but benignly–in effect, leavened by forty years of democracy, capitalism, and western integration. Countering the dour outlook described above, these analysts predicted a continuation of two trademark characteristics of West German foreign policy that flowed from memories of world war, the attendant crimes against humanity, and the punishing aftermath of total defeat: a reflexive multilateralism (or, put another way, a distaste for unilateral initiatives); and an innate willingness to pool national sovereignty to further the European integration project.

In retrospect, one might venture that history has been kinder to the positive prognosticators. Democracy in a unified Germany is still functioning, perhaps not better, but certainly no worse than it did prior to the fall of the Wall. Internationally, Germany has been content to continue swimming in the European sovereignty pool–indeed, more so, given the decisions in the early 1990s to commit to monetary union and to push for intensified political integration. As such, indeed almost by definition, the vast majority of its foreign policy actions have been multilateral–that is, defined and embraced by the joint decision-making processes that the European Union utilizes. Few if any of its policy positions in Europe have altered to any appreciable extent as a result of its larger territory and population, or the new interests and actors residing in the former German Democratic Republic (GDR) that came on board with unification. Although unified Germany is a changed country, it is the same country in the end.

Nevertheless, although this is a large part of the story, it is clearly not the whole story. For one, the political landscape in Germany bears the obvious marks of unification. Intergovernmental relations are now more complex and involved with the addition of five eastern Länder and a fully entitled (in a constitutional-administrative sense) Berlin. The party system has expanded to include a new grouping–the Left Party (die Linke, previously the Party of Democratic Socialism)–that can trace at least some of its roots back to the former communist party in the GDR, and which draws considerable support in eastern Germany (about 25 percent in the 2009 Bundestag election). The "Germany in Europe" we observe today, twenty years after the fall of the Berlin Wall, does not appear to be simply an older and larger version of the Bonn Republic. Germany cuts a different figure in Europe than it did twenty years ago, having grown more assertive and self-confident, and at the same time far less idealistic. We are fast approaching the tenth anniversary of the last time (2000) a heavyweight German politician (Joschka Fischer) called for a "United States of Europe." German enthusiasm for enlargement has cooled considerably, as sticker shock over the recent expansions to the east and the specter of Turkish accession to the EU have settled firmly in the minds of many politicians and an even higher proportion of the citizenry. The Federal Republic, which previously could be counted on among the larger member states reliably to push hard for widening and deepening, has adopted a much more cautious and self-regarding stance. Support for the first embattled and then ratified Lisbon Treaty has been tempered by an understanding among elites that the limits of what the public will tolerate from the European Union may well have been reached already, a conclusion that is underscored by the 2009 ruling on the Lisbon Treaty by the Federal Constitutional Court. One gets the feeling that, with a small number of necessary additions to the European space—specifically, the Balkans—and necessary institutional fixes—i.e., Lisbon—the *finalité politique* or *Endstation* sought by the Germans is actually quite near.

This new mindset has begun to inform Germany's dealings with the world outside of Europe as well. In fact, it is interesting that the two of the most prominent episodes in recent years where this new stance has been on display have involved relations with the United States. In 2003, the joint efforts of Germany and France to carve out a principled position to counter the U.S. drive to carry its global war on terrorism into Iraq can be interpreted as an early, and only partially successful, attempt to preserve a distinctive European position on international security affairs, one emphasizing diplomacy and restraint. More recently, Germany has emerged as chief spokesperson for a cautious and prudent approach to the global financial crisis, resisting American overtures to engage in additional stimulus spending and emphasizing the need to regulate the market excesses that sparked the crisis.

The Twentieth Anniversary Volume

The goal of this book is straightforward: to present a comprehensive portrait of German politics and society two decades after unification. As such, the twentieth anniversary of German unification is an occasion for stock-taking, and the ostensible common starting point—divided Germany circa 1990—suggests and obvious reference point for comparative statics. That said, unification is not necessarily a rigid frame or template for understanding each particular issue at hand. In other words, we asked the contributors to delve into their topics with open minds, allowing for the real possibility that whether they uncovered startling change, striking continuity, or something in between, unification—conceived as an historical event launching a process—was simply not a relevant theme in that particular area of inquiry.

We begin with two reflective essays by prominent historians–opening arguments that are not meant to serve as overarching frameworks for the essays that follow. Rather, they are meant to challenge the reader from the start to consider alternative and, at times, competing historical narratives of the postwar, post Wall, and postunification Germany(s).The volume opens with a *tour d'horizon* by Konrad Jarausch, who evaluates the two-decades-old Berlin Republic through the lenses of the sixtieth anniversary of the founding of the Bonn Republic. Jarausch concludes that at sixty, the Federal Republic has entered a comfortable middle age, having shed some of the drama of its younger years and now exuding a kind of competent normalcy. Problems and challenges abound, some of them connected to unification, but these are not unique to Germany–the much-discussed *Sonderweg,* he maintains, has finally come to an end. Next, Charles Maier examines the last twenty years through the pages of *German Politics and Society.* He observes irony, Angst and collective doubt permeating much of the scholarship on contemporary German affairs, regardless of academic discipline. The last twenty years have witnessed a gradual evolution of the paradigms through which academics interpret and analyze Germany. Indeed, by the twentieth anniversary of unification, that object of analysis has mellowed and is much less worrisome, "German" country.

We turn next to the overlapping realms of culture and society. A. James McAdams, in "The Last East German and the Memory of the German Democratic Republic," imagines what it would be like to meet the last defender of the *ancien* and now long defunct regime. How might this fictional character seek to portray the virtues and strengths of East Germany? Would there be any merit to this hypothetical testimonial, and if so, how might it inform the current leadership of unified Germany? Eric Langenbacher also takes up the theme of memory in "The Mastered Past? Collective Memory Trends in Germany since Unification." He examines three at times intersecting vectors of collective memory in Germany over the past two decades: the Holocaust, German suffering, and division. Langenbacher demonstrates that although the last twenty years saw a profusion of "memory work," the wave probably has crested, meaning that Germany (and Germans) will be much less beholden to pasts that refuse to pass. The final contribution in the vein of memory and discourse by Ruth Hatlapa and Andrei S. Markovits–examines long-standing continuities in German identity with reference to a usually negatively conceived "other:" the United States of America. In contrast to other aspects of German memory politics, this is a value dimension that has escaped the trials and tribulations unleashed by unification relatively unscathed, despite the adulation of U.S. President Barack Obama in Germany. Brad Prager, in "Passing Time since the *Wende*: Recent German Film on Unification," surveys German depictions of unification in film, with special emphasis on "cinematic time"–the way films have represented the difference between the passage of historical time and its subjective experience. Next, Dagmar Herzog's chapter examines the initial clash between, and later convergence of the sexual cultures of East and West Germans after unification, as well as the links between these discourses and debates on the one hand, and government public policies (e.g., age of consent laws, access to abortion, disability rights, etc.), on the other. Despite the persistence of traditional views in many areas, postunification Germany (especially the CDU) has evolved in many progressive directions.

Herzog's analysis is followed by three contributions that take up the question of citizenship, social integration, and gender in postunification Germany. Joyce Mushaben, in "From Ausländer to Inlander: The Changing Faces of Citizenship in Post-Wall Germany," tracks the fate and fortunes of foreigners and children of migrant descent under the Merkel government's new proactive measures to foster their education and integration. Mushaben argues that these new programs, paradoxically, have given the center-Right in Germany the opportunity to modernize its own identity. Complementing this chapter, Hilary Silver takes up the question of national integration in postunification Germany. Arriving at a perhaps less hopeful conclusion than Mushaben, Silver observes that a concern with national integration has a long history in modern Germany. She highlights the persistence of social cleavages in unified Germany (especially pronounced between oldtimers and newcomers), the higher degree of fragmentation in society and an ambivalence from all sides about the goals and measures involved with the integration process.

Finally, Myra Marx Ferree explores gender politics in the Berlin Republic, tracing four contested identity claims that inject gender meanings into politics: the cultural definition of the German nation in the face of immigration; the integration of the German state into the European project; the economic restructuring of unification and its impact on life chances and opportunities on either side of the former wall; and changes in the political representation of women in state offices and political parties. She outlines the continuities and changes in these four dimensions over the past twenty years, and shows how singly and in combination they engage passionate feelings about gender relations, and carry important implications for the lives of ordinary women and men in the new Berlin Republic.

The next section delves into politics and public policy. Although it is perhaps risky to draw firm conclusions, the picture that emerges from this set of contributions reveals starker discontinuities in comparison to the analyses of culture and memory from the first issue. My overview observes that Germans seem to be of two conflicting minds about unification—one is characterized by awe over the accomplishments of 1989-1990, the other by disappointment and even bitterness over unfulfilled ambitions and promises. This chapter examines the recurring themes, interpretations, and narratives about unification twenty years on through four vignettes. Public discourse on unification twenty years after the fact resembles a blind spot—look straight at it, and it disappears, replaced by blank spot—a seemingly irreducible gap between East and West. Avert one's gaze, and the spot fills in, almost seamlessly.

Russell Dalton and Willy Jou note that few aspects of politics have been as variable as partisan politics in the last two decades. In the East, citizens had to learn about democratic electoral politics and the party system from an almost completely fresh start, whereas in the West, voters experienced a changing partisan landscape and the shifting policy positions of the established parties as they confronted the challenges of unification. Analyzing voting results and the evolving links between social milieu and the parties, the chapter considers whether citizens are developing affective party ties that reflect the institutionalization of a unified party system and voter choice. Although there are broad similarities between electoral politics in West and East, the differences have not substantially narrowed in the past two decades. Next, Helga Welsh takes us on a tour of the German higher education system since unification. After the practice of wholesale West-to-East institutional transfer had begun to reach its natural limits in the mid 1990s, the federal government launched new higher education policies for unified Germany that in many ways have transformed the landscape for students, faculty, and administrators. Welsh argues that autonomy, competition, differentiation, performance, and Europeanization have become the building blocks of a new model of higher education in Germany, but their implementation is as yet incomplete, at times stymied by entrenched interests, existing institutions, and old modes of thinking. The old East-West divide in higher education has faded, but the system remains a long way from an all-German, uniform model.

Beverly Crawford and Abraham Newman close out the overview of politics and public policy with contrasting takes on unified Germany's foreign policy. Although the two authors agree that the country's approach to external relations today is quite different from its preunification incarnation, they disagree over the nature and implications of the changes. Crawford sees a great deal of continuity in Berlin's foreign policy, arguing that while the original aims of cooperative security and multilateralism guiding German policy was shaped by division, they have shown remarkable resilience, even as Germany has regained sovereignty, unity, and power. Unified Germany is more powerful, but still maintains a foreign policy vision that downplays the role of power. Crawford concludes that this paradoxical combination of power and vision in postunification German foreign policy has introduced a new and effective from of "normative power" in global politics. Newman, by contrast, maintains that– in Crawford's lexicon–both power and vision in German foreign policy have changed with unification. Newman argues that since the end of the Cold War, German leaders have acted in ways that suggest that the role of identity in shaping their approach to Europe and to global politics in general has weakened. He goes on to argue that rather than a shift to national self-interest, the postunification period has ushered in, and elevated, a set of beliefs in foreign policymaking circles associated with risk avoidance.

The final portion of this volume examines the impact of unification on political economy. Holger Wolf assesses the success of economic unification. Although authors differ depending on the criteria selected and the benchmark used, in many areas from productivity to infrastructure and housing, dramatic economic improvements are readily apparent in the new Bundesländer. Daunting challenges remain: the speed of productivity convergence has slowed, unemployment remains high, and net emigration continues. Stephen Silvia also investigates the progress that the eastern German economy has made since unification in two areas: unemployment and output. He finds that unemployment has remained persistently higher in eastern than in western Germany and output levels have remained extremely uniform across the eastern states. Neoclassical economists have put forth a convincing argument for the endurance of high unemployment in the East, which blames high initial wages in eastern Germany for producing a labor "trap," but this account needs to be augmented with attention devoted public policy, especially the content and volume of public investment. Economic modeling indicates that wage subsidies targeted at low-income employment would be the most effective means to break the current high-unemployment equilibrium in eastern Germany, but the political barriers to adopting such a policy are just as formidable as they were a decade ago, when such a policy was briefly considered.

Next, Anke Hassel argues that German unification acted as a catalyst for the substantial transformation of the German welfare and employment regime, changes that entail a process of a partial liberalization of the labor market within the boundaries of a coordinated industrial relations system and a conservative welfare state. Her chapter depicts the transformation towards a more liberal welfare and employment regime by focusing on the shifting boundaries between status and income maintenance and poor relief systems. Richard Deeg shows that since unification there have been dramatic and highly visible changes in the financial system and relations between banks and firms. The traditional *Hausbank* system has weakened, as securities markets have become more important for both borrowers and savers, and the demands of financial investors on how German firms manage themselves have become increasingly influential. Bank-industry relations in Germany became increasingly differentiated, with one set of (multinational) firms moving into an institutional environment readily characterized as market-based finance, but most remaining in a bank-based environment that, while not quite the same as the traditional model, is still easily recognized as such. These changes have had numerous consequences for the German economy, including increased pressure on firms to make greater profits and increased pressure on labor to limit wage gains and make concessions in the interest of corporate competitiveness

Christopher Allen concludes this section with a chapter entitled "Ideas, Institutions and Organized Capitalism: The German Model of Political Economy Twenty Years after Unification." He observes that the postunification economic literature has largely focused on the erosion of the German model of organized capitalism and emphasized institutional decline and the corresponding rise of neoliberalism. He inquires into why such a coordinated market economy was created in the first place and whether a renewed form of it might still be useful for Germany, the European Union, and other developed democracies in the early twenty-first century. Allen looks backwards articulating the origins of the institutional and ideational components of these coordinated market economy models, during both the Bismarckian and Social Market Economy periods before addressing whether the failure of the contemporary liberal market economy approach in the wake of the worldwide financial crisis and severe recession represents a possible opening for the creation of a third coordinated market economy not only for Germany but for a redesigned European Union.

This book concludes with a summary essay by Eric Langenbacher, "The Germans Must Have Done Something Right." Noting that the default setting for contemporary German studies seems to be harsh criticism and deep skepticism, he counters that the twentieth anniversary of unification should also be a time for calm reflection on the many accomplishments in and of contemporary Germany. Despite the many problems and many challenges that confront Germany in 2010 and beyond, there is much for Germans to be proud of, and much for the rest of the world to admire and to applaud–no more, but certainly no less than peer democracies in Europe and around the world. Langenbacher takes the reader full circle to the opening essay of this special issue project–Konrad Jarausch's conclusion that Germany has left the *Sonderweg*, and finds itself in a state of competent normalcy. Even the challenges that the country undoubtedly faces–a looming demographic crisis, high levels of debt, structural reforms to the economy–are unexceptional in the European or Western context.

PART I.
HISTORICAL REFLECTIONS

Chapter 1

$\mathcal{T}$HE FEDERAL REPUBLIC AT SIXTY

● ● ● ● ● ● ● ● ● ● ● ● ● ● ●

*Popular Myths, Actual Accomplishments and
Competing Interpretations*

Konrad H. Jarausch

The Federal Republic of Germany's (FRG) start was anything but auspicious. Exactly four years after the defeat of the Third Reich, fifty-three members of the Parliamentary Council voted to accept the "Basic Law," the constitution of a West German state, composed of the American, British and French occupation zones. Since they did not want to jeopardize the prospect of national unity, German leaders agreed only reluctantly to seize the chance of regaining a collective voice by creating a federal parliament and new government. They worried that the continuing oversight of the Western victors, specified in an occupation statute, would severely limit future sovereignty. While all democratic parties agreed on learning from Weimar's mistakes, the Social Democratic Party of Germany (SPD) and Christian Democratic Union (CDU) were at loggerheads about the extent of federalism. In spite of the provisional character of the document, the future Chancellor Konrad Adenauer was "deeply moved" during the simple ratification ceremony on 23 May, since it provided Germans a chance for a new and democratic beginning.[1]

This unwanted improvisation soon proved surprisingly successful in the eyes of conservative politicians, journalists, and an increasing number of citizens. During the election campaigns in 1953 or 1957 the CDU pointed primarily to the material recovery after the currency reform and Ludwig Erhard's return to a market economy, expanded by the adjective "social" to signal the growing welfare dimension of the state. Chancellor Adenauer could also claim visible progress in ending the Allied occupation and restoring a degree of sovereignty by integrating the FRG into Western institutions like the ECSC, NATO or the EEC. In their international comparison of "civic culture," U.S. social scientists Gabriel Almond and Sidney Verba also marveled at the domestic stability, citing the high voter participation and the smooth functioning of democratic institutions. Already in 1956, the Swiss journalist Fritz Rene Allemann pronounced a positive verdict with the book title which became a cliché: "Bonn is not Weimar."[2]

By contrast, intellectuals both at home and abroad, who had hoped for a radical moral redemption, remained skeptical of the integrative pragmatism of the "Rhenish Republic." One important irritant was the half-hearted process of denazification that had left many Nazi perpetrators or accomplices unpunished and allowed them to re-enter social and political life. Another widespread objection concerned the revival of capitalism that belied hopes for a more egalitarian society through socialization of industry and redistribution of land. In both East and West, some democratic thinkers also refused to be drawn into the hostilities of the Cold War and continued to promote peaceful neutrality between the power blocs. Many critics were finally suspicious of Western rearmament, Franz-Josef Strauss' nuclear ambitions, and a resurgence of German power.[3] The deep and abiding alienation of many intellectuals from the FRG raises some doubts about the accuracy of the simple success story promoted by bourgeois circles.

Constant comparison with the Communist rival German Democratic Republic (GDR) also complicated contemporary assessments of the FRG's development. Initially the Socialist Unity Party's (SED) project of creating a "better Germany" as a rigorously antifascist and egalitarian state appealed to a considerable section of the working class, intellectuals like the Jewish survivor Victor Klemperer, and many critics abroad. But, defenders of the FRG could point to the brutality of Soviet occupation, the erection of a Communist dictatorship, the persecution of the Churches, the dispossession of businessmen and landowners and the stifling of debate in order to defend Western democracy in spite of its own flaws. The intense East-West competition developed into an "asymmetrical entanglement," with the GDR more focused on the FRG than vice versa. The Cold War polarization forced commentators to take an ideological stand and endorse one or the other successor state, but with time their judgments gradually swung in favor of the freer and more prosperous West.[4]

Perhaps two generations after the modest beginning, the FRG's successes and failures have become amenable to a more balanced evaluation. From the vantage point of the "Berlin Republic," the key question has shifted from whether the second German democracy would survive at all to the reasons for its relatively positive course and to the extent of its lingering problems. In order to provide some tentative answers, the following chapter first addresses the emergence of popular myths that characterized the FRG's difficult search for identity. Secondly, it reviews some of the West's actual accomplishments in problem-solving, because such a comparison helps to explain why it won the competition with its rival in the East. Finally, it scrutinizes several of the competing interpretations so as to reveal their political agendas and discuss their analytical limitations.[5] Instead of presenting a simple success story, this reflection shall therefore strive for a critical appreciation.

Popular Myths

The development of the Federal Republic over six decades has left a trail of memories turned into myths that offer clues to its difficult struggle to evolve an accepted identity. Individual, group, and public recollections contained countless stories of wartime survival that metamorphosed into tales of postwar success, seeking to heal ruptures in life histories. Since the Nazis tarnished all older myths by abusing them, the FRG could not resort to earlier symbols in order to shore up its shaky legitimacy. Instead, ordinary people themselves transformed selected postwar memories into public myths, celebrating difficulties overcome and successes achieved, thereby reconstituting a sense of community. After the mid 1960s, intellectuals of the Left also began to sponsor critical counter myths in order to memorialize their struggles to transform a capitalist system which they felt needed fundamental reform.[6] How do such residues of memory and myth reflect the evolution of the FRG?

In contrast to British references to the Magna Carta or French invocations of the storming of the Bastille, the FRG lacked an inspiring founding myth. With its claim of an antifascist new beginning, its Eastern rival employed powerful historical justifications, based on a Marxist-Leninist master narrative that celebrated the struggle of the labor movement and the liberation by the Red Army. West German politicians like Konrad Adenauer, Theodor Heuss, or Kurt Schumacher also publicly distanced themselves from the crimes of National Socialism, but they could not invoke the Weimar Republic as it was too tarnished by its failure to serve as a general reference point. Instead, Western leaders felt compelled by the silent majority of Nazi sympathizers to engage in a memory politics that limited responsibility to a small group of high-profile Nazis and exonerated the rest.[7] Because it was burdened with shame and founded in chaos, the FRG was forced to prove itself to its citizens by actual performance rather than by ideological rhetoric.

While coping with bitter memories, individuals and groups created victimization narratives that emphasized German suffering without reference to its real cause. Since the demilitarization policy of the Allies suppressed public heroization of soldiers' or POWs' plight, it was rather the "bombing terror," witnessed by the elderly, women, and children that could be talked about freely. Refugee associations similarly promoted recollections of terrible experiences during flight and expulsion from the lost territories in the East that coalesced into a powerful call for a return to their homes. Similarly the "rubble women" who cleared away mountains of debris became deeply engraved in collective memory, even if some had collaborated previously with the Nazis. Taken together these private conversations, group representations, and public complaints inspired a role reversal in which former perpetrators turned into helpless victims, focused on their own pain rather than on the suffering they had inflicted on others.[8]

Government efforts to invent a progressive pedigree for the Bonn Republic largely failed, since the real past was too problematic to be used as a symbolic foundation of democracy. The anniversary of the revolution of 1848 showed that its tradition lived on only in a small region of Southwest Germany where the radicals had made their last stand. The 1918 revolution proved similarly inadequate, because bourgeois parties remembered it as military defeat, while the Left resented the SPD's recourse to soldiers in order to stabilize the Weimar Republic. Since the 1944 resistance remained controversial, the Adenauer government finally seized upon the 1953 workers' uprising in East Germany to enshrine 17 June as national holiday. This was a genuine grassroots revolt, had an anticommunist thrust and expressed a longing for reunification. But, in actual practice pious speeches to "our dear brothers and sisters in the East" lost their credibility when most West Germans used the day for a picnic in the woods.[9]

Yet from below, the Economic Miracle quickly assumed mythic proportions–it had a fascinating story, an appealing image, and a convincing representation. Its central tale recounts the miraculous filling of shop windows with scarce goods after the currency reform of 1948. Some narratives praised the caution of the Bundesbank that made the Deutsche Mark a symbol of stability and respectability when its value appreciated vis-à-vis other currencies. Yet other stories celebrate the success of the unpretentious and durable design which turned the modest Volkswagen Beetle into an icon of rising mobility at home and of peaceful German engineering abroad. Oral histories retell how the generous help of the Marshall Plan converted the U.S. image from occupier to friendly partner. Finally, opinion surveys demonstrate that the roly-poly, cigar chomping Ludwig Erhard was a persuasive advocate of his "social-market economy." In short, with the Economic Miracle slogan Germans could applaud their own hard work, regardless of political differences.[10]

The recovery of pride was reinforced by the unexpected success of the German national soccer team in the 1954 World Championship that also became an instant myth. After losing a preliminary group game with a partial reserve squad against the talented Hungarians, the Germans recovered from a two goal deficit in the final to beat the same favored opponent in the eighty-fourth minute with a third goal by left winger Helmut Rahn. The radio announcer Herbert Zimmermann's jubilant cry "*Toor, Toor, Toor*" triggered a wave of euphoric celebrations and waving of Republican black-red-gold flags that released much of the frustration after defeat, deprivation, and division. In retrospect, this surprising victory became known as "the miracle of Bern," since it helped restore self-confidence by showing that Germans could again succeed in peaceful competition.[11] In subsequent years, the coach, Sepp Herberger, and some players like Fritz Walter were heroized, contributing to the restoration of a visceral patriotism in the broader public.

In contrast, the Left's reconciliation with the Bonn Republic was a more protracted process, since it involved trying to transform a hated "system." Even if it failed to reach most of its proclaimed aims, the generational revolt of 1968 assumed mythic proportions with its frequent retelling during subsequent anniversaries. One inspiring story recalled the massive protests of unions, churches, intellectuals, and students in the Extra-parliamentary Opposition against the passage of the emergency laws. Another legend celebrated the creativity of the student movement against authoritarian education, bourgeois double standards, and the Vietnam War. Yet another heroic tale stressed the narrow election victory of 1969, which did bring a left-center social-liberal coalition into power and unleashed a barrage of long overdue reforms. Though deploring its later terrorist excesses, Jürgen Habermas applauded the revolt's contribution to "a fundamental liberalization," while some historians even talk about "a second founding" of the FRG.[12]

For a progressive mythologization, Willy Brandt's visionary enthusiasm was more suitable than the technocratic crisis management of Helmut Schmidt. The former's slogan of "daring more democracy" became a synonym for the Left's longing for social modernization and drew many student activists back into the system, encouraging their long march through the institutions. The domestic reforms of the welfare state and the education system as well as the foreign opening to a new *Ostpolitik*, symbolized by Brandt's kneeling in front of the Warsaw ghetto memorial, inspired an entire generation. Helmut Schmidt's halting of the reforms to combat the deleterious effects of the oil shocks, the nasty stagflation, and the rising unemployment of the 1970s were widely resented within the SPD. Therefore, the millenarianism of the peace movement and the Free Democratic Party's (FDP) neoliberal turn finally ended the "social democratic decade." But, the social-liberal coalition left a positive legacy of the reformist potential of a forward-looking *Modell Deutschland*.[13]

One fundamental irritant for the Left was the unresolved national question, because intellectuals were instinctively allergic to the Right's recourse to national myths. Dolf Sternberger therefore suggested a constitutional patriotism in order to provide a more rational basis for supporting the Federal Republic as a *Rechtstaat* without giving in to nationalist emotions. Nonetheless, Egon Bahr's opening to the GDR in the name of *Wandel durch Annäherung* retained a national component of preserving cultural and personal unity by retying ruptured connections to the East. To a generation born and socialized in the Federal Republic, such debates about national identity seemed old-fashioned, since many were ready to recognize GDR citizenship, thinking of themselves as entirely postnational and European in outlook. Ironically, the integration of the intellectuals into the FRG therefore proceeded largely through their critical questioning, in the philosopher's Luhmann's apt phrase by "participating and protesting."[14]

Forty years after its creation, the FRG had another opportunity to formulate a positive identity myth through the "democratic awakening" of the East Germans. As Timothy Garton Ash noted, the exciting events surrounding the fall of the Wall could be seen as a more successful repetition of 1848, since they involved a democratic rising from below, their course was surprisingly peaceful, and they reconstituted a German national state with internationally accepted borders. These attributes were comparable to the self-mythologizations of other Western states, offering the Germans in Fritz Stern's words a "second chance." Whether the national holiday, placed on 3 October, will eventually inspire a myth of democratic unity remains unclear, since the upheaval involved only the East Germans, many dissidents were disappointed in its results, and the new citizens faced a "unification crisis." Instead of repeating popular myths, the first task is, therefore, to deconstruct them and to make them the subject of scholarly analysis.[15]

Actual Accomplishments

In spite of such symbolic uncertainty, the Federal Republic gradually won over its citizens, because its problem-solving proved superior to the performance of the troubled Weimar Republic. Ironically, the circumstances after the second German defeat in 1945 were much worse than after the first–but it was precisely this desperate situation which triggered a more positive learning process after World War II. This time there was no denying defeat through a stab-in-the-back legend, because the Wehrmacht had been shattered and the capital had fallen; there was also no escaping from responsibility for Nazi crimes, since the Nuremberg Trials documented the atrocities beyond a doubt. The whole country was occupied, the territory drastically dismembered, the caretaker government rejected, and the Nazi Party with its auxiliaries dissolved. Probably it was the very depth of the caesura, captured in the controversial phrase "zero hour" (*Stunde Null*) that rendered a constructive renewal possible, because it barred a relapse into the past.[16]

As autobiographies show, the most basic accomplishment was a return of order, a recovery of normalcy that made it possible to resume a regular life. It is important to remember how much the chaos of the final fighting and the arrival of occupation disrupted work patterns, closed schools, and upset daily routines. Moreover, the hunger, cold, and disease that followed put a premium on mere survival from day to day. Only the restoration of basic services like water, electricity and public order in the streets and the resumption of reliable food supply as well as media information made it possible to return to a regular life. While the occupation powers created the framework, the local German authorities had to cope with these problems and find practical solutions. Their increasing success prepared the ground for the revival of organized politics and made new democratic leaders popular. This largely pre-political provision of basic necessities restored hope in an improving future that made it possible to go on living.[17]

Another signal achievement, closely identified with the FRG, was the revival of economic prosperity, ironically portrayed in the film *Wir Wunderkinder*. The currency reform implemented the necessary devaluation before the founding of the Bonn Republic and the policy of the Bundesbank prevented a repetition of run-away inflation. Erhard's gamble on the market reignited an astounding growth in production until the early 1970s, thereby banning the specter of another Depression. The labor-intensive rebuilding process gradually also absorbed the unemployed and GDR refugees, seeming to guarantee full employment. Moreover, rising prosperity created a new elite of wealthy businessmen whose suburban villas, Mercedes limousines, and consumer durables became icons of the Economic Miracle. Eventually labor unions succeeded in having some of the gains trickle down in the form of improved wages, the forty hour week, and longer vacations. In contrast to Weimar's straits, the FRG could take pride in offering consumption to its citizens.[18]

Equally important for pacifying the social conflicts that had torn the first democracy apart was the creation of an elaborate welfare state, second only to the Scandinavian countries. This *Sozialstaat* was a product of the electoral competition between the welfare-oriented SPD and the CDU that tried to follow Catholic social teaching. The government was responsible for a complex "Equalization of Burdens Law" that transferred over three dozen billion DM from those whose assets had escaped the war unscathed to the many victims such as disabled veterans, war widows, people with bombing losses, and refugees. With a shrewd eye for votes, Adenauer also instituted an indexing of pensions in 1957 in order to let the elderly participate in the rise of general prosperity. The opposition backed the union drive for co-determination in large coal and steel firms that offered workers a stake in their companies. Taken together, these and other measures gave Rhenish capitalism a human face which guaranteed labor peace.[19]

At the same time, the Federal Republic also reintroduced the Germans into the international community by embracing the West instead of continuing Weimar's revisionism. Chancellor Adenauer took much pride in speaking out for such German interests in negotiations with the victors as the ending of industrial dismantling. He seized upon the chance offered by the Korean War to propose limited rearmament as a lever to regain a greater measure of sovereignty, making German forces part of a Western defense structure in NATO in 1955. Similarly, he pressed for European integration through the ECSC and the EEC, making concessions in order to resolve the Ruhr issue and reassure the neighbors by Europeanizing a revived Germany. Finally, he worked tirelessly to overcome the hereditary enmity with France. Only the goal of national unity proved elusive and eventually the non-recognition policy of the GDR had to be abandoned. But on the whole, the population appreciated the benefits of his Westernization course.[20]

Due to the weakness of symbolic grounding, postwar democratization therefore required a gradual process of getting comfortable with representative institutions as well as Western values. To be sure, Allied victory and the cooperation of a liberal minority of Germans had already restored the framework of parliamentary government in the late 1940s. But many lingering effects of Wilhelmian authoritarianism, traces of Nazi racism, and anti-occupation resentment needed to be overcome before most Germans would wholeheartedly embrace the Federal Republic. After the establishment of formal institutions it took a cultural process of "inner democratization" to transform attitudes and behaviors which lasted several decades in order to turn skeptical Germans into true democrats. The SED dictatorship in the GDR also helped convince the defeated population to back the more liberal Rhenish Republic, since Communist repression formed a stark contrast to the participatory possibilities of self-government in the West."[21]

Critics could, however, point to several major areas in which the FRG failed to live up to its promise. One especially sensitive topic was dealing with the Nazi past. Though a minority of contrite democrats favored restitution payments to the Jewish community, an apologetic majority wanted to forget its own Nazi involvement and demanded the rehabilitation of former collaborators. Their reintegration produced many scandals such as the cases of the chief of the chancellor's office Hans Globke, who had written a commentary on the Nuremberg Laws, or the Baden-Württemberg premier Karl Hans Filbinger, who had been a naval judge–a predicament that the GDR was happy to exploit. It took until the Eichmann and Auschwitz trials in the early 1960s for the public to acknowledge the extent of Nazi crimes and for opinion to swing towards active coming-to-terms-with-the past (*Vergangenheitsbewältigung*). Since East German antifascism narrowed into a defense of SED dictatorship, the FRG seemed self critical in comparison.[22]

Another such problem area proved to be the lack of integration of foreigners. The Basic Law supported the return of ethnic German refugees and "resettlers" from the East, although it contained a remarkably liberal asylum provision. When the Wall was built, industrialists supported the invitation of temporary migrant workers, so-called guest workers (*Gastarbeiter*)–but some of them refused to go home as expected. Many Germans were unprepared for their remaining, because they thought of themselves as an emigration country, arguing that after World War II another 1.5 million had left for greener shores. Fearing to be overrun by foreigners, the parties of the Right turned xenophobic, while the Left embraced a multiculturalism that made no provision to help the newcomers integrate. As a result, primarily Turkish ghettos formed in some of the big cities. Neither the pleas of hybrid immigrant spokesmen like Cem Özdemir nor the recent liberalization of immigration and naturalization laws have so far been able to resolve the problem.[23]

A further example of continuing difficulties concerned the much debated issue of inner unification. In contrast to the international approval of the restoration of the German national state, the domestic response has been disappointing and contentious. No doubt the vote for quick unity, the fiscal collapse of the GDR and the small diplomatic time window left virtually no alternative to a wholesale transfer of functioning institutions from the West. But, the accession of the new states into the existing FRG made it virtually impossible to preserve positive Eastern institutions such as walk-in clinics and forced an overnight adjustment to unknown Western practices like tax returns or insurance policies. The media domination of the West, the scandalization of Stasi collaboration and the denigration of the GDR as *Unrechtstaat* created an impression of Western colonization which spawned an obdurate Eastern nostalgia.[24] Consequently, the euphoria of unification quickly dissipated, leaving a trail of mutual resentment between East and West.

A final disappointment referred to the FRG's inadequate response to globalization, which contrasts with the success of individual companies. The Social-Liberal coalition interpreted the abandonment of fixed exchange rates and the oil shocks as a problem of the business cycle to be combated by Keynesian measures. In spite of temporary recovery, long term unemployment rose and economic growth turned anemic, averaging about 2 percent per year after 1973. Limited neoliberal measures by the CDU-FDP coalition restored growth, but then the unification crisis destroyed the nimbus of German economic competence. Even a trillion DM of transfer payments in the 1990s were unable to cushion the double transition from plan to market and from protection to global competition. When the Red-Green government made a valiant effort to restore competitiveness with the "Agenda 2010," public uproar ensued.[25] The FRG therefore confronts a series of unresolved problems such as the reform of the universities that temper its claims to unqualified success.

Competing Interpretations

Long portraying itself as an escape from a terrible past, the FRG only gradually admitted to having a history in its own right. Its big intellectual controversies revolved more around the outbreak of World War I or the evaluation of the Third Reich than about its own development, which seemed like a kind of extended present. Moreover, Bonn's relative success, proclaimed by conservative commentators close to the ruling CDU, seemed too fragile to be endangered by probing analyses. Only the "restoration thesis" of the Left and the GDR's accusation of a fascist continuity injected a note of controversy, since they stressed the missed opportunities for a more radical new beginning. In contrast, social scientific recourse to "modernization theory" had a more ambivalent effect, since it acknowledged the evident departure from problematic traditions, while encouraging further changes in the future. Hence, it took until the 1980s for the FRG to historicize itself by building a museum of its own history (Haus der Geschichte) in Bonn.[26]

The reluctant self-recognition of the FRG involved a difficult effort to reconstruct a democratic master narrative out of the rubble of a shattered past. Rejecting the nationalist account discredited by the Third Reich and the Marxist counternarrative of the GDR, this Western version tried to tell the national story in a chastened fashion by focusing on one still somewhat provisional successor state. The quasi official history of the FRG in six volumes, edited by Karl Dietrich Bracher in 1982, therefore concentrated on the establishment of the Basic Law as a firm foundation for a more stable parliamentary democracy. Moreover, Hans-Peter Schwarz' many writings on Adenauer celebrated the first chancellor's astute leadership while other observers praised Erhard's courage in risking a return to a market economy.[27] Though partly convincing, this success narrative underplayed the many Nazi continuities, lingering authoritarianism, and social inequalities, ignoring the shortcomings of the Bonn Republic.

In contrast, the Left's understanding of the FRG admitted some progress in overcoming troubling legacies, but insisted on the necessity of further drastic changes. Critics like the concentration camp survivor Egon Kogon deplored the "restoration republic," objecting to the revival of bourgeois patterns and habits of obedience. Similarly, the sociologist Ralf Dahrendorf scorned the German incapacity for democracy, rooted in a heritage of illiberalism, insufficiently overcome. In the same vein the historian Fritz Fischer exposed the underlying continuities from World War I to the Third Reich, while his younger colleague Hans-Ulrich Wehler saw Imperial Germany as the source of authoritarian structures, still troubling the FRG. This critical view of postwar developments served as intellectual justification for supporting the reforms initiated by the Social-Liberal coalition. With these strictures in mind, progressive historians like Christoph Klessmann have produced a more complex account of restoration and new beginning.[28]

The democratic rising of 1989 ultimately settled the ideological dispute over the FRG's self-representation because the West won the ideological rivalry. In contrast to the decrepit SED dictatorship, the parliamentary democracy and social market economy looked attractive enough for GDR citizens to join it immediately. Even prior critics now had to admit the success of the Bonn Republic and start debating the reasons for its superiority instead. One leading explanation was the paradigm of Westernization, expressed by Heinrich August Winkler's book title "the long road to the West," which emphasized the end of the German *Sonderweg* through embracing Western institutions. On a more cultural level, other scholars like Axel Schildt began to explore dimensions of Americanization in popular taste and consumption. This approach accounted for the mental and stylistic difference from the former GDR, but remained somewhat uncritical of what was actually meant by "West," since it failed to probe its legacy of racism and slavery.[29]

As an alternative, I proposed an analysis of the process of recivilization, which sought to rehabilitate the East and West Germans after the barbarity of the Holocaust. Instead of just looking at the memory politics of *Vergangenheitsbewältigung*, this approach investigated the practical learning from Hitler's crimes in the many ways in which Germans tried to prevent a repetition of the Third Reich. This concept took up Dan Diner's suggestion of a genocidal rupture of civilization and looked at the efforts to undo the moral damage after 1945. Therefore, it acknowledged the crucial role of Allied intervention in the beginning, but then traced the growing involvement of Germans in the process of rehabilitation. This perspective had the advantage of using a generalized notion of civilization as a standard for measuring change and of transcending the caesura of 1989. Though the concept of civilization has been sharply criticized by postcolonial authors, its self-reflexive use might provide a more tempered understanding of success.[30]

In spite of agreement on the relative success of the FRG, a more complex explanation of its development still faces a number of challenges. The first unresolved problem is the integration of the parallel development of the two German successor states into one common postwar history. An unreflected Cold War triumphalism that asserts Eastern failure and Western superiority in black and white terms only reinforces accusations of colonization. Instead, it would be more productive to focus on the many ties which still linked the competing rivals after their increasing division, such as their comparisons with each other, mutual trade, social connections, and cultural exchanges. One might also want to look at cross-cutting developments such as occupation or globalization in order to discern the commonalities, as well as differences of their responses. It still has to be explained how two so different states as the GDR and FRG could arise from the same territory and people, but once again merge peacefully after half a century of competition.[31]

Another interpretative task is a more explicit engagement of the European context of postwar German development. Due to their central location, fluid borders, shifting population, and unstable politics, Germans are deeply entangled in the histories of their neighbors, but much of the writing still deals with Germany as a fixed and separate entity. Since the early 1950s, the process of European integration has, moreover, shifted many decisions to emerging authorities in Brussels, Strasbourg or Luxembourg, thereby rendering any purely national perspective on the past obsolete. An emphatically pro-European presentation, however, must seek to avoid the Treitschke trap of promoting a political agenda through scholarship on a higher level than the nation, since it conflates advocacy with analysis. Instead, the memories of mutually inflicted pain need to be acknowledged openly in order to transcend the heritage of conflicts by uncovering a multiplicity of prior connections and showing the potential of future cooperation.[32]

The more recent globalization debate has also begun to transform the interpretative framework by drawing attention to the transnational dimension of German history. The concept itself came into political usage only in the mid 1990s, but the reality described by it is much older. Before World War I, Imperial Germany was already so deeply involved in an international network of trade, popular migration, and exchange of ideas that Jürgen Osterhammel has located the "transformation of the world" in the nineteenth century. In the postwar period, it was the transnational impact of the Cold War that divided the Germans and drew them into a world-wide ideological conflict, while at the same time Americanized popular culture and mass consumption spilled across their frontiers. Though many younger scholars have called for a transnational history in order to explore the global dimension, this programmatic pronouncement has yet to have a noticeable effect on the writing of postwar history.[33]

The issue of periodizing a half century of development also requires more explicit reflection. Due to the collapse of the Nazi dictatorship, the caesura of 1945 functions as an unquestioned beginning, even if some scholars have suggested a broader transition period from 1943 to 1948 instead. The question of a dividing point that separates the Adenauer cum Erhardt era from the subsequent social democratic reform period is more complicated: Should one emphasize the generational rebellion of 1968 as a cultural watershed or follow a political chronology and stress the changeover to Brandt's Social-Liberal coalition in 1969? Perhaps the end of the postwar boom in 1973 might be an even more significant caesura, because the oil shock recession initiated the intractable problems of weak growth, long-term unemployment, and overburdening of the welfare state. While the collapse of communism heralded the end of the postwar era, by now narratives also need to account for two further decades of the Berlin Republic.[34]

Finally, the more fortunate development of the Federal Republic has to be placed into the perspective of the entire twentieth century. The stark contrast between the catastrophic first half and the more constructive course of the second half has been noted by contemporaries and historians alike. Yet, it took Peter Graf Kielmansegg to claim a direct causal connection: "It was the catastrophe which made Germany capable of democracy. It was the catastrophe which taught Germany to integrate itself into the community of European states. It was the catastrophe which forced Germany to define itself anew." In order not to yield to the temptation of further mythologizing through a redemption narrative, the complex and protracted process of collective learning from the disaster must be reconstructed in empirical detail. These methodological imperatives suggest that narratives of the Federal Republic ought to be integrated into broader geographic and temporal contests in order to prevent their renationalization.[35]

A Nation-Building Success?

In retrospect, the development of the FRG from its modest beginnings to the impressive present has been a qualified success, somewhat less stellar than its supporters claim but also more extensive than its detractors aver. The physical transformation of a battle-torn, rubble-strewn, and chaotic country into a manicured, prosperous and orderly land was impressive enough, but even more astounding was the mental transformation from bellicose nationalism to peaceful multilateralism. Nonetheless, this metamorphosis remains somewhat short of miraculous, because it did not come overnight, but involved lengthy struggles, witnessed repeated crises, and required contributions from the opposition that are often overlooked. Moreover, the FRG still faces serious long term difficulties such as the low birthrate or institutional gridlock, as well as short term problems such as rising unemployment and a vanishing export trade. Six decades after its founding, the FRG therefore has both cause for pride and reasons for caution.[36]

Should the postwar rehabilitation of the Germans be considered a text-book case of nation building as a "proconsul view" suggests? Certainly some aspects of the transformation seem to support this claim, advanced by the Bush Administration to justify its initial policies in Iraq. After the failure of the resistance in July 1944, only negative intervention from the outside could topple the Nazi dictatorship and clear the way for a new start by prohibiting National Socialism, proscribing militarism, and dis-crediting authoritarianism. At the same time, a more positive occupation policy of fostering reconstruction and reeducation was also needed in order to reorient the dispirited Germans by providing incentives to embrace democracy and capitalism. This combination of toughness and sympathy worked better than the exploitative effort of the Soviets to export a Stalinist brand of communism.[37] But creating a handbook of essential steps out of this unique experience to be applied during other occupations like Iraq was bound to fail.

The postwar lessons proved hard to transfer because the Germans made a crucial contribution their own rehabilitation and its success had specific causes that could not be replicated. While the Münchhausen myth that the Germans pulled themselves up by their own bootstraps is exag-gerated, it does suggest that a critical minority needed to be willing to par-ticipate from the inside in order to legitimize the desire for change and to sustain the process on its own. In spite of its limited duration, the nation state already existed as a frame of reference, leaving a legacy of commu-nity that did not need to be created. Both the Second Empire and the Weimar Republic provided experience with participatory politics that only had to be recovered, while the Third Reich served as cautionary example of dictatorship. Since they had lost for the second time around, many young Germans were quite willing to learn Western ways after 1945. These special circumstances indicate that Germany only needed to be redemocratized, not built up from scratch.[38]

Even if its particulars might be unrepeatable, the German case does send a hopeful message that with luck and statesmanship a recovery from self-inflicted catastrophe is possible. No doubt, fortunate circumstances such as the early reversal of occupation policy in the West, the help of the Marshall Plan, the effect of the Korean War or the survival of much indus-trial capacity, the existence of a hard-working population, and so on were instrumental in the positive outcome. But it also took the right political decisions such as Adenauer's daring Westernization course, Erhard's bet on the market, Willy Brandt's conciliatory *Ostpolitik*, and Helmut Schmidt's crisis management to seize such opportunities. In contrast to the

GDR's crumbling communism, the FRG's commitment to democracy and multilateralism was rewarded during the Bush-Gorbachev détente with the chance for unification which Helmut Kohl adroitly recognized. Since so many states face disasters, the example of such rehabilitation can be a powerful inspiration.[39]

At sixty, the FRG has, therefore, entered a comfortable middle age, leaving behind some of its earlier drama, but exuding a sense of competent normalcy. The mythical challenges of postwar reconstruction and recovery of international respectability have receded, followed instead by everyday concerns, the proverbial *Mühen der Ebene*, that are much less exhilarating. There are still plenty of problems, ranging from an aging population to a lack of full-day childcare, but they are shared by many other advanced industrial societies. After a century of first arrogant and then dejected difference, the German *Sonderweg* has finally come to an end. As a result of the meltdown of the Anglo-American version of unrestrained capitalism in 2008-2009, the German model of a socially responsive market economy has even regained some of its prior luster.[40] Hence the postwar record of cautious incrementalism inspires some confidence that the Germans will also manage to meet the unforeseen political and economic challenges of the future.

Notes

1. Konrad Adenauer, *Erinnerungen 1945-1953* (Stuttgart, 1965), 146-181. See also Christoph Klessmann, *Die doppelte Staatsgründung: Deutsche Geschichte 1945-1955* (Göttingen, 1982), 193 ff.
2. Fritz Rene Allemann, *Bonn ist nicht Weimar* (Cologne, 1956); Gabriel A. Almond and Sidney Verba, *The Civic Culture: Political Attitudes and Democracy in Five Nations* (Princeton, 1963). See also the invitation of the Konrad Adenauer Stiftung, 8 May 2009: "The history of the Federal Republic is a success story!," http://www.kas.de/wf/de/33.16426/
3. A. Dirk Moses, *German Intellectuals and the Nazi Past* (New York, 2007); Michael Geyer, ed., *The Power of Intellectuals in Contemporary Germany* (Chicago, 2001).
4. Victor Klemperer, *So sitze ich denn zwischen allen Stühlen: Tagebücher 1945-1949* (Berlin, 1999), ed. by Walter Nowojski; and Peter Bender, *Episode oder Epoche? Zur Geschichte des geteilten Deutschland* (Munich, 1996).
5. Axel Schildt, "Überlegungen zur Historisierung der Bundesrepublik," in *Verletztes Gedächtnis: Erinnerungskultur und Zeitgeschichte im Konflikt*, eds., Konrad H. Jarausch and Martin Sabrow (Frankfurt, 2002), 253-272; and Udo Wengst and Hermann Wentker, eds., *Das doppelte Deutschland: 40 Jahre Systemkonkurrenz* (Berlin, 2008).

6. Konrad H. Jarausch, "Survival in Catastrophe: Mending Broken Memories," in *Shattered Past: Reconstructing German Histories,* Konrad H. Jarausch and Michael Geyer (Princeton, 2003), 317-341; Herfried Münkler, *Die Deutschen und ihre Mythen* (Berlin, 2009), 9-30.

7. Jeffrey Herf, *Divided Memory: The Nazi Past in the Two Germanys* (Cambridge, 1997); Norbert Frei, *Adenauer's Germany and the Nazi Past: The Politics of Amnesty and Integration* (New York, 2002); Münkler (see note 6), 411-476.

8. Jörg Friedrich, *The Fire: The Bombing of Germany, 1940-1945* (New York, 2006); Elizabeth D. Heineman, *What Difference Does a Husband Make? Women and Marital Status in Nazi and Postwar Germany* (Berkeley, 1999); and Alon Confino, Paul Betts, Dirk Schumann, eds., *Between Mass Death and Individual Loss: The Place of the Dead in Twentieth Century Germany* (New York, 2008).

9. Wolfram Sieman, *The German Revolution of 1848* (London, 1998); Helga Grebing, ed., *Die deutsche Revolution von 1918/19* (Berlin, 2008); and Edgar Wolfrum, *Geschichtspolitik in der Bundesrepublik Deutschland: Der Weg zur bundesrepublikanischen Erinnerung, 1948-1990* (Darmstadt, 1999).

10. Anthony James Nicholls, *Freedom with Responsibility: The Social Market Economy in Germany, 1918-1963* (Oxford, 1994); Carter S. Dougherty, "The Language of Economics and the Creation of the Social Market Economy in West Germany, 1941-1961," MA thesis, Chapel Hill, 1995; Alfred Mierzejewski, *Ludwig Erhard: A Biography* (Chapel Hill, 2004); and Münkler (see note 6), 460-468.

11. Arthur Heinrich, *Toor! Toor! Toor! Vierzig Jahre* 3:2 (Berlin, 1994); Andreas Bauer, *Das Wunder von Bern: Spieler–Tore–Hintergründe* (Augsburg 2004); and Thomas Raithel, *Fußballweltmeisterschaft 1954: Sport–Geschichte–Mythos* (Munich, 2004). Fifty years after the event a popular movie reinforced the myth.

12. Elizabeth Peifer-Bostick, "1968 in German Political Culture: From Experience to Myth," PhD dissertation, Chapel Hill, 1997; Manfred Görtemaker, *Geschichte der Bundesrepublik Deutschland. Von der Gründung bis zur Gegenwart* (Munich, 1999); and Norbert Frei, *1968: Jugendrevolte und globaler Protest* (Munich 2008).

13. Peter Merseburger, *Willy Brandt 1913-1992: Visionär und Realist* (Stuttgart, 2002); Hartmut Soell, *Helmut Schmidt* (Munich, 2003); and Konrad H. Jarausch, ed., *Das Ende der Zuversicht? Die siebziger Jahre als Geschichte* (Göttingen, 2008).

14. Dolf Sternberger, "Verfassungspatriotismus," vol. x of *Schriften* (Frankfurt, 1990); Egon Bahr, *Zu meiner Zeit* (Munich, 1996); Niklas Luhmann, "Dabeisein und Dagegensein. Anregungen zu einem Nachruf auf die Bundesrepublik," *Frankfurter Allgemeine Zeitung,* 22 August 1990; and Dominik Geppert and Jens Hacke, eds., *Streit um den Staat: Intellektuelle Debatten in der Bundesrepublik 1960-1980* (Göttingen, 2008).

15. Charles S. Maier, *Dissolution: The Crisis of Communism and the End of East Germany* (New York, 1997); Fritz Stern, *Five Germanys I Have Known* (New York, 2006); Ilko-Sascha Kowalczuk, *Endspiel: Die Revolution von 1989 in der DDR* (Munich, 2009); and Konrad H. Jarausch, "Der Umbruch 1989/90," in Martin Sabrow, ed., *Die DDR als Erinnerungsort,* ed. Martin Sabrow (Munich, 2009).

16. Gerhard Weinberg, "Reflections on Two Unifications," *German Studies Review* 21 (1998): 13-25; Klaus-Dietmar Henke, *Die amerikanische Besatzung Deutschlands* (Munich, 1995); and Konrad H. Jarausch, "1945 and the Continuities of German History: Reflections on Memory, Historiography and Politics," in *Stunde Null: The End and the Beginning Fifty Years Ago,* ed., Geoffrey Giles (Washington, 1995), 9-24.

17. Christoph Klessmann and Georg Wagner, eds., *Das gespaltene Land: Leben in Deutschland 1945-1990* (Munich, 1993), 51-90; Klaus Naumann, ed., *Nachkrieg in Deutschland* (Hamburg, 2001); and Konrad H. Jarausch, *After Hitler: Recivilizing Germans, 1945-1995* (New York, 2006), 72 ff.

18. Werner Abelshauser, *Deutsche Wirtschaftsgeschichte seit 1945* (Munich, 2004); and Michael Wildt, *Am Beginn der "Konsumgesellschaft:" Mangelerfahrung, Lebenshaltung und Wohlstandshoffnung in Westdeutschland in den fünfziger Jahren* (Hamburg, 1994).

19. Michael L. Hughes, *Shouldering the Burdens of Defeat: West Germany and the Reconstruction of Social Justice* (Chapel Hill, 1999); Gabriele Metzler, *Der deutsche Sozialstaat: Vom bismarckschen Erfolgsmodell zum Pflegefall* (Stuttgart, 2003); and Hans-Günter Hockers et al., eds., *Geschichte der Sozialpolitik in Deutschland seit 1945* (Baden Baden, 2001), 11 volumes.

20. Wolfram Hanrieder, ed., *West German Foreign Policy, 1949-1979* (Boulder, CO, 1980); and Roland Granieri, *The Ambivalent Alliance: Konrad Adenauer, the CDU/CSU, and the West, 1949-1966* (New York, 2003).

21. Ulrich Herbert, ed., *Wandlungsprozesse in Westdeutschland: Belastung, Integration, Liberalisierung, 1945-1980* (Göttingen, 2002); and Arndt Bauerkämper, Konrad H. Jarausch and Markus Payk, eds., *"Demokratiewunder?" Transatlantische Mittler und kulturelle Öffnung Westdeutschlands, 1945-1970* (Göttingen, 2005).

22. Peter Reichel, *Vergangenheitsbewältigung in Deutschland: Die Auseinandersetzung mit dem Nationalsozialismus in Politik und Justiz* (Munich, 2007), 2nd. rev. ed; Philipp Gassert and Alan E. Steinweis, eds., *Coping with the Nazi Past: West German Debates on Nazism and Generational Conflict, 1955-1975* (New York, 2006); and Annette Weinke, *Die Verfolgung von NS-Tätern im geteilten Deutschland: Vergangenheitsbewältigung 1949-1969: oder eine deutsch-deutsche Beziehungsgeschichte im kalten Krieg* (Paderborn, 2002).

23. Ulrich Herbert, *Geschichte der Ausländerpolitik in Deutschland: Saisonarbeiter, Zwangsarbeiter, Gastarbeiter, Flüchtlinge* (Munich, 2001); Rita Chin, *The Guestworker Question in Postwar Germany* (NewYork, 2007); and Jarausch (see note 17), 239 ff.

24. Klaus Schroeder, *Die veränderte Republik* (Stamsried, 2006); Richard Schröder, *Die wichtigsten Irrtümer über die deutsche Einheit* (Freiburg, 2007); and Konrad H. Jarausch, "Anfänge der Berliner Republik," in *Kleine deutsche Geschichte*, eds., Ulrich Herrmann (Stuttgart, 2006) 477-510.

25. Konrad H. Jarausch, "Zwischen ‚Reformstau' und ‚Sozialabbau'. Anmerkungen zur Globalisierungsdebatte in Deutschland, 1973-2003," in Jarausch (see note 13), 330-349. See also Gerhard A. Ritter, *Der Preis der Einheit: Die Wiedervereinigung und die Krise des Sozialstaats* (Munich, 2006).

26. Klaus Große Kracht, *Die zankende Zunft: Historische Kontroversen in Deutschland seit 1945* (Göttingen, 2005); and Schildt (see note 5), 253 ff. See also Peter H. Merkl, *The Federal Republic of Germany at Forty-Five* (New York, 1995).

27. Karl Dietrich Bracher, ed., *Geschichte der Bundesrepublik Deutschland* (Stuttgart, 1982-2006), 6 vols; Hans-Peter Schwarz, *Die Ära Adenauer: Gründerjahre der Republik, 1949-1957* (Stuttgart, 1981) and *Die Ära Adenauer: Epochenwechsel, 1957-1963* (Stuttgart 1982).

28. Eugen Kogon, *Die restaurative Republik: Zur Geschichte der Bundesrepublik Deutschland* (Berlin, 1996); Ralf Dahrendorf, *Society and Democracy in Germany* (Garden City, 1967); Fritz Fischer, *Germany's Aims in the First World War* (New York, 1967); Hans-Ulrich Wehler, *The German Empire, 1871-1918* (Leamington Spa, 1985). See also Klessmann (see note 1), 11 ff.

29. Heinrich August Winkler, *Germany: The Long Road West* (New York, 2006), 2 vols; Axel Schildt, *Ankunft im Westen: Ein Essay zur Erfolgsgeschichte der Bundesrepublik* (Frankfurt, 1999); and Anselm Doering-Manteuffel, *Wie westlich sind die Deutschen? Amerikanisierung und Westernisierung im 20. Jahrhundert* (Göttingen, 1999). See also Eckart Conze, Die Suche nach Sicherheit: Eine Geschichte der Bundesrepublik Deutschland von 1949 bis in die Gegenwart (Munich, 2009).

30. Dan Diner, "Vorwort des Herausgebers," in Dan Diner, ed., *Zivilisationsbruch: Denken nach Auschwitz* (Frankfurt 1988), 7-13; Jarausch (see note 17); and Edgar Wolfrum, *Die geglückte Demokratie: Geschichte der Bundesrepublik Deutschland von ihren Anfängen bis zur Gegenwart* (Stuttgart, 2006).

31. Konrad H. Jarausch, "'Die Teile als Ganzes erkennen...' Zur Integration der beiden deutschen Nachkriegsgeschichten," *Zeithistorische Forschungen* 1 (2004), 11 ff. See also Christoph Klessmann and Peter Lautzas, eds., *Teilung und Integration: Die doppelte deutsche Nachkriegsgeschichte als wissenschaftliches und didaktisches Phänomen* (Göttingen, 2006).

32. Konrad H. Jarausch and Thomas Lindenberger, eds., *Conflicted Memories: Europeanizing Contemporary Histories* (New York, 2007), 1-20. See also John R. Gillingham, *European Integration 1950-2003: Superstate or New Market Economy?* (Cambridge, 2003).

33. Jürgen Osterhammel, *Die Verwandlung der Welt: Eine Geschichte des 19. Jahrhunderts* (Munich, 2009); and Hanna Schissler, "Navigating a Globalized World: Thoughts on Textbook Analysis, Teaching, and Learning," *Contexts* 1 (2009), 203-226. See also the debates about transnational history on H-German and HSK.

34. Hans-Günter Hockerts, ed., *Koordinaten deutscher Geschichte in der Epoche des Ost-West-Konflikts* (Munich, 2004); Anselm Doering-Manteuffel and Lutz Raphael, *Nach dem Boom: Perspektiven auf die Zeitgeschichte seit 1970* (Göttingen 2008); and Jarausch (see note 13), 10ff.

35. Peter Graf Kielmansegg, *Nach der Katastrophe: Eine Geschichte des geteilten Deutschlands* (Berlin, 2000), 10; Tonly Judt, *Postwar: A History of Europe Since 1945* (New York, 2005); and Jarausch (see note 17), 269 ff.

36. See the series "60 Jahre Bundesrepublik Deutschland" in the *Spiegel*, 9 February to 23 March 2009 with articles by Klaus Wiegrefe and others.

37. James Dobbins, Seth G. Jones, Keith Crane, and Beth Cole DeGrasse, *The Beginners Guide to Nation-Building* (Santa Monica, 2007), 21 ff. See also Reinhard Bendix, *Nation-Building and Citizenship: Studies of our Changing Social Order* (New Brunswick, 1996); Norman Naimark, *The Russians in Germany: A History of the Soviet Zone of Occupation, 1945-1949* (Cambridge, 1995).

38. American memoirs and accounts of the occupation tend to stress the U.S. role, while German recollections and scholarship emphasize their own contribution. See also Jarausch (see note 17), 269 ff.; and Alfred Stepan, "Paths Towards Redemocratization," in *Comparative Politics*, eds., Roger Macridis and Bernard Brown (Belmont, 1990), 143-153.

39. Especially Korean scholars have been interested in studying the reasons for German unification.

40. Helga Grebing, *Der „deutsche Sonderweg" in Europa 1806-1945: Eine Kritik* (Stuttgart, 1986); and Peter Merkl, ed., *The Federal Republic at Fifty: The End of a Century of Turmoil* (New York, 1999). See also Peter Steinbrück, "Warum diese Krise eine Zäsur ist," *Tagesspiegel*, 26 April 2009.

Chapter 2

"*A*LS WÄR'S EIN STÜCK VON UNS ..."
GERMAN POLITICS AND SOCIETY TRAVERSES
TWENTY YEARS OF UNITED GERMANY

• • • • • • • • • • • • • • •

Charles S. Maier

I.

Twenty years is not an insignificant time in remembered history–much
can change in two decades. Twenty years after the revolution of 1918
came Kristallnacht and twenty years after the signature of the Versailles
Treaty witnessed the preparations for the German attack on Poland that
launched World War II in Europe. Twenty years ago at the end of 1989,
my editor at Princeton University Press asked me if I might write a quick
book on what was happening in East and West Germany, and that book
(hardly quick) is already a dozen years old. For those of us who spent last
fall at one commemorative event or another we have been compelled to
think about that passage of time. The question I found pressing was not
"*was bleibt?*", but rather "*was bleibt zu sagen?*" What is left to say? After all
the discussions of Germany and its unification, its continuities and its
transformations, it seemed worthwhile to ask how "we"–observers
of contemporary Germany represented through our journal–had dealt
with these two decades. What preoccupations did we have and how have
they changed?

   This is a story about Germany-watching, not Germany. Some of us
were already academically in mid-career when the German Democratic
Republic (GDR) collapsed; others would begin their professional observation only during this interval. At the age of eighty, Fritz Stern could write
a memoir based on five Germanies he had known, whereas most of us

have been a younger crew and have had one–the Berlin Republic–or three–including the GDR and the "two" Federal Republics (FRG). What Germany represents has changed–and our scholarly and perhaps personal lives along with it. I have chosen as my title a paraphrase of the pun that playwright Carl Zuckmayer used for his memoir– *"Als wär's ein Stück von mir"*–lifted in turn from the last line of Franz Uhland's military lament, "Ich hatte einen Kamerad."

It is appropriate on two counts. The comrades no longer run East Germany; and *German Politics and Society* was a piece of our intellectual life, certainly for Andy Markovits, and owing much to Guido Goldman and Abby Collins in its early years at Harvard University, then, following Markovits, at the University of California, Santa Cruz and the University of California, Berkeley. After founding editor Markovits stepped down in 2003, the journal moved to the BMW Center for German and European Studies at Georgetown University under the editorship of Jeffrey Anderson.[1] It should be noted that the Harvard's Center for European Studies, along with Georgetown and Berkeley, were benefiting from Chancellor Helmut Kohl's initiative of the late 1980s to establish "Centers of Excellence" for German and European studies, and subsequently at the University of Wisconsin-Madison, the University of Minnesota–Twin Cities, Brandeis University, York University, and the Université de Montréal. Had this major commitment not been resolved before unification dominated the German government's agenda, it might well have never been funded. Most of the ongoing financial support went to train graduate students, but the journal, too, was a beneficiary; and helped, I believe on reviewing its record, to repay the expectations of that grant.

What follows is hardly scientific. It is not scholarship, but not just memory either. I have surveyed most of the almost eighty issues of *German Politics and Society* since 1989, or least their contents, extracted some essays that seemed symptomatic and have used them as the occasion for a highly subjective reflection. The underlying sensation relates not to the object of study but the observer–the confrontation with vanished time, expressed as the perhaps universally posed autobiographical question: Where have the years gone? The elision of time is an unremarkable experience, and yet it can take one's breath away. Has our journal conspired in that elision, that blurring? Or does it let us resist the smooth passage of time and mark every turn of event or cultural transition, such that we might feel we had experienced the years as if in a harshly fought retreat (or advance), contesting every interval like some trench to be defended?

As a group we have to face the fact that we nurture ambivalent interests for Germany. As commentators and teachers who often have to represent the German scene to a wider public, we are grateful for a country that is civic-minded, has a generous welfare state, seems to be a model democracy and (at least when the United States is itself acting rationally) a good ally. Nonetheless, most of us, certainly the historians, literary and cultural critics, also have a stake in its being slightly off-center–heir to a problematic politics, a picturesque cultural scene, a lingeringly imperfect unification, a sense of historical memory that is either too contrite or, conversely, too self-pitying. In short, where would be without some sort of *Sonderweg*? And, of course, exposing whatever uniqueness or whiff of deviance might exist was in the corporate interest of *GP&S*. Certainly no country is quite like any other, but our journal has been implicitly predicated, perhaps, on the expectation that Germany was to be a little more not like the others than the others from each other. Our job was to explain why that was so, or why it really was no longer so.

That's been a hard stance to maintain, however. Even before the events of 1989, we were faced with a country long since wealthy and equipped with a forty-year old political system that managed to filter out the impulses toward prejudice or parochialism we spent so much time dissecting. Occasionally we could take alarm at an ugly rightist resurgence, usually confined though to one regional setting or another.[2] Analysis of street demonstrations and police crack-downs generally represented the liberal academic call to ameliorate underlying grievances: "violence on a large scale will continue as long as an unresponsive, overly statist government does not deal with root causes–widespread unemployment among youth, poor housing, callousness of the prosperous two-thirds of the population toward the one-third less well off, ecological disasters, and the arms race."[3] And we could become moved by the memory wars, or perhaps better said, the amnesia struggle. We explored that moral and sometimes moralistic earnestness that could inform foreign policy or environmental concerns.

The end of the GDR and German unification brought the issues of historical responsibility that the Communist dictatorship raised to new salience. No longer did we as intellectuals just have to focus on the issues raised by the Nazi past, although that set of questions was never to disappear for long. What responsibilities must be assigned with respect to the SED state that disappeared before our surprised eyes? Before 1989, the occasional presence of the other Germany in our pages had not forced a fundamental moral scrutiny of the role of elites East and West, since the existence of two

German states seemed so inscribed for the ages in the postwar European order. To put it differently, we were hypnotized by Helsinki's "basket one" (stabilizing borders) that we (along with virtually all other observers in the West) underestimated the subversive impact of basket three" (human rights). *GP&S* was not home to those who harped on the repressiveness of the East German regime. Rather, we explored all the signs of evolution and dissent. There was certainly no Charter 77 or Solidarność in the GDR, but Christa Wolf could publish *A Model Childhood*. I cite her because her changing reputation signaled in our pages became symptomatic of the cultural climate of newly united Germany.

At the time of the 1989-1990 *Wende*–when in fact the term *Wende* still referred to the Christian Democratic-Liberal (CDU/CSU-FDP) replacement of the Social-Liberal coalition in 1982–our journal was six years old, published three times yearly out of the Minda de Gunzburg Center for European Studies. The Center in the months after November 1989 fizzed with the effervescence from the changes underway in Central Europe, as participants from the GDR or Czechoslovakia (still a country) arrived every few weeks to report on this most fantastic of transformations. John Connelly, now professor at Berkeley, then a Harvard graduate student, reported on the demonstrations and confrontations he had observed in early October in Plauen, where the trains filled with GDR citizens who had fled to the West German embassy in Prague passed through on their way to the West. By the time his article appeared as unification loomed, Connelly could already note the changed mood in Plauen as massive unemployment threatened and nostalgia, not for the old regime, but for the exhilaration of the autumn moment, was already encroaching.[4]

The same issue featured a long essay by Peter Schneider, based on a piece in *Die Zeit*, which chastised the Writers Union of the expiring GDR for their unwillingness to undergo needed self-criticism. Could Schneider have anticipated that within a couple of years Christa Wolf, whom he mentioned with admiration as an exception, would come under harsh attack by a newly fashionable *Frankfurter Allgemeine Zeitung* cohort around Frank Schirmacher, and such writers as Ulrich Greiner and the playwright Botho Strauss–similar in their zeal to instrumentalize the critique of a now defunct GDR for a neo-con-like discrediting of the social democratic Left? *GP&S* 27 reported on a 1991 Harvard conference covering politics and intellectuals in a special issue in the fall of 1992: "Getting over the Wall: Recent Reflections on German Art and Politics since the Third Reich." Did Judith Ryan fully perceive the elitist political implications of Strauss's aesthetic stance she refereed as postmodernism? Did our editors understand the implications and political valence of Greiner's supposedly neutral reporting on the *Literaturstreit* of 1990?[5] Or was it just too difficult to disentangle a social democratic variant of cultural politics in the old FRG of the 1980s and the new FRG after 1990 from the political liability of having tolerated and perhaps reinforced the GDR for perhaps a decade too long? As Greiner said, West Germany, at least the West Germany that had accepted Ostpolitik, had also ended (an observation this author made at a conference on the fortieth anniversary of the Basic Law in October 1989– but without the sharpening of knives that Greiner's essay portended). Nonetheless, the implications were becoming clear to the American *Germanisten* more sympathetic to GDR authors.

Just two issues after the one in which Ryan and Greiner appeared, Marc Silberman of the University of Wisconsin-Madison published his critique of the triumphalism of the West German intelligentsia.[6] Suitably hedged with claims of impartiality and the invocation of a postmodern sensibility, the piece nonetheless implied that there had been a viable tradition of subtle resistance among the East German literary establishment who had been coerced into silence by the triumphalism of unification. Looking back on the debate, the present historian recalls a certain distaste for the *mauvaise foi* on both sides: whether the politically correct apologetics on the part of the American academic Left; or the total lack of charity for the difficulties East German writers had faced on the part of a fashionable "smart set" in the West.

The editors' preface–and I was an editor–recognized that the euphoria of unification and Maastricht was giving way to "gloom and doom." But perhaps we were not initially prepared to recognize the powerful culture of reproach that was coming to prevail in both East and West, although the themes emerged in the following Autumn 1993 issue edited by John Torpey and A. James McAdams. And for better or worse, we were not prepared to act as critics of the debate, which as Americans we might, in fact, have been well positioned to do. Instead–let's face it–it was all too tempting to cast it into older categories of German politics that we often were tempted to conclude still lurked in the German psyche. Thus, John Ely in the summer of 1995 denounced a resurgent:

> intellectual spectrum of rightist thinking–the renaissance, one might say, of a "conservative revolution" at precisely the time when the boundaries between conservative views clearly within a liberal-democratic consensus and those outside are tendentially dissolving … One aspect of the new Right is the increasing dissolution of this dualistic distinction between liberal-democratic and antidemocratic conservatism, between "black" and "brown" politics.[7]

Of course, this seems alarmist, but looking back at the essays of the 1990s, we can discern in the pages of *German Politics and Society*, a trend that may have characterized political culture more broadly. The Wall had fallen, the twin towers still stood; political violence in the West was a bad memory from the 1970s or confined to the intractable peripheries of Europe. After so much hard work in winning the Cold War, concluding the Maastricht Treaty, and re-energizing capitalism; faced, too, with the troubling massacres in the Balkans and the unspeakable violence of Rwanda that neither Europeans nor Americans really wanted to deal with, wouldn't it be better if intellectuals took a brief vacation from historical responsibility, a happy holiday at the end of the century? Couldn't they (*hypocrites lecteurs, nos semblables, nos frères*) use the hiatus to revisit ideas that once seemed venomous, try them on like old clothes from the back of the closet? Alternatively, if Carl Schmitt was too much to swallow, mightn't we happily anticipate the advent of international civil society, doctors without frontiers, international criminal jurisdiction, and transitional justice? Germany had become a nation: the *FAZ* wanted it to become a state. Most Germans in fact weren't ready, and neither was *GP&S*.

II.

In the succeeding years some of these themes have continued, others have subsided, new ones have emerged. The reader who dips into the journal throughout the period encounters a number of recurrent preoccupations: first, that of cultural politics, including coverage of cinema and literature– a concern shared by our journal with the *New German Critique*, although *GP&S* brought a less cohesive, post-Frankfurt-school stance; second, V*ergangenheitsbewältigung* (coming-to-terms with the past) and memory wars; third, the transformation of German ideas of citizenship under the impact of immigration; fourth, politics, foreign and domestic (these last themes also marking the British journal, *German Politics*); finally, political economy–the future of Germany's industrial vocation and the role of labor and entrepreneurs. Each of these topical areas probably had its own constituency of readers and contributors although they all ran into each other. In what follows, however, I want to focus on the continuing reassessments that seem to have followed from the legacy of 1989.

It did not take unification to signal concerns about the Federal Republic's power (or the reluctance to wield power). Still, unification raised the stakes. Was united Germany likely to become a new European hegemon, or alternatively was it continually going to punch below its economic weight and large population? "Should Europe fear the Germans?" asked Andrei Markovits and Simon Reich in 1991 in a question that was more ominous than the answer, which argued that the united country had the responsibility to exercise more leadership.[8] Rather, wrote a friendly critic with respect to the Yuogslav crisis two years later, Germany was "not yet capable of formulating a European policy that matches ends and means."[9] Another two years on, Beverly Crawford's analysis of the disputed German decision to recognize the secession of Slovenia and Croatia from the Yugoslav federation came to a similar conclusion. Unilateral though it was, the policy reflected the upshot of German domestic political pressures on Chancellor Kohl and Foreign Minister Hans-Dietrich Genscher, and not a reversion to a nationalist agenda.[10] Indeed the issue was debated among American observers of Germany. I recall that my own misgivings of German recognition of the two states were contested sharply by Stanley Hoffmann, who, along with many others, felt that the federation was no more than a cover for Serbian ambitions. The paradoxical upshot of the protracted Yugoslav conflict (which became Bosnia's anguish, not Croatia's) was that in order to reintegrate its policy in a western framework, Germany was compelled to accept an initially unwelcome armed intervention outside its borders. Three articles in the summer of 1996 caught this transformation, so to speak, on the wing and endeavored to account for its halting evolution. Mary M. McKenzie appealed to the concept of "normality" in taking on an international military role (even while Kohl tried to make sure that the East European countries would remain welcomed in the projects of alliance and union). Jeffrey Lantis traced the acceptance of military deployments to shifts in domestic politics that pushed the CDU-FDP government toward greater activity (sanctioned also by the Constitutional Court decision of 1994 that found no legal impediment to intervention abroad and prodded, too, by Joschka Fischer's public rebalancing of German national obligations). Thomas Banchoff emphasized the continuing role of historical memory as a constraint, although one that demanded careful public rationalizing and did not impose paralysis.[11] The upshot, as noted six months later, was that for all the hesitation, by the end of 1996, Germany had decided to contribute to the Eurocorps and was prepared for intervention abroad, without, though, being tempted by any hegemonic vocation: "reflexive multilateralism, not hegemonic unilateralism will still be the rule for the foreseeable future"–and "only haphazardly and inefficiently, by frustrating fits and starts."[12]

The upshot was that by the 1996-1997 issues, united Germany—as reflected in the pages of the journal—was emerging as a nation less constrained by old hesitations and doubts. Although foreign policy responsibilities, as *GP&S* suggested, would remain conditioned by history and debated in its light, German policy makers no longer had to be constrained by formulaic lessons. So too, the debates over the historical relationship with the former GDR could move beyond pinning responsibilities on those who collaborated and those who fled; that is, it could leave behind the culture of reproach from the early 1990s. In the same issue of summer 1996 that featured, Mckenzie, Landtis, and Banchoff, Caroline Molina skillfully analyzed Wolf Biermann's career between East and West, by focusing on his poem, "Prussian Icarus," and could present him as neither martyr nor hero, while Renate Holub explained how Jürgen Habermas was updating his insistence on normative politics to argue for public intellectuals' engagement in the life of the Berlin Republic

The stimulating issue of Summer 1997, "One Nation—Which Past? Historiography and German Identities in the 1990s," took up for intellectuals and political culture the themes that had been pointed out in the debates on foreign policy. How did a country willing finally to say "*nie wieder Auschwitz*" rather than "*nie wieder Krieg*" (and commit forces to peace-keeping, or peace-imposing missions), manage to steer by the Habermasian course of postnationality and *Verfassungpatriotismus* (constitutional patriotism)? In effect, this was a re-run of the *Historikerstreit* (Historians' Dispute), but growing out of more subtle issue. No one in that controversy from a decade earlier had really wanted to rehabilitate the Third Reich into a constitutive part of the Bonn Republic. But, was the East German legacy to be similarly excised. "The East German past," Konrad Jarausch pointed out, "has become such a hotly contested terrain because of its implications for the identity of a united Germany." If it was simply totalitarian, "its legacy had best be obliterated and the FRG does not need to change." If it had a mix of bad and good elements, what was its contribution to be in reconstituting the FRG,[13] but now with a positive slant—not fear of reversion to bad old Germany, rather confusion about what sort of national structure in which to integrate the GDR.

III.

One might be forgiven for thinking that with respect to issues of German identity and intellectuals Heraclitus had it wrong: one plunged into the

---

same river over and over again. But, in fact, the identity issue was changing–certainly for the public and for intellectuals as well. Most notably, it was being inflected less as a debate over history than one over culture. As a participant-anthropologist who appreciated the Kreuzberg *Szene,* John Borneman wrote a provocative and humorous essay for the new millennium: "*Multikulti* or *Schweinerei* in the Year 2000." He included gender as well as ethnic issues, and concluded that:

> ... the national debate about German Kultur is now always a debate about Multikulti, since German monoculture occupies a shrinking part of the experiential landscape of Germany. German Kultur's major historical force is as utopia of dystopia ... Self-deception with respect to this empirical reality is perhaps the real joke, a self-inflicted Schweinerei.[14]

Further shifting sites for investigating the new Germany's culture was Patricia Anne Simpson's 2005 report on music groups that expressed wildly opposed views on inclusivity in the years after unification. Was German HipHop assisting "self-empowerment for people of color," or would rap, as promoted by major labels "effectively open the musical culture to recoding from the Right"? Simpson found that at least the German coding of masculinity was less misogynistic and homophobic than the American models. "Much German popular music questions the hegemony of military masculinity in the political sphere, but also the violent, aggressive practices of men in the street, on the dance floor, and in bed." As of 2005, however, one needed to ask whether Simpson's female singers were targeting the macho males looking for hook-ups in Berlin or those patrolling Baghdad.[15]

Culture is obviously a capacious, probably too capacious category. Perhaps it should be divided into Simpson and Borneman's Saturday night culture and Sunday civic culture. Sunday's was certainly less fun. In the same issue as Borneman, David P. Conradt offered social-survey take on the political culture that had crystallized in united Germany since 1990. In his major report, the alternative culture to be evaluated arose not in the gay scene or among Turks but in the persistence or non-persistence of former GDR values. Specifically, were citizens in the new Länder as committed to democracy as those in the West? Not surprisingly, living in a region that persistently seemed to lag economically tempered a commitment to abstract democracy, although the younger age cohorts were closer to West German levels of acceptance. Convergence into a single culture was occurring selectively.[16] A. James McAdams came to a similarly pessimistic conclusion from the view point of the controversy over Stasi files. The East German past had been thoroughly scrutinized, whereas West Germany's democratic leadership, as evidenced by the campaign financing scandals, had behaved evasively but with little sanction. Since this disillusioned observation was not a function of economic disparity, McAdams speculated, it was likely to persist, perhaps even across the generations.[17]

Yet, if such attitudes persisted, that did not mean the party alignments would remain static. The election of 1998 might be interpreted as one of democratic confirmation, but it could also be seen as a rejection of a chancellor who had stayed too long. In any case, the Gerhard Schröder governments ended in a disillusion that threatened to erode the traditional pattern of party change based on a bellwether center. Thus, David Conradt labeled his report on the 2005 national elections, "The Tipping Point," and suggested it might usher in a "deconsolidation" of the German party system. The report was prescient and valuably linked evolving electoral preferences to changing bases in society, including the decline of the SPD's core working-class constituency. He asked:

> Can the current [black-red] coalition save the old party system, or will it spark further de-consolidation and give the Federal Republic a multi-party system based on four or five parties of roughly equal strength? Is this the end of reform gridlock (*Reformstau*), or the continuation of the "catastrophic equilibrium"...?[18]

Still, the answer to his questions–"catastrophic equilibrium"–was not Conradt's own term, and indeed there were strong indications, through the economic shocks after 2008, that Germany had moved beyond gridlock. Indeed, the Schröder governments along with the successive Angela Merkel administration had compelled significant "reform." Reform might be reduced to the almost universal neoliberal sense of the capacity to reduce work forces and cap spending on welfare, an effort symbolized by the passage of Hartz IV. This was the initiative that could be counted on to arouse rallies for die Linke. But, there were other dimensions as well. Angelika von Wahl claimed that the Merkel government was making significant improvements to childcare policies that would allow women greater opportunity to combine work and family roles. Reform, too, was coming to the educational system, as Helga Welsh documented in her report of 2009.[19] Of course, even after the election of 2009 we don't know the answer to Conradt's question although the party system inched closer to the 1871-1930 pattern of multiple parties. As of this writing we have yet to see *GP&S*'s analysis of this last result, although the summer 2009 issue previewing the election anticipated the *Misere* of the SPD.[20] My own sense is that two implicit camps of voters confronted each other in German politics after a decade of political frustrations. There was a large group–a coalition for continuity–largely composed of older voters, seeking to vote for reliability, whether expressed by the diminishing SPD or by the CDU/CSU. In opposition was another group, a latent coalition for change, perhaps younger (although in eastern Germany sometimes elderly PDS voters) willing to wager on instability by voting for one of the three smaller parties–the coalition for change–of which the FDP profited most. The problem for the SPD was that there was "space" for only one of the Volksparteien to represent the coalition for continuity.

IV.

What conclusions can one draw from twenty years of reading our journal? What are the conclusions about Germany and what conclusions about the German watchers who filled its pages? It was natural enough that the writers had sought out and presented the most jagged and edgy aspects of culture and politics. How else to justify their vocation? We were invested in following an interesting country. Certainly, there was a great deal that promised interest: the momentous events of unification, the contradictory efforts at seeking to integrate and to master the former GDR, the claims of historical memory–which never were allowed to disappear. Eric Langenbacher and Frederike Eigler, insisted that they were still vital in the special issue on memory issues of Autumn 2005. They denied memory fatigue and cited the continuing controversies over German interpretations of their past as evidence of "a sustained and unabated memory boom." "Indeed 2005, like 1995, was a 'super' memory year."[21] Langenbacher's own essay argued for the legitimacy of the then-proposed center to remember the Germans expelled from Central Europe after 1945 and for a broad memory regime. Here, perhaps, was a sign of the evolution that the events of 1989 had helped to open up, because it is doubtful that the journal could have accepted such a plea so easily in the 1980s.

This has been a subjective journey. Other readers would emphasize different themes and essays. But, I am struck by what I read, by several aspects: first, by the vibrancy and size of the German-watching community in the United States. Some remained attracted by the laboratory of social challenges, represented above all, perhaps, by the issues of cultural identity and assimilation or non-assimilation of immigrants. Perhaps one could compare Germany and the United States. A faithful group sustained an interest in government and party politics. Whether the memory boom was flagging in Germany–or, perhaps more accurately, increasingly a function of interest-group contestation–could be debated. In any case, some of the most profound commentators, for instance Andreas Huyssen or Anson Rabinbach, wrote in other forums. For all the interest that our community had in exposing what was unique, problematic, or conversely highly successful in Germany, the contributions to *German Politics and Society*, I believe, revealed a society that had mellowed over two decades. The euphoria of 1989 had in some areas, such as economic integration, changed into disappointments. Germany had gone through a phase of deep recrimination; it had also experienced a period of real skinhead violence. It had pleaded its own brutal past to avoid the harsher international commitments of the early 1990s. But, that had changed. The country seemed more at ease with its own divisions. There was institutional stickiness–*eppure si muove*! In the fall of 2009, the United States gave signs of being a country far more bitterly divided than Germany, far more vulnerable to extreme political rhetoric and factional hostility, and perhaps more deeply caught in its own gridlock. And this despite the fact that a charismatic presidential candidate had captured the White House and generated tremendous enthusiasm–ironically, not least in Germany!

For all the essays, moreover, the German subject had become less unique. It had been a divided country–and the world spirit had seemed to descend on Germany on 9 November 1989. Yet, since then the issues, for instance, surrounding Islamic societies or the rise of China as an economic giant had reproportioned Europe. *German Politics and Society* produced a valuable series of reports in a special issue (vol. 24, 4) at the end of 2006: "Social Integration in the New Berlin," edited by Hilary Silver. But, the problems exposed and the communities observed were not particularly German–they were those of disadvantaged diasporas throughout the West, and exploded far more violently in the Paris banlieux two years later. On the other side of the social spectrum, more educated Germans spoke English easily–perhaps a class of American cultural mediators who were at home in its complex language appeared less necessary. Shortly after unification in Berlin, spooky large steel gray posters appeared throughout the city, each etched with a shadowy knife and the inscription *"Deutschland wird deutscher."* In fact, Germany had become less German.

This should be good news. But, it could also be unsettling. At every point in the postwar decades– 1949, 1968-1969, 1989, 2009–to take just some of the "nines," the community of Germanists has not necessarily feared the worst, but has traditionally remained alert to the country's vulnerability. This was part of our vocation. In the 1950s, would Germany revert to authoritarianism? Didn't antisemitism remain deeply rooted?

Didn't Adenauer harbor Nazis? Wouldn't the old FRG slip into neutralism and reinstate Rapallo? In the 1960s, weren't its professors authoritarian, its students intolerant? Wasn't Egon Bahr going to sell out the West? Wasn't the NPD on the threshold of power? In the 1970s and 1980s, wasn't Helmut Schmidt far too arrogant? Wouldn't the state destroy civil liberties in cracking down on terrorists? Wasn't the German economy too oriented toward industrial production to flourish in an age of services and software? Would it ever be able to integrate immigrants? Why was it so stingy in providing daycare? Wasn't its turn toward eroticism compulsive and devoid of joy? Weren't its museums and memorials insufficiently self-critical? Wasn't Fassbinder too nihilistic? Weren't half its historians apologists for the Third Reich? Weren't the other half its historians obsessed with permanent authoritarianism? And in the years since 1989, wouldn't Germany seek to claim a hegemonic role in post-1989 Eastern Europe? Wouldn't its move back to Berlin recreate Wilhelmian arrogance? Wasn't its federalism a recipe for paralysis? Wasn't it self-righteous and stingy about compensating former forced laborers? Wasn't it smarmy and self-righteous about intervention in the Balkans? Weren't the Ossis hopelessly self-pitying? Weren't the decrepit new Bundesländer a breeding ground for skinheads? Weren't the Wessis arrogant colonizers? Wasn't the German higher education system hopelessly dysfunctional? Weren't three opera houses in Berlin hopelessly self-indulgent? Wasn't Anselm Kiefer creepy and dangerous? Wasn't Gerhard Richter slick and opportunist?

Maybe in our worries we have been more German than the Germans. If we ask the question, *was bleibt?* we really need to ask it about united Germany not the former GDR. All of Germany has changed under our gaze, though not because of it. Of course much remains–foods, and art, evocative landscapes, soccer teams, great music and opera, the funky S-Bahn, countless places of personal memory. Much has changed. The purpose of our journal was not to capture a grand historical perspective but to track change underway. Such a task has to be undertaken in fragments, attaining fragmentary perspectives, applying fragments of expertise. In general I think the fragmentary reports we produced were discerning. Some were exaggerated, some over-emotional, some alarmist, but they provided orientation. When French statesmen or writers used to discuss their relationship with France they often personified her as a lover. I don't think our community would ever find that metaphor apt. When Heinrich Heine wrote about revisiting his home in Hamburg, he reckoned with his ageing Jewish mother. I think if we wanted a metaphorical personification, we might think of long-term, but contingent railroad companions. We shared a train compartment, some of us a first-class compartment, others a second-class. The train line, we knew had had a catastrophic accident long before we boarded, when drivers and passengers together had decided to drive really recklessly. But our trip was far calmer although we enjoyed at least one exhilarating passage in 1989. Different travelers got on, and indeed a whole family who hadn't been allowed to travel joined us warily at that time twenty years ago. We were curious about where we were going, but just as intrigued by the scenery along the way. It's gotten more familiar; we know what the passengers will talk about and the papers they'll read, and the sandwiches or döner kebab they'll open, but it's been an interesting ride and happily enough a surprisingly unpredictable one.

Notes

1. The journal is funded by a consortium of universities. In addition to Georgetown's BMW Center, current donors include the Canadian Centre for German and European Studies, Université de Montréal and York University; the Institute of European Studies, University of California, Berkeley; Center for German and European Studies, University of Wisconsin-Madison and University of Minnesota-Twin Cities; Joint Initiative in German and European Studies, University of Toronto; Minda de Gunzburg Center for European Studies, Harvard University; Center for German and European Studies, Brandeis University. The journal also benefitted from a five-year grant from the Kellen Foundation.
2. John Ely, "Republicans: Neo-Nazis or the Black-Brown Hazelnut? Recent Successes of the Radical Right in West Germany," *German Politics and Society* 18 (1989): 1-17.
3. Gerard Braunthal, "Political Demonstrations and Civil Liberties in West Germany," *German Politics and Society* 19 (1990): 41-54, here 53.
4. John Connelly, "Moment of Revolution: Plauen (Vogtland), October 7, 1989," *German Politics and Society* 20 (1990): 71-89. Connelly recently has revisited these events in an essay, "The Price of Freedom," *Commonweal,* 20 November 2009. The same 1990 issue featured a long essay by Peter Schneider, based on a piece in *Die Zeit,* which chastised the writers union of the expiring GDR for their ambivalence and unwillingness to undergo needed self-criticism. "Man kann ein Erdbeben auch verpassen," 1-21.
5. Judith Ryan, "Postmodernism as *Vergangenheitsbewältigung,*" and Ulrich Reiner, "*Die Mauer im Kopf.* Toward an Understanding of the 1990 German Literary Dispute," *German Politics and Society* 27 (1992): 12-24, and 61-68. In the spring of 1993, *German Politics and Society* would move to the University of California at Santa Cruz with Andrei Markovits as its primary and long-serving editor, and began identifying issues by annual volume and issue numbers.
6. Marc Silberman, "Speaking with Silence: The GDR Author in the New Germany," *German Politics and Society* 29 (1993): 87-103.
7. John Ely, "The *Frankfurter Allgemeine Zeitung* and Contemporary National-Conservatism," *German Politics and Society* 13, no. 2 (1995), 81-121, here 82. Although Ely was alarmist about encroaching fascist tendencies, he valuably documented the new-old national arguments that were tempting the intellectuals. He connected it to the debates on immigration at a time of rising alarm over asylum seekers. Just as important, though, was a willingness on the part of the *FAZ* editorial leadership to push the envelope, so to speak, ever since Joachim Fest's opened the paper's pages to Ernst Nolte's argumenta-

tion at the time of the *Historikerstreit.* Having discussed this policy with Fest, a courteous and historically engaged commentator, my sense was that he believed he was allowing a genuine debate. It says something about the Berlin Republic that Germany's two essential daily papers remain based in Frankfurt/Main and Munich, and the assorted print runners-up in Hamburg.

8. Andrei Markovits and Simon Reich, "Should Europe Fear the Germans?" *German Politics and Society* 23 (1991): 1-20; see also their subsequent book: *The German Predicament: Memory and Power in the New Europe* (Ithaca, 1997). Christa von Wijnbergen and Aaron Wildavsky argued, however, that such preoccupations had been both a major reason for the progress of European union and a way of justifying those advances: "A Rationale or a Reason? Institutional Consequences of Fear of German Power in Europe," *German Politics and Society* 29, (1993): 1-18.

9. See also Marten H.A. van Heuven, "Testing the New Germany: The Case of Yugoslavia," *German Politics and Society* 29 (1993): 52-63, here 52.

10. Beverly Crawford, "German Foreign Policy and European Political Cooperation: The Diplomatic Recognition of Croatia in 1991," *German Politics and Society* 13, no. 2 (1995): 1-34.

11. Mary M. McKenzie, "Competing Conceptions of Normality in the Post-Cold War Era: Germany, Europe, and Foreign Policy Change," *German Politics and Society* 14, no. 2 (1996): 1-18; Jeffrey S. Lantis, "Rising to the Challenge: German Security Policy in the Post-Cold War Era," *German Politics and Society* 14, no. 2, (1996): 19-35; Thomas Banchoff, "Historical Memory and German Foreign Policy: The Cases of Adenauer and Brandt," *German Politics and Society* 14, no. 2, (1996): 36-53

12. Michael E. Smith, "Sending the Bundeswehr to the Balkans: The Domestic Politics of Reflexive Multilateralism," *German Politics and Society* 14, no. 4 (1996): 49-67, here 65.

13. Konrad H. Jarausch, "The German Democratic Republic as History in United Germany: Reflections on Public Debate and Academic Controversy," *German Politics and Society* 15, no. 2 (1997): 33-48, here 43. The issue emerged from a Berkeley conference on German historiographies and identities and graduate students responded, very trenchantly, to the professors' major papers.

14. John Borneman, "*Multikulti* or *Schweinerei* in the Year 2000." *German Politics and Society* 20, no. 2 (2002): 93-114, here 111.

15. Patricia Anne Simpson, "'Manche Menschen werden Brüder:' Contemporary Music and new Fraternities," *German Politics and Society* 23, no. 2 (2005): 50-71, here 51-52, 60.

16. David P. Conradt, "Political Culture in Unified Germany: The First Ten Years," *German Politics and Society* 20, no. 2 (2002): 43-74.

17. A. James McAdams, "What Remains? The Political Culture of an Unlucky Birth," *German Politics and Society* 20, no 2 (2002): 26-42.

18. David P. Conradt, "The Tipping Point: The 2005 Election and the De-consolidation of the German Party System?" *German Politics and Society* 24, no. 1 (2006): 11-26, here 21. See also Kimmo Elo's critique of the parties, and particularly the SPD, for not being responsive to the fluid political and economic challenges of the last decades. He discerned therefore a growing possibility for a Left party and counseled the SPD to move toward the discontented voters the former communists represented. "The Left Party and the long-term Developments of the German Party System," *German Politics and Society* 26, no. 3 (2008): 25-49; but such a course certainly bore no fruit in the 2009 Hessian electoral catastrophe.

19. Angelika von Wahl, "From Family to Reconciliation Policy: How the Grand Coalition Reforms the German Welfare State," *German Politics and Society* 26, no. 3 (2008): 25-49; Helga A. Welsh, "Higher Education Reform in Germany: Advocacy and Discourse," *German Politics and Society* 27, no. 1 (2009): 1-23.

20. Christoph Egle, "No Escape from the long-term Crisis? The Social Democrats' Failure to Devise a Promising Political Strategy," *German Politics and Society* 27, no. 2 (2009): 9-27.

21. Eric Langenbacher and Frederike Eigler, "Introduction: Memory Boom or Memory Fatigue in 21st Century Germany?" *German Politics and Society* 23, no. 3 (2005): 1-15, here 3, 5. See also his own essay in the same issue, "*Moralpolitik* versus *Moralpolitik*: Recent Struggles over the Construction of Cultural Memory in Germany," *German Politics and Society* 23, no. 3 (2005): 106-134. See also Jenny Wüstenberg's review essay, "Berlin's Changing Memory Landscape: New Scholarship in German and English," *German Politics and Society* 24, no. 2 (2006): 82-88.

PART II.
CULTURE AND SOCIETY

Chapter 3

ℐHE LAST EAST GERMAN AND THE
MEMORY OF THE GERMAN DEMOCRATIC REPUBLIC

●●●●●●●●●●●●●●●

A. James McAdams

There's an old East German joke that goes like this: "Erich Honecker has been on a trip. He returns to East Berlin to find the city brightly illuminated, but the streets are empty, there's not a person in sight. In a panic, he drives around until he finally comes to the Berlin Wall where he discovers an enormous hole. There, on a handwritten note, he reads. 'Erich, you're the last to go. Please turn out the lights when you leave." Today, Honecker can no longer be the last East German to leave the territory of the German Democratic Republic (GDR). The general secretary of the Socialist Unity Party of Germany (SED) is no longer with us. Yet, others may still qualify to replace him. Twenty years after the fall of the Berlin Wall and the revolution of 1989, expressions of a certain east Germanness persist in the region. People convey their feelings in different ways: a wistfulness for the comforting niches of family and friends; a romantic attachment to the economic and political certainties of "real-existing socialism;" an outspoken frustration and resentment at the continuing burdens of national unification. Nonetheless, let us assume that these sentiments mellow with the passage of time, as they most likely will with each new generation. Who will be the last self-identifying East German? For that matter, will he or she have anything to say to us before leaving the region behind?

For two reasons, it is appropriate that we now begin thinking about this last East German. First, personal laments and nostalgia do not fully constitute an individual's identity. The longing for some part of the GDR past is real for most easterners, but this emotion is primarily a complaint about the consequences of unification, not a desire to turn back the clock.

Second, and just as important, the coming of the last East German raises profound questions about how future generations will interpret the fact that one part of Germany was ruled by a communist dictatorship for forty years. Is it possible that in another forty years, or even less time, no one will even care that the GDR existed? Indeed, will it matter to posterity that Germany was divided for much of its post World War II history?

To respond to these questions, we must begin by recognizing that one cannot speak about East Germans as a uniform bloc. Not long after the GDR's collapse, it quickly became clear that unification would mean different things to different people. In this chapter, I address this issue by distinguishing among three personality types: the ordinary citizen with little aspiration to attain political power or social notoriety; the enthusiast for certain aspects of the old regime with a vested interest in perpetuating its values; and the dissident activist with a long dedication to transforming that order. As the reader will see, I believe that the last East German will come from the ranks of this final type, the dissident. Once I have established this point, I will then seek to anticipate this individual's parting words. As I contend, our activist will have a lot to say about his or her contributions to the events of 1989. But even more significant, these words will call our attention to the ways in which a country, like modern Germany, can benefit from an underutilized legacy of defiance against dictatorship.

Three Types of East Germans

Let us begin with an ideal-typical person-on-the-street. In the years before 1989, this individual's defining quality, which he shared in common with all of his siblings, school friends, and fellow workers, was to be a realist. On the one hand, he did not have to watch West German television (although it was one of his regular pastimes) to know that Erich Honecker and his politburo colleagues would never live up to their promises of creating a world of socialist abundance and prosperity. He knew that he was destined to lead a life of hard work and low expectations. On the other hand, this East German recognized that there was nothing to be gained by openly voicing his dissatisfaction. Challenging his government's authority would have been foolhardy. Moreover, it would have been futile. Given that none of the SED's policies were likely to change in the foreseeable future, his safest bet was to make the most of what life had to offer, the city soccer club, a local pub, the market for Trabi parts, and above all, a carefree weekend at the family *Kleingarten.*

In drawing this characterization, I do not mean to suggest that our ordinary East German's feelings of attachment to his country were shallow or insincere. After all, it was inconceivable to him that he could choose any other life. But by the same token, when we consider how quickly the GDR fell apart after the opening of its borders, these feelings were unambiguously not deep enough. When tens of thousands of his compatriots poured into West Berlin in the first weeks after 9 November 1989, they were initially motivated by curiosity for the new and not yet opposition to the old. But, capitalism and the freedoms that went along with it quickly proved to be irresistible. Once the tangible benefits of life in West Germany were confirmed, there was no longer any point to preserving the GDR. Ironically, one of the SED's chief theorists, Otto Reinhold, had already acknowledged this fact in an interview with Radio DDR II on 19 August 1989. When asked why the Honecker government was not engaging in serious economic reforms like its Soviet counterparts, he emphasized that his country's sole reason for existence lay in its exclusive claim to represent a *socialist* alternative to West Germany. "What justification," Reinhold asked rhetorically, "would a capitalist GDR have next to a capitalist Federal Republic?" The answer, it became clear, was none at all.

This point is illustrated in a subtle way in the popular film, *Goodbye, Lenin!* (2003). On one level, the movie is about a mother and faithful Party member who has a heart attack and falls into a coma on the GDR's fortieth anniversary. Her family and friends are so worried about her fragile condition that when she wakes up just before German unification is to take place in 1990, they go to comical lengths to convince her that nothing has changed. On a deeper level, the story is really about her son, Alex, who along with everyone else around him, has lost no time in shedding his East German identity. While his mother sleeps, he clothes himself in western gear, exposes himself to the corrupting influences of Heavy Metal and degenerate art, and relaxes by smoking dope with his Russian girlfriend. Alex's only misfortune, it seems, is when he loses his job at a failed state-run television repair shop. Still, it is telling that this loss does not bother him at all. Indeed, what the film's director has him say as he leaves the building can hardly be coincidental: "I was the last one out. I turned off the lights."

What happens figuratively in *Goodbye, Lenin!* is taking place literally every day in the former GDR. East Germany is no longer a place to be; it is a place to leave. Between 1990 and 2008, the region's population shrank from 18.2 million inhabitants to 16.6 million. Demographers estimate that an additional 1 million departures will take place by 2020. This rapid rate of depopulation, combined with a persistent decline in birth rates, should not surprise anyone since there is no clear future in this part of Germany. Significantly greater numbers of eastern Germans are unemployed or underemployed than in the West. Making the situation worse, those who leave in search of jobs are the young and the skilled whose services are needed to turn the region's economy around. Some have even fewer reasons to stay because they were children or not yet even born when the GDR ceased to exist. In contrast, those who stay behind do so not because of affection but because they have no other choice. With the exception of the few who find work in growth areas, such as Leipzig and Dresden, many will only add to the region's problems rather than alleviating them. A steadily rising population of older and retired citizens will not only strain the region's social security system but also test the convictions of the gainfully employed who must pay the taxes to support it. Indeed, eastern Germany's economic prospects are regarded to be so uncertain that even immigrant workers steer clear of the area.[1]

If our ordinary, apolitical citizen is already in the process of leaving the region, psychologically but not yet physically, what about looking for signs of the last East German in the second group that I have mentioned above? Here, I refer to the individuals who have routinely cast their votes for the SED's successor party, the Party of Democratic Socialism (PDS) or, in the past few years, the amalgam of political groups known as The Left Party (Die Linke). In this case, let us say that our potential last East German was an idealistic young official in the Ministry of Culture who suddenly found herself out of work in 1990. Like many rising party members, she had never been enamored with all aspects of the Honecker government's policies, especially its disinclination to listen to new ideas. But, she still clung to the egalitarian and collectivist values that, she felt, had characterized her country in better times. Under these circumstances, it is hardly surprising that she would be attracted to the PDS. Thanks to the energetic leadership of people like Gregor Gysi and Lothar Bisky, here was a party that would guarantee her a job. At the same time, the PDS would be a defender of many of the social policies that she admired–full employment, inexpensive housing, and free health care. In the face of a seemingly constant assault by carpetbaggers and *besser Wessis*, she could hold onto the best of East Germany without having to put up with the old regime's bricks, mortar, and barbed wire.

The big question, though, is how long it will matter to this young woman that she identifies herself as an East German. In many ways, this issue has become a defining question for the PDS and Die Linke in the

2000s. When one considers the SED successor party's evolution, the source of its success has been its continuing ability to present itself as two types of parties. In its time, the PDS was simultaneously a protest party that represented East German interests and, in its new form as the cornerstone of Die Linke, a national party that attempted to speak for all Germans. Inevitably, these two identities will clash. By design or by default, I believe, the party's national aspirations will come out on top.

In its early years, the PDS was inconceivable as anything but an East German organization.[2] Precisely because of this limitation, however, it was the only party in the East that could effectively present itself as truly independent of western influence. This position virtually guaranteed its leaders the privilege of representing the case against unification. The party's good fortune was the key to its extraordinary showings at all levels of electoral competition. At times, the party's successes at the voting booth were tested by the intense, internecine battles among the hodgepodge of warring groups that made its existence possible. Still, by the late 1990s, the PDS had earned a reputation in the East of being dedicated to addressing the needs of its voter base and capable of working effectively with other parties.

Against this background, one might think that the party's transformation into Die Linke in the mid 2000s will bring a robust East German voice into national politics. In fact, the opposite is true. Almost by definition, the entire strategy of merging the PDS's distinctive political culture with the motley group of radical intellectuals, disaffected trade union activists, ex-Green environmentalists, and Fidelistas that comprise its western membership is destined to test the loyalties of its base. The results will be paradoxical. If Die Linke implodes due to its internal tensions, voters like our former SED official will lose faith in the efficacy of its leaders. Yet, ironically, if the party somehow succeeds in become a nationally competitive Volkspartei, it may inadvertently provoke these same supporters to look closely at the options presented by other all-German parties.[3]

For these reasons, I believe the last East German will come from the ranks of that small group of persons, the GDR's former dissidents and regime critics, who had the wherewithal to question their government's authority when opposition of any kind seemed pointless. The commemorations of the twentieth anniversary of the Wall's opening provided politicians, news organizations, and talk-show hosts with a pleasant occasion to reacquaint themselves with these heroes of yesteryear. Those who were once oppressed by a German dictatorship were momentarily given the opportunity to share their stories of ancient confrontations with the Stasi and the hardships of being ostracized by their own communities. Nevertheless, it is also part of the story of reunification that over the past two decades, these individuals have been among the most politically marginalized segments of the eastern German population.

How easy it has been to lose sight of the fact that these critics provided most of the moral substance and intellectual coherence that crystallized in fall 1989. Their record of defiance was long-standing. More than a decade earlier, activists had demanded that their country's leaders provide for precisely the democratic rights and free elections that were finally made possible with the fall of the Wall. After the signing of the Helsinki Final Accords in 1975, they openly campaigned for international support to pressure their government to reform its policies and live up to the civil rights guarantees in its constitution. For these efforts, many in their ranks, such as Wolf Biermann and Reiner Kunze, were expelled to the West or imprisoned, or both. Nonetheless, the threat of retaliation did not prevent others from stepping into their shoes. Because the dissidents' numbers were never large and because they were thinly spread out among a variety of opposition groups (e.g., in Lutheran parishes, women's circles, and pacifist bodies), most outsiders, including this writer, were disposed to dismiss these protests as ineffectual. Nonetheless, thanks to the opening of the files of the former Ministry of State Security, we now know that they had a profoundly unsettling impact on the communist regime.

To take just one episode out of many, consider the significance of the so-called Environmental Library which a handful of youthful idealists set up in September 1986 to call attention to the environmental dangers of East Germany's industrial policies. A year later, this little hole-in-the-wall office across from East Berlin's Church of Zion would become known throughout the country as a symbol of defiance to dictatorship when it was stormed by the secret police and its founders were arrested. Yet, imagine what its organizers must have thought about their activities during its short existence. Every day, when they entered the courtyard where it was located, they knew that they were at risk of being expelled from their school or losing their jobs. At the same time, they were exhilarated by the possibility of demonstrating what their country could look like as a free society. The library operated in full view of the authorities who patrolled it. But in one way or another, these idealists succeeded in making it a repository for forbidden texts, a distribution center for *samizdat* literature, and a gathering place for the disaffected. In their hearts, they were convinced that all one needed to change their society was to muster the will to demand it.

In this light, we can understand why the founders the Environmental Library, as well as others in their position, would still be heavily invested in their East German identity. For years, they sacrificed everything for principles whose time that had not yet come. At last, for a brief but glorious period in late 1989 and early 1990, they saw their dreams of a transformed GDR come to fruition: mass demonstrations against a seemingly unshakable dictatorship, a proliferation of independent opposition groups and nascent political parties, and a culture of civic engagement and dialogue that would have made Alexis de Tocqueville blush.

For these reasons, it makes sense that the last East German should come from those who could rejoice the most for *their* country in its final days. Unlike a majority of ordinary East Germans, their goal was to reform the GDR, not leave it. And unlike the followers of the PDS, they had no interest in compromising their principles for the sake of electoral gain. Thus, the loss of the GDR remains a nagging wound in the personal identity of each individual.

The Memory of the GDR

What will the last East German say when he or she turns out the lights? If this individual is one of the former dissidents, as I predict, the message will be simple: "don't forget what we accomplished." Of course, we would not want to deny any of the GDR's former citizens the right to make a similar claim. All human beings are entitled to have lives worth remembering. But our last East German merits special attention. This person's resilience in dangerous times demonstrated that the fight for basic freedoms and human rights was worth making in even the most desperate circumstances.

Will this bequest mean anything to Germany's leaders ten or twenty years from now? In my view, the answer to this question will depend upon how they choose to interpret the dissidents' historical impact. Until 1989, the closest that Germany had ever come to a democratic upheaval was the convening of the National Assembly in Frankfurt am Main on 18 May 1848. This event, too, was rooted in the determination of an assortment of regime critics to stand up to an oppressive government. What the new parliament's members lacked in experience, they made up for in bold demands for political representation and an expansion of suffrage. When their grand experiment with liberalism failed, it was followed by nearly 100 years of despair. But on a second occasion, on 23 May 1949, these aspirations were reawakened with the proclamation of the West German Federal Republic. The distinguishing characteristic of the new state was its constitutional commitment to the rule of law. The Basic Law obligated Bonn to become a "militant democracy," committed to the defense of human dignity. In one major respect, however, this achievement was wanting. Because it was founded under the auspices of foreign occupation, it lacked one feature that was manifestly present in East Germany in 1989. This was the legitimacy to be gained through popular acclamation.

We know that the opportunity to share in certain aspects of this legacy was not lost on West Germany's leaders. One full month before the GDR's accession to the Federal Republic, foreign minister Hans-Dietrich Genscher employed a verbal sleight of hand to inject his western compatriots into the discussion. "This was the first successful revolution in our history," Genscher proclaimed. "It was a peaceful revolution, which gave it particular historical value ... In these months, our people have demonstrated their political maturity."[4] I am not personally persuaded that these events constituted a full-blown revolution since, much like our ordinary East German, the hundreds of thousands of people who went into the streets throughout the fall had many different motives. But, we can account for Genscher's suggestive manipulation of the facts as a perfectly understandable attempt to establish a common bond between a long-divided people.

It is less easy to comprehend what has transpired in subsequent years. Once the historical import of these events was acknowledged, they have played an ever-decreasing role in the public articulation of Germany's official memory. In the immediate aftermath of the GDR's collapse, it is fair to say that there was a certain amount of *willful* forgetting on Bonn's part. Few of the Federal Republic's leaders had any confidence in the former dissidents' ability to meet eastern Germany's daunting challenges. They had good reason to be concerned. The representatives of a variety of eastern citizens' groups were determined to engage in elaborate negotiations over the terms under which national unity would be achieved. Yet, the Kohl government was not in the position to wait patiently. As the GDR's economy vanished into air, tens of thousands of the country's citizens were demonstrating with their feet how little they cared about their socialist identity. Unless Bonn wanted to see unification forced upon it through a massive rush to leave the GDR, it had no choice but to move the process along as quickly as it could. Accordingly, it was not to the heroes that the architects of unification turned for leadership but to people, such as Günther Krause and Peter-Michael Diestel, who had played little or no role in overthrowing the communist regime. In this regard, the dissidents were absolutely right when they claimed that their revolution had been hijacked from under their feet. "Please tell me, who was this Herr Krause," the outspoken activist Bärbel Bohley complained years later. "And who was this Herr Diestel? No one knew these people who were suddenly negotiating with Herr Kohl."[5]

These were the early days. Since then, the forgetting that has typified western German attitudes about East Germany in recent years does not appear to be consciously negligent. It is simply negligent. In 2010, one would expect to see a significant eastern German presence in the Federal Republic's most visible leadership positions. Yet, when German citizens went to the polls on 27 September 2009 to elect a new Bundestag, there were only two politicians from the East in the chancellor's cabinet. One was the former Social Democratic mayor of Leipzig, Wolfgang Tiefensee, whose *Ressort* was the not-so-scintillating Ministry for Transport, Building and Urban Development. The other was the chancellor herself, Angela Merkel, who bristles at the idea of being defined as an East German. After twenty years, can it still be that sufficient numbers of easterners with the qualifications for major political office cannot be found?

Symbolic tributes to the legacy of East Germany have been equally wanting. Indications of forgetting were present as early as June 1994, when Helmut Kohl presided over the opening of Bonn's National Museum of Contemporary German History (Haus der Geschichte). Long in gestation as one of the chancellor's pet projects, the museum was created to pay homage to the vitality of German democracy. Somehow, the East German opposition movement was left entirely out of the exhibition. Of the few highlights of East German history that were included, the museum's curators mysteriously found room for Erich Honecker's work desk. A decade and a-half later, forgetting has become a habit. This instinct was evident when, in May 2009, another chancellor, Merkel, opened a major art exhibit in Berlin that commemorated the sixtieth anniversary of the Basic Law. Here again, East Germany's existence was barely a whisper. Of the sixty paintings and sculptures in the collection, only one was from the forty-year history of the GDR.

Under these circumstances, one can easily understand why many of the former activists are inclined to replace their indignation with resignation. The East German author and playwright, Christoph Hein, was among those whom Merkel invited to the art exhibition. In a widely circulated letter in which he politely turned down his chancellor's invitation, Hein remarked about the peculiarity of celebrating a document, the Basic Law, which was written to protect freedom. How could one, at the same time, ignore the work of people who had once battled for this cause? "I belong to the excluded," he wrote, "and not to the excluders."[6] While Hein stayed home, others simply left the country. For example, Bohley went to Bosnia to work with the victims of genocide. She later explained that she did not intend to take leave of her East German identity. Rather, she hoped to preserve that identity by applying the principles of the citizens' movement to real life. "I didn't see any more purpose for me in Germany," she noted. "The lines were drawn after unification. I could put the new conditions behind me or simply sit in the corner and pout."[7] Although Bohley returned to Berlin in January 2009, one wonders whether the Federal Republic will be able to provide her with the sense of purpose she is seeking.

No Reason to Remember East Germany?

One cannot fault those, like Hein and Bohley, who are potentially last East Germans for their disgruntlement over Berlin's habit of forgetting. After all, the last thing either wants to happen is to go down in history as one of Friedrich Nietzsche's "last men," obsessed with memories that are both stagnant and devoid of meaning. But this fate is not preordained. As J. D. Bindenagel, the deputy U.S. Ambassador to the GDR at the time of the Wall's fall, argued in 2007, the Federal Republic has never had the option to pick or choose what it likes about its history. In this case, its leaders are morally obliged to remember that the events that led to unification provided Germany with a legitimacy that the old West German state could never have acquired on its own. For this reason, in Bindenagel's view, Berlin's failure to act on this principle has been one of its greatest "sins of omission."[8] I would add another point. Germany's tendency to downplay or ignore the dissidents' role in destabilizing the SED regime has been an equally substantial missed opportunity

Yet, Bindenagel and perhaps even Hein and Bohley would have been heartened by one recent exception to Berlin's forgetfulness. The occasion was a commemoration on 8 May 2009 of the efforts of the East German opposition to identify cases of SED voting fraud in the GDR's last municipal elections of 7 May 1989. In her address, Merkel pointedly praised the role of the individuals who put their commitment to justice ahead of their personal well-being. Their success in documenting instances of electoral malfeasance, she emphasized, generated the energy that transformed the GDR's small protest movement into a country-wide force. "Without May 7," she underscored, "no November 9 and no October 3. Without the civic courage of these independent groups of citizens on the day of the local elections and without the protests, the Wall would not have fallen and there would have been no reunification."9

Nonetheless, despite Merkel's noteworthy recognition of the all-too-infrequently-mentioned East German dissidents, there was one enormous hole in her argument. Although she advised in her speech that Germany as a whole owes the oppositionists a debt of respect for making national unity possible, she treated the protests in the GDR as though they had little relevance to West Germany before 1990. At the risk of exaggeration, it is as if the mass demonstrations and cries of "We are the people" had taken place on another planet. Hence, only when the dissidents had finished their work was Bonn prepared to transmit to the region the legal, political, and economic institutions that were required for reunification.

The problem with this conception is not only that it fails to satisfy Binde-nagel's moral imperative. It has also prevented Berlin from taking full advantage of an opportunity to incorporate the dissidents' actions into the Federal Republic's legitimating mythology. To cite one example of this missed opportunity, on 25 September 2007, Merkel gave a much-anticipated speech before the United Nations General Assembly in which she directly challenged the governments of Myanmar and Sudan to end their systematic violations of human rights.10 Yet, the speech was as empty as it was impor-tant. It was important because after years of equivocation by the chancellor's predecessor about such crimes, Germany was attempting to take a leader-ship role on a matter of global significance. But, the speech was empty because the chancellor provided no specific reasons for why her country in particular should be motivated to make these judgments. The opportunity was there had she drawn upon the bequest of the East Germans opposition-ists. By their actions, they had established the two facts that Myanmar and Sudan had most reason to fear. The first was that it was never acceptable to tolerate tyranny as a necessary evil and the second that it was always possi-ble to overthrow such a government when the will to persevere was evident.

What should we say when the last East German turns out the lights? We can reassure our protagonist that historians will not forget who really made the fall of the Wall possible. At the same time, we can point out that the loss will be borne by unified Germany instead.

Notes

1. Weert Canzler, "Transport Infrastructure in shrinking (East) Germany," in *German Politics and Society*, 26, no. 2 (Summer 2008): 76-82.
2. Heinrich Bortfeldt, *Von der SED zur PDS: Wandlung zur Demokratie?* (Bonn, 1992).
3. See Daniel Hough, "Success after Success, but Clouds loom on the Horizon: The Left Party in 2009," *AICGS Transatlantic Perspectives,* September 2009, available at http://www.aicgs.org/documents/pubs/hough.atp09.pdf.
4. Cited from Gregg O. Kvistad, "Parties and Citizens in the Western German Unification Debate," in *German Politics and Society* 30 (1993): 46.
5. *Süddeutsche Zeitung,* 10/11 January 2009.
6. *Der Freitag,* 6 May 2009.
7. *Süddeutsche Zeitung,* 10/11 January 2009.
8. *The Globalist,* 9 November 2007.
9. "Rede von Bundeskanzlerin Angela Merkel," 8 May 2009, available at http://www.bundeskanzlerin.de/nn_683608/Content/DE/Rede/2009/05/2009-05-08-bkin-friedliche-revolution.html.
10. Speech by Dr. Angela Merkel, Chancellor of the Federal Republic of Germany at the UN General Assembly, 25 September 2007, available at http://74.125.113.132/search?q=cache:gPFSsD8FlqcJ:www.un.org/webcast/ga/62/2007/pdfs/germany-eng.pdf+united+nations+speeches+merkel&cd=3&hl=en&ct=clnk&gl=us.

Chapter 4

$\mathcal{T}$HE MASTERED PAST?

Collective Memory Trends in Germany since Unification

● ● ● ● ● ● ● ● ● ● ● ● ● ● ● ●

Eric Langenbacher

Introduction

Attempts to periodize the past often abuse the historical flow and evolution of events, personalities, and processes. The decline of an industry, the rise of a political movement, or the dissipation of a generation's political influence rarely is connected nicely to a round date. Nevertheless, "critical junctures" do significantly affect political-cultural reality–sometimes with foundational impact, but often accelerating, decelerating, beginning, or ending processes. 1989/1990 in Germany was such a critical juncture in both senses. Yet, when looking specifically at cultural and collective memory trends, this caesura had delayed influence with processes begun before the watershed continuing and other incipient trends, "founded" by the juncture taking years to become manifest.

With these provisos in mind, looking back over the last twenty years, I discern two phases of German collective memories–divided loosely around the 1999 return of the capital to Berlin, which itself is another (albeit less-critical) juncture. Moreover, there have been three, at times, intersecting vectors of collective memory concerning the Holocaust, German suffering, and the period of division during the Cold War. In this chapter, I outline the major memory dynamics and debates, from both qualitative and quantitative perspectives. I argue that the last twenty years witnessed a period of vigorous memory work, but the zenith of such attention probably has passed and the German future will be much less beholden to "pasts that won't go away."[1] Indeed, Germany may be in the midst of a shift from an "unmasterable" to a "mastered" past.[2]

The History of Memories since Unification

Holocaust-centered Memory

The first postunification trend was the continuation, culmination, and institutionalization of Holocaust memory, what I elsewhere have called Holocaust-centered memory or the Bonn memory regime.[3] Rising slowly rose from subsequently much-criticized obscurity in the immediate post-war years—a period of silence, even repression towards the Nazi period during which a pervasive "amnesty mentality" allowed numerous perpetrators to escape justice[4]— the memory because increasingly prominent from the 1960s onward. This process was spurred by several factors including: generational change;[5] judicial proceedings, such as the Eichmann Trial in Jerusalem in 1961 and the Frankfurt Auschwitz Trial of 1963-1965; and a variety of cultural works including plays by Rolf Hochhuth (*Der Stellvertreter*, The Deputy, 1963) and Peter Weiss (*Die Ermittlung*, The Investigation, 1965), and, later, the NBC television miniseries *Holocaust*, which was aired in the Federal Republic in 1979 (and that one in two adults watched).[6] The rise of the local "history from below" and the history of everyday life (*Alltagsgeschichte*) movements from the 1970s onwards—part of a more general increase of interest in history, heritage, and memory internationally at this time—were additional facilitating factors.[7] Yet, despite heightening attention over several decades, this memory achieved cultural hegemony only in the years right before the fall of the Wall. Crucial were the great public and political debates surrounding the fortieth anniversary of the end of World War II in 1985: the Bitburg Affair, when Helmut Kohl and Ronald Reagan awkwardly celebrated Cold War unity at a German military cemetery that contained SS graves; President Richard von Weizsäcker's speech on 8 May; the Historians' Dispute (*Historikerstreit*) starting in 1986; and, later, the Jenninger Affair of 1988, where the Christian Democratic Union (CDU) Bundestag speaker was forced to quit after delivering an inappropriate speech on the fiftieth anniversary of the "Kristallnacht" pogrom.[8]

The continued ascendance of Holocaust memory post 1989 was especially visible in the institutionalization of unified German commemorations. "Round" anniversaries, especially 1995 and 2005, became significant political events, routinely producing important official pronouncements asserting responsibility and contrition for the crimes of the past, exemplified by former Chancellor Gerhard Schröder's speech at the sixtieth anniversary of the Warsaw Uprising in 2004. Other dates—like 8

May, 9 November (the anniversary of the fall of the Wall and "Kristall-nacht"), and 27 January (the date of the liberation of Auschwitz and, since 1996, an official commemorative day (*Gedenktag*))–have become annual commemorations replete with full media coverage. High-level visits of German politicians to Israel (e.g., Chancellor Angela Merkel's March 2008 trip) and stops by foreign dignitaries to former concentration camps (e.g., U.S. President Barack Obama at Buchenwald in June 2009) also have become expected rituals.[9]

Memorials have proliferated since 1990, continuing a trend that dates back to the mid 1980s in the Federal Republic.[10] Prominent examples include the Neue Wache memorial rededicated controversially (because various victim groups are not differentiated and their suffering seemingly is equated) to "all victims of war and tyranny" on Berlin's Unter den Lin-den in 1993, and the Memorial to the Murdered Jews of Europe, opened in 2005 near the Brandenburg Gate after fifteen years of debate mainly about proper commemorative forms and aesthetics in the "land of perpe-trators."[11] Other memorials in the capital include one on the Bebelplatz (site of the infamous Nazi book burning of 1933) erected in 1993; various "anti-monuments" especially in old Jewish districts like the Scheunenvier-tel (off Oranienburger Strasse) or the "Places of Remembrance" in Schöneberg's Bayerisches Viertel;[12] and at other sites such as the Haus der Wannsee Konferenz, Rathaus Steglitz and the train station in Grunewald (where many Berlin Jews were deported to Auschwitz). Additional memo-rials to other groups victimized by the Nazis commemorate gays (unveiled in 2008 across the street from the Holocaust memorial), Sinti and Roma (to be completed in late 2009 or 2010), and the "T4" euthanasia victims. Mention should also be made of the Jewish Museum in Kreuzberg with Daniel Libeskind's symbolic architectural "voids," the Museum of Ger-man History, re-opened in 2006, which comprehensively covers the Nazi period and the Holocaust, as well as the Topography of Terror, the site of Gestapo headquarters, where a new documentation center will open in 2010.[13] The proliferation of such sites has transformed the city into what some have called the "capital of remorse" (*Hauptstadt der Reue*) as the *Frankfurter Allgemeine Zeitung* memorably put it.[14]

These high-profile museums and memorials in the new/old capital are just the most prominent examples of the Holocaust memorialization trend that exists throughout the country beyond the memorials at the former Nazi concentration and labor camps on German soil (Bergen-Belsen, Neuengamme, Sachsenhausen, Ravensbrück, Buchenwald, Mittelbau-Dora, Dachau, Flossenbürg), as well as at the sites of destroyed synagogues (e.g., Worms, Altenkunstadt, Cologne) and former Jewish quarters (e.g. Augsburg, Rothenburg). Nuremberg, for example, installed a small museum and memorial plaques throughout the former Nazi Party Rally grounds–in time for the matches of the 2006 World Cup of Soccer that were played in the vicinity. It has declared itself a "city of human rights"[15] and is currently erecting a memorial and museum to the Nuremberg Trials (Courtroom 600).[16] Hamburg (the "Black Form" monument in Altona, dating back to the late 1980s and several others), Frankfurt (Judengasse), Kassel (Aschrottbrunnen), Stuttgart (Nordbahnhof) and many other places have installed memorials to the victims of the Nazis and to the centuries-old Jewish communities that were destroyed. There are also efforts to more fully commemorate Munich's "brown" past in a city notorious for its unwillingness to confront its Nazi legacy[17] and the East German city of Erfurt is erecting a museum at the former site of the Topf und Söhne factory, which produced the crematorium ovens used, for example, at Auschwitz and Buchenwald.[18] One of the most interesting commemorative efforts is the artist Gunter Demnig's *Stolperstein* (stumbling stone) initiative on-going since 1993. Individuals or groups research a victim of the Nazis (usually, but not always Jewish) and then can purchase a brass-covered cobblestone that is embedded in the sidewalk in front of the victim's former home as a memorial and admonition. By 2009, over 20,000 had been placed in 280 cities–including 1,400 in Cologne, 1,800 in Hamburg, and abroad, in Austria, Hungary, and the Netherlands.[19]

The postunification dominance of Holocaust memory shows in many other ways–for example, in the amount of pedagogical attention that German secondary schools (especially the Gymnasia) devote to it and the Nazi regime and the foregrounding of this history in adult political education (through the Bundes- and Landeszentralen für politische Bildung).[20] Official and civil societal actors have continued to support commemorative, compensatory, and reconciliatory efforts internationally. For example, the government and business community negotiated a compensation fund for individuals forced into slave labor during the Nazi years in 1999 funded with DM 10 billion, as well helping (albeit with a big impetus from U.S. courts) to compel insurance companies (in Germany and abroad) to honor Nazi-era policies.[21] Efforts also have continued to return looted art to Jewish owners and to complete the restitution process for property in the former German Democratic Republic (GDR).[22] The government was also a major force in the 2000 Stockholm Conference, which signified the European and even global resonance of the Holocaust,[23] and, more recently, contributed U.S. $6.31 million to the Museum of the History of

Polish Jews, which broke ground in the summer of 2009 in Warsaw.[24]

The impact of Holocaust-centered memory on postunification politics and public policy also has been marked. "Constructing Europe" became an overriding policy imperative, leading former Chancellor Helmut Kohl to justify European Monetary Union not on economic grounds, but as a means to avoid repeating Europe's genocidal twentieth-century history. Even more explicitly, former Foreign Minister Joschka Fischer, advocated the expansion of the European Union to the East, despite much opposition, as a "duty" due to crimes committed in that region by Nazi Germans.[25] Spurred by the worst ethnic warfare in Europe since 1945 in the Balkans, the 1990s also witnessed intense debates about foreign policy with two positions greatly influenced by Holocaust memory–"never again war" (*nie wieder Krieg*) versus "never again Auschwitz" (*nie wieder Auschwitz*)–vying for influence. The latter perspective largely prevailed, which helped to justify the deployment of over 7,000 troops abroad (especially in Afghanistan) as of 2009. More mundane policy also areas have been affected from the regulation of stem-cell research, to civil liberties (privacy rights, surveillance), to family policy (natalist polices have been difficult to implement because of Nazi abuse). The omnipresent fear of inflation–the hyperinflation of 1923 believed to have destabilized irrevocably the Weimar Republic and thus facilitated Hitler's rise–led the European Central Bank to adopt the Bundesbank's rigid anti-inflation mandate and during the 2008-2009 financial and economic crisis, probably helped motivate Merkel's resistance to a larger fiscal stimulus and bailouts of struggling neighbors.[26]

Numerous intellectual and political disputes also arose during this period, starting with a discussion about whether unification itself was allowable and whether Berlin–re-framed from Cold War *Frontstadt* to center of criminal Nazi decision making–should become the capital once again. In the middle of the decade, there were debates about the planned Holocaust monument in Berlin (regarding appropriate location, size and aesthetics); around Daniel Goldhagen's book *Hitler's Willing Executioners: Ordinary Germans and the Holocaust*, in which he argued that Nazi-era Germans long had been imbued with "eliminationist" anti-Semitism and that the Holocaust was the culmination of German history, a "national project;" and the *Wehrmachtaustellung*, a travelling exhibition of photos that tried to delegitimize the myth of the "clean" army and thematize the guilt of average Germans.[27] The controversial project was hugely popular–almost a million Germans and Austrians visited the original exhibition and the Bundestag even debated its merits in an open and emotional manner.[28] Later in the decade, the Walser-Bubis controversy broke out after novelist Martin Walser delivered an incendiary speech in which he called the Holocaust Memorial "a football field-sized nightmare," likened Auschwitz to a "moral cudgel" and noted his need to "look away" from the historical horrors. Then-leader of the Jewish community, Ignatz Bubis, responded by accusing Walser of "spiritual arson" (*geistige Brandstiftung*).[29] In the realm of popular culture, there were numerous milestones including *Schindler's List* in 1993 and, later in the decade, the re-publication of Victor Klemperer's diary that recounted the Nazi years from the perspective of a Jewish professor living in Dresden married to a gentile German. This string of very public and publicized "memory events" kept the Holocaust in public consciousness and each time, defenders of the status quo were rather successful, retaining *Meinungshoheit* or cultural hegemony.

All of these Holocaust-centered memory events from this first postunification phase represented a continuation and perfection of trends originating in the last years of the Bonn Republic. Yet, the 1990s also witnessed a growing impact on Holocaust-centered memories from several new factors that the 1989/1990 caesura–particularly the demise of communism–made possible. The experiences and the archives sealed behind the iron curtain led to a slew of new studies and a focus on other victim groups–such as Soviet prisoners of war, Poles, slave laborers, Eastern European civilians–and an outpouring of scholarship on Jewish communities in many of the former Eastern bloc countries in, for example, Galicia, Ukraine, or Hungary.[30] These new intellectual horizons have begun to produce a shift in historiographical perspective with the war in the East gaining more weight in overall assessments than hostilities in the West, which had dominated conceptions of the period during the Cold War. The consequences are increasingly visible. Conceptions of victimized groups have evolved with the almost exclusive attention on Jewish Holocaust victims being augmented by the inclusion of others. Related, many scholars are emphasizing more general racist doctrines (in contrast to a focus on antisemitism) as having animated the Nazi worldview. A sustained debunking of the myth of the "clean" Wehrmacht and a re-prioritization of the role of German industry and business have occurred, given that the most heinous economic and war crimes were committed in the East. Above all, there has been the foregrounding of the corruption, exploitation, and plunder–first of German Jews, later of the rest of (Eastern) European Jewry, and many others in conquered territories, including political opponents and slave laborers–that centrally motivated and sustained the Nazi regime.[31] Finally, the re-opening of the East also (eventually) increased the attention devoted to the memory of German suffering, insofar as the iron curtain sealed off the provinces lost at the Potsdam Conference (e.g., Silesia, East Prussia) physically and discursively.

In the second phase after about 1999, the string of such Holocaust-centered memory events continued, but with a decreased frequency and a different sense to them. For example, in the lead-up to the 2002 Bundestag election, Jamal Karsli, who had imputed "Nazi tactics" to Israel, was kicked out of the Green Party. Moving to the Free Democrats, then-party leader Jürgen Möllemann supported him and continued to criticize Israel in an election brochure widely perceived as antisemitic, a controversial tactic that some think decreased his party's vote share.[32] In 2003, there was a dispute over the firm Degussa, which was subcontracted to provide an anti-graffiti chemical for the Holocaust Memorial in Berlin because it was the same company that had produced the Zyklon-B gas used in Nazi death camps. Later that same year, CDU Bundestag backbencher Martin Hohmann delivered a speech in which he questioned references to present-day Germans as a *Tätervolk* (people of perpetrators) and asserted that the same could be said about Jews because of their disproportional influence on early Bolshevism. Conservative journalist Eva Hermann caused a stir in 2007 when she opined that Nazi family policy was not "all bad."[33] More recently, in 2008-2009 there was a wide-ranging debate about governmental plans to re-instate the iron cross service medal for the Bundeswehr. Critics pointed out that although the distinction dates back to 1813, it was forever sullied by the Nazis. The government then instituted alternative "bravery medals" (*Tapferkeitsorden*), the first of which were bestowed in July 2009.[34] Even though these more recent scandals appear less genuine and more hyped by the media compared to those of the 1980s or 1990s, they nevertheless reveal the continued influence of Holocaust-centered memory. Tellingly, Möllemann, Hohmann and Hermann all lost their jobs.

The Memory of German Suffering

The second empirical vector concerns the memory of German suffering–based on events from the end and aftermath of World War II–the flight/expulsion of 12-14 million Germans from the former Eastern provinces (e.g., Silesia, Neumark, Eastern Pomerania and East Prussia) and elsewhere in Central and Eastern Europe (Danzig, Hungary, Sudeten Germans from Czechoslovakia); the bombing of all sizable cities by the British and American Air Forces (e.g., Cologne, Hamburg, Berlin and Dresden); the mass rape of as many as 2 million German women by members of the Red Army; and the internment of millions of former Wehrmacht soldiers in the USSR, some for a decade.[35]

This memory was never absent from certain quarters of German society—especially among many (though not all) of the so-called expellees, who constituted between 16-25 percent of West and East Germany's postwar population (7 percent in Austria) and the interest groups that purportedly represented them, such as the Sudetendeutsche Landmannschaft and the national umbrella group, the Bund der Vertriebenen (League of German Expellees, BdV). In the early years of the Federal Republic, all parties competed for expellee votes, but, by the mid 1960s, the CDU and especially the Christian Social Union (CSU)—expellees constituted 21 percent of Bavaria's postwar population, overwhelmingly Sudeten Germans, who were even adopted as Bavaria's fifth "tribe" (*Stamm*)—increasingly monopolized expellee issues and the memory of German suffering.

In any case, this memory regime was clearly hegemonic in the immediate postwar decades, generating numerous cultural productions, especially the so-called *Heimatfilme* of the Adenauer era like *Grün ist die Heide* (The Heath is Green, 1951), but also in the Bonn Republic's later decades, in for example, *Die Ehe der Maria Braun* (The Marriage of Maria Braun, 1979), and *Deutschland, bleiche Mutter* (Germany, Pale Mother, 1980), and in many literary works. The memory also markedly influenced public policy. Domestically, an entire ministry was devoted to expellee issues until 1969, the controversial Lastenausgleich (equalization of burdens) helped expellees gain new homes and livelihoods by imposing an additional tax on those who had not sustained major losses in the war, and state funding for expellee groups' cultural programs was and remains substantial. Foreign policy, especially Konrad Adenauer's rigid non-recognition of communist regimes, the so-called Hallstein Doctrine, and the refusal to accept the Oder-Neisse line as Germany's unequivocal eastern border, were maintained long past their "best before" date largely because of the electoral power of expellees.[36]

By the 1970s and 1980s, this memory (and its representatives) rapidly lost influence and became increasingly "forgotten" in most of the political and societal mainstream. As postwar, "postnational" and more leftist generations (especially the 68ers) came of age,[37] the memory increasingly was perceived as revanchist, right-wing, and caught in the nationalistic past. The much discussed *Historikerstreit* of the mid 1980s not only determined the place and prominence of Holocaust-centered memory in contemporary German collective identity and culture, but also delegitimized the memory of German suffering.[38] Nevertheless, the expellee groups continued their efforts and the CDU/CSU maintained links to this still sizable constituency. The memory did erupt periodically on the national stage, for example, in 1985 when Kohl attended a rally of Silesian expellees (whose original slogan was "Silesia Remains Ours!") and when he equivocated for several months in 1990 on the final recognition of the Oder-Neisse border.

Largely absent in the first postunification memory phase, it came back unexpectedly and strongly after 2002, leading many to fret that this "return of German self pity" would relativize memory of the Holocaust and its progressive achievements.[39] Seven years later, however, these fears have not come to pass, not least due to the efforts of representative of the status quo to defend the hegemony of the Holocaust-centered memory regime. Today, the last years of intensive debate and interest appear to have crested and attention already is dropping off. Hence, the long-term place of this memory in German political culture is still unclear, but probably will be minimal.

In retrospect, already in the mid and late 1990s, an increase in attention to this set of memories was evident. For example, around the 8 May 1995 anniversary several high profile Germans sponsored the "Gegen das Vergessen" newspaper advertising campaign in which they appropriated the rhetoric of Holocaust-centered memory and admonished their fellow citizens for having forgotten the expulsion fifty years later. Also noteworthy was the on-going publication of Walter Kempowski's popular "history from below," *Das Echolot*, a collective diary, containing documents, letters, and diary entries that the author collected for decades in his "small library of the nameless" from a variety of people (victims and perpetrators) who witnessed the Nazi period.[40] Dieter Forte's *Der Junge mit den blutigen Schuhen* (The Youth with Bloody Shoes, 1995) and other literary treatments, including the original publication in 1999 of W.G. Sebald's *Luftkrieg und Literatur* (On the Natural History of Destruction) similarly increased the public visibility of these memories.[41] Mention should also be made of the continued efforts over the postunification period of groups like the Sudetendeutsche Landsmannschaft (and its CSU allies, notably Edmund Stoiber) to push their interests in Czech, German, and European courts, by, for example, advocating for the revocation of the Beneš Decrees, which had stripped Sudeten Germans of citizenship, rights, and property.[42]

All of this prepared the political-cultural ground, but the memory of German suffering returned forcefully only in 2002 with the publication of Günter Grass' *Im Krebsgang* (Crabwalk) and Jörg Friedrich's *Der Brand: Deutschland im Bombenkrieg, 1940-1945* (The Fire: The Bombing of Germany).[43] Over the subsequent years, an intensive memory discussion ensued–extensive print media treatment (*Der Spiegel, Bild Zeitung*), a series of television (and feature film) productions like *Downfall* (2004), *Dresden* (2006), *Die Flucht* (The Flight, 2007), *Die Gustloff* (2008) and *Anonyma: Eine Frau in Berlin* (Anonymous: A Woman in Berlin, 2008), as well as numerous "pop histories" in written and visual formats. Despite (or perhaps because of) the productions' mass popularity–*Dresden* garnered a 32.6 percent and 31.2 percent market share on the two nights that it was aired[44]–many intellectuals have been highly critical, deeming them, among other things, "Heimat kitsch."[45] Guido Knopp's numerous documentary productions for the ZDF television network, such as *Hitlers Helfer* (Hitler's Helpers, 1997) and *Die grosse Flucht* (The Great Flight, 2001) have been particularly popular and also greatly criticized as "Nazi kitsch," "knoppoganda," and even "historical pornography."[46]

The return of this memory was met with a marked backlash from much of the German Left and from abroad, notably Poland. Critics focused on efforts by the BdV and its leader, Erika Steinbach (a sitting CDU Bundestag deputy) to create a Zentrum gegen Vertreibungen (Center against Expulsions) in Berlin, which would memorialize the expulsion of the Germans, as well as many other victims of ethnic cleansing in the twentieth century, and sensitize individuals to the on-going potential of such terrible acts. Largely unnoticed when it first was announced in 1999, it became a major and on-going controversy after 2003. Many leftists–who after the late 1960s and Willy Brandt's Ostpolitik had ceased to represent expellee issues and who had come to embrace memory of the Holocaust[47]–such as Schröder and Fischer, and especially members of the cultural and political elite in Poland (notably Lech and Jarosław Kaczynski, leaders of the right-wing Law and Justice Party) eviscerated the initiative and Steinbach, who was depicted memorably as an SS officer riding Schröder on the cover of *wprost* magazine in 2003. Overall, critics felt these commemorative efforts signified a grave form of historical revisionism that was making the "perpetrators into victims" and would relativize the Holocaust and the crimes committed by Nazi Germans in Poland and elsewhere. The controversy finally ebbed in 2008 when the Grand Coalition decided to fund the Zentrum and find it space in Berlin.[48]

The amount of attention devoted to the memory of German suffering over the 2002-2008 period was unexpected, given the degree to which this memory had been de-emphasized publicly after the mid 1980s (if not earlier), even by the overwhelming majority of the mainstream Right. Yet, there is evidence that the crest of attention already has passed. For example, the viewership in March 2008 of the historical television miniseries *Die Gustloff* was well down from earlier works in the genre, which has led production companies to turn away from these historical themes.

Figure 1: Viewership of Television Productions (in millions)

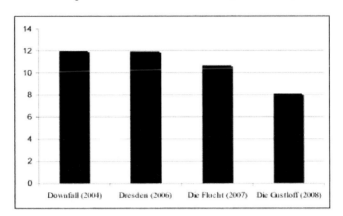

Source: "Feuersturm mit Millionenpublikum," *Spiegel online*, 7 March 2006; "'Gustloff' über-fährt Jauch," *Spiegel online*, 4 March 2008; Erik Kirschbaum, "'Die Gustloff' earns low ratings," *Variety*, 7 March 2008; John Bendix, "Facing Hitler: German Responses to Downfall," *German Politics and Society* 25, no. 1 (2007): 70-89.

Moreover, with the seeming resolution to the Zentrum dispute (similar to the opening of Berlin's Holocaust Memorial in 2005), a lot of the interest and invective from domestic and international critics has subsided. This is reminiscent of the "monumental invisibility" thesis associated with the writings of Robert Musil, and may indicate reduced influence of this memory in the future.[49]

Nevertheless, the situation with Poland is still tense. Over recent years, there have been a series of memory-related disputes, for example, on-going discussions about returning the "Berlinka" archival collection to the German capital, moved to Silesia for safe-keeping during the war. Polish officials have asserted their rights to possession because the documents were "abandoned by fleeing Nazis" as a former foreign minister once put it. Controversy erupted in 2006 when Grass admitted to having been briefly in the SS at the end of the war, which led several politicians such as Lech Walesa to threaten to revoke his honorary citizenship from the city of his birth, Gdansk (Danzig). Jarosław Kaczynski argued at European Summit in June 2007 that Poland should have a voting weight in EU institutions based on its hypothetical population had Nazi era depredations not occurred.[5] Most recently, there was the reaction to the May 2009 *Spiegel* cover story, "Die Komplizen: Hitlers europäische Helfer beim Judenmord" (The Accomplices: Hitler's European Helpers in the Murder of the Jews), which looked at French, Dutch, Lithuanian, Ukrainian, Polish, and other European collaborators in the Holocaust. Despite careful contextualization, clear acknowledgement of Nazi German responsibility, and little actual attention devoted to Polish collaborators, Jarosław Kaczynski asserted that "the Germans are attempting to shake off their guilt for a giant crime." Journalist Piotr Semka noted that "the article confirms the worst fears about the transformation taking shape in German thinking about World War II."[51] Given such widespread historical sensitivities and the continued influence of the Kaczynskis, it will take some time for memory issues between these neighbors to settle down.

Mention should also be made of the relationship with the Czech Republic. The 1990s were especially tense with repeated efforts by Sudeten Germans to press their issues in Czech and European courts (1995, 1999, 2002) and–with support from Bavarian CSU allies like Theo Waigel and Edmund Stoiber, threatening to hold up Czech ascension to the European Union.[52] Therefore, it was unsurprising in late 2009 when Czech President Vaclav Klaus refused to sign the Lisbon Treaty because of fears that the attached European Charter of Human Rights might facilitate additional legal actions from Sudeten Germans. After officials in Berlin and Brussels agreed to an explicit exemption, Klaus backed down.[53] Yet again, this incident speaks to the continued and deep influence that collective memories have on politics and policy in the region.

Cold War Memories

A third vector concerns memories from the period of postwar division. The more regionally specific memory of the German Democratic Republic is of obvious importance, especially efforts to come to terms with the Stasi (secret police) legacy. This "working-through" process was exemplified by the various laws passed granting citizens access to their Stasi files, two Bundestag Commissions of Inquiry (Enquete-Kommissionen, similar to truth commissions) in 1994 and 1998, which led to the establishment of a foundation (Stiftung zur Aufarbeitung der SED-Diktatur),[54] and various museums and memorials especially at the former Stasi Headquarters on Berlin's Normannenstrasse and at prisons such as those in Berlin-Hohenschönhausen and Bautzen in Saxony. Vowing to "get things right" this time, efforts were made to bring perpetrators of communist crimes to justice, including the trials of border guards (*Mauerschützenprozesse*) who had implemented the "shoot-to-kill" order when East Germans tried to escape to the West, as well as (more problematically given age, health, and evidence issues) some of the higher-ups such as Egon Krenz and Erich Mielke.[55] Culture also confronted this legacy early on with Christa Wolf's *Was bleibt?* (What Remains, 1990), and later, in works like Jürgen Fuchs's *Schriftprobe*

(2000) the critically acclaimed film *Das Leben der Anderen* (The Life of Others, 2006) that is about the tragic human toll wreaked by Stasi paranoia and spying, as well as the possibility to remain humane in such a system.[56]

There is also an on-going discussion about how East Germans and the GDR regime worked through Nazi crimes during the Cold War, as well as how easterners have done so in the aftermath of unification. Several scholars have shown that with the exception of a brief period of honest confrontation in the immediate postwar period–exemplified by DEFA film productions such as *Die Mörder sind unter uns* (The Murderers Are among Us, 1946), *Ehe im Schatten* (Marriage in Shadows, 1947), or *Die Affäre Blum* (The Blum Affair, 1948)–for most of the GDR's history, Nazism and the Holocaust were considered "dealt with" because the fundamental capitalistic cause of fascism was destroyed. Jewish victims were subsumed under the rubric of anti-fascist communist heroes.[57] Nevertheless, at the very end of the regime there were some incipient efforts to confront the Holocaust, recognize Jewish victims, and commemorate what was lost (e.g., partial rebuilding of the New Synagogue on the Oranienburger Strasse in East Berlin). The very first act of the short-lived East German Parliament in the spring of 1990 was an official apology for the crimes of the Holocaust. It should also be noted that many of the memorials and museums discussed above are located in the former East, which either had to start the commemoration process from scratch after unification, or had to revise propagandistic communist narratives (e.g., Neue Wache, German Historical Museum).

Other East German cities, particularly Dresden with its well-entrenched self-conception of having been victimized by the bombing of February 1945 ("anglo-amerikanische Terrorangriffe" as the communists put it), have had more challenges in confronting their Nazi pasts.[58] Interestingly, some authors have argued that the greater incidence of right-radical sentiment and violence in Eastern Germany today–for example, the attacks on hostels housing foreigners in Hoyerswerda in 1991 and Rostock in 1992, the success of the right-radical National Democratic Party (9.2 percent in the 2004 Saxon state elections, but only 5.6 percent in 2009), as well as the horrific murder of a pregnant Egyptian woman by a racist Russian-German immigrant in July 2009–is (partially) a consequence of the inadequate process of working-through the Nazi legacy.[59]

Shortly after unification, there were also intensive debates about the comparability of the Nazi and communist dictatorships and the alleged foregrounding of the East German legacy by conservatives, presumably in another attempt by the Kohl government (similar to efforts in the mid

1980s) to relativize the Nazi period and to make the Holocaust less exceptional.[60] Very quickly, however, representatives of the "incomparability" position (largely defenders of the Bonn memory regime) prevailed. Discursive efforts to downplay the nastiness of the communists (at least 500,000 Stasi unofficial informants and as many as 2 million) were buttressed by two additional trends in the East. First was the surprisingly rapid rise of nostalgic and positive memories of the GDR, *Ostalgie*, epitomized by films like *Helden wie wir* (Heroes Like Us, 1999), *Sonnenallee* (1999), and, even though directed by western German Wolfgang Becker, *Good Bye, Lenin!* (2003).[61]

Second, partially in response to the way that unification played out, resulting in perceptions of a Western "takeover" of the East, seemingly permanent economic immiseration–despite the massive amounts of governmental and private investment sent East–and the heightening of East-West differences (*die Mauer im Kopf*),[62] was the rise and sustained support of the regionally concentrated former communists, the PDS (after 2007 renamed the Left Party, *die Linken* after a merger with disgruntled western leftists). This party was both a cause and consequence of persistent regional differences and *Ostalgie*, whitewashing, even glorifying the communist period, and actively opposing many (political and cultural) efforts more fully to come to terms with the East German past.

Moreover, official efforts recently have intensified, including studies leading to an overarching concept for the commemoration of the Berlin Wall and an Expert Commission headed by historian Martin Sabrow, recommending to the Bundestag that commemoration of the GDR focus on three thematic areas: surveillance and persecution; wall and border; and leadership and society.[63] This work resulted in a new governmental concept for memorials (*Gedenkstättenkonzept*) in 2008, which increases the federal coordinating role (usually a state-level competence) and raises overall financing to EURO 35 million, divided two-thirds for memorials at former Nazi concentration camps and one-third for those pertaining to East Germany.[64] Finally, reminiscent of the 2001 academic project aimed at institutionalizing German memory places, *Deutsche Erinnerungsorte*, recent books are attempting to codify the collective memory of East Germany. Sabrow's *Erinnerungsorte der DDR* (Sites of Memory in the German Democratic Republic), includes highly political (Bautzen, Ständige Vertretung) and mundane (Intershops, Der Trabant) selections.[65] Finally, there are several dedicated museums such as the Dokumentationszentrum Alltagskultur der DDR in Eisenhüttenstadt opened in 1999 and the critically acclaimed DDR Museum in central Berlin unveiled in 2006.[66]

In sum, there was a brief period of rather intensive memory work regarding the GDR in the years immediately after unification, followed by a relative lull, and then in the last few years renewed attention. The recent rise in interest was pushed by popular culture, election campaigns and the looming twentieth anniversaries, as well as being a response to the continuing strength of the Left Party. For example, discussions flared up during the campaign for the federal presidency in the spring of 2009 as to whether the GDR should be classified as an *Unrechtstaat* (unjust state), a term long used to characterize the Nazi regime.[67] The fact that so many from both the East and the western Left (e.g., Gesine Schwan,[68] the SPD candidate) would not admit this, shows the power of the Left Party (and efforts to pander to its eastern base), as well as the continued resilience of Holocaust memory with the connected incomparability doctrine.

Other memories and historical episodes from the Cold War period are also starting to gain visibility. Broadly, one can discern the rise of memories based on the Bonn Republic–and its various phases and episodes–such as the Adenauer era. Especially noteworthy has been everything associated with "1968"–the generational rebellion, student radicals, the Social-Liberal coalition, Chancellor Brandt, the new Ostpolitik, left-wing terrorism (RAF), as well as these individuals' confrontation with their parents' complicity in the crimes of the Third Reich.[69] The media have been full of anniversaries and retrospectives, epitomized by the acclaimed 2008 film, *Das Baader Meinhof Komplex*. As the generation of '68–long having completed its "long march" through the Federal Republic's institutions and having made its mark on the memory politics of the country–begins to retire *en masse* and be replaced by younger cohorts, construction of such memories surely will intensify. This process probably will mirror that of the "Nazi" generation in the 1980s and 1990s as it struggled to institutionalize a cultural form of memory appropriate for the longer term. Nevertheless, one should not equate the two generations and sets of memories–the much greater existential and foundational importance of the Nazi period and Holocaust is not in doubt.

Substantiating the Trends

This narrative of postunification memory trends was based on an overview of the relevant qualitative primary and secondary sources.[70] A quantitative complement would be an additional check on the veracity of the trends–not just regarding overall interest in a given memory, but also the memories in competitive relation to each other. I now present the findings from a diachronic (based on year of publication, 1945-2008 inclusive) keyword analysis of the holdings of the Deutsche Nationalbibliothek (DNB), the national library of record.[71] These data are a useful indicator of how much scholarly and book market attention has been devoted to certain topics. In other words, these data can illuminate "supply" issues, as well as alluding to preferences within the scholarly, writing, and library communities—corresponding to what was (or not) a popular research or publication domain in a given year.

At the outset, I look at the overall number of books published per year (*Erst- und Neuauflage*)[72]—to control for the possibility that specific keyword trends are consequences of a secular increase in the number of titles produced. Overall, the total number of titles has fluctuated around the 55,000-70,000 mark since the late 1970s.[73] This rather constant level of book production over thirty-five years indicates that the specific trends discussed below are not artifacts of increasing overall production.

Figure 2: Book Production in the Federal Republic of Germany

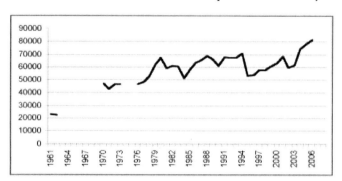

Source: Statistisches Jahrbuch für die Bundesrepublik Deutschland (Stuttgart, Wiesbaden 1962, 1975, 1980, 1981, 1983, 1986, 1988, 1990, 1992, 1994, 1996, 1998, 2000, 2002, 2004, 2007).

The two most significant memories—of German crimes and German suffering—can be captured by the keywords "Holocaust" and "Vertreibung" (expulsion/ethnic cleansing of Germans).[74] Although the "Holocaust" term was not in wide circulation before the 1970s and other terms like "Shoah" have become current more recently, the DNB (re-) categorized all relevant entries under the "Holocaust" keyword. Overall, the library has 3627 entries over the entire sixty-three year period examined for "Holocaust" and 1361 for "Vertreibung."

Figure 3: Frequency of Holocaust and Vertreibung Keywords

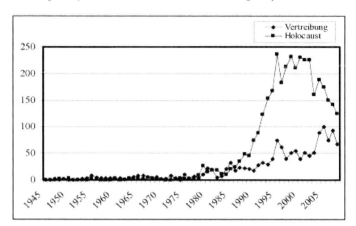

Especially visible is the dearth of attention devoted to the Holocaust until the late 1970s. But, it is also fascinating that there was so little attention devoted to Vertreibung—perhaps there was less working through of this memory than recent scholarship has asserted, and more silence, "repression," or an "inability to mourn." Moreover, in response to the critics who decried the return of the memory of German suffering especially over the last ten years (also clearly visible), from the late 1980s onwards the library's holdings on the Holocaust dominated those on Vertreibung, pointing to the (continued) hegemony of Holocaust-centered memory. Finally, it is noteworthy that the number of publications on both topics, markedly with the Holocaust, has decreased since 2002 (since 2005 for Vertreibung)—supporting the "end of intensive memory" argument.

This pairing is only a first cut—other keywords and concepts may reveal different dynamics and conclusions masked or excluded from this analysis. But first, I compare the evolution of publications on the Holocaust to a "benign" keyword, "Goethe," as a kind of control. In light of the rather constant interest in the famous classical author (200-400 publications per year, with exceptional "commemorative" years in 1949, 1982 and 1999),[75] the rise in books on the Holocaust once again does not appear to be an artifact.

As another kind of control, I compare publication trends in Germany to the United States Library of Congress (LOC). Four observations stand out: first, both curves have similar shapes; second, the number of publications that the LOC contains (vastly) exceeds the number in the DNB every single year—and over the period examined the LOC has 9,124 entries under the Holocaust keyword, versus 3,627 for the DNB; third, an increase in attention is discernible in the United States about fifteen years before a

Figure 4: Goethe versus Holocaust

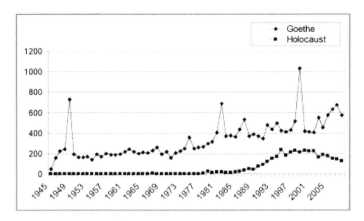

similar increase in Germany, which supports the hypothesis regarding American agency in thematizing the Holocaust and then prompting interest and action in Germany;[76] fourth, that after an immediate postwar blip, there were surprisingly few publications in the United States through the 1950s and until the late 1960s, which supports arguments about the rise of Holocaust consciousness in the U.S. only after this period and which coincides with the Adenauer era silence in the Federal Republic.[77]

Figure 5: Frequency of Holocaust Keyword in the United States and Germany

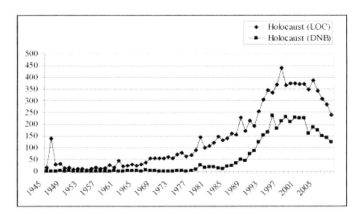

It is possible that publishing interest in the memory of German suffering does not appear in the relatively politicized keyword "Vertreibung." This, indeed, appears to be the case when this keyword (1,361 entries) is compared to the

more benign "Ostpreussen" and "Schlesien," (with 5,061 and 4,979 entries respectively) the two biggest former German provinces. The many publications, increasing over the years, categorized under these keywords seem to reinforce the much-observed popularity of nostalgic *Heimatliteratur.*[78]

Figure 6: Vertreibung, Ostpreußen and Schlesien

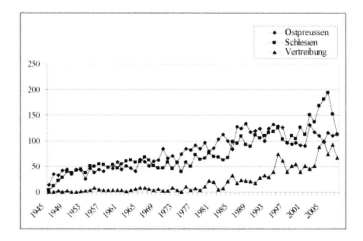

But, what about other related keywords that may capture important memory trends? Looking at "Weltkrieg 1939-1945" (4,122 entries), "Hitler" (5,840 entries), "Nationalsozialismus" (8,326 entries) and "GDR" it is evident that except for the last, all three only experienced a marked rise in the early or mid 1980s–probably part of the same memory and history wave that also increased publishing interest in the Holocaust and Vertreibung.[79] The number of publications on the GDR (25,976 entries) outnumbers by far all other keywords analyzed–even "Goethe" (with 21,619 entries). Starting around the time that the Berlin Wall was erected, publishing interest was maintained for decades–although the total number of publications declined every year since 1981 with the exception of the spike around unification. At least amongst West German authors and publishers, the division of the country was a major concern over these decades. Interestingly, the number of books published on the Stasi has been comparatively small since 1990 with 670 entries, peaking at 51 publications in 1997.

These publication data correspond to and substantiate the findings from other studies that used different methods. Although these data speak specifically only to trends in book publication and the purchasing choices of the German library of record, they also illuminate the evolution of interest among the scholarly and/or writing communities, as well as the reading public and/or book market because of the presumable (if only partial) correlation between publishers' supply and readers' (elite or mass) demand.

Figure 7: Competing Historical Keywords

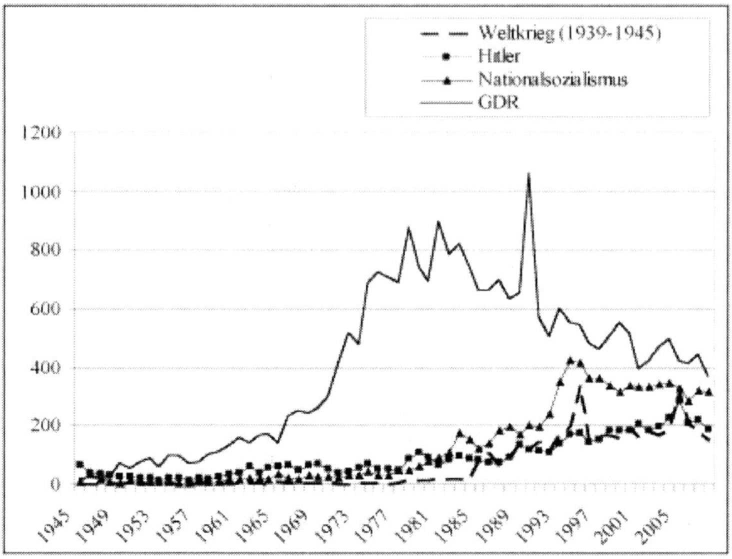

Discussion and Conclusion

The current state of collective memory appears more fluid and pluralistic in the Berlin Republic than in previous postwar periods, perhaps of necessity. Not only are there multiple collective memories circulating and vying for influence (based on the Holocaust, German suffering, and the GDR), but there is also evidence of diminishing interest in *all* collective memories. A quarter century of vigorous memory work may be coming to an end. This situation troubles many who believe in Holocaust-centered memory and who support its continued hegemony as a moral necessity for Germany, as revealed by the critical reaction to the Center against Expulsions initiative and to the more general resurgence of the memory of German suffering.[80]

Yet, it was always ambitious for authors and activists to expect that the hegemony of Holocaust-centered memory could be maintained with the same level of engagement and intensity almost seventy years and several generations after the demise of the Third Reich in an increasingly multicultural (almost 20 percent of the population has a "migration background"), Europeanized, and globalized country. This "new" Germany–so socio-struc-

turally different from the one that had unleashed world war and genocide–
may have increasing difficulties indentifying with this "older" Germany of
perpetrators and the memories based thereon. Arguably, there also comes a
point in time when almost all outstanding historical issues, lacunae, taboos,
and controversies have been discussed and/or addressed. The last twenty
years strike me as being concerned with the resolution of unfinished business
left over from the Nazi and in some cases the immediate postwar years–Ralf
Giordano's "second guilt" of repressing Nazi crimes and thus re-traumatizing
victims[81]–issues that kept Holocaust-centered memory on the public agenda.
Examples in postunification Germany include compensation for slave laborers, the establishment of a variety of museums and memorials to the victims
of the Nazi regime, property restitution and compensation in the former
GDR, and the opening of the International Tracing Service's archive in Bad
Arolsen in 2006, but also debates about the complicity of average Germans,
industry, and the Wehrmacht in Nazi crimes and discussions about appropriate commemorative aesthetics and representational forms.

Second, one of the unforeseen consequences of the rise of Holocaust-centered memory in Germany, throughout the West, and beyond is that the
Holocaust and the Nazi regime are increasingly becoming divorced from
their specific historical and cultural context. After looking at the increasing
currency of the historical thesis that conceives of the Holocaust and Nazism
not (just) as products of racist German hypernationalism and deep-seated
antisemitism, but as a product of the more general crisis of Western modernity, Daniel Levy and Natan Sznaider write: "… these memories have
become a measure for humanist and universal identifications. Hence, it is
precisely the abstract nature of 'good and evil' that symbolizes the Holocaust,
which contributes to the extraterritorial quality of cosmopolitan memory."[82]
Everything related to the Holocaust and Nazism–Auschwitz, Hitler, the SS–
have thus taken on almost mythical dimensions, becoming problematic
"floating signifiers" attached in an inflationary manner to completely unre-
lated and often base phenomena. For example, in the summer of 2009 when
opponents to the Democrats' health care reform initiative protested across
the United States, posters of President Barack Obama with a Hitler mous-
tache were ubiquitous.[83] Many point out that these transnational cultural
developments trivialize the actual historical phenomena and reduce the distinctiveness and "Germanness" of the Nazis and the Holocaust, thus diminishing their salience and impact on the Germans of the Berlin Republic.

Third, the country finally appears to have moved beyond the much-
observed transitional phase or "floating gap" between experienced communicative and institutionalized cultural memories[84] and is now firmly

within the realm of the latter. Cultural memory by definition is abstracted from the lived experiences of historical agents–of the victims, perpetrators, bystanders, and witnesses of the Nazi regime–and must struggle to maintain the emotional resonance typical of communicative memories. With the generations who actively planned, perpetrated, or witnessed Nazi crimes quickly passing away and the third and even fourth generations reaching adulthood, Nazi-era memories have been transmogrifying into cultural memory or even into Pierre Nora's less emotional history– like the Civil War in the U.S., the Ming Dynasty in China, or the heroic battles of World War I in France or Britain.[85]

In any case, for the first time in decades, it appears that the concerns of the present and the worries about the future have eroded the dominance of the past. Especially in light of the post 2008 global economic downturn, but also in the realm of European policy, where a more unconstrained pursuit of self-interest is apparent, and in foreign policy with the deployment of German troops in places like Afghanistan accepted as business-as-usual, a certain "normalization" (not in the bad sense) is evident. In September 2009, the government even erected a memorial to Bundeswehr soldiers killed in action since 1955–a gesture that would have been unthinkable twenty years ago. Moreover, it has been a long time since a major political figure used a Holocaust memory-based argument to justify a policy, like Kohl or Fischer did in the 1990s. And there are several examples of policy reforms (the Grand Coalition's family policy comes immediately to mind) that were rather unconstrained by historical arguments or analogies. Even pride in the German national community is no longer completely taboo, as the celebrations during the hosting of the World Cup of soccer in the summer of 2006 attest.

Perhaps Germany's Nazi past finally has been "mastered," as implied by the much-discussed process/concept of *Vergangenheitsbewältigung*–not in the constructed, elite-driven, and even manipulative manner of neoconservatives in the early Kohl era[86]–but rather, in spite of the good intentions to maintain memory and because of the inexorable power of time. Alternatively, active memory of the Holocaust (and German suffering) may be eroding because of its own success, which has, dialectically, "sown the seeds of its own destruction" so to say, making it redundant, even superfluous. Precisely because of the breadth and depth of Holocaust-centered (and other) memories, Germans have undergone successfully the transformation of values and social structures that made Nazi-era crimes possible. This is exactly what Theodore Adorno originally proclaimed "coming to terms with the past" to mean at the height of Adenauer-era silence and what many authors including Daniel Goldhagen believe has indeed occurred.[87]

Notes

1. This well-known phrase was originally used in response to the Historians' Debate in the mid 1980s by Ernst Nolte, "Vergangenheit, die nicht vergehen will," in *Historikerstreit: Die Dokumentation der Kontroverse um die Einzigartigkeit der nationalsozialistischen Judenvernichtung* (Munich, 1987).

2. See Charles Maier, *The Unmasterable Past: History, Holocaust and German National Identity* (Cambridge, 1988).

3. Eric Langenbacher, "Changing Memory Regimes in Contemporary Germany?," *German Politics and Society* 21, no. 2 (2003): 46-68; Eric Langenbacher, "*Moralpolitik* versus *Moralpolitik*: Recent Struggles over the Construction of Cultural Memory in Germany," *German Politics and Society* 23. no. 3 (2005): 106-134; Eric Langenbacher, "Twenty-first Century Memory Regimes in Germany and Poland: An Analysis of Elite Discourses and Public Opinion," *German Politics and Society* 26, no. 4 (2008): 50-81. Other excellent overviews include Andrei S. Markovits and Simon Reich, *The German Predicament: Memory and Power in the New Europe* (Ithaca, 1997); M. Anne Sa'adah, *Germany's Second Chance: Trust, Justice and Democratization* (Cambridge, 1998); and David Art, *The Politics of the Nazi Past in Germany and Austria* (Cambridge, 2006).

4. Alexander Mitscherlich and Margarethe Mitscherlich, *The Inability to Mourn: Principles of Collective Behavior* (New York, 1975); Ralf Giordano, *Die zweite Schuld oder Von der Last Deutscher zu sein* (Hamburg, 1987); Konrad Jarausch, *After Hitler: Recivilizing Germans, 1945-1995* (Oxford, 2006).

5. See most recently Mark Wolfgram, *"Getting History Right:" East and West German Collective Memories of the Holocaust and War* (Lewisburg, forthcoming 2009).

6. Mark E. Cory, "Some Reflections on NBC's Film Holocaust," *The German Quarterly* 53, no. 4 (1980): 444-451.

7. See for example Karen Till, *The New Berlin: Memory, Politics, Place* (Minneapolis, 2005)—especially her chapter on the Topography of Terror in West Berlin. On the international dimension see David Lowenthal, *The Past is a Foreign Country* (Cambridge, 1985).

8. See Maier (see note 2) and Richard J. Evans, *In Hitler's Shadow: West German Historians and the Attempt to Escape from the Nazi Past* (New York, 1989).

9. See Ruth Wittlinger, "The Merkel Government's Politics of the Past," *German Politics and Society* 26, no. 4 (2008): 9-27; Evelyn Finger, "Obama in Buchenwald: Gedenken ohne Pomp und Pathos," *Zeit online*, 6 June 2009.

10. See James E. Young, *The Texture of Memory: Holocaust Memorials and Meaning* (New Haven, 1993).

11. Ute Heimrod, Günter Schlusche, and Horst Seferens, eds., *Der Denkmalstreit–das Denkmal? Die Debatte um das 'Denkmal für die ermordeten Juden Europas.' Eine Dokumentation* (Berlin, 1999); James E. Young, "Berlin's Holocaust Memorial: A Report to the Bundestag Committee on Media and Culture," *German Politics and Society* 17, no. 3 (1999).

12. See Young (see note 10); Caroline Wiedmer, *The Claims of Memory: Representations of the Holocaust in Contemporary Germany and France* (Ithaca, 1999).

13. Till (see note 7); see also http://www.dhm.de/; http://www.juedisches-museum-berlin.de/site/DE/homepage.php?meta=TRUE; http://www.topographie.de/start.html; accessed on 16 October 2009.

14. Konrad Schuller, "Erinnerungsort deutscher Geschichte. Hauptstadt der Reue. Gedenkpolitik ist zu einer Hauptdisziplin geworden," *Frankfurter Allgemeine Zeitung,* 18 December 1996, 13.

15. Inge Manka, "A (Trans)National Site of Remembrance: The Former Nazi Party Rally Grounds in Nuremberg," *German Politics and Society* 26, no. 4 (2008): 113-133.

16. See http://museums.nuremberg.de/courtroom600/index.html; accessed on 13 July 2009.

17. Paul Jaskot and Gavriel Rosenfeld, eds., *Beyond Berlin: Twelve German Cities Confront the Past* (Ann Arbor, 2008).

18. See Aleida Assmann, Frank Hiddemann, Eckhard Schwarzenberger, eds., *Firma Topf & Söhne–Hersteller der Öfen für Auschwitz: ein Fabrikgelände als Erinnerungsort?* (Frankfurt/Main, 2002). See also http://www.topf-holocaust.de/; accessed on 23 July 2009.

19. See http://www.goethe.de/kue/bku/thm/idd/de78940.htm; accessed on 11 July 2009.

20. See Bodo von Borries, *Das Geschichtsbewußtsein Jugendlicher: Eine repräsentative Untersuchung über Vergangenheitsdeutungen, Gegenwartswahrnehmungen und Zukunftserwartungen von SchülerInnen in Ost- und Westdeutschland* (Weinheim, 1995); See also the numerous publications from the Georg Eckert Institute for International Textbook Reserach; http://www.gei.de/en/georg-eckert-institute-for-international-textbook-research.html.

21. Stuart E. Eizenstat, *Imperfect Justice: Looted Assets, Slave Labor, and the Unfinished Business of World War II* (New York, 2003).

22. See Mark Landler, "German company pays Jewish family for Nazi-era confiscation, *New York Times*, 30 March 2007; See also http://www.claimscon.org/index.asp ?url=looted_art; accessed on 23 July 2009.

23. Daniel Levy and Natan Sznaider, *The Holocaust and Memory in the Global Age* (Philadelphia, 2006).

24. See http://jta.org/news/article/2007/06/20/102550/polandmuseum; accessed on 11 July 2009.

25. See Thomas Banchoff. *The German Problem Transformed: Institutions, Politics and Foreign Policy, 1945-1995* (Ann Arbor, 1999), 178; Joschka Fischer, "Außenpolitik im Widerspruch," *Zeit online*, 3 February 2000, accessed on 12 October 2009; See also Markovits and Reich (see note 3).

26. Richard Tomlinson and Oliver Suess, "Merkel Makes Like Obama With German Stimulus Excluding Europe," www.bloomberg.com, 26 March 2009, accessed on 17 August 2009.

27. Daniel Jonah Goldhagen, *Hitler's Willing Executioners: Ordinary Germans and the Holocaust* (New York, 1996); Hannes Heer and Klaus Naumann, eds., *Vernichtungskrieg: Verbrechen der Wehrmacht, 1941-1944* (Hamburg, 1995).

28. Wolfgram (see note 5).

29. Frank Schirrmacher, *Die Walser-Bubis Debatte: Eine Dokumentation* (Frankfurt/Main, 1999).

30. See, for example, Omer, Bartov, *Erased: Vanishing Traces of Jewish Galicia in Present-day Ukraine* (Princeton, 2007).

31. Götz Aly, *Hitlers Volksstaat: Raub, Rassenkreig und nationaler Sozialismus* (Frankfurt/Main, 2005); Richard Evans, *The Third Reich in Power: How the Nazis Won over the Hearts and Minds of a Nation* (London, 2005).

32. See "Germany and its Jews," *The Economist*, 15 June 2002; Elihu Salpeter, "It doesn't pay these days to speak against the Jews in Germany," *Ha'aretz*, 10 September 2002.

33. For more details on these memory events see Langenbacher (2005, 2008, see note 3).

34. Nicholas Kulish, "Bid to revive the Iron Cross awakens Germany's angst," *New York Times*, 19 March 2008; Matthias Gebauer, "Merkel verleiht erste Tapferkeitsorden an Soldaten," *Spiegel online*, 6 July 2009.

35. See Jörg Friedrich *Der Brand: Deutschland im Bombenkrieg, 1940-1945* (Munich, 2002); Thomas Urban, *Der Verlust: Die Vertreibung der Deutschen und Polen im 20. Jahrhundert* (Munich, 2004).

36. See Robert Moeller, *War Stories: The Search for a Usable Past in the Federal* Republic of Germany (Berkeley, 2001); Pertti Ahonen, *After the Expulsion: West Germany and Eastern Europe, 1945-1990* (Oxford, 2003); Manfred Kittel, *Vertreibung der Vertreibenen? Der historische deutsche Osten in der Erinnerungskultur der Bundesrepublik (1961-1982)* (Munich, 2007).

37. Jarausch (see note 4).

38. Langenbacher (2003, 2005 see note 3).

39. See Bill Niven, *Germans as Victims: Remembering the Past in Contemporary Germany* (Houndsmills, 2006).

40. See Peter Fritzsche, "Review: Walter Kempowski's Collection," *Central European History* 35, no. 2 (2002): 257-267.

41. Walter Kempowski, *Das Echolot: Ein kollektives Tagesbuch, Januar und Februar 1943; Das Echolot: 18 Januar bis 14. Februar 1945: Fuga Furiosa* (Munich, 1997, 1999); Dieter Forte, *Der Junge mit den blutigen Schuhen* (Frankfurt/Main, 1995); W.G. Sebald, *Luftkrieg und Literatur* (Munich, 1999).

42. Steve Wood, "German Expellee Organisations in the Enlarged EU," *German Politics* 14, no. 4 (2005): 487–97; Jeffrey S. Kopstein, "The Politics of National Reconciliation: Memory and Institutions in German-Czech Relations since 1989," *Nationalism and Ethnic Politics* 3, no. 2 (1997): 57–78.

43. Günter Grass, *Im Krebsgang* (Göttingen, 2002); Friedrich (see note 35).

44. "Feuersturm mit Millionenpublikum," *Spiegel online*, 7 March 2006

45. Norbert Röttgen and Renate Künast, "Daheim zu Hause," *Der Tagesspiegel*, 12 July 2009; See also Andreas Kilb, "Kitsch und Vergewaltigung: 'Anonyma,'" *Frankfurter Allgemeine Zeitung online*, 22 October 2008; accessed 8 June 2009.

46. Sven Felix Kellerhoff, "Nur etwas dick aufgetragen," *Die Welt*, 14 October 2003; Tanja Dückers, "Alles nur Opfer," *Die Zeit online*, 7 March 2008; Wulf Kansteiner, *In Pursuit of German Memory: History, Television and Politics after Auschwitz* (Athens, 2006), 180.

47. See Ahonen (see note 36) and Kittel (see note 36).

48. Also important were the parliamentary elections in Poland in late 2007 that removed Jarosław Kaczynski from the prime ministership and brought the moderate conservative Donald Tusk to power. See Langenbacher (2008 see note 3).

49. See Andreas Huyssen, *Present pasts: urban palimpsests and the politics of memory* (Stanford, 2003); see also Young (see note 10), 13.

50. See Langenbacher (2008 see note 3).

51. Jan Puhl, "A Wave of Outrage," *Spiegel Online*, 21 May 2009; ""Die Komplizen: Hitlers europäische Helfer beim Judenmord," *Der Spiegel*, 21 (2009).

52. See Eric Langenbacher, "Ethical Cleansing?: The Expulsion of Germans from Central Europe during and after World War Two," in *Genocides by the Oppressed: Subaltern Genocide in Theory and Practice*, eds., Nicholas Robins and Adam Jones (Bloomington, 2009).

53. Edward Cody, "Europe's future, tangled by its past," The Washington Post, 23 October, 2009.

54. Andrew H. Beattie, *Playing Politics with History: The Bundestag Inquires into East Germany* (New York, 2008).

55. See A. James McAdams, *Judging the past in unified Germany* (Cambridge, 2001); see also http://www.stasimuseum.de; http://www.stiftung-aufarbeitung.de/; accessed on 12 October 2009.

56. Christa Wolf, *Was bleibt: Erzählung* (Frankfurt/Main, 1990); Jürgen Fuchs, *Schriftprobe* (Weimar, 2000). See also Bradley Prager's contribution in this issue.

57. See Jeffrey Herf, *Divided Memory: The Nazi Past in the Two Germanies* (Cambridge, 1997); Thomas C. Fox, *Stated Memory: East Germany and the Holocaust* (Rochester, 1999).

58. See Susanne Vees-Gulani, "The Politics of New Beginnings: The Continued Exclusion of the Nazi Past in Dresden's Cityscape," in Jaskot and Rosenfeld (see note 17).

59. "Egyptian Fury at Dresden Murder: Protestors Accuse Germany of Racism," *Spiegel online*, 7 July 2009; See also Art (see note 3). The fact that the perpetrator was a twenty-eight year-old Russian-German who immigrated in 2003 raises other issues about multicultural Germany. Note also that the tepid official response to the tragedy was also greatly criticized. See Kate Connolly and Jack Shenker, "The headscarf martyr: murder in German court sparks Egyptian fury," www.guardian.co.uk, 7 July 2009; accessed on 25 August 2009.

60. Klaus Suhl, ed., *Vergangenheitsbewältigung 1945 und 1989. Ein unmöglicher Vergleich? Eine Diskussion* (Berlin, 1994).

61. Anthony Enns, "The politics of Ostalgie: post-socialist nostalgia in recent German film," *Screen* 48, no. 4 (2007): 475–491; Paul Cooke, "Ostalgie's Not What It Used to Be: The German Television GDR Craze of 2003," *German Politics and Society* 22 (2004).

62. This phrase originally was coined by Peter Schneider, *Der Mauerspringer: Erzählung* (Darmstadt, 1988).
63. See http://www.berlin.de/sen/kultur/kulturpolitik/mauer/gesamtkonzept.html; and http://www.bundestag.de/presse/hib/2006_06/2006_204/02.html, accessed on 1 October 2009.
64. Interestingly, memorials concerning the memory of German suffering were not mentioned. Sven Felix Kellerhoff, "Deutsche Vergangenheit Kabinett beschließt neues Gedenkstättenkonzept," *Die Welt*, 18 July 2008.
65. Martin Sabrow, ed., *Erinnerungsorte der DDR* (Munich, 2009); Etienne Francois and Hagen Schulze, eds., *Deutsche Erinnerungsorte* (Munich 2001).
66. See http://www.alltagskultur-ddr.de/pages/home.html; http://www.ddr-museum.de/en/; accessed on 12 October 2009. See also Denny Lee, "36 Hours in Berlin," *New York Times*, 11 October 2009.
67. Peter von Becker, "Debatte um DDR-Äußerung: Rechts-, Halbrechts-, Unrechtsstaat," *Der Tagesspiegel*, 19 May 2009.
68. Gesine Schwan is a former academic who, interestingly, published *Politik und Schuld: die zerstörerische Macht des Schweigens* (Frankfurt/Main, 1997).
69. Joyce Marie Mushaben, *From Post-War to Post-Wall Generations: Changing Attitudes toward the National Question and NATO in the Federal Republic of Germany* (Boulder, 1998).
70. See, for example, Jenny Wüstenberg and David Art, "Using the Past in the Nazi Successor States from 1945 to the Present," *The Annals of the American Academy of Political and Social Science* 617 (2008): 72-87.
71. See http://www.d-nb.de/; research completed between 25 May and 12 June 2009.
72. These data are found in the *Statistisches Jahrbuch für die Bundesrepublik Deutschland* (Stuttgart/Wiesbaden 1962, 1975, 1980, 1981, 1983, 1986, 1988, 1990, 1992, 1994, 1996, 1998, 2000, 2002, 2004, 2007).
73. The last few years witnessed a discernable increase—2008 estimates put production at over 90,000, but the recession surely will reduce these numbers for 2009 and 2010). See http://www.buchmesse.de/de/networking/suchen_finden/buchmaerkte/europa/deutschland/00113/, accessed on 13 July 2009.
74. It should be noted that although the vast majority of the DNB's holdings are books, there are also films, catalogs, some audio recordings, etc. Also, although the preponderance of holdings is in the German language, there are foreign language works (as in the Library of Congress). Although this means that "German-language" interest may be less, it does not mean that Germans' interest is less (especially given transnationalization trends in scholarship and readership). The fact that the DNB would decide to purchase a Hebrew, Polish or English-language text, still shows interest in the topic.
75. These were the 200th anniversary of his birth, the 150th anniversary of his death and the 250th anniversary of his birth.
76. See Andrei S. Markovits, and Beth Simone Noveck, "West Germany," in *The World Reacts to the Holocaust*, ed., D. S. Wyman (Baltimore, 1996); Shlomo Shafir, *Ambiguous Relations: The American Jewish Community and Germany since 1945* (Detroit, 1999).
77. See, for example, Peter Novick, *The Holocaust in American Life* (Boston, 1999).
78. Moeller (see note 36). Note also that the totals listed here also correspond to the numbers compiled in two well-known bibliographies. Axel Dornemann, *Flucht und Vertreibung aus den ehemaligen deutschen Ostgebieten in Prosaliteratur und Erlebnisbericht seit 1945: Eine annotierte Bibliographie* (Stuttgart, 2005); Louis Ferdinand Helbig, *Der ungeheure Verlust: Gflucht und Vertreibung in der deutschsprachigen Belletristik der Nachkriegszeit* (Wiesbaden, 1988). Dornemann lists 1,894 entries in an "Alphabetisches Gesamtverzeichnis nach Autoren;" and an additional 87 "Sammelwerke und Anthologien"—note that many of the individual entries listed in the Gesamtverzeichnis are part of these edited volumes. Helbig's various bibliographical lists contain a total of 562 entries.
79. Many of the underlying concepts that one would think are caught in the Holocaust or Vertreibung keywords, may be categorized (additionally) under these rubrics.

80. See Langenbacher (2003, 2005 see note 3).
81. Ralf Giordano, *Die zweite Schuld oder Von der Last Deutscher zu sein* (Hamburg, 1987).
82. Levy and Sznaider (see note 23), 4.
83. See Kathleen Parker, "Summertime for Hitler," *The Washington Post*, 23 August 2009.
84. Assmann, Aleida and Ute Frevert, *Geschichtsvergessenheit, Geschichtsversessenheit: Vom Umgang mit deutschen Vergangenheiten nach 1945* (Stuttgart, 1999); The "floating gap between memory and history" notion comes from Lutz Niethammer, "Diesseits des 'Floating Gap.' Das kollektive Gedächtnis und die Konstruktion im wissenschaftlichen Diskurs," in *Generation und Gedächtnis. Erinnerungen und kollektive Identitäten*, eds., Kirstin Platt and Mihran Dabag (Opladen, 1995).
85. Pierre Nora, "Between Memory and History: Les Lieux de Memoire," *Representations* 26 (1989).
86. See Maier (see note 2).
87. Theodor Adorno, "What Does Coming to Terms with the Past Mean?" in *Bitburg in Moral and Political Discourse*, ed., Geoffrey Hartman (Bloomington, 1986); Daniel Goldhagen, "Modell Bundesrepublik: Nationalgeschichte, Demokratie und Internationalisierung in Deutschland," *Blätter für deutsche und internationale Politik*, 4, (1997); Jürgen Habermas, "Über den öffentlichen Gebrauch der Historie. Warum ein Demokratiepreis für Daniel Goldhagen?"*Blätter für deutsche und internationale Politik*, 4, (1997).

Chapter 5

OBAMAMANIA AND ANTI-AMERICANISM AS COMPLEMENTARY CONCEPTS IN CONTEMPORARY GERMAN DISCOURSE

● ● ● ● ● ● ● ● ● ● ● ● ● ● ●

Ruth Hatlapa

and

Andrei S. Markovits

Introduction

> ... [I]n Europe, there is an anti-Americanism that is at once casual but can also be insidious. Instead of recognizing the good that America so often does in the world, there have been times where Europeans choose to blame America for much of what's bad."[1]

In his speech in Strasbourg, President Barack Obama surprised his audiences on both sides of the Atlantic by being the very first American president to address in public a European resentment with a long history. To be sure, anti-Americanism–in Europe and worldwide–reached unprecedented proportions during the eight-year reign of the Bush Administration. Especially in the aftermath of the attacks of 11 September 2001 and the war against Iraq two years later, there emerged an unparalleled antipathy towards the United States government as well as American society that reached most social segments in many countries throughout the world.[2] Ivan Krastev, observing this tendency in 2004, predicted that the twenty-first century may well become known as the "anti-American century."[3] Andrei Markovits previously analyzed the pervasiveness and social acceptability of anti-Americanism in Europe as the continent's de facto "lingua franca," its most important inter- and intra-societal common discourse.[4]

The overwhelmingly positive reaction to the appearance of Barack Obama on the international political stage, however, seems to have run directly counter to this massive anti-Americanism. Indeed, Obamamania, as enthusiasm for Obama has been aptly termed, spread rapidly through Europe and the world seemingly negating the previously widely extant anti-Americanism. Thus, his being awarded the Nobel Peace Prize nary one year after having been elected President and barely ten months into holding this uniquely important office, testifies to this man's singular popularity among the world's publics, but most notably—and importantly—West (or, actually, in this case North) Europe's political and cultural elites who, after all, comprise the crucial decision makers that choose the recipients of this prestigious prize. Crudely put, had Barack Obama been less beloved by Norwegian, other Scandinavian and West European elites—and had George W. Bush not been as reviled and disdained—Obama would not have won this award so early in his presidential incumbency. This is not to say that Barack Obama is not a worthy recipient of this distinction. We emphatically believe that he is! But, we also argue that were he not to have benefited from such a high degree of affection among West Europe's publics and elites, it is very unlikely that he would have been bestowed this prize at this time.

Indeed, European audiences' love for Obama only has its parallels in their affection for John F. Kennedy with whom the current president has been serially compared.[5] Indeed, it is not only the president himself that benefits from this Camelot analogy, but his entire family. After all, Michelle Obama is constantly compared to Jacqueline Kennedy in terms of her style, beauty, panache, and composure, and the two Obama girls round out this poster-perfect family just the way Caroline and John-John did almost fifty years ago.

When Obama delivered a public speech in Berlin in July 2008—months before he was to be elected President of the United States—more than 200,000 people came to see him at an odd location that celebrates newly united and Prussia-led Germany's victory over France in 1871.[6] In contrast, a visit to the same city by George W. Bush in May 2002 witnessed a demonstration by 20,000 people against his presence.[7] Indeed, that was a relatively small affair when compared to the more than 200,000 demonstrators who brought the city to a complete halt and forced the authorities to convert it into a veritable fortress during the often violent demonstrations against Ronald Reagan's visits to Berlin throughout the 1980s, including his last one in which he implored Mikhail Gorbachev to "tear down this wall." In fact, every American president since John F. Kennedy was met with a much larger number of protesters demonstrating against him than audiences welcoming him in Germany and most West European countries (in notable contrast to Eastern Europe where Richard Nixon, for example, was accorded a hero's welcome after being scorned and excoriated in the continent's western part).

But, quite the opposite seems to be operative in Barack Obama's case. Thus, for example, according to opinion polls, 82 percent of the German population, 74 percent of the British, and 72 percent of the Spanish have "confidence in Obama to do the right thing in world affairs."[8] Obama is often–though neither exclusively nor without reservation–perceived as a source of hope and inspiration, a protagonist of political change. At first sight, this seems to contradict the notion of widespread anti-Americanism; the German print media as well as pundits have been quick to predict that European anti-Americanism will soon or may already have come to an end.[9] Our purpose in this chapter is to question such assumptions, rebut such statements, and present them as wishful thinking at best or–more likely–post hoc self-exculpatory statements designed to minimize a continuously extant anti-Americanism.

In this chapter, our data will hail only from Germany. In a subsequent publication, we fully intend to expand our horizon to include other West European countries. In the first section, we briefly address the entangled relationship between anti-Americanism and anti-Bushism, and gauge whether such positions and opinions are reasonable and fair criticism of American politics. In the next section, we demonstrate the continued presence of anti-Americanism by analyzing three particular instances: the financial crisis, the shooting in Winnenden, and the NATO summit. In the chapter's last section, we highlight the compatibility of German Obamamania with continued anti-Americanism. A brief conclusion ends our contribution in which we argue that anti-Americanism in Germany and Europe has not been altered by the amazing changes wrought in virtually every aspect of Europe's existence by the miraculous events that continue to characterize 1989, of which the fall of the Berlin Wall and Germany's subsequent unification was merely one piece of a still awe-inducing puzzle.

Anti-Americanism, Anti-Bushism, or reasonable and fair criticism of American politics?

The view of Obamamania's being the apotheosis of anti-Americanism and its obvious negation rests squarely on the premise that anti-Americanism did not so much exist sui generis, but was rather a justly expressed criticism of President George W. Bush's policies on every level, but particularly in foreign affairs, clearly the most salient for Europeans. Since disagreement–indeed disgust–with Bush's policies represented a completely legitimate and fair opposition to the policies enacted by the government of the United States, such sentiments ipso facto did not constitute resentment against the American people or things American, but rather a justified criticism of the United States government led by Bush. In countless instances, one would hear all across Europe that one was, of course, not in the least anti-American, merely anti-Bush. Indeed, very few, if any, Europeans declare themselves openly as anti-American. One can barely, if ever, find such people. Nevertheless, one can encounter many more who preface their remarks with the disclaimer that "I am not anti-American" followed by an emphatic "but," which, in turn, is an opening for an array of invectives against America and Americans that one would have a hard time viewing as anything but profoundly anti-American–ditto with antisemitism, racism, or most prejudices. Few people in this day and age readily admit to being antisemites or racists or misogynists; however many preface their negative opinions by the previously mentioned disclaimer of not being an anti-Semite, racist, or misogynist, but … and then commence with their negative views of Jews, blacks and other ethnic minorities, and women.

In order to separate resentment towards American policy and attitudes toward America–in other words to separate government from people– Markovits, in particular, centered his work on observing how Europeans reacted to American matters that were clearly non-political. His work demonstrates that while criticism of the U.S. government is directed against certain concrete political decisions, anti-Americanism is targeted against an imagined "American essence," an "American nature," and thus goes much deeper than a disagreement with a political strategy. Indeed, anti-Americanism disapproves of who Americans are and not what they do.[10] It centers on disdaining America's lifestyle, culture, habits and beliefs, and argues that America in its very essence represents an evil as well as inferior force in the world while at the same time being omnipotent and omniscient."Anti-Americanism rests on the notion that something associated with the United States, something at the core of American life, is deeply wrong and threatening to the rest of the world."[11] The "core markers" of anti-Americanism, according to Brendon O'Connor, are a "distorted or narrowcast focus, a reflexive dislike, an undifferentiated view of American behavior or politics and a tendency to conflate the nation's people with their government and its policies."[12] Pejorative attributions consist of viewing the United States as imperialist by "nature" and striving for world domination; it often includes economic arguments, identifying America with the negative aspects of neoliberalism; but it also focuses on perceiving American culture as artificial and lacking authenticity.[13] All of these negative views appear either on their own or bundled in a larger context of negativity, disdain, and dislike, if not always outright hatred. Like all powerful prejudices, anti-Americanism, too, resists any verification by empirical means. Prejudices, to those that hold them, are neither testable hypotheses, nor refutable by facts. Above all, they are always antonymous—everything and its opposite pertain in relation to the detested object. Thus, America is at once too powerful, yet also too weak; its soldiers are too Rambo-esque, yet also cowardly; Americans are too nationalistic, yet they do not constitute a proper nation; they are too religious, yet they are also too secular; their culture is pornographic, yet it is also prudish; their women are emasculating, yet they are also too domestic and traditional. Americans are slavish purveyors of Fordism and other methods of mass production and consumption while at the same time unable and unwilling to part with their outdated traditions and old-fashioned mores that bespeak their provincialism. America stands for unwanted and intrusive cosmopolitanism that destroys other cultures at the same time that it supposedly embodies an exclusive parochialism which is hostile to any influences from abroad. Examples abound. As Markovits has repeatedly pointed out, the nature of anti-Americanism's profound antinomies bear a striking resemblance to those that characterize anti-Semitism.[14] Thus, it is not by chance that historically and empirically speaking European anti-Americanism and antisemitism featured a considerable overlap in the essential ingredients of their concepts but also in the political reality of their social carriers.

Robert Singh has offered a detailed analysis pertaining to the crucial issue as to whether the Bush policies might be responsible for increasing anti-Americanism in Europe and the world. He concluded that the phenomenon of anti-Americanism constitutes a different occurance from a rational reaction to and critical assessment of U.S. foreign policy. Singh demonstrates that the widely shared criticisms of America's policies have been contradictory and selective. Thus, for example, while in the context of the war against Iraq the engagement of the United States has been denounced as too aggressive, in the context of the long-lasting wars conducted in Lebanon, the American reaction was criticized as being to meek and timid.[15] Once again, we have a fine manifestation of what Markovits has termed the "damned if you do, and damned if you don't" syndrome that is so crucial to the logic of any prejudice, that of anti-Americanism included.[16] Critics regard America as being too cowardly and self-interested by not preventing the genocide in Rwanda, and by rescuing the Bosnian Muslims and their brethren in Kosovo way too late. Yet, at the same time, often the very same critics blame America for being the actual culprit by exhibiting too much aggression even against bullies of the Slobodan Milosevic variety. One even hears criticism of America's passive-aggressive character, meaning that in its very passivity, America exhibits a sort of arrogance that is de facto aggressive. Singh observes this inherent contradiction quite well by stating that "many of those who claim that reasoned criticism of American foreign policy cannot be classified as anti-American nonetheless claim simultaneously that the recent growth of anti-Americanism is precisely attributable to a failed U.S. foreign policy."[17]

Bush's policies–as well as his entire being and very existence–have had a catalytic effect regarding the legitimizing of anti-Americanism in Europe and the world. Quite simply, Bush's presence "catapulted global and Western European anti-Americanism into 'overdrive'"in which a legitimate antipathy towards a person and his government's policies conveniently bled into a much more general prejudice against America and Americans.[18] After all, any prejudice can be displayed more openly, when it is legitimized by its object, as in the case of the "cowboy" Bush, who was such an ideal-typical target for the popular projection of all extant facets of negative characteristics attributed to America since 1776 that had Bush not been real, one would have had to invent him.[19] Like other forms of group-oriented hostilities, anti-Americanism, too, cannot be explained by attributes of the resentment's object and target. Instead, one needs to analyze the subject's disposition and the reason he/she feels compelled to express such resentment in order to best arrive at its roots. Jean-Paul Sartre put it correctly when he argued that anti-Semitism said little, if anything, about Jews but all the more about Christians, the bearers of such anti-Jewish prejudices. Thus, in anti-Americanism's case, too, we are likely to find its reasons and existence less in America's being and doing, but rather in this resentment's role and function in the subject societies, in this case Europe.

Notable in the case of anti-Americanism is, for example, the externalization of problems existing within European societies by projecting them onto the United States.[20] Using America as a scapegoat for global troubles, Europeans obscure their own responsibilities regarding social, economic and political problems besetting the world thus making America the sole culprit while at the same time establishing Europe's moral superiority vis-à-vis its American rival. Dan Diner identifies anti-Americanism as a general way of rationalizing complex and misconceived social processes defining all aspects of modern societies. "Resistive reactions to emblems of an incriminated time–modernity–convert into emblems of a denounced place–America."[21] Accordingly, anti-Americanism–like all prejudices–facilitates the substitution of a clear-cut explanation for a more nuanced understanding of the intricate structure of modern societies. By so doing, it offers a mindset leaving anti-American attitudes ever more resistant to rational arguments, differentiated interpretations, and empirical facts that point into an opposite direction.

Of course, this does not mean that a profound antipathy towards Bush as a president, a person, and a purveyor of certain policies always needs to be part of a larger resentment towards the United States and things American. Anti-Bushism surely existed widely without the presence of an acute anti-Americanism. And while the obverse was certainly much less prevalent, it is certainly conceivable that some Europeans actually did not mind Bush while disliking America and Americans. But our point here is to look at the overlapping–or orthogonal–rather than a purportedly identical nature of the two in which an overt anti-Bushism exacerbated, legitimated, manifested and articulated an extant anti-Americanism that lay dormant though was never moribund among Europeans. Bush impersonated the very essence of America to millions of Europeans–and the tally was decidedly pejorative and negative.

Anti-Americanism, though a prejudice like any other in terms of its structural characteristics, differs markedly from "classical" prejudices such as anti-Semitism, homophobia, misogyny, and racism, in that in these latter cases where Jews, gays and lesbians, women, and ethnic minorities rarely, if ever, have any actual power in and over the majority of the populations in most countries in which they reside, the real existing United States most certainly does have power and plenty of it. Markovits has argued that it is precisely because of this important (and actually quite unique) difference that–unlike these other prejudices, which, as a fine testimony to progress and tolerance over the past forty-five years, have by and large become publicly illegitimate in accepted discourse of most advanced industrial democracies–anti-Americanism remains not only acceptable in many fine circles, but has become commendable, indeed perhaps even a distinct icon of what constitutes a progressive these days. After all, by being anti-American, one adheres to a prejudice that ipso facto also opposes a truly powerful force in the world. Thus, in the case of anti-Americanism, one's prejudice partially assumes an antinomian, dissenting, or oppositional purpose, thereby attaining a legitimacy that most other prejudices–thankfully–no longer have. As such, anti-Americanism assumes the role of what one could term a "progressive resentment." But, since progressives by definition do not admit to having any such foul feelings for anybody and since all resentments are by definition the bailiwicks of reaction, the concept of "progressive resentment"– though for us an apt categorization of much of European anti-Americanism–would be dismissed as oxymoronic and hence nonexistent. Anti-Americanism has become the polite and accepted racism of the European chattering classes. Or, to speak with Mary Fitzgerald:

> it seems perverse, then, that anti-Americanism is the only face of xenophobia still broadly accepted in Europe. If, at a dinner party, you imitated the way Chinese people speak, laughed about their stupidity, their "slitty eyes" and their lack of grace, you could safely expect never to be invited back. But no one thinks twice about calling Americans dumb, fat and uncultured. How is it acceptable for one superpower, but not the other, to be the object for such derision?"[22]

The answer to Fitzgerald's question is simple and straightforward. First, Europeans at such dinner parties would never perceive China as having anywhere near the power that they ascribe to the United States, in other words, Europeans do not regard China as the true "Mr. Big" to use Joseph Joffe's apt metaphor of the United States. Second, articulating equivalently negative views of China as have become commonplace about America in polite European society would be construed as racist since China is a non-Western and postcolonial power, therefore, ipso facto not nearly as evil or dangerous as the United States. Depicting China in a pejorative manner would be construed as "reactionary resentment" whereas doing the same to America falls under the category of "progressive resentment," thus, de facto no resentment at all. To many Europeans, Americans are tantamount to white, middle-class, heterosexual males who–as the all-powerful–are subject to attacks that, accorded to any other group, would rightly be gauged to be sexist, racist, classist, hurtful, and discriminatory. But, a group's perceived power allows its opponents to rail against it in the most prejudicial manner without any worries of incurring any costs in the form of moral sanctions or reprimands.

Indeed, one of Obama's most powerful a priori reasons for legitimacy in the eyes of Europeans hails precisely from the fact that he is African-American and thus not the stereotypical American in European eyes. The fact that it remains inconceivable for anybody vaguely like Obama–with his name and his racial background–to be elected to a comparable position of head of state and/or government in any European society endears him to Europeans further still since, with their racism and continued de facto ethnic perception of community not permitting anything similar to happen in Europe for many years to come, Europeans experienced the election of a black in America as an overdue corrective to that country's racist past as well as a vicarious step in their own world that–luckily in their view, though sotto voce –they still do not have to confront.

If anti-Americanism derives primarily from a prejudiced worldview instead of a reasoned criticism of American policies, if it remains anchored primarily in what Americans are instead of what their government does, as we have argued, it is less likely that anti-Americanism will vanish in the context of the Obama presidency from one day to the next. To assess whether anti-Americanism prevails under the new president, two questions have to be asked. First, does America remain the recipient of negative attitudes and feelings despite the overwhelming enthusiasm directed towards Barack Obama by West European publics? And, second, how can the positive identification with Obama in Europe remain congruent with our arguments about anti-Americanism's continued existence in Western Europe? In this chapter, we offer answers for Germany alone. To that end, we analyzed reporting by German daily and weekly newspapers.[23]

The Continuing Presence of Anti-American Patterns in the German Press

To answer the question as to whether anti-Americanism continues to have a presence in German public opinion following Obama's ascendance to the presidency, we found a survey conducted by *The Wall Street Journal* that offers some interesting insights into this matter. Asked about the quality of America's political influence over the past five years, an overwhelming majority of the Germans–73 percent–considered it to be a negative force, while only 7 percent perceived it in a positive light. To be sure, 82 percent of the respondents believed that America's political influence will change for the better under the Obama presidency. Placed into its proper context, this number appears a lot less rosy than a first glance might reveal. Let us not forget the abysmally low baseline which the German public accorded American foreign policy nary six months prior to this survey and that an expected improvement from such a negative starting point need not mean a genuine embrace of the new. It merely states that compared to the old, things will hopefully improve. No more, no less. It most certainly does not mean that Germans will now come to see the

United States as a positive force for them, for Europe or for the world–merely as less negative than under the Bush years.

Turning to the data depicting Germans' views of America's cultural influence, the negative not only exceeds the positive but also remains steady and unchanged from the pre-Obama days. Thus, 36 percent perceive America's cultural influence as negative, only 16 percent as positive. As can be expected, Germans rate America's culinary impact as particularly horrid: 52 percent regard America's export in this realm as the absolute worst U.S. contribution to world culture. Showing yet again the abysmally low regard Germans (and other Europeans for that matter) accord American high-brow culture such as art/architecture and literature, only 3-7 percent believe that this aspect of American culture has any global influence, indicating yet again that there exists little, if any, knowledge of, let alone respect for, American culture beyond its mass aspects which, though disdained and hated by Germans, remains avidly consumed by them.[24] This patent contradiction, even hypocrisy, has never stopped a large percentage of Germans to express negative attitudes about America and things American without shame and any social sanctions. It has not done so prior to the election of Obama, and will not do so during his incumbency. While this survey demonstrates some changes in German public opinion resulting from Obama's ascendancy to the presidency of the United States, it also reveals convincingly the unabated perpetuation of the most common staples of traditional anti-American stereotypes.

In the following section, we will focus on press and media coverage of three important relatively recent developments: the global financial crisis, the deadly rampage in Winnenden, and the NATO summit held in Strasbourg in April 2009. Lest our analysis be skewed by data hailing from publications on either end of the German political spectrum–both of which, incidentally, have traditionally and consistently exhibited a rabid anti-Americanism which constitutes one of the very few items that actually unites them–we have confined ourselves exclusively to the mainstream outlets of the German media landscape.

"Made in America"[25]—The Financial Crisis

As the U.S. stock market crashed in September 2008, the severity of the financial crisis became obvious. Soon there commenced the inevitable search for a culprit. And, sure enough, the German (and European) media found one with alacrity and certainty: the collapse of the financial market was attributed virtually solely to the rapacious "acquisitiveness" of Wall Street bankers.[26] The bankers—now considered "hoodlums" und "criminals"[27]—were striving voraciously and ruthlessly for selfish profit maximization.[28] But the bankers were soon joined by the American people as the major culprits of this financial crisis since it was they—with their "American way"—that led them to live beyond their means and pursue their happiness with loans they could not pay back. Now, so the schadenfreude, the Americans had to pay the just price for their profligacy. "In America the recession is ending an era of excess that had united the nation so wonderfully beyond entrenched differences."[29] One article actually compared the U.S. president to a grower of narcotic-producing plants and the Wall Street bankers to his drug dealers.[30]

Much of the German media explained the financial crisis not so much in terms of global economic processes and various structural interdependencies, but rather by personifications that labeled the supposedly guilty persons as criminals and decidedly morally bankrupt. Of course, there occurred a demonization of the "American" economic system[31] thus implying that it was basically the "American character" that created this crisis.

This corresponds solidly with the centuries-old anti-American stereotypes of Americans' "materialist nature," their "egotism" hailing from their overvalued notion of the "individual," their penchant for an "excessive life style" and their profoundly asocial nature which essentially neglects the collective good, excepting those of nationalism and religiosity. Making matters worse still in the eyes of the German media was the fact that the Americans and their inherent profligacy did not only inflict this disaster upon themselves but also upon innocent others, like the Europeans. This notion can be found in a particularly graphic illustration in Germany's leading intellectual weekly *Die Zeit*, where we witness the American eagle in free fall, with one claw tightly holding onto the European flag, taking it down with it into the abyss.[32] Thus, the German press not only associates American behavior, thinking and modus operandi with dishonorable and self-destructive motives, but also considers them dangerous and destructive for the whole world.

To be sure, when the crisis persisted, many voices arose across Germany and Europe that implicated each nation's financial machinations and economically irresponsible behavior as culprits for the disaster. Nobody could claim clean hands anymore. For a brief moment, this self-reflecting introspection silenced the initially expressed facile attitude that the crisis was solely an "American problem,"[33] and initiated a process of reflection about the capitalist system as a whole. But, even during this more sophisticated phase of the analysis, the United States soon reappeared as the major, if not necessarily sole, culprit by dint of its being primus inter pares–or hegemonic–among all capitalist countries. Accompanying the condemnation of America's "casino capitalism" was an idealization of Germany's–and Europe's–"Rhenish capitalism," a supposedly cozier, more harmless, and certainly more humane variant that, among many of its virtues, was authentically "German," but had to succumb to the forces of the stronger and more pervasive "American model:"

> Most Germans probably share [Peer] Steinbrück's [Germany's Finance Minister, from 2005-2009] loathing of wild Wall Street capitalism. They have long regarded it with suspicion. Earlier, so much seemed certain, things were cozier in Germany. At that time, Rhenish capitalism prevailed ... But then the dream burst: The somewhat fossilized German Model with its low rates of return was Americanized."[34]

Apart from the fact that the Rhenish (i.e., German) model of capitalism never disappeared and remained hegemonic in Germany (for very good reasons and in many instances to the country's advantage) across regimes led by Social as well as Christian Democrats, the demon of its American rival had to be invoked not as a legitimate alternative, a different manner of organizing state, market, and society, but as an unwanted conqueror. The Rhenish model was made to succumb to its American counterpart by America's pernicious power and unwelcome influence.

This theme has not only become commonly accepted within much of the German media and journalistic circles, but has also come to enjoy considerable legitimacy in academic discourse. Thus, for example, in a free-wheeling dinner lecture on 20 September 2009, to eighteen visiting scholars from all over the world who were guests of the German Academic Exchange Service (DAAD) to observe the last week of the campaign for the 2009 Bundestag election, Hans-Peter Burghof, Professor of Banking and Finance at the University of Hohenheim in Stuttgart repeatedly and decidedly blamed the economic crisis solely on America, American banking methods and the irresponsibility inherent to American risk taking and profit obsession.

"The newest trend from America: to run amok"[35]— The Shooting in Winnenden

A second event in the discussion of which the prevalence of traditional anti-American attitudes became obvious was the tragic shooting rampage in Winnenden. On 11 March 2009, a student shot twelve of his peers and teachers at his school and three other persons before killing himself in the small town of Winnenden in Southern Germany. Even though this happened in a German town and a German student did the killing, the event was rapidly associated with America.This was not directly expressed by journalists or politicians, but articles quoted bystanders who immediately invoked the United States in their first reaction to this horror. Clearly, the associations with America were instantaneously negative: "It is worse than in America—and that here of all places, where everyone could be content."[36] The association is furthermore supported by the idea that a tragic event like this is threated with equanimity in the United States by dint of its being an everyday occurence.[37] As though American society were not just as shocked and concerned in the face of such an atrocity befalling it.

In online forums where this event was broadly discussed, many comments, in addition to considering the shooting a "typical American phenomenon,"[38] referred to the event as an alleged "Americanization" of Germany, thus making its cause not an inherent problem of German society, but solely the result of a harmful foreign import.[39] "Americanization" in this context pertains to an alleged loss of values, standards, and decorum in Germany, and a process of alienation within German society. "The rampage in Winnenden shows once more that the Americanization of our society is advancing to a catastrophe."[40] Clearly, America, and "things American" were solidly considered to be a negative force in the world and direct culprits for tragedies like the shooting in Winnenden.

The German reaction to the Winnenden incident had virtually identical precedents.[41] A similarly tragic shooting spree at an Erfurt secondary school in 2002 immediately led to a discussion about "American conditions" in German schools and blaming the incident on the "Americanization" of German youth, their culture, even the ills of German society in general. Across the political spectrum, the specter of the 1999 massacre at Columbine High School in Littleton, Colorado was pushed into the center of the political debate about the Erfurt incident. Edmund Stoiber, the conservative prime minister of Bavaria, called for a general regulation of Internet content, so that "violent videos" and "killer games" be forbidden: "This is something we have to achieve on a world-wide scale even though, of course, we face the problem that the Americans have a completely different conception of freedom."[42] Stoiber's remarks alluded to the Americans' purported deification of freedom that others have termed "freedom Bolshevism." It remains wholly unclear just how this American conception of freedom (too much, too little?) differs from that of the Germans and what this means for the issue at hand. But, to go into details would be too burdensome and completely unnecessary for Stoiber. There was a lot of discussion about the pathological effect of violent games, from the "Power Rangers" to the life-like simulations of war depicted on computer screens. Among the many thousands of games of this genre, one called "America's Army" was, of course, especially emphasized. And, naturally, Hollywood had to take the blame, starting with cult movies like *Friday the 13th* and Oliver Stone's *Natural Born Killers*. Otherwise, Stone is held in high esteem by European film critics and the cultural elite as a director who drastically depicts the hypocrisy and brutality of everyday life in America.

Even the German police union issued another warning about "American conditions" at German schools in the aftermath of the Erfurt tragedy. In a press release, it said:

> The German Police Union demands more security in German schools. There now exist those 'American conditions we always warned against,' said the federal vice-chairman of the union, Wendt ... This also means increasing security standards 'up to and including uniformed guard personnel.'"[43]

Although the police now wanted to protect their officers, if need be, "by carrying protective vests and, of course, a weapon," and to allow them ("in order to be able to react quickly") to handle their weapons outside their holsters and search persons and vehicles with weapons drawn, things would not be taking a turn for the worst, the police official reassured the German public: "But there will not be rigorously intervening 'sheriffs' here at home, because the police will remain public-friendly."[44] And public-friendliness is, as we know, as un-American as violence is American. In a long interview, the chair of the police union, Thomas Mohr, issued a reassurance that German police would not try to introduce American conditions under any circumstances.[45]

After the tragedy at Erfurt hardly anyone mentioned the catastrophe that happened in 1996 in the Scottish town of Dunblane, where a youth councilor had murdered sixteen children and a teacher. Not that "record-setting" ought ever to matter in tragedies like this, but the fact is that three more people died in Dunblane than was the case at Columbine. Nobody in Germany mentioned this tragedy, and nobody talked about a "Britishization" of German schools, German violence, or German youth. Conversely, the British media constantly featured the "Americanisation" of British youth culture as the main reason for the terrible incident in Dunblane. The fact that the Columbine incident could not be brought into play, because it happened three years after the Dunblane tragedy, did not prevent anybody discussing the Scottish tragedy from invoking America as a general bogeyman in this case as well.

But, not only in Germany is Dunblane as good as unknown. After a similar incident in the Parisian suburb of Nanterre in March 2002, the media, municipal city administration, and citizens talked exclusively about America, Americanization, and "American conditions." "'This isn't happening here. It's like America, not France. It's a pure nightmare,' said Germaine, a council secretary in her 40s, as police escorted relatives through the underground car-park into the building where the bodies of eight council members still lay in the meeting chamber."[46]

When it comes to violence and criminality, "Americanization" has played a central role in European discussions and notions since the 1920s. To this day, Chicago is associated with gangsters by Europeans. Europeans regarded leather-jacketed rowdies in the 1950s as wannabe Americans in the same way as the motorcycle gangs of the 1960s and subsequent decades. A documentary about *Kicking for Dunblane* would be totally unthinkable in Europe. *Bowling for Columbine*, however, became an icon of European anti-Americanism.

"Obama charmiert Europa in die Enge"[47]—"Killing Us Softly with His Song"

NATO Summit

Under the Bush presidency one of the most vehemently repeated reproaches of the United States voiced by Europeans was America's alleged unilateralism in global politics. As Federico Romero argues in regard to the disagreements over the "war on terror:"

> West Europeans by and large did not dispute the strategic or moral implications of the "war on terror"—at least prior to America's war against Iraq becoming this war's main focus—but its unilateral management by the Americans, the lack of consultation with European governments, and the fact that Washington did not perceive cooperation as a two-way street.[48]

The allegedly arrogant tone of the Americans' modus operandi was, if anything, an even greater irritant to the Europeans than its content. Nothing has filled the Europeans with greater hopes regarding the Obama presidency than a drastic change in his administration's tone and substance in the conduct of American foreign policy.[49] But the requisite skepticisms on the European side have accompanied these high hopes from the very beginning. The danger now perceived by the Europeans is that this president's charm and charisma will become irresistible thus potentially undermining European strategic interests and policy independence: "It is not so easy with this new President. Because he comes over as so persuasive, it is so hard to formulate German interests against his policies."[50]

In the context of the G20 and NATO summits in London and Strasbourg in early April 2009, Obama received a lot of positive press for his attentive listening, his general openness and his respect towards the European heads of state and government.[51] But, Obama's behavior also received negative marks, mainly for his being manipulative, for using his charm and seeming empathy to exact concessions from the Europeans. Of particular concern to the Europeans was Obama's implicitly demanding increased contributions to the battle against the Taliban and its allies in Afghanistan by saying in Strasbourg that America could not shoulder the problem of terrorism on its own without, however, explicitly requesting any additional help from the Europeans. Sure enough, some interpreted Obama's behavior as "pressure through charm:" "Without mentioning specific numbers or uttering the word 'troops' he [Obama] embellished his words so beautifully that Merkel was only left to smile. Obama's quiet tones are part of a strategy to which Europe can hardly deny any cooperation."[52] Thus, Obama's novel multilateralism is in this case not considered to be a positive quality and a welcome change to the arrogant unilateralism of the two Bush terms, but rather as a new, and somewhat devious, method to bamboozle the Europeans and get them to do what Obama and the Americans want via the president's seemingly irresistible charm. So, here we have it again: once more, the Europeans are victims of America's dominant position which, in this case, is exercised by a popular president's charisma instead of a hated president's brutishness. The results, however, appear to vary very little.

This criticism becomes even more contradictory. Obama is criticized for usurping and "Americanizing" the mission in Afghanistan, thereby depriving the European governments of the opportunity to influence the war in Afghanistan, even though the German chancellor and other European leaders have hardly shown any interest in doing so by increasing their commitment in that war.[53] Thus, by asking for more European support, Obama is seen as pressuring his allies. Given that the Europeans show little interest in an extension of their efforts, Obama is then blamed for monopolizing the mission. This is an example of how new argumentation schemes directed against the U.S. are evolving in European discourse, adapting to the new circumstances in American politics under the Obama presidency. One could call this "killing us softly with his song:" damned if you do, damned if you don't, damned if you are a bully, damned if you are a charmer.

The Integration of Obamamania into an Anti-American Perception

The effusive praise of Obama by Europeans in no way excludes the antipathies harbored by Europeans towards America, which received unprecedented amplification and legitimacy during the eight years of the Bush presidency. It seems as if the successful slogan of "change" promoted by Obama and the positive identification with Obama in Europe offered yet another pretext to voice once again one's displeasure with America and its ways while at the same time affirming–almost by definition–Europe's moral superiority. To many Europeans, Obama's election served as the first gambit in America's re-entry into the league of "civilized nations." The war against Iraq, as well as against terrorism, Guantanamo, Abu Ghraib, the refusal to sign the Kyoto Protocol, and many other American deeds and policies became prima facie evidence for the publics in Western Europe that Americans were inherently brutal and most assuredly different from Europeans, if not downright inferior. Thus, Obama's election was celebrated far and wide among Europe's chattering classes as the first American step in the country's long road towards being a civilized place, the criteria of which were, of course, solely a European prerogative. Obama's ascendance was a welcome sign for Europeans that there was some hope for America to return to its senses. "Welcome, America! For five years, the U.S. has been a stranger–if not an enemy–to us Germans. Now the nation is returning to the West; and to our hearts."[54]

We would be the first to join in the unmitigated condemnation of the illegal, unconstitutional and reprehensible policies and actions perpetrated by the administrations of Bush. Indeed, both of us continue to hope and work for the initiation of legal procedures that would bring the culprits for these errand ways to justice. But, while we see these reprehensible actions as an aberration in America's ways of dealing with the world, including its enemies, anti-Americanism in Europe has come to view them as exemplary and representative of America's very essence which Obama's presence could surely mitigate though not quite eliminate. Furthermore, few of the West European countries live up to the standards of human rights that they claim to uphold (just think of the treatment of immigrants among other cases) with Guantánamo and Abu Ghraib having made it easy for the Europeans to point their fingers at the United States, claiming moral superiority, instead of dealing with their own problems.[55] This view of the Obama presidency's having initiated the United States' return to the fold of the civilized club of the Western community has been accompanied by the idea of Obama as a "European."

"Un-American" Barack Obama

One way to integrate enthusiasm for and identification with Obama into an anti-American world view is to consider him an "honorary European."[56] Many of Obama's characteristics that Europeans value and cherish appear to them as genuinely "European." Seeing Obama as a de facto European constitutes one of the main reasons for his immense popularity in Germany and elsewhere in Europe. "Many in Europe wish for nothing more eagerly than having a European America. In all countries, Germany among them, in which public servants define the tone and content of political discourse, a former social worker from Chicago seems to fit the bill perfectly. This is the modern America we wish for: black, social and gentle."[57] Craig Kennedy, the president of the German Marshall Fund of the United States, reached the same conclusion when he commented on a 2009 Transatlantic Trends survey in which more than 90 percent of the Germans had a favorable view of Obama.[58] He stated that the viewing of Obama as "more European in his sensibilities than his policies" constituted the primary reason for the remarkable difference to the Europeans' assessment of Bush a year ago when only 19 percent of them supported Mr. Bush's foreign policy. "I suspect that as real political decisions have to be made, we will see 'Obama-Euphoria' fade as the Europeans begin to see him more as an American and less like themselves."[59]

The idea of Obama as "European" is ubiquitous in the German and European media, both print and electronic. It is interesting in this context to analyze what attributes are regularly assigned to "Europe" and which ones to "America." To wit:

> Obama is much closer to the Germans; despite his skin color, he seems less alien, you might say he appears so nicely European: not a cowboy from Texas, but a Harvard graduate with an urban background; instead of a 'straight shooter,' someone, who relies on dialogue and mutual understanding.[60]

Other articles construct the opposing pair of "bellicose American Mars" and "peaceloving European Venus," [61] or suggest that Americans are trying to be "Superpowermen." [62] Notably, "Americans" are considered to be like cowboys meaning uneducated, aggressive, uncouth, belligerent, and striving for global domination, while to be "European" in this view of the world entails being educated, polite, cultured, and having a multilateral approach to conflicts. Europeans now perceive Obama to share these European qualities which–ipso facto–render him non-American and a virtual European. Thus, the European love for Obama easily fits–indeed corroborates–the conventional anti-Americanism so widely shared as a European lingua franca during the years of the George W. Bush presidency, but also well before, of course.

A solidly common strategy of prejudice pertains here: what does not fit is thus made to fit. If Obama does not represent the "real" America, then his character and his actions do not contradict the idea that the "typical" America still remains deeply objectionable to Europeans and can thus be maintained as a marker of negativity and an object of antipathy. Obama, within this logic, constitutes part of the "other America" that, according to Diner, represents the very own "self" and therefore serves as a vehicle for positive identification.[63]

What makes the construct of Obama's being an idealized European truly reprehensible to us is the crucial fact that nobody vaguely similar to Obama in terms of skin color, name, personal history, family background, achievement, optimism, vivaciousness, and verve could come close to being elected to a mid-level position in regional politics, let alone to becoming head of state and government.[64] Europeans' hypocrisy on this issue appears to be boundless. Europeans thus usurp Obama's progressiveness and his very being to create an idealized European self-perception in pronounced contrast to a continued denigration of the "real" America which remains as uncouth as it has ever been despite electing Obama as its president. Far from lifting Europe's antipathy towards America, European Obamamania reinforces a dichotomous view of the world in which "Europe" represents a morally better place than "America." European Obamamania has not overcome the widely held perception in Europe of its being a morally more righteous place and a more benevolent force in the world than America.

The "Post-American Era"

Obama may be vigorously liked in Europe for one additional reason: his being the first president to preside over the so called "post-American era."[65] Tout court, many among West Europe's chattering classes delight in what they perceive to be a loss in America's global power and a clear weakening of its former reach in the economy, culture, politics and even military affairs. The schadenfreude could hardly be more emphatic. In the

German press, for example, there seems little doubt that America is in decline, though there is still no clear consensus as to whether the United States will continue to be a strong and important player or whether it is losing its power while helplessly clinging to the remains of its empire. "After the debacle of the past months [financial crisis] that is in the opinion of many not over yet, American authority is simply no longer accepted."[66]

Clearly, the constellation of global power structures changes constantly with the complex interplay of forces such as China, India, Brazil, Russia, Japan, and the European Union, adding hitherto unparalleled and completely incalculable dimensions, but the summary way in which German and European pundits blithely dismiss American power seems to be more the consequence of a wishful schadenfreude and a superciliousness rather than sober reasoning and the weighing of evidence. To wit: "Learning how to decline—is that possible? Can a superpower that is no longer capable of dominating the world find a new role without falling into a state of depression and anxiety; is there life after the brief moment of Empire?"[67] Furthermore, the transformation of power constellations is not explained by looking at intricate and multifaceted processes changing current global politics, but is attributed precisely to those political decisions which have been the major target of European criticism of the past ten years, namely the wars against Iraq and in Afghanistan, Guantánamo and the financial crisis.[68] Focusing the argument on these American missteps, the European position thus appears to receive solid confirmation by dint of the alleged decline of American power. No matter the national origin of the interlocutor, in this case Andrew J. Bacevich, the noted American foreign policy expert at Boston University, comments such as these remain ubiquitous in Europe and reflect the aforementioned schadenfreude regarding America's decline:

> As far as the art of governance is concerned, the Bush era teaches us basically three lessons: overbearing arrogance has shown the limits of American global leadership; carelessness and dilettantism revealed the limits of its military strength; and the foolish and immoderate refusal of the Americans not to build their wealth on tick and not to live beyond their means has demonstrated the limits of American prosperity.[69]

Obamamania has no bearing at all on views of America that the sentiment in this quotation expresses and that is widely shared in Europe. Accordingly, the role that Europeans consider appropriate for the United States in the future is no longer "to lead the world"—as Obama has repeatedly claimed—but to assume a more humble position: "The World President has to be in the first place a World Moderator."[70] European Obamamania might indeed diminish in the course of Obama's "real existing" presidency if the latter's deeds assume certain paths that will not conform to European preferences and expectations.

Conclusion

We argue in this chapter that antipathy towards America accompanied by anti-American language and attitudes have not disappeared in Germany and Europe due to the ascendancy of Obama to the office of the president of the United States. Obamamania has not become a magic wand that would annul overnight the resentment towards America on the part of Germans and other West Europeans. To be sure, Obama's America appears somewhat cleansed to Europeans, if only by dint of the new president's clear rejection of his predecessor's despised ways and means. America seems to be on the road to regaining its senses which, of course, means adopting a "European" approach to things which are not only morally superior to America's preferred modus operandi but also embody a more mature—i.e., nuanced—strategy of dealing with the world. None of these improved views, however, obviate the Germans' and Europeans' baseline disdain for America as the bastion of consumerism, violence, selfishness, and inauthenticity—in short of embodying an uncouth nation. Perhaps the only sound reason for Europeans' hope concerning America—other than the advent of Barack Obama—pertains to their rejoicing in America's real or alleged loss of power which is welcomed as a boon for Europe and the world. Furthermore, by rendering the popular Obama into a de facto European—sort of as an errand soul that appeared somehow miraculously in the American wasteland—Germans have easily decoupled Obama from the "real" America thereby allowing them to maintain their negative views of America without a moment's interruption and without experiencing any contradiction or dissonance between their love for Obama on the one hand and their disdain for America on the other. Thus, Obamamania offers no prima facie evidence of a changing European perception of the United States. Instead, it merely provides a new veneer of respectability for one's otherwise prominent antipathies towards America. Lastly, the identification with Obama perpetuates an idealized European self-perception, while still casting America as a morally and socially inferior Other. The fall of the Berlin Wall twenty years ago and the subsequent geopolitical earthquake that altered virtually everything in the contemporary post 1989 Europe as compared to its pre 1989 predecessor—from number of countries to political alliances, from economic systems to currencies, from ethnic compositions to migration patterns–seems not to have diminished the historically extant salience of anti-Americanism among this continent's chattering classes. If anything, its potency and immediacy attained a hitherto unknown dimension–that of enhancing Europe's very own identity.

Notes

1. See http://www.whitehouse.gov/the_press_office/Remarks-by-President-Obama-at-Strasbourg-Town-Hall/.
2. This observation is reflected in opinion polls as well as in academic research: Opinion Polls: Pew Global Attitudes Project (2002), *What the World Thinks in 2002: How Global Publics View: their Lives, their Countries, the World, America*, available at http://pewglobal.org/reports/display.php?ReportID=165; accessed 15 November 2007; Pew Global Attitudes Project (2006), *America's Image Slips, But Allies Share U.S. Concerns Over Iran, Hamas*, available at www.pewglobal.org/reports/display.php?ReportID=252; accessed 15 November 2007; Transatlantic Trends (2007), *Wichtigste Ergebnis 2007*, available at http://www.transatlantictrends.org/trends/index.cfm?id=62; accessed 15 November 2007. See also Russell A. Berman, *Anti-Americanism in Europe: A Cultural Problem* (Stanford, 2004); Andrei S. Markovits, *Uncouth Nation: Why Europe Dislikes America* (Princeton, 2007); Brendon O'Connor and Martin Griffiths, eds., *Anti-Americanism: History, Causes, and Themes*, 4 vols. (Oxford, 2007); Federico Romero, "The Twilight of American Cultural Hegemony: A Historical Perspective on Western Europe's Distancing from America," in *What They Think of Us: International Perceptions of the United States since 9/11*, ed., David Farber (Princeton, 2007), 153-175.
3. Ivan Krastev, "The Anti-American Century?" *Journal of Democracy*, 15, no. 2 (2004): 5.
4. Andrei S. Markovits, *Amerika, dich haßt sich's besser: Antiamerikanismus und Antisemitismus in Europa* (Hamburg, 2004), 15. See also James W. Ceaser, "A Genealogy of Anti-Americanism," *The Public Interest* 152 (2003): 4.
5. Instantaneously, Obama received the nickname: the "black Kennedy." Peter Gruber, "Barack Obama–Der schwarze Kennedy," *Focus online*, 26 May 2008, available at http://www.focus.de/politik/ausland/uswahl/usa-barack-obama-der-schwarze-kennedy_aid_303970.html; accessed 5 September 2008.
6. Corinna Edmundts, "Große Träume eines Weltverbesserers," www.tagesschau.de, 25 July 2008, available at http://www.tagesschau.de/inland/obamarede108.html; accessed 27 October 2008.
7. Holger Kulick, "Wasserwerfereinsatz gegen Demonstranten," *Spiegel online*, 23 May 2002, available at http://www.spiegel.de/politik/deutschland/0,1518,197314,00.html; accessed 14 March 2009.
8. Pew Global Attitudes Project, *Obamamania Abroad: The Candidate Can Expect a Warm Welcome in Europe, Not So in the Middle East*, available at http://pewresearch.org/pubs/900/obama-trip-abroad; accessed 5 September 2008.
9. Stefan Kornelius, "Im Dienst Amerikas," *Süddeutsche Zeitung*, 21 January 2009. ZDF Interview with Christoph Bertram, "Das Ende des Antiamerikanismus," www.zdf.de,

5 November 2008, available at http://uswahl.zdf.de/ZDFheute/inhalt/27/ 0,3672,7399419,00.html; accessed 10 November 2008.

10. See Paul Hollander, *Anti-Americanism: Critiques at Home and Abroad 1965-1990* (New York, 1992); Dan Diner, *Feindbild Amerika: Über die Beständigkeit eines Ressentiments* (Munich, 2002); Markovits (see note 2); Barry Rubin and Judith Rubin Colp, *Hating America: A History* (Oxford, 2004); Peter Katzenstein and Robert Keohane differentiate between fundamental sources of anti-americanism referring to what America *is* and ephemeral parts directed against what America *does*. Peter J. Katzenstein and Robert O. Keohane, eds., *Anti-Americanisms in World Politics* (Ithaca, 2007), 2.

11. Ceaser (see note 4), 4.

12. Brendon O'Connor, "What is Anti-Americanism?," in O'Connor and Griffiths (see note 2), vol. 1, *Causes and Sources*, 2.

13. Peter Lösche, "Antiamerikanismus in der Bundesrepublik? Stereotype über Ronald Reagan in der deutschen Presse," *Amerikastudien* 31, no. 3 (1986): 355-362. Rob Kroes, "Anti-Americanism and Anti-Modernism in Europe: Old and Recent Versions" in *Americanization and Anti-Americanism: The German Encounter with American Culture after 1945*, ed., Alexander Stephan (New York, 2005), 202; Markovits (see note 4).

14. Markovits (see note 2), especially Chapter 5.

15. Robert Singh, "The Bush Doctrine and Anti-Americanism" in O'Connor and Griffiths (see note 3), vol. 4, *In the 21st Century*, 67-91.

16. Markovits (see note 2).

17. Singh (see note 15).

18. Markovits (see note 2), 4.

19. The projection of traditional stereotypes onto the respective president has already been analyzed in regards to the perception of Ronald Reagan in 1986. See Lösche (see note 13).

20. Philipp Gassert "Amerikanismus, Antiamerikanismus, Amerikanisierung: Neue Literatur zur Sozial-, Wirtschafts- und Kulturgeschichte des amerikanischen Einflusses in Deutschland und Europa", *Archiv für Sozialgeschichte* 39 (1999): 561; Konrad Jarausch, "Missverständnis Amerika. Antiamerikanismus als Projektion," in *Antiamerikanismus im 20. Jahrhundert. Studien zu Ost- und Westeuropa*, eds., Jan C. Behrends, Árpád von Klimó and Patrice G. Poutrus (Bonn, 2005), 34-49.

21. Diner (see note 10), 9. This analogy of anti-Americanism and anti-Modernism can also be found in: Hollander, *Anti-Americanism*; Richard Herzinger and Hannes Stein, eds., *Endzeit-Propheten oder Die Offensive der Antiwestler: Fundamentalismus, Antiamerikanismus und Neue Rechte* (Hamburg: Rowohlt, 1995); Berman (see note 2); Kroes (see note 13).

22. Mary Fitzgerald, "Love to hate you," *The New Statesman*, 12 February 2007.

23. The analysis has so far been on the basis of examples rather than systematic, but is nonetheless revealing.

24. See Adam Cohen, "How Europe views America," *Wall Street Journal*, 19 June 2009, available at http://online.wsj.com/article/SB124534162608828017.html; accessed 19 June 2009.

25. John Gray, "Sternstunde der Bedeutungslosigkeit," *Süddeutsche Zeitung*, 2 April 2009.

26. "The acquisitiveness of the Wall-Street banker pulls down the financial markets at a pace that is making people dizzy." Matthias Nass, "Verrat am amerikanischen Traum," *Die Zeit*, 1 October 2009.

27. Kayhan Özgenc, "Nieten in Nadelstreifen? Nein, Ganoven," *Focus online*, 25 September 2008, available at http://www.focus.de/finanzen/news/oezgenc_oekonomie/ finanzkrise-nieten-in-nadelstreifen-nein-ganoven_aid_335699.html; accessed 19 October 2008.

28. Needless to say, the noun "Raffgier" appeared, as did its adjectival version "raffgierig" and/or "raffendes" which, of course, have antisemitic overtones since "Jewish," i.e., "financial" and "speculative" capital traditionally was depicted in Germany as "raffendes Kapital" in contrast to its German counterpart of "schaffendes Kapital" that was construed as being constructive and creative.

29. Jörg Häntzschel, "Gierige Bastarde," *Süddeutsche Zeitung*, 30 March 2009.

30. "Wall Street and the banks, the greedy of the financial industry, played an important, but not the decisive role. The bank managers were the dealer, who brought the hot speculation money to the people. But the poppy farmer sits in the White House"–here still referring to George W. Bush. Gabor Steingart, "Der goldene Schuss," *Spiegel Online*, 03 April 2009, available at http://www.spiegel.de/wirtschaft/0,1518,617151,00.html; accessed 12 April 2009.

31. For the "greedy American model" or "Wall Street racketeering" see Wolfgang Koydl, "Der erste unter zwanzig," *Süddeutsche Zeitung*, 2 April 2009. For "Anglo-Saxon turbo-capitalism" see Beate Balzli, et al., "Der Schwarze Herbst," *Der Spiegel* 42, 13 October 2008, 25.

32. *Die Zeit*, 1 October 2008.

33. As it has been voiced by former German minister of finance, Peer Steinbrück. "Peer Steinbrück sieht Finanzkrise als Zeitenwende," *Welt online*, 25 September 2008, available at http://www.welt.de/politik/article2490506/Peer-Steinbrueck-sieht-Finanzkrise-als-Zeitenwende.html; accessed 27 April 2009.

34. Wienand von Petersdorff, "Früher war es gemütlicher," *Frankfurter Allgemeine Sonntagszeitung*, 29 March 2009.

35. Comment of elphy90, available at http://www.youtube.com/watch?v=tMM6A6n6NFA.

36. An old women, cited by Hans Georg Frank, "Winnenden: eine Stadt trauert," *Südwest Presse online*, 11 March 2009, available at http://www.swp.de/Nachrichten/amoklauf/Winnenden+Eine+Stadt+trauert;art4200466; accessed 17 March 2009.

37. "In America people are always doing this. But I don't believe that this is happening at my school." Diane (fourteen), as quoted in "An unserer Schule passiert das nicht," Protocoll by Inge Kloepfer and Christine Ritzenhoff, www.faz.net, 17 March 2009, available at http://www.faz.net/s/RubF44DB96803344C01A48C93EDADCB0551/Doc~E078A616B63ED456D92675F2C5B0CF357~ATpl~Ecommon~Scontent.html; accessed 17 March 2009.

38. "This morning, I still thought, typical America (the same happened there)!! Now it's happened here too," Stephan1, available at http://www.wohnmobilforum.de/w-t37882.html.

39. "Before this, it has been said: such a thing only happens in America. Now it has to be said: America has come to Winnenden," Condolence of Fam. Wolny from Weiler zum Stein, available at http://www.kondolenzbuch-online.de/cgibin/2009/books/00172.pl?&action=view&start=1611.

40. Comment by Wolfslady, available at http://www.focus.de/politik/deutschland/sicherheit-an-schulen-diskussion-um-lehren-aus-dem-amoklauf_aid_379491.html#comment.

41. Similar discussions occurred following the shooting in Erfurt in 2002. See Markovits (see note 2), 123ff.

42. "Stoiber fordert generelle Reglementierung des Internet," www.heise online, 7 May 2002, available at www.heise.de./newsticker/meldung/27228; accessed 18 April 2009.

43. "27. April: Trauer, Entsetzen und Suche nach Konsequenzen," MDR, 4 July 2002, available at http://www.mediengewalt.de/_arc/pre/ard/001-7-1.htm; accessed 22 April 2009.

44. Ibid.

45. "Wir wollen keine amerikanischen Verhältnisse," *Die Rheinpfalz*, 14 July 2000.

46. Charles Bremner, "It's like America not France–a pure nightmare," *The Times*, 28 March 2002.

47. Matthias Gebauer, "Obama charmiert Europa in die Enge," *Spiegel online*, 3 April 2009, available at http://www.spiegel.de/politik/ausland/0,1518,617359,00.html; accessed 7 April 2009.

48. Romero (see note 2), 157.

49. "Isn't the whole world watching these weeks, as a new America is emerging? A peaceful, benign, compassionate one? The peoples of Europe, of Asia are waiting for such an America, one that will not always rely on military interventions, that can listen and welcomes his guests, an America, which respects and maybe even supports the United Nations and will strive for multilateralism because of its own interests." Klaus Brinkbäumer and Marc Hujer, "Der Menschenfänger," *Der Spiegel*, 11 February 2008, 90.
50. Ralf Beste, et. al., "Neue deutsche Teilung," *Der Spiegel*, 2 February 2009, 23.
51. Daniel Brössler and Paul-Anton Krüger, "Wiedersehen macht Freude," *Süddeutsche Zeitung*, 4/5 April 2009.
52. Gebauer (see note 47).
53. "With the replenishment of the troops in Afghanistan, Obama monopolizes the mission completely, he becomes commander in chief of the war in Afghanistan, the NATO-mission is Americanized ... The Europeans would only have marginal influence on the mission–they could command their own troops, but the USA could do as it pleases." Ibid.
54. Bernd Ulrich, "Willkommen, Amerika!" *Die Zeit*, 6 November 2008.
55. The refusal of admitting of Guantánamo inmates to Germany by the German Ministry of the Interior clearly demonstrated that there is little concern about the well-being of the prisoners. "Schäuble: Guantanamo-Häftlinge sind Problem der USA," *Der Tagesspiegel*, 21 January 2009, available at http://www.tagesspiegel.de/politik/deutschland/Guantanamo-SPD-CDU;art122,2711511; accessed 8 March 2009.
56. Andrei S. Markovits and Jeff Weintraub, "Some Blind Spots and Hypocrisies of European Obamamania," *The Huffington Post*, 10 June 2008, available at http://www.huffingtonpost.com/andrei-markovits-and-jeff-weintraub/some-blind-spots-and-hypo_b_106187.html; accessed 16 October 2008.
57. Gabor Steingart, "Das Ende der Obama Revolution," *Spiegel online*, 21 January 2008, available at http://www.spiegel.de/politik/ausland/0,1518,529824,00.html; accessed 23 September 2008.
58. Transatlantic Trends, Key Findings 2009, available at http://www.transatlantictrends.org/trends/keyfindings.html, accessed 12 September 2009.
59. As quoted in Peter Baker, "President's global image holds little sway," *International Herald Tribune*, 21 September 2009.
60. Ralf Beste, et al.: "Obama für Deutschland," *Der Spiegel*, 21 July 2008.
61. Jörg Lau, "Amerikas Hirn unter Schock," *Die Zeit*, 30 October 2008.
62. Josef Joffe, "Der Traum wird wahr," *Die Zeit*, 6 November 2008.
63. Diner (see note 10), 35.
64. Markovits and Weintraub (see note 56).
65. Jan Ross, "Helden des Rückzugs," *Die Zeit*, 1 October 2008.
66. Gray (see note 25).
67. Ross (see note 65).
68. "The miserable wars in Iraq and Afghanistan overburden the military power, the nation's *hard power* seems to have deteriorated. At the same time the financial crisis has ruined America's *soft power*." Christian Wernicke, "Amerikas einziger Trumph," *Süddeutsche Zeitung*, 30 March 2009. On Guantanamo, see Stefan Kornelius, "Gerechtigkeit nach Guantanamo," *Süddeutsche Zeitung*, 13 November 2008.
69. Andrew J. Bacevich: "Was kommt nach Amerika. Das Ende der Arroganz," *Zeit online*, 6 February 2009, available at http://www.zeit.de/2009/04/Post-Amerika-Bace; accessed 18 April 2009.
70. Patrick Schwarz, "Weltpräsident trifft Weltkrise," *Die Zeit*, 13 November 2008.

Chapter 6

$\mathscr{P}$ASSING TIME SINCE THE *WENDE*

Recent German Film on Unification

Brad Prager

Still today, it remains difficult to assess properly the consequences of the fall of the Berlin Wall, regardless of whether one is standing inside or outside of Germany. At the moment of the event itself, however, its consequences would have remained wholly obscure. In a critical assessment of the event, Susan Buck-Morss notes that "images of dazed and drinking Germans on top of the Berlin Wall gave the world a rush of freedom, but also provided little vision of the content of what was to come."[1] Antonio Negri likewise offers a reflective account of the events of that day, and notes the double-edged character of Germany's transformation:

> I saw these joyful people on television who came from the other side to buy themselves a pair of shoes. Fundamentally, they were miserable in the new consumerist ideology, but all of that was nothing compared to the true joy they felt upon exiting that totalitarian world in order to find a little freedom.[2]

Negri's speculative comments tend toward generalization–some Germans may have been miserable, others less so–but his version of events has the virtue of contradicting most of the traditional narratives.

Now that two decades have passed, the history books are beginning to make sense of matters. It is little surprise that cinema, which was likewise startled by the events of November 1989, continues to reconsider them as well. Film bears both conscious and unconscious witness to change and thus both constructs and is constructed by historians' narratives. Many films–including Oskar Roehler's *Die Unberührbare* (No Place to Go, 1999), Robert Thalheim's *Netto* (2004), and Christian Petzold's *Yella* (2007)–participate in recasting the past, engage in dialog about the fall of the Wall, and assess the *Wende's* consequences. They constitute part of the construction of what Jan and Aleida Assmann have referred to as cultural memory.[3] Cinema is a symptom of public discourse, but it is likewise an intervention in that discourse. Film has, however, a unique status in that it can mimetically or self-consciously engage with how history is mediated through images–for example, that most of the world saw footage of joyful Germans on their television sets–and, perhaps more important, cinema is itself always engaged with the passage of time because it provides the illusion of a moving image. In these respects among others, cinema has the potential to cut against the grain of conventional history.

Looking back, one may feel some degree of sympathy for the unreflected approach taken by Margarethe von Trotta's *Das Versprechen* (The Promise, 1994). This early feature film now appears as a banal staging of what its audiences were already supposed to know. Co-written by von Trotta and the West German writer Peter Schneider, its narrative is straightforward: a young East German couple, Konrad and Sophie, decides to flee to the West shortly after the construction of the Berlin Wall. At the last moment, Konrad demurs, offering the weak excuse that his shoelace came untied during their escape. The Wall thus separates him from Sophie. After several years of waiting for Konrad to conjure the courage to leave East Germany and his family, Sophie gives up and makes an independent life for herself in the West. Decades pass, the film's young actors are replaced by older ones, and, at the end, the Wall is opened. The two have the opportunity to be reunited along with Alexander, the son they conceived during a brief tryst, yet both acknowledge that it has grown too late–Germany's division permanently has etched itself into their lives. It was a wound that could not be healed for members of their generation.

Von Trotta's film, made in the wake of those events depicted at its climax, resonates profoundly with Christa Wolf's East German novel *Der geteilte Himmel* (The Divided Heaven, 1963), which also deals with a couple separated by the Berlin Wall. Although the gender roles are reversed–in Wolf's work Rita stays in East Germany, while Manfred emigrates to the West–there are numerous parallels. One key difference, however, is that Rita tells the story from the hospital in the wake of a breakdown, lending a literary irony to the narrative found nowhere in von Trotta and Schneider's earnest reconstruction. Von Trotta's film in some ways presents itself as even more ideological than Wolf's over-determined work insofar as the former consciously avoids ambivalences where the East German state is concerned. The message of *Das Versprechen* is clear, and it affirms the overall impression that East German history was wholly defined by a diabolical state and its Stasi (secret police). Much of this resonated with Germans–the film was acclaimed and won the Bavarian Film Prize for Best Director. Nevertheless, it also conveniently dovetailed with the most conventional historical narratives. Looking at the scenes of jubilation found in documentary films such as *Das war die DDR* (1993) and even the footage readily available on YouTube today, these images seem more or less reproduced wholesale in the final moments of von Trotta's film. With respect to the construction of cultural memory, her work dramatized what had been seen all over German television, reflecting the general sentiment, rather than taking the opportunity to cut against it.

Das Versprechen struck a chord, telling the story as many Germans wanted it told. Later films such as Leander Haußmann's *Sonnenallee* (1999) and Wolfgang Becker's *Good Bye, Lenin!* (2003) have been cited since then as examples of mainstream German films that, as a consequence of added time and their greater distance from the events of 1989, brought nuance to the subject. Each suggested that it was acceptable to praise life in the former East, even for those who had been entirely unsympathetic to the State.[4] Writing about *Sonnenallee* and *Good Bye, Lenin!*, Seán Allan notes that these films neither reject daily life in the German Democratic Republic (GDR) (as did *Das Versprechen*), nor do they lapse into outright sentimental idealization of that vanished lifestyle.[5] In light of their more ironic counterparts, *Das Versprechen* as well as the later, Academy Award winning hit *Das Leben der Anderen* (The Lives of Others, 2006) both can be seen to reproduce crass Manichean accounts wherein good people are juxtaposed with a bad police state. Both of these films, however, share with *Good Bye, Lenin!* the intention of placing the problems of the past squarely in the past, and leaving the bad old days behind. The narrative of Becker's film centers on a young East German, again named Alex (as in Alexanderplatz) whose mother's sudden fall into a coma takes place shortly before the fall of the Wall. Once she awakens Alex does all that he can to prevent her from confronting the possibly upsetting news that the GDR has collapsed. His charade leads to comic situations, many of which are premised on recreating the comforts of a lifestyle they have come to know and that is slipping away from them. Alex's mother dies at the film's end, and his farewell to her is presented as a farewell to East Germany itself. This summary of the film does not do justice to its thoughtful play with psychic investments–with the film's evident Oedipal thematic and with the clever notion that Alex was protecting his own inability to move beyond the past rather than his mother's–yet the film is mainly about mourning, or about how Germany would proceed into history's next stage. As Jennifer M. Kapczynski argues, *Good Bye, Lenin!* "enact[s] the mourning for the East, even as it shows the central characters preparing themselves to leave the GDR past behind and go boldly into the future promised by reunification."[6]

The choice between narratives that condemn the East German past as a stain on Germany's history, and those that (however self-reflectively) redeem the pace of GDR life along with the quality of its coffee, pickles, and other products, may be too narrow. Other complex engagements with questions raised by unification are possible, and one can continue down a road opened by Kapczynski in the interest of exploring still another tendency, one that dispenses with the binarism that has determined the reception of most post *Wende* feature films, analyzing instead those works that depict "a Germany that is decidedly 'un-unified' and cannot be rendered in the warm light of national nostalgia." Kapczynski writes: "Like their more wistful counterparts, [such films] catalog the disintegration of GDR culture after the fall of the Wall."[7] However, these films, among them *Lichter* (Distant Lights, 2003), *Schultze Gets the Blues* (2003), and *Berlin is in Germany* (2001), "refuse to look backwards and instead situate their central characters as adrift within newly accessible Western territories."[8] Investigations of how cinema contends with assimilating the East German part of Germany's national narrative thus must contend also with how cinema operates as a vehicle for the depiction of the difference between the subjective experience of history–the lived individual perception of time as depicted in narrative cinema–and hegemonic narratives of progress. In the films discussed below, by Roehler, Thalheim, and Petzold, subjective experience of historical events cuts in various ways against the grain of conventional history.

How can cinema be said to offer a counterpoint to the conventional representation of historical time? Because film appears as a temporal medium–despite the fact that it is a series of still frames–and because conventional feature films tend toward generally reproducing the apparently inexorable forward march of historical progress, its protagonists' inner lives or perception of time may be opposed with other movements of the narrative. Films may reference and even reproduce conventional histories while constructing parallel, subjectively defined encounters with the passage of time and diverse individual temporalities. Thus, they may orient themselves counter to the linear motion of progress, and specifically–in the context of East Germany's absorption into the West–with respect to the question of whether capitalism is depicted as a logical, inevitable, or positive consequence of history's vicissitudes. For some films, this confrontation consists only of the recognition that what has transpired as a result of the *Wende* is not progress, but is instead a stand still or, more likely, a regression. The difference between time as it is individually experienced and historical narratives of progress can highlight a protagonist's impression (and hence a viewer's own) that his or her existence is not thoroughly and consistently identified with the collective national story—that one's own experience may be contingent or even precarious.

Alongside mainstream cinematic trends—those that include the both the Ostalgia of *Good Bye, Lenin!* and the triumphal position taken by *Das Leben der Anderen*—a persistent post *Wende* cinema of disillusionment has been indexing the experiences of contingency, precariousness, and fragmentation associated with the new Germany and unification.[9] Long after 1989, cinema has continued to reflect on life in the wake of the fall of the Wall, and films, including those by Roehler, Thalheim, and Petzold, approach critically the *Wende*'s effects through their depiction of the disjunction between personal and historical time. They reflect on the disquiet produced by that confrontation. Distinct anxieties include accounting for the *Wende*'s effect on Germany's intellectual class (as embodied by the figure of Hanna Flanders in Roehler's *Die Unberührbare*); its effect on working class labor (as in Thalheim's *Netto*); and on the white collar working class (as in Petzold's *Yella*). To be sure, the tendency to depict disappointment, disenchantment, or merely the dysfunction associated with the *Wende* has long been apparent in cinema, in films such as Peter Timm's *Go, Trabi, Go!* (1990), in Christoph Schlingensief's *Das deutsche Kettensägenmassaker* (The German Chainsaw Massacre, 1990), and in numerous works by directors such as Andreas Kleinert and Andreas Dresen.[10] Here, however, I aim to examine how this tendency is negotiated in some recent films, and more specifically, how it expresses itself cinematically relative to the passage of filmic time.

Roehler's *Die Unberührbare* is somewhat loosely based on the life of its director's mother, the West German author Gisela Elsner, who wrote the novels *Die Riesenzwerge* (1964) and *Abseits* (1982), among others. Her quasi-fictional counterpart is a writer named Hanna Flanders, who, on the night the Wall falls, is working through a suicidal depression as she considers moving from Munich to Berlin. Hanna is a West German, but she harshly criticizes the West's bourgeois values and continues to articulate her support for the East, even as it collapses. Roehler's film problematizes Hanna's ideological position insofar as she is a character whose idealism is difficult to understand. She is stubborn, intellectually dishonest, and the contradictions between her lifestyle and her stated values are readily apparent. Her support for the East appears in the film as having been opportunistic, but Roehler's analysis of her is more concerned with her impending loss of control over her own life than with her political positions. Although there is nothing ostalgic in the film–Hanna is no *Ossi*, and the East German manner of living is presented only peripherally[11]–it can be seen as a narrative counterpoint to *Good Bye, Lenin!*. Hanna is a mother whose death comes as a consequence of the *Wende*, but in this case in the form of a suicide. Unlike Alex in *Good Bye, Lenin!*, Hanna's son, Viktor, offers his mother little comfort. Here, a member of the older generation–an adult at the time of the Wall's fall–is left entirely on her own to experience the forward movement of historical time as though she were walking directly into a storm.

More than a small distance separates Hanna from the jubilation experienced throughout Germany in November 1989. She lives through the *Wende* as a mediated event, seen on television, akin to the character Martin Schulz in Hannes Stöhr's *Berlin is in Germany*, who only had access to the fall of the Wall through the television in his prison cell.[12] For Hanna, the opening of the Wall is not associated with freedom. The crowds on television pile into the West and into the future, while Hanna complains that she can barely move. Her paralysis appears as an antipode to the general elation. Her identity was until that point defined by the existence of the two Germanys, and she now constructs herself as the very first one left behind by the national transformation. The sentiment that she cannot move tells an allegorical story: she believes that she is going to cohabitate with her publisher in Berlin, but soon sees that his romantic interest in her was an illusion; visits with her parents and her ex-husband are both disappointing; and, she is left feeling homeless once the Wall has fallen. She has–as the title of the English language release of the film tells us–"no place to go." The fact that she cannot move is recalled at the film's end, when she finds herself diagnosed with a vascular disorder such that one leg may have to be amputated. This physical ailment is, however, only nominally what is preventing her from getting closer to the center of things; it literalizes the metaphor that she is wholly divorced from the enthusiasm that seems to be sweeping Germany.

Roehler presents his mother's cinematic double in a harsh light and is well aware of the character's hypocrisy. In an interview with a journalist before she leaves Munich, Hanna expresses a cynical attitude about the rush to the West. She explains that the *Konsumgesellschaft* (consumer society) will likely gobble everyone up. We are, of course, not meant to give her critique much heft insofar as we have also witnessed her purchasing a Christian Dior coat in a fancy Munich boutique.[13] Roehler's point, however, is not whether her critique of capitalism is valid, but rather to under-score her newly precarious position. She feels that it is she not the state that is collapsing. A group of East Germans who welcome Hanna into their home speak with one voice about the freedom and truth now burst-ing forth, and show that they are caught up in the rush of freedom. Hanna plays the part of the party pooper, and has the poor taste to question whether this new situation will last. Her comment signals that she is dis-connected from the spirit of things, or, as one critic put it "nicht im Ein-klang mit der Zeit."[14] The effect of the *Wende* was to create in her a sudden dislocation, a fear generated by her profound social isolation. Andrew Webber conjectures that given what we know about Hanna, her "proper rite of sacrifice" would be to leap from the Berlin Wall in a public act of resistance contrary to the prevailing mood. Instead, however, as Webber points out, Hanna falls to what is likely her death in the virtual silence and near total isolation of a sanatorium.[15]

The film draws on the work of Rainer Werner Fassbinder insofar as films such as *Die Ehe der Maria Braun* (The Marriage of Maria Braun, 1978) tended to present female protagonists as allegories for Germany's transfor-mations–Fassbinder's heroines live and die with the nation's fortunes.[16] Most evident here, especially in the film's visual style, is an echo of Fass-binder's *Die Sehnsucht der Veronika Voss* (Veronika Voss, 1982), which deals with a formerly well-known actress whose career has fallen apart but who longs to return to the screen. Fassbinder's film is in black and white, as is Roehler's. Hanna's Dior coat with its dark spots reminds us that she has been rudely and misogynistically referred to as a cow more than once in the film, comments that tread upon her already bruised ego. More impor-tant, however, the film's retrograde black and white recalls the extent to which Hanna and historical time have fallen out of joint. Yet, the black and white also can be seen to function as a spectral allusion to German Expressionism. Hanna, who often casts a long shadow in the film, can be seen as a vampire crossing through dark territory. Although *Das Leben der Anderen* received much acclaim for depicting a colorless east, Roehler's depiction of recent history is more bloodless.

Among the excruciating final sequences of the film is a direct comment on Hanna's perception of the passage of time. As she sits in a sanatorium wondering whether she will lose her leg and whether she has any future at all, she stares at a large analog clock. The camera draws closer to her face, and then cuts to images of the face of the clock, each one closer than the last. The two reflect one another. The clock ticks away the seconds twice as fast as the time of the film passes (two clock-seconds appear to go by for every second of moving film). Hanna, who cannot sleep in the sanatorium, decides she can no longer tolerate the burden of the ticking and attempts to remove the clock from the wall. She stands beneath it in a large empty room, and, from the perspective of the low-angle shot, she appears tiny. The dimensions become suddenly surreal, and here more than elsewhere, Roehler draws upon Expressionists such as Robert Wiene and F. W. Murnau. Hanna succeeds in pulling the clock from the wall and it crashes upon the ground, but it is relentless–it neither breaks nor stops ticking. As a nurse enters the room, Hanna explains her actions, and the nurse admonishes her: "You're lucky, you could have broken it." Hanna replies: "What do you mean, lucky?" Her intention had been to break the clock and thereby stop time itself, but she failed. In order to depict its protagonist's feelings of fragmentation, Roehler's film contracts time.[17] It moves along a circuit created by Hanna's face and that of the clock, one in which the apparently actual passage of time comes up against the virtual time she perceives. Hanna feels herself diminished, but she fights back. As a precariously balanced subject in the new, post *Wende* Germany, it takes very little to send her falling off the ledge.

Die Unberührbare offers a third way, beyond contempt for the GDR and the sentimental idealization that rewrites Germany's past in the service of nostalgia. Robert Thalheim's *Netto* (also known as *Netto–Alles wird gut!*) can likewise be viewed as an abreaction to the success of *Good Bye, Lenin!* and other such films. Thalheim, who studied with the iconoclastic German director Rosa von Praunheim (credited as an artistic supervisor on *Netto*), later made *Am Ende kommen Touristen* (And Along Come Tourists, 2007). Thalheim's films have a languid pace, which is connected to the feeling of intimacy he constructs around his characters–the viewer gets to know them, especially while time passes them by. Akin to Roehler's film, *Netto* documents its main character's emergent feelings of instability in the wake of the *Wende*. Economic changes leave the film's protagonist, Marcel, feeling marginal, as though he were an outsider in Germany and left behind by history. He is suffering financially, his wife has left him for a man from Schöneberg (a man whom Marcel describes in terms of his Western auto), and he is growing estranged from his son, Sebastian, to whom he relates as though he were a child raised in a foreign country.

Thalheim's film gives voice to its protagonist's lost sense of security. Marcel's business has collapsed, and he describes the new economic climate as a "wild west." He is talkative and regularly riffs on his future business plans, returning repeatedly to the point that future opportunities will be in security services such as personal protection, which he describes as "das Thema der Zukunft" (the topic of the future). Anyone who doesn't understand that, he explains–as if to an Imbiss proprietor, but really to the viewer–has "echt den Zug verpasst" (truly missed the train). Marcel's claim speaks not only to the insight that the protection of private property will continue to increase in importance, but his exaggerated fascination with security, with personal protection (*Personenschutz*), and with threat assessment (*Bedrohungsanalyse*) simultaneously bespeak his own feelings of precariousness, his escalating anxieties, and his longing to be protected.

Marcel's son, Sebastian, is more at home in the new Germany than is his father. Having lived with his mother and her new husband, he now comes back to stay with Marcel in Prenzlauer Berg, partly as a rejection of his mother's consumer lifestyle, but also because he may perceive that his father could use some assistance. In this regard Thalheim's film can also be juxtaposed with *Good Bye, Lenin!* Here, however, a son needs to explain to his parent brutal truths about the *Wende*, rather than protect him or her from that knowledge.[18] Sebastian aims to help Marcel get a job, but his charitable disposition only intensifies the Oedipal crisis by further high-lighting Marcel's helplessness. Sebastian, who is fifteen in the film and was thus born shortly before the *Wende*, knows more than Marcel about resumé writing and about using computers. His mother, Angelika, wants Sebastian to join her out in the suburbs; she is now pregnant again, adding to the impression that the family is abandoning Marcel. This film, like *Die Unberührbare*, is about someone left behind, and again the concept of mobility is thematized. Although he refuses to admit it, Marcel is aware that the world is moving forward without him. All that remains for him is what can be described as a minor mobility, expressed, for example, in terms of bike riding. His ex-wife's new partner's Western auto thus signals more than merely financial success–Marcel can literally move less than those around him. For a young person, a bicycle might signify freedom, but for Marcel it signifies a lack of potency and that he plays the part of a boyish man trapped in a valley of giants. This is underscored by the size of the buildings around him in a sequence in which he rides his bicycle past the Reichstag, the Marie-Elisabeth-Lüders-Haus and other imposing land-marks. Although Milan Peschel, who plays Marcel, is an actor trained in the GDR who has worked with famous East German directors (such as Frank Castorf), he here seems to have been chosen for his diminutive sta-tus. Resembling a child in an adult world, he finds himself out of step.

The film is a rhapsody on the theme of isolation: Sebastian, who feels his father's disillusionment acutely, cannot connect with him. Although his son's support is constructive, there is little indication that Marcel's precarious position will change. He does not get the job for which he applies, and Thalheim intended to provoke audiences to consider the dangers that inhere in putting people into corners such as these. Thalheim explains:

> It was important for me to make clear that a person like this, with his fate, also represents a danger for us: a ticking time bomb—he has outbursts of rage, and he has a weapon. If we have succeeded in stripping people of their dreams—in letting five million people sit on the street—then this is a danger for us as well.[19]

In this respect Marcel is a ticking time bomb (*eine tickende Zeitbombe*). We see him handling a gun, and we know that the threat posed by his dissociation with Germany is real. Like a time bomb he is not moving with time, but against it, and may one day explode. Thalheim's film, however, travels a path distinct from the well-known Hollywood precarity film *Falling Down* (1993). *Netto* ends neither with violence nor with a shootout, perhaps because Marcel lacks confidence that even that project would turn out as planned.

By contrast with *Falling Down* this film's ending is quiet and consists only of Marcel's fantasy that he has finally been understood. The East German country singer and songwriter Peter Tschernig, whom Marcel describes in the film as the Johnny Cash of East Germany, suddenly appears, walking toward him as though he were fulfilling Marcel's wish. Marcel plays Tschernig's records throughout the film and a poster-size image of him hangs on the wall like an icon. This is not Ostalgie, but rather an expression of a utopian longing, a desire to be heard. Tschernig's lyrics are used throughout the film to underscore that Marcel feels out of step, especially the words that can be heard beneath the opening credits: "Ich bin immer nur in der falschen Spur./ Ich komm' und komm' einfach nicht voran/ Ich komm' nicht vorbei, keine Lücke frei./ Dabei liegt das nur/ An der falschen Spur." (I'm always on the wrong track./ I move and move, but never get ahead/ I don't get by, there are no openings for me./ The problem is just/ that I'm on the wrong track.) He remains out of sync with his son, who is, at the film's end, seeking but unable to find his father. Marcel does, however, feel himself connected with—and to an extent aided by—Tschernig, who likewise seems frozen in time.

Yet uncannier in its use of space and time is Christian Petzold's *Yella*. Petzold, who studied first at Berlin's Freie Universität and then at the Deutsche Film- und Fernsehakademie Berlin (DFFB) with the famous West German filmmaker Harun Farocki, has a distinctive style, and has been called an *auteur* (a label also attributed to Roehler).[20] His work has been seen in connection with a group of filmmakers referred to as the "Berlin School,"[21] but the uniqueness of his signature lies in his interest in hollowed out and modernized landscapes, in silences, and in depicting a world in which his protagonists are vexed by how one is meant to interact in an isolating and over-administered society. His film *Gespenster* (2005) has the mood of a science fiction film, even though it is set in what appears to be contemporary Berlin. *Yella* is considered part of a trilogy along with that film and *Die innere Sicherheit* (The State I Am In, 2000)– generally known as Petzold's "ghost trilogy"–but it also seems connected to *Jerichow* (2008), which takes place in similarly desolate spaces, along sparsely populated roads near the Elbe.

Like *Die Unberührbare* and *Netto*, *Yella* deals with the hopes and disillusionment that follow unification. Its protagonist, a woman named Yella, is moving to a job outside of the former East.[22] Although the film is not particularly insistent on its time frame, Germany seems to have been long united, making the characters' post *Wende* frustrations, by virtue of their persistence, that much more agonizing. Yella's former husband and business partner, Ben, feels abandoned. His wife is taking the train elsewhere, and Ben–as Marcel in *Netto* would have said–has *den Zug verpasst*. Time is moving on without him, and he calls out to her poignantly: "Yella, I miss you so." At the film's onset, she is returning to Wittenberge (not far from the former border between the two Germanys), where she and her husband once shared a life together. In these initial scenes, as in *Die Unberührbare*, the female protagonist becomes an object under the unflagging gaze of a dogged camera, one that is linked to Ben's desires.

The inhospitable space in which Ben finds himself makes him threatening. Like Hanna and Marcel, he has fallen out of step with the times, and his precarious condition creates the possibility of violence, either to the self (as in the case of *Die Unberührbare*), or to others. Akin to Marcel, Ben's business has gone under, and he now has nothing left but his plans. When we encounter him on the street, the surveilling pattern of the camera and the pace of the tracking shot suggest that an assault may be impending, and as Ben's hand gradually moves behind his back, we may falsely conclude that he is reaching for a gun. Later, as he comes to insist on giving Yella a ride to the train station–on trying to stave off her trip to Hannover, westward and away from him–a sound that may be a passing jet, which echoes like a gunshot, frightens Yella and her father, both of whom are already on edge. In the car, Ben reveals that he has a business plan, but it is one that turns out to be tied to the unlikely scenario that a new airport will be built in Wittenberge. He aims to win Yella back on that basis. In making many promises to her, he echoes the secondary title of Thalheim's film, pleading: *Alles wird wieder gut.*

Not long after having been introduced to these characters the threat of violence is realized. Ben deliberately drives the two of them off a bridge and into the water below. We are given to suspect that, following the crash, Ben has entered the realm of living dead, however we gradually uncover that it is Yella who is wandering in a netherworld.[23] The purgatorial spaces to which she has been sent resemble those found in Herk Harvey's *Carnival of Souls* (1962), a film Petzold explicitly references.[24] The subsequent images of Hannover and of this new Germany are similar to those of a vacated fairground; they contain unfulfilled promises of pleasure. The hotel that serves as her temporary home is reminiscent of a ghost ship. Petzold describes the type of architectural design he had in mind: "Wenn man diese Zimmer sieht: Das Hotel hat gar keinen Raum nach Innen, sondern so riesige Fenster mit Doppelscheiben. Man kann sie nicht mehr öffnen–das ist nur Blick. Man schaut hin und sieht eine Brücke zur Messe rüber, hinten ein Hügel mit über 70.000 Parkplätzen." (Look at these rooms: The hotel has no inner spaces, just huge windows with doubled panes of glass. You can't open them–they are only for the view. You look out and see a bridge to the exhibition center, and behind, a hill with more than 70,000 parking spots.) He concludes: "Hannover ist ja als Messestadt ein einziger Parkplatz." (As an exhibition space, Hannover is pretty much a parking lot.)[25]

The world of Western enterprise aims to overwhelm Petzold's protagonist. In an interview the director explains: "Ich wollte erzählen, dass das System so stark ist, dass man selber nicht mehr weiß, was man da anrichtet ... Ich glaube die Institutionen verändern einen. Man infiziert sich." (I wanted to show that the system is so strong that you yourself don't know what you are perpetrating ... I believe the institutions change you. You become contaminated.)[26] Yella's entanglement with corporate businessmen, the design of her hotel, and the stark boardrooms in which she finds herself recall the dynamics of Murnau's *Der letzte Mann* (The Last Laugh, 1924), which Gilles Deleuze refers to as an example of a silent film that employs "a physics of social degradation."[27] Deleuze concludes that the splendor of Murnau's silent film consists in the constitutive role of the hotel, and how its porter, who has lost his job and is stripped of his uniform, descends through its stations and functions. Likewise here (as in *Die Unberührbare*, which also recalls Murnau's film, and which consistently traps Hanna in small spaces), Yella is boxed into narrow confines and finds herself diminished by them. This world attempts to corner her and to reduce her to playing the part of its porter.

In Hannover, Yella's partner is Philipp, a venture capitalist. Because much of the film can be said to take place in Yella's imagination–insofar as we can infer that it is a vision she has before dying–it may be that Philipp is an alternative and more competent incarnation of Ben.[28] He and Yella are successful at their jobs, and she quickly picks up the performative language of business: Philipp tells her where her eyes should be focused, how she might use her glasses as a prop, and he even explains to her a ruse he describes with the English language phrase "broker posing." This routine suggests that much of the negotiation in which they are engaged is an empty façade, and the charade–perhaps because it is akin to a betrayal–seems to awaken the specter of Ben. Though she becomes a successful negotiator in this vision, she feels that she has become a cheat, like the man, Dr. Schmidt-Ott, who first hired her to come to Hannover and is subsequently revealed to be a fraud, and like Philipp, who admits that much of his own business practice is rooted in deception.

This new professional existence, or Yella's dream of it, comes to an awful end. Yella calls on a couple, one that she has strangely and improbably seen at an earlier point in the film, with the intention of blackmailing them into making a business deal. The body of the man she means to blackmail, Dr. Günthen, finds its way into the water. It seems he has committed suicide, and the manner of death serves as yet another indication that Yella herself is, in this moment, drowning. Ultimately, as her plans collapse, she finds herself transported back into the car with Ben, about to go over the bridge. The temporal circuit has now been closed, which allows the subjective experience of time to be set against its apparently objective passing. She returns to the "present" with the knowledge that there can be no moving forward, not for her. Perhaps for this reason Yella's death, in the second instance, resembles a suicide. In the earlier sequence, she struggled with Ben, pulling at the wheel and trying to save her own life. In this later sequence, she knows what she is facing; she appears to have thought it through and is either too exhausted or too cynical to fight. There is little redemption in this ending, in which the protagonist, like Hanna, acknowledges that there may be no place for her to go.

Of course there is no shortage of films that depict capitalism consuming its subjects, and not all of those are directly linked to the *Wende.* Indeed, *Yella* is itself an aesthetically groundbreaking film that concerns much more than merely unification. These films, however, bespeak a persistent tendency insofar as they resist redemptive readings, cut against conventional histories, and depict subjective experiences contrary to the general mood. In each of them, a character moves into the storm of history. The conflict between the subject and the storm often results in violence, and frequently, the violence is turned against the self. Today, two decades after the fall of the Wall, it seems that some of Germany's filmmakers have not bid a full farewell to the East German part of their nation's history. Film continues to contend with the Wall's fall as an ongoing transition that produces persistent fractures, disjunctions and disillusionment, rather than as a bright line that separates the past from the present.

Notes

1. Susan Buck-Morss, *Dreamworld and Catastrophe: The Passing of Mass Utopia in East and West* (Cambridge, 2000), 228.
2. Antonio Negri, *Goodbye Mr. Socialism: Antonio Negri in Conversation with RAF Valvola Scelsi* (New York, 2008), 9.
3. See Aleida Assmann, *Der lange Schatten der Vergangenheit: Erinnerungskultur und Geschichtspolitik* (Munich, 2006), 21-61.
4. On *Good Bye, Lenin!* see Roger F. Cook, "*Good Bye, Lenin!*: Free-Market Nostalgia for Socialist Consumerism," *Seminar*, 43, no. 2 (2007): 206-19; Jennifer M. Kapczynski, "Negotiating Nostalgia: The GDR Past in *Berlin Is in Germany* and *Good Bye, Lenin!*" *The Germanic Review* 82, no. 1 (2007): 78-100; and Michael D. Richardson, "A World of Objects: Consumer Culture in Filmic Reconstructions of the GDR," in *The Collapse of the Conventional: German Film and its Politics at the Turn of the Twenty-First Century*, eds., Jaimey Fisher and Brad Prager (Detroit, forthcoming). On *Sonnenallee*, see Paul Cooke, "Performing 'Ostalgie': Leander Haussmann's *Sonnenallee*," *German Life and Letters* 56, no. 2 (2003): 156-67.
5. Seán Allan, "*Ostalgie*, fantasy and the normalization of east-west relations in post-unification comedy," in *German Cinema: Since Unification*, ed., David Clarke (London, 2006), 105-26, here 123-24.
6. Kapczynski (see note 4), 89.
7. Kapczynski (see note 4), 81.
8. Ibid.
9. I am referring here to Eric Rentschler's notion that a "cinema of consensus" was prevalent in the 1980s and early 1990s. Disillusionment might be one way of naming a particular post *Wende* tendency in the German cinema. See Eric Rentschler, "From New German Cinema to the Post-Wall Cinema of Consensus," in *Cinema and Nation*, eds., Mette Hjort and Scott MacKenzie (London, 2000), 260-77.
10. See especially Laura G. McGee, "How Do We Tell Stories of What We Could Never Imagine? First East-West Encounters in German Feature Films from the Early 1990s by Andreas Dresen, Andreas Kleinert and Peter Kahane," *Colloquia Germanica* 40, no. 1 (2007): 51-66.
11. On *Die Unberührbare* as counterpoint to ostalgic films, see Mattias Frey, "No(ir) Place to Go: Spatial Anxiety and Sartorial Intertextuality in *Die Unberührbare*," *Cinema Journal* 45, no. 4 (2006): 64-80, especially 76. See also Paul Cooke, "Whatever Happened to Veronika Voss? Rehabilitating the '68ers' and the Problem of *Westalgie* in Oskar Roehler's *Die Unberührbare* (2000)," *German Studies Review* 27, no. 1 (2004): 33-44; and Johannes von Moltke, "*Terrains Vagues*: Landscapes of Unification in Oskar Roehler's *No Place to Go*," in Fisher and Prager (see note 4).

12. On the use of television in this sequence, see Frey (see note 11), 67-68.
13. Also discussed by Cooke (see note 11), 40; and Frey (see note 11), 74.
14. See Hans Schifferle, "Eine Sphinx in Deutschland. Porträt einer Verlorenen: Oskar Roehlers bedeutender Film *Die Unberührbare,*" *Süddeutsche Zeitung,* 20 April 2000.
15. Andrew J. Webber, "Falling Walls, Sliding Doors, Open Windows: Berlin on Film after the *Wende,*" *German as a foreign language* (2006); available at http://www.gfl-journal.de/1-2006/webber.html, accessed 5 October 2009, here 8-9.
16. On the connection to *Veronika Voss,* see Cooke (see note 11); and also Frey (see note 11), 74-5.
17. The concept of temporal contraction refers here to Gilles Deleuze, *Cinema 2: The Time-Image,* Hugh Tomlinson and Robert Galeta, trans. (Minneapolis, 1989 [1985]), 68-78.
18. On parallels between the films, see Anthonya Visser, "Simple Storys? Konstruierte Erinnerung an Leben in der DDR," in *Gedächtnis und Identität: Die deutsche Literatur nach der Vereinigung,* ed., Fabrizio Cambi (Würzburg, 2008), 74-75.
19. "Für mich war wichtig, klar zu machen, dass ein solcher Mensch, mit seinem Schicksal, für uns auch eine Gefahr darstellt: Eine tickende Zeitbombe–der hat Wutausbrüche, der hat eine Waffe. Wenn wir es uns leisten, die Träume der Menschen so abzuschneiden, also fünf Millionen Leute auf der Straße sitzen lassen, dann ist das auch eine Gefahr für uns." See Roberto Dzugan, "Mein bester Kumpel ist und bleibt mein Vater. Interview mit Robert Thalheim und Milan Peschel zu *Netto,*" *critic.de,* 28 April 2005; available at http://www.critic.de/interviews/detail/artikel/%E2%80%9Emein-bester-kumpel-ist-und-bleibt-mein-vater%E2%80%9C-1309.html, accessed 5 October 2009.
20. On his status as an *auteur,* see Michael Sicinski, "Once the Wall has Tumbled," *Cinemas-cope* 38, 2, no. 1 (2009), 6-9.
21. On the connections, see Marco Abel, "The Cinema of Identification Gets on my Nerves: An Interview with Christian Petzold" *Cineaste* 33, no.3 (2008); available at http://www.cineaste.com/articles/an-interview-with-christian-petzold.htm, accessed 5 October 2009; Marco Abel, "Intensifying Life: The Cinema of the 'Berlin School'," *Cineaste* 33, no.4 (2008); available at http://www.cineaste.com/articles/the-berlin-school.htm, accessed 5 October 2009; and Marco Abel, "Imaging Germany: The (Political) Cinema of Christian Petzold" in Fisher and Prager (see note 4).
22. According to Petzold, Yella's name is drawn from Yella Rottländer, the actress who played Alice in Wim Wenders's *Alice in den Städten* (Alice in the Cities, 1974). He explains, "Die achtjährige Alice wurde von einem Mädchen gespielt, das Yella Rottländer hieß. Dieses Kind öffnete die Sinne, es war in ständiger Bewegung. Im Arabischen heißt 'Jalla' ja auch 'Beweg Dich.' Und genau das ist ein Thema meines neuen Films." See Ralf Schenk "Auswandern aus Brandenburg: Regisseur Christian Petzold über seinen Wettbewerbsbeitrag *Yella* und den Gang von Nina Hoss," *Berliner Zeitung,* 14 February 2007; available at http://www.berlinonline.de/berliner-zeitung/archiv/.bin/dump.fcgi/2007/0214/feuilleton/0003/index.html, accessed 5 October 2009.
23. Petzold confirms: "das ist der Traum einer Sterbenden ... Ich habe den Film gar nicht dramaturgisch so angelegt, dass man am Schluss erstaunt sagt: 'Boah, die ist ja tot!' Im ganzen Film sind so viele Zeichen offen präsentiert, nicht einmal versteckt, dass jeder etwas aufmerksame Zuschauer begreift: Hier stimmt etwas nicht." See Rüdiger Suchsland, "Eine andere Erzählung des Kapitalismus ..." *artechock.de,* 20 September 2007; available at http://www.artechock.de/film/text/interview/p/petzold_2007.htm, accessed 5 October 2009.
24. Harvey's *Carnival of Souls* is referenced in Abel ("The Cinema of Identification" see note 20). Petzold also avows the influence of Ambrose Bierce's short story "An Occurrence at Owl Creek Bridge" (1890) in Suchsland (see note 23).
25. Suchsland (see note 23).
26. Suchsland (see note 23). Petzold is influenced, along these lines, by Marc Augé, whom he refers to in his "Regiestatement;" available at http://www.yella-der-film.de/

regiestatement.html, accessed 5 October 2009. He specifically is drawing upon Marc Augé, *Non-Places. Introduction to an Anthropology of Supermodernity*, John Howe, trans. (London, 1995 [1992]).

27. Deleuze (see note 17), 229.

28. On this point see Jens Hinrichsen, "Im Zwischenreich. Christian Petzolds Gespenster-Trilogie: Passagen in Schattenzonen deutscher Realität," *film-dienst* 60, no. 19 (2007): 6-8, here 6.

Chapter 7

$\mathscr{P}$OST COITUM TRISTE EST...?

Sexual Politics and Cultures in Postunification Germany

● ● ● ● ● ● ● ● ● ● ● ● ● ● ●

Dagmar Herzog[1]

We did it together–this act whose consequences are uncertain–after long years
of frustration-filled security partnership. By now the brief high of orgiastic unification festivities is over. After the climax one feels relief and exhaustion. The
bride, once called the GDR populace, feels, well: a little bit having achieved
exactly what she wanted (though she had always fantasized it turning out somewhat differently than it did), a little bit romantically seduced, a little bit taken
by force–sexists occasionally call the process "beneficial ravishing" or "compassionate violation" (*Vergewohltätigung*). But whining will do no good. Everyone knows that in *this* kind of situation it always takes two: He half-pulled her,
she half-succumbed; the spirit was unwilling, but the flesh was weak. Now she
has conceived, hopes she'll recover and that she'll have healthy children. She
worries about a weakened political-moral immune system. What the robust
rake can effortlessly handle, could seriously threaten the health of the bride.
Also, the eagle, once upon a time–just like, back in olden days, Leda's swan–
had seemed during the courtship phase a bit more financially giving than he
now, afterwards, after having had his lust satisfied, is proving himself to be:
post coitum triste est... ?

Konrad Weller, 1991[2]

In the brilliant, caustic opening pages of formerly East German social psy-
chologist Konrad Weller's 1991 classic, *Das Sexuelle in der deutsch-deutschen
Vereinigung* (The Sexual Element in German-German Unification), Weller
imagines unification as a sexual encounter between a powerful and self-
confident male Federal Republic (the "eagle," a stand-in for the Zeus-
turned-into-a-swan who once, in mythological times, seduced/coerced the
lovely Leda) and a not-quite-as-satisfied-as-she'd-hoped-to-be female German Democratic Republic (GDR).

Figure 1 Cover of Konrad Weller, *Das Sexuelle in der deutsch-deutschen Vereinigung.* Design: Dietmar Kunz. Reprinted with permission of Konrad Weller and the Forum Verlag, Leipzig.

To put it colloquially: She had wanted it; she was consenting, even eager. But then the sex itself was not as wonderful as she had imagined. And the morning after, the guy turned out to be something of an ungenerous jerk. In the book, Weller took careful stock of what was happening to the sexual culture of the former East under the impact of national unification on Western terms, as he also both mocked Western journalists' leeringly voyeuristic, frequently incoherent, and consistently condescending generalizations about East German sexual culture and documented the bewilderment and pain felt by Easterners as aspects of their lives that they had been most proud of were first belittled and then eventually vanquished.

Among the key points Weller highlighted as distinctive about East German sexual culture were: the sexual self-confidence and higher satisfaction rates of Eastern women as compared with Western German women (as scholarly studies conducted in the years before unification had documented); the comfort with nakedness that characterized the East, from the nude beaches to nudity within the family home—as contrasted with the stylized pornography of impossibly perfect and sanitized bodies and insistently provocative sex-chatter that saturated the media culture of the West; the sense that love and romance and joyful (as opposed to merely dutiful) fidelity were far more highly valued in the East, among homosexuals and heterosexuals alike, than in the always-calculating, competitive, achievement-oriented West; and the sense that people in the East actually took time for sex, rather than trying to squeeze sex into exhausted, multitasking lives. But Weller also recorded his outrage at the ways Eastern lifestyles were quickly both sensationalized and trivialized–and expressed concern that none of the (to him uniquely precious) qualities of Eastern sexual culture could long survive integration into a capitalist system. And Weller was certainly not alone among East German observers in taking umbrage at Western superciliousness–and returning it in kind.[3] As one formerly East German woman put it to me in 1998 with sublime self-assurance: "Everybody knows that East-women have more fun. Orgasm rates were higher in the East, all the studies show it."[4]

After all, not least among the reasons there had not been as large a feminist movement in East Germany as in the West was due to the state-sponsored advantages East Germany had offered women.[5] So many of the desiderata West German feminists had been fighting for since the 1970s–abortion rights, childcare facilities, economic independence, and professional respect–were things which East German women already by that point could largely take for granted. In addition, in the West, consumer capitalism functioned to a large degree via the (always distorted) representation of female sexuality, while the small amount of pornography available in the East, either in the monthly centerfold of *Das Magazin* or as surreptitiously circulated contraband, was typically remarkably tame compared with representations in the West. The sexual revolution that had taken the West by storm in the 1960s-1970s was matched by a quiet but therefore no less effective sexual evolution towards greater liberality in the East in the 1970s and especially the 1980s (a liberalization that was also carried by a strong lesbian and gay mobilization which found a home in the Protestant churches).

"Travel no, sex yes:" This was the message the SED sent its restive populace. At the same time, the sense of social security that the restrictive regime did manage to offer its citizens was accompanied by a strong popular as well as state-propagated consensus that career and motherhood (also single motherhood) were fully compatible. (By the end of the GDR, one in three children was born out of wedlock; in the Federal Republic it was one in ten.)[6] But most importantly, as numerous ex-GDR women have spontaneously asserted over the years, in print and in conversation: "In the East, sex was not for sale. Love was not for sale."[7] (Again in August 2009, a journalist from the former East who was twenty-four when the Wall fell, remarked impulsively to me when I observed in passing that she had been old enough still to experience the sexual culture of the East: "Yes–experienced it, and thoroughly relished it [*Jaja–erlebt, und genossen*]."[8] Rather than staying in undesired marriages or partnerships for the sake of the children or for economic support, women in the East felt free to break up with unsatisfactory male partners specifically because they possessed economic independence and because theirs was a social environment that treated single motherhood as utterly acceptable and feasible–and no barrier to further relationships. Indeed, a funny and telling thing that happened to me a few years ago (2006) was that several East German men (born 1961-62, so at that point in their mid forties) confided that it was really annoying that East German women had so much sexual self-confidence and economic independence. Money was useless, they complained. The few extra Eastern Marks that a doctor could make in contrast with, say, someone who worked in the theater, did absolutely no good, they explained, in luring or retaining women the way a doctor's salary could and did in the West. "You had to be 'interesting.'" What pressure. And as one revealed: "I have much more power now as a man in unified Germany than I ever did in communist days."[9]

Without a doubt, most devastating for citizens of the former East in the initial years after unification was a loss of economic security and the new idea that human worth would now be measured primarily by money. Easterners scrambled to acquire new job skills and a whole new style of comporting themselves.[10] The resulting shifts–also within intimate partnerships–were felt most acutely in the first decade after unification. Many long-term East German relationships went into crisis; couples first clung together despite conflicts and then crashed as they struggled with varying degrees of success to reinvent themselves under new conditions.[11] New East-West romantic relationships also became objects for intensive self-reflection as well as mass speculation, as first the inevitably more financially savvy Western men were thought to be snatching up the fabulously sexy Eastern women, but then eventually also Western women discovered the special appeal of the reputedly far less hung-up and narcissistic Eastern men.[12]

Above all, however, the disappearing social ethos of the GDR quickly became an especially important site for *Ostalgie.* "In the East the clocks ran more slowly," the East German journalist Katrin Rohnstock remembered with retrospective longing in 1995. In the West, in her view, lust for capital had replaced desire for another person. With reference to capitalism's competitive climate, she said: "Eroticism feels with its fingertips, elbows destroy that. The pressure to achieve makes human beings sick and has a negative impact on sexuality."[13] Others too spoke of "the difficult path of love in the market economy" and the negative effect of "cost-benefit analysis" in human interactions on the experiences of love and sex.[14] An initial curiosity about pornography and sex toys (which soon flooded into the East) gave way to unimpressed disinterest and ongoing perplexity.[15] In addition, commentators from the East wondered at the detachment of emotions from physical sensations that appeared to them to characterize so many Western sexual encounters, both within and outside of marriage. In the West, orgasms were seeming to function more as self-reassurance and trophies in a battle with the other body than as the pleasant effects of sexual encounters in the context of a powerful attraction to another, specific human being. In this dystopian vision of late twentieth-century Western culture, sex had become nothing but "two people somehow manipulating around on each other."[16]

Another way to think about these negative opinions about Western sex, however, is as Eastern fantasies about the West and about capitalism and what capitalism does, or can do, to interpersonal relations and even interbody relations. And there is no question that Westerners too had their share of fantasies about East German sex, especially with regard to the Stasi and its technological surveillance machinery–most vividly visualized in the scene in the 2006 movie *The Lives of Others* (Das Leben der Anderen, directed by Florian Henckel von Donnersmarck) in which a wire to record pillow talk was literally embedded in the bedroom wall–as well as the Stasi's extensive practice of encouraging citizens to inform on each other's secrets.

It may seem difficult after the fact to find credible the rosy image of East German sexual culture retrospectively described by those who experienced it with the added knowledge that–although the wiretapping of a bedroom wall was surely less frequent than of kitchens and living rooms where political discussions were held–the Stasi did engage in the most invasive surveillance of and intervention in GDR citizens' private lives. This could involve a husband's intimate betrayal of his wife by reporting to the Stasi on her opposition to the regime, as in the famous and much discussed case of Knud and Vera Wollenberger, or it could mean fabricating evidence of sexual malfeasance, spreading rumors, and sowing mistrust in order to cause difficulties for someone–for instance a pastor or a political dissenter–perceived as a problem by the regime.[17] Stasi files make note of individuals traipsing into each other's apartments as well as record when the informant believed intercourse had taken place. It could also mean active seduction by an informant of someone politically targeted by the regime, followed by extensive reporting to the authorities about the target's views and activities.[18] Nonetheless–and without in any way being an apologist for the dictatorship, its cruelties or its pettinesses–

it is important to recall the extent to which the work of the Stasi was integrated into GDR citizens' navigation of daily life, and also the ways mutual surveillance and horrifically punitive treatment of dissidents and nonconformists coexisted with considerable arbitration and compromise between government and citizens.[19] What bears emphasis is that while the Stasi certainly made use of sex, as of every other human vulnerability, the majority of GDR citizens appear to have experienced themselves as quite free to make their own self-determined romantic and sexual choices, already as teens and certainly as adults. Or to put it another way, in general the realm of love and sex was one of the few realms in which the government did not aggressively intervene. The idea that the Stasi controlled love and sex is, as the venerable East German sexologist Kurt Starke, who studied the sexual lives of GDR and post GDR citizens for thirty-seven years, put it, one of the "phantasms of the Cold War that stuffed the heads of well-meaning Westerners full of clichés."[20]

Since the 1990s–which saw the height both of *Ostalgie* and of affect-intensive anti-Stasi *Vergangenheitsbewältigung*–much has changed in unified Germany. And in that time as well, the sociologists and psychologists who study these matters have found, in comparing the two German societies over the long haul, also longer-term similarities. For example, on both sides of the wall, the tendency already since the 1970s has been towards earlier onset of coitus (but in the context not of indiscriminate promiscuity but rather of romantic coupledom) as, on both sides, serial monogamy became the social norm (and among the younger ones on both sides, relationships are shorter). Marriage is definitively in decline (of the 2,585 couples studied in a randomly generated multi-generational sample comparing "relationship biographies" in Hamburg and Leipzig whose results were published in 2005, 77 percent were unmarried). Yet, at the same time, fidelity is a seriously taken feature of relationships (50 percent of the sample were consistently faithful, and among the rest incidents of infidelity were fleeting and rare).[21] And while one formerly West German male sexologist once self-ironically summarized the difference between Western and Eastern women's attitudes about heterosexuality as the difference between "freedom from" and "freedom for" heterosexual coitus (with West German women complaining that men's ineptness left them cold during intercourse while East German women gloried in the pleasures of coital intimacy), there are increasingly fewer differences in attitudes and practices evident among the younger generations of women and men.[22] In the former East and in the former West alike, as Starke summarized it in surveying the cumulative results of the comparative study of which he was a coauthor–in the process also with great pleasure and relief letting go of his own (incorrigibly East German romantic's) erstwhile skepticism about Western sex: "The neoliberal or neosexual-revolutionary idea, that coitus is the continuation of masturbation with other means and that sexual lust is self-involved, egocentric, concentrated on the functioning of one's own genitality, neither needing nor succeeding in creating a partner-oriented intimacy, cannot be supported by our findings."[23] Meanwhile, however, in both East and West alike, as this and numerous other studies have found, children are ever less frequently part of unified Germans' partnership concept. While still in the 1980s in the East, the norm was early marriage (not least in order to access an apartment of one's own rather than continuing to live with parents) and early childbearing–with two children per couple as the expressed ideal–already then both parts of Germany had low birthrates. In unified Germany, the childbearing trend is (as media hype constantly reiterates) "below replacement levels."[24] Hovering just above 1.3, Germany has one of the lowest birthrates in the world. In terms of how women imagine and manage childrearing, there are still a few differences between East and West, with Eastern women still more likely to bear and raise children out of wedlock, with or without cohabitation, and with Eastern women more likely to find it unproblematic to rely on outside-the-home childcare as they pursue work.[25]

The present state of German sexual politics and sexual culture is complex. The overarching trends in unified German society have been towards ever greater sexual liberality–even as this liberality, significantly, is consistently accompanied by an ongoing interest in, and lived experience of, romantic love. German youth are infinitely less conflicted about their adolescent sexual experimentation than U.S. American youth, for instance–and there is no social movement calling for premarital abstinence in Germany–but they also tend to have fewer partners than American youth, higher levels of contraceptive use, and far lower levels of unwanted pregnancies and sexually transmitted diseases. Just to give one example, while 20 percent of sexually active female teens in the U.S. have been found to use no contraception whatsoever, that is true for only 1 percent of sexually active female teens in Germany; the unwanted pregnancies that do ensue are almost entirely due to the failure of contraception, whether in the form of slipped condoms or antibiotics having made contraceptive pills temporarily ineffective.[26]

In general, the main trajectory in unified Germany has been towards broad tolerance of diversity and strong defense of the ethical value of indi-

Figure 2 "Same-sex couples have a right to tolerance." CDU website page endorsing respect for gay and lesbian couples, May 13, 2009. Reprinted with permission of the Christlich Demokratische Union Deutschlands.

vidual self-determination. This is evident in such phenomena as the nonchalance with which openly gay and lesbian politicians and cultural figures are accepted across the political spectrum, and gay bathhouses and Christopher Street Day parades treated as just as unremarkable as gay and lesbian civil unions. In 2001, the "life-partner law" (*Lebenspartnerschaftsgesetz*) for same-sex couples went into effect, and in 2005 its benefits were further expanded. Lesbian couples are still barred from using sperm donor banks in Germany and must find volunteers or go outside the country; and there are ongoing skirmishes over adoption.[27] But there is no question that the direction of change is towards equalization of heterosexual and homosexual partnerships.[28] Even the Christian Democratic Union (CDU), while still opposed to gay marriage, decided a few years ago to include gay and lesbian families in its family-focused platform proposals.[29] The expansive mentality is also, if more prosaically nonetheless significantly, noticeable in such phenomena as the photos of fully naked male and female teenagers in the bestselling teen magazine *Bravo*–along with tips for gentle caressing and accounts of what it feels like to have intercourse "for the first time," as well as in the government-sponsored anti-HIV public health campaigns replete with consistently witty and explicit condom ads on billboards dotting the nation in train stations, city streets, and rural fields alike.

Figure 3 Condom ads from the Mach's Mit-campaign, 2000-2006. "Don't give AIDS a chance." Reprinted with permission of the Bundeszentrale für gesundheitliche Aufklärung, Köln.

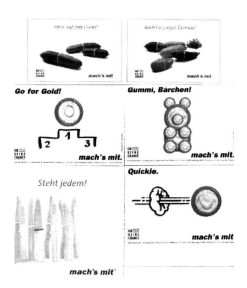

The broad-minded liberality is additionally evident in the 2002 decision to decriminalize prostitution—a striking contrast to such stereotypically sexually progressive cultures as the Netherlands (where Amsterdam has launched an effort to "clean up" the city's red light district) and Sweden (which since 1999 prosecutes not prostitutes but their johns—on the argument that any impersonal exchange of sex for money is shameful and perverse and not to be tolerated by the state).[30]

Germany's liberality is no less—and no less impressively—evident in the emergent energetic and creative commitment to defend such heretofore underrespected rights as the sexual and reproductive rights of the disabled—a clear and forceful rebuttal not only to the horrifically cruel and murderous policies of the Third Reich but also the far too long delayed postwar acknowledgment of those policies and the decades of ongoing postwar contempt.[31] The city of Berlin, in a recent public awareness campaign, promotes reproductive as well as partnership rights for individuals with Down Syndrome; sex advice and family planning clinics offer both workshops and confidential counseling on assistance in sexual encounters for the physically disabled.[32] It was remarkable and indicative of the transformed climate that in September 2007, at the occasion of the fifteenth anniversary of Balance, a family planning center in Berlin, an event

Figure 4 "In love, married, now we'd like to have a child. Some people think that's wrong, because we have Down Syndrome. What do you think?" From the poster competition "Anders in Gesellschaft," 2008, Lebenshilfe e.V., Berlin. Artist: Evelyn Kopp, Stein. Reprinted with permission of the Lebenshilfe e.V., Berlin.

attended by leading politicians and prominent medical doctors, one of the most loudly praised aspects of the center's work was its support precisely for the sexual and reproductive rights of the disabled.[33]

Moreover, it bears pointing out that the affirmative atmosphere and enumerated freedoms represent an achievement of long years of activist struggle and arduous post-fascist learning processes. A complicated interplay of transnational pressures and intranational conflicts over sexual mores and sex-related laws led first, in the Cold War 1950s, to the consolidation of a conservative sexual culture in the Federal Republic of Germany. Church and political leaders interpreted Nazism's barbarism as intrinsically connected to its frank promotion not only of sublime marital pleasures but also of pre- and extramarital libertinism for all those racially and ideologically approved by the regime to have sex (i.e., the majority of the population), and they avidly promoted the restoration of "family values" as an anti-Nazi imperative. In fact, "tidying up" German sexual mores recommended itself as an effective way to overcome the genocidal past, as a massive displacement of moral discourse occurred, away from the issue of popular complicity in expropriation and mass murder and toward a narrowed conception of morality as solely concerned with sex.[34] At the same time, the European Court of Human Rights, which began its work in 1959, grew out of a transnational commitment to secure the rights of the individual against an arbitrary and violent state, with several articles explicitly formulated in reaction against the experiences of Nazism's brutal invasions into bodies and relationships alike–among them the rights to found a family through marriage, to a private life free from state scrutiny, and to non-discrimination. The Court, as of the early twenty-first century, has come to understand its task as not only protecting individuals against sexual violence and abuse, but also in protecting the right to *desired* sexual activity (whether homo- or hetero) as well as the right to the freely chosen formation of intimate partnerships.[35] German law and public opinion largely coincides with the Court's stance. The process of political unification with the former GDR in the wake of the fall of communism, and the integration of the former East Germans with their generally strong commitment to the defense of sexual rights as human rights and pride in the culture of sexual freedom and romance they had been able to develop despite political repression con-tributed important impulses to the maintenance and further development of progressive legislation.

Along these lines, one of the interesting effects of unification was the compromise formation that evolved on abortion. While previously in the West, women needed to demonstrate that there was a medical, eugenic, criminological, or social "indication" that warranted the termination of a pregnancy, after unification and heated controversy, all German women can be granted first-trimester approval (standard in the East since 1972) as long as they agree to preabortion counseling (as had been required in the West).[36] (Technically, abortion remains a crime but it is not prosecuted when the legal conditions for approval are met.) And what is most notice-able in recent years–and this despite recurrent efforts on the part of abor-tion opponents to cut government funding to clinics that provide the counseling and the terminations–is the ongoing uncontroversial support given to the maintenance of legal access to abortion by Christian Democ-ratic Minister for the Family Ursula von der Leyen.[37]

In short, one of the major noteworthy trends of the postunification years is the internal sexual liberalization of the Christian Democratic Union–and this is at least in part due to the absorption into the party also of (in sexual matters generally less conservative) Christian Democrats from the former East. But the CDU (and the traditionally even more con-servative Bavarian-based sister party, the Christian Social Union, CSU) are definitely changing also in the West. (Minor but indicative signs of the newly expansive sensibilities were evident not only in the overall attitude of the media and public sympathy rather than outrage that greeted the story of prominent CSU politician Horst Seehofer after his adulterous love affair and illegitimate child were revealed in 2007, but also in the CSU's defiant ongoing defense of Seehofer and embrace of him as bringing the party a new "liberality" as well as a new "sexiness"—as of 2009, a second child with his lover was on the way.)[38]

In the meantime, however, and also noteworthy, there has been a countervailing turn towards greater conservatism within the Social Democratic Party—one that worries progressive sex rights activists greatly. Social Democrats have not only followed but have taken a lead in joining Christian Democrats in pushing newly restrictive legislation in the guise of concern either for adolescent safety or for the rights of the disabled. One instance is the 2008 law which (purportedly to accommodate new European Union guidelines about prostitution, though actually very much on the independent initiative of Social Democratic Minister of Justice Brigitte Zypries) raised the age of consent to eighteen for exchanging sexual contact for money or goods. Critics from the Free Democratic Party and the Green party had charged that sixteen- or seventeen-year-olds who offered a meal or a movie to someone with whom they were interested in having intimate connection would be making themselves liable to prosecution.[39] In defensive but immovable response, Zypries asserted that she had the young person's best interests at heart; he or she, in order to achieve "undisturbed sexual development," needed the state's protection from "experiencing sexuality as a purchasable commodity" (a somewhat hapless phrasing in view of feminists' longstanding efforts to point out that the conservative ideal of marriage in which only the man earned money while the woman stayed at home could also be interpreted as that kind of exchange—and also a peculiarly normative assumption that there was a standard of "good sex" from which consensual but emotionally depersonalized sex is an unacceptable departure).[40] Opponents of the new legislation remained insistent that the preexisting laws against sexual exploitation had been perfectly adequate, and they opined that what was really at stake was the restoration of a "repressive sexual morality" and a "European-wide trend towards a massive criminalization of the sexuality of adolescents up to the age of eighteen."[41]

Another and in some ways far more troubling instance because of its implications for assumptions about women's self-determination and moral maturity, was the 2009 law change (protested vehemently but unsuccessfully by reproductive rights activist groups like Pro Familia) in which pregnant women seeking later-term abortions in the wake of just having learned of a fetal disability will be subjected to a new three-day waiting and reflection period, and doctors who fail to counsel women appropriately on the matter are subject to prosecution and fines. The Vatican and anti-choice groups within Germany announced their delight at the change. Prior attempts led by Christian Democrats in 2001 and 2004 had failed; this time a quarter of the Social Democratic legislators (led by Andrea Nahles, Renate Schmidt, and Kerstin Griese) and a third of the Greens joined in voting for the new law, which was strategically pitched as an important advance for disability rights (rather than, as it will be experienced, an additional traumatization of an already traumatized woman—and in many cases also her partner; these are after all pregnancies which were desired, often fervently so).[42] Anti-choice activists feel newly empowered and are moving quickly to use the new wedge of disability rights to push for further restrictions on access to terminations.[43]

Already since the postunification compromise, abortions on the grounds merely of fetal disability have been illegal (an understandable postfascist stance, although a problematic one in view of the ongoing inadequacy of social support structures for disabled individuals and their families); instead, terminations of pregnancies due to fetal disability are handled as a subset of the maternal health indication—i.e., a doctor may endorse a termination if carrying the pregnancy to term would seriously harm the physical or emotional health of the mother. Many of the cases will concern women whose children's prospects for viability post-birth are grim. The biggest worry is that the new law will make doctors even more reluctant—for fear of being liable to prosecution—to attest that carrying to term a disabled fetus could be construed as a danger to maternal health. The ugly results of having women's reproductive rights increasingly being strategically posed as being in opposition to disability rights are already evident in journalistic controversies.[44]

Overall, however, it remains the case that Germany in the first decade of the twenty-first century has returned to its early twentieth-century status as one of the most—if not *the* most—liberal and "sex-positive" cultures in the world. In some ways, Germany is more progressive now than it was one hundred years ago. There is, for instance, the rise of Third Wave Feminism, which often mixes anger, humor, and graphically explicit sexiness in new ways. See for instance the just-launched *Missy* magazine, which covers such matters as polyamory and punk, but also the huge success of young writers and television celebrities like Thea Dorn or Charlotte Roche (the latter of whose outrageously graphic, Rabelaisian but ultimately deeply romantic story, *Wetlands* (Feuchtgebiete)—about hemorrhoids, pubic shaving, and masturbating-with-avocado-pits—was a runaway bestseller in 2008).[45] There is also the emergence of decidedly un-p.c. women's music like that of the Turkish German singer Lady Bitch

Ray (who complains openly about how unsatisfactory German men's penises are and thereby counters the aggressive misogyny of male rappers like Bushido with some misanthropy of her own).[46] And there is the quite a bit more marginal but nonetheless striking phenomenon of the recurrent closing-down of neo-Nazi internet dating sites–which forces those young "AntiAntifas" in search of love to use Facebook like everyone else.[47] Also essential to register is how many aspects of contemporary German sexual culture are no longer specifically German at all–from Internet dating sites and Internet porn, on the one hand, to conflicts over citizenship-acquisition marriages (*Scheinehen*) or, on the other, the prevalence of prostitutes, both female and male, hailing preeminently from the states of the former Eastern European bloc and the former Soviet Union.

Two conflictual areas that have become hot topics in the last decade all over postcommunist Europe do have special resonances in Germany. One is the rise of European Islam, especially its neofundamentalist strand and the challenge that that strand's hostility to both homosexuality and female sexual independence poses to non-Muslim German (and also moderate Muslim German) commitments to sexual freedom and the principle of individual self-determination. And the other is the matter of steadily declining German birthrates.

In the case of Islam, much of German public opinion is in a perpetual state of anxiety. It has become difficult to sort out what is by now a thoroughly snarled set of debates. On the one side are those who see the extreme phenomena of coerced marriages, honor killings, and female genital mutilation, as well as the more general effort to exert familial control over female–especially daughters'–sexuality as symptomatic of the inner truth of Islam and its purportedly backward-looking ethos. Many of these, whether themselves of Muslim or non-Muslim background, express outrage at what they perceive to be the taboos against criticizing others' religious beliefs or practices and/or express concern that Germans, after Nazism, are so afraid of being labeled racist that they, out of a misunderstood "cultural sensitivity," refuse to take an adequately strong stand against human rights violations. And some Muslim Germans have taken it upon themselves to be the "culture brokers" and spokespersons who dare to challenge neofundamentalism within Islam and use their authority as Muslims to do so. [48] On the other side are those who try–variously patiently or passionately–to point out that the vast majority of both immigrant and native-born Muslims in Germany are hardly militant Islamists, are well integrated into the society, and favor the separation of state and religion. In yet another variant, some commentators suggest that more conservative Muslims might have legitimate criticisms of what they see as Western hypersexuality and pseudo-freedom. Some above all express anguish that while antiracism had been the watchword among unified Germany's progressives as recently as the early 1990s, increasingly in recent years, leftists, liberals, and feminists have gone on something of an anti-Muslim rampage.[49] Whatever position one takes, there is no question that few debates have so powerfully shifted in their terms in the last ten years as this one.

Figure 5 Gayhane party at the SO36 club, Berlin, 2008, accompanying a story by Nicholas Kulish, "Gay Muslims Pack a Dance Floor of Their Own." From *The New York Times,* © January 1, 2008 The New York Times All rights reserved. Used by permission and protected by the Copyright Laws of the United States. The printing, copying, redistribution, or retransmission of the Material without express written permission is prohibited.

The New York Times

Europe

WORLD U.S. N.Y. / REGION BUSINESS TECHNOLOGY SCIENCE HEALTH SPORTS OPINION

AFRICA AMERICAS ASIA PACIFIC EUROPE MIDDLE EAST

Adve

BERLIN JOURNAL

Gay Muslims Pack a Dance Floor of Their Own

Jan-Peter Boening for The New York Times

The crowd at Gayhane, a monthly party for Arab and Turkish gay men, lesbians and bisexuals at SO36, a Berlin nightclub. The event's name is fashioned from gay and "hane," Turkish for home.

By NICHOLAS KULISH
Published: January 1, 2008

SIGN IN TO E-MAIL
OR SAVE THIS

BERLIN — Six men whirled faster and faster in the center of the nightclub, arms slung over one another's shoulders, performing a traditional circle dance popular in Turkey and the Middle East. Nothing unusual given the German capital's large Muslim population.

PRINT

SINGLE PAGE

REPRINTS

ARTICLE TOOLS
SPONSORED BY

In the middle of these debates are those who are often torn and truly not sure how to feel about such moves as Baden-Württemberg Christian Democratic politicians' insistence (as of 2006) that immigrants from predominantly Muslim countries wishing to become citizens not only demonstrate their knowledge of German history and language but also assert their comfort with both homosexuality and female sexual independence. It is after all also a kind of ironic achievement for sex rights activism to have these positions advanced by Christian Democrats (of all groups!) and there was extensive controversy over the "attitude test" across the Green, Social Democratic, and left-liberal "scenes" as well as in gay and lesbian activist communities. (As of 2007, the two questions about homosexuality were dropped, for unclear reasons–perhaps due to some Christian Democratic politicians' own qualms about the matter, despite the party's current emphatic official self-description as non-homophobic, but multiple questions surrounding women's and adolescent girls' rights to choose their own sexual activities and relationships free from familial interference remain.)[50] And meanwhile, gay and lesbian Muslims themselves are increasingly out of the closet, partying openly in clubs, negotiating tolerance with their families, and formulating alternative visions of Islam.[51]

Figure 6 "More Sex – Fewer Babies: Are the Germans dying out?" Cover of *Der Spiegel*, March 24, 1975. Reprinted with permission of *Der Spiegel.*

Figure 7 "Large guestworker family: Under the bedcovers…" (Photo: Inge Werth) is contrasted with "… We are a dying people: Small German family" (Photo: Kai Greiser). Photos accompanying the cover essay, "More Sex – Fewer Babies: Are the Germans dying out?" *Der Spiegel*, March 24, 1975, 41. The text of the essay explains: "For 'if one were to subtract the fruitful activity of our industrious guestworkers,' as the *Süddeutsche Zeitung* already last year wryly calculated, then every year only about 500,000 genuine Germans are born – whereby the birthrate within one decade has been cut by fully a half and the erstwhile Christian Democratic Minister for the Family Franz Josef Wuermeling could now think he was right when he once said: 'Under the bedcovers we are a dying people.'" Reprinted with permission of: *Der Spiegel*; Inge Werth, Haunetal; Kai Greiser, Kosel.

Gastarbeiter-Großfamilie: „Unter der Decke …

… sind wir ein sterbendes Volk": **Deutsche Kleinfamilie**

Developing their own independent views and lives are also countless Muslim women, both self-described Muslim feminists and the many Muslim women who are simply navigating the conflicting social and cultural pressures in their own ways (promiscuity and prayer, for instance, are not necessarily irreconcilable).[52] In addition, it is crucial to acknowledge that German sex and reproductive rights groups like Pro Familia as well as numerous progressive medical professionals involved in providing sex- and reproduction-related healthcare have definitely adapted to the new multicultural Germany and offer a plethora of culturally attuned services for migrants from all backgrounds, including various forms of Islam. Doctors and social workers alike are sensitized to deal with a wide range of issues–ranging from hymen repair to genetic counseling and fertility treatments.[53] What bears emphasis, in short, is how profoundly the purportedly premodern and the seemingly postmodern now intersect.

Meanwhile, the histrionic tone in media coverage of the birthrate issue raises echoes with a more recent past: that of the heyday of the sexual revolution of the 1970s in West Germany–and the striking ambivalences expressed at the time about women's eagerness to separate sex from reproduction. The topic, apparently, could not be disentangled from concern about the higher birthrates of Turkish guestworkers.[54] Moreover, the concerns about birthrates were then (and are again now in recent times) inseparable as well from irritation at feminism in general and a less-than-

Figure 8 "Woman '75: Back to Femininity." Cover of *Der Spiegel,* June 30, 1975. Reprinted with permission of *Der Spiegel.*

subtle plea that German women might "return to femininity."[55] And lest one think this was just a retrograde 1970s spasm—soon washed away by cheerful embrace of feminism as an erotic enhancement of men's lives and a boon also to children, a glance at the debates in the German media in the last three or four years will be curative. In Germany—with its long-standing paucity of good childcare facilities and lack of all-day schooling (in many regions children still come home for lunch)—it is especially difficult to combine career and motherhood (in contrast with France or Scandinavia); these are some practical reasons for the lower birthrate.[56] But the idea of German "childlessness" (*Kinderlosigkeit*) as an imminent demographic and cultural catastrophe is advanced with a whole range of aggressive arguments.[57]

One argument has been psychological: Germans are becoming egoists. This refers both to the parents who selfishly do not want any children or at best only one, as well as the only children who have no siblings from and with whom they can learn about human solidarity. This argument was put forward with particular vehemence by Frank Schirrmacher, co-publisher of the *Frankfurter Allgemeine Zeitung*, in his 2006 book *Minimum*.[58] A second argument is economic: Without children there will be nobody to pay into social security and pension plans (a misleading argument both because it blames the shakiness of entitlement plans on

Figure 9 "Everyone for Himself: How the Dearth of Children is Creating a Society of Egoists." Cover of *Der Spiegel*, March 6, 2006. Reprinted with permission of *Der Spiegel.*

reduced childbearing rather than wider global economic changes and not least because those same global economic changes have made population growth much less of an economic desideratum than it once was).[59] The third is either codedly or openly racist: Enlightenment-minded Europeans will be outnumbered by patriarchal and anti-Enlightenment populations both inside and outside of Europe.[60] Fourth, there is the pseudo-solicitous but ever-so-slightly eugenicist argument: In order to encourage especially those apparently child-averse career-oriented academic and professional women (but therefore also implicitly more intelligent and competent— that's where the eugenic implications come in) to have more children, one really should pay more child-money because it is somehow especially distressing that approximately 30 to 40 percent of these women will not become mothers.[61]

What becomes visible here is the incoherence of the current impasse. In the hostility to Islam, support for female sexual independence is central. In the distress over a declining German birthrate, female sexual independence is perceived as a problem, and a backlash against feminism is evident, replete with criticisms of German women's lamentable reliance on contraception. The endless commentary about the purported demerits of Islam keeps these contradictions from becoming too easy to decode.[62] For instance, in a 2009 flurry of upbeat government and media pronouncements due to a study showing a recent uptick in the German birthrate, from 1.33 to 1.37, it became clear not only that sometimes immigrant women are counted and sometimes not, but that when Muslim women stay at home with young children, that is deemed a sign of awful patriarchalism; when non-Muslim women do so, the Christian Democratic government of Angela Merkel congratulates itself for having developed improved family policies.[63]

In the constant exhortations to native-born German women to be more avidly reproductive, and even while the growth of a second- and third-generation native-born population that is both Muslim and German is variously either bemoaned or disavowed (of the three million Muslims living in Germany, 250,000 are citizens), there is a recurrent rehearsal of yet one more (faulty but nonetheless strategically effective) argument, in this case a historical one:[64] In the pre-pill 1950s, the story goes, women had more children and stayed home happily; the sexual revolution ruined all that. Now people just selfishly seek sexual pleasure—but all that does is spread anomie. It has become remarkably popular in the early twenty-first century to slam the sexual revolution of the 1960s-1970s for encouraging meaningless hedonism. This may seem gender-neutral, but it inevitably is meant as preeminently an attack on female self-determination. In addition, open animus against feminism and the yearning for a "little woman at the stove" (*Heimchen am Herd*) who will repair the ego of the husband when he comes home from his stressful day at work have returned with surprising forthrightness.[65]

And with that we come to a final point: the revival of antifeminism. The short answer to the rhetorical question "What's left of the man?" is: *Not much.* "My generation has been laundered into such softness by the women's movement," the Berlin cabaret comedian Horst Schroth says, and the T-shirts he sells for men are a huge hit: "In bed not so great. In other ways a fine mate." (*Schlecht im Bett. Sonst ganz nett.*) The joke is of course on the pressure women put on men to be better lovers. Already in the 1970s the threat was that if women expected more from their men, men would simply lose desire for women. Now the argument is that demanding women have ruined men entirely. The *Spiegel*–like countless other venues (the state of German masculinity is a hugely debated topic, showing up in the most diverse places, including for instance education policy, as the newly identified educational lag among German boys is variously blamed on single mothers or the preponderance of female teachers)–does note that younger men are choosing to develop new styles of masculinity, and are enjoying new roles as fathers and sharers in house-

Figure 10 "Emancipation: What's left of the man?" Cover of *Der Spiegel,* June 23, 2008. Reprinted with permission of *Der Spiegel.*

cleaning.[66] But the tone of displeasure and befuddlement at the current state of the battle of the sexes remains. Thus, the *Spiegel* declares authoritatively that women, those ever contradictory and irrational creatures, do not know themselves what they want, or secretly want the opposite of what they claim, and the magazine finds experts on psychology, masculinity, and couples counseling who opine that women these days complain when men do not change the baby's diapers and provide good foreplay to boot, but still tend to seek status-higher men who will provide for them financially. Or as an article in *Die Zeit* put it in 2006, women really are dreadful for not liking the very "whimpsters" and "emo boys" they initially demanded; men thus desperately try to recover their "'M-ness'" (i.e., masculinity)– to little avail. "Thus we see," the author sadly concluded, "the modern male lover engaging in the poignant project of attempting to have a politically correct, peace-loving, woman-friendly, totally spontaneous and self-ironically aware erection."[67] This may just be humorous carping, but it's not exactly pretty either. And while the authors could be dismissed–as a (German male) friend recently put it–as nothing more than "little wannabe alpha-males," there is indisputably also a large popular audience for these debates. I was earnestly informed in April 2009 by two male German journalists that "there are no more men in Germany."[68] If even a portion of these complaints are to be believed, then the gains of the last twenty postunification years are not secure. "Sex yes, equality no?" Post coitum triste est.

Notes

1. For their helpful critical readings and responses, I thank Jeff Anderson, Robert Beachy, Carola Dietze, Myra Marx Ferree, Eric Langenbacher, Till van Rahden, and Michael Staub, as well as audiences at Georgetown University and the German Historical Institute. For answering key questions and generously sharing crucial expertise, I thank Paul Betts, Gisela Notz, Gunter Schmidt, Sybill Schulz, and Kurt Starke.
2. "Wir haben den Akt, dessen Folgen ungewiss sind, gemeinsam vollzogen, nach langen Jahren frustreicher Sicherheitspartnerschaft. Inzwischen ist die kurze Hoch-Zeit orgiastistischer Vereinigungsfeten vorüber. Nach dem Höhepunkt spürt man Erleichterung und Ermüdung. Die Braut, einst DDR-Volk geheissen, fühlt sich, nun ja: ein bisschen am Ziel ihrer Wünsche (frau hat sich's immer etwas anders vorgestellt), ein bisschen verführt, ein bisschen gewaltsam in Besitz genommen–Sexisten nennen den Vorgang gelegentlich 'Vergewohltätigung'. Doch Jammern hilft nicht. Bekanntlich gehören *dazu* immer zwei: Halb zog er sie, halb sank sie hin; der Geist war unwillig,

doch das Fleisch war schwach. Nun hat sie empfangen, erhofft sich Genesung ihres Organismus und gesunde Kinder. Sorge bereitet ein geschwächtes politisch-moralisches Immunsystem. Was der robuste Freier mühelos wegsteckt, kann die Gesundheit der Braut ernsthaft bedrohen. Auch schien der Adler seinerzeit–wie damals Ledas Schwan– beim Werben spendabler, als er nun, hinterher, nach befriedigter Lust, sich zu zeigen bereit ist: post coitum triste est … ?" Konrad Weller, *Das Sexuelle in der deutsch-deutschen Vereinigung: Resümée und Ausblick* (Leipzig, 1991), 8-9.

3. See in this context also the testimonials in Wolfgang Engler, "Nacktheit, Sexualität und Partnerschaft," in *Die Ostdeutschen: Kunde von einem verlorenen Land* (Berlin, 1999); Uta Kolano, *Nackter Osten* (Frankfurt/Oder, 1995); Ina Merkel, "Die Nackten und die Roten: Zum Verhältnis von Nacktheit und Öffentlichkeit in der DDR," *Mitteilungen aus der kulturwissenschaftlichen Forschung* 18, no. 36 (1995); and Kurt Starke, *Schwuler Osten: Homosexuelle Männer in der DDR* (Berlin, 1994); as well as the insightful analysis by Josie McLellan, "State socialist bodies: East German nudism from ban to boom," *Journal of Modern History* 79, no. 1 (2007), 48-79.

4. Conversation with H. N., 1998.

5. This is not to minimize the fact that there was a vibrant feminist movement in East Germany, one significantly larger than in other East Bloc countries. See Myra Marx Ferree, "'The Time of Chaos was the Best': Feminist Mobilization and Demobilization in East Germany," *Gender and Society* 8, no. 4 (1994); Ingrid Miethe, *Frauen in der DDR-Opposition: Lebens- und kollektivgeschichtliche Verläufe in einer Frauenfriedensgruppe* (Opladen, 1999); and Anne Hampele Ulrich, *Der Unabhängige Frauenverband* (Berlin, 2000).

6. Hans-Joachim Ahrendt, "Neue Aspekte der Familienplanung und Geburtenregelung in Ostdeutschland," in *Sexualität und Partnerschaft im Wandel: Jahrestagung 1991 der Gesellschaft für Sexualwissenschaft, Leipziger Texte zur Sexualität* 1, no. 1 (1992), 6.

7. Conversation with T. T., 2001.

8. Conversation with A. U., 2009.

9. Conversation with Z. N., 2006.

10. Daphne Berdahl, "'Konsumrausch': The Production of Citizen-Consumers in the former GDR," paper delivered at a conference on Redefining the Nation in Europe: Germany and Austria, 1945-2000, Emory University, 13 April 2002.

11. Carmen Beilfuss, "Über sieben Brücken musst Du geh'n…': Der schwierige Weg der Liebe in der Marktwirtschaft," in *Sexualität und Partnerschaft* (see note 6).

12. Katrin Rohnstock, ed., *Stiefschwestern: Was Ostfrauen und Westfrauen voneinander denken* (Frankfurt/Main, 1994); Katrin Rohnstock, ed., *Stiefbrüder: Was Ostmänner und Ostfrauen voneinander denken* (Berlin, 1995).

13. Katrin Rohnstock, "Vorwort," in Rohnstock, ed., *Erotik macht die Hässlichen schön: Sexueller Alltag im Osten*, ed. Katrin Rohnstock (Berlin, 1995), 9-10.

14. Beilfuss (see note 11); and Dietrich Mühlberg, "Sexualität und ostdeutscher Alltag," *Mitteilungen zus der kulturwissenschaftlichen Forschung* 18, no. 36 (1995).

15. See Rohnstock, "Vorwort," (see note 13), 7-8: "Everywhere video stores opened, that tried to feed the supposedly starved Easterners with erotic Ersatz-fare. The owners were astonished that men and women arrived jointly. Together the partners watched the films–and were disappointed. They had expected eroticism and were instead supplied with cheap, crappy products. After the first curiosity was satisfied, two thirds of the video stores had to shut down." On Easterners' reactions to the sex toy offerings, see especially Dorothee Wierling, "Vereinigungen–ostdeutsche Briefe an Beate Uhse," *BIOS* 20 (2007).

16. Kurt Starke quoted in Mühlberg (see note 14), 21.

17. Marc Fisher, "East Germans Face Pain of Redefining Pasts; Secret Police Files Opened to Public; Woman Finds Out Even Her Husband Informed on Her," *The Washington Post*, 18 January 1992, available at http://voices.washingtonpost.com/rawfisher/2006/01/domestic_intelligence_buzzing.html.

18. See in this context the important essay by Belinda Cooper, "Patriarchy within a Patriarchy: Women and the Stasi," *German Politics and Society* 16, no. 2 (1998); as well as the revelatory little anecdote told by East German pastor and (since 1982) homosexual rights advocate Eduard Stapel: "During the years of the GDR, it was completely clear that the Stasi listens along and reads along. In other words, when I wrote a letter, it was obvious to me that it would be read or could be read. In the end the letters were brought to me still opened, nobody had even bothered to seal them shut again. We knew that. Or for instance when we were in groups and I noticed, someone is speaking beyond what is politically acceptable, then I always put on the brakes, so that he doesn't run directly into the knife. Insofar I am surprised that some people who were affected by it now act astonished about what all the Stasi did. Back then they would not have been surprised. It was totally clear to me. Besides, they let me know what they were up to. They once even packed a rather pretty boy into my bed and then had the bad luck that he fell in love with me and revealed the whole thing to me. Some people today find that 'terrible.' I think it's sort of funny. But not funny, of course, when it caused people pain." "Vom Arbeitskreis 'Homosexualität' der Evangelischen Studentengemeinde in Leipzig zum Schwulenverband in Deutschland," Eduard Stapel, interviewed by Kurt Starke, 19 April 1994, in Starke (see note 3), 101.

19. For general orientation, see the outstanding "Introduction" by Katherine Pence and Paul Betts to Katherine Pence and Paul Betts, eds., *Socialist Modern: East German Everyday Culture and Politics* (Ann Arbor, 2008), 1-34. The aggressive invasiveness of the Stasi is well described in Bürgerkomitee Leipzig, ed., *Stasi intern: Macht und Banalität* (Leipzig, 1998), 198-212; and Vera Wollenberger, *Virus der Heuchler: Innenansicht aus Stasi-Akten* (Berlin, 1992). On the Stasi's use of prostitutes, see Uta Falck, *VEB Bordell: Geschichte der Prostitution in der DDR* (Berlin, 1998). For a thought-provoking critique of the intensity of affect directed against the former collaborators with the Stasi, see Matthias Wagner, *Das Stasi-Syndrom: Über den Umgang mit den Akten des MfS in den 90er Jahren* (Berlin, 2001), 7-9, 174-87. See also the important commentaries in: Detlef Pollack, "Über die 68er und ihr Verhältnis zur DDR," *Leviathan*, no. 4 (1998); Konrad Jarausch, "Jenseits von Verdammung und Verklärung," *Frankfurter Rundschau*, 30 May 2000, 22; and the observations about the complex roles played by the several hundred thousand "informal collaborators" working for the Stasi—not just as functionaries of repression but also "paternalistic caregivers and privilege-distributors" and as mediums for the articulation of the infantilized citizenry's interests in Jürgen Habermas, "Bemerkungen zu einer verworrenen Diskussion: Was bedeutet 'Aufarbeitung der Vergangenheit' heute?" *Die Zeit*, 10 April 1992, 18. On the numerous romantic dramas and complexities that played out without any involvement from the Stasi, see the chapter on GDR divorce courts in Paul Betts, *Within Walls: A History of East German Private Life* (Oxford, 2010).

20. Kurt Starke, email to the author, 14 July 2009.

21. See Gunter Schmidt, Silja Matthiesen, Arne Dekker, and Kurt Starke, *Spätmoderne Beziehungswelten: Report über Partnerschaft und Sexualität in drei Generationen* (Wiesbaden, 2006); Kurt Starke, *Nichts als die reine Liebe: Beziehungsbiographien und Sexualität im sozialen und psychologischen Wandel: Ost-West-Unterschiede* (Lengerich, 2005).

22. Gunter Schmidt, "Emanzipation zum oder vom Geschlechtsverkehr?" *Pro Familia Magazin* 5 (1993).

23. Starke (see note 21).

24. Dirk Konietzka and Michaela Kreyenfeld, eds., *Ein Leben ohne Kinder: Kinderlosigkeit in Deutschland* (Wiesbaden, 2007).

25. Marina Adler and April Brayfield, "Gender Regimes and Cultures of Care: Public Support for Maternal Employment in Germany and the United States," *Marriage and Family Review* 39, nos. 3-4 (2006). See also Myra Marx Ferree's observations that as of the year 2000, "an absolute majority of all births in the ex-GDR occurred outside of marriage (52 percent versus 19 percent in the West) and in the new states 15 percent of women aged twenty-five to twenty-nine lived in non-marital unions with children (only 3 percent in

the West did)" and that "there are still [as of 2009] remarkably strong differences in women's preferred and actual work-family arrangements in the new and old federal states." Myra Marx Ferree, "Gender Politics in the Berlin Republic: Issues of Identity and Institutional Change," *German Politics and Society* (in this issue).

26. "Adolescent protective behaviors: Abstinence and contraceptive use," Advocates for Youth, available at http://www.advocatesforyouth.org/index.php?option=com_content&task=view&id=446&Itemid=336#references; Silja Matthiesen and Gunter Schmidt, "Sexuelle Erfahrungen und Beziehungen adoleszenter Frauen," *Zeitschrift für Sexualforschung* 22, no. 2 (2009).

27. Lisa Herrmann-Green and Monika Herrmann-Green, "Familien mit lesbischen Eltern in Deutschland, *Zeitschrift für Sexualforschung* 21, no. 4 (2008); Bernhard Hübner, "Bayern stoppt klage gegen Homo-Ehe," *die tageszeitung*, 10 August 2009, available at http://www.taz.de/1/politik/deutschland/artikel/1/bayern-stoppt klage-gegen-homo-ehe/.

28. No less symbolically significant is that recent years have seen not only the official acknowledgment, at long last, of the Third Reich's antihomosexual policies and practices but also the establishment of a memorial to the homosexual men tortured and murdered in the Third Reich, in close proximity to the mass graveyard of cement blocks that is the memorial to the murdered Jews of Europe. "'Eine Liebesszene, sonst nichts,'" *die tageszeitung*, 27 May 2008, http://www.taz.de/1/leben/kuenste/artikel/1/eine-liebesszene-sonst-nichts-1/.

29. See Wolfgang Keller, "CDU bewegt sich auf Schwule und Lesben zu," *gay-web.de–News* 405, 16 June 2006, available at: news.gay-web.de/njus/gay-webNews_ID405.pdf; and "Gleichgeschlechtliche Paare haben Anspruch auf Toleranz," CDU document, 31 July 2007, available at http://www.cdu.de/politikaz/gleichg.php. See also Sebastian Fischer, "CSU entdeckt Alleinerziehende und Schwule," *Spiegel online*, 20 October 2006.

30. For a useful discussion of the mixed results (decriminalization definitely has increased prostitute safety and independence from pimps, but the new law has been less successful in prompting prostitutes to pay taxes), see Bundesministerium für Familie, Senioren, Frauen, und Jugend, "Prostitutionsgesetz," 15 March 2006, available at www.bmfsfj.de/Politikbereiche/gleichstellung.did=72948.html. For a critique of the Swedish law, see Don Kulick, "Four Hundred Thousand Swedish Perverts," *GLQ* 11, no. 2 (2005): 205-235. For the contrasting view that the purchasing of sexual services deserves to be criminalized as well as culturally shamed, see Maria-Pia Boethius, "Das Ende der Prostitution in Schweden?" *Streit* 1 (2001): 6-10. On the Netherlands, see Laura Agustín, "What's happening in Amsterdam? An overview of changing prostitution law," *Border Thinking on Migration, Trafficking and Commercial Sex* (blog), 16 January 2009, available at http://www.nodo50.org/Laura_Agustin/whats-happening-in-amsterdam-an-independent-view.

31. On sex rights activism by and on behalf of disabled individuals, see Ernst Klee, *Behindert – Über die Enteignung von Körper und Bewusstsein: Ein kritisches Handbuch* (Frankfurt/Main, 1980); and Carol Poore, *Disability in Twentieth-Century German Culture* (Ann Arbor, 2007).

32. See for instance the presentations of Lothar Sandfort, Manuela Schmidt and Martina Lipp, and Lisa Roswitha Schuster at the workshop, "Sexualassistenz und Sexualbegleitung für Menschen mit Beeinträchtigungen," held at the Familienplanungszentrum Balance, Berlin, 16 September 2009, available at http://www.frauengesundheit berlin.de/index.php4?request= termine&topic=564&type=event.

33. Fifteen-year anniversary celebration at the Rotes Rathaus, Berlin for the Familienplanungszentrum Balance, 5 September 2007, available at http://www.fpz-berlin.de/.

34. Dagmar Herzog, *Sex after Fascism: Memory and Morality in Twentieth-Century Germany* (Princeton, 2005).

35. Helmut Graupner, "Das späte Menschenrecht (Teil 1)–Sexualität im europäischen und österreichischen Recht," *Sexuologie* 11, nos. 3-4 (2004): 119-139; Michele Grigolo,

"Sexualities and the ECHR: Introducing the Universal Sexual Legal Subject," *European Journal of International Law* 14, no. 5 (November 2003): 1023-1044; Dagmar Herzog, "'Das späte Menschenrecht': Auf der Suche nach einer nachfaschistischen Sexualmoral," in *Demokratie im Schatten der Gewalt: Geschichten des Privaten im deutschen Nachkrieg*, eds., Daniel Fulda et al. (Göttingen, forthcoming 2010).

36. See in this context the important essay by Eva Maleck-Lewy and Myra Marx Ferree, "Talking about Women and Wombs: Discourse about Abortion and Reproductive Rights in the GDR During and after the 'Wende,'" paper delivered at the conference on Gender and Reproductive Rights in Eastern Europe, Open Society Institute, Il Ciocco, Italy, June 1996.

37. Conversation with Elke Thoss, president of Pro Familia Germany, 2006. It is telling as well that significant funding for anti-abortion activists comes not from within Germany, but from the U.S., especially California.

38. Nikolaus Blome and Rolf Kleine, "Wofür entscheidet sich Minister Seehofer?" *Bild*, 17 January 2007, available at http://www.bild.de/BTO/news/2007/01/17/seehofer-geliebte-zukunft/seehofer-geliebte-zukunft.html; Joachim Peter and Peter Issig, "Seehofer soll die CSU liberaler machen–und sexy," *Die Welt*, 25 October 2008, available at http://www.welt.de/politik/article2626863/Seehofer-soll-die-CSU-liberaler-machen-und-sexy.html; Michael Stiller and Waltraud Taschner, "Seehofers Geliebte erneut schwanger?," *die tageszeitung*, 11 June 2009, http://www.taz.de/1/politik/deutschland/artikel/1/dringender-termin-in-berlin/.

39. See especially the interview with Green politician Jerzy Montag, "'Rückfall in den 50er-Puritanismus,'" *die tageszeitung*, 12 December 2007, available at http://www.taz.de/1/politik/deutschland/artikel/1/rueckfall-in-den-50er-puritanismus/?src=MT&cHash=362dc0afea; as well as Reinhard Müller, "Erste Liebe weiter straflos," *Frankfurter Allgemeine Zeitung*, 12 December 2007, available at http://www.faz.net/s/Rub77CAECAE 94D7431F9EACD163751D4CFD/Doc~E49B71E47053B4E0AB8247A2919907FBA~ ATpl~Ecommon~Scontent.html.

40. Brigitte Zypries quoted in "Besserer Schutz vor sexuellem Missbrauch von Kindern und Jugendlichen," press release of the German Ministry of Justice, 20 June 2008, available at http://www.bmj.bund.de/enid/0,ce78b5636f6e5f6964092d0935323239093a 095f7472636964092d0934393330/Pressestelle/Pressemitteilungen_58.html; on assumptions about "good" sex, see Kulick (see note 30).

41. Deutsche Gesellschaft für Sexualforschung and Pro Familia Bundesverband, "Stellungnahme zur geplanten Sexualstrafrechtsreform," *Zeitschrift für Sexualforschung* 21, no. 2 (2008), 181-84. The authors (Ulrike Brandenburg, Hertha Richter-Appelt, Lorenz Böllinger, and Gisela Notz) also deemed the legal change a "purely symbolic and populist" effort to pretend to get tough on crime while actually ignoring the conditions of poverty and unemployment that foster sexual exploitation.

42. See "Rückschritt im Abtreibungsrecht," Pressemitteilung des Pro Familia-Bundesverbandes, 15 May 2009: "True assistance for women, who after the twelfth week of pregnancy decide for a termination, which they will only receive with a medical indication, will not be provided by this new change in the law. To say that it will is nothing but hypocritical pretense. We ask instead, what difficulties will result from the change in the law for affected women in the future? Here it is important to differentiate between women who are pregnant in their thirteenth week and women who are, after the major ultrasound and later, pregnant after the twenty-second week. It will not be a relief for women, to be subjected to a fixed period of days, in order 'quietly' to be able to think about their decision–what an ignorant, contemptuous image of women lies behind such a concept! They will have three days of fear to worry about whether the doctor will grant them a medical indication. Also the doctor gains three days to reflect on whether he wants to subject himself to the risk of providing a–possibly contestable–medical assessment, additionally threatened with a fine of 5000 Euro if found guilty. He will tend only then to provide the medical indication if the patient is in danger of actually

losing her life. This division of the medical indication is a definitive setback for women's health politics."

43. See the call for counter-protest ("1000 Kreuze in die Spree!") to the "silent march" of the anti-abortion organization Bundesverband Lebensrecht ("1000 Kreuze für das Leben") on 26 September 2009: Antifaschistisches Bündnis Süd-Ost et al., "1000 Kreuze in die Spree: Abtreibungsverbote abschaffen–Gegen christlichen Fundamentalismus." The flyer notes that after the East-West compromise law was settled in 1995, public debate about abortion was practically nonexistent in Germany until the fall of 2008 and the discussions about late-term abortions in cases of fetal disability. Then, "although the law change affects the entire medical indication, the debate primarily turned on seemingly 'irresponsible women' who, purportedly in a 'panic reaction,' decide against 'disabled children.' These are the women who are deemed to need improved counseling." In the pro-choice counter-protesters' view, however, "The current law change was primarily pushed by opponents of abortion who want to use this as the breach in the wall in order to restrict further women's own decision-making process and the possibilities for access to a termination."

44. See the very important essays by Gisela Notz, "Guter Tag für 'Lebensschützer,'" *SoZ– Sozialistische Zeitung* 6 (2009), 6; and Oliver Tolmein, "Das Kind als Zeitbombe– Behinderung im 'Spiegel' der Nichtbehinderten," *Frankfurter Allgemeine Zeitung* online) 28 June 2009, available at http://faz-community.faz.net/blogs/biopolitik/archive/2009/ 06/28/ein-kind-ist-keine-zeitbombe-spiegel-und-behinderung.aspx.

45. For *Missy*, see http://missy-magazine.de/; on Roche, see Ingeborg Harms, "Sexualität ist Wahrheit" (review of *Feuchtgebiete*) in *Frankfurter Allgemeine Zeitung*, 14 April 2008, available at http://www.faz.net/s/RubCF3AEB154CE64960822FA5429A182360/ Doc~E8BC67AB932C047518A9F7391F1DAB131~ATpl~Ecommon~Scontent.html. A good introduction to Dorn are her essays: "Unnachgiebiger werden! Oder hinschmeissen!" *Spiegel online*, 18 October 2006, http://www.spiegel.de/kultur/ gesellschaft/0,1518,443223,00.html; and "Begrabt den Gebärneid!" *Spiegel online*, 20 October 2006, available at http://www.spiegel.de/kultur/gesellschaft/0,1518, 443728,00.html; as well as Thea Dorn, ed., *Die neue F-Klasse: Warum die Zukunft von Frauen gemacht wird* (Munich, 2006). On Third Wave Feminism more generally, see Sonja Eismann, ed., *Hot Topic: Popfeminismus Heute* (Mainz, 2007).

46. See http://www.last.fm/music/Lady+Bitch+Ray/+images.

47. Theodor Heisenberg, "Heimatlos im Weltnetz," *Jungle World*, 2 April 2009, 19.

48. See for example Necla Kelek, "Der menschliche Makel," *die tageszeitung*, 15 March 2009; Peter Schneider, "The New Berlin Wall," *New York Times Magazine*, 4 December 2005; Sylvia Maier, "Honour Killings and the Cultural Defense in Germany," in *Multicultural Jurisprudence: Comparative Perspectives on the Cultural Defense*, eds., Marie-Claire Foblets and Alison Dundes Renteln (Portland, 2009), 229-246.

49. See Eberhard Seidel, "Ihr und Wir," *die tageszeitung*, 18/19 April 2009, 14.

50. "30 Fragen für den Pass," *Zeit online* (2006), available at http://www.zeit.de/online/2006/ 02/gesinnungstest?page=3; Dr. Dienelt, "Gesinnungstest in Baden-Württemberg wird entschärft," *Migrationsrecht.Net*, 6 June 2007, available at http://www.migrationsrecht.net/ nachrichten-auslaenderrecht-politik-gesetzgebung/900-gesinnungstest-in-baden-wuerttemberg-wird-entschaerft.html.

51. Nicholas Kulish, "Gay Muslims Pack a Dance Floor of Their Own," *New York Times*, 1 January 2008, available at http://www.nytimes.com/2008/01/01/world/europe/ 01berlin.html. Note also the queer Muslim and migrant "Body-Check" and "Turkish Delight" parties held in Cologne.

52. Katrin Sieg, "Black Virgins and the Democratic Body in Europe," *New German Critique* 109 (2010); Katherine Pratt Ewing, "Between Cinema and Social Work: Diasporic Turkish Women and the (Dis)Pleasures of Hybridity," *Cultural Anthropology* 21, no. 2 (2006).

53. See *Integration von Migrantinnen*, special issue of *Pro Familia Magazin* 2 (2007); and Theda Borde and Matthias David, eds., *Frauengesundheit, Migration und Kultur in einer globalisierten Welt* (Frankfurt/Main, 2009).

54. See especially the *Spiegel* cover story, "Are the Germans dying out?," which also includes a cartoon with a doctor holding up a newborn in a hospital waiting room full of Turks and announcing elatedly: "It's a German!" "Mehr Sex – Weniger Babys: Sterben die Deutschen aus?" *Spiegel* 13 (1975). The cartoon is on 57.

55. See the cover story, "Frau '75: Zurück zur Weiblichkeit," *Spiegel* 27 (1975).

56. As of 2007, there were only preschool spots for 8.5 percent of children under age three; Family Minister Ursula von der Leyen is working to raise the percentage (against protest from her own party). See Mirjam Piniek and Marlene Riederer, "'Rabenmutter' contra 'Heimchen am Herd'" ARD, 14-21 April 2007, available at http://www.ard.de/zukunft/kinder-sind-zukunft/kinder-sind-gold-wert/hochqualifizierte-frauen-als-muetter/-/id=520620/nid=520620/did=550704/1s05pls/index.html. See in this context also Tonio Postel, "'Ein Kind kriegt man immer gross,'" *Spiegel online*, 22 September 2006; Joachim Rogge, "Der Babyboom macht keine Pause: Frankreich," *General-Anzeiger* (Bonn), 14/15 July 2007, 3; as well as "Cash Incentives Aren't Enough to Lift Fertility," *Wall Street Journal*, 17 August 2006, B1, B6.

57. For helpful overviews of the extraordinarily agitated state of debate, see the excellent website, available at http://www.single-generation.de/kritik/thema_gewollte_kinderlosigkeit.htm#zitate; and Konietzka and Kreyenfeld (see note 24).

58. See Frank Schirrmacher, *Minimum: Vom Vergehen und Neuentstehen unserer Gemeinschaft* (Munich, 2006); and the uncritically enthusiastic discussion of the book in Angela Gatterburg, Matthias Matussek, and Martin Wolf, "Unter Wölfen: Abnehmende Geburtenraten führen zur Vereinzelung der Kinder in unserer Gesellschaft. Nicht nur die finanzielle Zukunftssicherung ist davon betroffen–ohne Familie verlernt die Gesellschaft schlichtweg die Liebe," *Spiegel* 10 (2006), 76-84.

59. Useful analysis can be found in: Karl Otto Hondrich, "Die Bevölkerung schrumpft? Wunderbar!" *Cicero* (2005).

60. See the interview with the American author Phillip Longman, "'Die gehen Elche jagen,'" *Spiegel* 18 (2006), 148-50.

61. See "Akademikerinnen = erfolgreich = kinderlos,"ARD, 14-21 April 2007, available at http://www.ard.de/zukunft/kinder-sind-zukunft/kinder-sind-gold-wert/kinderlose-akademikerinnen/-/id=520620/nid=520620/did=571668/y4lk73/index.html; and "Der Familienkrach," *Spiegel online*, 24 February 2007; as well as the critical discussion in Gisela Notz, "Ist die Familie noch zu retten? Das Familienbild der Ursula von der Leyen," *SoZ–Sozialistische Zeitung* (September 2007), 10. For insight into all the comparable pronatalist argumentative strategies in Britain, see Jessica Autumn Brown and Myra Marx Ferree, "Close your Eyes and Think of England: Pronatalism in the British Print Media," *Gender and Society* 19, no. 1 (2005).

62. As Myra Marx Ferree notes, "Because the 'other' is seen as religious, patriarchal and oppressive to women, German national identity is being reconfigured to be the opposite–secular, egalitarian and supportive of women. On the other hand, this was not, and still is not, a fair reflection of the cultural identity of many individual Germans, who are happy to embrace Christianity as part of the national self-definition and are sure that a father-headed family is both natural and desirable." Marx Ferree (see note 25).

63. See E.S., "Ein Hoch auf Geburtenraten und Hausfrauenquoten," 18 February 2009, available at http://www.jurblog.de/2009/02/18/ein-hoch-auf-geburtenraten-und-hausfrauenquoten/.

64. Hamideh Mohagheghi, "Der Islam in Deutschland," *al-sakina,* http://www.al-sakina.de/inhalt/artikel/amg/mohagh/mohagh.html#2. Of the 15.3 million individuals with a "migratory background" living in Germany, 8 million are citizens. 18.6 percent of the population living in Germany has a "migratory background." They live primarily in the cities of the former West Germany; in Stuttgart, for instance, 40 percent of the

population has a "migratory background," and the percentages in Frankfurt/Main and Nuremberg are almost that high. Almost one in three children under the age of five in Germany has a "migratory background." See Sigrid Weiser, "Für ein Migrations-Main-streaming," *Pro Familia Magazin* 2 (2007), 4-6.

65. See the remarkably direct plea by Ulrich Greiner, "Was der Mann nicht kann," *Zeit*, 6 April 2006. Greiner opined: "As women conquer more and more male domains, there is no longer any pressing reason for the man to participate in raising children … Also scholarly professions are increasingly filled with women, so that in this area too men's former advantage and ability to win the prize and present it at home to the devoted wife, is rapidly disappearing … If the woman would recall herself to her difference from man, and resign herself to enduring all that belongs to that, then the man would be willing once again to resume his old role as self-renouncing protector." For an overview of the debate see Piniek and Riederer (see note 54).

66. On the boys' educational lag, see Detlef Fechtner, "Bildungsdefizite benachteiligen Jungen und junge Männer, "Politik, 31 May 2007, available at http://www.derwesten.de/nachrichten/nachrichten/politik/2007/5/31/news-656755/detail.html; and the discussion around Frank Dammasch, *Jungen in der Krise* (2008), available at http://www.pedocs.de/volltexte/2009/590/; and especially the very useful overview in Lotte Rose and Ulrike Schmauch, eds., *Jungen–die neuen Verlierer? Auf den Spuren eines öffentlichen Stimmungswechsels* (Königstein/Taunus, 2005).

67. Peter Kümmel, "Heimwerker des Trieblebens," *Zeit*, 20 July 2006.

68. Conversation with J. I. and B. A., 6 April 2009. The ongoing explosiveness of the debate about gender relations and as yet inadequate gender equality in present-day Germany was also evident at the taz-kongress held in Berlin, 18 April 2009. See especially the session on "Was nützt schon Geschlechterkampf?" with discussants Barbara Keddi, Detlef Siegfried, Barbara Höll, Ilka Quindeau und Judith Luig, available at http://tv.hobnox.com/#/en/CLTR-CTRL/taz/ntyoq.

Chapter 8

$\mathcal{F}$ROM AUSLÄNDER TO INLANDER

The Changing Faces of Citizenship in Post-Wall Germany

• • • • • • • • • • • • • • •

Joyce Marie Mushaben

> Citizenship is no longer a coherent discourse fixed in a particular framework. In short, it has suffered the fate of other 'meta-narratives' and is consequently open to new definitions: its core components–rights, duties, participation and identity–have become disjointed.
>
> *Gerhard Delanty*

In 1985, I commenced a five-year study of German identity in the Federal Republic (FRG), rooted in a belief that generational change had radically redefined "what it meant to be German" over a span of four decades. Although most of my ninety-plus interview partners denied that they possessed one back then, I discovered a wide assortment of (West) German identities, divided along three main axes. I characterized these groups as the Economic Miracle Generation, the Long March Generation and the Turn-Around Generation, respectively.[1] I initiated a parallel study of East German (GDR) identity in May 1989, at a time when few people on the other side of the Wall ascribed to a *DDR-Identität,* although several grudgingly admitted that such feelings arose when they compared themselves to distant FRG relatives. Less than a year later, the Wall had collapsed, the D-Mark had become the coin of the realm, and unification was set for 3 October 1990.

GDR citizens began their "Hot Autumn" protests with the chant *Wir sind das Volk!* ("we are the People"), shifting by December 1989 to *Wir sind ein Volk!* ("we are one people!"). Confronted with the cost of unity as a fait accompli, west German residents were heard to respond: *Wir auch!* ("so are we!").[2] The fact that blood lineage, shared borders, and a common currency do not make for a unified citizenry became increasingly apparent over the next five years.[3] There are few prescriptions beyond the Basic Law [Art. 16, 116] explaining what "being German" meant in a positive sense. So-called *Ossis* certainly did not think that it meant doing everything the *Besserwessi* way. By 1996, 62 percent of the Easterners felt that Germans had grown further apart, 30 percent among Westerners.[4] Almost a decade after the Wall's collapse, scholars were still unable to prove that the country's internal unity (*innere Einheit*) had been achieved.[5] The old Länder emerged as the ostensible winners of unification, due to western production and construction booms. New Länder residents saw themselves as the losers, as the regional jobless rate rose from 0 to 18 percent, even 20 to 35 percent in some parts by 2002.[6] The persistence of disparate opportunity structures as late as 2009 testifies that different "cultures" and identities are not easily integrated even when people who speak the same mother tongue come to share a single set of legal, political, economic and social institutions.[7]

This brings us to real losers of unification, given the events that followed: the so-called foreigners (*Ausländer*). By 1990, a majority of Germany's 7 million "foreigners" had lived there for over twenty years; accounting for 13 percent of all live births, over a million "aliens" comprise 30-40 percent of the elementary school enrolments in major cities. In 2000, over 60 percent of urban pre-schoolers had migrant families (67 percent in Nuremberg, 65 percent in Frankfurt/Main, 64 percent in Düsseldorf and Stuttgart). By contrast, 22 percent of Germans are sixty+; by 2035, half will be over fifty, and the population could decrease by 23 million through 2050. Social-cultural biases outweigh the legal and economic barriers to migrants' political incorporation.[8] Prior to 1990, most who met the formal requirements for naturalization could still be rejected at the discretion of bureaucrats (*Ermessen*) as "not in the best interest of German culture." Further discretionary criteria imposed by local or state authorities explained enfranchisement gaps from one Bezirk to another (e.g., Steglitz versus Kreuzberg in Berlin) as well as among the Länder. In 1993, for example, Berlin's naturalization rate was four times that of Bavaria.

An unprecedented wave of xenophobic attacks washed across Germany between 1990 and 1993, coinciding with a mass influx of "co-ethnic" repatriates from the former Soviet-bloc countries and thousands of Yugoslav refugees. While unification did not "cause" ultra-nationalist violence, it did serve as a catalyst for hostility towards foreigners (*Ausländerfeindlichkeit*), especially among young, disadvantaged males. The first year of unity saw 1,483 physical attacks against "foreigners," ranging from gang-assaults in subways to fire-bombings of temporary asylum quarters (hostels, container ships). Of the 2,368 violent incidents reported in 1991, 500 occurred between September and October; three-fourths of the arson attacks took place in the old Länder. The Office of Constitutional Protection registered a 54 percent increase in 1992, resulting in seventeen deaths–nine in the West, eight in the East; 1993 saw 1,814 acts of violence and eight more fatalities.[9] Attacks occurred in towns stretching from Aalen (Westphalia) to Zwickau (Saxony). The more sensational cases in Hoyerswerda (1991), Rostock-Lichtenhagen (1992), Mölln (1992) and Solingen (1993) led to copy-cat actions among youth in other cities. No other European state has witnessed comparable levels of xenophobic violence over the last two decades, despite the rise of radically anti-immigration "populist" parties in Great Britain, France, Belgium, the Netherlands and Denmark, inter alia.

From the onset of guestworker recruitment through the fall of the Berlin Wall, politicians and pundits erroneously referred to a lack of effective integration of resident aliens and their offspring as the "foreigner problem" (*das Ausländerproblem*). My earlier work on the nation's postwar identity conundrums, coupled with its refusal to adopt pro-active integration policies, convinced me that what was really at issue was "a German problem," rooted in political polemics, legal codes and notions of citizenship that had failed to keep pace with FRG social realities. Unification "proved" that Germany's adherence to a *jus sanguinis* paradigm is directly at odds with its own needs as a democratic polity. Its economic competitiveness, not to mention the solvency of its pension system, is intricately connected to migration and integration, past, present and future. I also came to recognize that economic marginalization and societal intolerance towards foreigners owes largely to a lack of positive identity among Federal Republicans themselves. I have long wondered how one could expect Turkish residents to "assimilate," given the reluctance of postwar citizens to specify the contours of their own German-ness. Even the *Leitkultur* debate invoked by conservatives in 1999, provides few clues.[10]

My argument here, however, is that Germany has seen a great leap forward over the last two decades, both as a land of immigration *and* integration–due to a little help from the European Union and the surprising policy advocacy of its first female/eastern Christian Democratic Union (CDU) Chancellor, Angela Merkel. Paradoxically, persons of migrant background who stood to lose the most in terms of educational and occupational opportunity–due to intensified competition from groups classified as "real Germans" (*DDR-Übersiedler* and post-Soviet *Aussiedler*)[11]–could become the winners of active social inclusion policies at two levels. Indeed, minority youth with hyphenated-identities may determine whether or not Germany can win "the race for the best brains" shaping the global economy. I first review efforts to redefine the parameters of "citizenship" based on post 1990 legislative reforms. Next, I offer short profiles of three "migrant" generations and the changing opportunity structure each has encountered, leading to different degrees of identification with the new homeland. Finally, I summarize key features of the National Integration Plan adopted in 2007, and speculate as to why Merkel could successfully blaze a trail in the perilous policy territory all previous chancellors had feared to tread.

Reconceptualizing German Citizenship, 1990-2000

From 1949 to 1999, German citizenship laws persistently trapped millions of human faces behind exclusionary masks of foreignness, by positing the nation as an organic community, contrary historical records notwithstanding.[12] The fall of the Wall precipitated not one but two historical breaks with the past regarding citizens' understanding of what it means to be German. The first major break, effected in grand style in 1989/1990, was territorial in nature: the opening of Central/East Europe significantly undermined Germany's insistence on ethno-national citizenship. Codified in the 1913 *Reichs- und Staatsangehörigkeitsgesetz,* an organic image of the German people was retained in the 1949 Preamble to the Basic Law and Article 116. Reliance on *jus sanguinis* throughout the Cold War supplied the fledgling Republic with new sources of political legitimacy. First, it defined German division as provisional, obliging lawmakers to work towards unification (affirmed in the Constitutional Court's 1973 *Grundlagenvertrag* decision). Secondly, the assertion that East and West nationals remained blood-brothers and sisters justified foreign policy mechanisms undermining the existential legitimacy of the other Germany, i.e., the Hallstein Doctrine and the *Alleinvertretungsanspruch.* Third, *jus sanguinis* kept open the question of Germany's final borders, through ties to "co-ethnics" throughout the eastern territories. Commencing with the Brandt Government under Ostpolitik, negotiations to improve the life-conditions of diaspora Germans (e.g., financial aid to secure minority rights or "exit" options for so-called *Aussiedler* in Poland, Romania, and elsewhere) served as the thin-edge-of-the-wedge for effecting slow changes in domains that otherwise would have been deemed "domestic affairs."

Unification turned millions of GDR "re-settlers" into everyday citizens, despite their self-perceived second-class status. The Treaty on Final Settlement ("Two plus Four," September 1990), coupled with the German-Polish Treaty (November 1990), drew a definitive line at the Oder-Neisse River, settling the border question once and for all. The end to territorial claims did not mitigate the influx of ever more *Spät-AussiedlerInnen,* hoping to "reactivate" their citizenship, most of whom were generations removed from the German nation.

Longer in the making, the second historical break is generational in nature, one that will carry the country through the new millennium. Here I contend that the "Long Marchers" ascension to national office in 1998 marks the final stage in bringing closure to fifty years of political re-education. Schooled in the street politics of the late 1960s involving many Third-World struggles, then professionalized by way of grassroots participation in new social movements, these Germans saw their radical aims legitimated by way of transnational human rights agreements (i.e., the 1975 Helsinki Accords). Citizen-activists of the Baby Boom era accept the Federal Republic as a *Staat der Gegenwart* rather than as a nation whose future rests primarily with the past.[13] "States of the present" redefine their national interests in accordance with changing global conditions. Modern and pluralistic in orientation, they rely primarily on *jus soli* to establish the parameters of membership in the polity; they willingly accord citizen status to persons who share constitutional values, a sense of community purpose, and rules of the larger economic game. *Staaten der Vergangenheit* fixate on the more exclusive *jus sanguinis* as the defining element of citizenship, reinforcing identity conundrums by imposing "unmasterable" historical burdens on all who follow.

That situation changed dramatically following revisions to the Alien Act in 1990. In theory, there are two categories of citizenship rules, one based on entitlement (*Anspruch*), the other on administrative discretion (*Ermessen*). In practice, there are multiple categories (see Figure 1). These "fine distinctions with major consequences" derive from legislative amendments stretching from 1913 to 1990, followed by the paradigm shift of 2000. Entitlement covers eleven categories of persons who meet formal requirements regarding length of residency or constitutional provisions reflecting disenfranchisements due to war, changing boundaries or statelessness. These persons have a "right" to citizenship, but secondary criteria regarding living conditions, ability to support dependents, employment status and even grammatical prowess can delay the process for years. Nine discretionary categories apply to foreign spouses, family unification, German descendants in foreign states, and offspring of civil servants or diplomats living abroad.

Table 1: Legal Bases of German Citizenship or Dual Nationality,
1949-1999

Acquisition	German Citizenship	Dual Nationality (German/Foreign)
By birth (jus sanguinis; birthright citizenship)	Children of German parents (at least one German parent)	Children of bi-national couples Children of dual citizen parents
By ethnic descent (constitutional right, legal claim)	Ethnic German expellees (Vertriebene) of 1944-48 without German citizenship (collectively naturalized in 1949) Ethnic German immigrants (Aussiedler) from central and eastern Europe (individually naturalized upon arrival in Germany since 1950)	Ethnic German immigrants (Aussiedler) who came since 1990 and were not forced to relinquish their original citizenship Ethnic German immigrants (Aussiedler) who successfully reclaimed their original citizenship
By ethnic descent (constitutional right, legal claim)	Former German citizens (stateless) who were expatriated and successfully reclaimed their original citizenship \	Former German citizens (meanwhile naturalized by another country) who were expatriated and successfully reclaimed their original citizenship Citizens of other countries who were naturalized by Nazi authorities (predominantly Volksliste III +IV) and successfully reclaimed German citizenship; children of this group of people.
By fulfilling residency requirements in Germany (legal claim, discretion of local authorities)	Foreigners (regardless of birthplace) who relinquished their original citizenship upon naturalization in Germany	Foreigners (regardless of place of birth) who are naturalized in Germany while maintain or (claming) their original citizenship
By place of birth (jus soli; birthright citizenship)		Conditional jus soli (After January 1, 2000): children born in Germany to legal foreign residents; option to become a German citizen or to remain German by renouncing other nationalities between the age of 18 and age 23

Sources: Basic Law (1949), Reich- and State Citizenship Law (1913), Aliens Act (1990), Citizenship Reform Law (1999), compiled by Rainer Münz and Ralf Ulrich, "Immigration and Citizenship in Germany," *German Politics and Society* 17, no. 4 (1999): 9.

Consisting of real "'68ers," the Red-Green Coalition effected a partial reconceptualization of citizenship by way of a new *Staatsangehörigkeitsgesetz.* Enacted on 1 January 2000, it offered a launching point for the incorporation of third-generation "migrants," albeit without accepting dual nationality beyond the age of twenty-three. Its rational counterpart, a bona fide immigration law, was rejected on procedural grounds by the Constitutional Court in 2002 but was eventually followed by a weaker version (*Zu-* not *Einwanderungsgesetz)* in 2004. This two-fold liberalization is the logical outgrowth of an extended national process of learning to live with difference. Despite hardliner protestations to the contrary, Germany has finally committed itself to becoming a state of immigration and integration; as anyone who visits Berlin, Frankfurt, Cologne or Stuttgart can attest, the FRG is already both.

Generational Dynamics and Hyphenated Identities

Composer Richard Wagner once observed: "*Deutsch-sein heisst die Sache, die man treibt, um ihrer selbst willen treiben*" (Being German means doing whatever one is doing for its own sake). Sixty years have passed since Germany was forced to incorporate over 12 million war refugees; two-thirds of its 7.3 million non-citizens have made the FRG the focal point of their lives for over twenty years; by 2000, 1.66 million (22.5 percent) had been born there, that is, 68 percent of all non-nationals under 18.[14] Ralf Ulrich estimates that 50 million people have crossed the border in both directions since the 1960s, some waves resulting in net losses (1967); roughly 31 million entered 1954 to 1999, while 22 million moved out.[15]

Obviously these people did "wander in" from somewhere, even without the benefits of an official *Einwanderungsgesetz*. Despite fluctuations across specific groups (guestworkers, repatriates, refugees), the influx has been continuous since 1949. What is really at issue here are the terms under which individuals, families, students, workers, professionals or refugees can, do or should enter the country. Although millions have lived in Germany for decades, enjoy substantial socioeconomic benefits and even permanent residency, they lack the participatory rights associated with a democratic polity. Here one could fault the Maastricht Treaty (Art. 8) for disaggregating citizenship into four distinct status-categories: legal, political, economic and social citizenship, subject to varying degrees of local, national and supranational regulation. Each construct carries its own set of benefits, duties and ties to the national community. Given the size of the community, I concentrate on Turkish migrants and their offspring, especially in Berlin, to highlight changes across three generations.

The first guestworkers, the Pioneer Generation, consisted largely of males born in Turkey between 1935-1955. Chain migration rendered this group the most homogeneous of the three, despite differences between Turks from the northern mountains or east Anatolia who settled in the *Ruhrpot*, and those from Kurdish areas or the southeast found in Berlin or Frankfurt. Although 40 percent (25 percent among women) held occupational certification, the German labor market did not offer jobs commensurate with their training.[16] Contractual agreements confined them to workers' barracks short on creature comforts, like familiar cuisine and music. Lacking language skills that would enable them to interact with the host society, they established soccer teams and private "mosques" (a single room in a run-down tenement), to overcome the intense isolation that fueled a desire to earn money quickly and go home.[17]

When employers extended their contracts, younger men rented apartments, often without central heating or bathrooms, bringing over wives and children between 1965 and 1975.[18] Social advances among the Pioneer Generation "were seldom tied to career mobility but were connected to extensive labor activity coupled with high savings and investment activity (mostly through property acquisition and entrepreneurship in the homeland), as well as through a shift to self-employment."[19] These years marked the Economic-Miracle phase, but guestworkers experienced self-imposed poverty in the host country in favor of accumulating wealth and proving their success back in the village. This led to resentment and inferiority complexes among the offspring, anxious to emulate the "material girl and boy" consumption of their young German peers. The former were in their teens/twenties when recruitment halted in 1973.

Roughly half of the migrant offspring, characterized here as the *Ausländer* or Outlander Generation, were born between 1955 and 1975 in Turkey, where they are labelled *Deutschländer* (Turkish: *Almancı*). Many entered the country as children, providing varying degrees of exposure to German schools. This group developed a different sensitivity to persistent discrimination, due to rising educational attainment, a lack of emotional identification with the "homeland," and exposure to New Left protests of the 1960s and 1970s. Political consciousness was bolstered by an influx of Turkish intellectuals after the 1980 military coup but also fractured by the fundamentalist revolution in Iran and human rights violations against Kurds back "home." Children acquired basic language skills at school, then challenged the authority of parents who depended on them when visiting doctors, service agencies, and registration bureaus. The only places offering formal instruction were the Koran schools financed by the Turkish, Saudi Arabian and Iranian governments.

These youth did not face as much legal uncertainty concerning residency, but lawmakers' refusal to promote active integration solidified indirect discrimination.[20] Economic restructuring did not offer equivalent earning opportunities, often rendering these cohorts more vulnerable. Family-based educational deficits meant parents could not help with homework nor decipher the complicated dual-system of vocational training. Facing prejudice and language problems, Turkish children were disproportionately channeled into the dead-end Hauptschulen. While the total number of "learning impaired children" declined nearly 50 percent between 1976 and 1990, the share of migrant children assigned to special-education schools rose to 4.3 percent, 5.8 percent in Baden-Württemberg.[21]

Members of this Outlander Generation integrated themselves at the lower end of the food chain or career ladder during an era of stagflation and mass unemployment. They were often urged to enter the labor force quickly, to "save" for the return home or to pursue occupations that would foster their re-integration in Turkey. They learned that the ethnic economy, providing starter jobs, did not hold the key to economic advancement. Initially confined to *Döner* stands, kiosks, restaurants, grocery stores, and small retail outlets, the fledgling ethnic economy did provide new jobs as mining and construction work declined, but takers also faced lower wages, benefits and promotional ceilings, restricting future mobility. They enjoyed better access to education, but the inequalities among types of schools increased rapidly over time. According to the 1996 micro-census, 56 percent of German-Turkish youth (50 percent of Italian parentage) did not finish Hauptschule.[22] By 2000, 40 percent of all "foreign" students at tertiary institutions had attended German schools; 77 percent of these "educational insiders" or denizens hailed from working class families, only 7 percent evinced high social standing.[23] The second generation continued the pattern of marrying and child-bearing earlier than average westerners.

Although two-thirds of the successor cohorts were born in Germany between 1975 and 1995, the Inlander Generation is more heterogeneous than its two predecessors. Socially disadvantaged groups, especially, seek to sustain family or religious ties–as well as to secure work permits beyond the recruitment freeze–by importing brides or grooms (often first cousins) from home villages.[24] According to Foreign Ministry data, 21,447 Turkish citizens entered Germany under "family unification" in 2001; the number of spouses "exported" back to Turkey is unknown. Even though at least one parent enjoys language fluency and permanent-resident status, this practice tends to reproduce the socio-cultural isolation and educational disadvantage witnessed during the early years, especially among women. Whereas the first generation had to learn German to keep up with current events through local radio, television and newspaper reports, new Internet and satellite-technology give migrants access to breaking news and entertainment in their mother tongue. This reinforces feelings of affinity with the country of origin, and hinders offspring from learning German prior to elementary school.

In terms of social integration, the youngest cohorts are doing quite well. Inlander Generation kids possess the kinds of intercultural competence that could contribute to the national economy in the face of EU enlargement. They casually switch back and forth between languages in public, admonishing Germans who make disparaging remarks (thinking they will not understand); they eat at Burger King, wear short skirts, baggy jeans, platform shoes, and anything else comprising the fashion *du jour*, sometimes combined with a headscarf. They pick and choose among elements of German culture, just as they identify selectively, consciously and self-confidently with the traditions of their parents and grandparents. Metropolitan surveys documenting stability, satisfaction, and identification with the host-society are clearly at odds with Heitmeyer's sensationalized 1995 study and the 1997 *Spiegel* issue ("Time-Bomb in the Suburbs") stressing disintegration, a "return" to fundamentalist values, and youth violence. Roughly 48,000 Turkish-Berliners became citizens between 1945 and 2000, as a function of liberalized requirements and generational change; young women outnumber men in naturalizations.

It is natural and, in many respects, necessary for Turkish workers, Greek exiles, Italian migrants, Russian Jews, Kazakh repatriates, Bosnian refugees and Iranian dissidents to build on ties to their own cultures, to develop organizational skills and practice democracy in familiar settings (e.g., in ethnic associations), in order to forge a new identification with the host-country. Community action and informal networking lies at the heart of civil society. Ethnic minorities capable of simply forgetting their own past–by divorcing themselves from their languages, customs and cuisines– will find it hard to understand why Germans hang on to their identity (as an alleged *Leitkultur)*, even when this runs counter to national interests and the realities of "Europeanization" in many cultural domains (e.g., daily television programming, student exchange programs, even limits on the "purity laws" with respect to imported beers). German "virtues" like obedience, discipline and even punctuality have lost their currency among the natives, while Polish *Putzfrauen* have replaced Turkish women in ensuring "cleanliness" in the country's middle-class homes.[25]

Berlin has become the focal point of existence for most Turkish residents: by the late 1990s, 63 percent viewed themselves as "part of German society." By 2001, only 22 percent owned a house in Turkey (39 percent in

1993). The number who return at least once a year dropped from 66 percent to 56 percent; those who only visit every other year rose from 22 percent (1993) to 36 percent (1999). About half would not retire in Turkey, because their children live in Berlin (48 percent) or because they "feel at home" in Germany (37 percent). Four-fifths feel good or very good about their lives in the capital city; half who do not cite unemployment. When troubles arise, they turn to local organizations or to the Integration Commissioner, not to the Turkish Embassy. As one interviewee declared, "These are not foreigner problems, they are integration problems!"

Younger cohorts see naturalization as a way to claim Germany as their homeland, not as a concession by authorities that they are fit to stay. Like adults, youth who evince strong skills in two languages, who are active in German and ethnic organizations, are more politically engaged than those who only participate in host-country clubs. Rather than yield to forced acculturation, they expand their behavioral options in order to derive benefits from both cultures. While 61 percent were prepared to naturalize in 1988 (provided they could keep Turkish passports), the figure rose to 74 percent in 1991.

Table 2: Naturalization Rates according to State, 1990-2003

Bundesland	1998	1999	2000*	2001	2002	2003	Rate (2003)
Baden-Württemberg	17,670	25,670	29,057	28,112	22,868	19,454	1.51
Bavaria	10,616	15,201	20,610	19,922	17,090	14,641	1.24
Berlin	6,794	9,508	6,730	6,270	6,700	6,626	1.48
Brandenburg	232	221	424	434	411	314	0.46
Bremen	1,568	1,817	2,083	1,857	1,936	1,656	1.97
Hamburg	5,221	5,586	8,640	9,832	7,731	6,732	2.67
Hessen	12,555	16,827	20,441	18,924	17,421	17,246	2.46
Mecklenburg-Western Pomerania	123	116	295	287	301	289	0.73
Lower Saxony	8,628	10,409	15,427	14,693	12,838	11,655	2.16
North Rhine-Westphalia	35,611	47,472	65,744	60,566	49,837	44,318	2.36
Rhineland-Pfalz	3,683	5,015	7,338	7,714	7,445	6,898	2.21
Saarland	975	998	1,833	1,235	1,287	1,473	1.63
Saxony	343	283	455	547	498	492	0.41
Saxony-Anhalt	202	197	461	447	482	447	0.88
Schleswig-Holstein	2,434	3,734	5,639	5,123	5,128	4,310	2.82
Thuringia	135	213	312	357	354	300	0.63
Total	291,331	248,206	186,688	178,098	154,547	140,731	1.92

* Citizenship Reform Law in effect.
Source: Destatis/GENESIS (Statistisches Bundesamt)

Multiple factors account for the rush to citizenship after 1990 beyond changes in the law itself. Unification and xenophobic violence rendered older migrants less secure but moved younger residents to seek greater legal protection as citizens. Automatic extension of citizenship to *Spätaussiedler*, unfamiliar with the German way-of-life, intensified awareness of the second-class status accorded aliens in residence for twenty-thirty years. A bigger force, I argue, is the third generation's coming-of-age: at eighteen, persons who have lived in Germany for eight years, attending school for six years, now have an independent right to citizenship. Over 90 percent were born there, so school attendance is a given. Changes enacted in 2000 apply retroactively to children born after 1990. Some parents acted immediately; others allow adolescents to decide for themselves, since they must declare either German or Turkish citizenship by age twenty-three. Should Turkey join the EU by 2013, that choice may become moot.

Berlin's entire population declined after unification, while the non-citizen total grew from 393,000 to 448,200 (14 percent). Naturalizations increased by 23.5 percent, from 9,903 (1994) to 12,228 (1995); German passports accorded on an entitlement basis rose 73 percent, while discretionary cases fell to 27 percent; almost half were Turkish. The number granted fluctuated between 10,200 and 12,300, 1996-1999, falling to 6,867 in 2000; these figures lag behind the applications filed, due to processing backlogs in districts like Neukölln and Kreuzberg. Applicants in non-integrated neighborhoods like Steglitz and Zehlendorf face delays of a different sort: Until 2004, if a resident became unemployed or dependent on social assistance while her application gathered dust on a bureaucrat's desk, she had to secure new documentation, and could become retroactively "ineligible" in that district.

Comparing 1,200 youth of Turkish and Italian heritage, Claudia Diehl found that the usual human/financial/social capital variables do not make a difference in shaping decisions to embrace German citizenship. Researchers focused on individuals who had lived in Germany for at least eight years, drew no welfare benefits, and displayed language competence, making them eligible for naturalization; 92 percent qualified in both groups.[26] Not surprisingly, FRG -born individuals who spoke German with their friends were more intent on attaining citizenship. Many Italians (13 percent) acquired citizenship at birth through binational marriages; more striking was that only 2 percent of the rest wanted to naturalize. Among Turkish youth, a third planned to naturalize, 17 percent completely rejected the idea (50 percent among Italians). Other studies likewise confirm that Turkish residents, allegedly "homeland" oriented and loathe to renounce their nationality, are more intent on naturalizing than Greeks, Italians, Spaniards, and Yugoslavs. They stress a craving for

political rights (23 percent Turks, 35 percent Italians), over a desire for
occupational opportunity (19 percent Turks, 15 percent Italians).[27] Meanwhile 7,000 Turks (18-25) applied in 1995, 9,130 in 1996, 7,433 in 1997
and 10,205 in 1998; rates among twenty-five to thirty-five year olds were
likewise higher than among Italians and Greeks.[28] Since naturalizations
"fell" nationally to 94,500 in 2008,[29] Berlin has taken its citizenship
recruitment campaign–"The German Passport has many faces...."–
directly into public schools.

Table 3: Berlin Naturalizations, by Sex and Legal Modus, 1991-2005

Year	Total	Male	Female	Entitlement	Discretionary
1991	7 515	4 149	3 366	1 844	5 671
1992	9 743	5 214	4 529	976	8 767
1993	9 458	4 766	4 692	1 482	7 976
1994	9 903	4 828	5 075	7 029	2 874
1995	12 228	5 677	6 551	8 904	3 324
1996	10 268	4 824	5 444	7 308	2 960
1997	10 485	5 057	5 428	7 698	2 787
1998	12 045	5 831	6 214	9 162	2 883
1999	12 278	5 910	6 368	8 162	4 116
2000	6 867	3 562	3 305	4 838	2 029
2001	6 273	3 260	3 013	5 103	1 170
2002	6 700	3 453	3 247	5 307	1 393
2003	6 626	3 440	3 186	5 279	1 347
2004	6 507	3 350	3 157	5 133	1 374
2005	7, 097	*	*	*	*
2006	8, 186	*	*	*	*
2007	7,710	*	*	*	*

Source: Statistisches Landesamt Berlin online.
* Information not available (as of this writing).

Turkish women out-naturalized men by 14 percent, 1994-1999, both
nationally and in Berlin; among eighteen to twenty-five year-olds, twice as
many became citizens. Diehl assumes that married women with children
are more "traditional," thus less "integration-oriented," although men with
children are also less likely to apply. She further posits that young women
naturalize in order to import husbands from Turkey more easily, enabling
the latter to acquire work permits. Spouses of employed migrants must
wait a year to resume paid labor, a provision biased against women since
importing grooms are more likely to hold jobs than brides, given higher
female unemployment. All partners of citizens, however, can naturalize
more quickly. About half of the entering brides but only 10 percent of the
grooms did so, implying that men are less integration-oriented.[30] Local
studies moreover show that fewer women import spouses.

Commissioner John (2002 interview) noted that Berlin men are recruiting brides from Turkey, due to a "woman shortage." Those born in Germany want to study, start careers and marry later; men want the comforts of home as soon as possible! Females also displayed higher naturalization rates after 2000, claiming 58.3 percent of the new passports issued to eighteen to twenty-three year-olds in 2003–suggesting a desire for self-determination, constitutional equality and protection against forced marriage under German law. Five citizens of Turkish descent now sit in the Berlin Abgeordnetenhaus. Dilek Kolat, Özcan Mutlu, and Evrim Baba became active by way of local educational concerns; Gyasettin Sayan was active in the Kurdish community; Jasenka Villbrandt (from Croatia) worked as a teacher and served a local women's organization. They represent their constituencies by way of three different political parties. Two Turkish-Germans have served in the Bundestag, Cem Özdemir and Lale Akgün; Özdemir won a seat in the European Parliament in 2004 and recently became the Greens' Executive Director. Nouri Omid (Greens) of Iranian descent is now a deputy as well. The fact that newly enfranchised minorities are more likely to vote for left-liberal, social-justice oriented parties makes it all the more amazing that a conservative female chancellor has now become their most formidable advocate.

Madam Chancellor and the National Integration Plan

As an easterner, Angela Merkel had no direct exposure to the millions of foreigners recruited to work in western industries as of the late 1950s. Although the GDR eventually recruited up to 190,000 temporary laborers from "fraternal socialist states" like Vietnam and Mozambique, the state replaced a "missing generation" after 1949 by pulling its women into the paid labor force. Merkel was catapulted onto the national stage just as the FRG found itself overwhelmed by new waves of GDR *Übersiedler,* co-ethnic *Aussiedler*, religious asylum-seekers and refugees from the Yugoslav wars. Merkel's dramatic learning curve with regard to EU policymaking has accorded her an unprecedented degree of influence over the framing and implementation of integration policies at two mutually reinforcing levels. Bucking fifty years of CDU/CSU anti-immigration politics, she has advanced a bold strategy for integrating minorities of migrant descent at home. Her proactive approach, evinced at both the national and European levels, reflects her scientific training as a physicist, mixed with an acquired gender sensitivity to social inclusiveness, and an eastern-bred, pragmatic-Protestant commitment to human rights.[31]

The last ten years have witnessed a paradoxical tendency on the part of EU members holding the Council Presidency. Although heads of state could be expected to block supranationalization in favor of preserving their sovereignty, since the 1990s each country has used its sixth-month term to make its mark on integration processes; "presidency conclusions" have increasingly been used to carve out new EU priorities, accompanied by agendas and action-items. The German Council Presidency (January-June 2007) was no exception. In addition to pushing EU members to address global warming and climate change, it added a number of foundation stones to the evolving EU framework on immigration and asylum policy. It is therefore possible to read a strong emphasis on migration/integration initiatives in the 2007 conclusions as policy advances personally supported by Chancellor Merkel. Laying the normative foundation for EU policies are the Hague Program (2004), the Common Basic Principles for Immigrant Integration Policy (2005), the Common Agenda for the Integration of Third-Country Nationals (COM (2005) 389 final), and the Commission's Policy Plan on Legal Migration (COM (2005) 669 final).

The 2000 Lisbon Strategy for Growth and Jobs (revised 2005) sets an overall employment rate target of 70 percent for the EU, 60 percent among women, to be met by 2010–despite a persistent gender pay gap of 16 percent. All EU employment and educational initiatives are subject to equal treatment (Council Directive 76/207/EEC) and gender mainstreaming mandates (COM(96) 67 final; COM(1998)122 final). The Commission's promotion of civic citizenship will gradually extend equal treatment, core rights and societal obligations to minorities even without naturalization. The Council has more recently adopted a package of antidiscrimination measures consisting of two directives and a Community action program.[32] German presidential "conclusions" embody and even extend the priorities codified in these initiatives, especially the chapter on "Freedom, Security and Justice" (Sections 14-35).[33]

Leading the Grand Coalition from 2005-2009, Merkel was directly exposed in the capital city to a wide assortment of integration initiatives, surveys and projects introduced by Berlin's veteran *Ausländerbeauftragte* Barbara John (CDU). Many activities date back to 1980, including the colorful Carnival of Cultures that parades its way through Neukölln and Kreuzberg into Mitte, attracting roughly 4,000 participants on floats each spring. Reigning Mayor Klaus Wowereit (SPD) convened the city's first Integration Summit in June 2006. Less than a month later, the chancellor opened the first National Integration Summit.

The second *Integrationsgipfel,* hosted by Merkel and federal integration commissioner Maria Böhmer assembled in July 2007. With great fanfare, the former introduced the first National Integration Plan (NIP) as a "central task for all society." The NIP relied on six expert task forces, deliberating on ten core themes: improving integration courses; promoting language acquisition; securing education, vocational training and labor mobility; improving conditions and opportunities for women and girls; fostering integration as a local responsibility; strengthening intercultural competence in public and private sectors; advancing integration through sports; promoting pluralism and diversity through the media; fostering integration through civic participation; and opening German scholarship and research facilities to the world. [34] Invoking the principle of "self-obligation," NIP authors solicited input from a wide assortment of federal, Länder and communal authorities, employers, ethnic associations, and integration "stake-holders." The Third *Integrationsgipfel,* attracting roughly 200 participants, was held on 6 November 2008, heralding the release of first "progress report" on the Plan's implementation.[35]

Another framework for ongoing dialogue emerged out of the first Youth Integration Summit convened by Böhmer in the Bundeskanzleramt on 7-8 May 2007. About 17 percent of ethnic youth still fail to complete secondary school; only 24 percent secure apprenticeships (57 percent among Germans). Eighty young adults, together with media reps and related organizations from across the country, discussed concrete proposals in workshops focusing on language and education, local integration and cultural diversity under the lead question: How should our society look in 2030? The Chancellor welcomed them back on 5 May 2008, where the adolescents likewise "committed themselves" to projects, benchmarks and deadlines.

The NIP (over 400 initiatives!) commits Germany to the "mainstreaming [of] integration policies and measures in all relevant policy portfolios and levels of government and public services ..." The themes articulated at national summits embody the EU's Common Basic Principles of 2005, recognizing integration as "a dynamic, two-way process of mutual accommodation," promote education and employment as central to the participation of minorities in the host society, irrespective of citizenship status. The chancellor's call for a multilevel dialogue at home replicates EU "multilevel governance." She rejected the idea of a single elected *Migranten- beirat,* a model (*Ausländerbeiräte*) used at local levels, to little effect, for thirty years. She prefers a "migrant council" based on rotating membership, depending upon the issue and expertise required, perhaps drawing on her experiences with the functional differentiation characterizing nine Councils of Ministers that deliberate, approve new directions and decide specific EU courses of action. The "self-obligation" and self-evaluation components of the National Integration Plan likewise suggest a willingness to utilize procedures comprising the Open Method of Coordination.

The chancellor's primary goal is "sustainable integration," under the motto *Einheit im Goal: Vielfalt der Wege* (analogous to the EU rubric, "unity in diversity.") Potential stakeholders are encouraged to create programs and initiatives replete with their own goals and integration "indicators" across an array of policy domains. The big questions center on legal status; early childhood education and language acquisition; elementary and secondary education; occupational training; labor market integration; social inclusion and income; societal integration and engagement in civil society; housing; culturally sensitive health care; demographic change; media utilization; "intercultural opening" of administration and social services; politics and participation; finally, working against criminality, violence and xenophobia.[36] The goals are qualitative, but the indicators are quantitative in nature.

Merkel thinks inductively, recognizes the heuristic value of plans, assesses probabilities, and advances through trial and error. She treats politics as an experiment requiring rational deliberation; in a natural world that follows observable rules, every decision involves an energy mass with a particular direction, strength, tempo, and significance. Her job is to scan the environment for new configurations, study the longer term "waves," then ask the right questions. Like the trained physicist who introduced the NIP, officials responsible for integration need to establish identifiable cause-and-effect variables before proceeding with program design. The "goal" tied to legal status, for example, is to facilitate and maximize naturalizations. The "indicator" builds on the number of naturalizations relative to the number of aliens with legal residency for ten or more years whose living circumstances have been primarily defined by employment in Germany. Educational policy rests on the goal of decreasing the number of migrant descendants lacking secondary school certification. The measure chosen is the ratio of all twenty to twenty-four year-olds to same age counterparts with migrant background who did not complete "Secondary Level I" and who had not participated in an occupational or continuing education program during the four weeks prior to the survey.

Not inclined to emphasize "gender" outside of personal interviews, the chancellor nonetheless prefers an ostensibly feminist concept of power with ("wheel and spokes") rather than power over (hierarchical command

and control), as demonstrated by the plethora of national, state and local officials, businesses, welfare organizations, educational institutions, and ethnic associations she has co-opted into implementing in the NIP. She also exhibits a "female tendency" to view integration problems as the result of complex social relations rather than as a static single issue (rooted in immutable "cultural differences") that lends itself to principled or legal regulation.[37] Rather than take the credit herself, Merkel employs (non-confrontational) negotiation skills to draw ever more partners, including private sector employers, into the integration process on a "voluntary" basis, creating a network of new stakeholders responsible for implementation and self-monitoring; in return, she expects inclusiveness, transparency, and self-accountability all sides. Integration failure can no longer be randomly or stereotypically attributed to the groups who have long been told to "integrate themselves." Rather, it will require the Germans *an und für sich* to adapt actively to new demographic realities.

Conclusion: A Paradigm Shift Indeed

Having accorded cabinet-level status to the Federal Integration Commissioner in 2005, Chancellor Merkel has turned migration related issues, along with education and climate change, into "high politics," against the wishes of CDU hardliners and CSU stalwarts. She has repeatedly stressed–and linked–three key themes in her efforts to modernize her own party, despite substantial resistance from within the Union: demographic change, the need for new family support structures, and holistic approaches to migrant integration. Usurping an issue usually monopolized by the Länder under German federalism, Merkel has prioritized educational reform as a long-term cure for unemployment (due to paradigmatic shifts in the labor market), a critical shortage of high tech workers (hindering national innovation and competitiveness), as well as the looming financial burdens of Baby Boomer retirements.

By doing so, Angela Merkel appears to have saved the "C-Parties" from themselves, especially since unification. As a result of that process, the party of Konrad Adenauer and Ludwig Erhard "lost" most of its core issues by 1998. First, the country has become overwhelmingly secular, undercutting the Union's traditional grip on "Christian" voters (despite the critical importuning of its Catholic bishops against abortion, stem-cell research and the replacement of religion classes with ethics courses in public schools). Secondly, the CDU long stood as the strongest proponent of unification, even though fewer than 12 percent of FRG citizens still believed in the prospect by the mid 1980s. When it finally occurred, conservatives opted to redefine ethnic minorities as new threat to German national identity–the very people who can rescue it from negative birth rates.[38] Third, the women's movement, higher educational attainment, and the need for dual incomes to sustain middle class life-styles has invalidated the Union's stubborn adherence to a "traditional" family model–especially among its own female voters! Fourth, the CDU/CSU's reputation as the party of "economic miracles" has been negated by twenty years of mass unemployment in the eastern states–despite unity Chancellor Helmut Kohl's promise to turn it into a "blossoming landscape." Finally, its claim to sound fiscal management and its turn towards neoliberal policies in the early 1990s has been thoroughly discredited by the magnitude of the current global financial crisis. Merkel's calls for educational reform and "opportunities for all" moreover infringe on heretofore uncontested "identity" claims espoused by the SPD.

As demonstrated above, motley waves of migrants encounter distinctive problems during resettlement, compelling them to develop new strategies of accommodation across time. As new waves of foreigners continued to pour in, German policy-makers repeatedly "switched codes," compelling successive cohorts to carve out their own paths to integration. The citizenship=ethnicity paradigm failed to explain successes of repatriate groups through the 1980s, compared to the failures of their co-ethnic counterparts after 1990; the latter still score poorly in terms of socioeconomic and political integration. Nor does the formula citizenship=legal status offer a clear explanation for the effective (self)integration of Berlin's non-national Turks versus the poor integration records of its EU-national Italians, and now Poles. The citizenship=religion paradigm that has arisen in the aftermath of 9/11 is even more tenuous. Muslims and Jews are being pushed back into identities many never actively embraced, rendering the former "unintegratable" and the latter privileged in their access to integration services and accelerated naturalization.

Ethnic minorities may yet emerge as winners of unification now that Germany has, at least legislatively, has "crossed that bridge to the twenty-first century" by recasting citizenship–made possible and necessary by the fall of the Wall. My longer study illustrated the reciprocal nature of lifestyle changes effected by the presence of foreign "co-citizens," including the gradual elimination of some negative character traits long deemed *typisch deutsch.* Most Germans have acquired multicultural tastes, valuing extended hours at Turkish shops or dining *bei meinem Italiener.* The myth of return, along with the mantra "*Deutschland is kein Einwanderungsland*" blocked integration from 1949-1999; the more politicians invoked exclusive images of German-ness, the more they forced average citizens to deny their own enlightened tendencies towards inclusiveness–and the more they misjudged a critical need for deeper socioeconomic reforms in *Modell Deutschland* per se. The Green Card's failure to generate an expected tidal wave of super-competent, information-technology specialists eager to uproot their families, relegate their wage-earning spouses to unpaid care-work, learn fluent German, pay outrageous rents, and then go back home after five years of rescuing the national economy from educational stagnation has helped to demonstrate the FRG's uncanny ability to hoist itself by its own petard regarding migration policy. It took another paradigm shift after unification–the election of the FRG's first woman chancellor, a protestant Easterner at that–to teach Germans how to "live with difference."

Merkel's dramatic learning curve with regard to EU policymaking has accorded her unprecedented policy influence not only with respect to climate change and environmental issues already popular among Germans. It has paradoxically converted her into an advocate of pro-active integration policies despite decades of opposition to such within her own party, allowing her to level the playing field for ethnic minorities at two mutually reinforcing levels. By 2002, most metropolitan Commissioners for "Foreigners" had changed their own job titles, to Commissioner(s) for Integration and Migration. On 12 May 2009 the Chancellor invited sixteen individuals from diverse countries of origin into her office, personally presenting each one with an official naturalization certificate. "I decided to hold this ceremony in order to give a clear signal," she declared. Though unanticipated, German unification and accelerated European integration combined have thus led to a genuine reversal of fortune for "foreigners"– although the proof will lie in the self-implementing pudding. There is now a much better chance that Federal Republic will not lose out in the global race for the "best brains" and for sustainable contributions to its soon-to-be baby boomed pension system. As many of us came to realize on the day the Wall "fell:" miracles happen.

Notes

1. The latter term reflected a neo-conservative *Wende* among western youth following Helmut Kohl's rise to the chancellorship in 1982. See Joyce Marie Mushaben, *From Post-War to Post-Wall Generations: Changing Attitudes towards the National Question and NATO in the Federal Republic of Germany* (Boulder, 1998).

2. Joyce Marie Mushaben, *Identity without a Hinterland? Continuity and Change in National Consciousness in the German Democratic Republic, 1949-1989* (Washington, 1993).

3. Although one reviewer objected to my claims regarding divergent East and West German mentalities, by the time AICGS issued my 1990 monograph, East German identity research had become a growth industry

4. "Umfrage: Daumen runter," *Der Spiegel*, 26 February 1996, 49.

5. Reinhard Höppner, Rede auf dem Rechtspolitischen Kongreß der Friedrich Ebert Stiftung, 20 April 1997, Rheingoldhalle-Mainz. Also, Eckhard Priller, *Ein Suchen und Sichfinden im Gestern und Heute. Verändern die Ostdeutschen ihre Einstellungen und Haltungen zur Demokratie und gesellschaftlichen Mitwirkung?* Working Paper FS III 97-411, Wissenschaftszentrum Berlin (1997).

6. East Germans had good reasons for seeing themselves as second-class citizens in the nation they caused to unite, despite billions in transfer-funds. See Heidrun Abromeit, "Die 'Vertrtungslücke.' Probleme im neuen deutschen Bundesstaat," *Gegenwartskunde* 3 (1993): 281-292; Peter Kirnich, "Forscher fördern langfristiges Konzept für Aufbau Ost," *Berliner Zeitung*, 19 June 2002; Jens Blankennagel, "Nur noch Schlafdörfer für Rentner," *Berliner Zeitung*, 29 May 2002.

7. Sebastian Wolff, "Der Osten ist ärmer dran," *Berliner Zeitung*, 9 July 2009.

8. Ralf E. Ulrich, "Die zukünftige Bevölkerungsstruktur Deutschlands nach Staatsanghörigkeit, Geburtsort und ethnischer Herkunft: Modellrechnung bis 2050," Gutachten für die Unabhängige Kommission "Zuwanderung" (Berlin/Windhoek, 2001).

9. Joyce Marie Mushaben, "A Crisis of Culture: Social Isolation and Integration among Turkish Guestworkers in the German Federal Republic," in *Turkish Workers in Europe: A Multidisciplinary Study*, eds., Ilyan Basgöz and Norman Furniss, (Bloomington, 1985): 125-150.

10. Mushaben (see note 1), ch. 7.

11. My earlier work on postwar identity exhorted policymakers to jettison the myth that the FRG was *kein Einwanderungsland* and criticized the inflamatory CDU/CSU rhetoric, e.g., Edmund Stoiber's declaration that a "flash flood" of immigrants would produce a "multinational society on German soil–*durchmischt und durchrasst*–of mixed, and by implication inferior, races.

12. The frequent exclusion of (feminist-) *Innen* forms here is deliberate insofar as the criteria used to recruit foreign workers, ensure the free flow of persons, extend legal protections, welfare benefits, permanent residency and asylum rights have been far from gender-neutral.

13. Klaus J. Bade and Jochen Oltmer, eds., *Aussiedler: deutsche Einwanderer aus Osteuropa* (Osnabrück, 1999).

14. On the Green Card, see Rita Süssmuth, et al., *Structuring Immigration, Fostering Integration* (Berlin, 2001), 63ff.

15. "Eklat im Bundesrat: Union wirft Wowereit Verfassungsbruch vor," *Berliner Zeitung*, 23/24 March, 2002; Werner Kolhoff, "Urteilsverkündung," *Berliner Zeitung*, 21 June 2002.

16. Süssmuth (see note 14), 14; Federal Commissioner for Foreigners, "Facts and Figures on the Situation of Foreigners in the Federal Republic of Germany" (Berlin, 2000).

17. Ulrich (see note 8), 19-20; Süssmuth (see note 14), 29.

18. Ertekin Özcan, *Immigrantenorganisationen in Deutschland* (Berlin, 1992), 31.

19. Gerdien Jonker and Andreas Kapphan, eds. *Moscheen und islamisches Leben in Berlin* (Berlin, 1999); Martin Greve and Tülay Cinar, eds., *Das Türkische Berlin* (Berlin, 1998); and Werner Schiffauer, *Die Migranten aus Subay: Türken in Deutschland. Eine Ethnographie* (Stuttgart, 1991).
20. I have lived in such places myself! Students installed plastic shower booths in their kitchens, hooked up to hot-water heaters over the sink, and used coal-fueled tile ovens to bake apples.
21. Bundesministerium für Familie, Senioren und Jugend, *Sechster Familienbericht*, Deutscher Bundestag, Drucksache 14/4357 (2000), 15.
22. Karin Schonwälder, "Zukunftsblindheit oder Steuerungsversage?" Zur Ausländerpolitik der Bundesregierung der 1960er und frühen 1970er Jahre," in, ed., *Migration steuern und verwalten*, ed., Jochen Oltmer (Göttingen, 2003), 129.
23. Bundesministerium (see note 21), 176, 180-181.
24. Michael Bommes, "Probleme der beruflichen Eingliederung von Zuwanderern–"Migranten in Organisationen," in *Integration und Integrationsförderung in der Einwanderungsgesellschaft* (Bonn, 1995), 12.
25. Bundesministerium (see note 21).
26. Zentrum für Türkeistudien, *Bestandsaufnahme und Situationsanalyse von nachreisenden Ehepartnern aus der Türkei* (Essen, 2003).
27. Joyce Marie Mushaben, "Up the Down Staircase: Reconfiguring Gender Identity through Ethnic Employment in Germany," *Journal of Ethnicity and Migration Studies* 35, no. 8 (2009): 1249-1274.
28. Rainer Ohliger and Ulrich Raiser, *Integration und Migration in Berlin. Zahlen–Daten–Fakten* (Berlin, 2005), 10.
29. Tables available at www. statistik-berlin.de/pms/2a1/1996/96-08-23b.html.
30. Claudia Diehl, "Wer wird Deutsche/r und warum? Bestimmungsfaktoren der Einbürgerung türkish- und italienischstämmiger junger Erwachsener" (unpublished paper), Bundesinstitut für Bevölkerungsforschung (2003), 14.
31. Ibid., 15-16; Alois Weidacher, ed., *In Deutschland zu Hause. Politische Orientierungen griechischer, italienischer, türkischer und deutscher junger Erwachsener im Vergleich* (Opladen, 2000), 50.
32. These figures exclude Hamburg. Ibid., 77-78.
33. *die tageszeitung*, 13 June 2009.
34. Diehl (see note 30), 22, 25.
35. Joyce Marie Mushaben, "Woman, Man and the National Integration Plan: Citizenship and Migration Policies under Merkel's Grand Coalition," paper presented at the Humboldt-Kolleg, University of Miami, 8-10 May 2009.
36. See Council Directive 2000/43/EC (29 June), implementing the principle of equal treatment between persons irrespective of racial or ethnic origin; Council Regulation (EC) No 1030/2002 (13 June), laying down a uniform format for residence permits for third-country nationals; Council Directive 2003/109/EC (25 November), concerning the status of third-country nationals who are long-term residents.
37. See http://www.consilium.europa.eu/ueDocs/cms_Data/docs/pressData/en/ec/94932.pdf.
38. Presse- und Informationsamt, "Nationaler Integrationsplan: Arbeitsgruppen schliessen Beratungen ab," 23 March 2007.
39. See the NIP website: http://www.bundesregierung.de/Content/DE/Publikation/IB/Anlagen/ nationaler-integrationsplan,property=publicationFile.pdf. Its effectiveness was marred in part by a boycott by leading roof organizations (i.e., Türkische Gemeinde in Deutschland, Türkisch-Islamische Union der Anstalt für Religion (DITIB), Rat Türkeistämmiger Staatsbürger, Föderation Türkischer Elternvereine) who chose this event to protest a sharpening of requirements under amendments to the 2005 *Zuwanderungsgesetz*.

40. "Culturally sensitive" health-care involves such issues as ensuring access to female doctors for devout Muslim women and male nurses for devout Muslim men; respecting holistic/spiritual health concerns (and the rejection of specific medical procedures) among Asian refugees, providing halal, kosher, or vegetarian meals in hospitals, etc.

41. In her own words: "*Zuerst ordnet man seine Gedanken. Dann ringt man mit sich, ob man es macht oder nicht. Das ist die Haderphase. Und dann ist es entschieden.*" Hajo Schumacher, *Die Zwölf Gesetze der Macht. Angela Merkels Erfolgsgeheimnisse* (Munich, 2007), i.

42. Carole Gilligan, *In a Different Voice: Psychological Theory and Women's Development* (Cambridge, 1982).

43. Margaret Heckel. *So regiert die Kanzlerin–eine Reportage* (Munich/Zurich, 2009), 227ff; further, Mariam Lau, *Die letzte Volkspartei. Angela Merkel und die Modernisierung der CDU* (Munich, 2009).

44. Mushaben (see note 1).

Chapter 9

THE SOCIAL INTEGRATION OF GERMANY SINCE UNIFICATION[1]

• • • • • • • • • • • • • •

Hilary Silver

Introduction

"We preach, punish, ignore, and exclude."
            Richard von Weizsacker

Social integration is a longstanding preoccupation of Germans. Late to form a unified nation-state, Germany was an idea before it became reality. Efforts to bridge the North-South, Protestant-Catholic rifts long preceded those of the last two decades to unite East and West. Persisting anxiety about the class polarization that wrecked the Weimar Republic produced the consensus model of the postwar welfare state (*Sozialstaat*). German aspirations to put World War II behind them at last brought down the Berlin Wall and united the two Germanys in a single democratic republic a mere twenty years ago.

Nevertheless, the preoccupation with social integration persists. Not only did Germany absorb those ethnic Germans expelled from the East after World War II, but since the Wende, also the *Spätaussiedler* (late resettlers) who had been trapped in socialist countries. Today, when Germans use the term "integration," they rarely have in mind the residents of the "new states" (neue Länder), but instead, former guest workers, immigrants, and refugees, especially Muslim immigrants from Turkey and their children. But the former citizens of the German Democratic Republic (GDR) are also poorly integrated in the united Germany. Furthermore, integration of the country into an expanding European Union and a global economy causes generalized nervousness about the potential decline of German distinctiveness and contributes to concerns about what holds Germans together.

The centrality of the theme of social integration reveals much about German politics and culture. Without falling into the essentialist trap of insisting on homogenizing diverse, ever-changing mainstream opinions into a dominant *Leitkultur*, it is fair to say that public discourse about social integration of "Ossis" and "Wessis," Germans and Turks, and social classes–three cleavages I consider in this chapter–offers lessons about Germany as a whole.

Germans devote an inordinate amount of attention to social integration not only because of their history of late national consolidation and the persistence of deep regional, religious, and class cleavages, but also because of a postwar taboo on addressing the content of nationhood. The questions of "what is German?" and "who belongs?" are silenced or deflected into other symbolic debates. Recent issues about commemorating the past served as an acceptable way of reconstructing national identity. The quest for a consensual narrative and for an ordered society after more than a century of conflict extends the long-term yearning for national unity and ethnocultural homogeneity precisely at a time that Europeanization and globalization make these goals elusive.

Yet, others maintain that this desire for social integration must be constrained. Between Bismarck and the Nazi interregnum, top-down efforts to force Germans to integrate threatened to erase valued differences. Germans want social order, but also the preservation of internal variation. Indeed, postwar institutions sustain the reality of diversity. The federal constitutional structure and the central principle of subsidiarity allow for compromise on some issues and agreement to differ on others. It is a principle that has influenced the development of the European Union (EU) as well.

In sum, Germans are inordinately preoccupied with the question of social integration. From the *Kulturkampf* to the Weimar Republic to the separation of East and West, social fractiousness is deeply ingrained in German history, giving rise to a desire to unify the "incomplete nation." Yet, the impulse to integrate German society has long been ambivalent. The twentieth anniversary of German unification is an occasion to assess the reality of and ambivalence towards social integration in contemporary Germany.

What is Social Integration?

Before trying to delineate what Germans mean by social integration, it is useful to consider some sociological definitions of the term. Traditionally, sociologists associate the concept with the classic "problem of order" that concerned Emile Durkheim, Talcott Parsons, and other theorists of modern industrial society. "What holds a society of individuals together?" they asked. Functionalists and system theorists assigned social actors differentiated, complementary roles that keep society running. In contrast, Karl Marx saw class conflict as the mirror image of class interdependence. The democratic class struggle lies behind the modern negotiation of the "social partners." More recently, Michel Foucault portrayed social mechanisms of integration as sources of discipline, enforcing dominant norms, keeping potential conflict in check, and punishing transgression. This perspective is not difficult to understand in light of the coercion and surveillance historically employed in the cause of unifying Germany.

In the Weberian theoretical tradition, social integration—the creation of a community—is related to state-building. Rather than imposed by capitalist class domination, nationalism is an enterprise of political elites who impose an imaginary historical narrative on the citizenry of a given territory in order to level, subordinate, or obliterate other differences among them. These myths of nationhood may appeal to common blood lines, place of birth, or other bases of belonging to forge a sense of unity among compatriots. Yet, the downside is that citizens can invoke their loyalty to these national images of an integrated society to exclude newcomers, hoard opportunities, or insist on adherence as a litmus test for membership.[2] Indeed, given the estrangement of the two Germanies in the early 1990s, there is some indication that the German government symbolically elevated the intrinsic value of being "German" to promote social integration of East and West Germans.[3]

The institutions that produce this sense of belonging—schools, armies, media, churches, and political parties—have tended to work better to promote common identity and broad interaction in societies divided primarily by social class than by religion, language, or culture. In more culturally plural societies like Belgium, Switzerland, or Czechoslovakia, territorial autonomy within a common nation encouraged social integration. German federalism was one such solution to multicultural regional difference. The Basic Law guarantees the uniformity of living standards and equalization of economic growth and capacity across the federal states. Transfers of revenue from richer to poorer Länder were a regular part of government functioning during the Bonn Republic. After unification, the West transferred to the five new Eastern states between EURO 80 and 150 billion a year in subsidies and unified social insurance funds. Even as late as 2005, one third of East German GDP derived from Western financial transfers.[4] Yet, the Basic Law's constitutional goal of similar living standards in all states remains far from met. Moreover, political unification and income redistribution does not insure social integration. East Germans who grew up under the GDR were socialized differently than West Germans, and stereotypes about each other are slow to disappear. As discussed below, social relations among those from either side of the Wall remain attenuated and *Ostalgie* resurgent.[5]

Similarly, legal citizenship says little about the social integration of immigrants. Granted, the democratic liberal basis of the German *Rechtsstaat* has produced a trend towards "de facto multiculturalism," greater accommodation and equal treatment of minorities.[6] The 1990s naturalization reforms, 2000 Citizenship Law, 2005 immigration reform, the creation of a federal Integration Office (*Beauftragte der Bundesregierung fur Migration, Fluchtlinge und Integration*), and the convening of an Islamic Summit are all indications that Germany is officially recognizing that integration is a "two-way process" of mutual accommodation between immigrants and citizens.[7]

Nevertheless, cultural, linguistic, and religious differences continue to challenge the dominant narrative that helped integrate the Federal Republic (FRG). The older *völkish* notion of German national identity lurks behind calls for acculturation as a condition of social acceptance. In contemporary Germany, "integration" is a codeword for cultural assimilation, with a strong emphasis on learning the majority language and history. No matter that Germany legally recognizes the Friesian and a few other indigenous communities whose languages are being protected from extinction.[8] No matter that, unlike the former guest workers, the *Aussiedler*, who arrived in the "homeland" speaking Russian or Kazak and knew no German, were provided with German language lessons and other support.[9] Until very recently, former guest workers and their children were left to fend for themselves in a country whose language differed considerably from their own.[10] An unspoken policy of benign neglect reflected the position that Germany was "not an immigration country" and that the migrant workers were unwanted and should return home.

Sociologists have long considered "assimilation" to be an inevitable, continuous, "straight-line" process in which successive generations became increasingly similar (if not identical) to the host country population.[11] Today, sociologists consider cultural assimilation, like learning German, to comprise only one aspect of a more complex process of becoming similar to the dominant society. Even Milton Gordon's classic statement included no fewer than seven dimensions of assimilation, including inter-marriage, identification, civic participation, and the group's reception or discrimination against it.[12] Legal theorist Ulrike Davy identified five indicators of integration—language; friends/spouses; participation; segregation; and identification–arguing that legal supports and rights were needed to accomplish these.[13] Clearly a more nuanced analysis of the assimilation process is called for. In addition to linguistic and behavioral "acculturation," social integration includes what Gordon called "structural assimilation"–entry into primary groups, friendship cliques, clubs, institutions, and neighborhoods of the host society. Finally, one must ask whether the socioeconomic profile of immigrants and ethnics comes to resemble that of the majority. While East Germans and immigrants enjoy equal rights to the German welfare state, they continue to work in different jobs and earn different wages than the majority. In sum, assimilation occurs differently and at different paces in various social domains.

In American sociology, there was a resurgence of "pluralist" approaches to social integration during the 1960s and 1970s. On the one hand, encountering group discrimination gave rise to "reactive ethnicity," greater salience of ethnic origins in reaction to mainstream devalorization. On the other hand, ethnic pride and the selective persistence of "symbolic ethnicity" rose in tandem with the civil rights movements of the time. Where discrimination was not encountered, the voluntary re-assertion of ethnic identity and practices–the exercise of "ethnic options"–could occur. Partly reflecting the need for political alliances to demand antidiscrimination protections and partly reflecting efforts to assimilate, there was a gradual rise of "pan-ethnicity." National origin boundaries blurred as white ethnic Catholics and Asians moved to the suburbs and increasingly intermarried, and as Latinos from multiple origins developed common cultural and political interests.

These more pluralist perspectives on social integration have been slow to take hold in Germany. The image of a society with separate communities has let loose a moral panic over potential "ghettos" and "parallel societies." Yet Germany is also witnessing some pan-ethnic developments. The state and society frequently lump together newcomers from multiple national origins under broad umbrella categories like "Ossis," "Aussiedler," and "Muslims." Differential treatment and official labeling can give rise to altogether new identities from the ones that people started with. In many respects, East Germans face obstacles to integration that are similar to those confronting ethnic groups.[14] Indeed, their identity is evolving from a national one to a quasi-ethnic one, posing similar problems of social exclusion as immigrants do. The insistence on remembering life in the GDR is a reaction to Western suppression of Easterners' former national identity and culture and to persistent socioeconomic disadvantage in the united Germany.

Social integration of ethnic groups is often complicated by visible signals of difference, such as "race," color, or religious practices. After the 1965 liberalization of immigration to the United States, the diversification of national origins gave rise to a questioning of assimilation possibilities among immigrants of color in a race-conscious society. Some argued that a combination of social class—human and social capital—and race would determine whether a particular group was likely to assimilate sooner or later than others. This "differentialist" impulse, sensitive to and supportive of difference, whether essentialist or constructed, was expressed in "multiculturalist" perspectives in political theory and "segmented assimilation theory" in sociology. In the latter, Alejandro Portes and Min Zhou proposed an alternative process of "segmented assimilation" in which some immigrants move up the social ladder and form good relations with the mainstream of the host society, but others remain mired in poverty or unemployment, melding into the native "underclass" or living in co-ethnic or multicultural "ghettos."[15] In Germany, there are indications of segmented assimilation in the differential integration of migrants from the European Union and those from other countries. In particular, there is some evidence of the racialization of Turks and Arabs. Even though the government has liberalized naturalization and expanded integration programs, European-origin immigrants appear to "assimilate"–close the socioeconomic and cultural gaps–faster than those from Muslim countries. The irony is that the groups encountering the greatest discrimination and obstacles to integration are sometimes blamed for their own social exclusion.

The debate around the potential rise of "parallel societies" suggests that a particular form of segmented assimilation is occurring in Germany. Differential group integration not only reflects the desires and capabilities of the newcomers. It depends too upon the context and institutional constraints newcomers face as well as the extent of accommodation and change in the larger society into which they are integrating. In discussions of social integration, what newcomers assimilate into is rarely questioned. The pervasive assumption is that integration occurs in one direction into a single national state and unitary society, the "imaginary community" of a culturally defined Deutschland.[16]

There is, however, no eternal, static host culture. Cultural boundaries between natives and immigrants, old-timers and newcomers, may themselves blur or shift to include others. With new people, national cultures selectively absorb their ideas and values, not to mention music, food, and other cultural practices. In this view, social integration is more or less a two-way street. Over the past twenty years since unification, Germany has been changing too.

To summarize, there are numerous conceptions of social integration, of the "glue" holding a cohesive society together. The nineteenth-century assumption of the nation-state still dominant in Germany, however, is mythical. Nations as "imagined communities" and the nationalist ideologies that are their clearest expression are projects of state-building, projects that exclude as well as include citizens.

In what follows, I consider the current state of German social integration in socioeconomic, regional, and cultural terms. The review of economic and social measures of East-West and immigrant integration provides many indications of progress. Nevertheless, political integration did not eliminate profound social cleavages. Indeed, in some aspects, including in the party system, fragmentation is greater now than it was two decades ago.

Socioeconomic Integration

The paramount concern at the outset of German unification was the political and economic integration of two systems of institutions—capitalist and communist, democratic and autocratic—in which the West, in the broadest sense, imposed its currency, laws, and ways of doing things on the East.[17] Article 23 of the Basic Law extended West German institutions and laws to the five new federal states, and the March 1990 election of the Alliance for Germany was taken as ratification of the union. After the initial euphoria of unification, all sorts of socialist institutions were shut down, partly because mergers were difficult logistically, economically, and culturally.

The economic situation in the former GDR quickly deteriorated as government jobs disappeared and factories closed. The Treuhandanstalt disposed of GDR state property, and many Eastern Germans resigned themselves to the collapse of local industry. Some 2.5 million jobs were lost and thousands of companies shut their doors immediately after unification. Between 1989 and 1993, jobs in the East fell by one-third. Unemployment, outlawed by the GDR constitution and virtually unknown before 1989, mushroomed. At 15 to 20 percent, it was twice that of West Germany, and these official unemployment figures excluded the women and youth who were discouraged from seeking work. Massive but temporary public job creation and subsidized retraining allowed some ten percent of the labor force to remain in their jobs. This raised real incomes, but came at the price of insecurity. Panel survey data show that, of the Easterners who remained in the labor force after the fall of the Wall, a fifth was unemployed in 1996 and 40 percent had been unemployed at some time between 1989 and 1996. One-third of those in the 1989 labor force changed occupation, and over two-thirds changed firms. Between 1989 and 1996, one-half of working East Germans switched firms, a rate of mobility considerably higher than in West Germany.[18]

Many in the older generation took early retirement, including many of the former GDR elites whose positions quickly were phased out. Perhaps surprisingly, compared to Russia, Poland, and other transition countries, GDR elites did not reproduce themselves after the Wende. The Treuhand undermined East German managers and public administrators. Stasi informers were purged, and West German elites moved in. After East and West German enterprises merged, cultural conflicts over work practices arose between managers. East German managers felt cheated when the West German ones occupied all the major positions.[19] Nor did entrepreneurship create a class of nouveaux riches. In fact, most self-employed East Germans worked in construction, which fell off after subsidies ended, and in marginal activities.

As unemployment mounted, younger, skilled workers fled from East to West. Indeed, some argue that the unification process was so swift and generous precisely in order to discourage mass migration of Easterners to the West. Since 1990, the dearth of good jobs and low wages pushed around 2 million people, many young and well-educated, to leave the former East.[20] Of 16.7 million people living in the GDR in 1980, 700,000 of them migrated to the West from 1980-1990, most in the fall of 1989, and from 1990 to 2001, one million more moved there, compared to 250,000 from other countries.[21] From 1990 to 2006, Saxony-Anhalt lost over a fifth of its people.[22] Some of the young men and women who went to the West for work have returned, even at the expense of income declines, because they did not fit in. Other easterners commute to western jobs. Economic uncertainty led east German women to halve their fertility, to a rate even lower than that of West German women.[23] In turn, the weak economy and falling birthrate in eastern Germany contributed to its further depopulation. Vacant housing, even the refurbished *Plattenbauten*, has been demolished. Eastern cities are planning for shrinkage, creating new parks and restructuring infrastructure for more compact urban living.

Contrary to promises made in 1990, the East German economic situation is still far from one of "flourishing landscapes." Both policy decisions and competition with West German workers contributed to the region's decline.[24] Unification aside, larger macro-economic changes have been creating a German "hourglass-shaped economy" that rewards highly educated workers and erodes the demand for, and wages and conditions of low-skill laborers, contributing to greater earnings inequality. After 1989, inequality of wages and household income rose in the East, although it remained lower than in West Germany where people had more assets. The gap in wealth between East and West persists.[25]

According to the German contribution to the *2009 Joint Report for Social Protection and Social Inclusion*,[26] the country's at-risk-of-poverty rate (60 percent of median income), based on the European Union's Survey of Income and Living Conditions (SILC) for 2007, was 15 percent: 14 percent for men, 16 for women, 17 for those sixty-five and older, and 14 for children under eighteen. Germany's rate fell slightly below the rate for the EU25 as a whole (16 percent), but had risen steadily since 2000 until the trend stopped in 2007. In 2007, Germany's long-term unemployment rate (the share of the unemployed who have been out of work for twelve months or more) was among the highest in Europe. While long-term unemployment was falling in all countries, the rate was below 1 percent in Denmark, Cyprus, and Sweden, but exceeded 4 percent only in Germany, Greece, Poland, and Slovakia. Thus, socioeconomic integration remains a challenge, regardless of regional and ethnic differences.

Similarly, class polarization and income inequality rose in the former GDR. According to the EU-SILC, the 2005 poverty rate (60 percent of median income) was 12 percent in the former Federal Republic, but 17 in the new states. Despite generous unemployment benefits, 40 percent of the unemployed lived in poverty. Since job growth was slow, the ranks of the unemployed accumulated. Long-term unemployment, which reached 1.3 million nationally, rose in the new states to a peak of 700,000 in 2004 before falling back to half a million in 2007. The excess unemployment in the East has not disappeared, and the current crisis may have exacerbated it. In 2007, when the unemployment rate in all of Germany was 10.1 percent, it was 17.4 in Saxony, 16.4 in Saxony-Anhalt, 18.1 percent in Mecklenburg Western Pomerania; 16 in Brandenburg; and 14.4 in Thuringia.

Regional cohesion, as reflected in variation in employment rates, was improving until recently. Although incomes in East and West converged, the trend ended in the mid 1990s.[27] Back in 1992, the collapsing former East German economy accounted for only 3.4 percent of unified Germany's GDP, which now has risen to 10 percent. Productivity also has improved: the gross value added per employee in the East had been less than 25 percent of that of their western counterparts in 1991; by 2008, it rose to 78.3 percent.

Twenty years after unification, the East German economy is still distinctive. DB Research, Deutsche Bank's think tank, found that many mid-sized firms were founded in, or relocated to East Germany, with both high- and low-wage jobs. The eastern states' emphasis on new technologies like renewable energy has paid off. The German Institute for Economic Research (DIW) has noted that eastern German manufacturing was restructured so that some of the industries that remain like chemicals have high capital intensity, productivity, and export potential. Almost every eastern state has some specialization or a so-called "cluster." While the chemical, automobile, or heavy-machinery and engineering sectors are vulnerable to the business cycle, health care has become more important in Berlin and tourism in sparsely populated Mecklenburg Western Pomerania provides the state a niche in the service sector. [28]

Despite these promising signs, private and public sector layoffs continue and GDP per capita in the East lags that in the West. During the 1990s, the two regional economies slowly converged, but at the turn of the century, the trend stagnated and since 2008, the gap slowly opened again. After western economic growth took off, the East had weaker growth and investment, and eastern firms are either dependent subsidiaries of western companies or small enterprises. Work hours are longer, promotion opportunities scarcer, employment less secure, and wages lower in the region. The east German labor market has taken on some of the insider-outsider problems of the West. Since the East has more precarious employment, however, some speak of "secondary integration" or "social exclusion" because many Easterners move among unemployment, training, and employment schemes, never to land a stable job. [29]

According to DIW, eastern Germany still faces structural problems, including a demographic slump and a shortage of better qualified young people and immigrants to keep its economy growing. At the same time, the employment rate in 2005 was 66 percent, 3.5 percent lower than in the Western states.[30] Hundreds of thousands of people commute to work in western states and those who do have jobs earn on average one-third less than their western counterparts. Experts estimate that the region needs another 1.5 million jobs. [31] Twenty years after unification, the unemployment rate in the East is about twice that in the West, adding to downward pressure on wages and impeding movement towards wage equilibrium.[32]

Despite the slowing of convergence, data from the German Socioeconomic Panel suggests that real household incomes rose substantially in East Germany following unification, increasing by over 40 percent between 1991 and 2001. Related to this trend, average life satisfaction in eastern Germany, which plummeted immediately after 1990, also increased considerably, back to its 1990 level. A closer examination of trends in satisfaction with specific domains of life in East Germany between June of 1990 and 1999 reveals improvements in the spheres of household income, standard of living, dwelling unit, and especially goods availability and the environment, but declines in satisfaction with health, work, and especially child care.[33] In contrast, western Germans, whose life satisfaction was fairly constant before unification, experienced a fall between 1991 and 1997, which was somewhat offset by improvements from 1998 to 2001.[34] The persisting gap, therefore, is a consequence of changes on both sides of the former Wall. Indeed, changes in life satisfaction among eastern and western Germans were more associated with relative than absolute income.

As income inequality in the East rose, one would have expected that health inequalities had too. In 1992, 47 percent of adult East Germans rated their health to be fair or poor compared with 54 percent in the West. By 1997, the regional gap in self-rated health had disappeared, with the prevalence of poor health increasing to 56 percent in both parts. Income and education were important determinants of perceived health in both regions, but unlike in the West, rising income inequality in the East between 1992 and 1997 did not produce a simultaneous increase in income-related health inequalities.[35]

In 1991, there were already signs of public disappointment with unification. The wholesale importation of western institutions and practices dashed expectations, and some easterners soon perceived the unification process as an imposed, almost authoritarian exertion of external control like the one faced during the GDR years. As in the socialist period, most coped passively and adjusted. As a legacy of national division and the experience of unification, attitudes towards political economy still differ between East and West. Germans in the new states, where privatization led to sharp increases in unemployment, oppose privatization of banks, electricity, and hospitals much more than do western Germans–not so much because of their personal interests, but because of their beliefs about the proper role of government.[36] In 2009, eastern Germans still fundamentally oppose reforms of the welfare state[37] and regard the social conditions and quality of life in the Federal Republic in a far more critical way than westerners.[38]

The traditional guarantor of social integration in the former Bonn Republic was the *Sozialstaat*, in which the social partners representing social classes reached a consensus about the distribution of national product. After the Wende, the welfare state was extended to the East to promote social integration. Special stimulus programs were introduced in the new states to absorb some of the jobless. The massive transfer of ABM subsidies from West to East created jobs, especially in construction, but could not stem the tide of disinvestment. Pensions were pegged to western standards, so easterners with much employment experience and two-earner households who retired actually enjoyed an increase in income. There is some reason to believe, however, that extending the FRG pension system to the former GDR did not strengthen easterners' identification with the state nor promote social integration.[39] As time wore on and eastern unemployment and welfare receipt remained stubbornly high, the socialist government instituted the Hartz reforms. Hartz IV reduced social benefits for the long-term unemployed, merging unemployment assistance with social assistance into *Arbeitslosengeld II* and enforcing work requirements.

In line with East Germans' traditional preferences for a strong welfare state, many opposed these reforms. Imitating the model of the Monday Demonstrations in 1989-1990 that brought down the Wall, tens of thousands of people mostly in eastern German cities began to demonstrate once again. In September 2004, as joblessness hit 10.5 percent nationally and peaked at 18.2 percent in Eastern Germany, close to 100,000 people came out to protest. Although the demonstrations eventually petered out as they failed to prevent the implementation of the reforms, they came to symbolize the deep disaffection that some in the former GDR were beginning to feel about unification.

As a consequence of rising inequality and long-term unemployment, the term *Unterschicht* (underclass) has crept into German political discourse. It refers to the intergenerational transmission of unemployment, poverty, poor education, and social assistance dependency and implicitly, the impossibility of overcoming this situation. In 2004 and 2005, *Stern, Die Zeit* and other mass publications ran feature stories on the *Unterschicht* and in the fall of 2006, a full-fledged debate took place between Social Democratic (SPD) party chief Kurt Beck, who used the term, and Franz Müntefering, farther to the left, who considered it unpleasant and stigmatizing. Politicians from the East blamed the SPD's Hartz IV reforms for the rise of the new poverty. Beck's remarks were based upon a Friedrich Ebert Foundation report that 8 percent of the population, or 6.5 million people, were living in "perpetual hopelessness." Four percent of western Germans and 20 percent of eastern Germans no longer believe that their children will be better off than they are.[40]

Since 2006, the refrain of a rising German "underclass" has become familiar. In September 2009, for example, Berlin's former Finance Minister and Bundesbank executive Thilo Sarrazin complained that the capital city has too big of an "underclass." Apparently that term now encompasses not only idle easterners, but also unproductive immigrants and leftists. He told the magazine, *Lettre International*, that Berlin has a disproportionate problem of "an underclass that does not take part in the normal economic cycle ... A large number of Arabs and Turks in this city, whose numbers have grown thanks to the wrong policies, have no productive function except selling fruit and vegetables." The city should attract highly qualified immigrants, Sarrazin said. "Anyone who can do something and strives for something with us is welcome. The rest should go elsewhere."

The evidence suggests that the socioeconomic integration of non European immigrants, many of whom have lived in western Germany longer than eastern German and ethnic German migrants, will be long in coming. Federal data show that the 2005 at-risk-of-poverty rate for men with "migration background" was much higher (28.2 percent) than for "other population groups" (11.6). In 2007, the employment rate of those with German nationality was 70.9 percent, of those with nationality from the EU 25 68.2 percent, but for those with nationalities outside the EU, it was only 49.6, up from 47 in 2005.[41] Integration of immigrants is greater in places with more labor market demand and problematic in depressed areas like the Ruhrgebiet. However, even in the regions with the best results, migrants are more than twice as likely to be unemployed as native Germans, and these persons are also more than two times more likely to be dependent on public social transfers. Foreigners, especially Turks, face widespread discrimination in employment. While the labor market disadvantages of the offspring of most labor migrants are accounted for by formal qualifications, young people with Turkish background suffer from an ethnic penalty. This may be the result of group-specific discrimination or fewer ethnic-specific resources. One analysis of the German Socioeconomic Panel Study found that the ethnic composition of friendship networks and German language proficiency could account for the Turkish penalty in the labor market.[42] Immigrants have lower rates of return in earnings for the same technical or vocational training than natives, although, with higher wage returns to experience, hours worked, years since migration, and Gymasium education, they did enjoy significant earnings mobility over time. A big problem is that immigrants in Germany are less able to get good first jobs than are German nationals with the same human capital, and over time, enjoy less upward job mobility, suggesting discrimination in the process of occupational attainment and a widening status gap.[43] Immigrant men are segregated in manual, mostly unskilled jobs. Moreover, longitudinal data from the German

Socioeconomic Panel show that employment career sequences of immigrants differ from those of native-born men due to long and frequent spells
of unemployment.[44] In this light, it is not surprising that since unification,
Turkish life satisfaction declined noticeably relative to that of Germans. As
with Germans, changes in life satisfaction for foreigners are most closely
associated with relative, not absolute income variables.[45]

The Social, Cultural, and Political Integration of East and West

Were socioeconomic differentials the only barrier to the social integration
of easterners, one might imagine that market forces would ultimately
erode the regional divide. As seen in the public opinion data about the
welfare state already presented, however, easterners and westerners are
far apart culturally, politically, and socially, as well as materially. Surveys
show that eastern Germans are more sensitive to inequalities and expect
more help from the state. They also feel relatively deprived and worry
more, regardless of age, than their counterparts in the West.[46] Eastern Germans, whatever their age and politics, agree they are better off in material
terms now than they were under the GDR, but there are clear cohort differences. Older easterners lost their status and identity with the Wende, and
now use the GDR as a touchstone for criticizing unified Germany.[47]

As high unemployment and western triumphalism fed a general disaffection with unification, some eastern Germans expressed a romantic
longing for the "good old days" of socialist full employment. Many "Ossis"
felt the West disrespected, devalued, and was trying to erase their history
and the lives they led under the GDR. For example, protests over the plan
to demolish the Palast der Republik and other socialist landmarks symbolized resistance to the demolition of GDR culture. Ironically, as part of the
2009 commemoration of unification, the FEZ's museum in Schöneweide, a
southeastern Berlin neighborhood, did launch an exhibit to give the
younger generation a look at life in the GDR and an appreciation of that
part of German identity, Stasi files included. [48]

This sentiment should nonetheless not be mistaken for a longing to go
back to the authoritarian days of the GDR. Rather, it is a reaction to the
imposition of west German utopian visions on a society that does not share
them.[49] East Germans expected that unification would bring more political
freedom, more democracy, and the guarantee of human and civil rights,
but as new institutions from the West were established, many easterners felt
that the legal system did not protect them nor treat them fairly, producing

greater dissatisfaction with democracy as well as the market than is expressed by westerners, and by easterners themselves immediately after the Wall came down.[50] Easterners are less likely to hold postmaterialist values than Westerners, but do support democratic values, even if they are more critical of the reality of democracy.[51] Data from the German Social Survey (ALLBUS) suggests that eastern Germans are less trusting than western Germans and that this social distrust has not declined since unification. In contrast, trust in institutions has converged toward Western levels.[52]

As one might expect from theories of "reactive ethnicity," eastern Germans feel deprived on multiple dimensions of quality of life relative to western Germans, and the greater this relative deprivation, the greater the "in-group bias" for easterners compared to westerners that they develop over time. In-group bias increases with greater east German identity too, suggesting this is a mechanism of "compensatory self-enhancement."[53] To be sure, one can exaggerate this trend toward an eastern consciousness. Some research suggests that eastern Germans "consciously and carefully negotiate their senses of belonging," avoiding exclusive identities and rather basing their attachments more on everyday local identities which still, as pan-ethnicity developed, included eastern Germany as a whole.[54]

Nevertheless, the "Wall in people's minds" has persisted and created a West German sensibility as well. After the Wende, western German discourse contained residues of Cold War concerns about eastern social integration. There is a refrain about the supposed lack of democratic values in the neue Länder. Even though neo-Nazi incidents also took place in the West, right-wing extremism in the East– election of NPD representatives, rise of young male skinheads, xenophobic attacks on foreigners, and reports of "no-go" zones–seemed to confirm the prejudices of many westerners that their eastern compatriots lacked democratic values[55]–in a country where incitement to racial hatred is a crime.

Regional Fragmentation in the 2009 Election

Ostalgie–an oppositional culture resisting western German hegemony, one which not only seeks to preserve the architecture and resurrect the consumer goods and popular entertainment of the GDR, but also to commemorate, yet not necessarily idealize the lives of its citizens–has attained political significance. Indeed, the East-West gap in political attitudes may have even widened over time.[56] The rise of a separate political party, the Party of Democratic Socialism (PDS), institutionalized the East's precarious social integration into western democratic culture. Individuals lost their "political capital" as the Communist party and government collapsed. For a while, the PDS remained a regional party in which east German biographies could be negotiated with the postunification encounter with German national identity and European integration. For some observers, the party helped smooth the integration of eastern Germans into these larger collectivities.[57] By acknowledging and confronting the past, the PDS hastened the adoption of a new critical perspective on the meaning of being German on both sides of the former Wall. The merger of the PDS into the Left Party (*Die Linke*) somewhat diluted the regional representation of eastern Germans and sent a wake-up call to the traditional "people's parties," especially the SPD, to address the new realities of unified Germany.[58]

By definition, elections reveal social cleavages, and the 2009 federal elections are no exception. The distribution of votes across political parties changed considerably, suggesting that the German party system is becoming increasingly fragmented. Some pundits saw in the results the rise of a "five party system" in which the two "people's parties" of the "grand coalition" no longer dominate the parliament as they did previously, losing ground to "protest parties" on the margins. Back in the 1970s, the center parties together garnered more than 91 percent of the votes, but in the 2009 election, the Christian Democratic Union (CDU) and SPD together barely reached 57 percent. In addition to rising party fragmentation, there has been an increase in the number of party combinations making up majorities. Since 1990, Germany has had more grand coalitions, particularly in eastern Germany, but in western German Länder too.

It is becoming more difficult to point to a stable political consensus or social integration achieved by means of German electoral politics. In the 2009 election, turnout hit an all-time low of 70.8 percent, down from a peak in 1972 of 91.1 percent. The increasing fragmentation of the German party system and growing political disaffection produced a center-Right coalition (33.8 percent to CDU and 14.6 percent to Free Democrats (FDP)). Angela Merkel's CDU promised to protect the welfare state, minimum wages, and other consensual institutions against her conservative partners' more extreme proposals. "I want to be the chancellor of all Germans to enable our country to do better and come out of this crisis," she said after her victory. But the existence of five medium-sized parties will make this integration difficult to achieve. The FDP was not the only small party to win big in 2009. The Greens, who at least have some migrant representatives despite the loss of party co-president Cem Özdemir in Stuttgart, increased their share of the vote to 10.7 percent. Those gains came at the expense of the Social Democrats whose support crashed to 23 percent, their lowest showing ever. The SPD won half the votes it received in 1998, and lost support among young people and blue-collar workers. Even in the East, the party came in third.

Perhaps the biggest surprise was the performance of the Left Party, which won 12.4 percent in 2009 compared to 8.7 percent 2005. Some might interpret this surge in support for Die Linke as an indication of a festering rift between eastern and western Germany. A look at the map of the 2009 election results by region reveals the persistence of older regional differences. The CDU/CSU tends to win in the historically Catholic parts of Germany (the South, much of the Rhineland), while the SPD tends to win in the historically Protestant parts of Germany and the old factory towns of former West Germany. As usual, the CDU/CSU carried the South in 2009, the most economically successful part of Germany, but SPD won control of only tiny pockets in Brandenburg, Bremen, Lower Saxony, and Hessen.

One should not exaggerate the limited regional appeal of the Left Party. Although the party made a strong showing in the new states, the plurality in Saxony and Mecklenburg Western Pomerania still went for the CDU. Similarly, in Berlin, the four eastern Bezirke went Linke, but two central wards were Green, and the West, CDU. Most importantly, the Left Party made inroads in the former West Germany too. The Left may be among the top three parties in all the new states, but it also expanded its support in western states, such as Saarland, over the last two years. Although in federal politics with respect to foreign policy, the Left is treated as an extreme fringe party, it has shared power at the local level, as in Berlin since 2001. Thus, further Red-Red amalgamation may occur in the foreseeable future. Moreover, comparing the Left in office in the eastern states to its leaders in the West, one could argue that the Left is in fact two parties. The eastern party bureaucrats are pragmatic, mainstream, even conservative, and concerned with holding on to power, while the Left Party in the West is made up of ideological protestors who do not mind being in the minority in opposition (except in Saarland under Oskar Lafontaine). Thus, the regional fragmentation among parties is also mirrored within them to some extent.

Social Relations

The tentativeness of political cooperation across the old border is not the only expression of lingering cultural estrangement between East and West. Personal relationships also reflect poor social integration. After the Wall fell, Easterners lost their "social capital," as the previously tight workplace-centered community offering security, solidarity, informal help, and little competition disappeared. The social structural and instrumental bases for friendships vanished, and people moved about. Rising inequalities increased social distance. In comparison with some other transition countries, eastern Germany has been slow to renew its civil society of associations, clubs, churches, and communities and secondary relations of middle distance.[59] The sense of social loss was real, not simply nostalgic.

In a society where Easterners were suddenly a minority at best in virtually all federal institutions, social relationships that were already emotionally close in 1989 were reinforced. According to the East German Life History Study, social networks turned inward toward the core family between 1989 and 1993, providing a haven of stability, helping people cope with the transformation, and compensating for the social losses in other spheres of life.[60] Four years after the Wende, people relied on long-term, trusted relations and dropped political and collegial ones. Personal networks, already small during the GDR, shrank further after the Wall came down. People clung to older, trusted relations, even as they recognized that friendships were more important in life and as people felt lonelier. It is hard to argue that eastern Germans were more socially integrated, even those who stayed in the East.

In the midst of so much change, what people could safeguard and control were their families. Divorces and fertility plummeted, and gender relations underwent change. The East German model of a two-earner, state-caring society gave way to the West German model of a two-earning, part-time homemaker model. Gender relations long differed between East and West Germany, reflecting eastern women's higher labor force participation and the greater availability of child care. Suddenly, older eastern women faced long-term unemployment or shorter hours. Although married women in both regions do more housework than single women, the greater number of hours that West German women spend in domestic labor is a difference that persisted after unification. Also in response to the socioeconomic changes since unification, the eastern German fertility rate has halved, falling well below western Germany's that was already among the lowest in the world.[61]

One might have conjectured that, with unification, a sense of unity between eastern and western Germans might develop over time. Existing evidence suggests, however, that social relations between Ossis and Wessis are minimal. According to polling data, almost half of all western Germans, especially younger ones, have not visited the East since unification, where only 12 percent of easterners have not yet visited the West. More tellingly, 79 percent of eastern Berliners and 68 percent of western Berliners do not have regular contact with people who live on the opposite side of the city.[62] Easterners who have migrated to western Germany report feeling isolated and experience problems establishing private relations with westerners. As the easy socializing in GDR workplaces disappeared, easterners encounter individualized and plural life styles in the West, finding it difficult to find their place.[63]

In sum, twenty years after unification, big differences in beliefs, values, and behavior between eastern and western Germans remain. The social integration of easterners has declined. As Martin Diewald, Anne Goedicke, and Karl Ulrich Mayer conclude, "it is not yet appropriate to speak of one German society."[64]

Conclusion

There are many ways to define and assess social integration. Usually, Germans speak of "integration" of immigrants, and have adopted an official "integration policy" to pursue this. But the same idea applies to other social cleavages as well. The evidence presented here (and by Joyce Mushaben in this volume) suggests that there has been some assimilation, in the sense of becoming similar, albeit at differential rates and on different dimensions. Nevertheless, there exists a danger that German society will develop some "durable inequalities" in which group identity and institutional categories overlap with socioeconomic position, mainly with respect to East Germans and Turks/Muslims.[65] Opening opportunities to members of these groups would seem the best way to forestall this outcome.

Socioeconomic integration is only part of the challenge. Cultural divides persist. In a unified Germany, eastern German identity is evolving from a national to an ethnic one, posing many of the same challenges to social integration as immigrants do. Twenty years after the Wende, Germans are still arguing over whether and how to commemorate the Wall that once separated East and West Germany. Apart from a memorial at Bernauerstrasse in Berlin, there is little of the concrete partition left. But, the Berlin Wall persists in people's minds socially and symbolically, reminding Germans of the unattainable perfection of an aspired-for national unity. The quest for integration of the imagined nation–both the unification of East and West and the mythic ingathering of the exiled *Aussiedler*–continues, only now within territorial boundaries. At best, unification was "a partial success. It will still take many years until full social and economic integration within a unified Germany will be reached."[66]

The social integration of the "new Germans" poses a particular challenge in a country preoccupied by national identity, cultural distinctiveness, and social order. Germans devote an inordinate amount of attention to social integration–of social classes, foreigners, Easterners–partly because of a history of late national consolidation, deep regional, religious, and class cleavages, and a postwar taboo on addressing the content of nationhood. Questions of "what is German?" and "who belongs?" are silenced or deflected into other symbolic debates.

The quest for an orderly society after a century of conflict contributed to a yearning for national unity and homogeneity precisely at a time that Europeanization and globalization make these goals elusive. Germans are feeling a loss of national identity as they integrate into Europe and the global economy. Subsidiarity, the traditional German solution to difference by decentralizing institutions to allow separate cultures to operate in their own sphere, is ironically a principle Europe has adopted. Unfortunately, it is a model of social integration that produces limited cohesion. This makes it difficult for Europe to pressure Germany to address social exclusion, unification with post-socialist societies, integration of Muslim immigrants, and antidiscrimination law. Since it is unseemly and may even be illegal to press for the preservation of their own national culture, Germans have projected the problems of social integration onto "others"–those who should "integrate themselves" by adopting traditional German practices, language, values.

German ambivalence about social integration is a major reason for the continuing social fragmentation of the society. Instead of embracing new members and adopting parts of their cultures to enrich their own, many Germans insist on the disappearance of difference, whether that difference arose from the experience of communism, minority religions, or foreign origins. Yet successful social integration is a two-way street, requiring the new and old Germans to interact and build social bonds.

Notes

1. An earlier version of this chapter was presented at the *German Politics & Society* Symposium on "The Bonn/Berlin Republic at 20: From Unification to Unity?" held at the BMW Center for German and European Studies, Georgetown University, Washington DC on 7 May 2009.
2. Anthony W. Marx, *Faith in Nation: Exclusionary Origins of Nationalism* (New York, 2003).

3. Reinhard Kreckel, "Soziale Integration und Nationale Identität," *Berliner Journal für Soziologie* 4, no. 1 (1994):13-20.

4. Martin Diewald, Anne Goedicke, and Karl Ulrich Mayer, eds. *After the Fall of the Wall: Life Courses in the Transformation of East Germany* (Stanford, 2006), 314-15. Concern about the redistribution led to the Constitutional Reform Act of 1994 that reconfirmed the role and autonomy of the Länder and Bundesrat vis-à-vis the federal government.

5. Dominic Boyer, "Ostalgie and the Politics of the Future in Eastern Germany, *Public Culture* 18, no. 2 (2006): 361-381; Martin Blum, "Remaking the East German Past: Ostalgie, Identity, and Material Culture," *Journal of Popular Culture* 34, no. 3 (2000): 229-54; Paul Cooke, "Ostalgie's Not What It Used to Be," *German Politics & Society* 22, no. 4 (2004):134-150; Daphne Berdahl, "(N)Ostalgie for the Present: Memory, Longing, and East German Things," *Ethnos: Journal of Anthropology* 64, no. 2 (1999):192-211.

6. Christian Joppke and Eva Morawska, *Toward Assimilation and Citizenship: Immigrants in Liberal Nation-States* (Hampshire, 2003).

7. Many of these reforms reflect a broader movement at the European level towards a common immigrant integration policy. Ryszard Cholewinski, "Migrants as Minorities: Integration and Inclusion in the Enlarged European Union," *Journal of Common Market Studies* 43, no. 4 (2005): 695-716.

8. Contrary to conventional wisdom, German law has some special group protections. One is the distinction in EU and German law between the protection of autochthonous minorities (Danish, Sorbian, Frisian, and Sinti-Roma) and the pressure for integration, indeed assimilation of long-term migrants. In these cases, the respect for diversity and the right to support for a distinctive language, culture, and ethnicity contrast sharply with the demand for third-country nationals who are long-term migrants to adapt to the majority German culture. See Ryszard Cholewinski, *Migrant Workers in International Human Rights Law: Their Protection in Countries of Employment* (Oxford, 1997).

9. Indeed, there is evidence that this unequal treatment is responsible for the disparity in educational attainment between the Aussiedler and other first-generation immigrants. Janina Söhn, "Bildungsunterschiede zwischen Migrantengruppen in Deutschland: Schulabschlüsse von Aussiedlern und anderen Migranten der ersten Generation im Vergleich," *Berliner Journal für Soziologie* 18, no. 3 (2008): 401-431.

10. In Germany, immigrant groups were educated in their native languages and provided services by particular voluntary associations in a "separate-but-equal" approach.

11. Homogenizing state projects are frowned upon. "In Germany, if anything, the word 'assimilation' has been even more strongly 'contaminated' and disqualified by its association with forcible Germanization," 533 in Rogers Brubaker, "The Return of Assimilation? Changing Perspectives on Immigration and Its Sequels in France, Germany, and the United States." *Ethnic & Racial Studies* 24, no. 4 (2001): 531-548. Brubaker distinguishes assimilation in a general, abstract sense (a process of becoming similar or treating as similar) from assimilation in a specific, organic sense of incorporation or absorption in total. Assimilationist policies, he argues, "rarely work, and ... are indeed more likely to strengthen than to erode differences, by provoking a reactive mobilization against such assimilatory pressures" (534). Rather, German policies now encourage "commonality" not sameness.

12. Milton Gordon, *Assimilation in American Life* (New York, 1964).

13. Ulrike Davy, *Die Integration von Einwanderern: Rechtliche Regelungen im europäischen Vergleich* (Vienna, 2001).

14. Marc Howard, "An East German Ethnicity? Understanding the New Division of Unified Germany," *German Politics and Society* 13, no. 4 (1995): 49-70.

15. Alejandro Portes and Min Zhou, "The New Second Generation: Segmented Assimilation and Its Variants," *Annals of the American Academy of Political and Social Sciences* 530 (1993): 7–96.

16. Richard Alba and Victor Nee, "Rethinking Assimilation Theory for a New Era of Immigration." *International Migration Review* 31, no. 4 (1997): 826–874. Tomatsu Shibutani and

Kian Kwan, *Ethnic Stratification* (New York, 1965) argued that assimilation is not the inevitable result of intergroup contact. Interaction can just as easily produce competition or even conflict. For that reason, the institutional framework in which groups interact matters considerably. Adrian Favell, *Philosophies of Integration: Immigration and the Idea of Citizenship in France and Britain* (New York, 1998).

17. Germans were supportive but also somewhat reluctant with regard to quick and comprehensive unification. The political leadership pushed for unification, rather than responding to grassroots sentiment. Considerations of economic gains and worries about mass migration seem to be more important than idealistic pan-German sentiments or national chauvinism. While East Germans displayed enthusiasm at first, their disappointment steadily rose. Manfred Keuchler, "The Road to German Unity: Mass Sentiment in East and West Germany." *Public Opinion Quarterly* 56, no. 1 (1992): 53-76.

18. Diewald et al. (see note 4), 195.

19. Jörg Roesler, "Aufsatze und Berichte," *Kultursoziologie* 15, no. 1 (2006): 7-26.

20. Joachim Ragnitz of the Ifo Institut in Dresden in "20 Years of Investment: Despite Progress, Former East Germany Still Lags Behind," *Der Spiegel*, 28 August 2009; available at http://www.spiegel.de/international/germany/0,1518,645596,00.html.

21. Diewald et al. (see note 4), 295.

22. *The Economist*, 12 April 2008, 60.

23. Witte, James C. and Gert Wagner, "Declining Fertility in East Germany After Unification: A Demographic Response to Socioeconomic Change," *Population & Development Review* 21, no. 2 (1995): 387-397.

24. Carsten Hefeker and Norbert Wunner, "Promises Made, Promises Broken: A Political Economic Perspective on German Unification," *German Politics* 12, no. 1 (2003): 109-134.

25. Diewald et al. (see note 4), 300.

26. Commission of the European Communities, Commission Staff Working Document, *Monitoring progress towards the objectives of the European Strategy for Social Protection and Social Inclusion* (Brussels, 6 October 2008).

27. Diewald et al. (see note 4), 314-15.

28. "20 Years" (see note 20).

29. Diewald et al. (see note 4), 62.

30. Commission (see note 26).

31. "20 Years" (see note 20).

32. Werner Smolny, "Wage Adjustment, Competitiveness and Unemployment: East Germany After Unification," *Jahrbucher fur Nationalokonomie und Statistik* 229, no. 2-3 (2009): 130-45.

33. Richard A. Easterlin and Anke Plagnol, "Life satisfaction and economic conditions in East and West Germany pre- and post-unification," *Journal of Economic Behavior and Organization* 68, no. 3-4 (2008): 433-44.

34. Paul Frijters, John Hasken-DeNew, and Michael Shields, "Money Does Matter! Evidence from Increasing Real Income and Life Satisfaction in East Germany Following Reunification," *American Economic Review* 94, no. 3 (2004): 730-740.

35. Ellen Nolte and Martin McKee, "Changing Health Inequalities in East and West Germany Since Unification," *Social Science & Medicine* 58, no. 1 (2004): 119-37.

36. Jerome Legge and Hall Rainey, "Privatization and Public Opinion in Germany," *Public Organization Review* 3, no. 2 (2003): 127-49, based on ALLBUS data.

37. East Germans strongly opposed the rise in retirement age to sixty-seven to qualify for a pension. Beatrice Scheubel, Daniel Schunk, and Joachim Winter, "Don't Raise the Retirement Age! An Experiment on Opposition to Pension Reforms and East-West Differences in Germany," CESifo Group Munich, CESifo Working Paper No. 275 (2009).

38. "Das Vereinte Deutschland: Eine Lebsenswerte Gesellschaft?" *Koelner Zeitschrift fuer Soziologie & Sozialpsychologie* 52 no. 3 (2000), 405-427.

39. imon Heglich, "Can Welfare Expansion Result in Disintegration? The Integration of East Germany into the German Pension System," *German Politics* 13, no. 1 (2004): 81-105.

40. Carsten Vokery, "Unterschicht-Debatte," *Der Spiegel*, 16 October 2006.

41. Commission (see note 26).

42. Frank Kalter, "Auf der Suche nach einer Erklärung für die spezifischen Arbeits-marktnachteile von Jugendlichen türkischer Herkunft," *Zeitschrift für Soziologie* 35 no. 2 (2006): 144-160.

43. Amelie Constant and Douglas Massey, "Labor Market Segmentation and the Earnings of German Guestworkers," *Population Research & Policy Review* 24, no. 5 (2005): 489-512. Based upon data from the German Socioeconomic Panel survey.

44. Irena Kogan, "Labour Market Careers of Immigrants in Germany and the United Kingdom," *Journal of International Migration & Integration* 5, no. 4 (2004): 417-447.

45. Easterlin and Plagnol (see note 33).

46. DIW 2002.

47. Diewald et al. (see note 4), 313.

48. Emma Bullimore, "Berlin Exhibit Gives Kids Glimpse of East Germany", *Der Spiegel*, 15 July 2009.

49. Dominic Boyer, "Ostalgie and the Politics of the Future in Eastern Germany," *Public Culture* 18, no. 2 (2006): 361-381.

50. Detlef Pollack, "Support for Democracy in Eastern and Western Germany: An Attempt to Explain the Differences," *European Journal of Sociology* 45, no. 2 (2004): 257-272.

51. Diewald et al. (see note 4), 62-63.

52. Helmut Rainer and Thomas Siedler, "Does Democracy Foster Trust?" *Journal of Comparative Economics* 37, no. 2 (2009): 251-69.

53. Manfred Schmitt, "Stereotypic Ingroup Bias as Self-Defense against Relative Deprivation: Evidence from a Longitudinal Study of the German Unification Process," *European Journal of Social Psychology* 32, no. 3 (2002): 309-326. At the same time, western Germans are biased against eastern Germans on the dimension of personal integrity. The study interprets this as a consequence of the guilty recognition of undeserved privilege via-a-vis eastern Germans. Whatever the psychological mechanisms, attitudes differ between the two regions.

54. Anselma Gallinat, "Being 'East German' or Being 'At Home in East Germany,'" *Identities* 15, no. 6 (2008): 665-686.

55. Klaus Farin, "Neue Studie: Rechte Szene auch im Osten out," *Neue Soziale Bewegungen* 19, no. 1 (2006): 101-07. For example, the neo-Nazi NPD, although initially only in the West, received its highest percent of votes in the 2005 federal elections in the new states (4.9 percent in Saxony, 3.7 percent in Thuringia, 3.5 percent in Mecklenburg Western Pomerania, and 3.2 percent in Brandenburg), while it won around 1 percent in the other states. The NPD vote in the federal election of September 2009 was 1.6 percent, compared to 1.5 percent in 2005. As before, it fared better in the east than in the west of the country. In the two eastern states where it already had regional parliament representatives, it even increased its support. In Saxony, the NPD received 4 percent and in Mecklenburg Western Pomerania, 3.3 percent of the electorate.

56. Heiner Meulemann, *Werte und Wertewandel: Zur Identität einer geteilten und wieder vereinten nation* (Weinheim and Munich, 1996).

57. Franz Oswald, "Negotiating Identities: The Party of Democratic Socialism between East German Regionalism, German National Identity, and European Integration," *Australian Journal of Politics & History* 50, no. 1 (2004): 75-85.

58. Kimmo Elo, "The Left Party and the Long-Term Developments of the German Party System," *German Politics & Society* 26, no. 3 (2008): 50-68.

59. Diewald et al. (see note 4), 294. On the other hand, eastern Germans adapted very quickly to the thousands of new rules and regulations and to the demands to upgrade their vocational and professional skills.

60. Diewald et al. (see note 4); and Beate Volker and Henk Flap, "The Effects of Institutional Transformation on Personal Networks, East Germany, Four Years Later," *Netherlands Journal of Social Science* 31 (1995): 87-111.

61. James Witte and Gert Wagner, "Declining Fertility in East Germany After Unification: A Demographic Response to Socioeconomic Change," *Population & Development Review* 21, no. 2 (1995): 387-397.

62. TNS-EMNID poll reported in *Der Spiegel*, 28 December 2006.

63. Manfred Gehrman "'Jeder lebt hier mehr fuer sich...' Zur Sozialen Integration von DDR-Zuwanderern in der alten Budnesrepublik Deutschland und West-Berlin," *Berliner Journal für Soziologie* 2, no. 2 (1992): 173-193.

64. Diewald et al. (see note 4), 315.

65. Charles Tilly, *Durable Inequality* (Berkeley, 1998).

66. Diewald et al. (see note 4), 317.

Chapter 10

$\mathcal{G}$ENDER POLITICS
IN THE BERLIN REPUBLIC

Four Issues of Identity and Institutional Change

● ● ● ● ● ● ● ● ● ● ● ● ● ● ● ●

Myra Marx Ferree

In the old joke, when the Lone Ranger and Tonto are surrounded by hostile Indians, the Lone Ranger says to Tonto "I guess we've had it" and Tonto replies: "who you calling 'we,' white man?" In European history, the question of who "we" are appears as the famous *deutsche Frage* of German national identity. It has also troubled feminists as they struggle with the differences among women and calls to global gender solidarity.[1] It is thus not surprising that German feminists face difficult questions of collective identity in the "new Germany." Many of these troubling questions of national identity are directly linked to the policies, institutions, and practices of the Berlin Republic.

These new political institutions are still very much in flux. The past two decades have seen not one, but two, massive reconstructions of German institutions, each of which has had considerable implications for ordinary people's gendered lives. On the one hand, national unification seems the most obvious discontinuity, and one whose anniversary is regularly celebrated. On the other hand, the widening and deepening of the European Union, while more gradual, may be an even more transformative "second unification" over the long run. Both German unification and transnational integration into the European Union have demanded considerable adjustment in state policies and practices. Although these institutional changes have largely been directed from the top down, they have also triggered shifts in political identities, personal practices, and popular culture from the bottom up. By looking at the different aspects of the "wir" of German politics, I attempt to connect these changes in macro-institutions of politics with the aspirations and practices of gender at all levels from the most collective and institutional to the most personal and individual.

As Tonto made clear to the Lone Ranger, no identity claim is uncontested. The assertions of who "we" are and what "we" need often come from more privileged groups, are challenged by those who see themselves as excluded, and provoke feminist debates both in Germany and transnationally about who and what any particular "we" claim represents for women, and for which women.[2] There are four such historically prominent assertions of the German "we" in the past twenty years that I select to consider as tropes for thinking about gender.

First, the claim that *wir sind wieder wer* (we are someone again) is a recurring theme of national pride that coexists with anxiety about the implications of nationalism for intolerance and violence. Overcoming the shame of defeat and of moral culpability in World War II has been a recurrent issue for German national identity, but a nationalism reflecting military and economic strength offers little attraction to feminists, given women's marginalization in both domains. At the time of unification, German feminists East and West not surprisingly emerged as vocal critics of nationalistic self-congratulation.[3] Today, however, pride as a dimension of national identity is more directed to the political "othering" of immigrants, and self-congratulation takes different forms, ones that perhaps are more appealing to ethnic German women and feminists. The headscarf plays a strong symbolic role, representing the contest over modernity and progress in gender terms.[4]

Second, the claim that *wir sind das Volk* (we are the people) originally characterized the East German mobilization against the German Democratic Republic (GDR). This was a participatory democratic critique of the state's top-down approach to politics, and assertion of a citizen's right to self-determination that found considerable resonance among movement activists in the West as well.[5] This democratic dimension of political identity suggests examining how the new Germany works to include women's concerns. Considering women as political actors in democratic mobilizations points both to feminism as a social movement and to the complex remaking of welfare state citizenship, as women's rights in social policy become increasingly intertwined with EU and transnational initiatives.

Third, the claim that *wir sind ein Volk* (we are one people) replaced the dissidents' call for participatory democracy in the GDR, and supported the rapid unification of the country on unequal terms. I use this wishful claim to a shared future in a single state to highlight the continuing divisions among women and men on both sides of the now invisible wall. As feminists have long argued, the gender relations that characterize the organization of daily life are political facts that both result from and lead to value differences and social policy constraints. The many ways that German "women" show no indication of becoming a single interest group are made especially evident by looking at the different family and work lives of younger women in both parts of a country that still has a "wall in its head."[6] While there are some signs of convergence, the issue of which set of norms will prevail is still uncertain.

Finally, and most recently, the feminist magazine *Emma* proclaimed *wir sind Kanzlerin* (we are the chancellor) when the GDR-raised Angela Merkel became Germany's first woman chancellor in 2005.[7] Here, I use the mixed and ambiguous identification of women with Merkel's success to consider the potential for women in party-based politics and institutional reforms in Germany, rather than to examine her as a political figure. Claims to what is now called "gender democracy" through the growing representation of women in leadership roles point to consideration of where and how the party structures of the Berlin Republic have succeeded and failed in bringing women into more fully empowered citizenship, and what prospects for more complete inclusion may emerge.

All four of these "we" claims are contested statements that invoke a German collective identity and so focus attention on specific dimensions of institutional change across the past twenty years. The cultural definition of the German nation in the face of immigration, the integration of the German state in a transnational project of making a single Europe, the economic restructuring of unification and its effects on the resources and opportunities available on each side of the former wall, and political changes in the representation of women in state offices, by parties and in national policy-making all reflect continuing struggles over the institutionalized boundaries of inclusion and exclusion as a nation, an imagined community.[8] These core political processes and the identities they mobilize are gendered for both men and women, because gender relations are invoked to mobilize their passionate attachments to the status quo as well as to legitimize institutional changes.[9] These struggles also point to how other forms of difference, power, and inequality are organized in and through gender relations.

Gender, Nationalism, and Headscarf

The recurrent phrase *wir sind wieder wer* expresses a renewed legitimacy for German pride, most recently stirred in the wake of unification. National pride is more problematic in post World-War-II Germany than in most countries, and the "economic miracle" of West Germany and the "anti-fascist principles" of socialist East Germany served in each case to anchor the identities of each postwar state in its respective bloc during the Cold War. United Germany needed a post Cold-War basis for legitimating its national self-congratulation and found this in part in the new coalition of "modern" states.[10] This new "West" sees itself in a new confrontation with militant Islam, the new "East." Taking its place as a powerful state in this new West bloc has led to re-normalized assertions of German authority, both in the cultural and military sense, including military engagements in Kosovo, Iraq, and Afghanistan. The moral claims to be an active sup-porter of human rights globally (*nie wieder Auschwitz*) have been used to override the moral claims of pacifism (*nie wieder Krieg*), and "women's rights as human rights" has been invoked in this "new West" to justify its military interventions.

Despite the remilitarization of both divided states during the Cold War, the collective memory of war remains a powerful source of resistance to imagining military power in positive terms. Even as the Green Party chose to endorse a renewed militarization of foreign policy in the German engagement in Kosovo and Afghanistan, the emphasis of all political parties has been more on peace-keeping and protecting human rights than on overt displays of power. Insofar as Germany is again "somebody," the national identity it seems most willing to embrace is a distinctly civilian one with economic power at the core. Yet, because of the identification of male-ness with competition, no less than with war, German national pride has an element of machismo that feminists have always been quick to criticize.[11]

Even more significantly, national identity has been reclaimed as a mat-ter of pride in upholding what are called "modern European" values, which now include gender equality and antiracism. The claim to being "modern" is central to nation-building projects in many parts of the world. In a reversal of Cold War moralism, the West is now presumed to be dis-tinguished from the backward East by its secularism and emancipation of women, precisely the "virtues" that the GDR had proclaimed as distin-guishing it from the bourgeois family politics of the West.[12]

Jessica Brown has particularly traced the emergence of a citizenship discourse that makes gender relations central to inclusion in the national community. Her study of local German culture courses for immigrants reveals that the lessons emphasize accepting the moral legitimacy of homosexual displays of affection, revealing clothing for women, and smoking and drinking in public spaces for both men and women. Despite some resistance to official tests proposed for ascertaining how well immigrants adopt such gender norms, she found considerable support in the curricula and classrooms for using gender relations as a focal point for teaching German-ness. Tolerance is emphasized, but tolerance in this instance, she argues, is understood as a one-way street in which displays of religion and of female inequality are now construed as threatening modernity and should not themselves be tolerated.[13]

This desire to be modern Europeans poses a paradoxical demand on Germans. On the one hand, they must embrace gender equality as a social norm that sets them apart from the backward and traditional "other," typically figured as a Muslim immigrant, often Turkish. Because the "other" is seen as religious, patriarchal and oppressive to women, German national identity is being reconfigured to be the opposite—secular, egalitarian and supportive of women. On the other hand, this was not, and still is not, a fair reflection of the cultural identity of many individual Germans, who are happy to embrace at least nominal Christianity as part of the national self-definition and are sure that a father-headed family is both natural and desirable.[14] By defining the "other" as backward, alien and threatening to what becomes defined as the cultural achievements of European modernity, the continuing patriarchal biases of the German state and society become obscured.[15] There is a new East-West myth-making at work here that seems not unlike the ways in which the GDR managed to fool itself, its citizens, and much of the rest of the world into thinking that it had achieved the emancipation of women.

Recreating system competition around gender equality poses several dangers. As Nira Yuval Davis has pointed out, women themselves become enlisted as the "border guards" for national identity, since variation in women's dress and demeanor is seen as expressing or attacking the normative boundaries of the community.[16] The focus on women's veiling as an expression of the inherent otherness of Muslim immigrants is a primary expression of this concern. It defines gender relations as political, where the state should intervene, and it also demonizes Muslim men (but only them) as the oppressors of women and thus as the appropriate targets for the disciplinary power of the state.[17] By allowing its federal states to exclude women wearing a veil from state employment, Germany uses women's clothing to express a "border" of otherness. Since representing the state defines full citizenship, this practice places religious women distinctively outside the boundaries of active membership: the state can act not through them but only on them, by deciding for them what is a political act. This contrasts with the framing of headscarves as uncontroversial symbols of religion in countries as diverse as Austria (where religion is accepted as part of the public sphere) and the United States (where religion is seen as private but protected from discrimination).[18]

Surprisingly, some German feminists have endorsed this exclusion of Muslim women from full citizenship, identifying strongly enough with the state as a defender of their secular values to want the state to enforce its norms against those of the local religious communities to which women themselves belong. In their view, being a modern state means standing for gender equality and acting to enforce the state's interpretation of the boundaries of inclusion on these grounds. The idea that Muslim women are incapable of self-determination in the face of familial patriarchy is remarkably inconsistent with the idea that German women have the right to be self-determining in matters of reproductive choice. Indeed, some feminists have taken the other side in the debate, arguing for the freedom of Muslim women to make their own choices about veiling without state interference.

The resulting "headscarf debate" among feminists in Germany has been vehement. In our analysis of feminist discourse, Susan Rottmann and I found that the symbolic weight of veiling in Germany reflected a division among German feminists between those who equated the headscarf with "forced marriages" and patriarchal coercion in the family, a private sphere of oppression from which the more modern and emancipated German state would free women, and those who had confidence that civil society would gradually assimilate and thus emancipate women without the state's help. But neither group of feminists expressed trust in the state as a guardian of gender equality, a skepticism also expressed in the minimal concern shown for the effects of discrimination by the German majority on Muslim women's ability to get jobs or rent housing on their own.[19]

As this example should make clear, the institutional politics of nationhood, religion, and sexuality centrally engage gender relations. The reconfiguration of states after the Cold War into a new international order in which the secular West confronts the patriarchal and religious Islamic "East" has become increasingly significant to the new imagined community of Germany. A focus on women's emancipation as a symbol of national modernity is not central to political discourse in states that have a more ambivalent relationship to modernity and secularism such as Austria, Poland or even the United States, but plays an important part in states that imagine themselves as "post-patriarchal" and secular such as the Netherlands, France and Denmark.[20] For Germany in particular, the false dichotomy of "us" as modern and "them" as backward, using gender equality as an emotionally loaded indicator of modernity, may be appealing precisely because it offers both East and West Germans a chance to embrace a vision of their future in which gender relations no longer divide them, as they did throughout the Cold War.

Gender Equality as Societal Transformation

The second identity claim, *wir sind das Volk*, remains an unfulfilled democratic aspiration for an empowered citizenship. This idealistic affirmation encourages political engagement, greater social equality and political freedom for both women and men. The extent to which either has been translated into actual policy and practice is debatable. With regard to translating gender equality aspirations into real political arrangements in unified Germany, feminist movements have found only mixed success. The contours of feminist effects are not only or perhaps even primarily shaped by the unification process, but have followed a transnational course of development in gender politics.

The Berlin Republic emerged in a time of global gender transformation. It is nearly fifteen years since the United Nations World Conference on Women was held in Beijing in 1995, affirming women's equality and political empowerment. This was itself the cumulation of twenty years of transnational feminist mobilization.[21] The Platform for Action that was broadly endorsed in Beijing challenged all signatory states to bring consideration of gender equality into all policy making by all decision-makers, an approach called gender-mainstreaming. As a mandate for states to transform gender relations, the Platform for Action reached first from Beijing to Brussels and then to Berlin. In contrast to the feminist politics of autonomy in the 1980s in West Germany, the postunification version of feminism redefined women as citizens rather than as mothers, and expressed a growing determination to use feminist organizations and influence to achieve more equality in and through state channels of policy making.[22]

In German political discourse, this feminist entry into the state has become familiar as the claim to "gender democracy" as a matter of full inclusion of women and men in decision-making roles as well as gender-mainstreaming in the considering all policy as having gendered outcomes.[23] While still controversial as being insufficiently radical, critical and transformative, the "mainstreaming" approach has been quite successful in bring feminists into policy positions. The Federal Republic of Germany responded to the Platform for Action by legally endorsing the goal of gender mainstreaming in 1998 and by funding an independent institute at the Humboldt University, the Gender Expertise Center, to teach bureaucrats throughout the system how to "mainstream gender" into their policy work.[24] Gender mainstreaming (GM) means paying attention to the disparate impacts on women and men of any policy decision. Although women are no longer to be the only ones responsible for bringing a "gender perspective" to policy making, GM deems including women's perspectives in the process of considering policy options to be essential. The Gender Expertise Center has specialized in "training the trainers" and has built out a wide network of gender consultants who are working at the state and local level as well as in federal ministries on topics from sports budgets to transportation planning.

In addition, several of the party-related foundations have begun to get much more involved in the gender mainstreaming business since 2000. The Hans Böckler Stiftung, close politically to the Social Democratic Party (SPD), has helped a number of unions do gender assessments and encouraged their own endorsement of gender equality as a goal and gender mainstreaming as means (a position unions as different as IG Metall and ver.di have endorsed). As part of the process of reaching that goal, a recent demand has been to ensure that all members of corporate governing boards are gender-mixed (no more than 40 percent of one gender).[25] The Heinrich Böll Foundation made "gender democracy" its watchword, and has not only sponsored a great deal of gender training itself, but has committed the organization to the principle that the equal engagement of women and men in political decision-making is a sine qua non of a fully realized democracy[26].

How to approach this goal remains controversial. The state-centered and corporatist style of German politics was open to a constitutional amendment to give the state the positive duty to take steps to advance gender equality, which was adopted in 1994. This feminist success reflected an effort in the East to advance some of the goals of the failed Social Charter of the dissidents in the GDR.[27] In the West, feminists were determined to make sure that the EU definition of equal treatment of men and women did not block efforts toward affirmative action, as the *Kalanke vs. Bremen* decision of the European Court of Justice threatened.[28] Like the compromise abortion law that passed in 1992, the revision of the equal rights amendment reflected the active lobbying work of an East-West cross-party coalition of women in parliament and in civil society in the early 1990s.[29]

The positive action called for in the gender mainstreaming approach has received some of its impetus from the EU level. The EU is certainly not intrinsically a pro-feminist force, but the accession of Sweden and Finland helped feminists to win a set of more supportive provisions in the Treaty of Amsterdam in 1995. Similarly, German unification and the widening of the EU to the East helped to define gender equality as part of the modernization and liberalization agenda the EU endorses.[30] The main EU policy direction has been to both demand national laws prohibiting discrimination on grounds of gender, language, religion, sexuality, disability, and age, which Germany has been notably reluctant to accept, and to endorse a strategy of "activation" of all potential workers, which has met with mixed success in Germany.[31] Both of these were to be combined with policies making gender equality a practical state goal, not just a matter of modern values, by adopting such measures as a parental leave directive and equalization of employment conditions between full and part-time workers.[32]

This has meant that EU integration has contributed significantly to concrete policies "activating" women workers and recognizing gender equality as an appropriate target of public policy. Policies that aim for gender equality in Germany now include both anti-discrimination law and family policies. Both of these have proved quite controversial.

The degree of German resistance to passing an anti-discrimination law (ADG) is actually remarkable.[33] Initially introduced by the Red-Green coalition in 2002 as a response to the EU demand that all member states prohibit discrimination on the basis of gender, language, religion, age, disability, and sexuality, the bill foundered in 2004-2005, in part because even members of the government proclaimed it a bureaucratic nightmare and job-killer.[34] The Grand Coalition that was in office from 2005-2009 was finally able to pass a broad but weaker anti-discrimination law (AGG, or Allgemeines Gleichbehandlungsgesetz) that would cover all employers and also at least those portions of civil society that were judged to have broad impact (thus only landlords with more than fifty units and who also lived off-site were to be covered). This met the minimum EU standard but lacked any of the mechanisms for collective pressure for enforcement that the Red-Green bill had offered, such as the class action suit.

Even among feminists, neither the ADG or AGG mobilized the same sort of popular engagement that either the headscarf or abortion issues did, and was instead defined by most women's groups as "really more about race," especially the desire to continue to allow landlords to refuse to rent to Turkish or other non-ethnic German families.[35] Women's groups preferred the affirmative action approach taken in the constitutional amendment. This positioned the state as the actor rather than the enforcer and targeted women for state help. The active policy of gender mainstreaming that feminists preferred included an extension of affirmative action hiring plans into private industry. The 2001 voluntary measures, all that the women's lobby had been able to secure, however, were widely deemed a failure, even though pronounced a success by then Chancellor Gerhard Schröder–a judgment widely seen as reflecting his personal view that women's equality concerns were a *Gedöns* (fuss) rather than the government's serious assessment that any real progress had been made.[36]

Moreover, the so-called Hartz IV reform package introduced under the Red-Green government included measures such as the *Bedarfsgemeinschaft* that have precisely the kind of disparate negative impact on women's unemployment benefits and job training that gender mainstreaming was supposed to identify and prevent.[37] This represents a step backwards in a country already perceived to be lagging the rest of the EU: in Germany, women are slightly less likely to be in leadership roles (28 percent versus 32 percent in the EU 27), earn less (23 percent less than men working similar hours compared to 17 percent less in the EU 27) and are much more likely to be working part-time (47 percent versus 31 percent).[38] Overall, the effect of the Hartz reforms has been to decrease the total hours per week that women spend in employment, which is precisely opposite to what the EU has been seeking to achieve in its "activation" approach.[39] Also, few cases of gender discrimination have made it successfully through the courts, and the damages paid by discriminating companies are not large enough to be a deterrent.[40] Overall, labor policy seems not to have done much to help women, and feminist engagement has been relatively ineffective.

For family policies, the verdict is more split. Optimists see the family policies now being introduced as heralding the remaking of the longstanding institutionalization of a strong male-breadwinner family policy.[41] This more "modern" approach, which is typically cast as "Nordic," paradoxically resembles the policies of the supposedly "backward" East and allows alliances among feminists in eastern Germany with EU and Scandinavian feminist networks.[42] But pessimists argue that even a more generous rate of pay and the ability to work part-time during the leave still will not be enough to induce men to take leaves and still attenuates women's attachment to the labor force.[43] Both pessimists and optimists agree that Germany is slowly moving in the direction of a "Nordic model" of encouraging a "daddy month" for men, expanding childcare to cover more of the three to five year-olds, and institutionalizing a more continuous but often part-time career orientation for women.[44] At a minimum, family policy that actively tries to bring men into taking leave can have effects on public consciousness well beyond its actual and immediate changes in sharing domestic labor.

The EU has endorsed this direction of reconfiguration of gender relations in the family as a step toward greater equality, but most feminists remain skeptical. In Germany, any move away from the strong male-breadwinner model is hailed as a sign of feminist progress, but in other European countries the issue is whether such modernization is not simply a re-institutionalization of gender inequalities on new terms. Some worry that work-family policy is displacing rather than enhancing gender equality as a state goal, seeing these changes in law as just reflecting the state's need for women's paid and unpaid labor to meet the demographic challenges of an aging and declining population.[45] Within Germany, even the labor force activation and modernization impulses coming from the EU are still blocked by both the income-splitting provisions of the tax code and the erratic hours of the school system.[46]

To sum up, there are unmistakable signs of a changing gender regime that is "activating" women as workers and citizens. With the impetus for redefining women "from mothers to citizens" coming from Beijing and Brussels, feminists have had some successes in Berlin, but remain concerned about how little commitment they see toward modernizing the German welfare state as an egalitarian one, rather than institutionalizing a one and a half earner family that still leaves women in an economically precarious position. Women's individual choices of how much paid work to do, how many children to have, as well as collective feminist struggles form an important part of the story, as women are seeking more actively than ever to have their desires respected and their needs met. The closer to these grassroots one goes, however, the more the question of whether German women are part of one people or remain two different "nations" arises.

Unification and Diversity among Women

The third phrase on which I focus is the claim that *wir sind ein Volk*. This, ironically, highlights the continuing sharp division between the lives that women and men are leading east and west of the now invisible wall. What Irene Dölling called East German women's "stubbornness" has kept alive a different regime of gender in the new states that is in some ways more modern and egalitarian than that institutionally anchored in the West.[47] Yet, the West's framing of the East as backward and patriarchal hampered real collaboration among feminists within Germany in the years following unification. Feminists in the West were scornful of the "Muttis" of the East while the East German women who wanted more gender equality were put off by the personal and organizational style of the "Emanzen" in the West.[48] Mutual devaluation has become less significant today, in part because of the active work of women's organizations, including women's affairs offices at the state and local levels, to bridge divides of experience and identity.

But, as the Berlin Republic adopts more "mommy politics" of its own, by bringing more women into higher education, keeping mothers in the labor force more continuously, but still looking the other way in the face of continuing discrimination against women, the differences in how women respond to these incentives in both parts of the country remain.[49] Despite convergences in matters such as deferring children until education is complete, there are still remarkably strong differences in women's preferred and actual work-family arrangements in the new and old federal states. In fact, because many of the differences are seen among young people, there is every reason to see gender norms and identities as being transmitted across generations and institutionalized as parts of the local collective identities of both women and men.

For example, by 2000 an absolute majority of all births in the ex-GDR occurred outside of marriage (52 percent versus 19 percent in the West) and in the new states 15 percent of women aged twenty-five to twenty-nine lived in non-marital unions with children (only 3 percent in the West did). The reasons that women in the ex-GDR give for putting off children remained notably different from those in the West too—the former emphasizing the difficulty of achieving sufficient financial security and finding a husband who will participate in childrearing and the latter naming a desire for travel, fun and self-realization. Women in the ex-GDR continued to prioritize getting a job and supporting themselves over being married, and they make decisions—like deferring births—that help them to fit children into that model.[50]

Right from the start, polls indicated a much higher level of support for a two-earner family, greater awareness of discrimination against women, and less support for the idea that a stay-at-home mother has a warmer relationship with her child in the East than in the West.[51] The idea that wifehood and motherhood are just two sides of the same coin—an idea that was characteristic of the West but not of the GDR—has also not exactly caught on in the East, even among the younger generation. Germans under age thirty in 2000 who had been raised in the East were less likely to consider having a child together as a reason to marry (24 percent versus 38 percent).[52] In 2000, there were higher proportions of four to six year-olds in full-time daycare (56 percent versus 20 percent), infants in any out of home child-care (34 percent versus 7 percent), and higher levels of husbands' participa-tion in housework (sixteen hours versus twelve weekly) and childcare (10.5 hours versus 8.5) in the new states than in the old ones.[53]

The "East" perspective, while different from that of the Federal Repub-lic, is not unusual internationally. Even in 1991, ex-GDR women were closer to the European and American norms than the women raised under the strong-breadwinner/housewife division of labor in West Germany were.[54] Women in the East continue to struggle to sustain a worker-mother identity across generations, sometimes with the help of their state and local govern-ments. But, in the terms internationally defined as more "modern," West Germany falls behind. Thus, Katja Guenther finds that the EU-oriented local women's groups in Rostock, which benefit from their Baltic regional ties with Scandinavia, are more engaged in helping women succeed eco-nomically and in supporting families' needs than are the local women's organizations in Erfurt, a city more closely connected by the transportation grid and political parties to its adjoining West German sister states.[55]

In sum, the claim of being "ein Volk" is still far from true. The gender relations that characterize Germany today are not unified and show no signs of becoming so. While there are secular trends toward smaller fami-lies and fewer marriages, the gulf between East and West in what consti-tutes a good life continues to be huge. Even as one generation is replaced by another, the collective element of a distinctively Eastern set of gender norms remains visible, not only in women's and men's stated attitudes but in the family arrangements of the generation that came of age in an osten-sibly unified Germany. As individual as these decisions might seem to those who make them, they add up to a different approach to gender that creates facts on the ground for future policy-makers.

Making a New State with Women

The feminist organization that emerged in the course of the unification process, the Independent Women's Association (Unabhängiger Frauen-verein, UFV) had as its slogan "Ohne Frauen ist kein Staat zu machen" (one can't make a state without women). In the years since unification, it appears that to some extent they were correct. The final phrase *wir sind Kanzlerin* highlights this reality. On the one hand, it points to the electoral successes women have experienced, but on the other, it points to the con-tinuing role of partisanship and electoral campaigns in defining what gender means and how equality is understood. The phrase, used by Alice Schwarzer, the public face of feminism for the German media and publisher of *Emma,* the feminist magazine, loosed a storm of outrage among some feminists and most journalists. Most framed this as Schwarzer's capitulation to the mere fact of Merkel "having breasts" rather than a political judgment that "feminism lite" as she called it, was an improvement over supporting more left parties, such as the SPD and Greens, which had repeatedly shown themselves untrustworthy on feminist issues.[56]

Like other aspects of changing gender relations since unification, the expansion of women's political representation has been a secular trend visible around the world rather than a German *Sonderweg.* It is most obvious in countries where there is proportional representation and electoral quotas or party quotas for women, but it is observable even in single member, winner-take-all systems such as the U.S.[57] Of course, the selection of Angela Merkel as chancellor is a symbol of this greater inclusion of women in positions of authority, but it is more useful to consider the rise of women as candidates and representatives as a broader phenomenon. This does not mean that unification itself had no effect.

As the table shows, in the preunification national elections of 1987 only 16 percent of the SPD seats and less than 8 percent of the Christian Democratic Union/Christian Social Union (CDU/CSU) seats were held by women. In just three years, in the first postunification election, this jumped to 27 percent for the SPD and 14 percent for the Union parties. The introduction of party quotas helped, and one can see the time lag between the SPD and CDU/CSU in this regard (see Table 1).[58] As one also can see in Table 1, another important factor was the introduction of a "zipper list" (alternate listing of male and female names on the party list) by the Green Party in the 1986 campaign. This highly visible commitment to a principle of gender equality in representation had a effect on other parties as well, since the parties that had been resisting demands from their own women members for some sort of quota rule themselves more or less quickly capitulated, although not to the extent of also adopting a 50 percent rule. The PDS/Linke also embraced the zipper list, and variation in the numbers of seats won by the Green and PDS/Linke lists overall thus has a disproportionate effect in the overall representation of women. The proportion of women has hovered in the vicinity of 36 percent (+/- 2 percent) for the SPD and 20 percent (+/- 3 percent) for the Union parties through most of the Berlin Republic.

Table 1: Women's Share of German Parliamentary Seats by Party and Party Alliances 1987-2005 (in percent)

	CDU/CSU	SPD	FDP	Greens /Alliance'90)	PDS/Left Party
8th Legislative Period 1976-1980	7.5	6.7	10.0	-	-
9th Legislative Period 1980-1983	7.6	8.3	13.3	-	-
10th Legislative Period 1983-1987	6.7	10.4	8.6	35.7	-
11th Legislative Period 1987-1990	7.7	16.1	12.5	56.8	-
12th Legislative Period 1990-1994	13.8	27.2	20.3	37.5	47.1
13th Legislative Period 1994-1998	13.9	33.7	17.0	59.2	43.3
14th Legislative Period 1998-2002	18.3	35.2	20.9	57.5	58.3
15th Legislative Period 2002-2005	23.0	37.8	25.5	58.1	100
16th Legislative Period 2005-2009	20.4	35.6	24.6	56.9	46.3
17th Legislative Period 2009-	20.6	38.4	24.7	54.4	52.6

Source: www.bundeswahlleiter.de

What Angela Merkel as chancellor represents is not mere representation of women, however, but of a different model of governing. Brigitte Zypries, the SPD Justice Minister in the Grand Coalition, praised Merkel's collegial style with thinly veiled jabs at her chancellor and fellow cabinet ministers in the previous Red-Green coalition.[59] As a childless woman with a professional career in science and politics who only married when about to run for national office, Merkel does not embody the wife-mother ideal that even many German feminists still invoke when speaking of women.[60] Her family politics, however, follow the line laid out by the equally exceptional Ursula von der Leyen, a mother of seven who has also maintained her employment when her children were young, and who enjoys an even greater level of personal popularity. Controversial as their policies have proved in terms of actually shifting the German gender relations away from idealized motherhood, as discussed earlier, their unquestioned competence and quiet exercise of power have had the same type of counter-stereotypical effects in Germany as "no-drama Obama" has had in the United States. While there is obvious ambivalence about such an ambiguous symbol of emancipation as Merkel herself, the shifts of political representation and family policy are connected. The attempt to modernize the welfare state–not merely in family politics, but in part-time jobs creation, flexible and precarious working conditions, and privatization for both women and men–reflects some of the concern for the future that is part of the "second demographic revolution" that is sweeping Europe, namely its declining birth rates and aging population.[61]

This significant demographic change has multiple political consequences for all European countries, and Germany's gender politics reflects this broader transformation as well. Among other things, it returns to the question of immigration as a source of a new tax-paying workforce that can support the pensions that Germans are hoping to collect, but also is bringing in increasing numbers of non-German women–more or less legally–to serve as caregivers for the elderly. Policies that the government adopts about immigration, pensions, retirement, and paying for eldercare, all ostensibly gender neutral, are therefore key elements in defining where and how gender relations will change in the future.

Angela Merkel's selection as chancellor and the policies being adopted by the Grand Coalition she has led may point to a broader shift in the meaning of modernity and conservatism in Europe. As the Grand Coalition brought the CDU and SPD together in a common project of modernization, it has also radicalized both the right and left wings. On the right, the traditional nationalist voices in the CDU/CSU and the protectionist defenders of the male-headed family in the SPD as well as CDU are being challenged by the realities of ethnic, family and sexual diversity; on the left, the advocates of gender, class, and race equality are challenged by the embrace of neo-liberalism, the weakening of social protections for low-wage workers, and the realities of an economic crisis in a globalized economy. While Merkel and her supporters have initiated a reform process within the CDU that may have discomfited many of its "traditional values backers," the SPD faces considerable difficulty in competing for votes with the left alliance, Die Linke, which has taken up many of its unfulfilled promises of gender equality. As the Green party previously challenged the mainstream parties and changed their representation of women by forcing them to compete for the loyalties of young women voters, the generational and gender divides of the electorate will surely play some role in the policy-making of the CDU-FDP coalition that emerged from the 2009 elections.

It seems unlikely for the CDU to be captured by "traditional values voters" and move backward away from its gradual embrace of modern families. The family reform tack taken by Merkel and von der Leyen is, after all, a continuation of family policy shifts begun already under both Rita Süssmuth and Heiner Geissler in the 1980s. But such regression is not unthinkable: the "pro-family" moral tone that is taken about gender in the current webpages of the Federal Ministry for Families, Seniors, Women and Youth is notably out of line with the actual policy directions that its minister, Ursula von der Leyen, repeatedly has taken. There is also evidence of a press-driven antifeminist mobilization of men and conservative women.[62] The practical family agenda is one of modernization, including support for two-earner couples, gay relationships, and shared parenting.[63] But will such a modernized work-family system be any better in the long run for women than the single male breadwinner model it is replacing?

Part of the modernizing process for politics evident globally and in Germany is the growing importance of non-state, non-elected actors in the political process. Even as women are becoming more visible and powerful in electoral positions, the non-elected bureaucrats and technocrats are increasingly important in laying down policy directions, whether through the EU's comparative "best practices" models of governance (the so-called Open Method of Coordination), the decentralization of policy to local administrators, and the growth of transnational advocacy groups who have an important role in making domestic and foreign policy.[64] Some have argued that shift toward "modern" neoliberal governance–stronger administration and weaker, less clearly defined parties, privatizing of public services, fragmentation and consolidation that makes regions and transnational actors more influential than individual states–has been facilitated in Germany by unification and concomitant need to rapidly remake the politics of the GDR, which has had spillover effects on the old federal states as well.[65] Sonia Alvarez calls the engagement of feminists in nonpartisan, typically transnational, expert networks as a form of activism for women the "NGOization" of the women's movement.[66] Sabine Lang has documented the shift toward the NGO form in West Germany before and after unification, while Katja Guenther also points to the "lobby" style adopted with some success by feminists in Rostock.[67]

The use of NGOs as advocacy networks can be seen as a valuable political innovation or as a threat to either social protest movements or conventional party politics or both.[68] This process of "NGOization" provides opportunities for access and influence outside the party system, using resources of expertise and organizing at which women have historically excelled, but it also implies a loss of power in and through democratic means, suggesting that women may be coming in ever greater numbers into a parliament that is ever more constrained by the demands of the European Commission, the Council of Europe, the G20 and other transnational governance mechanisms that are less democratically accountable.

Challenges for the Next Decade of the Berlin Republic?

In the twenty years since unification, the changes in gender relations are complex, and can neither be called good or bad for women. When looking at gender, it becomes clear that unification cannot be seen in isolation from the processes of European Union growth and global processes of liberalization. These include such complex issues as the definition of modernity as part of a new East-West system competition between the Muslim countries and the secular West, and the uses of gender equality as a legitimizing myth, a global norm and a policy objective as part of modernization. This does not make unification unimportant, but places it as a thread in a broader tapestry of gender change that has been underway for generations.

On the one hand, feminists might welcome the present modernization of welfare state toward an adult worker model, one that defines the state's role as supporting "the child and its parents" rather than "the worker and his dependents." The normative power of the EU has worked toward making discrimination illegal even over German resistance. On the other hand, the modernization of Europe has gone along with a shift toward neoliberal politics that leave more women and men in precarious economic circumstances and at the mercy of administrative rather than democratic decision-making. The global dimensions of the issues facing the Berlin Republic, from gender mainstreaming to the NGOization of politics, point to the need to engage in a transnational debate about what modernity can and should mean.

These debates are, as I hope to have shown above, very much about gender relations and what form they will take in future even when they seem to be about ethnicity (immigration) or class (the welfare state). Whether that future is described as the fuller realization of the promises of modernity or the more challenging and unstable ideal of a post-modern society, the restructuring of gender relations is inseparable from the overall reconstitution of the nation through the remaking of inequalities and borders. The gendered governance practices of the Berlin Republic regulate people's access to and rewards from membership in the national community, their means of economic and social support, and their ability to participate in and influence the political decision-making process itself. In this context, the incorporation of diversity—between east and west, among the EU 27, and within and among native-born and immigrant people—becomes the central challenge for contemporary politics.

Moreover, there is a challenge not only to the state but to German feminists to diversify their own imaginations of what kinds of life plans women and men find fulfilling. This is a matter of importance not only for those who are still looking at the divide produced by the old east-west system competition but for those who are concerned about the opportunities for full inclusion of "traditional" women, both Muslim and Christian and secular conservatives, in the polity. The model of using the state to institutionalize a particular family-work model and then expect all women and men to fit their lives into the age, gender, and religious boxes that it produces will never be able to accommodate the diversity of life plans that actual women and men try to follow. When the state is seen as the active guarantor of one model of gender equality, it may be unable or unwilling to defuse either the "mommy wars" or the "headscarf debates." The ultimate gender question is whether any state can be a site for inclusive citizenship practices, and the next decade will show more clearly if the Berlin Republic is willing to try.

Notes

1. The "sisterhood" question is explored, for example, in Myra Marx Ferree and Aili Mari Tripp, eds., *Global feminism: Transnational women's activism, organizing, and human right* (New York, 2006).

2. This process of differentiation and exclusion is traced very clearly in the feminist literature on intersectionality. One of the defining early works of this genre bore the trenchant title *All the women are white, all the Blacks are men but some of us are brave*, eds., Gloria Hull, Patricia Scott, and Barbara Smith (Old Westbury, 1982) and this concern has become a central one for German feminist theorists today. See for example, Cornelia Klinger and Gudrun-Axeli Knapp, eds., *ÜberKreuzungen. Fremdheit, Ungleichheit, Differenz* (Forum Frauen- und Geschlechterforschung, Band 23) (Münster, 2008).

3. Criticism of nationalist self-assertion as machismo can be found in Ingrid Miethe, "From 'Mother of the Revolution' to 'Fathers of Unification: Concepts of Politics among Women Activists Following German Unification," *Social Politics* 6, no. 1 (1999): 1-22. Other early 1990 German feminist discussions problematizing national self-congratulation are discussed in Myra Marx Ferree, *German feminism since the sixties* (Palo Alto, forthcoming).

4. The headscarf issue is addressed as key issue of European feminist politics in Joan Wallach Scott, *The Politics of the Veil.* (Princeton, 2007) while the specific feminist debates in Germany are reviewed in Susan B. Rottman and Myra Marx Ferree, "Citizenship and intersectionality: German feminist debates about headscarf and anti-discrimination laws," *Social Politics* 15, no. 4 (2008): 481-513.

5. There was considerable resonance of social movement participatory democratic mobilization for feminists in both East and West Germany. See, for example, Ingrid Miethe, *Frauen in der DDR-opposition: Lebens- und kollektivgeschichtliche verläufe in einer frauenfriedensgruppe* (Opladen, 1999) and for the West, Ute Gerhard, *Atempause: Feminismus als demokratisches Projekt* (Frankfurt/Main, 1999).

6. "Die Mauer im Kopf" was a trope made familiar in the media in the years immediately postunification, and continues to be a focus of attention. See for example, retrospectives from the ten year anniversary: "Die Mauer im Kopf." *Die Zeit*, 38/1999, and Heinrich Senfft, *Die sogenannte Wiedervereinigung* (Berlin, 1999).

7. The gender issues raised in the election period around 2005 are reviewed in Myra Marx Ferree, "Angela Merkel: What does it mean to run as a woman?" *German Politics and Society*, 24, no. 1 (2006): 93.

8. Benedict Anderson, *Imagined communities: Reflections on the origin and spread of nationalism* (London, 1983) initiated the upsurge of scholarly interest in the imagined community idea of nationhood through his study of nation-making by the spread of common media, but other scholars have built out from his argument to show how the imaginations of communities are gendered as well. Nira Yuval Davis, *Gender and nation,* (London, 1997) has been among the most influential of these.

9. Susan Gal and Gail Kligman, *Reproducing gender: Politics, publics and everyday life after socialism* (Princeton, 2000) offer a powerful analysis of the intertwining of gender and reproduction in the political claims-making process, particularly in times of national restructuring. In their account, women and their bodies symbolized moral purity (in times of corruption), tradition (in times of rapid social change), order and control (through patriarchal families) and national renewal (in giving birth) that Eastern European politicians exploited in the 1990s.

10. The shift to a politics of "modernity" in both Germany and the EU is evident in Jane Jenson, "Writing women out, folding gender in: The European Union 'modernises'," *Social Policy* 15 (2008): 131 – 153; Teresa Wobbe, "From Protecting to Promoting: Evolving EU Sex Equality Norms in an Organisational Field," *European Law Journal* 9, no. 1 (2003): 88-108, and Angelika von Wahl, "Gender Equality in Germany: Comparing Policy Change across Domains," *West European Politics* 29, no. 3 (2006): 461 - 488. See also Hae Yeon Choo, "Gendered Modernity and Ethnicized Citizenship," *Gender & Society,* 20, no. 6 (2006): 576-604, on images of North Koreans in South Korea as an interesting parallel to the remaking of Cold War citizenship language in Germany.

11. Feminist pacifism has been an important element of German postwar feminism, see Jennifer Anne Davy, "Pacifist Thought and Gender Ideology in the Political Biographies of Women Peace Activists in Germany, 1899-1970," *Journal of Women's History* 13, no. 3, (2001): 34-45.

12. The establishment of the GDR version of women's emancipation is outlined in Myra Marx Ferree, "The Rise and Fall of 'Mommy Politics': Feminism and German unification," *Feminist Studies* 19, no. 1 (1993): 89-115, and the vision of restored religious and male authority and female domestication in the postwar FRG version is detailed in Robert Moeller, *Protecting motherhood: Women and the family in postwar West Germany* (Berkeley, 1993).

13. Jessica Autumn Brown, "Making citizens: Educating Germany's immigrants on the ideological, emotional and practical aspects of belonging," PhD thesis, University of Wisconsin-Madison, Department of Sociology, 2010.

14. The claim to a German *Leitkultur* was more often than not expressed in terms of the central role of Christianity and Christian values, despite the obvious discontinuity

between the gender relations chosen to symbolize this in German classrooms for immigrants and the gender relations espoused in international relations, at least by the Catholic Church. See Doris Buss and Didi Herman, eds., *Globalizing family values: The Christian right in international politics* (Minneapolis, 2003). In Germany this power is clear in Angelika von Wahl's discussion of the continuing impact of the right in the form of the CSU and Catholic Church in "From family policy to reconciliation policy: how the Grand Coalition reforms the welfare state," *German Politics and Society* 26, no. 3 (2008): 25-49.

15. For example, the resistance to extending school days for older children and providing childcare for younger ones revolves around continuing claims that a mother should be home with her children and resistance to eliminating income-splitting is tied to fathers having the primary obligation for financial support. Karin Hagemann, "Between Ideology and Economy: The 'Time Politics' of Child Care and Public Education in the Two Germanys," *Social Politics* 13, no. 2 (2006): 217-260; Sabine Berghahn, "Der Ritt auf der Schnecke. Rechtliche Gleichstellung in der Bundesrepublik Deutschland,"(2003) http://www.gender-politik-online.de; also available an abbreviated version in *Recht und Geschlecht. Zwischen Gleichberechtigung, Gleichstellung und Differenz*, eds., Mechthild Koreuber and Ute Mager (Baden-Baden, 2004), 59-78.

16. Nira Yuval Davis, *Gender and Nation* (Thousand Oaks, 1997).

17. This tension is explored in detail in Susan B. Rottmann and Myra Marx Ferree "Citizenship and Intersectionality: German Feminist Debates about Headscarf and Anti-discrimination Laws," *Social Politics* 15, no. 4 (2008): 481-513. See also Sabine Berghahn, "Verfassungspolitischer Streit um ein Stück Stoff: Das Kopftuch der Lehrerin im Konflikt zwischen Grundrechtsschutz, staatlicher Neutralität in Glaubenfragen und föderaler Gesetzgebung," *femina politica: Schwerpunkt: Verfassungspolitik–verfasste Politik* 13, no. 1 (2004): 45-56. The entire October/November 2009 issue of *Emma* is devoted to articles making the case that a headscarf ban in German schools is necessary for women's rights, with references to the French approach as a positive model.

18. Nora Gresch, Leila Hadj-Abdou, Sieglinde Rosenberger, and Birgit Sauer, "Tu felix Austria? The Headscarf and the Politics of 'Non-issues'", *Social Politics* 15, no. 4 (2008): 411– 432, and Joyce Marie Mushaben, "'Die Freiheit, die ich meine …': An American View of the Kopftuch Debate," *femina politica: Zeitschrift für feministische Politik-Wissenschaft* 13, no.1 (2004): 98-104.

19. The experience of being discriminated against is certainly not rare. See Umut Erel, "Gendered and Racialized Experiences of Citizenship in the Life Stories of Women of Turkish Background in Germany," in *Gender and Ethnicity in Contemporary Europe,* ed., Jacqueline Andall, (Oxford, 2003), 155-176, and Rob Euwals, Jaco Dagevos, Mérove Gijsberts, and Hans Roodenburg, "Immigration, Integration and the Labour Market: Turkish Immigrants in Germany and the Netherlands," *IZA DP Discussion Paper Series*, no. 2677 (2007). Consider, too, the publicly expressed willingness of landlords to discriminate: Ulrike Herrmann, "Vermieter wollen diskriminieren dürfen; Die SPD streitet um das Anti-diskriminierungsgesetz. Die Gegner erhalten Auftrieb bei einer Bundestagsanhörung," *taz, die tageszeitung*, 8 March, 2005. Although noting that good data on experiences of discrimination is rare, Heike Gleibs points to an increasing percentage of immigrants who report school or workplace discrimination (65 percent in 1999 and 77 percent in 2004) and a plurality who report housing discrimination (49 percent). Heike Gleibs, "Haben Anne und Ayshe gleiche Chancen?" *Themenblätter im Unterricht*, no. 59, (Bundeszentrale für politische Bildung, 2006), available at http://www.bpb.de/publikationen/LPYWGT,0,Gleiche_Chancen_f%FCr_Anne_und_Ayshe.htm.

20. Gresch et al. (see note 18).

21. See Margaret Snyder, "Unlikely Godmother: The UN and the Global Women's Movement," in Marx Ferree and Tripp (see note 1), 24-50.

22. The long transformation of the UN's approach to women "from mothers to citizens" is well documented in Nitza Berkovitch, *From Motherhood to Citizenship: Women's Rights and International Organizations* (Baltimore, 1999) and Snyder (see note 21). This transformation of the EU is followed by Rachel Cichowski, "Women's Rights, the European Court and Supranational Constitutionalism," *Law & Society Review* 38 (2004): 489-512, and Rachel Cichowski, *The European Court and Civil Society: Litigation, Mobilization and Governance* (Cambridge, 2007).

23. Halina Bendkowski is credited with coining the term "gender democracy" but it passed into more general use through its adoption by the Heinrich Böll Institute in the 1990s, see Helga Braun, *Geschlechterdemokratie wagen!* (Königstein/Taunus, 2002). It has been a controversial idea among feminists, as evidenced in Halina Bendkowski, Sabine Hark und Claudia Neusüß, "Geschlechterdemokratie–ein Streitgespräch: Feministischer Aufbruch oder institutionelle Anpassung?" *femina politica, Zeitschrift für feministische Politikwissenschaft* 11, no. 2 (2002): 29-40. Unlike "Geschlechterdemokratie" the term "gender mainstreaming" remains in use only in English, reflecting its transnational origins.

24. See the website of the GenderKompetenz Zentrum at the Humboldt Universität zu Berlin, available at http://www.genderkompetenz.info/.

25. Birgit Riegraf, "Geschlecht und Differenz in Organisationen: von Gleichstellungspolitik und erfolgreichem Organisationslernen," *WSI-Mitteilungen* (2008). For more regional details on the implementation and effects of gender mainstreaming, see http://www.gender-index.de/.

26. Gabrielle Schambach and Barbara Unmüßig, "Geschlechterdemokratie–das Konzept der Heinrich-Böll-Stiftung," *femina politica, Zeitschrift für feministische Politikwissenschaft* 11, no. 2 (2002): 11-28.

27. Dagmar Schiek, "Die Schnecke Fortschritt kriecht rückwärts: Das zweite Gleichberechtigungsgesetz," *Streit: feministische Rechtszeitschrift* 13, no. 1 (1995): 3-13.

28. Case 450/93 Eckhard Kalanke v Freie Hansestadt Bremen; available at http://eur-lex.europa.eu/LexUriServ/ LexUriServ.do?uri=CELEX:61993J0450:EN:HTML.

29. See more extensive discussion and interviews in Myra Marx Ferree (see note 3).

30. Silke Roth, *Gender politics in the expanding European Union: Mobilization, inclusion, exclusion* (New York, 2008).

31. Von Wahl (see note 14); Ursula Degener and Beate Rosenzweig, eds., *Die Neuverhandlung sozialer Gerechtigkeit: Feministische Analysen und Perspektiven* (Wiesbaden, 2006). See also Ines Hofbauer and Gundula Ludwig, "Gender Mainstreaming–ein Thema für die Wissenschaftsforschung–Geschlechtergerechtigkeit limited? Eine politische Strategie auf dem Prüfstand?" *femina politica, Zeitschrift für feministische Politikwissenschaft* 14, no 2 (2005): 32-42.

32. Council Directive 96/34/EC of 3 June 1996 on the framework agreement on parental leave concluded by UNICE, CEEP and the ETUC, *Official Journal of the European Union*, L 145, (1996): 4-9, available at http://eur-lex.europa.eu/LexUriServ/LexUriServ.do?uri=CELEX:31996L0034:EN:HTML; Council Directive 97/81/EC of 15 December 1997 concerning the Framework Agreement on part-time work concluded by UNICE, CEEP and the ETUC, *Official Journal of the European Union*, L 14 (1998): 9-14 available at http://eur-lex.europa.eu/LexUriServ/LexUriServ.do?uri=CELEX:31997L0081:EN:HTML.

33. This continues the resistance expressed in the "EU conformity law" of 1981 that mandated non-discrimination but set up such weak sanctions as to make it no deterrent to actual practice, as the ECJ finally ruled. See also Wiebke Hennig and Susanne Baer, "Europarecht als Chance–Zu den Richtlinien 2000/43/EG vom 29 June 2000 und 2000/78/EG vom 27 November 2000 gegen Diskriminierung," *Streit: feministische Rechtszeitschrift* 21, no. 4 (2002): 169-175; and Barbara Degen, "Das Allgemeine Gleichbehandlungsgesetz (AGG)–Tanzschritte auf dem Weg zur Gerechtigkeit im Erwerbsleben," *Streit: feministische Rechtszeitschrift* 25, no. 1 (2007).

34. Prominent SPD politicians cited in the CDU/CSU position paper against the Red-Green anti-discrimination proposal included the following: (NRW Ministerpräsident Peer)

Steinbrück hingegen übte scharfe Kritik an dem Entwurf. Das Gesetz sei in seiner jetzigen Form "eine zusätzliche Belastung für die Wirtschaft," und erschwere"die Konkurrenzfähigkeit unserer Unternehmen." Er wünsche sich, dass es "so nicht in Kraft tritt" und werde der gegenwärtigen Form im Bundesrat nicht zustimmen, sagte der SPD-Politiker der *Bild am Sonntag* (Meldung AFP, 5 March 2005). "Bundesinnenminister Otto Schily (SPD) hat Presseinformationen zufolge bei der Kabinettssitzung am Mittwoch die Rücknahme des Entwurfes für ein Antidiskriminierungsgesetz gefordert. Schily habe seinen Vorstoß mit den Worten begründet:"Das wäre ein echter Beitrag zum Bürokratieabbau," berichtet das Düsseldorfer *Handelsblatt* (Donnerstagausgabe) unter Berufung auf Regierungskreise (Meldung DDP, 2 March 2005). "Ich sehe das genauso wie der Kollege Schily," (Wolfgang Clement nach einer Meldung von Reuters, 3 March 2005). See "Kritikpunkte der CDU/CSU-Bundestagsfraktion am Gesetzentwurf des Antidiskriminierungsgesetzes (ADG)," 16 March 2005, available at http://www.cducsu.de/ upload/ 2B64476570ACCC6D0B861AB66B230F7211376-n4pjldai.pdf. See also Karl-Otto Sattler,"Geschichten vom verregelten Völkchen," *Das Parlament,* no. 11 (14 March 2005), available at http://www.das-parlament.de/2005/11/ThemaderWoche/001.html.

35. Rottmann and Marx Ferree (see note 17).
36. Chancellor Gerhard Schröder's hostility to feminism was seen as best captured in his widely cited comment about "Frauenpolitik und so Gedöns" on the occasion of the swearing in of his cabinet in 1998. *Bild,* 14 January 2002. The failure of the 2001 compromise is detailed in "Frauen in Führungspositionen: Je höher, desto seltener," available at http://www.box2.boeckler-boxen.de/5437.htm, which concludes that there was no change to be observed.
37. Feminist assessments of the consequences of Hartz IV can be seen in Ursula Degener and Beate Rosenzweig, eds., *Die Neuverhandlung sozialer Gerechtigkeit: Feministische Analysen und Perspektiven* (Wiesbaden, 2006) as well as Sabine Berghahn and Maria Wersig, "Vergemeinschaftung von (Ehe-)Partnern durch die Reformen der Agenda 2010–eine Rückkehr zum Geschlechtervertrag" des 19. Jahrhunderts?" *femina politica, Zeitschrift für feministische Politikwissenschaft* 23, no. 2(2005): 21-32; Sabine Berghahn,"Geschlechtergleichstellung und Bedarfsgemeinschaft: Vorwärts in die Vergangenheit des Ernährermodells?" *Vortrag im Institut für Arbeitsmarkt- und Berufsforschung der Bundesagentur für Arbeit (IAB)* (Nuremberg, 2005); available at http://web.fu-berlin.de/ernaehrermodell/ IAB.pdf. Silke Bothfeld, Ute Klammer, Christina Klenner, Simone Leiber, Anke Thiel, and Astrid Ziegler, *WSI-FrauenDatenReport 2005: Handbuch zur wirtschaftlichen und sozialen Situation von Frauen* (Berlin, 2005; available at http://www.boeckler.de/169_91922.html) report that the percentage of employed women who worked only part time in the old federal states rose from 34 percent to 45 percent and in the East from 17 percent to 28 percent between 1991 and 2004, while the numbers of women in full time employment fell, shifting more women to marginal positions in employment.
38. A sobering assessment of how far behind the European norm Germany falls is provided by Birgit Breese, "Frauenverdienste–Männerverdienste: wie weit liegen sie auseinander? oder: Wie breit ist der 'gender pay gap' in Deutschland?" *Streit: feministische Rechtszeitschrift* 25, no. 3 (2007): 99-107; and for women in management, Elke Holst, "Women in managerial positions in Europe," *Management Revue* 17, no. 2 (2006): 122-142.
39. Between 2001 and 2006, women's total average hours of work fell from 31.5 to 30.2. Statistisches Bundesamt, *Frauendatenreport* (Wiesbaden, 2008).
40. The disappointments of the three most widely known cases are reviewed in *Emma.* Chantal Louis, "Antidiskriminerungsgesetz: Ein Sieg und zwei Niederlagen," *Emma,* no. 2 (March/April 2009), available at http://www.emma.de/anti_dis_2009_02.html.
41. The most optimistic reading of family law reform is von Wahl (see note 14).
42. Katja Guenther, *Places of resistance: Feminism after socialism in eastern Germany* (Palo Alto, forthcoming).

43. Sabine Berghahn, "Von der Familienpolitik zur Frauenpolitik und zurück ..." *Streit: feministische Rechtszeitschrift* 24, no. 2 (2006): 51-56) is one of the most eloquent and least ideological of the pessimists.

44. For fuller discussions of the Nordic model as such, see Kimberly Morgan, *Working mothers and the welfare state: Religion and the politics of work-family policies in Western Europe and the United States* (Palo Alto, 2006), Wiebke Kolbe and Mechtild Veil, "Schweden–idealisiertes Vorbild für Gleichstellungspolitik und familienpolitische Reformen in Deutschland?" *Feministische Studien* 25 (2007): 86-91, and Janet Gornick and Marcia Meyers, eds., *Gender Inequality* (Cambridge, 2009).

45. Jane Jenson, "Writing Women Out, Folding Gender In: The European Union 'Modernises,'" *Social Policy* 15 (2008): 131-153, and Berghahn (see note 43) are among the most prominent of these critics, but hardly the only ones.

46. Ulrike Spangenberg, "50 Jahre Ehegattensplitting! Gute Gründe für eine Reform der Besteuerung der Ehe," *Streit: feministische Rechtszeitschrift* 26, no. 4 (2008): 161-167, and Hagemann (see note 15).

47. Irene Dölling, "Structure and Eigensinn: Transformation processes and continuities of Eastern German women," in *After the wall: Eastern Germany since 1989*, ed., P. J. Smith (Boulder, 1998), 183-202.

48. Ulrike Helwerth and Gislinde Schwarz, *Von Muttis und Emanzen: Feministinnen in Ost- und Westdeutschland* (Frankfurt/Main, 1995).

49. Marina Adler, "Child-Free and Unmarried: Changes in the Life Planning of Young East German Women," *Journal of Marriage and Family* 66 no. 4 (2004): 1170–1179; note also that Lynn Price Cooke finds continuing differences in how much housework male partners contribute, with the East German men being more participatory. See "Persistent Policy Effects on Gender Equity in the Home: The Division of Domestic Tasks in Reunified Germany," *Journal of Marriage and Family* 69 (2007): 930-950.

50. Adler (see note 49); and Karsten Hank and Michaela Kreyenfeld, "A Multilevel Analysis of Child Care and the Transition to Motherhood in Western Germany," *Journal of Marriage and Family* 65, no. 3 (2003).

51. The wifehood-motherhood connection at the time of unification is explored in Myra Marx Ferree, "Patriarchies and Feminisms: The Two Women's Movements of Unified Germany," *Social Politics* 2, no. 1 (1995): 10-24.

52. Statistics on reasons for marrying are found in Adler (see note 49).

53. Childcare use statistics are based on regional differences in use, which reflects both local availability as well individual decisions to enroll children, while the domestic division of labor is calculated for married couples based on where the wife was educated. Both structural availability (311 public childcare places/1000 children aged zero to three in the East and 19/1000 in the West) and individual choices reflect the persistence of a different gender culture in the ex-GDR. See Hank and Kreyenfeld (note 50).

54. Consider the level of agreement in 1991 with the statement "an employed mother can give a child just as much warmth and security as a mother who does not have a job." While 66 percent of East Germans agreed, only 39 percent of West Germans did. In this regard, it is the East Germans who were closer to the European average (61 percent agreement). Institut für Demoskopie (Allensbach, 1993).

55. Katja Guenther, "Understanding Policy Diffusion across Feminist Social Movements: The Case of Gender Mainstreaming in Eastern Germany," *Politics & Gender* 4, no. 4 (2008): 1-27; Katja Guenther, "A Bastion of Sanity in a Crazy World: A Local Feminist Movement and the Reconstitution of Scale, Space, and Place in an Eastern German City," *Social Politics* 13, no. 4 (2006): 551-575.

56. Marx Ferree (see note 7).

57. Aili Mari Tripp and Alice Kang, "The Global Impact of Quotas: On The Fast Track to Female Representation," *Comparative Political Studies* 41, no. 5 (2008): 338-61.

58. Table adapted from Beate Hoecker, "50 Jahre Frauen in der Politik: späte Erfolge, aber nicht am Ziel," *Aus Politik und Zeitgeschichte (APUZ), Beilage zur Wochenzeitschrift Das*

Parlament, no. 24-25 (2008): 10-18; available at http://www.bundestag.de/blickpunkt/104_Spezial/0402020.html, and author's additional calculations.

59. Alice Schwarzer interview with Justizministerin Brigitte Zypries, "Bei uns zu Hause waren die Rollen umgekehrt," *Emma* (July/August 2006), available at http://www.emma.de/zypries_2006_4.html.

60. Marx Ferree (see note 7).

61. Ron Lesthaeghe, "The Second Demographic Transition in Western Countries: An Interpretation," in *Gender and family change in industrialized countries,* eds., Karen Oppenheim Mason and Ann-Magritt Jensen (New York, 2003), 17-62.

62. Elisabeth Klaus, "Antifeminismus und Elitefeminismus–Eine Intervention," *Feministische Studien* 26, no. 2 (2008): 176-186.

63. On issues of sexual modernity and gay rights in particular, see Dagmar Herzog, "Post coitum triste es...? Sexual Politics and Cultures in Post-Reunification Germany," *German Politics & Society* (this issue).

64. Brigitte Young, *Triumph of the fatherland: German unification and the marginalization of women* (Ann Arbor, 1999) pointed soon after unification at the paradoxes of women becoming more vocal in making claims on government and more visible in representative roles in politics and government administration just as the powers of the state were being hollowed out by the increases in corporate influence transnationally. See also Heike Kahlert and Antonia Kupfer, "Mehr Markt, weniger Staat und (ungelöste) Ungleichheitsfragen: Perspektiven der Wohlfahrtsstaatsforschung im Neoliberalismus?" *femina politica, Zeitschrift für feministische Politikwissenschaft* 14, no. 2 (2005): 2-20; and Marion Löffler, "Transformation des politischen Feldes als Chance für feministische Politik?" *femina politica, Zeitschrift für feministische Politikwissenschaft* 17, no. 2 (2008). Much more optimistically, Roth (see note 30) and Kathrin Zippel, *The politics of sexual harassment: A comparative study of the United States, the European Union and Germany,* (New York, 2006) see women as benefiting in the long as well as short term from the political opportunities of expert networks and expanded administrative authority that vie with classic forms of partisan conflict management.

65. Sünne Andresen, Irene Dölling, and Christoph Kimmerle, *Verwaltungsmodernisierung als soziale Praxis. Geschlechterwissen und Organisationsverständnis von Reformakteuren* (Opladen, 2003). See also Ingrid Kurz-Scherf, Julia Lepperhoff, and Alexandra Scheele, "Modernisierung jenseits von Traditionalismus und Neoliberalismus? Die aktuelle Arbeitsmarktpolitik als Ausdruck eines verkürzten Modernisierungskonzepts," *femina politica, Zeitschrift für feministische Politikwissenschaft* 14, no. 2 (2005): 62-74.

66. "Advocating Feminism: The Latin American Feminist NGO 'Boom,'" *International Feminist Journal of Politics* 1, no. 2 (1999): 181-209 is her classic argument, more recently nuanced in her article "Beyond NGO-ization?: Reflections from Latin America," *Development* 52, no. 2 (2009): 175-184.

67. For "NGOization" as a trend in both eastern and western parts of Germany and in Europe see Sabine Lang, "The NGO-ization of feminism," in *Transitions, environments, translations: Feminisms in international politics,* eds., Joan Wallach Scott, Cora Kaplan, and Diane Keats (New York, 1997), 101-120, and Guenther (see note 42). See also Birgit Locher, "Wissenschaft, Politik und NROs: Strategische Allianzen für frauenpolitische Belange am Beispiel neuester EU-Politiken gegen Frauenhandel," *femina politica, Zeitschrift für feministische Politikwissenschaft* 13, no. 2 (2003): 51-60.

68. For the tension between German inequality politics and transnational equality aspirations see, for example, Birgit Sauer, *Die Asche des Souveräns: Staat und Demokratie in der Geschlechterdebatte* (Frankfurt/Main, 2001) and Zippel (see note 64).

PART III.
POLITICS AND PUBLIC POLICY

Chapter 11

THE FEDERAL REPUBLIC AT TWENTY

Of Blind Spots and Peripheral Visions

• • • • • • • • • • • • • • •

Jeffrey J. Anderson

Twenty years after all the excitement, Germans seem to be genuinely of two minds about unification. As amateur historians, they look back on the events of 1989-1990 with pride and a kind of awe typically associated with the witnessing of miracles. The coming together of civic courage and elite wisdom to produce a peaceful and relatively consensual path to a Germany whole and sovereign surely qualifies as one of the more remarkable achievements of the twentieth century. As citizen pundits, however, Germans appear to have arrived at a much more nuanced and far less euphoric conclusion about the state of union. Everywhere they look, they see a persistent East-West divide. In social relations, eastern and western Germans are separated to this day by the "wall in the head" (Mauer im Kopf). The economy is a tale of two Germanys, one rich and prosperous—the other essentially a ward of the state. And in the political realm, citizens and their representatives seem to operate within different coordinate systems and seek to realize very different visions, depending on whether they hail from one side or the other of the former wall.

These contrasting interpretations and assessments of unification, often held by the same person and quite clearly clustered according to an East-West divide, are fluid, but surface repeatedly in crystallized form in the quality print media. There are recurring themes, interpretations, and narratives, sometimes complementary and reinforcing, other times conflicting and juxtaposed, about unification twenty years on. What follows is very much in the mold of an interpretive essay—a plausible accounting of the major currents of thought in what educated Germans read about unification's balance sheet of success and failure. I have a strong sense that these public musings matter. Of course, it would be useful to know whether what appears on the printed page and on the Internet is cause or symptom—that is, whether these media offerings and exchanges influence elite and/or mass opinion, or whether they simply reflect the discourses that are already under way in society. In examining these stories, though, one can trace the interconnections between the social, economic, and political dimensions of unification. As such, these contemporary printed narratives can tell us a great deal about how a people views its recent past, what its priorities are, and how it is facing the future.

In the pages that follow, I present four representative "vignettes" that capture important aspects of contemporary Germany's encounters with a very recent past, and what this all means for the present. These are, in order, the failed attempt to commission a national monument to unification; the end of solidarity over the "Soli;" the strange case of Karl-Heinz Felgner; and the challenges of coming-to-terms with the past (*Vergangenheitsbewälti-gung*) within the Left Party. Individually and as a group, these stories reveal something curious. Unification is akin to a blind spot—look straight at it, and it disappears, replaced by blank spot—a seemingly irreducible gap between East and West. Avert one's gaze, and the spot fills in, almost seamlessly.

Memorializing History

In November 2007, on the eighteenth anniversary of the fall of the Berlin Wall, the Bundestag voted to build a monument to freedom and unity. The Nationales Freiheits- und Einheitsdenkmal was to be erected in Berlin in 2009, to commemorate the twentieth anniversary celebrations of the peaceful revolution in East Germany, the collapse of the Wall, and the subsequent uniting of the two Germanys. The German parliament set aside EURO 15 million for the project (including EURO 160,000 in prize money for the winning entry), and designated a choice parcel of land along the Spree River in Berlin, just in front of the soon-to-be rebuilt Hohenzollern Castle (Stadtschloss), as the site of the national monument.

The Bundestag's decision authorized a formal competition to select the winning design for the national monument. The official call for design proposals indicated that the memorial was intended to speak to several themes simultaneously: the peaceful revolution of 1989 and unification; the principles of unity, freedom, and democracy; and peaceful movements and efforts toward unity of centuries past, which presumably included the failed revolutions of 1848 and 1918. Last but not least, the national memorial in Berlin was supposed to signify in some way the events of October 1989 in Leipzig. This would have been a tall order for a book or film, to say nothing of an art installation.

The government decision to memorialize the events leading up to the unification of Germany provoked a mixed reaction from the public and from political cultural elites. Many welcomed the decision, pointing out that most of Germany's European neighbors had erected similar national monuments, and that it was high time for Germany to commemorate the sacrifices and achievements of those who forged a democratic, unified Germany in the twentieth century. Others voiced support, but added that one should not overdo the focus on a national monument residing in Berlin, since this would divert attention from worthy sites of historical memory elsewhere in the country, such as Leipzig. Wolfgang Tiefensee, Federal Commissioner for the New Federal States, observed: "The peaceful revolution of 1989 took place throughout the entire German Democratic Republic (GDR) and it is only right that it be remembered in other places. I call upon the people, local councilors, and mayors to erect memorial sites in their own cities, towns, and villages."[1]

Opponents of the monument initiative cautioned that the time was not yet ripe for such a formal gesture–Germans on both sides of the former wall were still working out the implications of unification in their daily lives, and for the country to fix the symbolic meaning of unification in 2009, less than a generation after these seminal events, was more than a little presumptuous. Others, notably the historian Alfred Grosser, remarked pointedly that a monument to unification would inevitably constrain the focus of memory and interpretation, thereby omitting the important contributions of East German dissidents, many of them devout communists, who had been striving for laudable objectives that did not come to pass.

It is worth noting that the characteristic zeal with which the Berlin city government permitted the wall to be dismantled, piece by piece, over the course of the 1990s almost certainly contributed to the perceived need to erect (anew) a structure to commemorate its dismantling. By 2009, less than a quarter of the original wall was still standing, and observers noted that there were more *Berliner Mauer* fragments overseas than in all of Germany, to say nothing of Berlin proper.[2] Where portions of the wall remain intact, they are often inconspicuously marked, and many of the sites are unprotected by city or federal ordinances. Only recently has there been anything like a movement to preserve for posterity the remains of this notorious structure. Apparently, the drive to unify and to normalize was accompanied by at best an indifference, and in many instances outright hostility to any vestigial reminders of what had kept the two German peoples apart. As Petra Roland, spokesperson for the city's Department for Urban Development, observed matter-of-factly: "It was a border, it was a reminder of an uncomfortable past and everyone just wanted to get rid of it ... which I think can be hard for outsiders to understand."[3]

The prize jury for the Nationales Freiheits- und Einheitsdenkmal competition, comprised of nineteen prominent historians, architects, politicians, and artists, was supposed to announce a winner by the anniversary date of 9 November 2009. The jury received a total of 532 entries, which were winnowed down to twenty finalists in early April 2009. Then, in a stunning development, the jury announced on 30 April that by unanimous decision, it could recommend none of the finalists, and so no prize would be awarded. Jan Otakar Fischer, in an essay written for the on-line site "The Design Observer Group," commented:

> The competition failure was splashed onto the front pages of the German newspapers, where some of the journalists were give a chance to explain why the process had flopped. A chorus of critics joined in. Two fundamental complaints emerged: the program was impossibly overloaded and the site was inappropriate. The competition had been doomed from the start. Several competitors smelled unethical conduct, countering that the scandal was not in the decision to reject the work, but in the fact that the jury understood the weaknesses of the brief but participated anyway. Within two weeks, the public was able to judge for itself, when all the designs were briefly exhibited in Berlin's Kronprinzenpalais. Remarkably few people came.[4]

In a wry and understated style, Fischer goes on to discuss the process and entries. Media commentators calculated that jury members must have spent an average of ninety seconds reviewing each proposal. Fischer notes that "such a concentrated barrage of images must have provoked strange dreams."[5] He goes on:

> There were familiar motifs, both realistic and abstract, from the realm of popular sentiment: rainbows; flowers; flags; trees of life; parents and children; hands holding hands, clocks or balls; dancing children; doves of peace; people carrying keys; torches; maps of Germany; broken walls. There were essays in simple geometry: rings; cubes; spheres; pyramids; obelisks; stelae; Möbius strips; labyrinths. There were architectural elements, often cueing the Wilhelm monument: columns; plinths; towers; arches; colonnades; stairs. There were German national colors in every combination of gold, glass, metal, and stone. There were meta-text installations, usually employing the words "Einheit" and "Freiheit" or "Wir sind das Volk" ..., in projected or solid form. There were patently silly entries, often cloaking a more pointed social commentary: a golden banana; a lone giraffe; a spiked helmet; a company of Smurfs; a giant figure pushing a shopping cart. There were mysteries: shards; piles of sticks; blobs; turds.[6]

Perhaps, as some commentators concluded, this episode suggests little more than that if one gives talented people an impossible assignment they will (alas) fail. And perhaps it also says that despite the undeniable quality present amidst the spate of entries, no one is truly capable of capturing a complex feeling or a memory that has yet to gel in the minds of the German people (or at least these particular nineteen Germans). In early 2010, the prize jury, newly charged and reconstituted, announced a second competition, which is ongoing. This time around, entries are to address a more Spartan, stream-lined theme: the peaceful revolution of 1989 and unification. This time around, failure is most likely not an option.

The "Soli" and Mezzogiorno Ost

If the reader had been able to collect a EURO each time Helmut Kohl's ill-fated prediction of "blossoming landscapes" (*blühende Landschaften*) in the eastern Länder[7] has been quoted in the press over the past eighteen months, a nice dinner for two at a four-star restaurant would certainly be within reach. The facts on the ground, twenty years after German Economic and Monetary Union (GEMU, for connoisseurs of mothballed acronyms), are well known. Indeed, one can find an-up-to date balance sheet in the chapters by Stephen Silvia and Holger Wolf in this volume. The region remains a net exporter of inhabitants; since 1991, approximately 1.1 million people (almost 6.5 percent of the original East German population) have left for western Germany. After making up considerable ground in the early years after unification, labor productivity languishes at around 70 percent of the western German average. Unemployment rates are twice those registered in the West.

Economists and geographers caution against the temptation to make blanket statements about "the east German region," pointing out that these rather depressing statistics conceal a great deal of variation in conditions and performance and, quite logically, many examples of real success stories. A few sectors, like chemicals, are actually more technologically advanced and therefore more competitive than their counterparts in the old Germany. Several conurbations–usually mentioned are Dresden, Leipzig, and the Berlin-Brandenburg ring–have achieved commendable levels of prosperity. The region has staged a remarkable environmental comeback, and is now poised to reap the benefits of renewable energy, both on the production and consumption sides.

The fact remains, however, that the tail on the other end of the curve in eastern Germany is much longer, and far more worrisome, then anything ever seen in the west. And the general perception both in the public domain and within political circles is that eastern Germany, despite taking in over EURO 1.3 trillion in direct transfers from the federal government since 1990, shows few signs of a robust and self-sustaining growth dynamic. The specter of an eastern German Mezzogiorno looms large. In a much publicized stock-taking exercise on the twentieth anniversary of the fall of the wall, the Institut der deutschen Wirtschaft (IW) predicted that the eastern German economy would require another decade even to approximate western levels of growth and prosperity.[8]

As in other unification discourses and debates that received particularly close attention during this period, though, there was little if anything new about the actual numbers or the larger trends that they helped constitute. Framed in the context of the twenty year milestone, however, the political discussion of these numbers and trends produced some novel twists. One issue in particular is worthy of note here—the flap over the "Soli," or *Solidaritätszuschlag* (solidarity surcharge). This special surcharge on personal and corporate income taxes, with proceeds earmarked for financing the reconstruction of the eastern German economy, has gone through several phases since it was first introduced in 1991; in 1998, the levy was set at 5.5 percent. Up through the end of 2009, the solidarity surcharge had generated EURO 185 billion in transfers to eastern Germany.

The Soli found itself in the political crosshairs twice in 2009. During the first part of the year, as the political campaign season began to slowly heat up with an eye toward parliamentary elections in September, Thomas Strobl, a senior official in the Christian Democratic Union (CDU), announced that his party would seek an end to the Soli should the CDU find itself in a position to form the government after the election. "This would provide rapid, tangible relief for all employees and all taxpayers in the east and the west, with a minimum of bureaucratic overhead," claimed Strobl.[9] Although his announcement soon disappeared in the avalanche of proposals and counterproposals on tax reform advanced by the major contenders for power, it provided an indication of the where the limits of solidarity were to be found in the twenty-year-old unified Germany.

The Soli was back in the news in November, when the tax court (*Finanzgericht*) of the western state of Lower Saxony ruled that the solidarity surcharge was unconstitutional because a tax instrument of this nature, which is designed to address short term budgetary needs, cannot be used to meet ongoing or long-term needs. The state court ruling provoked a pained and sharp response not only from eastern German politicians but also from the highest levels of the Berlin coalition government; critics questioned why judges deemed it necessary to call into question an eighteen year-old political decision that had originally emanated from a strong sense of national solidarity. The ruling currently awaits final arbitration before the Federal Constitutional Court (*Bundesverfassungsgericht*)–a decision is expected sometime in 2010.

Unlike many other issues covered here, this discussion was not simply a ramped up version of an old debate. Rather, the Lower Saxony court ruling vaulted the Soli onto the national agenda almost out of the blue. The attention devoted to the issue seemed to embolden others to call into question the overwhelming focus of government economic policy on the eastern Länder. The day before the twentieth anniversary of the fall of the Berlin Wall, Federal Minister of Transportation Peter Ramsauer (Christian Social Union, CSU) gave an interview to *Welt am Sonntag*, in which he stated that one should not overlook the fact that there was a significant need for the modernization of infrastructure in the western parts of Germany, and the federal states there were certainly justified in demanding an "Aufbau West" program as compensation for their years of support for the ongoing "Aufbau Ost" efforts aimed at their eastern counterparts.[10] Ramsauer's comments earned him a swift rebuke from his coalition partners in the Free Democratic Party, who spoke of a "tasteless contribution by the federal minister" to the public discussions surrounding this important anniversary. Nevertheless, it appears that taboos have been weakened or even broken, and the outer limits of solidarity have come into view. For many in western Germany, unification is over, even if it remains an unfulfilled objective.

The Stasi and the Unrechtsstaat

On 9 February 2010, Karl-Heinz Felgner went on trial in Düsseldorf for robbing a drugstore at knife-point six months before. A former East German boxer who had won titles in both the featherweight and lightweight classes, Felgner was unemployed and living in a homeless shelter at the time of the alleged holdup. The trial was noteworthy not for the outcome– Felgner was convicted of the crime and sentenced to a prison term of six and one half years–but for the startling revelations contained in his testimony before the court. Felgner maintained that he left the GDR for West Germany in 1980 while in the employ of the East German secret police

(Stasi). He claimed that his mission was to kill Lutz Eigendorf, a former star soccer player for Dynamo Berlin who had defected to West Germany in 1979 while on a trip with Dynamo to play a friendly against FC Kaiserslautern. Even more remarkable, Felgner claimed that his assignment came directly from the top–specifically from Erich Mielke, Minister of State Security for the GDR, who was honorary chairman of Dynamo Berlin and a huge fan of the club. Felgner stated under oath: "I was supposed to kill Lutz Eigendorf. He played for Mielke's favorite club, then bunked off illegally. I accepted the murder contract but didn't fulfill it."[11]

To many, Lutz Eigendorf was nothing more than a poignant footnote in the sporting history of the Federal Republic. When he broke off from his Dynamo teammates and jumped into a get-away cab in Giessen, Eigendorf left behind a wife and two-year-old daughter whom he would never see again (his wife immediately filed for divorce, which was granted three months later by an East German court). Under the prevailing rules of the international governing body of soccer (FIFA), Eigendorf served a one-year suspension, during which time he was not permitted to play professionally for any other team other than Dynamo (which refused to sell his contract, presumably out of pique as the hard currency would undoubtedly have been welcomed in the east). He first signed on with Kaislerslautern, and then his contract was sold in 1982 to Eintracht Braunschweig, but injuries and inconsistent play on the field limited his appearances and overall impact. On 5 March 1983, the twenty-six year-old Eigendorf totaled his sports car on a very dangerous curve near Braunschweig. He succumbed to severe head injuries two days later. Tests revealed a significant amount of alcohol in Eigendorf's blood, and the police declared the cause of death an accident. Case closed.

Or perhaps not? Eigendorf's death raised suspicions immediately within East German dissident circles, where the East German regime and particularly its Stasi arm were regarded as ruthlessly efficient operators. In West Germany, by contrast, the official police explanation of his death was accepted with little or no comment. After the fall of the Wall, those who harbored doubts about the official version of Eigendorf's death were able to pursue their suspicions in the files of the now-defunct Stasi. Heribert Schwan, a Cologne journalist and filmmaker, took interest in the case a decade after unification, eventually producing both a film and a book on the subject. Based on files that Schwan uncovered in the Stasi archives, Mielke's intense interest in Eigendorf is indisputable; the Stasi chief assigned at one point or another over fifty agents to monitor the defector's whereabouts in the West, and went so far as to order some of his officers–

so-called "Romeos"–to seduce Eigendorf's wife and thereby keep her from maintaining contact with him. One of these Romeos eventually became her husband; another Romeo, it so happens, was Felgner himself! In fact, Schwan's research revealed that when Felgner failed in his role as Romeo, he was sent over to the West to report on Eigendorf from a close distance, even striking up a friendship with the professional footballer that brought them together on many an occasion. Although Schwan could find no smoking gun among the files–indeed, it appears that the files from the last few months of Eigendorf's life were destroyed–he claimed that there was strong circumstantial evidence that Eigendorf was poisoned, and that the automobile accident was caused by a hidden car "flashing" its high beams at the sports car as it was traversing this notorious stretch of highway. Moreover, Schwan claimed that two Stasi agents were involved in this assassination, one of whom was Felgner, whose contacts with his Stasi handlers increased in frequency in the run-up to the accident, and whose bank account swelled by DM 2,300 shortly after Eigendorf's death. Schwan's film and book, as well as a subsequent television documentary, prompted authorities to reopen the case, but the investigations came to nothing. Felgner was questioned at the time, but admitted to nothing more than being a Stasi agent at the time, and produced an alibi for the night of the automobile accident.

The renewed public attention on this long-forgotten case came about solely because of Felgner's assertion–or, in light of Schwan's decade-old charge, admission–at his trial that he had been sent to the West in 1980 on a Stasi contract not simply to monitor the whereabouts of a *Staatsfeind*, but in fact to kill a man who had had the temerity to cross the Minister of State Security over a personal matter: Dynamo Berlin. Whether or not Felgner is lying when he claims that he never intended to carry out the contract on Eigendorf's life is in many ways beside the point. His acknowledgment that he entered the West with a license to kill underscored in harsh terms not only what the GDR regime was capable of, but also the depths to which it was capable of descending. Public discourse was grappling not so much with new facts as with a new and chilling idea–there really were no limits to what the GDR regime could or would do. Back in the news, Heribert Schwan was joined by Hubertus Knabe, director of the Berlin-Hohenschönhausen Memorial (dedicated to victims of the Stasi), in calling for Eigendorf's body to be exhumed so it can be tested for the presence of neurotoxins. The case may not be closed after all.

The public's fascination with an otherwise unremarkable armed robbery trial must be seen in the context of the East Germany as an unjust state (Unrechtsstaat) a debate that has been running for twenty years more or less in academic channels, but has reached a curious kind of public crescendo as the twentieth anniversary season approached. The opposing sides are well known, and to maintain that they split the country neatly along East-West lines is to overlook the profoundly deep disagreements within eastern Germany over this question. The running dispute turns on what many outside of Germany would consider a largely legal-semantic distinction. Although most eastern Germans would readily agree that the GDR was not a regime bound by the rule of law ("die DDR war kein Rechtsstaat"), many bridle at the notion that the GDR was an unjust regime ("die DDR war ein Unrechtsstaat"), as this term locates their former regime squarely in the camp with the Nazi regime, the Ur-Unrechtsstaat in German legal circles. As such, the term carries a strong judgmental quality that eastern Germans generally reject–it tars their memories of their personal lives in GDR times, and also implicitly makes of them accomplices: ordinary Germans who tolerated the institutionalized injustice of Germanic Stalinism, much as their grandfathers and grandmothers permitted the Nazi Unrechtsstaat to flourish for a terrible time.

Although this was not a new controversy, it took out a new lease on life in 2009. In March, Erwin Sellering (Social Democratic Party, SPD), the minister-president of Mecklenburg West Pomerania, cautioned against damning the GDR as an Unrechtsstaat in a public interview, arguing that this had the effect of denigrating the many good things about life in the GDR, and moreover concealing the existence of the many weakness of the Federal Republic. His populist outburst, which played well in his home state, the poorest of the poor in eastern Germany, was echoed a few months later in the race for the office of President of the Federal Republic, when Gesine Schwan, SPD candidate for the post, refused to describe the GDR as an Unrechtsstaat in an interview with the *Tagesspiegel* in May. She rejected the use of the term, arguing that it was "too diffuse" and moreover it

> ...implies that everything that happened in this country was unjust. Looking back on the GDR, I would not go so far as to say that. The GDR was not a state based on the rule of law, there was no system of checks and balances on the use of power, and arbitrariness and uncertainty reigned. The justice system was expressly an instrument of the communist party, and as such not independent. This led to a general unsettling [*Verunsicherung*] of the population. But this does not mean that every single state action, for example in labor law or transportation law, was unjust.[12]

Reaction from within the SPD, even in the East, was sharply negative. Recalling the pervasive oppressiveness of the Stasi, the barbed wire and death strips, fellow party members wondered openly why the term

Unrechtsstaat was so inappropriate. Schwan's statements resonated, however, drawing favorable reactions from the Left Party as well as being reflected in public opinion currents in the East. Despite the best efforts of cooler, rational heads,[13] the discussion quickly settled around the traditional impasse, dividing those who see this as a straightforward case of describing reality with precise terms on the one hand, and those who see a thinly veiled political agenda intended to rob them of their right to remember and to claim a significant portion of their past.

Ironically, then, a debate launched by a noun, and one that is certainly subject to resolution based on a common understanding and acceptance of both the connotation and denotation of the word in question, has become irresolvable because the discussion has become bound up with identity and even individual psychology. Many ordinary eastern Germans react warily at best to news events like the Felgner trial, or to the earnest musings of the Feuilleton set over the Unrechtsstaat label, because they are tired of feeling like strangers in a strange land, deprived of legitimate access to a part of their past. According to public opinion surveys conducted in mid 2009 by the Emnid Institut, over half of eastern Germans held a positive outlook on the GDR; 49 percent believed that the good aspects of the GDR outweighed the bad.[14] It is perhaps no surprise that the attention devoted to the Unrechtsstaat debate was matched by media coverage of the Ostalgie[15] phenomenon–the sometimes wistful, sometimes defiant efforts of eastern Germans to look back fondly on life in the GDR. To some this represented an honest ability to parse personal experience–to separate out the good and the meaningful from the bad and the unjustified. To others, the phenomenon is nothing more than a shameless collective reach for the rose-tinted glasses, or simply mistaking "die guten alten Zeiten" of one's youth for laudable qualities of one's country of origin. A measure of the significance of the discussion of Ostalgie is the fact that Chancellor Merkel, typically very cautious about staking out positions on anything to do with possible East-West divides in unified Germany, chose to comment:

> The impression has mistakenly arisen, that both life in the GDR and the GDR regime itself were equally bad. We celebrated Christmas and Easter and Whitsun, and experienced anger and fights in our families as well as joy and desire. Everyone in the west thinks that those "over there" must be beside themselves with joy over unification because their lives were so awful. I'm struck by the absence of curiosity in the west about the positive experiences in those times.[16]

It is important to underscore that the positive sentiments expressed by ordinary eastern Germans about East Germany are typically not linked to any strong desire on their part to turn back the clock. In fact, overwhelming majorities among eastern Germans support the notion that the events of 1989/1990, which brought an end to the GDR, were a good thing.[17] But these complex bundles of attitudes on display in eastern Germany indicate that old reference points—and presumably values connected with them such as solidarity, security, and so on—are still very much alive in this region of the Federal Republic, and as such distinguish it from the older regions of the country and contribute in all likelihood to its enduring political, economic, and social distinctiveness.

Stasi Links and the Left Party

The Stasi and the Unrechtsstaat are ongoing themes for the Left Party, which has become a lightning rod for the ongoing debate about the GDR and the past. It seems that hardly a day goes by without an article appearing in a major German media outlet that chronicles the Stasi past and controversial present of a leading figure in this party. Not surprisingly, such stories have accumulated as it has taken on governing functions at the Land level, in coalition with the SPD (the so-called red-red governing formula). Since examples are legion; only a few will be mentioned here. In November, the news was full of accounts of the new red-red coalition in Brandenburg. Matthias Platzeck, leader of the SPD in this eastern Land, had announced his decision to form a governing coalition with the Left Party instead of the CDU; a condition for the coalition, however, was that the leader of the Left Party's Landtag caucus, Kerstin Kaiser, would not be appointed to a ministerial post in the SPD-Left Party state government because of her past association with the Stasi.

In virtually every way, this was a very ordinary case. During the 1980s, Kaiser was recruited by the Stasi at age eighteen as an *inoffizielle Mitarbeiterin* (unofficial co-worker, IM) code-named "Kathrin," during a study abroad stint in Leningrad. Her Stasi past came to light in 1994, and the revelations ultimately forced her to step down as a member of the Bundestag. Kaiser went on to considerable political success at the Land level, but her climb up the political ladder halted on the basis of these previously known revelations in 2009. What gave this by now familiar narrative a curious angle was the contrition Kaiser demonstrated in the years after the story first broke. Kaiser personally contacted all the individuals on whom she had informed, and expressed her sincere regret for her actions; most of those she contacted accepted her apology, according to news sources.[18] It all seemed to suggest that whatever the circumstances of the Stasi involvement and whatever the aftermath–stubborn denial or a real effort to confront one's past–there were strict limits on what is considered *salonfähig*. It also suggested that in unified Germany, however completely and profoundly an individual works through his or her past (*Vergangenheitsbewältigung*), broader acceptance, to say nothing of forgiveness, may not be forthcoming.

The story–and one possible moral–did not end there, however. In a sign of how quickly narratives can change, the attention devoted to the Brandenburg coalition negotiations, in which the Kaiser case featured prominently, turned up additional instances of prominent Left Party politicians with Stasi pasts. The defensive, combative reactions of those involved did little to help the image of the new party[19]–indeed, it reinforced the prevailing mindset on both sides of the "Mauer im Kopf."

Viewed from a broader perspective than this particular debate frame, the Left Party is either a sign that something is profoundly amiss in unified Germany, or it is a sign that democracy in Germany 2010 is healthy and functional. Or perhaps, more accurately, it is a bit of both. The surging fortunes of the party, most recently confirmed in the September 2009 federal elections, as well as its remarkably strong base in the eastern Länder,[20] suggest that the party has established itself at least for the time being as the voice of a distinctive region within the Federal Republic. One might say this is nothing new for Germany–after all, the CSU has dominated Bavarian politics from the very inception of the Federal Republic of Germany. The difference, of course, is that the CSU has operated within the broad mainstream of postwar German politics, whether it be in economic, social, or foreign policy. The same cannot be said–at least not yet–about the Left Party. On issues ranging from fiscal policy to social policy to NATO and the European Union, the Left Party has staked out positions that call into question decades of cross-party political consensus.

There is much one could ask about the Left Party. As it strives to be regarded as a viable junior coalition partner with the ailing SPD, will it be forced to abandon portions of its PDS policy legacy, becoming in the process less connected to the eastern German experience? Will it be able to withstand the inevitable onslaught of competition from the Social Democrats who, shorn of the constraints of governing, are now free as an opposition party to concentrate their fire on their left flanks? How will the party cope with the sudden departure of Oskar Laftontaine, the iconic figurehead of the left who many believe is largely responsible for the party's success in establishing a secure foothold outside the of the eastern Länder?

These are all important questions, but somewhat off the subject here, which is how and to what effect the Left Party phenomenon has become part of the complex public narrative about unification twenty years on. In no small way, the party's enduring presence, combined with its feisty public presentation of self, is a clear barometer of lingering singularities in the former GDR: a place where the values of equality and justice still resonate strongly; a place where the politics of resentment plays well; and a place where an almost ahistorical German nationalism flourishes. As such, the fortunes of the party in the new Länder will tell us a great deal about the state of the region, and by extension the state of the state.

Conclusions

According to Günther Grass, the complex processes set in motion twenty years ago have yet to come to closure: "To this day, unification hasn't happened yet. Unity is completed, but only on paper."[21] As a recent *Zeit-Online* op-ed observed in pointed fashion, neither the current ruling cabinet of the federal government nor soccer's Bundesliga boasts a single member from the former GDR, underscoring the political and economic feebleness of the eastern piece of the all-German puzzle as well as Grass's broader point.[22] The vignettes discussed in this chapter, which range across politics, economics, society, and culture in contemporary Germany, reveal that when the eye is trained directly on some variant of the question "Is Germany unified twenty years after the events of 1989-1990?," the signs of progress on unification seem to vanish into thin air, much in the manner of the proverbial blind spot. The reason why is quite clear—the discourses on economic development, *Vergangenheitsbewältigung,* and related themes revolve around benchmarks and reference points that originate in frames developed within the Federal Republic—for example, the extent to which eastern German economic progress measures up against the "Made in (West) Germany" standard. Measured against these frames, the dominant impression is naturally one of shortfall, even failure, whether the metric is economic, political, or even moral. Viewed straight on, unification does not exist.

From a different vantage point—looking away from the blind spot, in other words—unification is complete. Eastern Germany's apparently stubborn refusal to "regress to the mean" or to converge to the western German norm is an unalterable fact. As a result, unified Germany is a fundamentally different country than the pre 1990 Federal Republic. Its expanded borders capture a broader range of experiences and outcomes. Perhaps this is the lasting legacy of unification: dehomogenization, and consequently a broadening of the sense of what is, and what it means to be, German. Just look slightly away, and you'll see it.

Taking a further step back, it is a little sad that the failures, tensions, and bitterness–the perspective of the citizen pundit–have come to dominate the discourse on the twentieth anniversary of unification, instead of the more optimistic and celebratory stance of the amateur historian. Moreover, it is even sadder, or at least ironic, that such a dour mood persists at a time when Germany's international stature has grown, as Eric Langenbacher argues in the conclusion, and as the country's normative influence increases, as in Beverly Crawford's analysis. Perhaps this is simply another dimension of the blindspot–if only Germans could see in themselves what so much of the rest of the world recognizes from the outside.

Notes

1. "Germany to Build Monument for Peaceful Revolution of 1989," *REGIERUNGonline/ Die Bundesregierung*, 6 November 2007; available at http://www.budesregierung.de/ nn_919412/Content/EN/Artikel/2007/11/2007-11-06-denkmal-dt-einheit_en.html; accessed 23 February 2010.
2. Cathrin Schaer, "Little is Left Today of the Cold War's Most Famous Monument," *Spiegel Online*, 16 July 2009; available at http://www.spiegel.de/international/germany/ 0,1518,druck-636586,00.html; accessed 23 February 2010.
3. Ibid.
4. Jan Otakar Fischer, "The Art of Reunification," The Design Observer Group, 9 November 2009; available at http://www.designobserver.com/places/entryprint.html?entry= 11707; accessed 23 February 2010.
5. Ibid.
6. Ibid.
7. "Durch eine gemeinsame Anstrengung wird es uns gelingen, Mecklenburg-Vorpommern und Sachsen-Anhalt, Brandenburg, Sachsen und Thüringen schon bald wieder in *blühende Landschaften* zu verwandeln, in denen es sich zu leben und zu arbeiten lohnt." Helmut Kohl in a televised speech 1 July 1990. Emphasis added.
8. As referenced in "Ostdeutschland schließt frühestens 2020 zum Westen auf," *Zeit Online-Deutschland*, 3 November 2009; available at http://www.zeit.de/wirtschaft/ 2009-11/ost-west-vergleich-studie-iw?page=all&print-true; accessed 23 February 2010.
9. "CDU will nach Wahl Soli abschaffen," *Süddeutsche Zeitung*, 17 April 2009; available at http://www.sueddeutsche.de/politik/752/465344/text/print.html; accessed 23 February 2010.
10. "FDP nennt Ramsauers Vorschlag eine ‚Provokation,'" *Zeit Online-Deutschland*, 8 November 2009; available at http://www.zeit.de/wirtschaft/2009-11/fdp-ramsauer- aufbau-west?page=all&print-true; accessed 23 February 2010.

11. Uli Hesse-Lichtenberger, "The Curious Case of Lutz Eigendorf–Part 1," *ESPNsoccernet: Europe*, 23 February 2010; available at http://soccernet.espn.com/print?id=745905& type=story&cc=5901; accessed 23 February 2010.

12. Direct quote taken from Stephan Haselberger, „Gegenwind aus der Ost-SPD für Gesine Schwan," *Zeit Online-Deutschland*, 19 May 2009; available at http://www.zeit.de/online/ 2009/21/ddr-spd-schwan?page=all&print-true; accessed 23 February 2010.

13. See for example Marianne Birthler, "Liebe Ossiversteher!," *Zeit Online-Deutschland*, 8 July 2009; available at http://www.zeit.de/online/2009/28/op-ed-Unrechtsstaat?page= all&print-true; accessed 23 February 2010.

14. "Ostdeutsche haben positives DDR-Bild," *Zeit Online-Deutschland*, 26 June 2009; available at http://www.zeit.de/online/2009/27/ddr-bild-positiv=2?page=all&print-true; accessed 23 February 2010.

15. Ost + Nostalgie = Ostalgie.

16. Stephan Lebert, "Es gab us wirklich," *Zeit Online-Deutschland*, 11 November 2009; available at http://www.zeit.de/online/2009/46/DDR-46?page=all&print-true; accessed 23 February 2010. For a scholarly account, see Timothy Barney, "When We Was Red: Good Bye Lenin? and Nostalgia for the 'Everyday GDR,'" *Communication and Critical/Cultural Studies* 6, no. 2 (2009): 132-51.

17. "Ostdeutsche haben positives DDR-Bild." Polls taken around the same time by other organizations produced similar results, although it should not be overlooked that small but significant minorities in eastern Germany (upwards of 13 percent) profess a desire to see the wall reinstated. "Jeder achte Deutsche will die Mauer zurück," *Spiegel online*, 8 November 2009; available at http://www.spiegel.de/politik/Deutschland/0,1518,druck-660034,00.html; accessed 23 February 2010.

18. Tina Hildebrandt, "Die Grenzen der Schuld," *Zeit Online-Deutschland*, 12 November 2009; available at http://www.zeit.de/online/2009/47/Linke-Brandenburg-Kaiser? page=all&print-true; accessed 23 February 2010.

19. A Left Party official in Mecklenburg-Vorpommern, while distancing himself from the apparent efforts of some of his compatriots in Brandenburg to whitewash their biographies, complained that what was going on in Potsdam was not an overcoming of the past (*Vergangenheitsbewältigung*), "but a witchhunt ... intended to torpedo the red-red model." Matthias Meisner,"Die Linke zeigt sich fon Stasi-Vertrickungen geplagt," *Zeit Online-Deutschland*, 3 December 2009; available at http://www.zeit.de/politik/ deutschland/2009-12/brandenburg-stasi-linkspartei?page=all&print-true; accessed 23 February 2010.

20. The Left Party received 11.9 percent of the vote, a 3.2 percentage point increase over their previous federal election result and only 11.1 percentage points back of the SPD, which registered its worst election tally in the history of the Federal Republic. At the Land level in eastern Germany, the Left Party is now generally speaking the second strongest party in the region, just behind the CDU but comfortably ahead of the SPD. In the 2009 election, the Left Party won sixteen *Direktmandate* (all in the east), twice as many as the SPD.

21. Christoph Dieckmann and Christof Siemes, "Großer Hofferei hing ich nie an," *Zeit Online-Literatur*, 29 April 2009; available at http://www.zeit.de/2009/05/Grass-Interview?page=all&print-true; accessed 23 February 2010.

22. Angela Merkel was born in Hamburg. Helmut Schümann, "20 Jahre danach: Was ist Deutschland?," *Zeit Online-Zeitgeschehen*, 8 November 2009; available at http:// www.zeit.de/politik/2009-11/was-ist-deutschland?page=all&print-true; accessed 23 February 2010.

$\mathcal{I}$s There a
Single German Party System?

• • • • • • • • • • • • • • •

Russell J. Dalton and Willy Jou

Few aspects of politics have been as variable as electoral politics in the two decades since German unification. In the East, the collapse of the communist state led to the emergence of new political parties and citizen groups in 1989-90, which were soon usurped by parties from the West. Thus, easterners had to learn about democratic electoral politics and party competition from an almost completely new start. In the West, voters confronted a changing partisan landscape with the addition of the Party of Democratic Socialism (PDS) and then the Left Party (Linke), and the variability in the established parties' policy positions as they faced the challenges of unification.

The centrality of elections and political parties to democracy and the governing process makes it especially important to study changes in partisan politics since unification. This chapter first provides a brief history of the voting results in Bundestag elections up through the 2009 election, raising the question of whether there is one party system or two. Then, we examine voters' ties to political parties, analyzing the evolving class and religious bases of party support in West and East. Next we consider whether citizens are developing affective party ties that reflect the institutionalization of a party system and voter choice. This leads to a concluding discussion about the prospects for the German party system in the immediate future.

The Evolution of the Party System(s)

The 1990 Bundestag election signaled the initial formation of two similar, but distinct, party systems in West and East. At one level there was a basic commonality. Already by the March 1990 Volkskammer election in the East, the larger, established, and well-funded political parties from the Federal Republic took over the electoral process in the new Länder. By the October 1990 Bundestag election, the eastern party system had essentially become an extension of the party system from the West (with the addition of the PDS).

Even at that time, however, there were major contrasts between parties in both regions. The Christian Democratic Union/Christian Social Union (CDU/CSU) captured a nearly equal vote share in the West and East, as a reaction to Chancellor Helmut Kohl's successful negotiation of the unification process (see Table 1).[1] While others, especially Oskar Lafontaine and the Social Democrats (SPD), looked on the events with wonder or uncertainty, Kohl quickly embraced the idea of closer ties between the two Germanies. Yet, the CDU's strength in the East ran against the leftist tendencies of the region dating back to the Weimar Republic and the Kaiserreich. In addition, the social bases of the CDU vote in class and religious terms were in stark contrast to their voter base in the West.[2] The Party of Democratic Socialism also emerged as a distinct regional and ideological party to represent the East, and the SPD fared poorly among eastern voters.

The CDU-led governing coalition lost votes and seats in the 1994 election, although Kohl retained a slim majority. The different centers of gravity in West and East, however, were becoming more apparent. The Free Democratic Party (FDP) initially appealed to easterners, due in part to Hans Dietrich Genscher's eastern roots, but its bourgeois liberalism and conservative economic policies eroded its support by 1994. From 12.9 percent of the eastern vote in 1990, the party fell to only 3.5 percent in 1994 (see Table 1). Similarly, the Greens were becoming a predominately western party as they increased their vote share in the West and lost support in the East. The Greens' postmaterial program was at odds with an eastern electorate that was more concerned with their own materialist needs. In addition, the PDS evolved from a postcommunist successor party into a major voice for eastern voters, capturing nearly a fifth of the eastern vote.

Table 1: Election Results in West and East, 1990-2009 (in percent)

Party	1990 West	1990 East	1994 West	1994 East	1998 West	1998 East	2002 West	2002 East	2005 West	2005 East	2009 West	2009 East
CDU/CSU	44.3	41.8	42.1	38.5	37.1	27.3	40.8	28.3	37.5	25.3	34.6	29.8
SPD	35.7	24.3	37.5	31.5	42.3	35.1	38.3	39.7	35.1	30.4	24.1	17.9
FPD	10.6	12.9	7.7	3.5	7.0	3.3	7.6	6.4	10.2	8.0	15.4	10.6
Greens	4.8	6.2	7.9	4.3	7.3	4.1	9.4	4.7	8.8	5.2	11.5	6.8
PDS/Left Party	0.3	11.1	1.0	19.8	1.2	21.6	1.1	16.9	4.9	25.3	8.3	28.5
Other parties	4.3	3.7	3.9	2.4	5.2	8.6	2.8	4.0	3.5	5.8	6.1	6.4

Source: Der Bundeswahlleiter (www.bundeswahlleiter.de).

Note: Table presents Zweitstimmen vote percentages; the West is the earlier Federal Republic and West Berlin, the East is the new Länder and East Berlin.

While change in 1994 primarily affected the smaller parties, regional forces began to affect the major parties more clearly by the 1998 election. The accumulation of sixteen years of governing and the special challenges of unification had taken their toll on the CDU/CSU and Kohl. There had been dramatic improvements in living conditions in the East, but nothing close to the blooming landscapes and tax-free growth that Kohl had promised in 1990. The CDU/CSU thus fared poorly in the election, especially in the eastern Länder that were frustrated by their persistent second-class status. From 41.8 percent of the eastern vote in 1990, the CDU/CSU dropped to 27.3 percent in 1998, indicating the re-emergence of the East's leftist history. The Social Democrats' vote total increased by nearly half over its share in 1990, and the PDS doubled its vote share compared to 1990. If one includes the SPD, PDS and Greens, more than 60 percent of the eastern electorate voted for leftist parties in 1998, compared to 51 percent in the West. This facilitated the formation of a new SPD-Green government with Gerhard Schröder as Chancellor. The FDP, Greens and PDS also deepened their distinct regional bases.

The CDU made some gains after the 1998 election and seemed poised to win several state elections in 1999 and 2000–and then lightning struck. Investigations showed that Kohl had accepted illegal campaign contributions while he was chancellor. His allies within the CDU were forced to resign, and the party's electoral fortunes suffered. The CDU/CSU chose Edmund Stoiber, the head of the Christian Social Union, as its chancellor candidate in 2002. Even though the CDU/CSU gained votes in the West, along with their potential FDP allies, the SPD-Green coalition retained control of the government.

When early elections were called in 2005, the CDU/CSU offered Angela Merkel as their chancellor candidate. As an easterner, one might have expected that she would have special appeal to eastern voters. The CDU/CSU, however, lost vote shares in both West and East. Lafontaine's efforts to link leftists in the West and the PDS voter bloc in the East severely eroded support for the SPD as well, which led the CDU by only five percent in the eastern Länder. The PDS/Linke appeared to be a cross-regional alliance, yet it gained only 4.9 percent of the vote in the West compared to 25.3 percent in the East. Conversely, the Greens and FDP drew greater support from the western electorate. With such a fragmented electorate and party system, the second coming of the "Grand Coalition" between CDU/CSU and SPD formed the post election government.

Merkel and the CDU/CSU retained power after the 2009 election in coalition with the resurgent FDP. Yet, both Volksparteien lost votes in 2009, especially the SPD.[3] This probably reflects a negative reaction to the Grand Coalition and Germany's current economic problems, which generated new support for the three minor parties. The FDP, Greens, and the Left Party all won more votes than in any prior election. Yet, even in this election, the East-West gap is apparent. Leftist parties won a majority of votes in the East–where the Left Party received almost the same vote share as the CDU. In contrast, the FDP and Greens gained significantly larger vote shares in the West than in the East, albeit from different voter bases. The CDU/CSU also garnered a substantially larger vote share in the West, so that a majority of Westerners voted for parties in the new center-right government.

In formal terms, the Federal Republic has a single party system that spans the East-West divide. But below this surface similarity exists a persisting difference between the parties in East and West, and to a degree this difference has persisted in the two decades since unification. The East has become a bastion of support for leftist parties. Nearly all the parliamentary parties have significantly greater support in one region than the other. This is most clearly evident in the Left Party, but applies to the CDU/CSU, FDP, and Greens as well. If one simply sums the differences in West-East support across all the parties, the last two elections have averaged more than a 20 percent gap in party support–a difference that has not narrowed over time.[4]

Alignment and Realignment in Party Support

The differences in party vote shares in West and East are an initial sign of the contrasts in the party systems across regions. This contrast may run deeper in terms of the bases of party support. Party choice in West Germany long has been structured along class and religious lines.[5] Thus, we ask how these two cleavages are related to party support. In the former East Germany, where parties lacked core constituencies rooted in longstanding occupational and confessional affiliations, the first few postunification elections saw unexpected patterns with respect to class voting.[6] Accumulated electoral experience in the East, however, may have led to convergence with Western trends. Moreover, the large differences in the religious composition of the electorate between the two regions may affect levels of party support.

Class Voting

Following previous studies, we analyze class voting by identifying three major categories based on the respondent's occupation: working class, old middle class, and new middle class.[7] The last category, which includes white collar employees in both the public and private sectors, constitutes the largest occupational group, comprising around 60 percent in the West and 50 percent in the East (civil servants make up a larger proportion in the West). About one-quarter of respondents in the West belong to the working class compared with over 40 percent in the East during the 1990s, though the latter figure declined in the 2000s. The percentage of the old middle class is very stable in the West at around 10-15 percent. There were few entrepreneurs or free professionals in the East at the beginning of the 1990s, but this group has since increased to a level comparable to the West. It is important to keep these shares of the overall population in mind as we examine data on class voting.

Space constraints preclude presentation of data on the class voting pattern for each party over time across both regions.[8] To summarize the broad patterns, we created a voting index for each class category by subtracting the vote percentage for leftist parties (SPD, Greens, PDS/Linke) from votes for the Right (CDU/CSU and FDP). Positive values indicate a preference for rightist parties. Figures 1a-c show this index for all three class categories, separately for East and West to compare whether and how each class votes differently in the two regions.

As expected, old middle class voters consistently prefer rightist parties (see Figure 1a). Although the overwhelming advantage that rightist parties enjoyed among this group in 1990 has since eroded, the voting index remains positive. With the exception of the 1990 election, the CDU/CSU and FDP perform better among the old middle class in the West than in the East. This difference has widened during the 2000s in the West, as the conservative parties regained old middle class support at a higher

Figure 1: Class Voting Patterns over Time

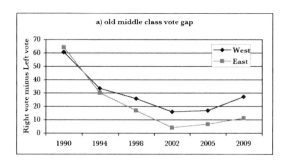

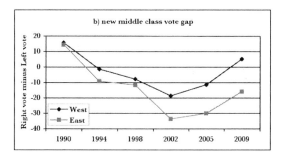

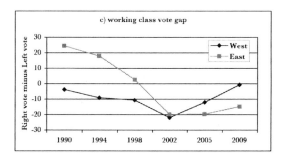

Sources: Forschungsgruppe Wahlen, Politbarometer surveys, 1990-2009 (see endnote 7).
Note: The figure plots the vote gap calculated by subtracting vote share of Left parties (SPD + Greens + PDS/Linke) from vote share of center-Right parties (CDU/CSU + FDP).

rate. An examination of the two largest parties reveals that while SPD vote shares are nearly the same for this stratum in both parts of the country, the CDU generally receives slightly less support among the old middle class in the East.

Leftist parties have generally commanded a larger share of the new middle class vote (negative values in Figure 1b) in both parts of the country. Their failure to do so in the West in 2009 is attributable to the collapse in support for the SPD. We can once again observe trajectories trending in the same direction, but the vote gap has widened since 2002, with leftist parties winning higher vote shares among white collar workers in the East. The Greens have performed particularly well among western civil servants in recent elections. The Volksparteien were competitive over the new middle class vote during most of the 1990s, though the SPD achieved greater success in 2002 and 2005 before declining sharply in 2009. In 2009, the Left Party nearly matched the CDU vote among the eastern new middle class, leaving the Social Democrats well behind in third place.

East-West differences are most clearly exposed when we examine working class voting patterns (see Figure 1c). In the West, the SPD has long received a clear plurality from these voters (whereas the Greens do poorly among this class). In stark contrast, the Social Democrats' share of workers' votes in the East is similar to–in fact often lower than–its share among new middle class voters. During the first several postunification elections, blue collar voters in the East supported rightist parties more than the left by a significant margin–an unexpected reversal of not only western patterns but also our traditional understanding of class voting. This anomaly is probably attributable to the weak bonds between eastern workers and the SPD, an initial attraction to Kohl as a result of unification, and negativity toward the Left in reaction to experiences under the German Democratic Republic.

If we use the standard Alford class voting index, namely the difference in support for leftist parties between the middle class (both old and new) and the working class, we find mostly positive values in the West for each election in conformity with traditional models of class voting (see Table 2).[9] The level of class voting, however, is a shadow of what it was in the Federal Republic 1950s and 1960s, and becomes essentially insignificant in recent elections.

Table 2: The Alford Index of Class Voting in West and East

Region	Election					
	1990	1994	1998	2002	2005	2009
West	13.3	7.0	4.3	5.2	3.2	2.0
East	-3.5	-13.0	-6.3	-4.4	-2.1	-1.0

Sources: Forschungsgruppe Wahlen, Politbarometer surveys, 1990-2009 (see endnote 7).

Note: The table presents the Alford class voting index that is calculated by subtracting vote share of left parties (SPD + Greens + PDS/Linke) among the middle class (combined old middle class and new middle class) from the leftist vote among the working class. A positive value means the working class leans toward leftist parties.

Regional patterns in workers' vote that had converged over the first four postunification elections are now diverging. Eastern workers have leaned toward leftist parties in recent elections. Moreover, the composition of the leftist vote also varies across regions. The SPD's percentage of votes among eastern workers consistently lags behind its share in the West, but there is disproportionate support for the PDS/Left Party in the East. The Left Party not only attracted increased blue collar support in 2009 in the East, but actually won a plurality among working-class easterners for the first time. In broader terms, leftist parties in the East achieved greater success among white collar employees and civil servants than workers with the exception of 2009 (see Table 2). Whether the narrowing of this gap in the last two elections portends a continuing trend awaits confirmation in future elections.

Religious Voting

In addition to class, religious affiliation (or the lack thereof) is another long-standing factor in structuring voting behavior.[10] Catholics and deeply religious voters in the Federal Republic have strongly favored the CDU/CSU. However, there are dramatic differences in the religious composition of both regions. Catholics comprise approximately 40 percent of the population in the West, but have a small presence in the East (slightly over 5 percent). Protestants are more sizeable in the West (around 40 percent) than in the East (below 30 percent). Finally, whereas less than one-fifth of the Western public claim no religious affiliation, this is true of up to two-thirds of easterners, most of whom were socialized under the atheist doctrine of communism.

Similar to our class voting analyses, we compare religious groups in their support for the rightist and leftist party blocs with a vote difference index.[11] Figures 2a-c shows the gap in rightist minus leftist vote share among each group. As expected, Catholics display a clear preference for the Right (Figure 2a), specifically the CDU/CSU (the FDP usually receives below-average support from this group). The magnitude of this advantage is practically the same in both regions in the 2002 and 2005 elections. This advantage, however, only translates into a large lead in actual votes in the West, since Catholics constitute a small minority in the East. Unusually, in 2009 the rightist parties led their opponents by a considerably wider margin among Western Catholics thanks to increased support for the FDP among this group.

Since Christian Democrat support among Protestants traditionally has been lower than Catholics in the Federal Republic, many anticipated that unification would bring about a decline in CDU/CSU fortunes by adding many more Protestants than Catholics to the electorate. Election results in the first decade of unified Germany confounded such expectations. Figure

Figure 2: Religious Voting Patterns over Time

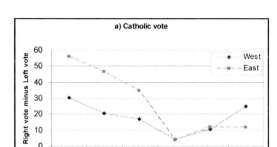

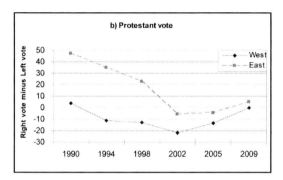

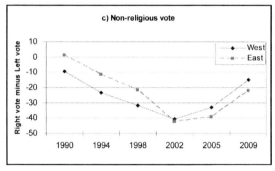

Sources: Forschungsgruppe Wahlen, Politbarometer surveys, 1990-2009 (see endnote 7).

Note: The figure plots the vote gap calculated by subtracting vote share of Left parties (SPD + Greens + PDS/Linke) from vote share of center-Right parties (CDU/CSU + FDP).

2b shows a distinct difference in vote patterns among eastern and western Protestants. Throughout the 1990s, leftist parties did better than the Right in the West, but the reverse was true in the East. In the 2002 and 2005 elections, leftist parties finally managed to win a plurality among eastern Protestants, but they still enjoyed less support among this constituency than might have been predicted based on western voting patterns. Results in 2009 saw a plurality of eastern Protestants casting their ballots for right-ist parties. Also noteworthy is the convergence of Protestant voters in both parts of the country over the last decade. In terms of the two large parties, the Christian Democrats have always won a greater share of the Protestant vote in the East, while the Social Democrats have achieved greater success among western Protestants.[12]

Finally, leftist parties are dominant in both East and West among voters who profess no religious affiliation. The magnitude of their leftist prefer-ence has increased over time, and regional differences are generally mod-est (see Figure 2c). Within this party bloc, the Greens perform particular well in the West. Similarly, the PDS/Left Party finds its core constituency among eastern voters without religious attachment. For example, fully one-third of non-religious easterners voted for the Left Party in 2009. This translates into a greater advantage for the Left Party than the Greens, con-sidering the much larger size of the non-religious group in the East. While the CDU/CSU vote share among non-religious voters is similarly low in both regions, the SPD typically secures a slightly higher proportion of non-religious vote in the West. Similar to the two confessional groups, differ-ences in voting behavior between eastern and western non-religious voters have diminished since the 1990s.

In sum, this section leads to three general observations. First, long-term dealignment in sociostructural cleavages notwithstanding, occupational and confessional classifications still modestly influences voting behavior. The CDU/CSU still counts on solid Catholic support, while the leftist parties (par-ticularly the Greens and PDS/Left Party) appeal to non-religious voters. The self-employed favor the right (the FDP consistently draws above-average support among this group), while blue collar workers in the East have grad-ually come to join their western counterparts in supporting leftist parties.

Second, the differing proportions among occupational and confessional categories across regions affect party fortunes. For instance, the large num-ber of non-religious voters in the East strongly benefits leftist parties, par-ticularly the Left Party. Even the CDU has a significant percentage of non-religious and Protestant supporters among its eastern voter base. In contrast, the new middle class is somewhat larger in the West, and this benefits parties such as the Greens and FDP that appeal to these voters. The shrinkage of the blue collar constituency in both parts of the country and the increase in the proportion of old middle class voters in the East could adversely affect the fortune of leftist parties.

Third, there are some persisting voting differences between East and West. Left/Right patterns of voting have widened among each occupational category in the most recent elections, although religious voting patterns have narrowed.[13] These patterns are even more striking if one disaggregates leftist and rightist party blocs and compares support for specific parties over time. We find a negative Alford index in the East and a positive class voting index for the West. To a significant degree, party constellations in East and West remain distinct.

Party Attachments and the Evolution of the Party System

The electoral experiences of the past two decades should have influenced Germans' deeper orientations toward partisan politics. One important trait is the development of long-term psychological attachments to political parties or "party identification." This concept has proven to be one of the most important concepts in understanding electoral behavior in contemporary democracies.[14] Party attachments link voters to their preferred party, provide cues on how to evaluate the political issues and politicians of the day, and stimulate partisans to participate. The existence of such party ties also creates a stable basis of party competition, ensuring the political parties of a core base of support and limiting the potential for new parties to form.

We should expect that these party attachments would strengthen in the East in the years since unification. Party attachments arise from inherited family loyalties and accumulated electoral experience, and both were initially lacking in the East.[15] Few easterners initially should (or could) have displayed the deep affective partisan loyalties that constitute a sense of party identification. Overnight easterners became participants in the Federal Republic's electoral system and had to learn about democratic elections and party competition. Social learning theory would suggest that these party ties should strengthen after twenty years of electoral experience, which would be a positive sign of the institutionalization of electoral politics in the East.

Previous electoral research focused on the extent of party attachments in the West.[16] In the 1960s, the party system consolidated and party attachments strengthened. Starting in the mid-1970s, however, a decreasing proportion of Westerners express strong feelings of partisan identity, and a growing number do not feel close to any political party. Several factors seem to account for this decline in partisanship in the West. After the decades of postwar growth and policy accomplishments, starting in the 1970s the political parties have struggled with economic recession and the rise of new political issues that create new bases of political competition. Other political institutions–such as citizen action groups and public interest lobbies–arose to represent these new political interests and challenge the political parties. A series of political scandals at the national and state levels also tarnished party images. In short, these developments created doubts about the ability of political parties to represent the public's interests effectively.

In addition, the growing sophistication of the western electorate should weaken individual party ties.[17] With increased interest and knowledge about politics, people are better able to make their own political decisions without a habitual dependence on party attachments. Furthermore, as voters began to focus on issues as a basis of electoral choice, they became more likely to defect from their normal party predispositions, which then erodes these predispositions. This general pattern is described as a dealignment of long-term party attachments in the Federal Republic. Unification appeared to accelerate this dealignment process in the West, creating major new policy challenges for the Federal Republic. Parties of both the Left and Right struggled to deal with the new political issues of globalization, European integration, and multiculturalism that confront the country today. At question is whether party ties have restabilized twenty years after unification.

Table 3 tracks party identifications among western and eastern voters from unification to the 2005 election (2009 results are not yet available). The western data indicate a slight erosion in the strength of party attachments since 1990. Back in the 1972 election, 75 percent of the electorate indicated attachment to their preferred party. By 1990 this group of partisans fell to 71 percent of the public, and by 2005 only 63 percent. The postunification pace of dealignment has continued the long-term erosion of party ties in the West, and today, fewer Germans now have partisan ties compared to other established democracies.[18] This suggests that Germany's special problems of unification may have reinforced a more general dealigning process affecting other democracies.

Table 3: The Strength of Partisanship (in percent)

Partisan Strength	West					East				
	1990	1994	1998	2002	2005	1990	1994	1998	2002	2005
Very Strong	11	12	9	12	10	4	6	7	7	7
Strong	29	24	22	25	28	22	19	17	21	24
Weak	31	31	31	27	27	35	34	30	26	26
No party/Don't know	27	31	36	32	34	37	40	44	45	40
Refused	2	2	2	3	2	3	1	2	2	2
Total	100	100	100	100	100	101	100	100	101	101

Source: Data from German election studies collected by the Forschungsgruppe Wahlen; several pre-election and a post-election survey are included for most time points.

Regular measurement of partisanship in the East began in 1991. By then, most voters already had some direct electoral experience with party competition, having participated in two national elections (the March 1990 Volkskammer and December 1990 Bundestag elections), as well as regional and local contests. Still, easterners were less likely to express a sense of party attachment (61 percent in the East versus 71 percent in the West). A decade and half later, eastern partisanship remains essentially unchanged.

What does the lower level of partisanship in the East imply for the development of electoral politics among these citizens? In one sense, the level of partisanship in the East in 1991 was probably higher than one might expect in a 'new' party system, possibly because most easterners had watched West German electoral politics from afar for decades. In addition, they began their democratic experience with established, efficient, and well-organized parties (in part because the western parties dominated electoral politics in the East). Still, partisan ties are not significantly increasing in the East as social learning theory would predict. The past two decades have been a period of dramatic political change for easterners, having yielded four different government coalitions (1990, 1998, 2005, and 2009). Party positions and party leadership have been relatively volatile, including the addition of the PDS to the party system and its later reformation into the Left Party. Many easterners also feel overlooked by the partisan politics of the Federal Republic. Moreover, many of the dealigning forces present in the West probably carry over to the East.

Scholars have argued that the rapidity with which easterners form party attachments is an important measure of their development of stable political orientations and their integration into the Federal Republic's party system.[19] For instance, partisan attachments encourage individuals to participate in electoral politics and form positive images about the process. Partisans generally are more stable in their voting preferences, since they enter elections with standing party predispositions. Therefore, splitting one's party support on the *Erststimme* and *Zweitstimme* (first and second votes) as well as shifting voting preferences between elections, are more common among non-partisans. Various pre-election polls in 2009 suggested that as many as a quarter of the electorate was unsure about their vote a week before the election, and ticket-splitting again appeared high.[20]

Detailed survey data on party attachments are not yet available from the 2009 Bundestag election, but we can demonstrate the continuing differences in party connectedness with evidence from the 2005 election study (see Figure 3).[21] For instance, the stronger partisan ties in the West are a stimulus to electoral participation. Turnout has been significantly lower in the East, and this continues in 2009.[22] Similarly, even with an easterner running as chancellor in 2005, interest in the election was slightly lower in the East. Additional multivariate analyses (not shown) demonstrate that about half of these regional differences are attributable to the weaker party ties in the East.

Figure 3: Evidence of Weak Party Ties in West and East

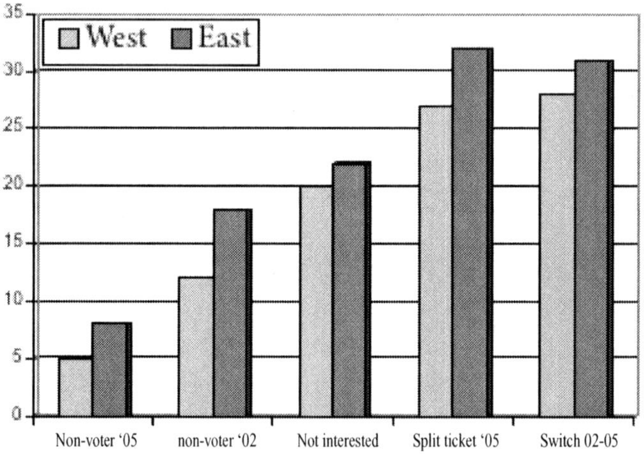

Source: 2005 Germany Election Study (CSES)

Partisanship also shapes the stability and predictability of voting choices. The percentage of voters who change party votes between elections has been steadily growing in the Federal Republic, reaching 28 percent of voters in 2005. This pattern of partisan change is strongly related to the strength of party ties, with only 18 percent of strong partisans changing parties between 2002 and 2005, compared to 42 percent among non-partisans. This contributes to a slightly higher proportion of fluid voters in the East in 2005 (and in prior elections). One example from the 2005 Bundestag election clearly illustrates the impact of party attachments: 11.1 percent of non-partisans voted for the new PDS/Left Party alliance in all of Germany, compared to only 6.7 percent among strong partisans. This is not because non-partisans are substantially more liberal in their views. Instead, they are available for mobilization because they lack previous party loyalties. Similarly, the percentage of voters who split their *Erststimme* and *Zweitstimme* between different parties has been steadily growing in the Federal Republic since the 1960s, reaching 27 percent of the voters in 2005. Split-ticket voting remains higher in the East (5 percent more than in the West).

The figure illustrates the direct and indirect consequences of the differing party attachments in West and East.[23] Despite dealignment trends since the 1980s, westerners retain stronger party attachments. Consequently, strong partisans enter elections with their decisions already made: they will vote for "their" party as they have in prior elections. In large part, these voters are unswayed by the dynamics of the campaign except insofar as this mobilizes them to vote. By comparison, easterners have weaker party ties, and thus they are more likely begin the election cycle unsure about how they will vote, possibly shifting their vote since the last election, and are less likely to vote.[24] Greater partisan volatility seems likely to continue in the East, unless differences in party attachments eventually converge with the West. These East-West differences are modest, but in an electoral context where a few percentage points may shape coalition outcomes, even modest differences can have large potential implications.

Party Politics in a Unified Germany

This chapter has considered how the German party system fits Willy Brandt's famous statement about German unification: "What belongs together will now grow together." At least in formal terms, Brandt's description applies to the German party system. Residents of the eastern Länder were very quickly integrated into the party system of the Federal Republic, and the same set of parties now competes in both West and East.

Yet, this is not so much growing together, as being overtaken by the well-established parties in the West. With the exception of the PDS/Left Party, the current German party system developed through the eastern expansion of the western parties. Moreover, even if the same party names generally appear on the ballots in West and East, this article has highlighted the continuing differences across regions. Most parties have developed a distinct regional bias in their share of the electorate. The CDU/CSU, FDP, and Greens receive a significantly larger share of their vote from the West; the Left Party (and previously the PDS) draws disproportionate support from the East. The regional differences in party support have not narrowed over time.

Moreover, many of these parties have significant differences in their voter clientele across regions. Western working class voters lean toward the SPD (or now the SPD and Left Party), but in the East this social stratum has given greater support to the CDU and FDP. The 2009 Bundestag election marked a convergence of overall middle class-working class Left-Right gap in voting patterns across regions, and if this continues is may foretell greater partisan similarity overall. But easterners from all classes are distinctly more leftist and this gap has widened over time. Religious voting has grown more similar across the two regions. Because religious attachments differ so greatly across regions, however, even similar voting patterns for religious groups have different implications for party strength across East and West. For instance, about a third of the Christian Democratic voters in the East say they have no religion, in marked contrast to core CDU/CSU voters in the West.

Many of these differences sprang from the unique set of political circumstances and party positions that accompanied unification. What is surprising is the persistence of these patterns over time, and in some cases a widening of regional differences. In addition, social learning theory would predict a gradual growth of party attachments among new voters in the East, but this individual level institutionalization of party ties has not occurred. In short, an important regional gap still persists in the party system, even two decades and six elections after unification.

Such regional contrasts are not entirely new to German politics–think of the CSU and the party traditions of many western Länder. Nevertheless, these differences run deeper in the current West-East contrast. Parties have distinct regional strengths, but the same party also has different voter clienteles across regions. This brings party representatives together in the Bundestag with different political constituencies and identities. The CDU Bundestag deputy from the East has a different voter base than one from the Catholic West. The SPD partisan in the East is more middle-class than in the West. This diversity can erode party cohesion, and the SPD-Left Party split may be attributable partially to such tensions. Specific policy issues are also likely to heighten these tensions, such as cultural issues or policies affecting East-West economic policy. German federalism provides a vehicle to address these regional differences, but it probably also has worked to institutionalize these differences, so that Germans have not come together fully in terms of party support.

Notes

We would like to thank Andreas Wüst, Christian Welzel, Steve Weldon, and Robert Rohrschneider for their assistance and advice in preparing this essay.

1. Public opinion polls from early 1989 suggested that the Kohl government lagged behind the SPD by more than ten percent and was headed toward defeat in the next Bundestag election. But, the CDU/CSU's standing in the West dramatically improved as a result of unification. See Russell J. Dalton and Alexandra Cole, "The peaceful revolution and German electoral politics," in *The New Germany Votes*, ed., Russell J. Dalton (Providence, 1993).
2. Russell J. Dalton and Wilhelm Bürklin, "Two German electorates?: The social bases of the vote in 1990 and 1994," *German Politics and Society* 34 (1995): 79-99.
3. As a further sign of the public's disillusionment with politics, turnout dropped to 70.8 percent, the lowest level in the Federal Republic's electoral history.
4. This is calculated as the net difference (summing up the gap for parties that gained a greater percentage in the West) based on Table 1:

1990	1994	1998	2002	2005	2009
14.5	18.9	23.9	18.4	22.7	20.5

5. There is an abundant literature on class and religious voting in Germany; see Russell J. Dalton, "Voter Choice and Electoral Politics," in *Developments in German Politics 3*, eds., Stephen Padgett, William E. Paterson, and Gordon Smith (Basingstoke, 2003); Wolfgang G. Gibowski, "Who Voted for Whom—and Why," in, *Power Shift in Germany: The 1998 Election and the End of the Kohl Era*, eds., David P. Conradt, Gerald R. Kleinfeld, and Christian Soe (New York, 2000; Franz Urban Pappi, "Die politisierte Sozialstruktur heute: Historische Reminiszenz oder aktuelles Erklärungspotential?" in *Das Ende der politisierte Sozialstruktur?*, eds., Frank Brettschneider, Jan van Deth, and Edeltraud Roller (Opladen, 2002); Bernhard Weßels, "Gruppenbindung und Wahlverhalten. 50 Jahre Wahlen in der Bundesrepublik," in *50 Jahre Empirische Wahlforschung in Deutschland*, eds., Markus Klein, Wolfgang Jagodzinski, Ekkehard Mochmann, and Dieter Ohr (Wiesbaden, 2000).
6. Dalton and Bürklin (see note 2); Martin Elff and Sigrid Roßteutscher, "Die Entwicklung sozialer Konfliktlinien in den Wahlen von 1994 bis 2005," in *Wahlen und Wähler: Analysen aus Anlass der Bundestagswahl 2005*, eds., Oskar Gabriel, Jürgen Falter, and Bernard Weßels (Wiesbaden, 2009).
7. Data for this section are based on Politbarometer surveys conducted by Forschungsgruppe Wahlen in election years (Zentralarchiv study numbers 1920, 1987, 2546, 2559, 3160, 3849, 3850, 4258, 4259). Only surveys conducted after each election are used in the analysis. We measured class by respondent's occupation. Working class includes manual jobs (*ungelernt oder angelernt/Landarbeiter*, *Facharbeiter*, and *Meister*). New middle class comprises all categories classified under *Angestellte* (white collar employees) and *Beamter* (civil servants). Old middle class refers to the category *Selbständig* (self-employed). The 2009 data are from a Forschungsgruppe exit poll conducted on election day.
8. Further data on the class voting patterns for all parties for the 1990-2009 elections is available from the authors upon request.
9. These values are recalculated from the data used in Figure 1. If the Greens, who are not a workers' party judged by either programmatic appeals or membership profiles, are excluded from the calculation, the Alford index for both East and (especially) West increases considerably, but the contrast between the two parts of the country remains the same.
10. See Wolfgang Jagodzinski and Markus Quandt, "Religion und Wahlverhalten in der längsschnittlichen Entwicklung," in Klein et al. (see note 5); Franz Urban Pappi, "Die konfessionell-religiöse Konfliktlinie in der deutschen Wählerschaft. Enstehung, Stabilität und Wandel," in *Wirtschaftlicher Wandel, religiöser Wandel und Wertwandel. Folgen für das politiche*

Verhalten in der Bundesrepublik Deutschland, eds., Dieter Obernodörfer, Hans Rattinger and Karl Schmitt (Berlin, 1985).

11. Further data on the religious voting patterns for all parties for the 1990-2009 is available from the authors upon request.

12. Kai Arzheimer and Harald Schoen find that denominational affiliation rarely was a significant factor in the 1994-2005 elections in distinguishing between CDU/CSU and SPD voters after controlling for frequency of religious attendance. This holds true in both regions of the country, except in 1998 when western Protestants were more likely to support the SPD, and in 1994 when both Catholics and Protestants in East significantly favored the CDU. See Kai Arzheimer and Harald Schoen, "Mehr al seine Erinnerung an das 19. Jahrhundert? Das sozioökonomische und das religiös-konfessionelle Cleavage und Wahlverhalten 1994-2005," in *Der gesamtdeutsche Wähler: Stabilität und Wandel des Wählerverhaltens im wiedervereinigten Deutschland*, eds., Hans Rattinger, Oscar W. Gabriel and Jürgen W. Falter (Baden-Baden, 2007).

13. See Kai Arzheimer and Jürgen W. Falter, "Ist der Osten wirklich rot? Das Wahlverhalten bei der Bundestagswahl 2002 in Ost-West-Perspektive," *Aus Politik und Zeitgeschichte* 49-50 (2002): 27-35; Harald Schoen and Roland Abold, "Zwei Wählerschaften in einem Land? Wahlverhalten im vereinigten Deutschland," in *Sind wir ein Volk? Ost- und Westdeutschland im Vergleich*, eds., Jürgen W. Falter, Oscar W. Gabriel, Hans Rattinger and Harald Schoen (Munich, 2006).

14. Sören Holmberg, "Party identification compared across the Atlantic," in *Elections at Home and Abroad*, eds., M. Kent Jennings and Thomas Mann (Ann Arbor, 1994); Dieter Ohr, Markus Quandt, and Hermann Dülmer, "Zur Funktion und Bedeutung der Parteibindung für den modernen Wähler," in *Wahlen und Wähler. Analysen aus Anlass der Bundestagswahl 2002*, eds., Jürgen Falter, Oscar Gabriel und Bernhard Weßels (Wiesbaden, 2005).

15. Max Kaase and Hans-Dieter Klingemann, "The cumbersome way to partisan orientations in a 'new' democracy," in Jennings and Mann (see note 14).

16. Kai Arzheimer und Harald Schoen, "Erste Schritte auf kaum erschlossenem Terrain. Zur Stabilität der Parteiidentifikation in Deutschland," *Politische Vierteljahresschrift* (2005) 46: 629-654; Rüdiger Schmitt-Beck.and Stefan Weick, "Die dauefhafte Parteiidentifikation– nur noch a Mythos?" *Informationsdienst Soziale Indikatoren* (2001) 26:1-5; Russell Dalton and Wilhelm Bürklin, "Wahler als Wandervogel: Dealignment and the German Voter," *German Politics and Society* 21 (2003): 57-75; Carsten Zelle, "Social dealignment vs. political frustration," *European Journal for Political Research* 27 (1995): 319-45.

17. See the contrasting views in Russell J. Dalton and Robert Rohrschneider, "Wählerwandel und die Abschwächung der Parteineigungen von 1972 bis 1987," in *Wahlen und Wähler: Analysen aus Anlass der Bundestagswahl 1987*, eds Max Kaase and Hans-Dieter Klingemann. (Opladen, 1990); and Dieter Ohr, Hermann Dülmer, and Markus Quandt, "Kognitive Mobilisierung oder nicht-kognitive De-mobilisierung" in Gabriel, Falter, and Weßels (see note 6).

18. Kaase and Klingemann (see note 14); Russell J. Dalton and Steve Weldon, "Partisanship and party system institutionalization," *Party Politics* 13 (2007): 179-196.

19. Bernard Wessels, "Re-Mobilisierung, 'Floating'oder Abwanderung? Wechselwähler 2002 und 2005 im Vergleich," in *Die Bundestagswahl 2005: Analysen des Wahlkampfs und der Wahlergebnisse*, eds., Frank Brettschneider, Oskar Niedermayer, and Bernard Wessels (Wiesbaden, 2009); Dalton and Bürklin (see note 16); Harald Schoen, "Stimmensplitting bei Bundestagswahlen: Ein Spiegelbild des Verhältnisses zwischen Bürgern und Parteien?" in Klein et al. (see note 5).

20. Another sign of the lack of party ties is the emergence of the Pirate Party in 2009, a youth oriented party that opposes restrictions on internet usage and file sharing on the internet. Even as a narrow single-issue party, it gained 2 percent of the vote nationally or approximately 845,000 *Zweitstimmen*.

21. Bernhard Wessels, "Post-election study of the Bundestagswahl 2005," Wissenschaftszentrum Berlin; available at www.wzb.eu/zkd/dsl/download.en.htm.
22. Turnout was 72.3 percent in the West in 2009 versus 64.8 percent in the East.
23. Region is based on the current region of the interview rather than the respondent's residence in 1989. Given mobility since unification, the differences between western-born and eastern-born voters are probably larger.
24. Except for 2009 when volatility in the West nearly doubled, the net amount of voting switching between elections has been greater in the East (based on net aggregate vote switching in Table 1):

	1990-94	1994-98	1998-02	2002-05	2005-09
East	15.9	11.6	6.2	12.3	10.8
West	5.6	6.5	5.2	7.2	13.9

Chapter 13

$\mathcal{H}$IGHER EDUCATION IN GERMANY

Fragmented Change amid Paradigm Shifts[1]

● ● ● ● ● ● ● ● ● ● ● ● ● ●

Helga A. Welsh

Unification of the two German states in October 1990 initiated comprehensive institutional, policy, and personnel transfer from West to East.
The political, economic, and social transformation of East Germany was
fashioned after West Germany, yet, by the middle of the decade, the need
for an overhaul of many cherished aspects of the West German model
became palpable. Although most attention focused on restructuring social
and labor policies, other areas that came under scrutiny included education in general and higher education in particular, the focus of this article.
After a long period of inertia, starting in the mid 1990s, myriad reform initiatives transformed the higher education system in unified Germany.

The term paradigm shift, borrowed from Thomas Kuhn's theory of scientific progress to signify a profound, radical change in understanding, has
a firm place in the policy discourse of many countries. Germany is no
exception.[2] Paradigms are frameworks that include ideas, goals, and instruments by which experts in the field seek solutions—when they shift, a new
system replaces the old one. The concept is applied with amazing regular-
ity to highlight breaks with tradition in Germany's higher education system. Prominent among them are the curricular restructuring associated
with the Bologna Declaration to introduce tiered study programs; diversification trends within the two main categories of higher education institutions in Germany—the research-oriented universities, which can grant
doctoral degrees, and universities of applied sciences (Fachhochschulen);[3]
and the implementation of steering and funding mechanisms to modify
state/university partnerships. Much of the discourse has focused on the

key terms "competition" and "performance" to pave the way for reform.[4] They are the seeds around which other ideas coalesce, including diversification, internationalization, autonomy, and accountability.

While paradigm shifts originally alluded to radical breaks with past practices, recent studies emphasize more evolutionary change and the co-existence of paradigms. Looking at economic policy in the United Kingdom, Michael J. Oliver and Hugh Pemberton speak of paradigm evolution rather than revolution, arguing that "one can envisage a subset of the new ideas being incorporated into the prevailing policy paradigm and being used in further experimentation with new instruments and settings."[5] Such a long-term perspective, with its emphasis on gradual development, corresponds to German reform of higher education: old paradigms have staying power, and the elaboration of new ones can be lengthy.

Change has been pressured by Europeanization and globalization, reinforced by feedback mechanisms from unification. They have empowered newly formed advocacy coalitions to advance a reform agenda. Nevertheless, existing institutions and firmly rooted values condition and limit changes, which are contested, and outcomes vary; critique and reforming the reforms are commonplace. In higher education, paradigmatic change connects with elements of tradition. The system has become more fluid and more varied.

Agenda-Setting amid Domestic and Global Change

Unification and Its Consequences

After unification, the tendency to eliminate old East German systems and to transplant West German systems was pronounced in areas where differences and perceived inefficiency met ideological reservations. The higher education system in the former German Democratic Republic (GDR) was among them. It was ideologically tainted, highly centralized, and regimented. Compared to the West, the institutions were small, and only about 12 to 13 percent of the student-age population was enrolled. In comparison, the academic personnel structure was bloated. A marked separation between research and teaching was supported by research centers outside the universities–the academies.[6] A comprehensive institutional, policy, and personnel transfer from West to East was accompanied by import of West German academic culture. As in so many other areas, the overload of decision making combined with real and perceived time pressure reduced complexity and helped to cement the prevailing notion of "no experiments."[7]

Overall, unification did not spark major reform initiatives in higher education, but in contrast to other policy areas, it did not stall reform efforts already under way—the reform discourse had not yet advanced to action. Yet, as institutional and policy transfer is never an exact copy of the blueprint, feedback mechanisms played out, most of them unanticipated.[8] For example, the evaluation of research and higher education institutions in the former GDR exerted pressure on western institutions to show that they could withstand similar evaluations. External advisory and assessment bodies, in particular the German Council of Science and Humanities (Wissenschaftsrat; henceforth referred to as Science Council), elevated their profiles and promoted innovation.

Substantial financial transfers from West to East moved the renewal process along. New universities, such as those in Erfurt and Frankfurt/ Oder, were explicitly created as "reform" universities and experimented with governance structures and degree programs. Many small institutions of higher education in the former GDR were restructured as Fach- hochschulen. By the mid 1990s, the first phase of the transformation of the eastern German higher education system was largely completed, yet rather than consolidating, policy change continued and now grips the country as a whole.

International Factors

In higher education, as in other policy realms, Germany was not alone in having to evaluate its system. The emergence of an international educa- tion market, demand for a skilled workforce that can adapt to changing environments ("knowledge society"), and resource scarcity have launched new initiatives in all industrialized countries.[9] They may agree on broad goals, but outcomes remain strongly influenced by national values and structures. International assessments became an important strategic resource. The German higher education model, once widely exported and cher- ished, was under competitive pressure, a fact not lost on experts. In the aftermath of communism's collapse, many countries in Central and East Europe initially reformed their higher education systems by returning to Humboldtian ideas of self-governance that rely on a strong professorial chair system but weak university management—a model that had been prominent before communist takeover. Soon, however, market-oriented models started to make important inroads.[10]

The OECD Program for International Student Assessment (PISA) has become a coded reference to dilemmas in the German education system and fears that it is falling behind its international competitors. First in

2000 and then every three years, PISA surveys the reading, math, and scientific competencies of fifteen year-old students. The 2000 PISA results attested to German students' only average performance: out of thirty-two countries, they ranked twentieth. Although the test results in science categories have improved in recent PISA studies, Germany is still not in the top ten tier. The evaluations may be restricted to secondary education, but the findings have jolted the German education system as a whole and intensified the reform debate, with spillover effects to all areas of education, calling for greater transparency in educational outcomes.

PISA was soon joined by a plethora of other evaluations that sparked public debate and acquired political relevance. For example, the yearly OECD publication "Education at a Glance" receives wide attention beyond the circle of education experts. It regularly highlights some of the shortcomings of the German system, especially crowded institutions and high dropout rates; comparatively fewer students in the tertiary sector; low public appropriations; and social class as the main determinant of access and performance. Although less noted by the general public, international evaluations of world-class universities, such as the Shanghai and Times HES rankings, still upset German stakeholders and frustrate academics: no German university is among the world's top fifty. Two seemingly contradictory trends have emerged; while international evaluations unveil structural deficiencies in the German higher education system, German academics are integrated into the international scholarly community, and their work is respected and cited.[11]

The term *Europeanization* has various meanings but is used here to emphasize transnational interactions and policy processes.[12] The aim of creating a European Higher Education Area as part of the Bologna Process is the most prominent; the number of participants has grown from twenty-nine to forty-seven European countries. The European Union has also elevated its own profile in education and research.[13] The Lisbon Strategy, agreed upon by the European Council in 2000, highlights the role of research and development in keeping Europe competitive, aiming to make it "the most dynamic and competitive knowledge-based economy." Although the 2010 target rate of 3 percent of GDP for research and development will not be met by most countries, including Germany, such programs have acted as an important benchmark and agent for change. The European Union has also become an important source of research funding; currently, it allocates about EURO 7 billion annually to the Seventh Framework Program for Research (2007-2010). Europeanization, within and outside of the European Union, is linked to a transnational network of political actors that meets regularly; participants share information, learn from each other, and develop a common language.

Domestic actors actively drew international organizations into the discourse, and they emerged as influential actors in domestic politics.[14] Take the Bologna Process. As Katrin Toens shows, the introduction of MA and BA degrees was not the result of endogenous pressure imposed on reluctant German players but shaped by domestic players, such as the German Rectors' Conference.[15] Carolin Balzer and Alessandra Rusconi echo this finding: "[T]he key to success lay in close cooperation between domestic actors and an IO." In the case of the Bologna Process, it was the European Union. Representatives of the four signatory states of the 1998 Sorbonne Joint Declaration (France, Germany, Italy, and the United Kingdom), which set the Bologna Process in motion, were motivated by "the desire to justify and push reforms in national systems."[16]

In agenda setting, a special role emerged for policy entrepreneurs who became idea carriers.[17] Articulated by a newly emerging advocacy coalition of national science organizations–the German Science Council, the German Research Foundation (DFG), the Max Planck Societies, the German Academic Exchange Service (DAAD), and the Center for Higher Education Development (CHE), a think-tank created explicitly to bring in new concepts and advance reform–ideas that had been simmering for a long time surfaced and began to dominate the discourse. The German Rectors' Conference (HRK), as the "voice of the universities," has more difficulty presenting unified reform proposals but has joined the reform advocates in important initiatives.

At this point, the vocabulary of power politics and resource scarcity enters the discussion. The complexity of the multilevel decision-making network is notorious, not least because education is mostly the policy prerogative of the sixteen Länder, but also because it is complemented by many national players. Starting in the late 1960s, the federal government assumed a greater role in higher education. The reversal of the process began in 1998 with the fourth Amendment to the Higher Education Framework Act. By 2006, the Länder legally reclaimed their exclusive right to govern the cultural domain (*Kulturhoheit*). This move was spurred by distributive conflicts over financial contributions that became more pronounced due to the merging of East and West and a creeping power shift from the Länder to the Federal Ministry for Education and Research (BMBF). The reshuffling of power, however, has not been nearly as dramatic as the constitutional changes imply. The need for national policy coordination and planning, as well as resource scarcity, secure the federal government's continued influence through seed money and incentive-based grants.

How to increase efficiency and performance in view of limited funds also has motivated the major political parties to tackle reforms. Conservative and Social Democratic governments differ in their emphasis on equality of opportunity, for example, in admission to tertiary education. Nevertheless, they have asserted distinct profiles only in politically sensitive cases, such as when the topic of tuition fees captured policymakers' attention and aroused heated controversy. More often, their policies have been pragmatic rather than ideological with the result that, across the federation, principles are generally agreed upon with great variation in detail and practice. Leaders and laggards among the Länder vary, depending on the reform under consideration, although regional variations in the population and the economic strength account for the unequal distribution of resources, institutions, personnel, and students. In 2009, only about 15 percent of all students are enrolled in the five Länder in the former GDR's territory, and the higher education institutions there constitute about one-fifth of the total 394.

One outcome of recent developments is obvious: education and higher education have emerged as a topic of public debate and political relevance, accompanied by intensive media coverage. Myriad new initiatives have taken off, reflecting curricular changes, new steering and funding mechanisms, and personnel structure. This process continues unabated.

Building Blocks of a New Model

Competition and Performance

International competition has been elevated in recent years, but the principle of national competition has long been on the political agenda. At the beginning of the 1980s, the Federal Ministry for Education and Science and the Science Council advocated policies that aimed to promote competition among Länder and institutions of higher education for academic personnel and students. To this end, institutions of higher learning would be granted more autonomy, the system of financing changed, incentives provided, and differentiation encouraged to allow specialization and enhanced reputation.[18] It took until the 1990s, however, for these ideas to be incorporated into actual policies. From then on, political actors "created competition" by including benchmarking as a central point in the newly emerging discourse.[19]

International rankings, complemented by those offered by science associations, such as the CHE, the German Research Foundation, the Humboldt Foundation, the Science Council, and the DAAD, took off and are used as strategic tools in the battle for money, talent, and international visibility. Major weeklies like *Die Zeit* and *Der Spiegel* and newspapers (for example, the *Hochschulanzeiger* of the *Frankfurter Allgemeine Zeitung*) have expanded their media coverage on higher education and serve as guides for prospective students. Since 2004, the Initiative New Social Market Economy (Initiative Neue Soziale Marktwirtschaft, INSM), a think tank financed by employers' associations, adds its voice to the reform debate by monitoring educational achievements in the Länder (*Bildungsmonitor*).[20]

The choice of indicators to measure and to interpret performance is crucial. There is no agreement on best practices, differing ideas vie for attention, and the value of international and national assessments remains disputed. International evaluations and rankings often fail to reflect adequately the special characteristics of the German education system. Its emphasis on specialized apprenticeship-based vocational training (the "dual system") contributes to the lower enrolment of students in the tertiary sector, while the strength of research centers outside the universities, such as the Max Planck Institutes, Helmholtz Association, and Fraunhofer Gesellschaft, is not assessed, excluding their major contributions to research and graduate training.

Diversification of the Higher Education Landscape

A striking recent development has been the diversification of higher education and its prominence in the discourse. It was triggered by the "Excellence Initiative" (*Exzellenzinitiative*), which is often portrayed as a break with tradition, as it awards money to selected universities.[21] The old mantra that German universities are equal in standing and, by implication, quality, has been shattered officially. Peer Pasternack dismisses the paradigmatic status of the initiative and describes it as a creeping development from the mid 1990s that places greater emphasis on grant-based research.[22] The difference may be more etymological than real, as his interpretation supports the prolonged nature of paradigmatic changes.

First introduced in 2005, the initiative, coordinated by the DFG and the Science Council, aims to strengthen the international competitiveness of German universities by targeting research and graduate training. It is jointly funded by the federal government and the Länder, with the former covering three-fourths of the total cost of EURO 1.9 billion. Scheduled to expire in 2011, the program was renewed in summer 2009; new funds in the amount of EURO 2.7 billion will be made available, and funding extended to 2017. In 2007, nine universities—now colloquially referred to as "elite universities," although the program deliberately avoided the term—were awarded funds based on their "future concepts for project-related top-level research." The initiative has had a profound effect in multiple and, at times, unanticipated ways,[23] creating new momentum even among institutions that were not selected. It has fueled functional differentiation, encouraged Land ministries to initiate their own competitive grant programs, and led to new networks between universities and research centers outside of universities, among them, the Jülich-Aachen-Research Alliance and the Göttingen Research Council.[24]

East/West differences remain pertinent. Four of the nine chosen universities are located in southern Germany and none in the former GDR. Thirty-nine institutions were successful in the graduate-program competition, Humboldt University in Berlin, the universities in Jena and Leipzig, and the Technical University Dresden among them. Dresden was awarded one of the thirty-seven clusters of excellence. All remaining institutions were in the "old" Federal Republic. The grants entered the East/West division into the discourse again but, more broadly, asserted the principles of competition and differentiation among regions and universities.

Political interest in supporting eastern German institutions of higher education remains high. For example, the BMBF has launched special pilot programs to fund research and innovation in the region. The newly instituted Higher Education Pacts between the Länder and the federal government earmark funds to encourage and cushion the anticipated significant rise in tertiary enrolment in Germany. Allocated funds are per student and disbursed only if a student enrolls. While all states profit from the program, it gives special attention and funds to the eastern states where enrolment numbers lag.[25]

They face an uphill battle due to an expected decline in enrolment between 2011 and 2015, resulting from the rapid drop of birth rates in the East in the first half of the 1990s and continued East/West migration. Approximately 22 percent of eastern German students are admitted to western institutions; only 4 percent of western students move east.[26] New marketing strategies promote moving east.[27] After all, when criteria such as teaching, faculty-to-student ratios, length of study, student satisfaction, and cost of living are considered, eastern institutions rank high. Continued high unemployment in the East (in June 2009, the East was at 12.9 percent; the West, at 6.9 percent), coupled with the need for a broad-based, skilled workforce, have also redirected the discourse. Higher education institutions not only provide individual benefits to students but are crucial for regional economic development.[28] The initial impetus for functional variation and marketing may differ between East and West, but the strategies and outcomes display many similarities.

Another kind of diversification has also received renewed attention: the underrepresentation of women in the upper echelons of the academic hierarchy. Special programs to decrease gender inequality have been in place since the 1990s,[29] and the Excellence Initiative added new incentives.[30] As part of the application process, institutions had to stipulate how their proposed programs would address gender equality. In 2007, women comprised one-half of graduates from higher education institutions; among PhD recipients, 42 percent were women. However, the higher up the career ladder, the greater the decline in female representation: 24 percent of those who completed a Habilitation were women, but their representation among the professoriate is only 11.9 percent for the professorial rank (C4/W3 salary classification) and somewhat better at 33.5 percent among junior professorships.[31] Progress is visible, but the glass ceiling has not shattered. Quota regulations are still rejected, but all political actors acknowledge the need for action. The emphasis has also shifted to reforming family policy to allow academics more leeway in fulfilling their parental duties. The impact of the eastern states on these changes is difficult to measure, but awareness of gender issues and child care has clearly been heightened as a result of unification.

Internationalization and Europeanization

In Germany, the self-image of elites and public is closely tied to excellence in education. Germany wants to be a leader in science and education and a player in the international higher education market. Consequently, the average or low standings in international comparisons hit a raw nerve. Herfried Münkler's suggestion that Germany should diversify its soft power resources by increasing its international attractiveness in culture and science reflects concerns about its standing in the world.[32] Internationalization strategies have become a priority for governments and higher education institutions. They are not new; support for international research and education cooperation has a long tradition. The Federal Foreign Office, for example, yearly allocates about EURO 250 million to this endeavor. Efforts have been stepped up to meet new challenges. According to Max Hägler, about one-half of higher education institutions participate in international marketing programs; one-third advertise their programs internationally; many maintain offices abroad; and some institutions offer English-language instruction, although only 6 percent of students take advantage of those courses. To make real impact, he says, more work must be done.[33]

Numerous initiatives are under way to assure that Germany remains one of the top destinations for foreign students; depending on the year, it ranks as the third or fourth most popular destination worldwide, with 9-10 percent of foreign students.[34] Attracting foreign academic personnel has been more challenging. In 2007, only 9.6 percent of all academic positions were occupied by foreigners; of those, less than 10 percent were professors. In the eastern states, enrolment rates and foreign academic employment reflect the small percentage of foreigners in the overall population; the East/West gap is significant, although within the eastern region, there is considerable variation.[35]

One reason why relatively few foreigners pursue an academic career in Germany is the lengthy traditional career process, which is fraught with uncertainty about whether it will result in a professorial position. The junior professorship is accepted in all Länder, but so far they comprise only about 4 percent of all professorships, and tenure options remain severely circumscribed. [36] Cultural, language, and immigration barriers also contribute to the halting progress in attracting foreign scholars.

The Bologna Process highlights internationalization and Europeanization and the accompanying pressures of competition and performance.[37] The new tiered degree structure aims to facilitate credit transfers, recognition of degrees across Europe, and greater student mobility. Within Germany, the restructured three-year BA and two-year MA programs aim to lower drop-out rates, cut the length of studies, and increase student employment options. Curricular changes associated with the Bologna Process have been in motion since the program's inception in 1999 but hampered by structural and psychological barriers.

The introduction of BA and MA degree programs constitutes a radical departure from the traditional degree structure and is seen as a paradigmatic change. Not only does it replace the traditional diploma degree, but, more importantly, it restructures the curricula in radical ways. The BA focuses on skill development and employability and took its inspiration from the British model, diverging from the BA degree in the United States, which celebrates the idea of general education. New degree programs were slow to emerge but have taken off; in summer 2004, only 19 percent of all study programs led to a BA and MA. By summer 2009, the number increased to 76 percent. Variation among the Länder is high, with Lower Saxony having converted nearly 95 percent of all programs and Saarland only 55 percent. Leaders and laggards are spread throughout the country.[38]

The curricular changes have elicited strong reactions among the academic community. In particular, the understanding of *Bildung* in juxtaposition to training in particular skills remains crucial to many contemporary debates. Old practices are routinely defended by reference to the ideas of Wilhelm von Humboldt. No matter how often they have been exposed as myth, an idealistic leitmotif removed from reality or, at the very least, inadequate to meet the demands of the mass universities of the twenty-first century,[39] they have remarkable staying power. "Freedom of teaching and learning," "unity of teaching and research," "unity of science and scholarship," and the "primacy of 'pure' science over specialized professional training"[40] are central to the discourse. The clash between *Bildung* and *Ausbildung* may have been preprogrammed, but it was amplified by the way the new curricula were structured. Old programs were crammed into the new, shorter ones and many assert that "old wine was put into new bottles" instead of taking on the real challenge of curricular reform.

Harsh critique of the new system emerged as soon as the first preliminary data came in. The easing of transfer credits and increased student mobility have not materialized, and how many students and under what conditions advance from the BA to the MA level is contested. Drop-out rates are lower in the humanities but increased in engineering studies. To what extent employers are accepting graduates with the new degrees is not yet known, but detractors have not waited to undermine their value. The initial goal of completing the Bologna Process by 2010 is off. Indeed, a reform of the reform is under way.[41]

Autonomy and Accountability

Practices that emphasize accountability, efficiency, and performance have a prominent role in many policy areas, including higher education. Ideas and principles associated with New Public Management and the entrepreneurial university took time to root in German higher education but have spread rapidly in the last decade.[42] They involve new funding mechanisms, lump-sum budgets, contract management, and indictor-based funding schemes that link appropriations to output. These new steering schemes have profoundly reshaped the interaction between regional governments and higher education institutions. For example, newly established university councils, modeled after company boards, have evolved from advisory to co-decision-making bodies. [43] Power is no longer solely concentrated in the Land ministries, but they retain important functions, driving competition, change, and quality assurance. Not least, they contribute about three-fourths of all funds to public higher education institutions.

Enhanced autonomy in decision-making and flexibility in operating procedures come at a price, linked to new accountability and transparency systems.[44] A prominent example is the new accreditation system. Facilitated by the shift to a tiered degree structure as part of the Bologna Process, it was pioneered jointly by the German Rectors' Conference and the Standing Conference of State Ministers of Educational and Cultural Affairs (Kultusministerkonferenz, KMK) in 1999 and expanded in 2004-2005. Accreditation agencies have assumed the role of the Land ministries in program approval, yet, in keeping with Germany's federal structure, the process remains decentralized, with the Foundation for the Accreditation of Study Programs in Germany assuming the roles of coordinator and monitoring agency, among others.[45]

The autonomous university has become a model, albeit with many variations. Some Länder emphasize central regulation, and others take a more pro-active role in deregulation.[46] No reform is without controversy and mistrust about the actual workings of the new structures lingers and hampers reforms. Many academics fear decreased self-governance, external stakeholders with too much influence, and a loss of academic freedom. Civil servants in the top levels of science ministries wonder whether university managers are up to the job, and politicians want to maintain influence and control. Establishing trust remains a crucial variable in building new, multilevel power configurations.

Development towards the autonomous university cannot be divided from the perennial resource scarcity that plagues education, particularly, higher education. Germany's expenditures have not matched its aspirations as a global education player. Measured as a percentage of GDP, the 2005 OECD average was 3.8 for education generally and 1.5 for tertiary education specifically. Germany trailed in both categories, with 3.4 and 1.1 respectively.[47] According to Frieder Wolf, part of the gap can be explained by looking at private contributions. Compared to some of its international peers, especially the United States, the United Kingdom, and Japan, German private expenditures in elementary and secondary education are high, but the reverse is true for the tertiary sector. Public monies have not been able to compensate for the difference. Since expenditures for research institutes outside of higher education institutions are not included in the OECD data, Germany consistently ranks low in tertiary education spending among its peers.[48]

Cost-cutting measures and pressure to increase public funding are constants, but their urgency has heightened since the 1990s–they have been a veiled force driving some reform efforts. For example, the introduction of tiered BA and MA programs as part of the Bologna Declaration reflects the homogenizing trends of Europeanization, but the regulation to limit BA programs to three years signals that financial considerations were not far from the minds of the Land ministries. The 2002 restructuring of salary schemes for academic positions came into effect in 2005, introducing flexibility and performance criteria for newly hired academic positions while lowering basic compensation. The 2006 federalism reform entitled Land governments to institute their own remuneration schemes for civil servants, a move that may well amplify existing regional and within-region salary variations to attract world-class researchers.

The introduction of general tuition fees is another sign of cost considerations, even if their overall contribution is relatively modest–per student semester fees cannot exceed EURO 500. They are levied in most CDU/CSU-governed Länder in the western part of the country, and the fact that no tuition fees have been introduced in the East reflects social considerations and the already low enrolment of students; in fact, the lack of tuition fees is used as a marketing tool to attract students. The break with cost-free education has ignited heated debates, and strong opposition by the parties on the Left keeps it on the political radar screen.[49] The high visibility of education, including the topic of tuition fees, in the 2008 and 2009 Hesse Landtag elections sensitized politicians of all parties and re-introduced a measure of uncertainty about the future of tuition fees.

Fragmented Change amid Paradigm Shifts?

Globalization, Europeanization, efficiency, and performance have become catchphrases to explain and justify reform in higher education. Reforms take time, and outcomes are varied, not least because of the multilevel character of decision-making. The perception of reform often clashes with perceptions of inertia and ambivalence. Change is easier to accomplish when there is clear agreement on the deficiencies of the old system and the contours of the new system. In the case of German higher education, such agreement is missing, allowing core elements of the old system to survive relatively unscathed. While some claim that recent changes have transformed the German university system, others are more skeptical and emphasize an ambivalence that undercuts reforms and reduces them to face-lifts rather than radical changes.[50] Profound change and persistence of established traditions coincide and, at times, collide. Reforms are questioned, and reforming the reforms has become commonplace.

The degree of change in the German higher education system depends on the area of investigation. I have emphasized movement and continued pressure for reform. At the policy level, myriad new initiatives have left their mark, and some of the most important have been outlined, but long-standing problems persist and were highlighted in the student protest of summer 2009. For example, looking at enrolment levels and the social composition of the student body, the system remains conservative and elitist,[51] although–in view of overcrowded seminars and lecture halls–this characterization is not without irony. Despite increased allocations for higher education budgets, Germany still lags behind many other European countries. The academic culture is characterized by status hierarchy, and the introduction of the junior professor as an alternative career path has done little to break the mold. Women and international scholars remain underrepresented. Political awareness, however, has grown, and pressure for reform has not abated.

The German higher education system has been reformed in ways that were unforeseen at unification, and eastern institutions have been subject to a dual transformation–one revolutionary, the other evolutionary. Twenty years later, they can be viewed as a means to reduce crowding in western institutions by absorbing students, a regional provider of skills and training, or perennial recipients of financial subsidies. In those accounts, East/West differentiation in prestige and visibility remain central. Another perspective is more nuanced, highlighting fragmented developments.[52] There are pockets of research excellence in the East, in particular in Thuringia and Saxony, and the North/South dimension is sometimes as important as East/West differences.[53]

Do multiple paradigmatic changes amount to a new model of higher education in Germany? Do they represent cracks in a monument, or are we seeing new buildings and renovation of older buildings in the same complex so that, ultimately, no paradigm reigns? While the higher education system is "under construction," the architecture of the envisioned new university campus remains in flux. International comparisons, in particular with the United States, the United Kingdom, the Netherlands, Canada, Switzerland, and the Scandinavian countries, are routine; they serve as source of ideas and provide benchmarking criteria. Plans are drawn and redrawn; some buildings are remodeled substantially; some touched up; new buildings are added. Much of the structural work has been accomplished, yet recalibration continues. The process is intentional–adaptive pressures will prevent petrifaction of a system that combines distinctive traditional and modern features.

Notes

1. My analysis has greatly benefitted from interviews with German academics, members of science organizations, as well as representatives of Land ministries and parliaments and the BMFB. The interviews were conducted in 2001, 2008, and 2009. Misinterpretations or errors remain, of course, my own.

2. Gila Menahem, "The Transformation of Higher Education in Israel since the 1990s: The Role of Ideas and Policy Paradigms," *Governance: An International Journal of Policy, Administration, and Institutions* 21, no. 4 (2008): 499-526. Fenwick W. English assumes a radical stance and asks, "What paradigm shift?" He disavows efforts to locate one new paradigm in the study of educational administration; rather, higher education change should be viewed with "truly *multi*-paradigmatic approaches" in mind. "There will no longer be paradigm shifts because there are no paradigms." See "What paradigm shift? An interrogation of Kuhn's idea of normalcy in the research practice of educational administration," *International Journal of Leadership in Education* 4, no. 1 (2001): 37. The term originates in Thomas Kuhn, *The Structure of Scientific Revolutions* (Chicago, 1962).

3. In 2008-2009, there were 104 universities and 189 universities of applied sciences.

4. Klaus Hüfner, and Klaus Landfried, "Guest Editorial: German Higher Education: A System under Reform," *Higher Education in Europe* 28, no. 2 (2003): 141-43.

5. "Learning and Change in 20th Century British Economic Policy," *Governance: An International Journal of Policy, Administration, and Institutions* 17, no. 3 (2004): 419.

6. Nina Arnhold, "The Transformation of Higher Education and Research in Eastern Germany: A review 10 years after the *Wende*," *Education in Germany since Unification*, ed., David Phillips (Oxford, 2000), 95-96.

7. See, for example, the work of Rosalind M.O. Pritchard, "Was East German Education a Victim of West German 'Colonisation' after Unification?" *Compare*, 32, no. 1 (2002): 47-59; *Reconstructing Education: East German schools and universities after unification* (Oxford, 1999).

8. Helmut de Rudder, "The Transformation of East German Higher Education: Renewal as Adaptation, Integration and Innovation," *Minerva* 35 (1997): 99-125.

9. See John W. Moravec, "A New Paradigm of Knowledge Production in Higher Education," *On the Horizon*, 16, no. 3 (2008): 123-36.

10. Michael Dobbins, and Christoph Knill, "Higher Education Policies in Central and Eastern Europe: Convergence toward a Common Model?" *Governance: An International Journal of Policy, Administration, and Institutions* 22, no. 3 (2009): 397-430.

11. "Es reicht noch nicht," *duz Magazin,* 21 November 2008, 22-24.

12. The concept of Europeanization is now widely used to describe the integration process associated with the European Union but also Europe-wide developments independent of the European Union. The literature on the topic is abundant and growing. For a primer of its multiple meanings, see Robert Harmsen and Thomas M. Wilson, "Introduction: Approaches to Europeanization," *Yearbook of European Studies* 14 (2000): 13-26.

13. Heiko Walkenhorst, "Europeanisation of the German Education System," *German Politics* 14, no. 4 (2005): 470-86; Jarle Trondal, "The Europeanization of Research and Higher Education," *Scandinavian Political Studies* 25, no. 4 (2002): 333-55.

14. See, for example, Kerstin Martens et al., eds., *New Arenas of Education Governance. The Impact of International Organizations and Markets on Educational Policy Making* (Houndmills, 2007); Stephan Leibfried and Kerstin Martens, "PISA—Internationalisierung von Bildungspolitik: Oder: Wie kommt die Landespolitik zur OECD," *Leviathan* 36 (2008): 3-24.

15. Katrin Toens, "Policy Change in German Higher Education," in *Education in Political Science. Discovering a Neglected Field*, eds., Anja P. Jakobi et al. (London, 2009).

16. Carolin Balzer, and Alessandra Rusconi, "From the European Commission to the Member State and Back—A Comparison of the Bologna and the Copenhagen Process," *New Arenas of Education Governance,* Martens et al. (see note 14), 65, 70.

17. Menahem (see note 2).
18. Klaus Hüfner, "Differentiation and Competition in Higher Education: recent trends in the Federal Republic," *European Journal of Education* 22, no. 2 (1987): 133-43.
19. For an interesting discussion of the political significance of benchmarking, see Antonia Kupfer, "Diminished States? National Power in European Education Policy," *British Journal of Educational Studies* 56, no. 3 (2008): 299-301.
20. The findings can be viewed at http://www.insm-bildungsmonitor.de/; accessed 30 August 2009.
21. Michael Hartmann, "Die Exzellenzinitiative–ein Paradigmenwechsel in der deutschen Hochschulpolitik," *Leviathan* 34, no. 4 (2006): 447-65; Richard Münch also introduced the term "differentiation paradigm;" cited in Peter Strohschneider, "Über Voraussetzung und Konzeption der Exzellenzinitiative," *Beiträge zur Hochschulforschung* 31, no. 1 (2009): 14.
22. "Die Exzellenzinitiative als politisches Programm–Fortsetzung der normalen Forschungsförderung oder Paradigmenwechsel?" in *Making Excellence. Grundlagen, Praxis und Konsequenzen der Exzellenzinitiative,* eds., Roland Bloch, et al. (Bielefeld, 2008), 13-36.
23. See, for example, Stefan Hornbostel et al., eds., "Exzellente Wissenschaft. Das Problem, der Diskurs, das Programm und die Folgen," *iFQ-Working Paper,* no. 4 (2008); available at http://www.forschungsinfo.de/.
24. Strohschneider (see note 21).
25. For details, see the web page of the BMBF "Higher Education Pact;" available at http://www.bmbf.de/en/6142.php, accessed 19 August 2009.
26. "Bund und Neue Länder werben für den Hochschulstandort Ost," *Pressemitteilung,* 19 December 2007; available at http://www.bmbf.de/press/2206.php, accessed 20 August 2009.
27. Some marketing slogans refer to the former GDR as the "Near East," alluding to the "foreign" and exotic nature of the former GDR for many West Germans.
28. See also Peer Pasternack, "Jenseits der Exzellenzinitiative. Alternative Optionen für die ostdeutsche Hochschulentwicklung," *die hochschule. journal für wissenschaft und forschung* 18, no. 1 (2009): 142-54.
29. See also Rosalind Pritchard, "Gender inequality in British and German universities," *Compare* 37, no. 5 (2007): 651-69; *Empfehlungen zur Chancengleichheit von Wissenschaftlerinnen und Wissenschaftlern,* ed. Wissenschaftsrat, Drs. 8036-07 (Berlin, 2007).
30. *Bundesbericht zur Förderung des Wissenschaftlichen Nachwuchses (BuWiN),* ed. Bundesministerium für Bildung und Forschung (BMBF), (Bonn and Berlin, 2008), 25-28.
31. Statistisches Bundesamt, ed., *Hochschulen auf einen Blick. Ausgabe 2009* (Wiesbaden, 2009), 26-27; Bund-Länder-Kommission: Chancengleichheit in Wissenschaft und Forschung. Elfte Fortschreibung des Datenmaterials (2005/2006) zu Frauen in Hochschulen und außerhochschulischen Forschungseinrichtungen. Materialien zur Bildungsplanung und zur Forschungsförderung, no. 139 (Bonn, 2007).
32. "Die selbstbewußte Mittelmacht. Außenpolitik im souveränen Staat," *Merkur* 60, no. 9/10 (2006): 854.
33. "Deutsche bleiben unter sich," *duz Magazin. Das unabhängige Hochschulmagazin,* 21 November 2008, 27.
34. *Education at a Glance. OECD Indicators,* ed. OECD (Paris, 2008), 354.
35. German Academic Exchange Service, ed., *Wissenschaft weltoffen 2009. Facts and Figures on the International Nature of Studies and Research in Germany* (Bielefeld, 2009), 10.
36. Helga A. Welsh, "Higher Education Reform in Germany. Advocacy and Discourse," *German Politics and Society* 27, no. 1 (2009): 5-7.
37. See Johanna Witte et al., "European Higher Education Reforms in the Context of the Bologna Process: How did we get there, where are we and where are we going?" *Higher Education to 2030 (Vol. 3): Globalisation,* ed. OECD, (Paris, forthcoming).

38. The Rectors' Conference regularly publishes reports on the Bologna Process. For the lastest, see "Statistische Daten zur Einführung von Bachelor- und Masterstudiengängen. Sommersemester 2009," *Statistiken zur Hochschulpolitik* 1 (2009).

39. Olaf Bartz, "Bundesrepublikanische Universitätsleitbilder: Blüte und Zerfall des Humboldtianismus," *die hochschule. journal für wissenschaft und bildung* 2 (2005): 99-113; Mitchell G. Ash, "Bachelor of What, Master of Whom? The Humboldt Myth and Historical Transformations of Higher Education in German-Speaking Europe and the US," *European Journal of Education* 41, no. 2 (2006): 245-67; Konrad H. Jarausch, "Demokratische Exzellenz? Ein transatlantisches Plädoyer für ein neues Leitbild deutscher Hochschulen," *Denkströme. Journal der Sächsischen Akademie der Wissenschaften* 1 (2008): 34-52; Martin Spiewak, "Falsches Vorbild," *Die Zeit*, 18 June 2009, 35.

40. Ash (see note 39): 246.

41. The debate peaked in summer 2009. Among the many media contributions see, for example, Hans Joachim Meyer, "Nur Mut zu einer Reform der Reform," *Frankfurter Allgemeine Zeitung*, 6 July 2009, 7; Jan-Martin Wiarda and Martin Spiewak, "Klüger werden," *Die Zeit*, 25 June 2009, 31-32.

42. For an up-to-date account of the new steering mechanism, see *Neue Steuerung von Hochschulen. Eine Zwischenbilanz*, eds., Jörg Bogumil and Rolf G. Heinze (Berlin, 2009). Funding mechanisms are addressed, among others, by Michael Leszczezenky, "Paradigmenwechsel in der Hochschulfinanzierung," *Aus Politik und Zeitgeschichte* B25 (2004):18-25; Dominic Orr, et al., "Performance-based funding as an instrument of competition in German higher education," *Journal of Higher Education Policy and Management* 29, no. 1 (2007): 3-23.

43. Sascha Gerber et al., "Hochschulräte als neues Steuerungsinstrument," *Neue Steuerung* (see note 42), 93-122.

44. For a good general introduction to the subject, see Jeroen Huisman, and Jan Currie, "Accountability in higher education: Bridge over troubled water?" *Higher Education* 48 (2004): 529-51.

45. Accreditation Council, *Evaluation Report. Self-evaluation report for the external review of the Foundation for the Accreditation of Study Programmes in Germany*, no. 61 (Bonn, 2007); available at http://www.akkreditierungsrat.de, accessed 5 August 2009.

46. For an overview, see Ute Lanzendorf and Peer Pasternack, "Landeshochschulpolitiken," in *Die Politik der Bundesländer. Staatstätigkeit im Vergleich*, eds. Achim Hildebrandt and Frieder Wolf (Wiesbaden, 2008), 43-66; Barbara Kehm and Ute Lanzendorf, "Germany−16 Länder Approaches to Reform," in *Reforming University Governance. Changing Conditions for Research in Four European Countries*, eds., Barbara Kehm and Ute Lanzendorf (Bonn, 2006), 135-86.

47. OECD, ed., *Education at a Glance 2008: OECD Indicators* (Paris, 2008), 240.

48. Frieder Wolf, *Bildungsfinanzierung in Deutschland* (Wiesbaden, 2008).

49. Welsh (see note 36), 1-23.

50. Hans N. Weiler, "Ambivalence and the Politics of Knowledge: The Struggle for Change in German Higher Education," *Higher Education* 49 (2005): 177-95; Hans Ulbrich Gumbrecht, "Facelifting als Dauertherapie. Historische Thesen zur deutschen Universität," *Merkur* 60, no. 9/10 (2006): 917-28.

51. Ben W. Ansell, "University Challenges: Explaining Institutional Change in Higher Education," *World Politics* 60 (2008): 189-230.

52. Peer Pasternack and Reinhard Kreckel, "Die Ost-Hochschulen: Teil des Problems oder der Problemlösung? Fragestellungen und Ausgangspunkte," in *Stabilisierungsfaktoren und Innovationsagenturen. Die ostdeutschen Hochschulen und die zweite Phase des Aufbau Ost*, ed., Peer Pasternack (Leipzig, 2007), 21-30.

53. See, for example, Institut der deutschen Wirtschaft Köln, ed., *Bildungsmonitor 2008*; available at http://www.insm-bildungs.monitor.de/, accessed 7 August 2009, which ranks the educational achievements of Thuringia and Saxony highly.

$\mathcal{T}$HE NORMATIVE POWER OF A NORMAL STATE

Power and Revolutionary Vision in Germany's Post-Wall Foreign Policy

● ● ● ● ● ● ● ● ● ● ● ● ● ● ●

Beverly Crawford[1]

Introduction

Germany's growing weight on the world stage is indisputable, and its foreign policy stance is exceptional among powerful states. Remarkably, as German power has grown, the vision guiding policy has not returned to assumptions of international anarchy and the use of traditional power politics that bolster short-term self interest. Instead, that vision emphasizes multilateralism, integration, diplomacy, and antimilitarism. It is a vision that accepts the necessity of cooperation in pursuit of its international goals, sees military means to secure its interests abroad as a last resort, and accepts the governance of international institutions in the regulation of its international affairs. It is a radical departure from the traditional aims and goals of power politics. With regard to the latter, Regina Karp has written: "This vision (Weltanschauung) rests on deeply held assumptions about the possibilities and opportunities for progress in international relations; the mechanisms by which peace and stability can be achieved and sustained; the civilizational potential of treaties, rules, and norms; and the inevitable decline of the state as the single most important locus of political organization."[2]

For most international relations theorists and foreign policy observers, this is either the vision of a weak state or a paradigm shift in the international aims of a powerful one. For Germany, it began as the former and has now become the latter. Devised as a pragmatic international strategy for a defeated state, this Weltanschauung has become a sincere commitment that has been stamped deeply into the decision-making system of every foreign ministry since the founding of the Federal Republic of Germany (FRG).

Not only has this vision curiously endured as German power has grown, it has become a fitting paradigm for international behavior in the twenty-first century. Postwar German foreign policy was forced to renounce many sovereignty claims, but at the moment sovereignty was regained, its usefulness in international relations was called into question. The postwar Federal Republic was tied to Western Europe by the victors of war, but at the moment of recouping the freedom to loosen those ties, the European Union–and Germany's role in it–grew in strength. The postwar Federal Republic renounced militarism, but at the moment when a growing German military power became acceptable, international problems increasingly defied military solutions. Formulated for pragmatic reasons in one era, the vision is again pragmatic, but for very different reasons in the current period. A great power policy that was once considered "idealistic" has now become "realistic."

This paper explores the meaning of Germany's strange twenty-year marriage between traditional state power and a foreign policy vision which transforms the meaning of that power. I begin with a brief discussion of the intellectual debates over continuity and change in German foreign policy since unification. I place my own view within the context of those debates and argue that German practices have historically both adhered to that vision *and* deviated from it, both before and after unification. It is the discourse that changed after 3 October 1990. German power began to grow before that date and continued afterwards. And power now backs the radical vision. Furthermore, Germany's vision seems ideally suited to steer policy in a world where rigid notions of power, sovereignty, and the "national interest" are everywhere in evidence but they are failing as guides to foreign policy. I further discuss the current manifestation of power and vision in Germany's foreign policy. Finally, I look to the future, suggesting that Germany's vision seems ideally suited to steer policy in a world where rigid notions of power, sovereignty, and the "national interest" are failing as a guide to foreign policy.

Beyond Continuity and Change

During the "Bonn Republic," German foreign policy practices were seen as largely consistent with the Weltanschauung of a weak, divided, and occupied state. But with Germany's rise to power and achievement of sovereignty, the question of consistency between practice and vision became a matter of intense academic debate.[3] Does continued alignment with its vision characterize Germany's postunification international practices? Or has German foreign policy "changed" to reflect more narrow self-interested behavior, both inside and out of multilateral institutions? Do decision-makers' references to Germany as a "great power," signal this change? Have we seen the weakening of antimilitarism as German power has grown? Behind the divergent answers to these questions stands a larger debate about theories of international relations and whether those theories can guide foreign policy analysis.[4]

The "Realist" View

Proponents of the "change" thesis usually adhere to realist theories of international relations and believe that foreign policy is guided by a state's power position and its "national interest" in maintaining power in an anarchic world. Some speculate that, as its power has increased, Germany is indeed returning (or should return) to the practices of traditional power politics.[5] For realists, Germany's foreign policy practices were expected to conform to its new power position, and each policy decision was interpreted as an exercise of self-interested behavior. Realist sentiments were particularly prominent in the media. For example, some cited the unilateral recognition of Croatia as an instance of a more powerful Germany recreating its World War II alliance with an independent Croatia as part of a divide-and-conquer strategy in order to assert power in the Balkans.[6] The Bundesbank's startling interest rate hike in 1992, which briefly derailed the progress toward monetary union, was cited as an example of Germany's effort to undermine the project of European integration. The country was said to be flexing its "deal-breaking" muscle, by raising interest rates at precisely the time when the French government faced a referendum on the Maastricht Treaty. Germany's breach of the Eurozone's Stability and Growth Pact accompanying EMU was interpreted as evidence of a weakened "European identity" and an assertion of national self-interest. The American media criticized Gerhard Schröder's refusal to participate in the invasion of Iraq as a break "with the caution of postwar [German] policy" and urged that "the focus in Berlin ought not to be on Germany's 'great power.'" Many analysts interpreted the growth of Germany's military participation in the wars of the Yugoslav succession and in Afghanistan as a sign that Federal Republic's unique vision had expired.[7]

The Constructivist View

On the other side stand the "constructivists" who believe that power politics in international relations can be transcended. Pointing to Germany's deepened participation in the process of European integration, they argue that, incidents of deviation notwithstanding, united Germany clearly has engaged in practices that are, for the most part, consistent with the continuity of the Bonn Republic's normative vision.[8] And although Germany's military force has grown, it is largely limited to missions of peacekeeping, crisis management, and humanitarian aid. The refusal to participate in the Iraq invasion is seen as a political tactic that appealed to the German populace and therefore was a testament to Germany's commitment to antimilitarism.

At its heart, these differing interpretations and choice of emphasis are more about the viability of competing theories of international relations than about German foreign policy itself. Each side musters pieces of evidence to support its position, and opposing interpretations of similar evidence have kept the debate alive. Does the bid for a seat on the UN Security Council suggest an even greater commitment to multilateralism or does it show that Germany seeks recognition of its powerful *national* position in international politics and the symbolic status of a great power? Was Germany's refusal to participate in America's Iraq war in 2002/03 evidence of a break with multilateralism or of a fundamental commitment to antimilitarism? Does any *one* breach of a multilateral agreement signal a fundamental break with multilateralism itself? Is the essential German policy vision still alive but simply adapting to changing circumstances?

A Mighty Vision: Regional Hegemony and Normative Power

My thesis does not fit particularly well on either side. It claims that Germany has changed the way it has pursued its original vision as its power position in Europe and in international politics has grown. More importantly, it emphasizes the importance of the vision as a practical guide to the policy of powerful states as the twenty-first century advances. In emphasizing the importance of the original vision, I suggest that 1990 does not represent a significant break: continuity characterizes both vision and practice. The vision remains, but practices since 1949 have both conformed to the vision and deviated from it. The assertion of self-interest is not unique to the post Wall period—Germany often exhibited moments of self-interested behavior both early in the life of the Federal Republic, and later, as its power grew. Practices that either conform to or deviate from the vision are not easily correlated with the rise in power and achievement of sovereignty.

Change is crucial to my argument in three respects. First, at the analytic level, interpretations of the significance of practices that deviated from the vision have changed. Before unification, most observers either ignored or tolerated deviations. Flexing muscles as power grew was not seen as a return to power politics. After unification, however, each deviation was magnified and exaggerated as a significant departure from the unique vision of cooperation and antimilitarism. The interpretations changed because Germany's power had grown and expectations of behavior were grounded in traditional paradigms and in Germany's "new" international power position.

Second, my own interpretation is that power indeed has changed things, but differently than most analysts suggest. As German power has grown, the impact of practices based on the original vision has changed. In this argument, I have dusted off the old tenets of "hegemonic stability theory."[9] I argue that Germany has become a "regional hegemon" in Europe and one of the "great powers" on the international stage. The country has asserted its power, but, for the most part, the assertion of power has been on behalf of the vision. Power tied to vision has meant an assumption of leadership in Europe and in international diplomacy that have only strengthened the practices based on that vision and made them more effective. In short, vision is now backed by power.

As this vision of multilateralism, antimilitarism, and supranationalism is married to an increasingly wealthy, and, by traditional measures, powerful, state, Germany has began to successfully exercise what Ian Manners called "normative power,"[10] or the effort to tame anarchy with civilian (as opposed to military) practices and attract others to join in the effort.[11] Germany has used normative power backed by its material resources to tackle many of the new international crises that have arisen since the end of the Cold War and to foster and enhance international cooperation to resolve new global problems.

Third, and perhaps most importantly, fundamental change has taken place in the very nature of the international system itself, a change for which Germany's foreign policy vision is particularly appropriate. It is a change in which new threats throughout the world undermine sovereignty and cannot be vanquished through national "power," traditional practices of power politics, or even traditional international diplomacy. This does not mean that traditional power politics will not be exercised–far from it. But, the exercise of that power will become increasingly ineffective in achieving policy aims. The point is that Germany's foreign policy vision seems ideally suited to steer effective policy in a world where rigid notions of power and sovereignty are failing as a guide to successful foreign policy and where traditional conceptions of the "national" interest are increasingly irrelevant. Germany may have become a "normal" power after unification, but that by and large, it exercises "normative power" on the world stage.

A Vision Born in Weakness but Bolstered by Strength

Ironically, Germany's foreign policy vision was born in weakness as a strategy for survival in its postwar world of defeat, division, and occupation. Firmly in the grip of occupying powers, the Federal Republic had few policy options in defeat after the carnage it had left behind in the first half of the twentieth century. Until 1955, as William Paterson suggests, Germany could be called a "pre-sovereign" state.[12] It is well known that the core of Konrad Adenauer's legendary foreign policy was focused by necessity on the abandonment of unilateral sovereignty claims and the dissolving of German foreign policy into European institutions, identity, and multilateral regimes. Most striking was the stance on the role of military power. In the absence of national control over military force, German leaders began to hold the belief that military means to solve foreign policy problems should be a last resort. With no real foreign policy of its own, Germany's international behavior was based on civilian practices: trade, foreign aid, peacekeeping, international monitoring, and international law. These practices led to a view of "cooperative security" that linked classic security elements to economic, environmental, cultural and human-rights concerns. "Cooperative security" was seen as *indivisible*, in the sense that Germany's own security was seen as inseparable from that of other states in an interdependent world. It was *cooperative,* in the belief that security is based on confidence building, the peaceful resolution of disputes, and the work of mutually reinforcing multilateral institutions. Adenauer's vision was perhaps the only practical strategy that would allow Germany to hold on to the last shreds of "national interest" in the absence of traditional state power and national sovereignty.[13]

That strategy of maintaining the national interest by abandoning it and giving up the forces that previously had propped it up, was accompanied and bolstered by a stunning transformation of both society and political culture within the Federal Republic. West German society changed from one that was complicit with the barbarism and inhumanity of the concentration camps to a one that became deeply imbued with a commitment to liberal democracy, collective security, human rights, and antimilitarism—values that utterly reshaped German political identity.[14]

Even after 1955, when the FRG attained partial sovereignty, this culture was bolstered by a political structure which Peter Katzenstein described as "semi-sovereign," a structure in which the state was unable to act autonomously from the many social and institutional networks that attempt to influence political outcomes. Clogged with competing interests in a decentralized federal system, decision making was slow and incremental, making any policy change—including change in foreign policy—difficult. It would also be difficult for any one social or political group to capture the state to change the direction of German foreign policy. Unlike Britain or the United States, West German policy was unlikely to be subject to wide policy swings, even as sovereignty was restored.[15] This important aspect of semi-sovereignty supported the FRG's unique foreign policy vision and protected the West German state from counterproductive delusions of grandeur still held by other states.

The fact that West German leaders chose that particular strategy is unsurprising. The strength of a nation's commitment to international law and organizations, collective security, and international norms has usually been inversely proportional to its power. The weaker and more vulnerable a state, the more important are international institutions that protect its rights. Conversely, as a country grows in power, the more foreign policy options it has, the less it must conform to the views of its partners in international organizations and the more it can afford to ignore them if it sees fit. Thus, the view that Germany's foreign policy vision was only appropriate for a weak state and the speculation that Germany would revert to the practice of traditional power politics as it grew more powerful.

Power and Practice before 1990

1990 was clearly a watershed, but West German power had grown throughout the postwar period, and the policies based on the vision of "civilian power" and the submergence of national power in international institutions were increasingly backed by growth in the traditional measures of national power. No one will deny the significance of the postwar *Wirtschaftswunder* that permitted the FRG grew to become the third largest economy in the world and the largest economy in Europe.[16] And few observers will contest the fact that the economic gap between

West Germany and its neighbors began to grow before unification. Germany has long and successfully defended its title as one of the world's leading exporters.

By the 1980s, West Germany, together with France, exercised power in shaping the European integration process. The Single European Act of 1985–the first major revision of the Treaty of Rome–largely reflected French and German preferences. The Deutschmark was the backbone of the successful European Monetary System, the precursor to European Monetary Union.[17] French officials declared that they considered the FRG to be the West's industrial leader, and despite U.S. military preeminence, the French government would therefore follow West German policies on export control. And West Germany was becoming Europe's "patron." In the 1980s it contributed the most to the European Community budget of any member state, almost one-third more than France, the second largest contributor, and its receipts were lower than any other state.

But, even in the absence of power conferred by sovereignty and unity, Bonn was assertive in pursuit of its policy vision, even when that assertiveness was often risky and against the grain of traditional power politics. During the Cold War, the FRG could have remained passive in the shadow of its occupiers, but instead often rose to the occasion in times of crisis by acting as an "honest broker" in conflicts and disputes among partners and between partners and adversaries.

Successive postwar West German governments played the honest broker in transatlantic quarrels, in Cold War disputes between the U.S. and Russia, and in rancorous Middle East conflicts. They followed Otto von Bismarck, allying with old friends in the West and building bridges to new ones in the East, developing better relations with each of them than they had with each other.[18] But this time, the aim was not to simply keep conflicting parties apart as Bismarck had done, but rather to bring them closer together in cooperative arrangements.

Ostpolitik was a bold policy initiative that would prove to be the most risky of West Germany's postwar honest broker policies: an assertive act not entirely consistent with its power position. Certainly, during the cold war years, commitment to Atlanticism always trumped any policy that would reach out to the East. But at the very height of the Cold War, West German leaders single handedly laid down the foundations for rapprochement with the Eastern bloc. And when the Soviet Union invaded Afghanistan, the German government, while condemning the offensive, emphasized–to the displeasure of the United States–that conflict management in the East-West relationship demanded continuing the dialogue across the Iron Curtain rather than reducing the ties that had been so carefully built throughout the decade.

Indeed, the FRG was often assertive before unification—and not always in the service of its policy vision. Even in a state of "semi-sovereignty" before 1990, the Federal Republic sometimes exhibited behavior that can be interpreted as narrowly self-interested. As part of the strategy to increase exports, for example, Germany—in its role as a "trading state"—sold dual-use goods and technology abroad—even to unstable countries.[19] In 1989, a West German firm, Imhausen Chemie, had provided Libya with the goods and technology to produce poison gas in significant and dangerous quantities. In the thick of the Cold War, the FRG broke with the United States when it chose to assist the Soviet Union in building a pipeline to transport natural gas to Europe.[20] From the 1970s until the creation of EMU, West Germany riled its European partners by raising interest rates to counter domestic inflation.

For the most part, however, Bonn adhered to the old vision. The fact that leaders chose that particular strategy is unsurprising because the strength of a nation's commitment to its allies, international law and organizations, collective security, and international norms usually has been inversely proportional to its power. The weaker and more vulnerable a state, the more important are the allies for security and the international institutions for the protection of its rights. Conversely, as a country grows in power, the more foreign policy options it has, the less reliant it is on those same allies and international organizations and the more it can afford to ignore them if it sees fit. These assumptions gave rise to the view that Germany's foreign policy vision was only appropriate for a weak state and to the speculation that Germany would revert to the practice of traditional power politics after it achieved full sovereignty.

Power and Practice since Unification

Clearly, the Soviet Union's collapse and America's declining European presence enhanced Germany's *relative* political weight in Europe and in the world. Germany's economy grew to become the largest in Europe, and the gap between German economic strength and that of its neighbors remains large. The EU is dependent on German goods, and the country maintains a competitive advantage in the production of the most highly valued goods in Europe. In 2008, Germany retained its position as the world's number-one exporter, even against a far more rapidly growing China, and despite having fewer than a tenth as many inhabitants. Moreover, since unification, Germany has grown in the traditional indicators of military power. Despite declining defense spending, Germany's army is the largest in Europe and it has the sixth largest defense budget in the world[21] It has stationed more troops abroad than any country except the U.S.

This strength has affected policy in two ways. First, Germany has been able to become a regional hegemon, providing stability to an increasingly integrated Europe. Although they would not use the term "hegemon," most observers would accept Simon Bulmer, Charlie Jeffrey, and William Paterson's claim that Germany exercises "institutional power"[22] in the EU, and through that form of power, steers the course of European integration. In exercising leadership to deepen European integration, Germany has relinquished important aspects of national sovereignty and independence. Yet, my argument goes further. True to its foreign policy vision and backed by growing power, Germany has taken on a disproportionate share of the regional burden of European integration. A few examples suffice to illustrate: Germany is still the largest net contributor to the EU budget, consistently paying in almost twice as much as it has received; in contrast, France and the UK have managed to maintain relative parity between payments and receipts. In the realm of nonproliferation policy and export control, Germany continues to be the leader in cooperative efforts to stem the tide of weapons proliferation. Within the EU, Germany took the lead in creating a regime to curb the spread of technology that can be used to create WMD. And as noted above, German leadership ushered in European Monetary Union, an unprecedented step in European integration. The German economy now stabilizes the EURO and is the driving force behind the currency's strength.[23] In short, Germany took the lead in creating European institutions, provided these institutions with stability, and has paid a price to maintain cooperation. As Adam Posen writes, Germany has played the role of the "nice guy who picks up the check and turns a blind eye to others' free-riding on him ..." [24] Ironically, it is the very fact that Germany is seen as Europe's patron that permits acts that deviate from that role to be magnified out of proportion and interpreted as a return to self-interested behavior.

Of course, Germany was not alone in these accomplishments, but European integration and multilateralism have long been pillars of German foreign policy, and as its economic power grew, Germany was able to take a leadership role in cementing that cooperation. As a counterfactual exercise, it would be difficult to imagine the creation and enlargement of the European Union, the deepening of European integration, and

Europe's exercise of "normative power" on the international stage in the absence of German power and leadership. German practices in comparison with those of its strongest European partners seem to bear out Katzenstein's claim that Germany's identity has become "European," and that its European identity is more pronounced than that of its neighbors.[25]

Secondly, Germany has exercised normative power to the international stage, and it has underwritten its policy aims with material support. It has taken responsibility for the largest proportion of the EU obligation to reduce greenhouse emissions under the Kyoto Treaty and is the third largest contributor to the UN budget (with a larger contribution than four of the five permanent members of the Security Council). In absolute terms, it is the third largest contributor to international development assistance.

There has been much debate about the role of the German military since unification and full sovereignty.[26] By most traditional measures, the German military has become more powerful since 1990. Since the beginning of this century, Germany has taken over the command of multilateral military operations in Afghanistan, Kosovo, and Bosnia, as well as the naval deployment to Lebanon. Nonetheless, in the years after unification, German defense spending fell by roughly 15 percent, and Germany cut its armed forces from 670,000 troops to 340,000.[27] Twenty years after unification, the German military remains the least "deployable" of NATO's armies. Its structure is still not geared toward power projection but rather on territorial defense.[28] One third of all potential conscripts are conscientious objectors. Although the German military is involved in eight peacekeeping and crisis management operations around the world, and all of its army units are assigned to multinational units, the rules of engagement for troops limit their use of force far more than the rules for other NATO countries.[29]

Germany also has continued in its role of the "honest broker," a role that has become increasingly important as international crises have changed and multiplied in the past twenty years. Eerily, the Balkans proved again to be the testing ground. This time it was the wars of Yugoslav secession. The great powers picked sides in the Bosnian war: Russia (and France) supported Serbia, and the U.S. supported Bosnia and Croatia. Despite its support for Croatia's independence, Germany quickly became the mediator between Russia and the West, knowing that the former Yugoslavia could not be stabilized without Russian participation. German negotiators crafted a compromise between opposing sides in the war in order to prevent an escalation of global tensions.[30]

In the Middle East, Chancellor Gerhard Schröder and Foreign Minister Joschka Fischer became "bridge-builders" between the West and the Arab world. Declaring Germany's intention to forestall a "clash of civilizations" between the West and Islam while continuing to support Israel, Schröder intensified relations with leading Muslim nations. In particular, Germany played an important role in negotiations to end Iran's nuclear threat. The United States had excluded itself from negotiations early on–its position was that the West should isolate Iran and threaten war if Iran continued along the nuclear path. Germany took the lead in the successful effort to bring the Americans on board.[31] When the case was taken to the UN Security Council where Russia and China joined the negotiations, Germany became the only party to the negotiations that was not a permanent member.

One could argue that the roles of honest broker and member of a negotiating team are the only roles fitting for Germany's position on the international stage; by the lights of traditional power politics, Germany does not have the capability to threaten Iran. Germany is only one of the European negotiating team (EU 3). Nonetheless, as the strongest country in Europe, Germany is in a position to lead the team. Indeed, its preferred language has prevailed in all of the negotiating packages offered to Iran. Furthermore, the other two members of the EU 3 have been weakened: Britain's role in the Iraq war has undermined its credibility in the Arab world, and France's ties to Algeria, Syria, and Lebanon raise suspicions in both Israel and the United States about its objectivity. Indeed, Germany is in a material position to influence Iran. Not only is it Iran's largest trade partner, but 75 percent of Iran's small and medium industries rely on imported goods and technology from Germany. Germany is also Syria's most important trade partner. While far from breaking ranks with the United States, Chancellor Angela Merkel has made it clear that military action against Iran is "not an option."

Despite its sustained role in European integration, its constructive role in international diplomacy, and its shaping of the military for the primary purpose of peacekeeping, there are instances in which Germany has also deviated from its radical vision, just as it did many times *before* unification. For example, the recognition of Croatia in 1991 broke an agreement with European partners to act in concert with regard to the wars of the Yugoslav secession. The brief abrogation of the Eurozone's Stability and Growth Pact violated the agreement on European Monetary Union. Perhaps most troubling–and most damaging to my argument–the growth of German arms exports both before and after unification violates and trivializes the norms of antimilitarism and cooperative security.

Nonetheless in a larger sense, Germany *has* adhered to its foreign policy vision as its power grew. Why? A thorough answer would require another essay and a closer look at Germany's domestic political system. The Federal Republic's internal political "semi-sovereignty" may have been compromised in several ways after unification, but incrementalism has continued to characterize the making of foreign policy, and political structures still prevent rapid change.[32] Sometimes domestic forces and culture have shaped Germany's preferences in opposition to the policy vision and in ways that are narrowly self-interested. But, what is crucial is that German leaders did not abandon their commitment to multilateralism and antimilitarism as their country began again to exhibit the traditional markers of state power. And they did not abandon that commitment when full sovereignty was restored to the united country. Moreover, German society did not revert to the nationalism and militarism that was its signature in the first half of the twentieth century.

Power and Vision in the Face of New Challenges

The abrupt and astonishing fall of the Berlin Wall on 9 November 1989 ironically heralded the beginning of a painful process of global transformation. International politics, long dominated by stable bipolar confrontation and governed by well-defined rules and hierarchies of power, unraveled overnight. Until 8 November 1989, while the world continued to focus on the behavior of states and their rulers, social, technological, economic, and political forces were at work below the radar. When the Berlin Wall was cracked open, analysts were caught completely off guard. The focus on the East German "state" and Soviet domination, the belief that powerful international actors would keep Germany divided, and the conviction that power politics would always determine outcomes, acted as blinders. Old paradigms blinded statesmen and analysts alike to the reality of the East German state's "Wizard of Oz" character, the importance of non-state actors and the power of non-violent citizen action. This primary focus on the state has continued. Symbolically true to the old paradigm, 3 October was chosen as the day to celebrate this transformation, in the continued belief that a unified and sovereign *state* was the most significant outcome of these revolutionary changes.

   Joyful events in Germany were followed by sudden death of Yugoslavia and then the death of one of the world's two superpowers–other "Wizard of Oz" states unmasked. Breathtaking ethnic and sectarian violence erupted across the globe, leaving gross human rights violations and millions of refugees in its wake. Nimble and lethal non-state challengers emerged in force, exclusive and well-armed "isms" grew, and states continued to respond with more militarization. Nuclear weapons have proliferated both horizontally and vertically, and even if they were to be abolished, there are huge stockpiles of conventional arms around the world, some so devastating as to be comparable to nuclear alternatives.

Predictable practices of power politics–still entrenched in the foreign policy bureaucracies of powerful and weaker states alike–continue, but are maladapted to this new, unpredictable environment. Analysts have failed to understand new challenges because they are locked in a brittle nineteenth-century vision of the world that is long out of date. Both analysts and policy-makers are baffled by a world where overwhelming modern force cannot defeat tribal combatants living in caves, where computer hackers can potentially shut down a nation, where threats to the national interest, can come from the earth's atmosphere, where a global financial crisis, like the fall of the Berlin Wall, can happen overnight, and where, as Konrad Jarausch has written, "havoc created by global capitalism ... is beginning to rival the suffering caused by the nation state."[33] Experts and politicians will continue to be blind to a host of other lurking problems that were once unthinkable, but now inevitable, unless the paradigm changes.

The German foreign policy vision was freed from the old paradigm when it was forced to abandon the practice of traditional power politics after 8 May 1945. Of course, in the face of many current problems, Germany's foreign policy vision is still limited. But among all the great powers in the twenty-first century, the country is equipped with a transformative foreign policy Weltanschauung, which can give birth to practices that can meet the challenges of a transformed world. These practices may represent the beginning of a new form of power that is not based on the use of raw material force to compel others into compliance. Rather, it is based on the ability to attract them as partners in solving big problems often obscured by outdated assumptions of what constitutes interest and power in the international system.

Conclusion

The debate over continuity and change in foreign policy emerged because of Germany's rise in the traditional sources of power that caught the world's attention when unity and full sovereignty were restored in 1990. This particular debate emerged because the paradigm of power politics is still dominant in both analytic and policy circles. In the early years of the

Federal Republic, the foreign policy vision described here was the only choice in the face of defeat and widespread experience of the havoc that the country had wrecked on the first half of the twentieth century. But, as noted above, the more power a state amasses, the more options it has in its foreign policy choices. For powerful states, the options chosen reveal the relationship between vision and practice. After 1990, Germany could have taken a more self-interested path–as Britain did–with regard to European integration. Yet, German leaders chose to integrate more deeply into Europe and to underwrite the integration process. Of course, Germany does not always agree with the means its partners have chosen to solve collective problems, and will attempt to steer collective decision making in directions that its leaders prefer. Nevertheless, disagreement on means does not mean rejection of cooperative ends. Claims to the contrary neglect the larger picture. After 1989, Germany had the option to shed the role of the honest broker and assert unilateral self-interest as it had had done in the beginning of the twentieth century. German leaders from Kohl to Merkel have taken the path consistent with its vision of diplomacy, and have provided leadership in international negotiations. Allies and critics, for example, have called on Germany to drop its restrictive rules of combat in Afghanistan, but it has refused to do so.

There is no question that Germany could revert to traditional practices of power politics in many issue areas. But, the assumptions that guide those practices are likely to render them increasingly useless in the face of the revolutionary changes of the twenty-first century. So far, the vision of cooperation, integration, and antimilitarism has largely prevailed in practice, and Germany's normative power has continued to grow. The twenty-first century international environment presents a clear hurdle to the cooperative vision guiding German foreign policy, and it challenges Germany's power to back that vision. Germany's vision is still focused on international, not "global" issues. I have suggested, however, that on the positive side, Germany's normative power is still amplified by material power, and there are many twenty-first century problems that it *has* successfully confronted. Even then, though, thorny questions remain: Can the exercise of normative power alone reduce human rights abuses and manage ethnic and sectarian conflict? Can the country maintain its status as a "civilian power" and its commitment to antimilitarism when it has grown to become the third largest arms exporter in the world? Can Germany's vision of cooperation lead to the construction of new international governance structures that include new actors and are fashioned to meet the challenges of a new century? Let us revisit these questions in another twenty years' time, on a future anniversary of change in Germany.

Notes

1. I gratefully acknowledge the assistance of Ronny Clausner in the preparation of this chapter.
2. Regina Karp, "The New German Foreign Policy Consensus," *The Washington Quarterly* 29, no. 1 (2005-2006): 61–62. Similar arguments are made by Thomas U. Berger, "Norms, Identity and National Security in Germany and Japan," in *The Culture of National Security: Norms and Identity in World Politics*, ed. Peter J. Katzenstein (New York, 1996), 317–356; Peter J. Katzenstein, ed. *Tamed Power: Germany in Europe* (Ithaca, 1997); John S. Duffield, *World Power Forsaken: Political Culture, International Institutions, and German Security Policy After Unification* (Stanford, 1998); Thomas Banchoff, *The German Problem Transformed: Institutions, Politics, and Foreign Policy, 1945–1995* (Ann Arbor, 1999); Adrian Hyde-Price, *Germany and European Order: Enlarging NATO and the EU* (Manchester, 2000), 116–117; Volker Rittberger, ed. *German Foreign Policy Since Unification: Theories and Case Studies* (Manchester, 2001); Kerry Longhurst, *Germany and the Use of Force: The Evolution of German Security Policy, 1990–2003* (Manchester, 2004).
3. For overviews of this literature, see: Benjamin Herborth and Gunther Hellmann, "Taking Process Seriously: Concatenations of Continuity and Change in German Foreign Policy," paper presented at the Annual Meeting of the International Studies Association, 22 March 2006; Rainer Baumann, "'The German Way'–Germany's policy in the Iraq Crisis and the Question of Continuity and Change in German Foreign Policy," paper presented at the annual meeting of the International Studies Association, 17 March 2004; Thomas Risse, "Kontinuität durch Wandel: Eine 'neue' deutsche Außenpolitik?" *Aus Politik und Zeitgeschichte* 11, no. 3. (2004): 24-31; Sebastian Harnisch, "Change and continuity in post-unification German foreign policy," *German Politics* 10, no.1 (2001): 25-60; Eva Gross, "German Foreign Policy and European Security and Defense Co-Operation–The Europeanization of National Crisis Management Policies?" paper presented at the Annual Meeting of the International Studies Association, 28 February 2007 available at http://www.allacademic.com/meta/p180815_index.html.
4. See Gunther Hellmann, "Fatal attraction? German foreign policy and IR/foreign policy theory," *Journal of International Relations and Development* 12 (2009): 257–292.
5. See, for example John Mearsheimer, "Back to the Future," *International Security* 15 (1990); Christopher Layne, "The Unipolar Illusion: Why New Great Powers will Rise," *International Security* 17 (1993): especially 41-45; Kenneth Waltz, "The Emerging Structure of International Politics," *International Security* 18 (1993); Philip H. Gordon, "The Normalization of German Foreign Policy," *Orbis* (1994). Max Otte with Juergen Grewe, *A Rising Middle Power? German Foreign Policy in Transformation, 1989-1999* (New York, 2000); Christian Hacke, "Mehr Bismarck, weniger Habermas. Ein neuer Realismus in der deutschen Außenpolitik?" *Internationale Politik* (2006): 71. Some realists see a continuation of the old practices and believe that Germany should engage in power politics but is not doing so. They argue that Germany's continued emersion in Europe, the rules of engagement that limit Germany's participation in combat, and a "pacifist popu-

lation" restrict its capabilities and that the country should marry its material power to decisive military leadership, matching "rhetoric with risk." Germany is often seen as consistently punching below its actual political and diplomatic weight when it plays that role. Those who urge Germany to take on a "leadership" role or pursue a truly independent foreign policy often interpret this policy as one that hides behind its "culture of reticence," or a policy that refuses to leave its "reflexive comfort zone," lacks the courage to "take sides in international disputes," and is afraid to leave its "safe house of moral comfort and limited involvement." For the most recent expressions of this view see John C. Hulsman and Nile Gardiner, "After Schroeder: U.S.-German Relations in the Merkel Era," Heritage Foundation Backgrounder #1907, 11 January 2006; available at http://www.heritage.org/Research/Europe/bg1907.cfm; John Vinocur, "Ms. Merkel Becomes Ms. Soft Power," *International Herald Tribune*, 17 September 2007; Karl-Heinz Kamp and Julian Lindley-French "Big power, little will," *New York Times*, 14 June 2008; Stephen Walt, "Over-achievers and under-achievers," 21 April 2009; available at http://walt.foreignpolicy.com/posts/2009/04/21/over_achievers_and_under_achievers

6. Pierre Gallios, "Vers une predominance allemande," *Le Monde*, 16 July 1993.

7. For these accounts see Beverly Crawford, *Power and German Foreign Policy: Embedded Hegemony in Europe* (Houndmill, 2007): 14, 108, 132-133, 140.

8. See note 2.

9. See Charles Kindelberger, *The World in Depression* (Berkeley, 1973); Charles Kindelberger, "Dominance and Leadership in the International Economy: Exploitation, Public Goods, and Free Rides," *International Studies Quarterly* 25 (1981): 242-54, and Robert Keohane, *After Hegemony: Discord and Cooperation in the World Political Economy* (Princeton, 1984).

10. Ian Manners, "Normative Power Europe: A Contradiction in Terms?" *Journal of Common Market Studies* 40, no. 2 (2002): 235-58.

11. François Duchêne, "The European Community and the Uncertainties of Interdependence," in *A Nation Writ Large? Foreign-Policy Problems before the European Community*, eds., Max Kohnstamm and William Hager (London 1973), 1-21; Kalypso Nicolaïdis and Robert Howse, "'This is My EUtopia ...': narrative as power," in *Integration in an Expanding European Union*, eds., J. H. H. Weiler, Iain Begg, and John Peterson (Oxford, 2003), 341-66; and for a popularization of this view Andrew Moravcsik, "The Quiet Superpower," *Newsweek*, 17 June 2002.

12. See William E. Paterson, "European Policy-making: Between Associated Sovereignty and Semi-sovereignty," in *Governance in Contemporary Germany: The Semisovereign State Revisited*, eds., Simon Green and William E. Paterson (Cambridge, 2005), 261-282.

13. Banchoff (see note 2).

14. See Katzenstein *Tamed Power* (see note 2); Thomas U. Berger, *Cultures of Anti-Militarism: National Security in Germany and Japan* (Baltimore, 1998); Konrad H. Jarausch. *After Hitler: Recivilizing the Germans, 1945-1995* (New York, 2006).

15. Peter J. Katzenstein, *Policy and Politics in West Germany: The Growth of a Semi-sovereign State* (Philadelphia, 1987).

16. By 1990, Germany's share of all European imports and exports was 25.6 percent, compared to France's 16 percent, the next highest. Cited in Andrei Markovits and Simon Reich, "Should Europe Fear the Germans," in *From Bundesrepublik to Deutschland: German Politics after Unification*, eds., John Huelshoff, Andrei Markovits and Simon Reich (Ann Arbor, 1993), 278.

17. William Wallace, "Is Germany Europe's Leading Power?," *World Today* 51 (1995): 162-5; Jeffrey Frieden, "The Dynamics of International Monetary Systems: International and Domestic Factors in the Rise, Reign, and Demise of the Classical Gold Standard," in, *Coping with Complexity in the International System*, eds., Jack Snider and Robert Jervis (Boulder, 1993), 137-62; Markovits and Reich (see note 16); Michael E. Smith and Wayne Sandholtz, "Institutions and Leadership: Germany, Maastricht, and the ERM Crisis," in, *The State of the European Union: Building a European Polity?*, eds., Carolyn Rhodes

and Sonia Mazey (Boulder, 1995), 245–65; Helen Milner, "Regional Economic Cooperation, Global Markets, and Domestic Politics: A Comparison of NAFTA and the Maastricht Treaty," *Journal of European Public Policy* 2 (1995): 337–60.

18. In 1877, Bismarck's "iron rule" for German foreign policy was to create "political situation in which all the powers need us and are kept as much as possible from forming coalitions against us." He thus balanced commitments to Britain, Austria-Hungary, and Russia with the aim of preserving peace in Europe, which would, in turn, permit German power to grow. When crises among opposing sides threatened to tear fragile alliances apart, Bismarck interceded as the honest broker to settle disputes. See A. J. P Taylor, *Bismarck: the Man and the Statesman* (New York, 1969).

19. Beverly Crawford, *Economic Vulnerability in International Relations* (New York, 1993); Julian Perry Robinson and Jozef Goldblat. "Chemical Weapons I," Stockholm International Peace Research Institute, SIPRI Fact Sheet (1984); Harald Müller, Matthias Dembinski, Alexander Kelle, and Anette Schaper, *From Black Sheep to White Angel? The New German Export Control Policy*, Peace Research Institute, Report no. 32 (Frankfurt, 1994); Michael Rietz, "Germany's Export Control Law in the New Millennium" (2002); available at http://www.isis-online.org/publications/expcontrol/ rietz2002.html; Amnesty International, "Who Armed Iraq?" *Terror Trade Times* (2003); available at http://web.amnesty.org/pages/ttt4-article_7-eng.

20. In 1982, the United States imposed an embargo on all U.S. technology bound for the USSR to be used in the construction of a natural gas pipeline from Siberia to the FRG. European firms had contracted to build this pipeline with U.S. technology and equipment in exchange for increased supplies of Soviet natural gas. With the embargo of equipment, the U.S. attempted to halt the construction of the pipeline, arguing that its supply of gas to Europe would create unacceptable NATO dependence on Soviet energy supplies. The embargo triggered bitterness and discord within the Western alliance because European allies refused to comply with U.S. embargo requirements and stubbornly refused to halt the pipeline construction.

21. SIPRI Yearbook 2008: Armaments, Disarmament and International Security (2008); available at http://www.defencetalk.com/sipri-yearbook-2008-armaments-disarmament-and-international-security-15581/.

22. See Simon Bulmer, Charlie Jeffery and William Paterson, *Germany's European Policy: Shaping the Regional Milieu* (Manchester, 2000). For a recent statement of Germany's EU leadership role see Gunther Hellmann, "Ein fordernder Multilateralismus. Deutschlands Fortschreibung seiner außenpolitischen Traditionslinie ist gefestigter als gemeinhin unterstellt," *Frankfurter Allgemeine Zeitung,* 4 February 2009.

23. For a more detailed empirical account of Germany's leadership, contributions to stable cooperation, and adherence to the German policy vision under Merkel (albeit from a critical perspective), see Christian Hacke, "Germany's foreign policy under Angela Merkel," *The AICGS Advisor*, 8 August 2008; available at http://www.aicgs.org.

24. Adam S. Posen "If America Won't, Germany Must" *Internationale Politik* 6 (2005): 32–37.

25. Katzenstein (see note 15).

26. This debate started almost immediately after unification and continues today. See, for example: Hanns W Maull, "Zivilmacht Bundesrepublik Deutschland: Vierzehn Thesen für eine neue deutsche Außenpolitik," *Europa-Archiv* 47, no. 10 (1992): 269-78; Hans-Peter Schwarz, *Die Zentralmacht Europas: Deutschlands Rückkehr auf die Weltbühne* (Berlin,1994); William Wallace, "Deutschland als europäische Führungsmacht," *Internationale Politik* 50, no. 5 (1995): 23-8; Christian Hacke, *Die Außenpolitik der Bundesrepublik Deutschland: Weltmacht wider Willen?* (Berlin, 1997); Rainer Baumann and Gunther Hellmann, "Germany and the Use of Military Force: 'Total War,' the 'Culture of Restraint,' and the Quest for Normality," *German Politics* 10, no. 1 (2001): 61-82; Piotr Buras and Kerry Longhurst, "The Berlin Republic, Iraq, and the Use of Force," *European Security* 13, no. 3 (2004): 215-245; Ole Wæver, "European Integration and Secu-

rity: Analysing French and German Discourses on State, Nation, and Europe," in *Discourse Theory in European Politics*, ed. David Howarth (Basingstoke, 2005): 33-67; "The Berlin Stonewall," *The Economist*, 30 October 2008; Hacke (see note 23).

27. It is commonly agreed that NATO members should spend 2 percent of their national wealth on defense. This target is also a minimum requirement for the EU's European Security and Defense Policy to be credible. Germany has refused to spend more than 1.4 percent on defense.

28. See Hacke (see note 23).

29. In Afghanistan, for example, German Tornado aircraft are limited to unarmed reconnaissance; German Medevac helicopters have to be back at base by dusk; German rules of engagement prevent German soldiers from firing if the targets may be civilians. No other member of NATO and no other member of the coalition in Afghanistan must adhere to these restrictions.

30. Beverly Crawford "The Bosnian Road TO NATO Expansion," *Journal of Contemporary Security Policy* 21, no. 2 (2000).

31. Press reports cited Germany as the "most aggressive of the European three" in the effort to bring the U.S. into the negotiations. See Garath Porter, "Iranian Crisis in the Wilderness," *Asia Times Online*, May 2006; available at http://www.atimes.com/atimes/ Middle_east/HE02Ak04.html.

32. See the essays in Green and Paterson (see note 12).

33. Konrad H. Jarausch, "Reflections on Transnational History," 20 January 2006; http://h-net.msu.edu/cgi-bin/logbrowse.pl?trx=vx&list=hgerman&month=0601&week=c&msg=LPkNHirCm1xgSZQKHOGRXQ.

Chapter 15

$\mathscr{F}$LIGHT FROM RISK

Unified Germany and the Role of Beliefs in the European Response to the Financial Crisis

● ● ● ● ● ● ● ● ● ● ● ● ● ● ● ●

Abraham L. Newman

Introduction

Since the end of World War II, scholars have attempted to make sense of German policy makers, who repeatedly sacrificed their nation's sovereignty for highly ambiguous and uncertain goals of multilateralism and European integration.[1] Many concluded that this sacrifice resulted from a deeply ingrained political identity that stressed international cooperation and shunned parochial national politics.[2] Since the end of the Cold War, however, German leadership has suggested a willingness to weaken its role as global altruist and reassert its interests in Europe and abroad.[3] A string of policy moves seem to signal this policy shift including German demands for a reallocation of the European Union (EU) budget, strict adherence to the Stability and Growth Pact, and most recently a refusal to bail out financially stressed member states in Eastern Europe. Several scholars have thus concluded that the role of German identity in European and global politics has waned, replaced by a more interest-based agenda.[4]

This chapter indeed concludes that German foreign economy policy towards regional and global cooperation has shifted. The identity/self-interest dichotomy, however, obscures the driver and character of this shift. In short, I argue that the unification process elevated long-held beliefs about policy conservatism that now compete with the postwar multilateral policy frame within the foreign policy elite. In addition to the pro-European, multilateralist agenda, a second powerful lesson of the interwar period emphasized the dangers associated with sudden change, loss of control and the benefits of incrementalism. This flight from risk is embedded both in the institutional logic of the Federal Republic (e.g., the five percent rule in parliament, the independent central bank, the requirement that a new government must be proposed before a vote of no confidence is possible, cooperative federalism) and in the public narrative concerning the Nazis' rise (e.g., hyperinflation, cycling governments, emergency rule). Such attitudes increasingly are finding their way into Germany's policy towards the EU, with the reverence for the Stability and Growth Pact probably the most infamous example.

This shift within German foreign policy is in part a product of the transformative effects of German unification. It is hard to imagine that an event as dramatic as reunification would not shape policy makers' beliefs about the world. In particular, unification has undermined the primary narrative supporting German multilateralism that stressed a resurgent German military threat to the continent. In fact, the economic drag imposed by unification severely weakened Germany's position within Europe and globally.[5] Dubbed a civilian power in the late 1980s,[6] the country retreated into high unemployment, low growth, and sizable deficits through the 1990s. Unified Germany faced the shock of sudden integration and, in response, has returned to a core belief in caution and policy conservatism.

Such beliefs matter because policy making is embedded within highly uncertain environments.[7] Leaders are frequently in a position where they are unable to calculate the probability that a particular action will result in a specific outcome. In the run up to unification, for example, an equal number of scholars predicted a resurgent German nationalism as those who predicted a continuation of cooperative multilateralism.[8] In a much more mundane, but equally important way, the prevalence of "unanticipated consequences" associated with public policy underscores the tenuous relationship between means and ends. Owing to this uncertainty, decision makers must rely on causal and normative beliefs about how the world works to guide their decisions. These beliefs are conditioned by sociohistorical experience and often compete with one another over time.

To demonstrate the importance of policy conservatism in Unified Germany's European and foreign policy, I examine two recent decisions by the German leadership–the role of economic stimulus as a European response to the global economic crisis and the need for a European initiative to resolve the bank crisis in Eastern Europe. The two examples initially seem to reflect a national interest story as Germany forgoes cooperative, regional solutions and asserts its preferences. Germany's foreign economic policy (blocking European stimulus efforts and regional support for stumbling Eastern European member states), however, stands in direct opposition to the cornerstone of Germany's primary economic engine–European export markets. Therefore, the empirical narrative must explain the puzzling insistence by the German leadership for a regional response to the post 2008 financial crisis based on stability instead of export market stimulus. Understanding the German position on these issues is not only critical to explain the specific policy maneuvers, but also lay at the crux of both resolving the global economic crisis and the future of European integration. Theoretically, the chapter contributes to a growing research agenda that examines the role of historical context for understanding causal relationships.[9]

The chapter is organized around three sections. The first builds the core argument of the paper, emphasizing the role of beliefs in policy making and highlighting competing beliefs within German policy elite. The second section examines the argument within the debates on regional economic stimulus and the Eastern European banking crisis. The final section concludes by drawing out implications for German policy within Europe and the role of beliefs in international affairs more generally.

From Partner to Scrouge?

Scholars interested in the role of identity in international relations have frequently turned to the case of Germany as an important example. This was driven among other reasons by the German political elite's deep commitment to sovereignty-reducing strategies in the postwar period. Under the auspices of *Einbindungspolitik* (the policy of cooperative self-binding) Germany repeatedly pursued multilateral cooperation within Europe even though it constrained its ability to act independently.[10] Running counter to traditional realist predictions about state behavior, research examined the role of the German past in the creation of a distinct foreign policy identity to make sense of this empirical puzzle.[11]

Since unification, however, German European policy has subtlety shifted. Far from abandoning the European project, Germany has been more critical of potential free riding by other members.[12] In a series of high profile debates including EU budget negotiations and the Stability and Growth Pact, Germany has signaled its unwillingness to continue integration at any cost. This has led a number of scholars to conclude that the role of postnational German identity is waning and that it is moving towards a more self interest- based politics.[13]

Rather than positioning identity concerns in opposition to self-interests, the argument in this paper is that ideas and interests are largely inseparable. It would be difficult to construct a theory of politics in which actors repeatedly acted irrationally. This does not mean, however, that context does not pay a role in interest construction for two primary reasons. First, meaning is socially and historically embedded. An actor's understanding of her environment shapes how she calculates her interests and the factors that go into that calculation.[14] In the imperial era, for example, heads of state had to consider (and often preferred) direct colonization as a foreign policy tool. Similarly, rational economic policy meant very different things during periods dominated by mercantilism, Keynesianism, and monetarism.[15]

Second, in situations of uncertainty, beliefs play a critical role in interest construction.[16] Following work on the sociology of markets and recent research on constructivism in international relations, uncertainty refers to those situations where an actor is unable to calculate the probability that a certain action will produce a specific outcome. This contrasts to risk, in which probabilities can be assigned.[17] Given the complexity of social relations, decision makers frequently find themselves in conditions of uncertainty. Unlike the natural sciences, most policy debates center on contested cause and effect relationships. The empirical reflection of this fact is the widely documented (and often ignored) unintended consequences of policy actions. Given such high levels of uncertainty, decision makers must rely on beliefs and narratives about how the world works to adjudicate disputes and guide their behavior. In short, there are often multiple self-interested solutions depending on one's socially embedded self-conception. From this perspective, postwar German multilateralism should not be contrasted to interest-based politics, but rather should be seen as the product of a period when German preferences were embedded in a specific set of historically rooted beliefs. Faced with the daunting task of postwar reconstruction and managing its position on the front line of the Cold War, German beliefs about regionalism offered a straightforward path to make sense of a highly complex and uncertain environment.

It seems clear that unification has tempered the narratives that long supported and maintained the multilateralist frame.[18] On the one hand, militarism and nationalism have not been stoked by unification. There has been no debate about proliferation, still one of the key great power status symbols.[19] Nor has Germany attempted to develop an offensive military capability outside of the NATO or European defense architectures.[20] Economically, Chancellor Helmut Kohl's promise of "blooming fields" in the East never materialized. Instead, the economic powerhouse of the postwar period has been struggling over the last decade to manage rising public debt and high unemployment, producing serious reflection on the country's long term economic competitiveness.[21] The experience of unification, a product of geostrategic structural changes, has undermined the resonance of beliefs focusing on international law and regional cooperation.

At the same time, unification has reinforced another set of beliefs held by German elites centered on policy conservatism. A central narrative in German political debates rests on notions of caution and incrementalism. Reflecting the rapid downward spiral into economic chaos and fascism during the interwar period, societal and political lesson-drawing stressed the dangers of high public debt, rapid inflation, and quick political change. The founders of the Bonn Republic promoted reform-adverse decentralization that spread political decision making among a number of actors, fostering the diffusion of power.[22] These ideas are embedded in a host of political institutions such as the independence of the central bank, the five percent rule for parties to enter the parliament, cooperative federalism, rules on no-confidence votes, and strong judicial review.[23] In the private sector, similar beliefs prevail within the coordinated market economy privileging incremental change and gradual adjustment.[24]

These institutional sites of caution and conservative policy making are tied to a parallel set of economic ideas–ordoliberalism–with a long history in German policy making. Embodied in the economic policies of Ludwig Erhard and the work of the Freiburg School, ordoliberalism focuses on the critical role of the state in providing the necessary stability in society and the economy to permit the efficient functioning of markets.[25] Known under the rubric of *Ordnungspolitik*, economic policy in Germany has long privileged monetary and fiscal stability as important preconditions for effective capitalism. Clearly, this strain of economic liberalism buttresses a set of more general political beliefs that promote sociopolitical incrementalism.

In many respects, then, unification was quintessentially un-German. It happened with little preparation and proceeded in the most radical of forms. The painful reality subsequently has elevated the narratives surrounding policy conservatism to the top of the public policy agenda. With mounting deficits and escalating unemployment reaching their highest levels of the postwar period, triggers for these alternative beliefs reverberated through the public sphere. In terms of the role of ideas in politics, the unification process had the simultaneous effect of undermining self-reinforcing narratives of a revitalized Germany (which would necessitate further cooperation) and raising the salience of beliefs in caution and policy incrementalism.

The following section explores the role of beliefs in the German position vis-à-vis the European response to the post 2008 financial crisis. The crisis offers a useful set of cases to explore the argument for both empirical and theoretical reasons. Empirically, the German position has stood out as the key to the European and perhaps global response. Theoretically, the cases offer interesting examples that appear to conflict with both a standard explanation focusing on self-interest and an identity-based argument centering on regional cooperation. According to the former, one reasonably would have expected Germany to act swiftly to prop up this important export market, which accounts for roughly half of the country's GDP. Under the latter, one would have predicted that Germany would emphasize regional solutions to the problems, embedding its response within the institutional structures of the European Union. Instead, German elites have ignored calls for both and emphasized caution, even when such a policy could undermine its national economic interests and broader solidarity within Europe.

A Teutonic Approach to the Global Financial Crisis

German policy makers have repeatedly taken a strong and unique position with regard to the financial crisis that struck the global economy starting in 2008. Generally speaking, they have downplayed the domestic sources of the crisis, highlighted irrational lending promoted by the United States as its primary cause, and been reluctant to promote global economic stimulus via Keynesian economic policies as a plausible solution. On all accounts, German policy seems guided by a deep belief in the danger of quick action and loss of control. Importantly, much of this caution is focused on European decision makers outside of Germany, where institutional constraints are perceived to be weaker.

The clearest example of the role of risk aversion in German foreign economic policy came in the debate concerning the use of economic stimulus to revive the European and global economy. The United States and the United Kingdom, supported by projections from the World Bank and IMF, were strong advocates for large scale domestic spending packages as a means to kick start the global economy. These efforts were augmented by large spending packages in China and other developing economies.

By contrast, Germany repeatedly denounced the strategy as short-sighted with former Finance Minister Peer Steinbrück infamously denouncing British policy as "crass Keynesianism" and Chancellor Angela Merkel receiving the nickname "Madame Non" in the French press.[26] While the German government committed itself to a significant stimulus at home, it blocked large-scale European efforts at a stimulus and argued against similar policies by its neighbors.[27]

German opposition to European stimulus seemed particularly puzzling as Germany depends heavily on other European consumers to purchase its exports (nearly 65 percent of its products travel to other EU markets).[28] A persistent failure to reignite the European market will have significant ramifications for the German economy and bring widespread unemployment. By late 2009, German exports fell 20 percent from their 2008 level and over half a million workers had been placed on short hours (where the government picks up roughly 60 percent of the wage bill to prevent job cuts). Projections by Commerzbank expect German GDP to fall 6 percent because of the crisis and the World Bank expects global growth to fall by at least 2 percent. Given the immensity of the crisis for the German economy, it was at least a plausible argument that a broad-based European stimulus would be in Germany's self-interest.

The German argument against a regional stimulus solution rested on two basic arguments both of which are steeped in causal beliefs focused on caution. The first concerned the long-term macroeconomic consequences of pumping enormous amounts of money into the global economy—inflation. Merkel dubbed this the "crisis after the crisis."[29] In short, the economic meltdown was the product of loose monetary policy in the U.S. that led to an undervaluation of risk in the global economy. A European stimulus would have a similar effect by throwing money on the fire. Both the government's rhetoric and analysis seemed embedded within policy conservatism and the fear of losing control. Speaking in the Bundestag in November 2008, Merkel argued: "Excessively cheap money in the U.S. was a driver of today's crisis ... I am deeply concerned about whether we are now reinforcing this trend through measures being adopted in the U.S. and elsewhere and whether we could find ourselves in five years facing the exact same crisis."[30] Steinbrück concurred: "So much money is being pumped into the market that capital markets could easily become overwhelmed, resulting in a global period of inflation in the recovery."[31] Far from a cynical move by Germany to free ride on U.S. policy, the German policy elite held a unified view that U.S. policy might in fact augment the crisis and vocally opposed further efforts in this direction. It is important to remember that while many bemoaned the German effort, between emergency spending and automatic stabilizers, the German government committed around 3 percent of GDP to stimulus spending in 2009. Merkel continued: "We were living beyond our means ... After the Asian crisis and after 9/11, governments encouraged risk taking in order to boost growth. We cannot repeat this mistake."[32]

Second, the German government feared the potential loss of control that might result if other European governments became unshackled from the Stability and Growth Pact. Promoted by Germany as a condition of monetary union, the Pact commits EURO members to a 3 percent debt ceiling.[33] A pan-European stimulus would give countries like Italy and Greece free license to expand already bloated government deficits. Axel Weber, the Bundesbank President, warned that this would be the wrong time "to lose sight of the sustainability of public financing."[34] Once again, this scenario played on a deeply rooted caution within Germany to public debt and violated the commitment of Ordungspolitik to monetary stability. If other countries lost control of their budgets, the potential exists that the Euro could be destabilized. This would, in turn, realize German fears about giving up the D-Mark, the holy grail of postwar German stability.[35]

Finally, the German counter proposal based on expanded regulation of the financial services sector smacked of the more general set of conservative policy beliefs. Through new rules on hedge funds, credit rating agencies, and other non-bank alternatives, Germany hoped to bring a sense of renewed stability and calm to the sector. Banking (as opposed to securities markets) lies at the center of the German political economy. "Patient" capital focused on reasonable rates of return underpins a large small-to-medium-sized industrial sector, which plays a critical role in wage growth and job stability.[36] The financial services boom of the last decade placed tremendous pressure on German banks to increase their profitability or face acquisition.[37] Similarly, hedge funds, which take advantage of short-term shifts in market positions, further exacerbated such pressures. The German strategy to restrain non-bank activity deemphasizes a return to rapid economic growth through financial services and instead emphasizes the stability provided by a more traditional banking sector. *Der Spiegel* summarized nicely the German risk aversion approach to the financial crisis: "Mrs. Merkel is crawling across the slippery surface on all fours, slowly and cautiously."[38]

Trouble on the Eastern Front

German caution seemed to be playing a similar role in its response to the banking crisis in Eastern Europe. During the last decade, West European banks lent Eastern European citizens money in foreign denominated loans. This seemed like a good bet while Eastern European currencies were strong and their economies were growing at a brisk pace. The global slowdown, however, revaluated Eastern European currencies, instantly increasing loan payments. Western banks ignoring this danger offered an exorbitant number of these loans. Austrian banks alone made loans in the region equivalent to 70 percent of Austrian GDP. Over 50 percent of consumer loans in Hungary and Poland are foreign denominated. The first wave of loans has already gone bad and foreign investment has withered. Several new member states have seen double digit declines in GDP with Hungary, Latvia, and Romania negotiating rescue packages from the IMF.

Importantly, Germany took a rather aloof policy stance to the crisis, refusing a European bailout package promoted by Hungary at a spring 2008 European summit and waffling on its commitment to the region if the situation should worsen.[39] A chorus of German elites including the head of the central bank and the finance ministry denounced proposals that new members quickly rush to join the EURO.[40] Counter to the Germany-through-Europe identity, German policy rejected both European initiatives and direct bilateral aid to the new member states.

Some have argued that Germany's stance reflects the relatively small exposure of its banks to the crisis and thus supports a self-interest story.[41] While this might be the belief of German elites, it is difficult to imagine that the German economy truly is decoupled from what transpires on its eastern borders. In terms of exports, German sales in 2007 to just the Czech Republic, Hungary, and Poland surpassed exports to the United States. Additionally, a meltdown of the Austrian and Swedish banking systems would have severe repercussions for the Eurozone and two of Germany's main export destinations.[42]

Politically, the German position also undermines solidarity within the European Union for its newest members and stands in sharp contrast to traditional *Einbindungspolitik*. The idea that member states in the East must negotiate with the IMF stands in stark contrast to regional rescue packages negotiated in the early 1990s during the last currency crisis. It is hard to imagine Germany having pressed new member states Spain or Portugal into the hands of the IMF in the face of the European Monetary System crisis.[43] Already, Polish and Hungarian leaders have questioned the German position in such terms with Polish Prime Mister Donald Tusk arguing: "We see the biggest risk in crumbling solidarity in Europe, and in growing national egoism."[44]

Underlying German policy were concerns that a German-led bailout would reward risk taking by others. Over the last decade, Germany has dealt with the difficulties associated with unification by enacting a number of austerity programs and suffered slow growth and job loss. They emerged as the largest among a small group of economically responsible member states and attribute this success to their focus on stability and economic order. In order to check the potential of moral hazard, Germany turned to the IMF to oversee and manage the bailout of Hungary, Latvia, and Romania. While these packages limited the short term instability in the countries, they came with strict austerity packages. As a result, all three countries will see domestic spending contract in the coming years. While the IMF provides a useful institutional mechanism to externalize German risk aversion, this reverse stimulus will do little to jump start demand for German exports or deepen trust within the European Union.

Conclusion

German foreign policy, especially European policy, has long interested scholars of international relations. Upsetting standard realist logics, German elites repeatedly have sacrificed their own sovereignty for the potential long-term benefits of European integration. Whether due to a deep-seated postnationalism or an alternative path toward power, German policy makers believed in the slogan "Germany through Europe." In the face of a number of highly uncertain situations–postwar reconciliation, cold war reemergence, and unification–they returned to this regional identity to guide their behavior. This has led scholars of foreign policy to identify a unique German power resource based on international law and multilateralism (see Beverly Crawford's contribution to this volume).

Since unification, however, a competing narrative has been elevated, which emphasizes policy conservatism and stability. Long part of the German domestic policy discourse, it has emerged as a fundamental feature of its European policy. In both the case of the regional stimulus debate and the Eastern European banking crisis, Germany rejected European solutions and instead followed a politics of austerity, emphasizing monetary stability, moral hazard, and institutional constraints. They have pursued this policy strategy even in the face of dramatically falling exports, the lifeblood of the German economy. Rather than a free-riding strategy, German elites have cast the debate as an instance where they are on the right side of ambiguous economic terrain. While definitive proof of either a self-interest or identity explanation is difficult, policy makers in Germany seem to hold a clear set of beliefs that run through the narratives they chose to justify their actions: a narrative that relies on a flight from risk.

If this shift in ideas persists, it will mark an important turn for European politics more generally as Germany remains its largest and most economically powerful member. Above all, the country could become an important counterpole to those advocating a swift return to fast growth strategies. By contrast, Germany could push for a set of policies that prioritize stability and minimize business cycle fluctuations. This would set it on a different path than past U.S. and UK policy. It will be interesting to watch how the German position resonates with emerging markets that long privileged growth, but that recently have come to respect the violence of market volatility. The rise of risk aversion does not necessarily mean the end of multilateralist Germany. Rather, it indicates the values and concerns that will motivate German leaders as they sit at regional and international negotiations.

Theoretically, this chapter builds on a growing constructivist literature that stresses the role of beliefs in shaping national preferences. National preferences remain one of the least understood workhorses in political economy.[45] While the majority of research in this area relies on arguments stressing materialist claims of self interest, the literature on uncertainty argues that such self-interests are embedded within sociohistorical contexts. Far from static, the case demonstrates the role that major historical events–such as unification–can have in altering the resonance of competing belief sets. Now, in the face of a global financial crisis, as means-end relationships become attenuated, policy makers face conflicting explanations of the problem and the solution. They (intentionally and unintentionally) employ their beliefs to make sense of the world. Politics is thus not a debate about rational versus irrational or material versus appropriate, but distinct (and often competing) beliefs about what is materially and normatively appropriate.

Notes

1. Gunther Hellmann, "Goodbye Bismarck? The Foreign Policy of Contemporary Germany," *Mershon International Studies Review* 40 (1996): 1-39.
2. Peter Katzenstein, *Tamed Power: Germany in Europe* (Ithaca, 1997); Thomas Banchoff, "German Identity and European Integration," *European Journal of International Relations* 5 (1999): 259-289.

3. Adrian Hyde-Price and Charlie Jeffery, C. (2001) Germany in the European Union: Constructing Normality. *Journal of Common Market Studies,* 39 (2001): 689-717; Jeffrey Anderson, *German Unification and the Union of Europe: The Domestic Politics of Integration Policy* (Cambridge, 1999).
4. Charlie Jeffery and William Paterson, "Germany and European Integration: A Shifting of Tectonic Plates," *West European Politics* 26 (2003): 59-71.
5. Hans-Werner Sinn, "Germany's Economic Unification: An Assessment after Ten Years," *CESifo Working Paper Series* (2000): 1-24.
6. Hanns Maull, "Germany and Japan: The New Civilian Powers," *Foreign Affairs* (Winter 1990/1991); available at http://www.foreignaffairs.com/articles/46262/hanns-w-maull/germany-and-japan-the-new-civilian-powers.
7. Cornelia Woll, *Firm Interests: How Governments Shape Business Lobbying on Global Trade* (Ithaca, 2008);.Mark Blyth, *Great Transformations: Economic Ideas and Institutional Change in the Twentieth Century* (Cambridge, 2002); Frank Knight, *Risk, Uncertainty and Profit* (Boston, 1921).
8. John Mearsheimer, "Back to the Future: Instability in European after the Cold War," *International Security* 15 (1990): 5-56.
9. Blyth (see note 7); Abraham Newman, "What You Want Depends on What You Know: Firm Preferences in an Information Age," *Comparative Political Studies* (forthcoming, 2010).
10. Karl Kaiser, "Deutsche Aussenpolitik in der Aera des Globalismus," *Internationale Politik* 50 (1995): 27-36.
11. Peter Katzenstein, "United Germany in an Integrating Europe," *Current History* 96 (1997): 116-123; See also Katzenstein (see note 2); Banchoff (see note 2).
12. Anderson (see note 3); Hyde-Price and Jeffery (see note 3).
13. Jeffery and Paterson (see note 4); Beverly Crawford, *Power and German Foreign Policy* (Hampshire, 2007).
14. See, for example, Kathleen Mcnamara, *The Currency of Ideas* (Ithaca, 1998).
15. Kathleen Mcnamara, "Rational Fictions: central bank independence and the social logic of delegation," *West European Politics* 25 (2002): 47-76.
16. Woll (see note 7); Blyth (see note 7).
17. Knight (see note 7).
18. Herbert Kitschelt and Peter Katzenstein, "From Stability to Stagnation: Germany at the Beginning of the Twenty-First Century," *West European Politics* 26 (2003): 1-34.
19. Mearsheimer (see note 8).
20. Simon Bulmer and William Paterson, "Germany in the European Union: Gentle Giant or Emergent Leader?" *International Affairs* 72 (1996): 9-32.
21. Wolfgang Streeck, "German Capitalism: Does it Exist? Can it Survive" in *Modern Capitalism or Modern Capitalisms?*, eds., Colin Crouch and Wolfgang Streeck (London, 1995); Helmut Wiesenthal, "German Unification and 'Model Germany': An Adventure in Institutional Conservatism," *West European Politics* 26 (2003): 37-58.
22. Fritz Scharpf, Bernd Reissert and Fritz Schnable, *Politikverflechtung* (Anthenaeum, 1976).
23. David Currie, *The Constitution of the Federal Republic of Germany* (Chicago, 1994).
24. Peter Hall and David Soskice, *Varieties of Capitalism* (Oxford, 2001).
25. Edward Megay, "Anti-Pluralist Liberalism: the German neoliberals," *Political Science Quarterly* 85 (1970): 422.
26. Carter Dougherty, "Allies See Germany Trying Bailout with a Thimble," *New York Times,* 17 December 2009, availanle at www.nytimes.com.
27. See Carter Dougherty and Judy Dempsey, "Leery of Debt, Germany Shuns a Spending Spree," *New York Times.* 10 March 2009; available at www.nytimes.com.
28. World Trade Organization Statistics Portal; http://stat.wto.org/CountryProfile/WSDB CountryPFView.aspx?Language=E&Country=DE.
29. Bertrand Benoit, Quentin Peel, and Chris Bryant, "We All Want to Put the Global Economy Back on its Feet," *Financial Times,* 28/29 March 2009, 2.

30. Richard Tomlinson and Oliver Suess, "Merkel Makes Like Obama with German Stimulus Excluding Europe," *Bloomberg*, 26 March 2009; available at www.bloomberg.com.
31. Bertrand Benoit, "Germany warns on 'Crisis after Crisis,'" *Financial Times*, 12 April 2009; available at www.ft.com.
32. Robert Marquand, "Germany's Hard Line on the Stimulus: Why Merkel says 'Nein,'" *Christian Science Monitor*, 31 March 2009, 6.
33. Martin Heipertz and Amy Verdun, *Ruling Europe: The Politics of the Stability and Growth Pact* (Cambridge, 2010).
34. Ralph Atkins, "Where are the Star Economists to Defend German Policy?" *Financial Times*, 20 April 2009, 2; Carter Dougherty and Judy Dempsey, "Leery of Debt, Germany Shuns a Spending Spree," *New York Times*, 10 March 2009; available at www.nytimes.com.
35. McNamara (see note 14).
36. Richard Deeg, *Financial Capitalism Unveiled: Banks and the German political economy* (Ann Arbor, 1999).
37. Richard Deeg and Susanne Luetz, "Internationalization and Financial Federalism," *Comparative Political Studies* 33 (2000): 374-405.
38. Suzanne Fields, "Germany's Approach: An Empty Shoe for Mrs. Merkel," *Washington Post*, 18 December 2009, A23.
39. "EU-Gipfel laesst Traum von Osteuropa-Hilfe platzen," 1 March 2009; available at www.welt.de.
40. "German Finance Minister says Conditions for Adopting Euro should not be Changed-Extended," 9 April 2009; available at www.econews.hu.
41. "Osteuropa-Krise bedroht deutsche Banken nicht," 2 March 2009; available at www.reuters.com.
42. Ambrose Evans-Pritchard, "Failure to Save East Europe will Lead to Worldwide Meltdown," *Telegraph*, 15 February 2009; available at www.telegraphy.co.uk; "Die Krise in Osteuropea reisst Deutschland mit," 19 February 2009; available at www.welt.de.
43. McNamara (see note 14).
44. Jan Puhl, "Eastern Europe's Economic Crisis," *Spiegel Online*, 23 March 2009; available at www.spiegel.de; Steven Erlanger and Stephen Castle, "Growing Economic Crisis Threaten the idea of One Europe," *New York Times*, 2 March 2009; available at www.nytimes.com.
45. Jeffry Frieden, "Actors and Preferences in International Relations," in *Strategic Choice and International Relations*, eds., David Lake and Robert Powell (Princeton, 1999).

PART IV.
POLITICAL ECONOMY

ᵍᵉᵣ GERMAN ECONOMIC UNIFICATION
TWENTY YEARS LATER

• • • • • • • • • • • • •

Holger Wolf

Introduction

Has German economic unification succeeded?[1] The twentieth anniversary of 1989 invites a look back at the experience of economic unification and a glance forward to new and remaining challenges. The rearview mirror reveals dramatic economic improvements. While both subjective assessments of material well-being and some measurable indicators still display gaps, the increase in such measures since the early 1990s has been remarkable (see Figure 1).

Yet, a closer look reveals downsides as well. In contrast to the "economic miracle" in the postwar Federal Republic (FRG), the economic success in the new states did not include an employment boom. Almost two decades of GDP growth following the 1990-1991 economic collapse have not undone the employment collapse of the early postunification period. Despite significant convergence in labor productivity, a sizable gap remains and appears to be quite persistent, raising the specter of a permanent difference with implications for future migration patterns.

Fiscal challenges raise another concern. Over the last two decades, the new states have benefitted from sizable transfers supporting the economic unification process in manifold ways, from financing infrastructure investment and housing modernization, to raising demand for locally produced goods and services. Looking forward, transfers are set to diminish as Solidarity Pact II winds down, placing additional pressures on already funding-strapped and (except Saxony) significantly indebted state and local

Figure 1: Comparison of New and Old States 1991 and 2008

	New States as % of Old States 1991	New States as % of Old States 2009	New States 2006	Old States 2006	New States as % of Germany 1991	New States as % of Germany 2009
GDP per capita	42.9	73.0				
GDP per hour worked	68.1	77.9				
Satisfaction (1-10) with						
Life generally			6.3	6.9		
Housing			7.5	7.7		
Living standard			6.6	7.1		
Work (Employed Only)			6.8	6.9		
Household Income			5.2	6.2		
GDP					11.1	15.5
Population					22.6	20.0
Unemployed					39.1	32.2

Source: Economic data from Bundesministerium für Wirtschaft und Technologie, Wirtschaftsdaten Neue Bundesländer (Berlin 2010), 3. Survey data from DESTATIS, GESIS-ZUMA and WZB in *Datenreport* 2008, Bundeszentrale für politische Bildung (Bonn, 2008), 403.

governments just as they have to confront the myriad adjustment challenges of an unfolding demographic transition.

The chapter takes up some of these issues in more detail. The next section begins with a brief review of economic developments since unification. The chapter then turns to a discussion of three core issues set to play a major role in future economic performance–the ability to close the remaining productivity gap, the challenges posed by the demographic transition and the fiscal situation.

A Short History of Economic Unification

The planned economy left a daunting legacy in the new Länder. Much of the capital stock proved to be technologically out-dated, the physical infrastructure and the housing stock dilapidated, the monetary and trading systems in disarray and environmental damage widespread.[2] The cumulative impact was reflected in labor productivity standing at less than half the level in the old states at the time of unification. Institutionally, economic unification extended the monetary, social, and economic arrangements of the Federal Republic to the new Länder (GEMSU).[3] Separately, the Treuhandanstalt embarked on the task of privatization, largely completed by 1994.

Following unification, the new states faced a dramatic decline in demand, reflecting both the dissolution of the CMEA and the switch of domestic consumers to imported goods. Declining demand mapped into a collapse of manufacturing sector output and employment, and sharply rising unemployment. Rapid wage increases partly motivated by concerns about large-scale out-migration of skilled workers raised unit labor costs and accelerated the move to a capital-intensive manufacturing sector, reflected in high investment ratios and rapidly rising labor productivity.

Following two years of dramatic decline dispelling any hopes for an immediate second economic miracle, economic activity bottomed and then strongly rebounded. A booming construction sector fueled by generous fiscal incentives provided support for output and employment. In the spate of a few years, the housing stock was substantially modernized and replenished, while gaps in transportation and communication infrastructure were reduced. Manufacturing sector production and exports began a lasting rebound, though from a much-diminished base. More promising economic dynamics found their reflection in net emigration rates declining from 165.4 thousand in 1991 to 24.9 thousand in 1996.[4]

Figure 2: Sectoral Growth 1996 to 2007

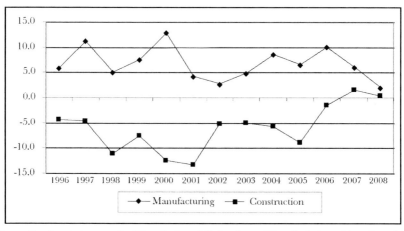

Source: Bundesministerium für Wirtschaft und Technologie, Wirtschaftsdaten Neue Laender, November 2009, 5. Growth in gross value added, price adjusted.

Following the initial rebound, convergence in labor productivity and GDP per capita slowed in the second half of the 1990s, and has remained subdued since. On the sectoral level, the boom in the construction sector ended, giving way to a prolonged decline. Manufacturing sector output and exports continued to expand but could not fully compensate.[5]

Figure 3: *Unemployment in the New Länder*

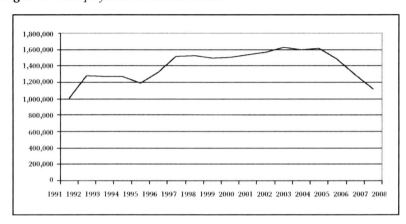

Source: DESTATIS, Statistical Yearbook 2009, 94.

Though declining in recent years, unemployment has remained high, prompting the continuation of a broad array of active labor market policies.[6] Net migration began to rise again, in recent years standing at about 50 thousand a year.[7] Wage setting arrangements have seen a marked trend towards differentiated firm-level agreements; moderate wage increases coupled with further productivity gains found their reflection in steadily declining unit labor costs.

Economic Unification Twenty Years Later

The economic unification experience provides rich pickings for both optimists and pessimists. On the positive side, measures of material well-being have improved markedly; gaps between the old and the new states have diminished. Yet, unemployment remains high, transfers continue to provide important support and convergence has slowed.

Looking forward, many factors will jointly determine the economic prospects of the new states. The following focuses on three specific issues. The first concerns convergence. Are there reasons to suspect that labor productivity in the new states will remain permanently below the levels in the old states? The answer matters both for the future of migration flows and for the fiscal transfer system. The second concerns the impact of the demographic transition, which will be much more dramatic and immediate in the new states. The final aspect concerns the fiscal challenges facing both states and municipalities as they address these issues.

Convergence

At unification, relative productivity in eastern Germany–subject to a range of measurement challenges–stood at less than half of the western level. By the mid 1990s, the gap had closed dramatically. Since then, however, further convergence has been slow, and a persistent residual gap has emerged. For the entire economy, the gap in hourly productivity amounts to about a quarter, with significant variation across broad sectors and across sub-sectors within industry.[8] This gap remains despite the diminution of the most apparent initial challenges–the capital stock has been modernized, the communications and transportation infrastructure is comparable, property rights largely have been settled, and trade and distribution relations reshaped. Has catch-up indeed ended, with implications for both migration and transfers?

Figure 4: Firm Creation in the New Länder

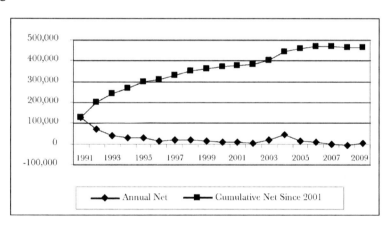

Source: Bundesministerium für Wirtschaft und Technologie, Wirtschaftsdaten Neue Länder, November 2009, 18.

The causes of the productivity gap–and thus the likely future dynamics–have been actively debated. One focus has been on features related to the smaller average size of firms in the new states, ranging from a reduced demand for high-end business services (in turn related to the scarcity of headquarters) to the relative lack of branded products and a lower R&D intensity. Looking forward, to the extent that continued growth of firms–many created after unification and thus still quite young–stands to resolve some of these obstacles to further convergence, a cautiously optimistic outlook seems warranted. The prospects for additional convergence are however likely to differ spatially between the dynamic urban centers and innovation clusters and some of the sparsely populated rural areas facing a more difficult challenge attracting investment and retaining skilled workers. The traditional east-west distinction will thus increasingly have to be complemented by a more spatially disaggregated view.

Demographic Transition

The demographic transition driven by the combination of a declining fertility rate and rising life expectancy results in an ageing and eventually declining population. While the broad trends are shared in the old and new states, the new states face more immediate and pronounced demographic changes, reflecting both the dramatic decline in the fertility rate in the early 1990s and ongoing net emigration.[9] Over the next decades, forecasts for the new states (excluding Berlin) predict significant declines both in the overall and in particular in the working age population (see Figure 5). While the broad trends are similar, the declines are likely to be particularly pronounced in the more remote rural counties suffering net emigration, less so in the urban centers. The three stylized features—a declining labor force, a shrinking population, and a shift in the age structure of the population and the labor force—in turn have first order and often quite complex economic implications.[10]

Figure 5: Population Trends, 1987-2050 (in millions)

	Brandenburg	Mecklenburg West Pomerania	Saxony	Saxony-Anhalt	Thuringia
1987	2.667	1.974	5.032	3.007	2.721
1995	2.542	1.823	4.567	2.739	2.504
2008	2.522	1.664	4.193	2.382	2.268
2020	2.410	1.538	3.875	2.113	2.053
2030	2.206	1.427	3.591	1.927	1.886
2040	2.008	1.316	3.318	1.745	1.716
2050	1.790	1.194	3.047	1.562	1.538

Source: For 1987, 1995, 2008, DESTATIS Statistical Yearbook 2009, 35. Forecasts for 2020 to 2050, DESTATIS, "Bevölkerung Deutschlands nach Bundesländern bis 2050, Ergebnisse der 11. Koordinierten Bevölkerungsvorausberechnung nach Ländern" (Wiesbaden, 2007).

Apart from the direct effect of a declining labor force, the effects of the demographic transition on the core aggregate measures of economic activity and material welfare—the growth rates of GDP and of GDP per capita—depend, inter alia, on the relationships between the age composition of the labor force skill levels based on formal education and experience, productivity, the propensity to create firms, mobility, and innovation. While these relationships are complex and often nonlinear, the evidence suggests that the fraction of the labor aged twenty-five to forty (set to decline sharply) may play a crucial role, as both mobility and the propensity to create firms are currently highest in this age group.[11]

An important caveat arises, however, in that forward-looking assessments are by necessity based on past experience. In a number of areas, changes in public policy and firm-level practices have the potential to alter these features. For instance, the challenges for knowledge diffusion created by the traditional concentration of formal vocational and tertiary education at the start of an individual's working life as the size of the groups newly entering the labor force declines can be addressed through a more determined move towards life-long learning. The net effect will thus depend not just on the demographic change itself, but also on the ability of both policy and firm-level practices to adjust to the challenges. The marked increase in labor market flexibility in the new states provides some comfort in this respect.

Transfer and Fiscal Outlook

Over the last two decades, the new states have benefitted from significant net transfers through programs specifically oriented at the new states (notably the German Unity Fund followed by the Solidarity Pact I and II), through other fiscal programs–that due to their specific characteristics, resulted in net transfers to the new states–and through the net beneficiary status of the new states within the social insurance system. On the private side, the transfers support demand for the non-traded sector, with a non-negligible aggregate effect.[12] On the public side, the transfers have enabled remarkable improvements in infrastructure and other public amenities.

While transfers significantly raised per capita state revenues in eastern Germany, an even more pronounced increase in per capita expenditures found its reflection in rising debt levels. Twenty years after unification, per capita debt levels in the new states (except Saxony) exceed levels in the old states (see Figure 6). Similar fiscal challenges arise on the municipal level where the daunting investment challenges of repairing and upgrading infrastructure were partly financed through debt.

Figure 6: Debt Levels 2008 (EURO per capita)

	State	Municipalities
Saxony-Anhalt	8,259	1,610
Brandenburg	6,773	874
Thuringia	6,759	1,116
Mecklenburg West Pomerania	5,927	1,257
Germany	*5,888*	*1,392*
Saxony	2,279	885

Source: Based on DESTATIS, Statistical Yearbook 2009, 595.

Looking forward, both the new states and the municipalities[13] face significant fiscal pressures. On the national level, the new deficit limits will impose fiscal constraints on all levels of government. Specific to the new states, targeted transfers under Solidarity Pact II are declining and set to end by 2019. The fiscal equalization system (Länderfinanzausgleich) limiting divergences in fiscal resources across states (and associated intrastate equalization systems across municipalities) will limit the effect of these changes on per capita, but not on total revenues.[14] The significant fixed cost component associated with many public services will require tough choices to minimize the likelihood of negative feedback effects in which cutbacks, in turn, affect investment and migration decisions. Again, the challenges are likely to be most pronounced in the rural areas.

Conclusion

Looking back twenty years after economic unification, is the glass half-full or half-empty? The list of economic accomplishments achieved in the last two decades is remarkable indeed. Today, the new states enjoy a world class communications and transportation infrastructure. A desolate housing stock has been thoroughly modernized and a technologically dated capital stock has been replaced. Labor productivity has jumped dramatically. In fact, labor markets in the new states are more flexible than in the old states. The revitalization of traditional strengths is complemented by the emergence of new sectors. Dynamic urban cores have emerged, notably in the southeast. Following the initial decline, manufacturing has recorded steady growth, and exports have rebounded strongly.

This general positive assessment is tempered by a number of factors, and by challenges to sustained dynamic performance. Looking backward, the sharp increase in productivity brought about by the rapid move to a capital-intensive manufacturing sector was accompanied by a sharp reduction in manufacturing employment and two decades of high–though recently declining–unemployment. Growth is unequal. Dynamic industrial urban cores emerging primarily in the south-east contrast with more stagnant developments in some rural areas experiencing persistent emigration. Productivity convergence has stalled after the initial jump, though the aggregate picture hides more positive disaggregated dynamics.

Looking forward, the ability of the new states to sustain growth and re-accelerate convergence depends on their ability to sustain the good recent performance and to address the challenge of the demographic transition under constrained fiscal conditions. Over the last decade, the new states have developed a remarkable level of flexibility, providing room for optimism that the serious challenges will be successfully addressed.

Notes

1. Over the last two decades, a sizable literature has explored prospects and performance of the new states. See Horst Siebert, *Das Wagnis der Einheit* (Stuttgart 1992); Gerlinde Sinn and Hans-Werner Sinn, *Jumpstart: The Economic Unification of Germany* (Cambridge, 1992); Gerhard Ritter, *Der Preis der deutschen Einheit* (Munich, 2007); and Karl-Heinz Paqué, *Die Bilanz–Eine wirtschaftliche Analyse der Deutschen Einheit* (Munich, 2009).

2. For an economic history of the German Democratic Republic, see André Steiner, *Von Plan zu Plan* (Munich, 2004).

3. Ritter 2007 (see note 1).

4. Statistisches Bundesamt Deutschland DESTATIS, Pressemitteilung Nr. 375 "Wanderungssaldo von Ost- nach Westdeutschland andert sich wenig," 1 October 2009. For recent studies exploring migration patterns and determinants see Herbert Brücker and Parvati Trübswetter, "Do the best go west? An Analysis of the self-selection of employed East-West Migrants in Germany," *Empirica* 34, no. 4 (2007): 371-395; Jennifer Hunt, "Staunching Emigration from East Germany: Age and the Determinants of Migration," *Journal of the European Economic Association* 4, no. 5 (2006): 1014-1037; Alexander Kubis and Lutz Schneider, "IM Fokus: Ist Abwanderung typisch ostdeutsch? Regionale Mobilität im West-Ost Vergleich," *IWH Wirtschaft im Wandel* 4 (2009): 152-157.

5. Since the turn of the millennium, export growth in the new states has substantially exceeded growth in the old states, though in terms of exports per capita a gap remains.

6. For an assessment of active labor market policies see Eckhard Wurzel, "The Economic Integration of Germany's New Länder," *OECD Working Paper* no. 307, September 2001, 39; and Dennis Snower and Christian Merkl, "The Caring Hand that Cripples," *American Economic Review* 96, no. 2 (2006): 375-382.

7. See DESTATIS (see note 4).

8. See Joachim Ragnitz, "Zur Diskussion um den Produktivitätsrückstand Ostdeutschlands," Institut für Wirtschaftsforschung Halle (2005). For a discussion of the spatial aspects of convergence see DIW, IfW, IAB, IWH and ZEW, "Erster Fortschrittsbericht

wirtschaftswissenschaftlicher Institute über die wirtschaftliche Entwicklung in Ost-deutschland," 17 June 2002.

9. For a comparative assessment on occasion of the fifteenth anniversary of unification, see Michael Berlemann and Marcel Thum, "Blooming Landscapes in East Germany?" *CESifo Forum* 4 (2005): 16-22. For recent papers exploring aspects of the convergence debate see Margarethe Quehenberger, "Ten Years after: Eastern Germany's convergence at a halt?," EIB Papers 5 (2000): 117-136; Michael Burda and Jennifer Hunt, "From Reunification to Economic Integration: Productivity and the Labor Market in Eastern Germany," *Brookings Papers on Economic Activity* 2 (2001): 1-71; Hans-Werner Sinn, "Germany's Economic Unification: An Assessment after Ten Years," *Review of International Economics* 10 (2002): 113-28; Joachim Ragnitz, 2005, "Fifteen Years After: East Germany revisited," *CESifo Forum* (2005): 3-6; and Michael Burda, "What kind of shock was it? Regional Integration and Structural Change in Germany after Unification," *Journal of Comparative Economics* 36, no. 4 (2008): 557-567. See also DIW et al. (see note 8) and Ragnitz (see note 8) for discussions of network effects; Harald Uhlig, "Regional Labor Markets, Network Externalities and Migration: The Case of German Reunification," *The American Economic Review* 96, no. 2 (2006): 383-387 for a more cautious view.

10. The fertility rate has since rebounded and currently slightly exceeds the level in the old states.

11. See Institut für Wirtschaftsforschung Halle, Technische Universitaet Dresden (Helmut Seitz), and ifo Institut Dresden, *Demographische Entwicklung in Ostdeutschland, Forschungsauftrag des BMWi, Endbericht* (Halle, 2006) for a detailed assessment.

12. Ibid.

13. See Harald Lehmann, Udo Ludwig and Joachim Ragnitz, "Originäre Wirtschaftskaft der neuen Länder noch schwächer als bislang angenommen," *Wirtschaft im Wandel*, IWH, (2005): 134-145 for an assessment.

14. The structure of municipal financing, including the reliance on the cyclical *Gewerbesteuer*, is currently under review.

15. For a detailed asessment see Institut fuer Wirtschaftsforschung Halle et al. (see note 11).

Chapter 17

THE ELUSIVE QUEST FOR NORMALCY

The German Economy since Unification

● ● ● ● ● ● ● ● ● ● ● ● ● ●

Stephen J. Silvia

Introduction

Early on, the project of German unification came to be defined as the elimination of economic and social differences between East and West. A combination of western triumphalism and caution–expressed succinctly in the omnipresent mantra of the day, "no experiments"[1]–quickly specified the task more tightly. Germany would unify through the East adopting without modification the economic and social structures of the West, which would provide the material and technical assistance needed to implement the changes. The argument in favor of this approach was highly compelling. There had been five German regimes during the twentieth century: the Second Empire, the Weimar Republic, the National Socialist dictatorship, the German Democratic Republic and the Federal Republic of Germany. Only the latter proved viable. It would be foolhardy, therefore, for a united Germany to depart from the institutions and practices of the Federal Republic, since they were the only ones that had worked and earlier failure repeatedly had proved catastrophic.

Twenty years have passed, so we are now in a good position to assess the impact of adopting wholesale the institutions of western Germany to achieve unification. Specifically, this chapter focuses on two economic outcomes in eastern Germany–namely, unemployment and Land (state) output. Unemployment and Land output are good proxies for overall economic performance and progress in recovering from four decades of central planning. Explaining the performance of these factors also entails analyses of other core economic variables, including growth, income, and productivity.

Unemployment has remained disproportionately high in eastern Germany well after the unit labor cost reached a level roughly comparable with that of the west. Keynesian and neoclassical economists have proffered alternative explanations for the persistence of eastern unemployment. The latter have the more convincing argument, which blames high initial wages in eastern Germany for producing a labor "trap," but this explanation is not without flaws. Turning to the second outcome under investigation, Land output per employee in eastern Germany is extremely uniform, a pattern that contrasts with both western Germany and prewar eastern Germany. The best explanation here is both the sheer volume and specific content of public investment in eastern Germany since unification. The volume and uniformity of a government program contrasts with the disaggregated and uneven pattern characteristic of private investment. The concentration of public investment in structures was also not conducive to producing enduring advances in productivity.

The anomalous patterns for unemployment and output have persisted for some time. Public policy in the years immediately following unification is in large part responsible for both outcomes. Yet, even when the conditions and policies that initially produced disproportionately high unemployment in eastern Germany had changed, two factors produced hysteresis that hindered adjustment: productivity traps for low-skilled and unemployed workers, and the reality that factor adjustment takes time. Per capita investment rates over the past decade, which have actually been lower than in western Germany, have further hindered progress toward convergence. Economic modeling indicates that wage subsidies targeted at low-income employment would be a promising way to break the current high-unemployment equilibrium in eastern Germany. Nevertheless, the political barriers to implementing such a policy have been insurmountable in the past. The current experience with subsidized employment through short-time work offers an opportunity to rethink taking similar measures at the lower end of the labor market, but the political barriers to adopting such a policy are just as formidable as they were a decade ago.

The next two sections present in detail data and explanations for developments in unemployment and Land output per employee. The subsequent section discusses the implications of the findings for future developments in German unification and economic integration.

Unemployment in Eastern Germany: Trends and Contending Explanations

The single most politically salient economic variable in any discussion of German unification is unemployment. Both the eastern unemployment rate and the ratio of eastern to western unemployment are important. The full-employment policy of the German Democratic Republic (GDR) set the initial joblessness figures at an unsustainably low level (see Figure 1). During the third quarter of 1990, which was the opening quarter of German economic and monetary union, the eastern unemployment rate was just 3.5 percent, which was 2.9 percentage points *lower* than the western rate.[2] Eastern joblessness surged quickly, however, and by the fourth quarter of 1990, the unemployment rate in eastern and western Germany had already converged at 6.1 percent. Two quarters later, eastern unemployment reached 9 percent while the western rate fell to 5.6 percent. In the final quarter of 1991, joblessness topped 11 percent in eastern Germany but was only 5.7 percent in the West.

Figure 1. Eastern and Western Unemployment Rates.

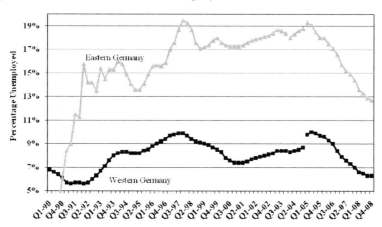

Series breaks starting in 2004 and 2005 indicate substantial redefinitions of unemployment.

Source: Bundesagentur für Arbeit

In the first quarter of 1992, the eastern unemployment rate spiked to 15.8 percent while unemployment fell in the west back to 5.6 percent. The divergent trends produced the largest gap ever between eastern and western unemployment. The eastern unemployment rate expressed as a percentage of the western rate reached 282 percent (see Figure 2). In subsequent quarters, the relative difference in eastern versus western unemployment rates shrank substantially, falling to 166 percent in the first quarter of 1995. This progress was principally the product of two developments: first, the western jobless rate rose to 8.2 percent when the brief unification boom came to an abrupt end, and second, the unemployment rate actually fell in the East because hundreds of thousands of employees retired early, migrated to the West, or participated in job-creation programs. Still, the eastern unemployment rate stood at 13.6 percent in the first two quarters of 1995 (see Figure 1). The eastern unemployment rate deteriorated badly thereafter for several reasons. First, the Treuhand Anstalt, which was the government agency in charge of privatization of the former state holdings of the German Democratic Republic, accelerated its activities. Second, the government cut the funding for numerous employment creation measures (*Arbeitsbeschaffungsmassnahmen*). Third, the western German economy softened. As a result, eastern joblessness peaked at 19.5 percent in the fourth quarter of 1997.

Figure 2. Eastern Unemployment as a Percentage of Western Unemployment, 1991-2008

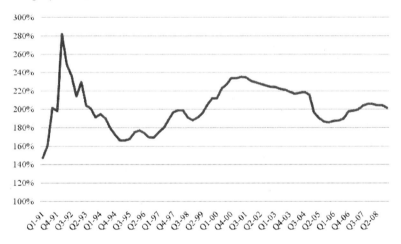

Source: Bundesagentur für Arbeit and own calculation.

The 1998-2000 "dot com" bubble stimulated the western German economy, but it had a much smaller impact on the East, because that region was far less deeply articulated into the international economy than the West.[3] As a result, the relative eastern unemployment rate grew disproportionately once again, reaching 235 percent of the western rate in the second quarter of 2001. Problems persisted during the first half of the 2000s. The exceptional softness of the western German economy led the unemployment rate to drift upward on both sides of the Elbe (see Figure 1). Relative joblessness in eastern Germany did not dip below 200 percent until the first quarter of 2005 (see Figure 2). It reached 186 percent in the fourth quarter of 2005, but then began to drift back upward. The unemployment picture in both East and West brightened in the second half of the decade; by the end of 2008, eastern unemployment had fallen below 13 percent for the first time since 1991. In contrast, the relative East-West unemployment rate deteriorated, returning to 200 percent in the second quarter 2007 and remaining over twice the western rate throughout 2008 (see Figure 2).

To recapitulate, convergence in the area of unemployment has been elusive. Unemployment has remained stubbornly high in eastern Germany and has only improved significantly in the last few years. Despite recent progress, which is noteworthy to be sure, the relative eastern unemployment rate still stands at roughly double that of the West. What accounts for the persistence of the gap?

A close examination of the relative wage-rates, productivity, and unit labor costs in eastern Germany does not resolve the question, but instead produces a new quandary. In the first five years after unification, East-West gaps in compensation and productivity narrow significantly, with eastern Germany reaching approximately 80 percent on both measures. In subsequent years, however, further progress comes to a virtual standstill (see Figure 3). It is also worth noting that initially, the relative wage in eastern Germany exceeded productivity by a wide margin, which put eastern unit labor costs at more than 125 percent of those in the West. Such elevated unit labor costs are consistent with the unemployment gap, but they did not last.[4] In 1994, eastern unit labor costs had dropped to 109 percent and by 2002, they had fallen to less than 104 percent of western unit labor costs, where they have remained ever since.[5] In several significant sectors, eastern Germany's unit labor costs have remained well below those of the West for some time. In goods sectors (*produzierendes Gewerbe*) excluding construction, for example, eastern Germany's relative unit labor costs fell from 133 percent of western levels in 1991 to rates well below those of the west (i.e., 96.2 percent in 2000 and 85.2 percent in 2008).[6] Economic theory and considerable evidence from cross-national comparisons leads to the expectation that the gap between eastern and western unemployment rates should have closed soon after relative eastern unit labor costs began to fall.[7] Instead, the gap actually widened. This outcome is particularly perplexing because microeconomic studies suggest a reasonably fluid German labor market.[8] What accounts for this anomaly?

Figure 3. Eastern German Compensation, Productivity and Unit Labor Costs as a Percentage of the Western Rate

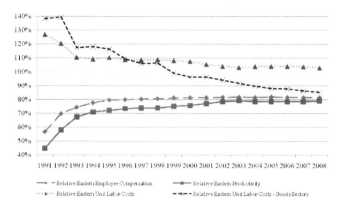

Source: Arbeitskreis volkswirtschaftliche Gesamtrechnungen der Länder

Economists have put forward two contending arguments to explain the persistence of the unemployment gap in eastern Germany. One alternative is neoclassical and the other Keynesian. Christian Merkl and his colleague Dennis Snower from the Kiel Institut für Weltwirtschaft have written a series of papers outlining a neoclassical explanation.[9] They argue that high compensation rates in eastern Germany—which were set through negotiations between westerners in the employers associations and trade unions—coupled with the eastward extension of the Federal Republic's "generous unemployment provisions and associated welfare benefits," and "generous job security provisions and costly hiring regulations," produced the steep drop in eastern German employment and "raised the persistence of employment (i.e., made current employment depend more heavily on past employment)," which "was mirrored in long-term unemployment." The long-term unemployment produced a "trap." "The longer workers are unemployed, the more prone they are to attrition of skills and work habits. ... As their productivity falls, it is more difficult for them to find a new job, even if labor costs fall relative to the average productivity of the employed workforce." [10]

Merkl and Snower present a model to capture this phenomenon. They partition the labor market into "primary" and "trapped" sectors, with employed and unemployed workers in each portion. Employment status (i.e., does a person in the labor market currently have a job?) determines whether a worker's productivity is improving or deteriorating, which in turn affects the likelihood of an employee moving up or down within the labor market. The model shows a persistence of joblessness for the unemployed in trapped sectors even when relative unit labor costs–and the costs of hiring and firing–fell by rates comparable to those found in eastern Germany since the early 1990s.[11]

Similarly, Michael Burda presents a "constant-returns" neoclassical model to account for the persistence of East-West differentials in the rate of return for both capital and labor, even after an equilibrium path had been reached. Burda argues that unification triggered a factor "mobility race," that is, integration consisting of the weaker region experiencing simultaneous capital inflow and labor outflow. Burda's model is far more sophisticated than that of Merkl and Snower. It covers both East and West, uses two factors and contains adjustment costs in the East, which include regulations, property rights disputes, and the impact of bureaucracy. Burda's results are consistent with Merkl and Snower (i.e., disproportionately high unemployment can persist for some time in eastern Germany despite factor mobility), but his causal mechanism differs. Burda points to the adjustment costs of factor movements–that include conforming to regulation, untangling contested property rights, and bureaucratic drag–as impediments that constrict the flows of factors across borders sufficiently to "reconcile finite rates of factor movements with persistently low wages and high rates of return in Eastern Germany."[12]

Both the supply-side human capital account of Merkl and Snower and Burda's adjustment cost explanation for the persistence of disproportionately high unemployment in eastern Germany are credible and the two explanations are broadly compatible. They do share two shortcomings, however. First, the authors of both models have not undertaken additional empirical research to confirm some of their "mildly heroic assumptions."[13] For example, Merkl and Snower do not attempt to establish the actual development of human capital in eastern Germany since unification, nor do they include school leavers from the secondary and university levels in their analysis. Other scholars at the authors' institute show that this research is possible, having undertaken more in-depth investigations of human capital trends.[14] Burda's adjustment cost model suggests that the East-West unemployment differential should shrink over time, yet the data instead show persistence. To be sure, collecting the additional empirical data needed to confirm the models would be difficult and time consuming. In their absence, the two neoclassical models stand as well-argued and plausible based on stylized data and back-of-the-envelope estimations, but are not quite *quod erat demonstrandum*.

What do the Keynesians have to say? John Hall and Udo Ludwig have been most prominent in pursuing a Keynesian approach. Hall and Ludwig have criticized Merkl and Snower, arguing that the latter's findings are "both interesting and, in principle, scientifically accurate. However, … at best secondary factors affecting levels of employment and causing unemployment."[15] Hall and Ludwig point to alternative explanations for the persistence of high unemployment in eastern Germany, namely, rapid privatization and labor shedding resulting from huge capital inflows. Hall and Ludwig proceed to provide a stylized account of privatization that consists of managers from western firms buying eastern workplaces, shutting down the production of products similar to those the western firm already makes, and taking advantage of ample subsidies to make heavily capital-intensive investments that produce few jobs. They also argue that the dearth of corporate headquarters in eastern Germany has turned it into a "branch plant" periphery, which hurts the employment prospects for the region. The result of rapid privatization and "a curious pattern of regional reindustrialization," they assert, has been "stagnating levels of effective aggregate demand and slack labor demand."[16]

The arguments of Hall and Ludwig also have their shortcomings. They argue that wage rates in eastern Germany have been too low to sustain aggregate demand and that the capital intensity of some investments may have been excessive. Yet, capital-intensive investment is necessary in order to bring eastern German productivity closer to western levels, which is a prerequisite to being able to afford western wage rates. Although the capital intensity of investment may have been extreme in a few sectors (e.g., chemicals and auto assembly), it is hard to argue that capital investment has been excessive at an aggregate level because eastern Germany's relative productivity has stagnated at four-fifths of the western rate for a decade. Moreover, paying higher wages without greater productivity improvements would not have expanded aggregate demand, but rather would have simply depressed investment in some sectors and deepened the capital intensity of others.

Hall and Ludwig never provide evidence from Germany or elsewhere to back up their second argument, which is an old red herring from the widely discredited dependency literature, that the presence of corporate headquarters has a significant impact on regional employment. They also never substantiate their assertion—either empirically or through a model—that the productivity-trap argument is secondary. Moreover, Merkl and Snower responded in a subsequent article, showing convincingly that the productivity trap potentially has a substantial impact on the eastern German labor market.[17] In sum, Burda and Merkl and Snower present far more compelling explanations for the persistence of disproportionately high unemployment in eastern Germany than Hall and Ludwig. Labor market traps and constraints imposed by adjustment costs are likely the principal factors hampering convergence, although further research is still needed to verify these conclusions, since they are based largely on models and stylized evidence.

What are the policy implications of these findings? Burda's model does not suggest means for accelerating adjustment, but the findings of Merkl and Snower indicate that the quickest and most cost-effective solution to the persistence in unemployment in eastern Germany would be wage subsidies, particularly if they can be targeted to the trapped portion of the labor market. Such payments would help workers to escape the unemployment trap and get back into paid employment where they could start once again to raise their productivity. It is worth noting with some irony that in 1999 the benchmarking group, which was part of Chancellor Gerhard Schröder's Alliance for Jobs initiative, produced a draft proposal (leaked to the media), suggesting the use of wage subsidies in the form of waiving payroll taxes for employees with low incomes. [18] Trade union and business association leaders quickly denounced the proposal as too expensive and an excessive distortion of the labor market. [19] Some observed that the social partners actually disliked the proposal because their core clientele–that is, highly paid employees in the manufacturing and public sectors–would not be the prime recipients of the wage subsidies. [20] In the end, the benchmarking group's wage-subsidy proposal was never implemented. Some years later, the Schröder government instead pursued, through the Hartz reforms and Agenda 2010, what Merkl and Snower find to be a second-best solution: reducing the employee "replacement ratio" (i.e., hiring and firing costs) through cuts in social benefits. Merkl and Snower judged decreasing the replacement ratio to be a less effective alternative for reducing unemployment because it requires tremendous reductions in social benefits to have a significant impact on the labor market, it takes a long time to implement fully, and it has the side effect of increasing inequality. Merkl and Snower dismissed a third option–training subsidies–because they would take the longest to implement and it would "be a challenge to design training measures in a way that they can effectively improve workers' upward mobility." [21] Evidence from eastern Germany supports this conclusion. About a decade ago, the German government ramped down support for training as an employment-creation measure in the East because it proved costly and relatively ineffective. [22]

The 2008-2009 global financial crisis complicates an already difficult employment situation in eastern Germany. The substantial employment subsidization through short-time work at the high end of the western German labor market has contained immediate increases in unemployment there. Once the German government begins to unwind these subsidies, relative East-West unemployment is likely to go down initially as a result of the crisis, but that is only because the denominator–that is, the western unemployment rate–will rise disproportionately, owing to the West's greater export dependence. The underlying problems with adjustment costs and the labor market trap–which the neoclassical analyses identify–will persist well beyond the recovery from the financial crisis. Moreover, the post 2009 conservative coalition government has given no indication that it would consider adopting wage subsidies for the low end of the eastern German labor market. As a result, the East-West differential in unemployment rates is likely to persist for some time to come.

The Absence of Intraregional Variance in the Eastern German Economic Output

A second striking peculiarity of the eastern German economy twenty years after unification is the absence of intraregional variation in economic output. Economic performance typically diverges considerably across regions in most countries, generated by differences in access to raw materials, infrastructure, skill sets, and external economies of scale.[23] The western German economy always has exhibited substantial regional variance. In 2008, for example, Hamburg stands out with the highest output per employee at slightly above EURO 80,000, followed by Hesse and Bremen, which are almost exactly EURO 10,000 lower (see Table 1). Hamburg and Bremen are city-states, skewing the results upward for them, and Hesse's strong performance can be attributed at least in part to Frankfurt's position as a major global financial center and the Land's manufacturing hub. The southern manufacturing powerhouses of Baden-Württemberg and Bavaria fill out the next tier, with output per employee at EURO 64,914 and EURO 66,983 respectively. The old industrial states of North Rhine-Westphalia and the Saar follow at EURO 62,153 and EURO 60,872, and the bottom tier consists of the more rural states of Lower Saxony, Rhineland-Palatinate, and Schleswig-Holstein whose output per employee ranges from EURO 58,400 to EURO 57,900. Berlin's output per employee holds up the rear at EURO 53,400 in 2008–an unsurprising outcome because it is the only state that contains eastern and western parts. Excluding the two city states and Berlin, output per employee of the top three western Länder exceeded that of the bottom three by 23 percent.[24]

In contrast, the pattern for eastern Germany is much more uniform. No eastern state has an output per employee higher than a western state, which is no surprise, although Berlin has stagnated since the mid 1990s to

Table 1. Nominal Gross Product per Employee: German States

Year	Baden-Württemberg	Bavaria	Berlin	Bremen	Hamburg	Hesse	Lower Saxony	North Rhine Westphalia	Rhineland Palatinate	Saar	Schleswig-Holstein	Brandenburg	Mecklenburg West Pomerania	Saxony	Saxony-Anhalt	Thuringia
1991	23 430	22 724	18 427	26 838	33 845	24 419	18 890	21 184	19 301	19 231	19 304	7 660	7 470	7 597	7 139	6 625
1992	24 274	23 946	20 185	27 772	35 015	25 566	19 803	22 069	19 801	19 921	20 188	9 638	9 497	9 618	9 146	9 083
1993	23 729	24 012	21 545	27 900	35 848	25 663	19 981	22 035	19 588	19 561	20 463	11 758	11 550	11 784	11 319	11 215
1994	24 564	24 896	22 246	29 100	37 022	26 422	20 716	22 688	20 262	20 557	21 089	13 719	13 617	13 875	13 144	13 208
1995	25 358	25 523	23 024	29 805	37 977	27 146	20 858	23 443	20 940	21 527	21 800	15 036	14 965	15 287	14 038	13 933
1996	25 749	25 907	22 707	29 980	38 761	27 728	20 883	23 441	20 918	21 011	22 058	15 656	15 586	15 934	14 680	14 532
1997	26 180	26 472	22 560	31 081	40 010	28 117	21 186	23 929	21 277	21 484	22 359	16 017	15 940	16 087	15 261	15 167
1998	26 948	27 563	22 721	31 702	41 106	28 580	21 884	24 545	21 576	22 015	22 379	16 257	16 073	16 371	15 642	15 587
1999	27 700	28 405	22 970	32 083	41 493	29 720	22 197	24 802	22 108	22 383	22 859	16 822	16 605	16 871	16 041	16 232
2000	28 343	29 487	23 161	33 426	42 423	30 223	22 767	25 236	22 587	23 125	23 309	17 298	16 859	17 031	16 437	16 638
2001	29 309	30 090	23 244	34 419	44 403	31 204	22 904	25 622	22 531	23 566	23 775	17 695	17 342	17 731	16 937	17 212
2002	29 350	30 671	23 210	35 277	44 907	31 407	22 795	25 944	23 042	23 691	23 331	18 015	17 624	18 632	17 848	17 666
2003	29 521	30 797	23 035	35 892	44 980	32 145	22 961	26 073	23 165	23 938	23 544	18 213	17 906	19 188	18 166	18 221
2004	29 887	31 552	22 914	36 600	45 620	32 690	23 403	26 726	23 831	25 189	23 892	18 796	18 449	19 873	18 790	18 883
2005	30 078	32 095	23 361	37 401	46 725	33 240	24 075	27 063	23 862	26 538	23 966	19 132	18 750	19 960	19 042	19 136
2006	31 677	33 077	24 023	38 937	47 566	34 244	24 943	27 869	24 727	27 585	24 677	19 935	19 383	20 875	20 028	20 076
2007	33 274	34 630	24 873	40 349	48 852	35 437	25 976	29 132	25 825	29 133	25 312	20 921	20 621	21 903	21 262	21 110
2008	33 876	35 530	25 554	41 918	50 640	36 382	26 902	30 113	26 623	30 168	25 945	21 721	21 439	22 620	22 427	21 875

Source: Arbeitskreis volkswirtschaftliche Gesamtrechnungen der Länder

the point where it is converging with Brandenburg and Saxony-Anhalt. Table 1 shows two tight groupings of eastern Länder. Within these two groups, less than EURO 500 separate the output per employee of Mecklenburg-West Pomerania and Thuringia, (with Saxony in between the two); and the gap between Brandenburg and Saxony-Anhalt is slightly more than EURO 300. The output gap between the best performing state (Saxony-Anhalt) and the worst (Thuringia) is only slightly less than EURO 4,000 (EURO 52,473 versus EURO 48,491). Excluding Berlin again, output per employee of the top two eastern Länder exceeded that of the bottom two by only 8.5 percent. Table 1 also indicates that during the first half of the 1990s, the eastern German states made substantial progress toward converging toward the German average, but then progress stalled at about EURO 10,000 below the German mean.

The homogeneity within eastern Germany is unusual and unprecedented. Before World War II, greater Berlin, Saxony, and parts of what are now Saxony-Anhalt and Brandenburg ranked among the highest in terms of output per employee, whereas West Pomerania and Thuringia were among the lowest. The economic policies of the GDR reduced regional differences in output. GDR policy-makers promoted economic specialization across the country's fifteen districts (Bezirke), and took care to place some industry in each. As a result, output per employee was extremely close across the five eastern Länder in the early 1990s. Targeted investment since unification in the steel and chemicals sectors, which are located in Saxony-Anhalt and Brandenburg, accounts for much of the gap in output per employee between those two states and the remaining three eastern Länder.

A comparison of output per capita of each Land instead of output per employee adjusts the ranking for differences in labor-force participation. This modification produces even starker results (see Table 2). The per capita output gap in 2008 between the three largest and three smallest western German Länder, excluding the city states, is much wider, increasing by more than ten percentage points to 33.1 percent. In contrast, the per capita output gap between the two largest and two smallest eastern Länder narrows by more than half to just 4 percent. There is also movement among the eastern states. Brandenburg and Mecklenburg-West Pomerania fall from the top to the bottom of the table in eastern Germany and Saxony rises to the top. This reordering reflects the lower labor-force participation rates of Brandenburg and Mecklenburg-West Pomerania when compared to Saxony. Since the differences among the states are so small, however, too much significance should not be placed on any shifts. In this data series, Berlin maintains a position among the lowest tier of western states,

Table 2. Nominal Gross Product per capita: German Statese

Year	Baden-Württemberg	Bavaria	Berlin	Bremen	Hamburg	Hesse	Lower Saxony	North Rhine Westphalia	Rhineland Palatinate	Saar	Schleswig Holstein	Brandenburg	Mecklenburg West Pomerania	Saxony	Saxony-Anhalt	Thuringia
1991	45 409	43 553	37 875	45 742	55 232	48 393	42 489	45 942	43 749	43 150	42 307	16 450	16 905	15 940	15 874	13 993
1992	45 381	45 930	42 323	46 960	56 818	50 737	44 522	47 915	45 392	44 770	44 404	23 171	23 604	22 916	22 698	22 238
1993	47 613	47 043	45 594	47 788	59 211	52 059	45 738	48 854	46 033	44 891	45 831	29 177	28 987	28 715	28 598	27 871
1994	50 055	49 142	47 550	50 346	61 520	54 157	47 745	51 022	48 093	47 277	47 628	33 055	32 977	32 664	32 340	31 836
1995	51 884	50 731	49 233	52 591	64 038	56 047	48 101	53 135	49 817	49 179	49 365	35 504	35 170	34 851	33 858	33 067
1996	52 782	52 093	49 310	53 509	65 897	57 370	48 657	53 246	50 004	47 872	50 156	37 147	36 953	36 216	35 809	34 786
1997	53 640	53 363	49 703	55 035	68 407	58 398	49 533	54 156	51 079	48 924	51 258	38 308	38 287	36 920	37 711	36 556
1998	54 562	54 505	49 958	56 057	69 259	58 836	50 896	54 556	51 102	48 952	51 710	39 348	38 512	37 343	38 370	36 515
1999	55 536	55 518	50 216	56 227	69 032	60 441	50 853	54 109	51 611	48 475	51 756	40 874	39 450	38 085	39 485	37 184
2000	55 567	56 826	49 753	57 062	69 615	60 205	51 092	53 620	51 604	48 802	52 049	42 282	40 098	38 377	40 892	38 171
2001	57 021	57 719	50 079	58 176	72 365	61 646	51 398	54 270	51 345	49 473	53 042	43 935	41 639	40 258	42 331	39 749
2002	57 520	59 424	50 878	60 072	73 939	62 432	51 364	55 337	52 500	49 906	52 806	45 453	42 545	42 448	44 787	41 257
2003	58 575	60 445	51 194	61 925	75 056	64 707	52 003	56 222	53 113	50 584	54 271	46 369	43 627	43 602	45 703	43 029
2004	59 303	61 928	50 415	63 231	75 900	65 544	52 790	57 278	54 240	52 684	55 146	47 510	44 794	44 763	46 937	44 129
2005	59 712	62 832	51 336	65 133	77 413	66 895	54 524	58 032	54 253	55 082	55 404	48 533	45 363	45 108	47 733	44 637
2006	62 589	64 278	52 047	67 704	78 228	68 474	56 104	59 497	55 712	57 087	56 691	50 164	46 088	46 510	49 381	46 295
2007	64 692	66 197	52 841	68 849	78 967	69 678	57 368	61 141	57 066	59 595	57 376	51 392	47 776	47 719	51 030	47 452
2008	64 914	66 983	53 418	70 558	80 395	70 597	58 371	62 153	57 903	60 822	57 918	52 473	48 982	48 518	52 790	48 491

Source: Arbeitskreis volkswirtschaftliche Gesamtrechnungen der Länder

and does not converge toward the eastern states. The bottom line from analysis of these output data is the lack of divergence among eastern states, which is highlighted when they are compared to the western states.

What accounts for the persistence of uniformity in output across the eastern Länder? Several scholars over the years either have analyzed the efficacy of investment in eastern Germany as a whole or have undertaken East-West investment comparisons,[25] but no one has investigated this specific question. The remainder of this article endeavors to uncover the reasons for this uniformity. It is important to begin with a snapshot of the aggregate state of eastern investment, and then proceed to a disaggregation of the data into regions and sectors.

The scale of the investment transfers from West to East since 1990 must be reiterated. Michael Burda summarizes it well: "over the period 1991-2007, EURO 1.2 trillion in new investment (1995 prices) was undertaken on behalf of about 16.5 million residents in the East, making this episode one of the most intensive periods of net per-capita capital formation in modern economic history."[26] The large volume of western investment coming principally out of a single program, the Aufschwung Ost assistance plan for eastern Germany, injects a dimension of uniformity that would easily overwhelm private investment decisions und helps to explain the absence of divergence among the eastern Länder.

The data on gross capital formation per employee disaggregated by Land exhibit a pattern consistent with the output and productivity trends presented above. From the early 1990s to 2000, gross capital formation per employee in all five eastern Länder exceeded that for Germany as a whole, peaking at mid decade (see Figure 4). Since 2001, however, gross capital formation per employee in eastern Germany has been about the same as in the country as a whole. The trend in all eastern Länder runs closely together; the two states with concentrations in heavy industry, Brandenburg (steel) and Mecklenburg-West Pomerania (ship building), have the highest gross capital formation per employee. It should be noted that developments in relative unemployment do not appear to be related to gross fixed capital formation per employee. Other factors also appear to be influencing the pattern of relative unemployment in eastern Germany, including the rise and fall of the construction sector and the use of employment creation measures during the 1990s.

Figure 4. Annual Gross Capital Formation per Employee

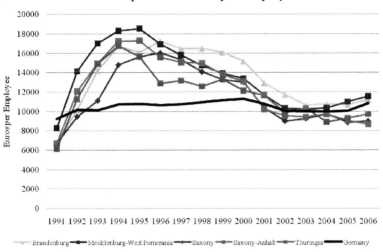

Source: Arbeitskreis volkswirtschaftliche Gesamtrechnungen der Länder

Investment data are also useful for addressing a question that arose earlier in this investigation, that is, why the productivity gap between East and West has persisted. The type of investment was not the most efficacious for closing the productivity gap and the volume of investment from West to East has been by no means constant: two-thirds of the total investment was used to build residential and business structures, which is an extraordinarily large share (see Figure 5). At its peak in the mid 1990s, per capita investment in structures in the East was double that of the West, money that was used principally to repair and to modernize dilapidated buildings. Although improving the eastern building stock did contribute to enhanced living conditions and may have helped boost productivity at the margins, it was not the best way to produce an enduring increase in productivity. Nevertheless, the surge in construction investment during the early 1990s is no surprise, reflecting the priorities established in the federal government's Aufschwung Ost program. In the latter half of the 1990s, the German government decided to ramp down this program with a telling impact. By 2002, per capita investment in structures in eastern Germany had come down to the western rate and has remained there since.

Figure 5. Per Capita Investment in Structure and Equipment

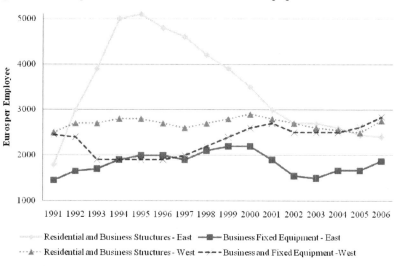

Source: Bundesministerium für Verkehr, Bau und Stadtentwicklung

Investment in business fixed equipment comprises the remaining third of eastern investment since unification, but it follows a markedly different pattern (see Figure 5). Eastern per capita investment in business fixed equipment only exceeded the western rate in two years: 1995 and 1996. Since then, western per capita fixed equipment investment has exceeded eastern investment by between 40 and 67 percent each year. The relative overinvestment in buildings and underinvestment in equipment in eastern Germany is not the optimal mix for achieving convergence in productivity rates. If anything, it is remarkable that the eastern Länder have managed to maintain their productivity relative to western Germany over the last ten years despite the significantly lower investment rate per capita in equipment when compared to the West.

Conclusion

Three conclusions follow from the material presented in this chapter. First, in several important respects, two of which were highlighted above, eastern Germany is still far from achieving anything that can be considered normalcy. Second, over the last ten years, the eastern economy has made virtually no progress toward convergence with the West. Third, government policy choices about how to pursue unification are at least partly responsible for the difficulties and the lack of recent progress in resolving them.

To be fair, it would be difficult to say how effective many of the widely suggested policy alternatives would have been if they actually had been tried. For example, a lower set of Ostmark-Deutsche Mark exchange rates may have left a higher percentage of eastern German firms more competitive in the short run, but they would have reduced the value of property in eastern Germany and left many more firms vulnerable to outside take-overs. Moreover, any short-term gains in competitiveness most likely would have been eroded away quickly simply by steeper increases in wages and prices. Changing the means to resolve property claims from restitution to compensation would have raised the cost of unification considerably and opened an extremely complex and no faster process to price eastern German assets fairly.

Given the shortcomings of the initial set of policies surrounding unification, which have had enduring legacies, as Merkl and Snower point out, there is a case to be made for the introduction of more carefully developed policies to assist particularly those who have come out on the short end of the process. For example, wage subsidies for employees earning low incomes should be reconsidered, even if some thoughtful critiques do suggest caution before enacting them.[27] Germany's current experience with short-time work for mostly high-income employees may change some attitudes regarding the use of wage subsidies, but there are few other indications that the political tide has turned since the late 1990s. Moreover, the current short-time payments go to the core constituents of the social partners, whereas wage subsidies to low income employees would not. As a result, the social partners are likely to remain far less interested in them. Still, it should not be forgotten that a decade of making little progress toward convergence or normalcy has not been good economically or politically for the Federal Republic in general and eastern Germany in particular. Something more needs to be done. Otherwise, the lost decade of economic progress that eastern Germans have just endured could easily become a lost score.

Notes

1. It is worth noting that this slogan was a cautious borrowing from the Christian Democratic Union's federal election campaign of 1957. Konrad Adenauer used it during the Wirtschaftswunder to raise caution about adopting the Social Democratic ideas of the day. In the 1990s, the slogan was used to parry leftist calls to write a new German constitution from scratch, and to adopt a new economic model that would be a "third way" between capitalism and central planning.

2. This article uses unemployment data reported by the German government (i.e., Bundesagentur für Arbeit) because they include separate reporting for eastern and western Germany. The German methodology for calculating unemployment results in an unemployment rate that is roughly one percentage point higher than an unemployment rate calculated using the International Labor Organization's standardized definition of unemployment. These data do have some shortcomings. The German government substantially changed the definition of unemployment twice since unification, once for the start of 2004 and again for the start of 2005. Since this article is not undertaking cross-national comparisons and focuses on the relative East-West unemployment rate, the definitional issues do not pose significant analytical problems.

3. Bundesministerium für Verkehr, Bau und Stadtentwicklung, *Jahresbericht der Bundesregierung zum Stand der deutschen Einheit 2009* (Berlin, 2009), D12.

4. The initially high unit labor costs in eastern Germany were a product of the excessive optimism that pervaded the first years of unification and a political calculation on the part of trade union leaders, heads of employers association, and top government officials that paying wage rates above the immediate productivity levels would stave off a massive East-West migration and ruinous interregional competition among firms. See Gerhard A. Ritter, *Der Preis der deutschen Einheit. Die Wiedervereinigung und die Krise des Sozialstaats* (Munich, 2006), 312-17.

5. The East's relative unit labor costs fell for two reasons. First, when economic performance in eastern Germany failed to meet initial expectations, trade union officials increasingly accepted more modest agreements and often even consented to the inclusion of "opening clauses" in contracts, which permitted workplace-level derogations that reduced compensation. Second, the infrastructure of collective bargaining in eastern Germany, which never was very stable, began to crumble. After the first few years of unification, association avoidance and flight plagued many employers associations and trade union membership fell swiftly. Employees at many workplaces proved willing to accept surreptitiously compensation packages well below the minimum union rate for their sectors. Other firms simply set compensation unilaterally, or through individual negotiations with employees. See Stephen J. Silvia, "German Trade Unionism in the Postwar Years: The Third and Fourth Movements," in *Trade Unions since 1945: Towards a Global History*, ed., Craig L. Phelan (Oxford, 2009), 84-88. See also Anke Hassel and Richard Deeg in this issue.

6. Bundesministerium (see note 3), D8.

7. See Organization for Economic Cooperation and Development, *The OECD Jobs Strategy: Technology, Productivity and Job Creation. Best Policy Practices* (Paris, 1998).

8. See Jennifer Hunt, "Convergence and Determinants of Non-employment Durations in Eastern and Western Germany," *Journal of Population Economics* 17, no. 2 (2004): 249-66.

9. See Dennis J. Snower and Christian Merkl, "The Caring hand that Cripples: The East German Labor Market after Reunification (Detailed Version)," IZA Discussion Paper No. 2066, April 2006; Christian Merkl and Dennis J. Snower, "East German Unemployment: The Myth of the Irrelevant Labor Market," *Journal of Post Keynesian Economics* 31, no. 1 (Fall 2008): 151-165; and Christian Merkl and Dennis J. Snower, "Escaping the Unemployment Trap: The Case of East Germany," *Journal of Comparative Economics* 36 (2008): 542-56.

10. Merkl and Snower, "Escaping" (see note 9), 543.
11. Ibid., 548-49.
12. Michael Burda, "What Kind of Shock is it? Regional Integration and Structural Change in Germany after Unification", *Journal of Comparative Economics* 36 (2008): 560-66.
13. Ibid., 565.
14. Joachim Ragnitz, "Explaining the East German Productivity Gap–The Role of Human Capital," Kiel Working Paper, no. 1310, January 2007.
15. John B. Hall and Udo Ludwig, "Explaining Persistent Unemployment in eastern Germany," *Journal of Post Keynesian Economics* 29, no. 4 (2007): 605.
16. Ibid., 608-11.
17. Merkl and Snower, "Escaping" (see note 9), 554-55.
18. *Der Spiegel*, 8 May 1999.
19. See, for example, *Frankfurter Rundschau*, 12 May 1999.
20. It is worth noting that the social partners did support a wage-subsidization policy in the form of short-time work (*Kurzarbeit*) in response to the 2008-2009 financial crisis. This time, the wage subsidies were targeted at higher paid employees in the core of the manufacturing sector.
21. Merkl and Snower, "Escaping" (see note 9), 550.
22. See, for example, Michael Lechner, Ruth Miquel, and Conny Wunsch, "The Curse and Blessing of Training the Unemployed in a Changing Economy: The Case of East Germany," IZA Discussion Paper, no. 1684, Institut zur Zukunft der Arbeit (Bonn, 2005).
23. See, for example, Michael Porter, *The Competitive Advantage of* Nations (New York, 1990); and Annalee Saxenian, *The New Argonauts: Regional Advantage in a Global Economy* (Cambridge, 2006).
24. Statistische Ämter der Länder, *Volkswirtschaftliche Gesamtrechnungen der Länder*, table 3.3.
25. See, for example, Ullrich Heilemann and Wolfgang H. Reinicke, *Welcome to Hard Times: The Fiscal Consequences of German Unity* (Washington, 1995); Horst Siebert, *Das Wagnis der Einheit: eine wirtschaftspolitische Therapie* (Stuttgart, 1992); Gerlinde Sinn and Hans-Werner Sinn, *Jumpstart: The Economic Unification of Germany* (Cambridge, 1992), and Paul J. J. Welfens, ed., *Economic Aspects of German Unification* (Berlin, 1992).
26. Burda (see note 12), 557-58.
27. See, for example, *IAB Kurzbericht*, no. 6, 14 June 1999.

$\mathcal{T}$WENTY YEARS
AFTER GERMAN UNIFICATION
The Restructuring of the German Welfare and Employment Regime

● ● ● ● ● ● ● ● ● ● ● ● ● ● ●

Anke Hassel

Introduction

The fall of the Berlin Wall was a catalyst for a major transformation of the German welfare state and labor market. The adjustment process that started in the early 1990s was prompted by multi-layered challenges of unification and the consequent institutional adaptation, the changing role of Germany in European Monetary Union, the recession prompted by unification, and the long-term structure problems of the Bismarckian welfare state, which had been building up since the early 1970s. In this adjustment process, many facets of the traditional welfare and employment institutions have remained remarkably stable and probably will remain in place for a long time to come. If one scratches the surface, however, it becomes clear that Germany has been, and is, changing more rapidly and radically than is often perceived. Two areas of change—the regulation of the labor market and the unemployment benefit system—are used in this article to illustrate this phenomenon.

This transformation has two defining characteristics. First, traditional German institutions remain in place, but are nevertheless undergoing processes of change. Indeed, this combination of continuity and change is key—it is as if the institutions are being gutted while their walls and ceilings remain in place.[1] Second, changes in underlying expectations, attitudes and values in business, policy-making, and in the wider society are fundamental forces driving the country away from its traditional model towards one that remains essentially German, but that draws on a much wider range of social, economic, and cultural influences than thirty years ago. Both features are driven by the challenges of unification. While political reassurance and policy continuity were central to managing the transition of the 1990s, the economic challenges to German business increased dramatically. Political continuity and economic restructuring could only work if the institutions were hollowed out and replaced by new meanings.

From the mid 1990s onwards, it was popular to criticize Germany for its failure to adjust to economic, social, and demographic challenges. The urgent need for "reform" appeared frequently in newspaper headlines, in reports by expert commissions and high-flying economists, and even in newspaper adverts placed by German "citizens' campaigns." The basis for the call to action was Germany's low–and partially negative–growth rate, its high level of unemployment and steadily rising public deficit.

The Agenda 2010 reforms from March 2003 and the subsequent adoption of the proposals have exemplified the government's awareness of the necessity to react. Whether these reforms present a break with the German model is still the subject of intensive debate, but certainly changing attitudes and expectations already have had a marked impact on these institutions. Globalization, in particular the internationalization of companies and of business standards, has forced German managers to adopt more open, international approaches. They have adapted the workings of the traditional corporate governance institutions to their own needs–including the role of employees in codetermination procedures. Similarly, changing attitudes towards work and towards the often-conservative role played by centralized unions and employers' bodies have fuelled an approach among the wider population towards trade unions that is largely instrumental and stripped of traditional political motivations. Such changes add up to a gradual transformation of the old German social market model established during the postwar period, to something that is indeed more liberal than before.

This chapter is divided in four parts. The first portrays the problems of the Bismarckian welfare state as the reference point to which the changes over the last two decades are compared. It discusses the increasing fiscal constraints on the state generated by increasing long-term unemployment and heightened levels of inactivity. This coincided with a harsher competitive climate in the 1990s, the introduction of European Monetary Union, and the deep recession early in that decade. Moreover, the collapse of the eastern German labor market put further strain on the welfare state. The second and third sections discuss the changes regarding labor market regulation and transfer policies respectively. In both areas, however, change can be observed within a given regulatory framework. The final section discusses the politics of the adjustment process and provides a prognosis of what is to come.

The Bismarckian Welfare State and its Challenges

By the end of the 1980s, most observers of German social and employment policies agreed that the welfare state had run out of steam and had accumulated numerous structural problems.[2] These consisted of:

1) **A steady decline of the employment rate**: from the onset of the oil crisis in the early 1970s, government responses consisted of incentives for employees who were made redundant to leave the labor market. Early retirement schemes–initially designed for problems in the mining and steel industry–were expanded to other sectors and then to the labor market as a whole. Similarly, work creation schemes renewed access for the long-term unemployed to relatively generous benefits, but did little to reintegrate the schemes' participants back into the labor market. As a consequence, Germany achieved one of the lowest employment rates for elderly males in the OECD.[3]

2) **A steady increase in the rise of payroll taxes**: between the late 1960s and the late 1980s, social security contributions rose from 27 to 35 percent of gross wages. As a highly regressive tax on labor, these contributions increased labor costs of the unskilled resulting in an exceptionally high unemployment rate for unskilled compared to skilled workers.[4]

3) **A complex structure of shared responsibilities for the long-term unemployed**: involving local authorities and the labor agency (Bundesanstalt für Arbeit), rather than trying to bring the unemployed back into work, the administrative structure gave incentives to shift them into a new scheme.[5]

The problems embedded in these policy responses were all well known under the center-Right government of Helmut Kohl. In fact, the policy-measures that led to the situation had been carried by an overwhelming majority in parliament and by all political stakeholders, particularly the unions and employers. It was a form of corporate restructuring at taxpayers expense which was, however, widely approved by political actors and the public at large, since it cushioned the negative effects of redundancies and unemployment.[6] Nevertheless, a rising number of observers–from both politics and economics–started to criticize the low activity that the welfare system had generated.[7]

Nevertheless, adjustments to the system were minor, rather haphazard, and largely in the interest of balancing the budgets of various social security funds. Benefit entitlements were lengthened and then shortened. Entitlements to pensions and health insurance for the unemployed were changed at will by the government to balance the budget. Neither the Conservatives nor the Social Democrats had a strong desire for change.

It was only in regard to the pension system that the government realized the unsustainable nature of the pay-as-you-go system, combined with an aging population and a continuing trend towards lower retirement ages. The Kohl government had contemplated a law to adjust pension entitlements with demographic changes on the eve of the fall of the Berlin Wall. But, as is well known, German unification put an end to the pension reform, as well as to other discussions on policy reforms in the area of social and employment policies.[8]

During the 1990s, the features and the structural problems of the West German welfare state were transferred to the new Länder and were exacerbate in the process. As unemployment exploded in the East, social protection was needed. In 1991, unemployment levels in eastern Germany stood at 10.2 percent and rose to 19.2 percent in 1998. In western Germany, unemployment also rose in the same period from 6.2 percent to 10.2 percent. Within four years after 1989, the number of employees in the East shrank by 36 percent (- 3.5 million). 7.3 million out of 9.8 million employees lost their previous jobs, only 25 percent of all employees remained in their workplaces. Particularly hard hit were farming jobs (declining by 77 percent) and manufacturing (reduced by 51 percent).[9] In the service and public sectors, less than a third of employees lost their jobs. While employment in private services increased steadily, the numbers were not sufficient to compensate for the job losses elsewhere.

At the same time, the continuation and expansion of the social provisions for the unemployed catalyzed change. Companies reacted to the recession of the early 1990s and governments confronted fast-rising public debt. Both responses led to adjustment strategies that ultimately contributed to fundamental change, while institutions and structures remained largely in place.

Increasing Flexibility in a System of Tight Employment Protection

In many accounts by the IMF and the OECD, labor market regulation is seen as a stumbling block limiting the growth potential of the German economy. According to the OECD, Germany is near the top in a ranking of employment protection measures, in fourth place behind Italy, France, and Sweden. Recipes for overcoming economic stagnation usually start with proposals to deregulate the labor market, including Germany's labor relations regime. The most recent survey of Germany by the OECD states: "The government should thus consider easing employment protection legislation for regular job contracts, which is strict by international standards, in order to use the current upswing to create as many regular job contracts as possible."[10]

Indeed, despite continuous recommendations by the OECD since the 1994 "Jobs Study,"[11] Germany has done very little to change its system of labor market regulations, including employment protection and the collective bargaining framework. Political proposals to reduce employment protection and to decentralize collective bargaining were often on the political agenda. In Gerhard Schröder's Agenda 2010 speech, for example, both items were mentioned as potential reforms if the social partners were unable to find their own ways of making the labor market more flexible. The social partners did find their own ways, and, as a result, the core elements of this model are still in place—centralized, industry-wide collective bargaining, co-determination, and sectorally-based union and employers' bodies operating in a tight legal framework in which dismissals are highly regulated.

At the same time, the image of tight regulation enforced by strong trade unions holding a firm grip on companies is a partially distorted view. In fact, the employment landscape in Germany has changed much more significantly than is commonly perceived. Companies today are generally much more able to determine wages and working conditions for their employees than they were a decade ago.

During the recession of 1992/1993, half a million jobs in the manufacturing sector were shed. Redundancies were negotiated with the help of unions and plant-level representatives. "Concession bargaining" at the plant level now takes place in the majority of big companies in industry. Longer working hours, pay cuts, and flexible work organization has spread throughout the economy. Today, plant-level agreements exist in a third of private sector companies, producing terms and conditions that deviate from industry-wide collective agreements. Another 15 percent of companies simply violate the agreements, according to a survey by the union-based research institute WSI.[12]

The price that companies paid for plant-level agreements was, however, a move towards tighter dismissal protection for the existing workforce, rather than a more flexible regime of hiring and firing. Firms pledge in plant-level agreements to refrain from any collective dismissal for a period of several years. In a recent bargaining agreement, for instance, Deutsche Bahn, the German railway firm whose goal is to be listed on the stock exchange, has committed itself to forego any redundancies until the year 2023.

The flexibility firms gained from concession bargaining is internal cooperation rather than external adjustments. Unions and employers adjusted collective agreements to allow for plant-level deals. They have introduced "opening clauses" that allow for local bargaining, if the business situation is bad. In the chemical sector, pay grades were widened by introducing a "pay corridor" reaching down to 10 percent below agreed rates, following pressure from tire manufacturer Continental. Therefore, pay grades have become more differentiated and lower pay grades have been introduced. Even the trademark of German trade unionism, the thirty-five-hour week, has been effectively shattered. Studies show that the majority of white-collar employees in the car industry does not work the thirty-five-hour week but has returned to a forty-hour one. In a face-saving exercise, the IG Metall engineering union now negotiates over annual working time accounts, in which an average of thirty-five hours for blue-collar workers must be reached over a period of two years. In reality, the issue for IG Metall is not the length of the working week, but overtime bonuses. The fight for a shorter working week has long been lost. According to data from the Federal Statistical Office, the share of German employees who work forty hours or more has increased steadily since 1993. At the same time, the share of those that work between thirty-five and forty hours is decreasing.[13]

Many companies design new work arrangements with their works councils at the plant level without even informing the associations. Moreover, it is virtually impossible for unions to monitor and police violations of collective agreements at the plant level. Hardly any employee is prepared to sue a company for breaking an agreement, and unions do not have the staffing capacity to enforce or negotiate agreements in small- and medium-sized companies.[14]

Those firms unhappy with the general state of labor market regulation left the system–having chosen exit, rather than voice. Firms are generally less willing than previously to participate in the industry-wide collective bargaining system. Indeed, the share of firms that belong to employers' associations and are thereby obliged to apply industry-wide collective agreements has diminished to 45 percent in western Germany. In eastern Germany, only 23 percent of companies are members of associations. The share of private-sector employees that work in companies that are part of a collective agreement has declined to roughly 60 percent.[15]

The remaining firms chose to reform the system from within. Changes in legislation often would not have increased flexibility, since collective agreements propped up labor laws. For instance, the framework collective agreements in the metal sector have clauses that forbid dismissals for elderly workers above the age of fifty-three.[16] Looser employment protection legislation would not have changed this. Rather, firms hoped that competitive pressure, stubbornly high unemployment, and weaker trade unions would allow them to change the conduct of these agreements and give them internal flexibility to reduce labor costs as needed.

With regard to union cooperation, this strategy worked. While unions rarely block workplace deals aimed at providing job security and competitiveness, they usually do not talk about these deals in order to avoid other firms following suit. This has led to a further worsening of the unions' public image and tended to undermine their own authority. IG Metall's failed strike for the thirty-five- hour week in the eastern metal industry in mid 2003 showed how much the union misjudged the effects of these deals.

In sum, the labor market that has emerged from these micro-level processes is less regulated than is commonly assumed. One should recall that big manufacturing companies in the U.S. and UK also have strong union representation. The regulatory power of the unions in these countries does not, however, extend beyond these plants. It has been a feature of the German model of labor market regulation that agreements were forged that set universal rules for the vast majority of employees. This system is being eroded by company opt-outs and concessionary bargaining.

Tight labor laws that regulate dismissals and workers' participation still exist. Nevertheless, they increasingly divide workers into those who enjoy such protections and those who do not. Employment expansion has taken place among workers on temporary contracts, in temping agencies, and in so-called precarious jobs. More than 30 percent of young workers between twenty and twenty-four years of age (and who are not on vocational training contracts) are employed on temporary contracts, forestalling employment security and dismissal protection.[17] In the first quarter of 2009, there were 6.7 million workers employed in so-called mini-jobs— low wage jobs that largely are exempted from social security charges.[18] Temping agencies are now widespread, even in the manufacturing sector. Deregulation is spreading to the fringes of the labor market, and unions have little power to do anything about it.

Protection for the core of the workforce and instability for fringe workers (the well-documented insider-outsider problem) are complementary to each other. Firms argued that the only way to protect core workers was to look for other options to lower labor costs—coming at the expense of other parts of the workforce. Flexibility was thereby achieved in an uneven or segmented pattern. Thus, the German case shows that flexibility has increased, but in a patchy and not-universal way.

Activation: Addressing the Public Funding Crisis by Increasing Work Incentives

The German welfare state always has been a mixture of an Anglo-American lean benefit system for the needy poor, and a contribution-based insurance system covering periods of unemployment and old age that linked benefits to previous pay. In the past, however, the focus was firmly on the latter component, centered on the idea of *Lebensstandardsicherung* (securing of living standards) both now and in the future. Once a certain living standard was reached—say that of a skilled worker—the system guaranteed the maintenance of this standard, also during periods of unemployment and in retirement.[19]

Until 2005, there was a third category between the means-tested poor relief benefit and the regular unemployment benefit, which was specifically designed for the long-term unemployed. Those still unemployed after the unemployment benefit entitlement had expired received tax-financed "unemployment assistance,." which was lower than unemployment benefits, but still connected to previous earnings.

The three different benefit systems for the unemployed produced complex administrative procedures. Partly in order to streamline these processes, the Hartz reforms proposed to merge unemployment assistance and parts of the coverage of social assistance into one benefit, called Arbeitslosengeld II (ALG II), essentially for the long-term unemployed. (Social assistance remains for those unable to work). The philosophy that underlies the reform previously had been used by the Blair government in Britain for activating the unemployed. Here, the state provides opportunities, but also asks for commitment and personal effort to find a new position. It aims to toughen the rules for entitlement to social assistance and to increase the incentives to look for work for those on unemployment assistance. Importantly, these incentives include tougher sanctions for the unemployed—jobless people face cuts in benefits if they refuse job offers—and increased pressure to be more geographically mobile in the job search.

Labor economists and sociologists frequently make the point that after a year of unemployment, the value of previous qualifications is significantly reduced, and the long-term unemployed only will find new work in areas that are markedly worse paid than their previous job.[20] Therefore, linking unemployment benefits to previous earnings in the past was seen as creating a disincentive for people to accept a new job. In contrast to the Nordic countries where long duration periods of unemployment benefits are also common, the German system had additional features that prevented the unemployed from looking for work. In particular, the protection of skills was a major hallmark of the system. Unemployed individuals with a specialist trade could not be asked by the job centers to move into a different profession. Up until the 1990s, job agencies could only offer vacancies that matched the skills of the unemployed. The high level of skill protection gradually eroded during the adjustments in the 1990s. Still, when it came to implementation, many professionally trained unemployed workers insisted on pursuing their trade or remaining unemployed, even when the chances of being reemployed were slim.

The 2004 reform of the unemployment system therefore targeted the incentive structure of benefits and the level of skill protection. In order to reduce the incentives to remain unemployed rather than taking lower-paid jobs, the maximum duration of unemployment benefits also has been cut. Unemployment benefits are still available, but are now limited to the first year of unemployment (eighteen months for those over fifty-five).[21] A new benefit (ALG II) was introduced for the long-term unemployed (exceeding twelve months of unemployment). This is a means-tested flat rate payment set at what is universally seen as a low level, that of social assistance (it can be topped up temporarily if a claimant previously received considerably higher unemployment benefit). Those receiving ALG II usually must prove that partners and close family members living in the same household are unable to support them, and that most of the recipient's savings are used up. Moreover, ALG II recipients will be required to take any job that is offered to them to prove their willingness to work.

The reforms shifted the relationship between means-tested flat rate benefits, which are available universally and not tied to entitlements, and contribution-based, status-oriented unemployment benefits clearly towards an increase of the former. As the data in Table 1 show, before the reform, the ratio of recipients of earnings-related benefits to flat rate recipients was well in favor of earnings-related benefits, while after the reform, the flat rate recipients clearly outnumbered the others.

Table 1: Recipients of Benefits Due to Unemployment (in millions)

	Earnings related benefits		Universal benefit, no eligibility test
	Unemployment benefit	Unemployment Assistance	Social Assistance
2004	1.84	2.19	2.91

	Earnings related benefit	Universal benefit, no eligibility test, means tested	
	Unemployment Benefit	Unemployment Benefit II	Social Assistance
2005	1.72	4.98	0.27

Source: Bundesagentur für Arbeit, *Arbeitsmarkt in Deutschland: Zeitreihen bis 2006* (Nuremberg, 2007); Statistisches Bundesamt, *Sozialleistungen: Statistik der Sozialhilfe*, Fachserie 13/ Reihe 2.1. (Wiesbaden, 2004).

At the same time, the benefit system reform has not altered some of the most important obstacles towards a more employment-friendly system—the high tax-wedge that burdens low-skilled and low-paid work disproportionally. Germany remains the OECD country with the highest marginal tax rate for low-paid employment. While a number of social security exemptions were introduced for part-time, low-paid employment (the so-called mini jobs), full-time employment for low- paid workers is taxed at a rate of 36 percent.[22] Combined with strong pressure on the unemployed to take up low-paid employment and a new system of topping up income with partial benefits, the recent reforms have created strong incentives for low-skilled workers to take up part-time employment for very low wages and simultaneously draw social security benefits. As a consequence, Germany has now moved to the top of the list within the European Union as the country with the highest share of working poor.

Unlike the labor market regulation example discussed above, this benefit system reform has been driven largely by politicians, but with economic and financial factors—in particular high structural unemployment, the state's severe budgetary problems, and the financial crisis of local authorities—playing a vital role in forcing political decision makers to act. The motivation for a comprehensive restructuring of the benefit system was a mixture of wanting to provide more financial incentives for work, as compared to non-work, and a deep financial crisis of local authorities, which were increasingly forced to take care of the long-term unemployed.[23] As a result, the distinction between skill-specific and unspecific benefits has become sharper. Insiders—those with permanent employment—tend to worry even more about employment security. Firms are therefore even more under pressure to avoid major lay-offs.

The Process of Adjustment

As these two examples make clear, Germany is moving towards more flexibility and liberal policies, but it is doing so gradually and more-or-less within the framework of the established institutions of a conservative welfare state and a coordinated market economy. Increased labor market flexibility has been achieved by a two-tier system in which the insiders are forced to make concessions regarding pay and working time in order to achieve job security, while the outsiders experience relatively unstable employment conditions. The move towards a more employment- friendly benefit system accordingly provides temporary skill-specific benefits for the insiders, which increases the pressure on firms to provide job security or facilitate the transition to new employment if the firm has to lay-off workers.

Segmentation is therefore a defining characteristic of the transformed German model, with the inner core smaller than before and the outer fringe under stronger pressure to adapt to a flexible labor market.[24] As a result, liberalization is taking place in the context of a German regulatory framework and German institutions. The driving forces for liberalization are twofold. First, firms were confronted with the postunification recession, an increase in labor costs, and a worsening of their competitive position. Second, the government budget quickly became overburdened by social expenditure. Indeed, social expenditure as part of total government spending stood at 22 percent in 1990, but increased to 57 percent in 2000.[25] Fiscal spending was therefore squeezed by social spending.

For both developments, unification was the key catalyst. While the financial burden and the negative effects of low activity in the labor market were visible before the fall of the Berlin Wall, the simultaneous necessity to keep the main framework of social security and labor market institutions for political reasons while adjusting to the economic shock of unification and European monetary integration facilitated the pattern of adjustment. It is hard to see how this pattern will be broken in the future.

Germany certainly is moving. It is moving towards more flexibility and more employment-oriented policies–albeit in the framework of traditional corporatist, conservative, and coordinating institutions. Therefore, the changes will not necessarily produce similar outcomes as in more liberal and flexible countries. Rather, political and economic actors in Germany have dealt with their local problems by adjusting local institutions in their own way and according to their own interests.

Notes

1. See Anke Hassel and Hugh Williamson, "The evolution of the German model: How to judge reforms in Europe's largest economy," Paper prepared for the Anglo-German Foundation, 2004.
2. The problems of the Bismarckian welfare state are analyzed in an exemplary way by Phillip Manow and Eric Seils, "The Employment Crisis of the German Welfare State," *West European Politics* 23 (2000): 137-160; Fritz W. Scharpf and Vivian A. Schmidt, "Adjusting Badly: The German Welfare State, Structural Change, and the Open Economy,"in *Welfare and work in the open economy*, volume 2, eds., Frtz Scharpf and Vivian Schmidt (Oxford, 2000), 264-308; and Werner Eichhorst, Stefan Profit, et al., "Benchmarking Deutschland: Arbeitsmarkt und Beschäftigung," Bericht der Arbeitsgruppe Benchmarking und der Bertelsmann Stiftung an das Bündnis für Arbeit, Ausbildung und Wettbewerbsfähigkeit (Berlin, 2001).
3. Eichhorst et al. (see note 2).
4. See Wolfgang Streeck and Christine Trampusch, "Economic Reform and the Political Economy of the German Welfare State," *German Politics* 14, no. 2 (2005): 174-195.
5. On the complex system of shifting the costs for the long-term unemployed between different social security systems see Christine Trampusch, "Ein Bündnis für die nachhaltige Finanzierung der Sozialversicherungssysteme: Interessenvermittlung in der bundesdeutschen Arbeitsmarkt- und Rentenpolitik," Max-Planck-Institut für Gesellschaftsforschung -Discussion Paper 03, no. 1, (Cologne, 2003); available at http://www.mpifg.de/pu/mpifg_dp/dp03-1.pdf; and Christine Trampusch, *Der erschöpfte Sozialstaat Transformation eines Politikfeldes, Schriften aus dem Max-Planck-Institut für Gesellschaftsforschung,* 66 (Frankfurt/Main, 2009).
6. On the fiscal implications see Wolfgang Streeck, "From State Weakness as Strength to State Weakness as Weakness: Welfare Corporatism and the Private Use of the Public Interest," Max-Planck-Institut für Gesellschaftsforschung Working Paper, (Cologne, 2003).
7. Particularly in the comparative and international debate Germany's performance was seen critically. See Manow and Seils (see note 2) and Anton Hemerijck, Philip Manow, und Kees van Kersbergen, "Welfare without work? Divergent experiences of reform in Germany and the Netherlands," in *Survival of the European Welfare State*, ed., Stein Kuhnle (London, 2000), 106-127.
8. On the initial policy effects of unification see Gerhard Ritter, *Der Preis der deutschen Einheit. Die Wiedervereinigung und die Krise des Sozialstaats* (Munich, 2007).
9. Data are based on Klaus Funken, "Keine Wende am Arbeitsmarkt in Ostdeutschland: Eine Zwischenbilanz im Jahre 1996," *Wirtschaftspolitische Diskurse* 89 (1996); available at http://library.fes.de/fulltext/fo-wirtschaft/00323toc.htm.
10. OECD Policy Brief (2008); available at http://www.oecd.org/dataoecd/24/9/40367952.pdf.
11. OECD, *The OECD Jobs Study, Facts, Analysis, Strategies* (Paris, 1994).
12. Reinhard Bispinck and Thorsten Schulten, "Verbetrieblichung der Tarifpolitik?–Aktuelle Tendenzen und Einschätzungen," *WSI-Mitteilungen* (2003): 157-166.
13. Statistisches Bundesamt, "10 Jahre Erwerbsleben in Deutschland," (2002).
14. On concession bargaining in the aftermath of unification see Britta Rehder, "Betriebliche Bündnisse für Arbeit in Deutschland. Mitbestimmung und Flächentarif im Wandel," Schriftenreihe des MPI für Gesellschaftsforschung 48 (Frankfurt/ Main, 2003); and Anke Hassel and Britta Rehder, "Institutional Change in the German Wage Bargaining System–The Role of Big Companies," Max-Planck-Institut für Gesellschaftsforschung Working Paper 01, no. 9 (Cologne, 2001).
15. Available at: http://doku.iab.de/kurzgraf/2008/kbfolien16082.pdf.
16. Framework Agreement for the Metal Sector in Baden-Württemberg.

17. Press release by the Statistische Bundesamt, "40% der Erwerbstätigen unter 20 Jahren haben einen Zeitvertrag," (2005); available at http://www.destatis.de/jetspeed/portal/cms/Sites/destatis/Internet/DE/Presse/pm/ 2005/04/PD05__193__133,templateId= renderPrint.psml.

18. Press release of the Minijob-Zentrale, (2009); available at http://www.minijob-zentrale.de/nn_10152/sid_291. A824859FE226BC8F05965705DE450/nsc_true/DE/ 5__Presse/09__06__03.html.

19. The importance of status maintenance in the Bismarckian welfare state led to its classification as a conservative welfare state by Gosta Esping-Andersen,. *The Three Worlds of Welfare Capitalism* (Princeton , 1990).

20. Markus Gangl, "Welfare states and the scar effects of unemployment: A comparative analysis of the United States and West Germany," *American Journal of Sociology* 109, no. 6 (2004): 1319-1364.

21. See for a detailed discussion of the Hartz IV reforms see Anke Hassel and Christof Schiller, "Sozialpolitik im Finanzföderalismus. Hartz IV als Antwort auf die Krise der Kommunalfinanzen," forthcoming in: *Politische Vierteljahresschrift* 1 (2010).

22. Herwig Immervoll, "Minimum Wages, Minimum Labour Costs and the Tax Treatment of Low-wage Employment," *OECD Social Employment and Migration Working Papers* 46 (2007).

23. For a full explication of the argument see Anke Hassel and Christof Schiller, "Bringing the state back in–the role of fiscal federalism in welfare restructuring," Paper prepared for the 21st annual meeting of the Society for the Advancement of Socio-Economics, Sciences-Po, Paris, 16-18 July 2009.

24. Bruno Palier und Kathleen Thelen, "Dualizing CMEs: Flexibility and change in coordinated market economies," Paper presented at the Sixteenth International Conference of the Council for European Studies, Chicago 6-8 March 2008.

25. OECD, Social Expenditure Database; available at http://www.oecd.org/document/9/ 0,3343,en_2649_34637_38141385_1_1_1_1,00.html.

Chapter 19

$\mathscr{I}$NDUSTRY AND FINANCE
IN GERMANY SINCE UNIFICATION

• • • • • • • • • • • • • • •

Richard Deeg

Introduction

Since unification, there have been dramatic and highly visible changes in
the German financial system and relations between banks and firms. While
at the beginning of this era the transformation of the German financial system had already begun, it was still much closer to the traditional postwar
Hausbank model characterized by close bank-firm ties. Today, however, the
financial system is characterized by a stronger orientation to securities markets and bank-industry relations have become far more variable. The
demands of financial investors and markets on how German firms manage
themselves have–for better or worse–become increasingly influential in
this time. This transformation has neither been smooth nor continuous.
During the 1990s the federal government, along with the financial sector
and key industrial firms, promoted the growth of securities markets and an
"equity culture" (*Aktienkultur*) among German investors and firms alike.
Politicians were hoping to support Germany as a global financial center
and to provide German firms with diverse sources of finance, while financial institutions were looking for new sources of profit and to keep up with
the transformation going on in the rest of Europe and especially the U.S.
Many large industrial firms were happy to reduce dependence on the large
banks and turn to new sources of capital. In many respects, the Social
Democrats under Gerhard Schröder became even more ardent promoters

of an equity culture than the Christian Democrats.[1] In its efforts to foster financial market integration in Europe, the European Union also promoted reforms intended to stimulate market-based finance.

The market crash of 2001 proved to be only a temporary setback in this transformation. Despite some growing misgivings within Germany about the rapid changes in finance, as exemplified most famously by the "locust debate" in 2005 (*Heuschreckendebatte*) over the desirability of private equity investment in firms, the transformation of the financial system marched on. The crisis of 2008/2009 will likely have more effects on German finance, but it is unlikely to reverse the direction of change witnessed over the last two decades. Given that the West German financial system was duplicated in the East after unification, the general contours of change just described apply there as well. Indeed, the process of rapidly privatizing firms in eastern Germany during the early 1990s gave a huge boost to the growth of private equity activity overall.

Since unification the German financial system broadly has moved to a significant degree away from a bank-based towards a market-based financial system. In the former, banks provide the overwhelming portion of external capital to firms, often control securities markets that are relatively small, and practice "relationship banking" with firms based on a mutual expectation that the relationship will be long-term and persist through good times and bad. In market-based systems, by contrast, firms utilize securities markets to a much greater degree, banks and firms sustain arms-length relationships based on explicit contracts, and savers direct a greater portion of their assets into the various securities that firms use to finance themselves. While the changes in Germany have been profound, when compared to other leading economies, the country is still notably more bank-oriented. My interest in this chapter, however, is to analyze the transformation within Germany and its broader implications for the economy. Specifically I advance the thesis that bank-industry relations became increasingly differentiated, with one set of firms moving into an institutional environment readily characterized as market-based finance. Meanwhile, most German firms remain in a bank-based environment that, while not quite the same as the *Hausbank* model that prevailed at the time of unification, is still easily recognized as such.

I start with a simple typology of two ideal-types of firm financing models. The first *Hausbank* model, which embodies the traditional unlisted firm, relies on domestic bank financing, has concentrated ownership, makes little effort to comply with shareholder value principles, and uses national financial reporting and accounting standards. I call the other the "international" firm model. The ideal-typical "international" firm is publicly listed, relies on market finance for its external financing, pursues a shareholder value orientation in management and corporate governance, has dispersed ownership, and utilizes international financial reporting and accounting standards. Between these two is a set of hybrid firms. This type may be a firm that is publicly listed but has concentrated ownership and complies with only some of the international standards and norms on corporate governance. My main empirical contention is that despite all of the changes in the last two decades, the large majority of German firms still falls into the traditional *Hausbank* model, while only a relatively small number closely approximate the international model and a slightly larger number fall into the hybrid category. The economic significance of firms in these last two categories, however, leverages the broader impact of these changes on the general German economic model.

There are two primary firm characteristics that appear to play a major role in determining a firm's categorization: size and ownership (private versus public listing). These characteristics have long distinguished firms in their financing patterns, but changes in financial markets and other regulations have altogether amplified diversity within the German financial system since the early 1990s.

Some firms have embraced the international model, while others seek to limit financial market pressures by various means such as retaining concentrated ownership, especially by families. Diversity among smaller firms is rooted partly in divergent preferences among them and partly in barriers to their participation in the "international" model. For many modes of market finance they are simply too small (e.g., bonds or even private equity). Mediated financing, whether by banks or other financial institutions, remains the most cost-effective. German Mittelstand firms (SMEs) in some cases also have strongly resisted efforts to force elements of this international model on them. For example, in 2007 when the European Commission attempted to extend the requirement to use international accounting standards to non-listed firms, a groundswell of opposition began with German SMEs that feared it would undermine their traditional reliance on bank borrowing in which owner capital plays a crucial role as collateral. The revolt soon spilled over into the European Parliament and the Commission backed off.[2]

In the next two sections, I provide more empirical material on changing patterns of firm finance and bank-firm relations, first for large firms (the 'international') model and then for Mittelstand firms. The final section discusses briefly the impact on the German economy more generally.

The Changing Context of Large Firms in Germany

The "international" firm model can be characterized by four general features. First, there is a general shift in firm financing from bank to market finance, including international finance. Second, firms are increasingly subject to a common set of rules of financial transparency and sound financial practice. Third, firms are subject to increasingly common corporate governance rules and practices, such as shareholder value, minority shareholder protection, etc. Fourth, firm strategies and restructuring are increasingly subject to influence outside of firm management or corporate insiders, especially by financial market actors (notably institutional investors, hedge, and equity funds), which leads to a more active market for corporate control and restructuring via takeovers, mergers, and acquisitions.

Changing Patterns of Firm Finance: Shift to Market Finance

For more than thirty years there has been a broad trend toward increasing self-finance and market finance by European corporations, a dynamic that has been most pronounced among larger firms. Federico Galizia[3] shows the percentage of total capital formation self-financed by German firms rising from about 72 percent in the 1970s to more than 86 percent in the 1990s. Across Europe, there is also a shift in corporate finance from loans to marketable securities (notably bonds), though this shift is largely confined to larger firms.[4] Evidence for this can be found in the data on corporate borrowing: from 1989 to 1998, outstanding domestic corporate debt rose from 40 percent to 63 percent of GDP, a reflection of the heavy restructuring by German firms due to reunification and new post Cold War economic conditions. From 1998 to 2005, however, corporate debt declined to 26 percent of GDP, reflecting not only the economic malaise of the early 2000s, but also the shift to market and private equity finance by many firms.[5] That said, banks are still the single most important source of external finance in most European countries, including Germany.[6] In Germany the there has been no clear long-term structural shift in the aggregate from bank loans to securities.[7] When broken down by firm size, however, the picture is different: large firms have always relied much less bank and external debt than smaller firms, and this divergence has own over time.[8] It is also the large firms that have turned to international securities markets for borrowing: from 1993 to 2005 international corporate debt rose steadily from 0.3 percent of GDP to 3 percent of GDP–a tenfold rise in little more than a decade.[9]

Changing Rules and Norms of Financial Management

Since unification, there have been numerous market and regulatory developments in Germany and Europe that have considerably increased the external transparency of the financial practices and condition of large firms. Altogether these changes have made many German firms more subject to the influence of external financial market actors, as well as opened the door to increased ownership and influence by non-traditional financial firms such as hedge and equity funds.

In Germany, lawmakers and regulators advanced these developments in numerous steps. In addition to several financial market promotion laws promulgated since the early 1990s, in 1998 the Law on Control and Transparency in Enterprises (Gesetz zur Kontrolle und Transparenz im Unternehmensbereich, KonTraG) sought to support the growth of securities markets by limiting the influence of banks in firms and instead increasing corporate transparency, management accountability and protection for minority shareholders.[10] The KonTraG made German corporate law among the more shareholder-friendly ones in Europe. For example, it eliminated unequal voting rights and abolished voting caps in shareholders meetings–two features still common in other European Union member states.[11] Also in 1998, the Law to Facilitate Equity Issues (Kapitalaufnahmeerleichterungsgesetz, KapAEG) was promulgated which, among other things, allowed German firms to balance their books using the international (IAS) or American accounting standards.[12] This was a step sought by several large German firms eager to list their shares in New York.

As part of its broad program to modernize corporate Germany, in 2000 the Federal Government passed a corporate income tax taw that made the sale of long-term equity stakes held by large firms and banks in other firms tax free after 1 January 2002. This measure gave further impetus to the already ongoing sell-off of big industrial shareholdings–most notably by the large banks–and large-scale reshuffling of corporate assets.[13] Even before these tax changes, the 1990s had twice the level of mergers and acquisitions as during the 1980s–due in no small part to transactions in eastern Germany.[14] The number of capital ties among the 100 largest corporations declined from 169 in 1996 to 80 in 2000;[15] the percentage of corporate equity held by other German non-financial firms fell from 45.8

percent in 1995 to 32.5 percent by 2003.[16] Banks have also greatly reduced their direct involvement in corporate governance via board representation. In sum, the traditionally tight financial and personal linkages among German firms and banks have been greatly reduced. To be clear, though, many large German firms still have large, long-term shareholders–the difference is that now many also have a large number of institutional and retail investors who are interested in shareholder value.[17]

At the European level, there have also been many Directives passed that have fostered the growth of the international firm model in Germany. More recently, since 2005 the EU has required all listed firms in member states to begin publishing consolidated financial statements in accordance with International Financial Reporting Standards and International Accounting Standards, which were based on fair value or "mark to market" accounting principles. The shift added further pressure on German managers to give greater weight in their decisions to financial profitability.[18] Second, increased transparency and common financial disclosure rules were furthered by regulatory changes and listing rules in European stock exchanges during the 1990s. Third, and only recently receiving attention due to the 2008 crisis, is the growing influence of bond rating agencies on corporate financial practices. Any firm that issues bonds or other debt securities is likely rated by at least one of three major bond rating agencies that tend to spread Anglo-American norms about financial practices.[19]

Altogether, common accounting standards, stock listing regulations, and ratings agencies make corporate balance sheets more directly comparable across national settings. Among other things, this facilitates the ability of international investors to compare corporate performance across borders and to apply pressure on firm management. In short, then, German firms following the "international model" are part of an emerging, common global orthodoxy about financial practices and transparency (and the knock-on implications for general management practices).

Corporate Governance Norms and Rules

By the early 2000s, Germany and other European countries had by and large completed a wave of corporate governance reform. Shareholder value as a set of norms and practices has come to be the umbrella concept deployed both in public discourse and management practices to reflect the broad sweep of corporate governance changes. For shareholder value advocates, a central path to its achievement is through enhanced minority shareholder protection, such as rules that prevent or eliminate unequal voting and control rights and strengthened disclosure and transparency rules.[20] Germany, like other nations, has also made efforts to empower supervisory boards to oversee and control managers in the interests of shareholders. Finally, we can point to an increased use of performance-related pay for managers as a common corporate governance trend. The objective of these measures is to make the interests of shareholders and managers coincide by linking managers' remuneration with the performance of the firm through performance-related forms of compensation such as stock options.

The impact of such corporate governance reforms on German firms is quite variable. First, corporate governance reforms have so far had relatively little consequence for the vast majority of small and medium-sized firms, since such firms are not typically listed and the EU has made little effort to change corporate governance rules for SMEs. Even among large German firms, many are relatively unaffected because they have some degree of choice in the extent to which they change their corporate governance practices. Like many other nations, Germany regulates corporate governance in part through a voluntary code rather than a full regime of mandatory corporate governance rules. In practice, it is enterprises that are more globally oriented or whose shares are widely held which have generally made the most changes, i.e., have come closest to the "international model."[21] Second, firms have chosen diverse ways to satisfy the corporate governance demands of institutional investors. German firms commonly appease investors through increased transparency of management and company finances, rather than by selling off weakly performing divisions as is common in France.[22] In Germany, corporate reforms also left intact key elements of its traditional corporate governance model such as codetermination and works councils, which are typically viewed as antithetical to shareholder value.[23]

Enterprise Ownership, Control and Restructuring

For much of the postwar period, large firms in Germany were controlled by large blockholders (bank, families, other firms). The control of such "insiders" was also frequently strengthened through a variety of control enhancing mechanisms (CEMs) such as dual voting shares, cross-shareholdings, pyramids, etc. As result of efforts to foster financial market growth and securities markets in particular, various pressures have emerged to reduce blockholding ownership Europe-wide.

Indeed, across Europe there is a notable trend toward the unwinding of cross-shareholdings, most strikingly in the cases of France and Germany.[24] A decline in the role of banks as industrial shareholders is readily apparent in Germany, and non-financial enterprises also have displayed a reduced interest in holding large shares in other companies.[25] Gregory Jackson shows that during the 1990s the proportion of shares held by "stable investors" (banks, insurance firms, corporations, and the state) declined from 60.2 percent to 52.8 percent, while shares held by individuals, institutions and foreigners–who are much more likely to actively trade shares– rose from 39.8 percent to 47.1 percent.[26] The change is greatest among large firms. Of the twenty largest publicly traded firms in Germany, only a quarter have a shareholder with more than a 20 percent stake.[27]

The dispersion of ownership is generally viewed as leading to more pressure on firms to maximize shareholder value–i.e., manage their share prices for maximum gain–and greater influence of outside investors over firms. The rapid recent growth of hedge and private equity funds that are taking large stakes in, or buying outright, firms in Germany and then restructuring them, pushes this process even further.

SME Finance in Germany

Germany has long been seen as the paragon of a bank-based financial system and the picture for SMEs generally bears this out. First, Germany historically has had the highest level of bank loans as a percentage of company liabilities. Aggregate corporate borrowing declined dramatically beginning in the 1990s (as elsewhere), but still remains comparatively high.[28] As noted earlier, this decline is accounted for largely by declines in bank borrowing by large firms. Thus, German SMEs are now substantially more indebted than large firms,[29] though bank debt as a percentage of balance sheet totals has remained steady for SMEs since the mid-1990s.[30] Compared to other European cases, bank borrowing by German SMEs has also been composed to a much greater degree of long-term debt, reflecting the long-term *Hausbank* relationship.[31] Trade credits and especially leasing have become important alternative sources of external funds, but bank borrowing is still dominant.[32] Thus, the historic *Hausbank* relationship appears largely intact for SMEs. This stability in bank borrowing and relationship is attributable to a number of factors, including the tax system, the unique character and stability of the banking system marked by the role of strong savings and cooperative banks focused on SME finance, strong public support programs for SME lending, and the strong aversion of SME owners to outside interference and equity.[33]

The low equity ratios of German SMEs compared to large firms and SMEs in other countries suggests that they are relatively undercapitalized.[34] This ratio has been declining for a long time,[35] often precipitating worries over an "equity gap" and reformers' demands for more private equity investment. In the 1980s and 1990s, public authorities established numerous publicly financed equity funds to address this concern, and also efforts to stimulate the growth of private equity. In the 1990s, equity funds played a small but significant role, especially in the restructuring of eastern Germany. Nonetheless, equity ratios remained comparatively low and thus the potential market for private equity and venture capital in Germany is quite large. Following the general European pattern, private equity did grow dramatically in the late 1990s, declined equally dramatically after the stock market peak in 2001, then rebounded in recent years, making Germany the third largest market in Europe.[36] Nevertheless, on a GDP basis Germany remains well behind the UK, France, the Netherlands, and Sweden. In short, despite an apparently higher "need" for external equity, German SMEs are not rushing to it. During the 1990s, there was also a marked trend toward initial public offerings (IPOs) among German firms–a welcome development by government and financial market actors. The number of listed firms in Germany rose from 436 in 1983 to 933 in 1999.[37] The IPO trend was fostered by dynamics in eastern Germany but also the Neuer Markt, created in 1997 to encourage more small firms to go public. But, after peaking in 2000, the number of listed firms began to decline and the number of IPOs dropped back to levels of the early 1990s.[38]

The Meaning of Changing Bank-Industry Relations

How do these changes in bank-industry relations affect the broader German model of organized capitalism? In the comparative capitalisms literature, it is posited that essential complementarities exist between the financial system and other key institutional domains of the economy.[39] In coordinated market economies like Germany, long-term finance ("patient capital")–notably *Hausbank* practices and concentrated ownership–is hypothesized to support production strategies based on long-term relations and investment, as well as incremental innovation.[40] The leading German firms, for example, have long emphasized technical criteria as much as financial ones as a basis for investment decisions.[41] Similarly, traditional German accounting rules enabled firms to amass large hidden reserves that helped managers smooth out fluctuations in reported earnings and thus facilitate long-term investment. The required use of International Accounting and Financial Reporting Standards, along with strengthened financial disclosure rules, greatly reduces the capacity of German firms to engage in such "smoothing," thus forcing them to focus more on shorter-term financial performance measures.[42] The varieties of capitalism school predicts that national capitalisms that mix institutions with different logics–such as short-term market finance with inflexible labor markets–will underperform relative to economies whose institutions uniformly follow either a liberal market or a coordinated logic. In short, to the extent that capital has become less "patient" in Germany, we would predict two outcomes: increased pressure on unions and labor markets for greater flexibility and a reduction in the ability of German firms to engage in long-term cooperation with other firms, whether for research or production purposes.[43] There is ample evidence for the first outcome, as attested by the recent literature on German industrial relations. Though to be clear, pressures on the labor market are likely due more to increased product market competition than changes in the financial system.[44] For the second outcome, evidence is still anecdotal.

On one side of this issue stand those who argue that financial system changes are not fundamentally altering the coordinated or organized character of the German economy. In this view, the institutional changes observed in Germany since the early 1990s represent a normal process of adjustment to altered market environments that preserve basic patterns of strategic coordination among firms.[45] Thus, the increased shareholder value orientation of large German firms, for instance, has not undermined codetermination (labor-management coordination) because new complementarities have been generated.[46] The return of booming exports by German firms in the mid 2000s and the comparative resilience of the German economy during the current recession support such a conclusion.

On the other side of this issue are those who argue that the consequences of increased financial market influence are still working their way through the country.[47] While codetermination remains formally intact, its character has shifted to "comanagement" in which labor's goals take second place to those of the corporation.[48] Viewed this way, the rise of private equity and hedge fund investors may also be seen as mechanisms forcing the erosion of the traditional *Hausbank* system for Mittelstand firms as well. If such investors apply strict cost-cutting and profit maximization standards while loading the firm with debt in order to fund the acquisition, then firms may be more likely to disengage from the strategic coordination regimes that have been essential to Germany's advantage in incremental innovation. While there is anecdotal evidence to support this erosion hypothesis, there is also evidence that the German institutional context often modifies the behavior of such investors.[49] At this point in time, resolving this debate requires much more empirical research.

The financial crisis of the late 2000s had major and obvious consequences for Germany in the short term. Over the long-term, however, it is less clear whether the developments of the past twenty years will resume their forward march. A number of the large German banks have been chastened by the huge losses sustained in the crisis and the pitfalls of fancy financial products. Although Commerzbank never went as far down the road toward Anglo-American banking as Deutsche Bank, after the crisis, it strengthened its commitment to more conventional German banking with industry. As elsewhere, the crisis also laid low private equity and activist hedge funds that had relied heavily on bank borrowing to fund their acquisitions. Thus the "locusts" are not swarming Germany, at least for a while. Moreover, the effort to create an "equity culture" among German investors has had moderate success at best. That said, there is no way back to the financial industry and bank-industry relations present at the time of unification. Many of the new financial products and opportunities that emerged for banks, firms, and investors since then are still useful, desired, and now embedded in German and European laws and regulations. The persistence of diverse financial models in Germany seems to be the likely future for some time to come.

Notes

1. John Cioffi and Martin Höpner, "The Political Paradox of Finance Capitalism: Interests, Preferences, and Center-Left Party Politics in Corporate Governance Reform," *Politics & Society* 34 (2006): 463-502; Richard Deeg, "Change from Within: German and Italian Finance in the 1990s," in *Beyond Continuity: Institutional Change in Advanced Political Economies*, eds., Wolfgang Streeck and Kathleen Thelen (Oxford, 2005).
2. Andreas Nölke and James Perry, "The power of transnational private governance: financialisation and the IASB," *Business and Politics* 9, no. 3 (2007); available at http://www.bepress.com/bap/vol9/iss3/art4; accessed 8 February 2007.
3. Federico Galizia, "Measuring the 'financing gap' of European corporations. An update," Economic and Financial Report 2 (Luxembourg, 2003); available at http://www.eib.org/attachments/efs/efr03n02.pdf; accessed 14 May 2007.

4. Joseph Byrne and E. Phillip Davis, "A comparison of balance sheet structures in major EU countries," *National Institute Economic Review* 180 (2002); Victor Murinde, Juda Agung and Andy Mullineux, "Patterns of corporate financing and financial system convergence in Europe," *Review of International Economics* 12 (2004): 693-705.

5. Richard Deeg, "The Rise of Internal Capitalist Diversity? Changing Patterns of Finance and Corporate Governance in Europe," *Economy & Society*, 38 (2009): 552-579.

6. Dorothee Rivaud-Danset and Valerie Oheix, "Do corporate financial patterns in European countries converge and testify for disintermediation?" MPRA Paper No. 40, (Munich, 2006); available at http://mpra.ub.uni-muenchen.de/40/; accessed 14 May 2007.

7. Sigurt Vitols, "Changes in Germany's bank-based financial system: A varieties of capitalism perspective," Discussion Paper SP II 2004-03 (Berlin, 2004), 20; Reihard Schmidt, Andreas Hackethal and Marcel Tyrell, "The convergence of financial systems in Europe," Johann Wolfgang Goethe University, Working Paper Series No. 75 (Frankfurt/Main, 2001).

8. Rivaud-Danset and Oheix (see note 5); Andreas Hackethal, Reinhard Schmidt and Marcel Tyrell, "Banks and German corporate governance: On the way to a capital market-based system?" Johann Wolfgang Goethe University, Working Paper Series No. 146 (Frankfurt/Main, 2005), 9.

9. Deeg (see note 5).

10. John Cioffi, "Expansive Retrenchment: The Regulatory Politics of Corporate Governance Reform and the Foundations of Finance Capitalism in the United States and Germany," in *The State After Statism: New State Activities in the Age of Globalization and Liberalization*, ed. Jonah Levy (Cambridge, 2006).

11. Ibid.

12. Ibid.

13. Martin Höpner, "Corporate governance in transition: Ten empirical findings on shareholder value and industrial relations in Germany," Max-Planck-Institut für Gesellschaftsforschung Discussion Paper 01/5 (Cologne, 2001); Jürgen Beyer, "Deutschland AG a.D.: Deutsche Bank, Allianz und das Verflechtungszentrum grosser deutscher Unternehmen," Max-Planck-Institut für Gesellschaftsforschung Working Paper 04/4 (Cologne, 2002).

14. Martin Höpner and Gregory Jackson, "Political Economy of Takeovers in Germany: The Case of Mannesmann and its Implications for Institutional Change," Max Planck Institute for the Study of Societies, Discussion Paper 01/5 (Cologne, 2001).

15. Beyer (see note 13).

16. Vitols (see note 7).

17. The median size shareholding (as a per cent of all shares) held by the single largest shareholder in a DAX 30 firm was 21.5 percent at the end of 2002; this compared to 5.3 percent for the Dow Jones 30. Vitols (see note 7).

18. Nölke and Perry (see note 2).

19. Timothy Sinclair, *The new masters of capital: American bond rating agencies and the politics of creditworthiness* (Ithaca, 2005); A non-trivial number of SMEs are also seeking external ratings in order to secure loans at better rates. With modifications to the new Basel Capital Adequacy rules, however, most banks are expected to use internal rating methods to assess creditworthiness of SMEs.

20. Peter A. Gourevitch and James Shinn, *Political power and corporate control: The new global politics of corporate governance* (Princeton, 2005).

21. See Höpner (see note 13); Alexander Börsch, *Global pressure, national system: How German corporate governance is changing* (Ithaca, 2007).

22. Michel Goyer, "Varieties of institutional investor and national models of capitalism: The transformation of corporate governance in France and Germany," *Politics and Society* 34 (2006): 399-430.

23. Vitols (see note 7); Gregory Jackson, "Stakeholders under pressure: corporate governance and labour management in Germany and Japan," *Corporate Governance: An International Review* 13 (2005): 419-428.

24. European Commission, "Report on the proportionality principle in the European Union," (June 2007); available at http://ec.europa.eu/internal_market/company/docs/shareholders/study/final_report_en.pdf; accessed 25 June 2007.

25. Jürgen Beyer and Martin Höpner, "The disintegration of organised capitalism: German corporate governance in the 1990s," *West European Politics* 26 (2003): 179-98. Pepper Culpepper, "Institutional change in contemporary capitalism: Coordinated financial systems since 1990," *World Politics* 57 (2005): 173-99.

26. Gregory Jackson, "Corporate Governance in Germany and Japan: Liberalization Pressures and Responses during the 1990s," in *The End of Diversity: Prospects for German and Japanese Capitalism*, eds., Wolfgang Streeck and Kozo Yamamura (Ithaca, 2003). Aggregate equity holdings by banks held steady during the 1990s, but from 1999 to 2003 they dropped from 13 percent to 9 percent of all outstanding equity in German firms; insurance companies and other financial firms (mostly investment funds) more than doubled their holdings, from 6.6 percent to 13.2 percent and 6 percent to 13.5 percent respectively, but this was largely portfolio investment. Vitols (see note 7).

27. European Commission (see note 24).

28. Byrne and Davis (see note 4), 89.

29. Dorothee Rivaud-Danset, Emmanuelle Dubocage and Robert Salais, "Comparison between the financial structure of SME versus large enterprise using the Bach database, UMR 604, Centre National de la Recherche Scientifique (1998); available at http://papers.ssrn.com/sol3/papers.cfm?abstract_id=141478; accessed 15 May 2007.

30. Ulrich Hommel and Hilmar Schneider, "Financing the German Mittelstand," *EIB Papers* 8, no. 2 (2003): 52-91, here 84.

31. Rivaud-Danset et al. (see note 29), 32-33; Hommel and Schneider (see note 30), 62-63.

32. Hommel and Schneider (see note 30), 72).

33. Rien Wagenvoort, "Are finance constraints hindering the growth of SMEs in Europe?" *EIB Papers* 8, no. 2 (2003): 22-51, here 31; Hommel and Schneider (see note 28).

34. European Commission, "2003 Observatory of European SMEs: 2003/2 SMEs and access to finance" (Brussels, 2003); available at http://ec.europa.eu/enterprise/enterprise_policy/analysis/doc/smes_observatory_2003_report2_en.pdf; accessed 4 May 2007; and Rivaud-Danset et al. (see note29), 31.

35. Hommel and Schneider (see note 30), 60.

36. European Venture Capital Association, "European fundraising reaches new record," 12 June 2007; available at http://www.evca.com/images/attachments/tmpl_13_art_107_att_1149.pdf; accessed 20 June 2007.

37. Beyer (see note 13).

38. Deeg (see note 5).

39. See Richard Deeg and Gregory Jackson, "Towards a more dynamic theory of capitalist variety," *Socio-Economic Review* 5 (2007): 149-179.

40. Peter A. Hall and David Soskice, "An Introduction to Varieties of Capitalism," in *Varieties of Capitalism: The Institutional Foundations of Comparative Advantage*, eds., Peter A. Hall and David Soskice (Oxford, 2001), 1-70.

41. Börsch (see note 21).

42. Nölke and Perry (see note 2).

43. Knut Lange and Florian Becker-Ritterspach, "International private equity investors as an emerging transnational community and their impact on the German business system," Paper presented at the 23rd EGOS Colloquium, Vienna, Austria, July 2007.

44. Roger Barker, *Corporate Governance, Competition, and Political Parties: Explaining Corporate Governance Change in Europe* (Oxford, 2010).

45. Peter A. Hall and Kathleen Thelen, "Institutional Change in Varieties of Capitalism," *Socio-Economic Review* 7 (2009): 7-34.; Börsch (see note 21).

46. Martin Höpner, "What connects industrial relations and corporate governance? Explaining institutional complementarity," *Socio-Economic Review* 3 (2005): 331-358.

47. Christel Lane, "Institutional transformation and system change: changes in the Corporate Governance of German corporations," in *Changing capitalisms? Internationalization, institutional change, and systems of economic organization,* eds., Glenn Morgan, Richard Whitley and Eli Moen (Oxford, 2005), 78-108.

48. Jackson (see note 23).

49. Lange and Becker-Ritterspach (see note 43).

Chapter 20

$\mathcal{I}$DEAS, INSTITUTIONS
AND ORGANIZED CAPITALISM

*The German Model of Political Economy
Twenty Years after Unification*[1]

● ● ● ● ● ● ● ● ● ● ● ● ● ●

Christopher S. Allen

Introduction

At the time of German unification, *Modell Deutschland* was considered to be
the primary reason for the health and stability of the Federal Republic's
forty-year record of strong economic performance. Many observers
thought it would be an excellent foundation for incorporating the five new
Länder of the former German Democratic Republic. For much of the past
two decades since unification, however, the literature on the German
economy has largely focused on the erosion of the German form of organized capitalism (*Modell Deutschland*) and emphasized institutional decline
and the corresponding rise of neoliberalism, which the first part of this
essay briefly reviews.[2] But, since mid 2008, the worldwide financial crisis
has challenged the virtues of the apparent neoliberal hegemony and perhaps opened up once again a debate regarding appropriate economic policy models. In short, the crisis has suggested that a coordinated market
economy (CME) might yet have some considerable virtues.

The second part of this chapter takes up this possible shift in focus
toward a renewed CME, but it argues that in order to explain adequately the
erosion of the German model in the two decades since unification, we need
to pose a question that is seldom asked in the literature that chronicles its

apparent demise. This purpose of this chapter is to investigate why such a model was created in the first place and whether a renewed form of it might still be useful not only for a Germany still struggling with unification issues, but perhaps also for the European Union (EU) and other developed democracies in the early twenty-first century. Specifically, it argues that the formation of this organized capitalist model (CME), not only in the postwar period, but also during Germany's rapid industrialization in the late ninteenth century arose because an Anglo-American free market model was inappropriate for generating the economic growth that each epoch required. It also argues that the creation of this policy regime was comprised of dynamic, flexible institutions and a clear set of visionary ideas in the context of either state-building or state-rebuilding.[3] In light of the recent crisis that has produced sharp challenges for liberal market economy (LME) approaches, might there be opportunities for a revived CME?

The third part of this chapter articulates the components of these coordinated market economy models during both the Bismarckian and Social Market Economy periods. It also suggests that the context of state formation (Imperial Germany) and state reformation (the Federal Republic and the Social Market Economy) were fundamental processes that made the institutions and ideas greater than the sum of the parts.

The final section inquires into whether the failure of the neoliberal model in the wake of the worldwide financial crisis and severe recession represents a possible opening for the creation of a third organized capitalist model not only for Germany but for a redesigned European Union. It outlines three possible scenarios: a renewed LME, in spite of its apparent demise; a hybrid LME-CME formation in which neither dominates, but elements of both are clearly present; or a path that contains institutional and ideational elements recognizable from earlier CME models that would extend beyond Germany to other continental Western European countries and perhaps to the EU itself.

Before proceeding further, it is important to clarify terminology. Through significant portions of the postwar period, the German CME has been called *Modell Deutschland.*[4] As much as this term has been used, one thing is clear: economic policy "models" are characterizations of institutional arrangements that only are recognized fully after their creation, sometimes many years thereafter. In other words, economic policy models are the institutional landscapes that we can only see through the rearview mirror. Since this chapter focuses primarily on the origins of Germany's CME experiences and only secondarily on their decline, it is more important to identify both the specific institutional and ideational components that shaped these two CMEs, as well as the processes with which they were formed. Thus, while the paper examines the origins of these two earlier periods, it will generally avoid using the term "model." As Kathleen Thelen and Wolfgang Streeck[5] have argued, the creation of these CME regimes was an iterative, experimental, trial-and-error process that owed much to the innovative capacities of the economic and political actors and the institutions they were creating. They also had unintended consequences, for example, being created to serve a specific purpose at one moment, only to serve a very different purpose as circumstances changed and institutions adapted. In this context, this paper stresses that a more free-market LME was never a serious option as Germany industrialized in the late nineteenth or reindustrialized in the mid twentieth centuries. Thus, what came to be recognized as a CME "model" was not visible from the outset of either period. Yet, what all of these cooperative and institutionally dense experiments shared is that they were not embarking on a laissez faire path. There was no "system designer" for this CME, but, given the pressure to industrialize, develop, and, politically, provide access to resources, markets, and capital, these material pressures forced forms of cooperation as the only way to industrialize rapidly since the LME option was off the table. To extent that Otto von Bismarck or Konrad Adenauer/Ludwig Erhard "planned" these particular CME regimes, they were in the context of state formation and reformation, respectively.

The Demise of *Modell Deutschland*

By now, the litany of shortcomings of the postwar form of German organized capitalism is well known. Since the 1990s, the German economy has been beset with increasingly uncompetitive industries, persistent structural unemployment, and continued stagnation in eastern Germany.[6] In addition, the large German banks, which for more than a century served as a guardian for dozens of German firms, began to sever their *Hausbank* relationships with large German firms in favor of focusing on global opportunities and global profits.[7] For more than a decade, within the formerly cooperative corporatist industrial relations system, German employers have been deserting their employer associations in favor of "going it alone" when negotiating with unions.[8] In addition, the latter have fared poorly in the past twenty years with the share of German workers in trade unions dropping by almost half, now representing less than 20 percent of the German workforce. Finally, the Social Democratic Party (SPD), once the exemplar of "capitalism with a human face" after its first years as the leading party in government in the 1970s, recently has turned to serious retrenchment in the form of the Hartz IV labor market reforms that victimized many of its own supporters during the Gerhard Schröder governments of the early 2000s,[9] only to lose control of government in the 2005 election[10] and then suffer its worst postwar defeat in the 2009 election.

The inglorious end of the German organized capitalist "model" came to be characterized as one comprised of cumbersome, limiting, and sclerotic institutions incapable of adaptation. The conventional wisdom was that only a turn to neoliberal market approaches could pull the German economy out of the doldrums[11] and address the continuing costs of unification that the postwar system was never able to accomplish. While the 2008 financial crisis and subsequent severe recession clearly had cut short the enthusiasm for neoliberal solutions both in Germany and elsewhere, the standard consensus by mainstream economists still remains that the current version of the organized capitalist economy does not offer much promise. This view suggests that the neoliberalism proposed by the Free Democrats, the new junior coalition partner of the Christian Democrats (CDU/CSU) following the 2009 election, is a more appropriate policy model. Specifically, this party argues that an economy dominated by older manufacturing industries with comparatively high-priced labor may not be agile enough to remain competitive in an increasingly harsh economic climate.

Institutional Innovation, Visionary Ideas, & State (re)building

One can tell a great deal about the organization of a nation's economic policy by understanding the country's timing of industrialization and democratization.[12] Countries that industrialized early tended to have laissez-faire, free market economies that gradually evolved into the world's leading economies because their good fortune and path-breaking industrialization allowed them to have relatively easy access to resources, markets, and capital. The UK and the U.S. are the prime examples of this pattern. Countries that industrialized later, such as Germany and Japan, faced a different set of choices.[13] Lacking ready and predictable access to resources, markets, and capital, they needed to construct a different set of institutions if they were to catch up to the earlier industrializers. In short, they needed to construct a model that maximized efficient access and use of resources, targeted foreign markets since their own domestic markets were so underdeveloped, and allocated capital so that each investment had a high probability of success. Unlike the "trial and error" economies of the earlier industrializers, the latecomers had much less margin for error.

Thus, with neither classical liberalism nor dirigisme (in the post World War II period) possible what other option was there? The most likely alternative was one that organized and mobilized major producer groups via the framing guidance of the state. This was not an easy task. Rather than waiting for capitalism to evolve slowly as it had in the Anglo-American world, it needed to be "force-fed" quickly to produce the most profitable paths.[14] Thus, in both the late nineteenth and mid twentieth centuries, the state both encouraged and allowed large firms to form with tight coordination from their financial partners. Resources had to be acquired and used efficiently, foreign markets had to be identified and targeted (since domestic demand in the early years of both models was quite underdeveloped), and capital investment had to have a high expectation of success. "Trial-and-error" capitalism was simply not sufficient or fast enough. Moreover, because production for domestic consumption was a second order priority, providing some sort of social protection for the majority of citizens who were not favored in these top-down CME systems was crucial. In essence, this was an "all eggs in one basket" economic policy model–especially during the nondemocratic Bismarckian era–that required close coordination or all major producers and the emphatic provision of social order. To be sure, in the democratic Federal Republic, the prospect for dissent and social disturbance was less regime-threatening than it was during the late nineteenth and early twentieth centuries.

In essence, to make this form of capitalism work at both the economic and political levels the founders of these two models developed a conception of institutions that were both dynamic and flexible. Such a path was only possible with visionary ideas to imbue institutions with innovative, transformative policies that could also evolve over time. Theoretically, this is captured much more effectively by institutional characteristics closer to the views of Albert O. Hirschman than those of Mancur Olson.[15] The former believed that institutions could be more flexible and dynamic with the effective use of "voice." The latter saw institutions as impediments to individual action and often produced suboptimal outcomes at the macro level. But in a larger sense, what enabled these institutions and ideas to achieve and then transcend the very effective incremental adaptation at the beginning of these regimes was the specific process of state formation and reformation. This larger geopolitical perspective gave the respective sets of leaders a broader tableau upon which to make their case for these institutional and ideational innovations.

Most contemporary scolars working in the varieties of capitalism and comparative historical institutional fields focus on the decline of these coordinated market economies or models. To understand the synergy of ideas, institutions, and state (re)building, this article argues that we also need to see the origins, as well as the decline of these organized capitalist regimes. It draws heavily on the major "historical institutionalist" and path dependence literature such as that of Paul Pierson and Thelen, which examine both the decline and the origins of such regimes. But, the value-added to this project is connecting this institutional analysis to the literature on ideas[16] and to selected literature on state formation.[17]

Latecomers such as Germany–and other continental western European nations–were forced to create a set of institutions that could accomplish economic and political development quickly because following the gradual, evolutionary path of the UK and the U.S. would have been disastrously insufficient, and ultimately too late.[18] While Bismarck was able to use the state as an entrepreneur,[19] that option was not possible in the post World War II period due to the Nazis' colossal abuse of state power. Both epochs, however, did share the use of a universal banking system and close coordination among major producer groups as significant entrepreneurial forces.[20] They were called cartels in the nineteenth century and the more palatable *Verbände* in the mid twentieth. The larger point here is that neither the universal banks nor organized German business were decisive individually. But, together they anchored a set of economic policies that could industrialize–and re-industrialize quickly–and make maximum use of resources, target markets, and use capital efficiently. Not surprisingly, rapid economic transformation based upon industrial development and largely export-led growth did not offer much immediate benefit to ordinary Germans. Both Bismarck and the "fathers" of the Social Market Economy, Adenauer and Erhard, realized that such social dislocation required protective social policies.[21] These leaders did not offer such policies altruistically, rather, they were preventive policies aimed pragmatically at minimizing social tension and political opposition while the economy grew. Bismarck's creation of the first social insurance schemes (while simultaneously banning the then revolutionary SPD) was one mechanism.[22] Another was the less draconian implementation of the Social Market Economy,[23] which provided the beginnings of the postwar welfare state in Germany's first stable democracy.

Unlike more open free-market oriented economic policy models that had few constraints in terms of resources, markets, and capital, an organized capitalist or coordinated market economy requires close coordination. Making this work required people with visionary ideas to imbue these institutions (banks, firms, *Verbände*, works councils, unions, parapublic service providers, etc.) with innovative and transformative policies, providing a total that was greater than the sum of the parts.[24] Institutions may turn into inefficient Weberian bureaucracies when allowed to atrophy. But, when imbued with a larger public purpose such as invigorating an economy when the usual market approaches are not available or when building or rebuilding a nation state, in the right hands and with far-reaching vision, they can be much more dynamic than conventional wisdom holds.[25] In fact, we have the proof of the capacity of institutional transformation in the presence of Germany's largest banks (Deutsche, Commerz, and Dresdner which in 2008 merged with Commerzbank) and firms (Siemens, Daimler-Benz, BASF, Bayer), all of which have existed for over a century amidst periods of great turmoil.

Bismarck and the First Organized Capitalist Model

What specifically were the institutions, ideas and state-building context that made these two epochs possible? During the latter half of the nineteenth century, first Prussia, and then a united Germany created a universal banking system—an the idea borrowed from Louis Napoleon's *Credit Mobilier* that focused on long-term, targeted investment in the dominant industries of the "second industrial revolution" (coal, steel, chemicals, machine tools, railroads, and industrial electronics).[26] This required large sums of money, but the newly created firms in these sectors were unable to raise the funds themselves from the primitive stock markets of the time. By virtue of loans, ownership of company stock, holding proxies for the firms' shareholders, and having seats on the board of directors, the banks—aided by the state— played a significant role in the industrial direction of these firms.[27] By having deep pockets and a longer term horizon, this strategy enabled firms to establish their position in world markets. The *Verbände* (cartels) were essential since members did not see themselves as competitors of one another.[28] Rather, they viewed their principal competition as other industries abroad, hence collaboration allowed them to maximize their respective strategies. Skilled labor was also increasingly important for most of these industries and these firms were able to build on the legacy of the guild system that produced workers of exceptionally high skills.[29] Finally, Bismarck used the state more as an architect, rather than in an interventionist, micro-managing way. It supervised and facilitated—but did not direct—the evolution and growth of an organized and coordinated set of economic experiments that later was to be called a *Modell*.

What were the visionary ideas that embodied these institutions? One was the "marriage of iron and rye" that Bismarck forged between the feudal Prussian lords (*Junker*) who needed a way to get their grain to market and the new money industrialists who needed cargo to transport on the new rail system.[30] The second was Bismarck's "iron fist in a velvet glove" that saw him first ban the SPD in 1878, but then initiate one of the party's major demands, namely the creation of a welfare system in the 1880s.[31] When the SPD was made legal again in 1890, they were a much less revolutionary party because Bismarck's governments had co-opted much of the party's platform. Significantly, both Karl Marx (1883) and Friedrich Engels (1890) had died before the SPD became legal once again. By that time the revolutionary socialism of the movement's founders had been replaced by Eduard Bernstein's "evolutionary" socialism.[32]

This juncture of ideas and newly created institutions took place in a context of state building that made many of these actions possible. To be sure, Bismarck had not built the most stable foundation when Germany unified, since he had to rely on aggressive nationalism and considerable political repression as major tools. This autocratic version of the organized capitalist model was successful economically and politically for a time, but it contained the seeds of its own destruction as World War I, Weimar, the Great Depression, and the Third Reich painfully show.

This model was ultimately undermined by a series of exogenous and endogenous challenges, all of which were due to the particular timing and character of the rapid growth of the German economy in the nineteenth century and the specific form that the German state took as it unified the country in 1871. Because Germany was late to industrialize, it was

Table 1: Rise of the Bismarckian Era

Institutional Innovation & Rapid Industrialization
– Banks and long-term, targeted investment
– Verbände–heart of organized capitalism
– Modernized guild system–skills foundation
– State as framing architect not "model builder"

Visionary Ideas
– Marriage of iron and rye
– "Iron fist in velvet glove" (banning spd and creating beginnings of first welfare state)

State Formation via Nationalism and Political Repression

also late in acquiring imperial possessions. When it attempted to do so, it used aggressive nationalism to mobilize support for challenging those countries that had acquired imperial possessions in Africa, and to acquire the material resources that a rapidly growing German industry needed. World War I was the truly unfortunate result. The combination of one other exogenous event (the Russian Revolution in 1917) and endogenous phenomena comprised the ultimately fragile foundation upon which Bismarck built the Second Reich. Grafting modern industry upon a society that had never dislodged feudal institutions, a sharp division of the German Left in the wake of the Bolshevik Revolution, the lack of deep societal commitment to democracy, and dysfunctional economic policy (i.e., hyperinflation in 1923) in the wake of the Allies' insistence of massive war reparations produced catastrophe as the institutional structures exploded within a decade.

Table 2: *Decline of the Bismarckian Era*

Exogenous Challenges
– Late imperialism – Russian Revolution
Endogenous Challenges
– World War I – Unstable industry-agriculture coalition – Division of the Left – Too few believed in democracy – Dysfunctional economic ideas
Institutional Collapse and National Socialist Ideas

But if Germany was to industrialize and unify successfully in the nineteenth century, it is hard to see another viable path. This first iteration of an organized capitalist model suggests that imposing this framework upon one's neighbors and one's own citizens may produce the initial goals of industrialization and state formation. But, without adapting these ideas and institutions to subsequent conditions (both inside and outside the country), which encompass both peaceful relations with neighbors, as well as genuine political accountability and democratic representation, it is highly unlikely that such a model would be sustainable.

The Social Market Economy:
The Second Organized Capitalist Model

Many observers of contemporary Germany characterized the post World War II period as *Stunde Null* (zero hour) and the 1949 founding of the Federal Republic as a sharp departure from all that had happened in Germany over the previous century. Politically, this was true in the sense that the Federal Republic of Germany (FRG) was the country's first stable democracy. With respect to the postwar economy, one scholar suggests that the reason for the rapid growth in the mid 1950s was a legacy of the Nazi period.[33] Yet, for those who looked closely at the foundational elements of the political economy of the FRG, there was an unmistakable, deeper continuity with the late nineteenth century.[34] The Allies' original plan for Germany after the war as proposed by U.S. Secretary of the Treasury Henry Morgenthau was to deindustrialize Germany and emphasize agriculture. The Cold War and imperatives to restore a functioning German economy, however, trumped such fanciful concerns. Thus, both public and private-sector actors chose familiar patterns of industrial organization to rebuild the country since a trial-and-error free market model once again was off the table. Not only did Germans have no experience with large-scale laissez-faire economic practice, but the imperative to rebuild the German economy quickly with the onset of the Cold War took precedence. Since speed of industrial development was paramount, German banks and large German firms adopted familiar organized patterns. Universal banking, with its deep ties to larger German firms was re-established quickly, providing a stable and profitable link between finance and manufacturing.

Table 3: Rise of the Social Market Economy

Institutional Innovation
– Bank-firm links and long-view investing
– *Rahmenbedingungen* regulatory framework
– Democratic corporatism: *Mitbestimmung* and *Betriebsräte*
– Personalized proportional representation electoral system
Visionary Ideas
– Freiburg School *Ordoliberalismus*–between market and state
– Incremental adaptation via high skills
State Re-formation with Mixed Economy and Stable Parliamentary Democracy

Nevertheless, since this form of organized capitalism was now implemented under democratic auspices, other institutions re-emerged to act as a check on arbitrary power by the financial and manufacturing community. German unions, for instance, expanded the concept of the earlier *Betriebsräte* (works councils) to establish a democratic corporatism in which labor played a much more prominent role than it did under Bismarck. The trade unions and their allies in both the SPD and the CDU/CSU agreed to *Mitbestimmung* (codetermination), which gave trade unions membership rights on the boards of all large German companies.[35] This second organized capitalist model in Germany also saw a unique form of framework regulation (*Rahmenbedingungen*) that acted not like American-style regulation, which tries to belatedly address specific market failures like a fire brigade. Rather, *Rahmenbedingungen* regulated the general rules of the game, more like an architect.[36] Significant examples of this included encouraging banks to maintain high capital adequacy reserves and vetting all of those who held responsible positions in the financial sector. These framing regulations proved crucial for the health of the economy since, once again, Germany was creating an "all eggs in one basket" set of institutions in which finance and manufacturing were deeply intertwined and were mutually dependent for their—and the country's—economic success.

The visionary ideas that animated this second iteration of a coordinated model came from a group of economists who were collectively known as the Freiburg School.[37] Acknowledging that a laissez-faire policy would not work in a country with no history of it, and that the use of the state as an entrepreneur had been compromised fatally by the Third Reich, the Freiburg School economists developed a theory that refused to frame economic policy as a stark choice between state and market—a view that was most succinctly articulated by Wilhelm Röpke during the early years of the Social Market Economy:

> ....(our program) consists of measures and institutions which impart to competition the framework, rules, and machinery of impartial supervision which a competitive system needs as much as any game or match if it is not to degenerate into a vulgar brawl. A genuine, equitable, and smoothly functioning competitive system can not in fact survive without a judicious moral and legal framework and without regular supervision of the conditions under which competition can take place pursuant to real efficiency principles. This presupposes mature economic discernment on the part of all responsible bodies and individuals and a strong impartial state...[38]

The second visionary idea that emerged as a guiding principle of the Social Market Economy was the conception of innovation. In liberal market economies that celebrate the role of the individual, innovation is generally characterized by lone individuals or small firms discovering new products. In coordinated market economies without this laissez-faire tradition, by contrast, innovation came to be defined in very different ways. Rather than inventing new products, the large German firms would adapt inventions developed elsewhere and then integrate them into the production process and improve existing products.[39] Perhaps that most obvious manifestation of this pattern is the long-running television commercials (shown in the U.S) of the German chemical firm BASF that conclude: "We don't make (product x); we make (product x) better."

These renewed institutions and context-specific ideas took place at a time when Germany could not function as a "normal" nation state and when many questioned its ability to "behave" as a democratic polity. The country's ability to renew these nineteenth century economic institutions, but frame them in a way that enhanced rather than retarded political democracy, enabled Germany to emerge over succeeding decades as the economic, and eventually, the political lynchpin of Europe. To put this more directly, Germany's "economic giant, political dwarf" period in the early years of the postwar period, allowed it to rebuild a state that would be anchored solidly in a democratic Western Europe yet not project the centralized power that its neighbors feared for much of the previous half-century. By building a semi-sovereign federal state that diffused strong central power but still produced economic growth and political accountability, state reformation provided an overarching context for the specific mix of ideas and institutions that produced the second variation of a German CME.[40]

Table 4: Decline of the Social Market Economy

Exogenous Factors
– Globalization – European Union – Unification
Endogenous Factors
– What happens when a "late" model catches up? – "Siren song" of deregulation – Loss of institutional memory
Institutional Atrophy and "keine Ahnung"

The erosion of this second model of Germany's organized capitalist economy did not go the way of the first, with a "bang," rather, it eroded more with a "whimper." Ideas and institutions that were once congruent to specific purposes and needs do not always maintain their efficacy as Thelen has powerfully argued in several of her works. In some cases, they contained the seeds of their own destruction, and, in their failure to adapt to changing conditions, can precipitate catastrophe as was the case with the first model. In other cases, such as the time of German unification in the early 1990s, they erode slowly and almost imperceptibly. Without a conscious effort by the actors that inhabit these institutions to find organizational and ideational renewal, a once coherent policy model can erode.

To be sure, at the beginning of the 1990s, Germany faced three exogenous shocks that contributed to the erosion of the efficacy of this second iteration of organized capitalism. The combination of accelerated globalization, the expansion of the EU with its neoliberal directives that whittled away the nationally specific German coordinated market institutions, and finally (and most importantly), the stresses of unification[41] constituted powerful forces challenging this model.[42] There also were endogenous forces at work. First, this particular model thrived in both epochs as one that was created to "catch up" with economic powers that were more advanced. Yet, by the 1980s, Germany was seen as rivaling Japan as the two leading candidates to displace the U.S. as the leading capitalist country. This did not come to pass, of course, but it raises the larger issue of whether this model is suitable once it "catches up." Part of the problem here is that while non-Germans could see and articulate how this model worked, Germans themselves were remarkably reticent about touting it as an explicit model. They were also complacent about assuming that their Social Market Economy would keep working, even though the Freiburg School economists whose ideas animated the model long had expired. This ambivalence prevented them from understanding how much a threat the neoliberalism of the Anglo-Americans in the 1980s, and later the EU itself were a threat to Germany's nationally specific economic and political institutions.[43] In a sense, the Kohl government lost its "institutional memory" regarding the functioning of the Social Market Economy with respect to the challenges of unification.[44] Specifically, in the policy areas of property, currency, and state-market relations–pressing issues in the late 1940s and in the early 1990s–the Kohl government's policy ignored the Adenauer/ Erhard governments' policies on these issues. In the 1990s and 2000s, much of the architecture of the German model, while still physically present, had lost much of its original functionality due to the above stresses (as well as unification), and, more importantly, the ideas that once animated it.

Economic policy models can erode in different ways: dramatically and catastrophically, such as at the end of the first model, but they also slowly and quietly such as the end of the second model. What is similar in both forms of erosion is that the institutions that once were their foundation and the ideas that once animated them were no longer capable of responding to newer challenges. The larger lesson to take from the rise and decline of these coordinated market models is that they are intrinsically neither superior nor deficient to liberal market ones. Rather, their success or failure depends on the capacity of actors within these coordinated market models to use well-articulated and appropriate ideas in order to imbue the institutions with the dynamism and flexibility to respond to ever changing challenges.

Towards a Third Organized Capitalist Model?

One of the virtues of writing an chapter that attempts to extrapolate from the past to the future is that it is very difficult to know what the outcome will be, thus leaving the writer somewhat "off the hook." Nevertheless, if using frameworks that embrace historical institutionalism and path dependence (two schools of thought upon which the larger project of which this article is drawn) are to be useful, there should be some reasonable expectation of a payoff. This conclusion offers three scenarios that assess the likelihood (or not) of Germany and the EU developing a policy model that bears some resemblance to the first two models articulated above.

1. Neoliberalism Renewed

The first scenario would hold that, for all of the financial crisis and attendant economic dislocation, the neoliberal agenda, particularly as instituted by the EU and apparently embraced by most European social democratic parties, has simply progressed too far. This scenario would argue further that the age of national models has passed and that globalization is too powerful a force to allow for the social protections that the older models embodied. Together with the hypermobility of capital and labor, the erosion of the core organized capitalist institutions, "hard" laissez-faire policies, and the European Union's role in eroding national sovereignty through its dominance of monetary and fiscal policy, it is simple to make the case that the easy "exit" from these institutions has destroyed the capacity for use of the "voice" necessary to rebuild them.

Among the key indicators for the resilience of neoliberalism would be:

- Continued hypermobility of capital and labor
- Minimal effective re-regulation of market activity
- Increased liberalization of the EU and continued loss of national sovereignty
- Erosion of core CME labor market and social protection institutions
- Continued push for laissez faire economic policies
- Policies encouraging "exit" from organizations and lack of "voice" as institutional renewal mechanism
- Fundamental challenge to comparative historical institutionalism and adaptive institutions

Specifically, in Germany and Europe we would see the re-emergence of pre-crisis patterns in terms of corporate behavior (such as a continued emulation of Anglo-American business practices) and ineffective attempts to reintroduce government regulation of business, especially the financial sector. Theoretically, this would represent a sharp challenge to comparative historical institutionalism and its foundational core insight of adaptive institutions. But, the great unknown in the wake of the international financial crisis and serious recession that began in 2008 is whether the power of neoliberal forces within the EU and among many of the national governments of Europe is as durable as it was before the crisis.

2. Hybrid Patterns

The second scenario would see no dominant model emerge. Even now within Germany, one can see evidence of this trend. While the large German banks have "gone global" (to the recent consternation of some of them), many of the smaller regional and local banks still maintain a *Hausbank* relationship with firms in their local regions. This second scenario would see a number of unfocused experiments with no coherent policy. In other words, there would be regional and sectoral examples of both organized and laissez-faire economic policy models with neither becoming hegemonic in Europe. Indicators of this scenario would include:

- No dominant hegemonic model
- Unfocused experimentation with incoherent policy
- Regional, sectoral examples of organized and laissez faire policies
- Implication that path dependence and comparative historical institutionalism not generalizable beyond a few favorable cases

The context that would indicate that this outcome was occurring would be patterns of experimentation in different CME countries and regions in Germany and Europe. These outcomes would likely be driven by such variables as the kinds of sectors and industries in particular regions, the types of governments in specific areas, and the inability of private and public-sector policy makers to impose (or generate) either a dominant LME or CME pattern of governance of the political economy. A spirit of pragmatism rather than ideological hegemony would shape the dominant discourse.

3. Towards a Third (European) CME

Finally there could be a third scenario that would produce an organized capitalist model reminiscent in the spirit–but not the letter–of the first two models. Until the financial crisis exploded in mid 2008, this was the least likely of the three scenarios. But, looking back, the conditions under which these two earlier organized models tended to thrive in the late nineteenth and mid twentieth centuries were when markets either were not available or had failed. We are now, once again, in one of these moments. When the essential features and core assumptions of liberal market economies (unfettered access to resources, markets and capital) are no longer easily attained, then neoliberalism looks far less hegemonic, or even attractive as an economic policy model. The very act of proposing this third scenario argues that Germany–and the EU–may represent a potentially critical case of third-generation CME ideas, institutions and state reformation. Among the indicators that might suggest such a scenario was developing would be:

- Continued uncertainty about access to resources, markets and capital
- Serious discussion about the purpose of capitalism–financial innovation or production of needed goods and services?
- Human capital formation–long-term investment and productivity growth
- Social welfare to soften harsh economic dislocation
- From single market to a democratic polity–democratic deficit overcome by empowered EU citizens
- Only successful with twenty-first-century set of ideas to transform European political institutions towards a polity

Among the questions that have not been asked during the neoliberal ascendancy of the last two decades, are existential ones about the purpose of capitalism itself. Is capitalism concerned only with financial innovation for its own sake with little concern for the production of needed goods and services in the "real economy"? Is long-term oriented investment necessary for larger projects with slower expectations of profitability no longer important? Is human capital formation essential for productivity growth—no longer seen as a collective good for all firms or is it proprietary only for those firms that can afford it at the moment? Is a functioning social welfare state that can soften the blow for those who are displaced by this economic transformation no longer necessary?

If these are important goals for modern twenty-first-century developed economies, then adapting the spirit of earlier organized models might be of much greater use than continuing to press for a neoliberalism that has shown some extremely serious shortcomings at the end of the first decade of the century and apparently offers no better options for the near future. But, there is one large problem that a third generation of organized capitalist "model builders" must face: the age of national models in Europe is over. Any such construction would have to confront the redoubtable architecture of the EU, i.e., state (re)building. In the late1980s "Europhoria" days, many Europeans believed that they could embrace the advantages of Europeanization without any serious consequences. Yet, when increasingly neoliberal treaties and directives were adopted and individual nation states saw their sovereignty eroded in the form of reduced control over fiscal policy (the 3 percent mandate regarding deficit spending) and monetary policy (for those sixteen countries that have joined the Eurozone), political power had essentially been transferred to Brussels without the possibility of return.[45] This transfer was not literal of course, but the decreasing domestic control over fiscal and monetary policy meant that EU policies in these areas often pre-empted domestic ones. If these policies are to be changed and a coordinated market economy is to replace it, Europeans would need to tackle the lack of political accountability that the EU has not yet addressed—namely a democratic polity and not just a market. By early 2010, political tensions in Greece, Spain and Portugal over deficit spending to maintain social benefits produced the first serious questions concerning the long term role of the EURO among countries with very diverse fiscal policies This third scenario is clearly a long-term project, but if Europe wishes to avoid economic catastrophe and create a stable political environment, then there are clearly options that offer more promise than the neoliberalism that no longer seems to be a panacea for developed democracies.

Notes

1. I would like to thank Jeffrey Anderson and Carolyn Forestiere for comments on an earlier version that appeared as a working paper at Johns Hopkins American Institute for Contemporary German Studies in December 2008; available at http://www.aicgs.org/documents/advisor/callen1208.pdf. Additional versions were presented at: "The Bonn/Berlin Republic at 20: From Unification to Unity?," a symposium organized by the editors of *German Politics and Society* at Georgetown University, 7-8 May 2009, for which I would like to thank Richard Deeg, Anke Hassel, Konrad Jarausch, Eric Langenbacher, and Stephen Silvia; the 35th Annual Conference of the International Association of the Study of German Politics, Aston University, Birmingham, UK, 26-27 May 2009, for which I would like to thank Dan Hough, Wade Jacoby, Philipp Klages, Stephen Padgett, and Peter Pulzer; and the 21st Annual Meeting of the Society for the Advancement of Socio-Economics (SASE), Sciences Po, Paris, France, 16-18 July 2009. Thanks also to Leah Langford, my research assistant during the Fall 2009 semester. Finally, special thanks go to Wolfgang Streeck and Martin Höpner for their support of my research in 2008 and 2009 as a Visiting Research Affiliate at the Max Planck Institute for the Study of Societies in Cologne. This paper is part of a larger book manuscript in process; for a more extensive working paper on this theme, please consult my website (http://csallen.myweb.uga.edu) or contact me at csallen@uga.edu. Comments are welcome.
2. Wolfgang Streeck, *Re-Forming Capitalism: Institutional Change in the German Political Economy* (New York, 2009).
3. Peter A. Hall and David W. Soskice, *Varieties of Capitalism : the Institutional Foundations of Comparative Advantage* (Oxford, 2001); Paul Pierson, *Politics in Time: History, Institutions, and Social Analysis* (Princeton, 2004); Kathleen Thelen, *How Institutions Evolve: The Political Economy of Skills in Germany, Britain, the United States and Japan* (New York, 2004).
4. Herbert Kitschelt and Wolfgang Streeck, *Germany: Beyond the Stable State* (London, 2004); Andrei S. Markovits, *Modell Deutschland : The Political Economy of West Germany* (New York, 1982).
5. Wolfgang Streeck and Kathleen Thelen, *Beyond Continuity: Institutional Change in Advanced Political Economies* (New York, 2005).
6. Jeremy Leaman, *The Political Economy of Germany under Chancellors Kohl and Schroeder: Decline of the German Model?* (New York, 2009).
7. Richard Deeg, "Industry and Finance in Germany in the Heyday of Financialization," in this issue.
8. Stephen J Silvia, "From Unification to Fragmentation: The German Economy since Unification," in this issue.
9. Anke Hassel, "Labor Markets and Labor Market Reform since Unification," in this issue.
10. Christopher S. Allen, "'Empty Nets:' Social Democracy and the 'Catch-all Party Thesis' in Germany and Sweden," *Party Politics* 15 (2009): 635-653.
11. Alberto Alesina and Francesco Giavazzi, *The Future of Europe: Reform or Decline* (Cambridge, 2006).
12. Barrington Moore, *Social Origins of Dictatorship and Democracy* (Boston, 1966).
13. Wolfgang Streeck and Kozo Yamamura, *The Origins of Nonliberal Capitalism: Germany and Japan in Comparison* (Ithaca, 2001).
14. Gregory Jackson, "The Origins of Nonliberal Corporate Governance in Germany and Japan in Comparison," in Streeck and Yamamura (see note 13), 121-170.
15. Albert O. Hirschman, *Exit, Voice, and Loyalty: Responses to Decline in Firms, Organizations, and States* (Cambridge, 1970); Mancur Olson, *The Logic of Collective Action: Public Goods and the Theory of Groups* (Cambridge, 1965).

16. Sheri Berman, "Ideas, Norms, and Culture in Political Analysis," *Comparative Politics* 33 (2001): 231-250; Mark Blyth, *Great Transformations: Economic Ideas and Institutional Change in the Twentieth Century* (Cambridge, 2002); Peter A. Hall, *The Political Power of Economic Ideas: Keynesianism Across Nations* (Princeton, 1989). J. Nicholas Ziegler, *Governing Ideas: Strategies for Innovation in France and Germany* (Ithaca, 1997).

17. Pepper D. Culpepper, *Creating Cooperation: How States Develop Human Capital in Europe* (Ithaca, 2003); Geoff Eley, *Society, Culture, and the State in Germany, 1870-1930* (Ann Arbor, 1996); Peter B. Evans, Dietrich Rueschemeyer and Theda Skocpol, *Bringing the State Back In* (Cambridge, 1985); Isabela Mares, *The Politics of Social Risk: Business and Welfare State Development* (Cambridge, 2003); Charles Tilly, *The Formation of National States in Western Europe* (Princeton, 1975), Daniel Ziblatt, *Structuring the State:The Formation of Italy and Germany and the Puzzle of Federalism* (Princeton, 2006).

18. Alexander Gerschenkron, *Bread and Democracy in Germany* (Ithaca, 1989).

19. Richard H. Tilly, *Financial Institutions and Industrialization in the Rhineland. 1815-1870* (Madison, 1966).

20. Richard Deeg, "On the Origins of Universal Banking in Germany," in *Origins of National Financial Systems: Alexander Gerschenkron Reconsidered*, eds. Douglas Forsyth and Daniel Verdier (London, 2002), 87-104; Caroline Fohlin, *Finance Capitalism and Germany's Rise to Industrial Power* (Cambridge, 2007); Gary Herrigel, *Industrial Constructions: The Sources of German Industrial Power* (Cambridge, 1996).

21. E. P. Hennock, *The Origin of the Welfare State in England and Germany, 1850-1914: Social Policies Compared* (Cambridge, 2007); Alexander M. Hicks, *Social Democracy & Welfare Capitalism: A Century of Income Security Politics* (Ithaca, 1999); Anthony James Nicholls, *Freedom with Responsibility : The Social Market Economy in Germany, 1918-1963* (Oxford, 1994); Wilhelm Röpke, *A Humane Economy* (Chicago, 1960); Mark E. Spicka, *Selling the Economic Miracle : Economic Reconstruction and Politics in West Germany, 1949-1957* (New York, 2007).

22. Philip Manow, *Social Insurance and the German Political Economy* (Cologne, 1997).

23. Alfred Müller-Armack, "The Second Phase of the Social Market Economy: An Additional Concept of a Humane Economy," in *Standard Tests on the Social Market Economy*, ed. Horst Friedrich Wünche (Stuttgart, 1982), 49-61.

24. Gerhard Lehmbruch, "The Institutional Embedding of Market Economies: The German 'Model' and Its Impact on Japan," in Streeck and Yamamura (see note 13), 39-93.

25. Charles Tilly, *Trust and Rule* (New York, 2005).

26. Manfred Pohl, *Entstehung und Entwicklung des Universal Bankensystems: Konzentration und Krise als wichtige Faktoren* (Frankfurt/Main, 1986).

27. Hugh Neuberger, *German Banks and German Economic Growth from Unification to World War I* (New York, 1977).

28. Wilfried Feldenkirschen, "Competition and Cartelization: Concentration in German Industry and the Banks' Influence on their Development, 1870-1939," (Boston, 1984).

29. Kathleen Thelen and Ikuo Kume, "The Rise of Nonliberal Training Regimes: Germany and Japan Compared," in Streeck and Yamamura (see note 13), 200-227.

30. Colleen A. Dunlavy, *Politics and Industrialization: Early Railroads in the United States and Prussia* (Princeton, 1994).

31. Philip Manow, *Social Protection and Capitalist Production: The Bismarckian Welfare State and the German Political Economy: 1880 - 1890* (Amsterdam, 2007).

32. Eduard Bernstein and Edith C. Harvey, *Evolutionary Socialism: A Criticism and Affirmation* (New York, 1909).

33. Simon Reich, *The Fruits of Fascism: Postwar Prosperity in Historical Perspective* (Ithaca, 1990).

34. Volker R. Berghahn and Sigurt Vitols, *Gibt es einen deutschen Kapitalismus? Tradition und globale Perspektiven der sozialen Marktwirtschaft* (Frankfurt/Main, 2006).

35. Barry J. Eichengreen, *The European Economy since 1945: Coordinated Capitalism and Beyond* (Princeton, 2007).

36. Kenneth H. F. Dyson, *The Politics of German Regulation* (Aldershot, 1992).

37. Agnès Labrousse and Jean-Daniel Weisz, *Institutional Economics in France and Germany: German Ordoliberalism versus the French Regulation School* (Berlin, 2001); Philip Manow, "Ordoliberalism as an Economic Theology of Order," *Leviathan: Zeitschrift fur Sozialwissenschaft* 29 (2001): 179-198.

38. Wilhelm Röpke, "The Guiding Principles of the Liberal Programme," in Wünche (see note 23), 188.

39. Bruno Amable, "Institutional Complementarity and Diversity of Social Systems of Innovation and Production," *Review of International Political Economy* 7 (2000): 645-687; Andrew Chadwick and Christopher May, "Interaction between States and Citizens in the Age of the Internet: 'e-Government' in the United States, Britain, and the European Union," *Governance* 16 (2003): 271-300.

40. Peter J. Katzenstein, *Politics and Policy in West Germany: The Growth of a Semi-Sovereign State* (Philadelphia, 1987); Renate Mayntz and Fritz W. Scharpf, *Policy-Making in the German Federal Bureaucracy* (Amsterdam, 1975).

41. Andreas Busch, "Shock Absorbers Under Stress: Parapublic Institutions and the Double Challenges of German Unification and European Integration," in *Governance in Contemporary Germany: The Semisovereign State Revisited*, eds. Simon Green and William E. Paterson (Cambridge, 2005), 94-114.

42. German unification here is initially viewed as an exogenous shock, but it has now become endogenous. The European Union is viewed principally as an exogenous shock, even though Germany's role as a founding member of the organization suggests and endogenous role. The point here is that the neoliberal ethos of the EU's economic policy was very much at variance with that of Germany's organized capitalism.

43. In a series of interviews on an earlier project in 1990-91 with economic elites from the former *Sprecher* of the Deutsche Bank (F. Wilhelm Christians) to economists with the German Greens, virtually all of them believed that the German CME would be able to withstand the new challenges of neoliberalism. To a person, a common theme emerged, namely that they expected German institutions to behave has they had for much of the previous decades. But, none of them offered specific reasons for how and why this would take place.

44. Christopher S. Allen, "Institutions Challenged: German Unification, Policy Errors and the 'Siren Song' of Deregulation," in *Negotiating the New Germany: Can Social Partnership Survive?*, ed. Lowell Turner (Ithaca, 1997), 137-156.

45. Fritz W. Scharpf, "Legitimacy in the Multilevel European Polity," *European Political Science Review* 1 (2009): 173-204.

*C*ONCLUSION

The Germans Must Have Done Something Right

Eric Langenbacher

Cognitive Dissonance

Almost twenty years after the fall of the Berlin Wall, a 2009 survey found that Germany was the most positively assessed country cross-nationally with a score of 61 percent–ahead of the perennial, non-offensive, universal-health-care-providing favorite, Canada with 59 percent (the UK scored 58 percent and Japan 57 percent).[1] This finding (for the second year in a row) was rather surprising–at least to the community of intellectuals interested in Germany, where a certain pessimism since (and before) the 1989/1990 caesura has been typical. Such negativity may be unavoidable with scholars trained always to direct a critical eye towards their object of study. But, it is also true that many authors especially in the English-speaking world long have viewed the country through the lens of the Nazi past and its purported continuities in the present. Andrei Markovits and Simon Reich, for example, wrote that the memory of Nazism "'crowds out' all others in the way Germans are viewed by the world."[2] Or, when asked about the existence of stereotypes in journalism, former *New York Times* correspondent Roger Cohen responded very frankly: "For Italians, we think of pasta, for the English, of the remarkable sexual practices of their aristocracy and for Germans, of Nazis."[3]

Indeed, in almost all of the subfields of German studies, critical sentiments have been apparent, and often well-founded. Those who deal with migration and diversity issues, have long decried Germany's anachronistic and excessively restrictive immigration, citizenship, and integration policies,[4] failings that have exacerbated the challenges that "indigenous"

Germans face accepting new multicultural realities. Moreover, ever since unification, observers have noted and feared a resurgence of German ethnic nationalism and xenophobia, as a consequence of immigration (many, not all, from Muslim-majority countries) and the achievement of national unity. These attitudes sometimes resulted in violent acts against newcomers, such as the wave of arson attacks on "foreigners" in the early 1990s (Hoyerswerda, Rostock, Mölln, Solingen) and on-going individual attacks—especially in eastern Germany—related to the right-radical scene.[5] The 2009 Transatlantic Trends survey of the German Marshall Fund of the United States found that 60 percent of German respondents believed that:

> immigrants' unwillingness to integrate is the greatest barrier to integration, as opposed to 27 percent who believe that discrimination by society is the greatest challenge. Germany has the largest majority of people who support the view that [the failure to integrate] … is the immigrants' fault.[6]

According to another 2009 poll, only 23 percent of Muslims in Germany feel German, versus 78 percent in Britain and 49 percent in France.[7] Related is the problem of terrorism—not just the Hamburg cell involved with the 9/11 attacks, but the "home-grown" terrorists behind thwarted attacks in 2007.[8]

Nevertheless, a comparative perspective shows that the situation in Germany is not particularly worse than in other European countries. A recent Gallup poll found that 40 percent of Muslims living in Germany felt a connection to the Federal Republic (versus 32 percent of the population as a whole).[9] As troubling as the ethnic/racial/religious dynamics are in contemporary Germany, where almost 20 percent of the population now has a "migration background" (*Migrationshintergrund*),[10] they have not produced race-related riots such as those in the French banlieux in the fall of 2005, in the UK in 2001, or in southern Italy in early 2010. There have not been assassinations like in the Netherlands or (successful) terrorist attacks as in the United Kingdom or Spain. And there is no ban on minaret construction, as a referendum in Switzerland determined in late 2009. Moreover, a wave of liberalizing reforms implemented after the 1998 change in government resulted in citizenship policy moving from the most illiberal in western Europe to the middle of the pack.[11] Years of discussion about "parallel societies" and integration also have produced major policy initiatives, especially under the Merkel governments (see Joyce Mushaben and Hilary Silver in this volume).

Likewise, scholars of the German economy have long been pessimistic, deeming the country the newest "sick man of Europe" in the 1990s with GDP growth rates well below European or OECD averages and an unemployment rate that hovered around 10 percent.[12] As Richard Deeg, Anke

Hassel, Stephen Silvia, Holger Wolf, and Christopher Allen show in this volume, the identified problems were legion—caused both by the postunification recessionary environment and by much deeper structural issues: high unit labor costs; an exorbitant tax burden on higher earners; labor market rigidities; excessive bureaucratic regulation (e.g., the seemingly endless debates about store hours, liberalizing the labor market, or the red tape involved with trying to open a new business); the antiquated industrial/manufacturing nature of the economy where almost 30 percent of the workforce is still employed; excessive dependence on exports at the expense of domestic demand; overly powerful and self-interested unions; and the rigors and costs of European Monetary Union—to name just a few of the many criticisms. Rheinish capitalism and the once-lauded social market economy, which Geoffrey Garrett a decade ago called an "incoherent political economy" with dim prospects,[13] seemed doomed and the political system in the 1990s and early 2000s appeared unable to implement the needed (neoliberal) reforms to get things back on track.

But then, partially as a consequence of the poor economy that forced down unit labor costs and eroded the power of unions and centralized bargaining, and partially due to the Red-Green government's implementation of the neoliberal Agenda 2010 and Hartz IV reforms in the early 2000s, the situation changed rapidly. Today, the World Economic Forum places it seventh (behind Switzerland, the U.S., Singapore, and the Nordic countries) in its Global Competitiveness Report.[14] Other rankings show that the country is ranked twenty-fifth for the ease of doing business—above France, the Netherlands, and Israel, but well below the U.S. and UK. One can hardly speak of a complete transformation, however. Germany places eighty-fourth out of 183 countries in terms of starting a new business and a dismal one hundred-fifty-third regarding the ease of letting workers go, which the OECD in March 2010 recommended the government take immediate action to redress.[15]

In any case, these (partial) reforms produced an unprecedented volume of high value-added exports and some of the most competitive and profitable companies in the world. The bugaboo of unemployment seemed tamed, per capita incomes began to rise, and a veritable economic boom characterized the post 2003 period—that is, until the financial and economic crisis began to hit in late 2008. In 2009, GDP contracted nearly 5 percent with unemployment expected once again to top 10 percent in 2010.[16] Nevertheless, the German economy has proven more resilient during the crisis than many feared—even if higher unemployment, fallout in the financial sector (Landesbanken), and problems in the Eurozone with highly indebted countries such as Greece, Portugal, or Spain may prolong instability through 2010 and beyond. The Merkel governments' policy responses appeared right-on: highly effective, targeted stimulus–the original cash-for-clunkers program (*Abwrackprämie*); reasonable and controllable deficit spending and borrowing; schemes that incentivized companies not immediately to lay off workers, etc.[17] The 2009 Bundestag election rewarded Chancellor Angela Merkel with a more desirable center-Right coalition government, and there were no hints of political instability. More generally, the social market economy once again has regained its luster (see Allen above).

Pessimism also has long been apparent among scholars who deal with collective memory and culture. Perhaps by definition, attention devoted to the Nazi regime, the Holocaust, and all of the related political cultural aspects–such as heightened sensitivity towards and combating right-wing extremism and related antisemitic and xenophobic attitudes–fosters very high standards of assessment and, often, disappointment. Indeed, over the postwar and postunification decades, observers constantly have noted unwillingness from Germans to express sufficient contrition, collective responsibility, compensation/restitution, or simply *Betroffenheit*.[18] For example, as I wrote in the Spring 2010 issue of this journal, one of the biggest cultural and memory trends of the last decade has been the return of the memory of German suffering to the political and cultural mainstream–a development that spurred vehement reactions to such alleged "historical revisionism," "revanchism," and "self-pity"–and that confirmed the fears of the many critics who have observed fragility in Germany's Holocaust-centered memory culture of contrition. Yet, despite periodic antisemitic incidents and some right radical successes at the Land level,[19] no right-wing xenophobic party or social movement has arisen, in contrast to other European countries. Moreover, many observers increasingly have lauded the character of Germany's efforts to work through its Nazi legacy and construct an exemplary memory regime.[20]

The German Soul

In short, the empirical record shows more positive developments than scholars have acknowledged over the last twenty years. Does the intrinsic academic proclivity for critical analysis suffice to explain the degree of negativity among observers of Germany? Or, as Charles Maier implies above, maybe it takes a while to assimilate more positive findings and to update the paradigms through which we observe the country–to reduce cognitive dissonance so to say.

But, it may also be true that Germany specialists have "gone native" and have adopted the serious, often pessimistic demeanor so often associated with the people who created the words *Angst* and *Schadenfreude*, and whose classical literary effervescence was captured by the phrase "storm and stress" (*Sturm und Drang*). Thomas Mann even said that "a collective inclination towards self-criticism, leading to self-disgust (*Selbstekel*)" was "typically German" (*kerndeutsch*).[21] Although such descriptions are reminiscent of old-fashioned national character studies, there is something to the brooding, self-critical reputation of the self-proclaimed "land of poets and thinkers" (*Dichter und Denker*). Certainly, as public opinion polls constantly reveal, Germany is among the least patriotic nations on earth, having internalized the postwar critique of nationalism and seemingly embracing Habermasian notions of postnationality, constitutional patriotism (*Verfassungspatriotismus*), or "European" identity.[22]

In any case, Germans themselves probably are even more negative about their country than observers from abroad. Recent finds on bookstore shelves include: *Betrügter Republik Deutschland, Die Dilettanten: wie unfähig unsere Politiker wirklich sind, Der Deutschland-Clan: Das skrupellose Netzwerk aus Politikern, Top-Managern und Justiz,* or *Der gekaufte Staat: Wie bezahlte Konzernvertreter in deutschen Ministerien sich ihre Gesetze selbst schreiben.* Every year, the Society for the German Language (Gesellschaft für deutsche Sprache) publishes its word of the year. Recent winners include: *Finanzkrise* (2008), *Klimakatastrophe* (2007), *Teuro* (2002), *Schwarzgeldaffäre* (2000), *Reformstau* (1997), *Sozialabbau* (1993), and the perennial favorite, *Politikverdrossenheit* (1992).[23] There was a marked absence of joy as the twentieth anniversary of the fall of the Berlin Wall approached–despite the best efforts of governmental cheerleaders to drum up enthusiasm (through "build and then destroy your own wall" programs or the effort to commission a unification memorial). Even though international press coverage was quite positive, the anniversary itself was a muted, even somber affair (poor November weather also compounded the situation). Admittedly, the circumstances in 2009-2010 were inauspicious with the big anniversaries falling in the midst of the worst economic crisis since World War II. Yet, even had the overall economy continued to boom, a depressed mood would have been likely for one massive reason: the continued socio-economic problems in the East.

As Stephen Silvia, Jeffrey Anderson, and Holger Wolf discuss in this volume, whatever indicators one looks at–unemployment, crime, productivity, demographics, income, xenophobia, political radicalism–it is still a rather bleak picture twenty years after unification, even though easterners' quality of life and basic freedoms are incalculably better than during the communist period and compared to any other former communist country. Challenges persist despite the political promises–Helmut Kohl's blossoming landscapes (*blühende Landschaften*)–and the massive sums of money that have been transferred from West to East. This redistribution has amounted to about 4 percent of western GDP or over EURO 80 billion (constituting 30 percent of eastern GDP) per year.[24] Unemployment in the region is double the rate in the West, although the differences between the truly depressed areas and those of modest growth–Dresden, Leipzig, Eisenach, the "bacon belt" around Berlin–are also significant. The region has lost almost 2 million people since unification (16 million versus 14.4 million today), particularly in the rural and old heavy industrial areas of Mecklenburg West Pomerania, Saxony-Anhalt, and Brandenburg. Youth (especially women) have abandoned the region, leading to fewer births (a big drop in the fertility rate over the 1990s, but some convergence with the West in recent years), a graying population, and, consequently, daunting challenges to provide basic infrastructures.[25]

The entrenched problems have helped the former/reformed communist party (Party of Democratic Socialism, PDS, since 2007 renamed the Left Party, *die Linken* after a merger with rogue western SPD elements led by Oskar Lafontaine before his recent retirement) gain a seemingly permanent 20-30 percent electoral foothold in the region–and a share of governing power in coalitions at various points in time in Brandenburg, Mecklenburg West Pomerania, and Berlin, as well as at the local level. Even though it has governed rather pragmatically,[26] the PDS/Left Party has adopted a left-populist profile, campaigning in 2009 on issues like "tax wealth" and "wealth for everyone." This party has been both cause and consequence of another trend in the region, the rise of *Ostalgie*–an overly positive and tendentious view of the German Democratic Republic (GDR), which arguably has inhibited a fuller confrontation with that legacy. Radical right parties (the DVU and more recently the NPD especially in Saxony) also have gained strength in the region and representation in several Landtage at various points over the last twenty years. Many areas have witnessed violent attacks on foreigners and parts of the region were declared "no-go" areas for foreign fans during the 2006 World Cup. The problems appear intractable and there is no end in sight for the region's challenges, especially in light of predicted further demographic contraction, as Holger Wolf shows above.

Yet, nation-wide, almost all of the problems that afflict the East–migration, integration, antiquated economic sectors, rigid labor markets, red tape, not even to mention the demographic time-bomb, the still second-class status of many German women (see Myra Marx Ferree and Dagmar Herzog above), and, despite some recent progress, a mediocre school system—afflict the western portion of the country as well. One should not forget the older but still salient developmental gradient in the West—booming Bavaria, Baden-Württemberg, Hessen (at least around Frankfurt), and Hamburg, versus the persistent problems in the "rust belt" Ruhrgebiet (despite the region's designation as a European cultural capital in 2010)[27] and many rural areas in Lower Saxony, Hessen, and even Bavaria (Upper Franconia, Upper Palatinate), for instance. Germans have fretted over these issues—rightfully—even more than outside observers have, contributing to the current *Angst.*

Why the World Likes Germany

All of this said, maybe the poll mentioned at the outset should be mulled over by those interested in Germany, as well as by Germans themselves. Admittedly, one of the very reasons that Germany may be so well-respected worldwide is precisely the self-critical tradition that often has spurred constant improvement—so an uncritical stance is certainly never to be advocated. But, perhaps we should all pause and reflect upon the multitude of reasons—serious and mundane—for Germany's current popularity and respect during this twentieth anniversary season.

Engineering is still at the top of the list of things the world likes about Germany. People everywhere dream about driving a Mercedes-Benz, BMW, Audi or Porsche, (perhaps even an Opel!), and many do so on the legendary Autobahn. Siemens-built subway systems; Bosch tools, Miele dishwashers; Gaggenau stoves; Braun coffeemakers; SAP software; and, behind-the-scenes, the machines that make machines are all highly valued. Yet, there are also Bechstein pianos, Heckel bassoons, Birkenstock sandals, Nivea cream, Meissen porcelain, Augustinerbräu beer, and Hugo Boss clothes. Indeed, Germany was the "world's export champion" for many years until 2009 when China overtook it.

Culturally, Germans continue to have worldwide impact—especially in photography with artists such as Andreas Gursky and Thomas Demand. The country has three of the top ten symphony orchestras, some of the best opera companies, the Wagner Festival in Bayreuth, and, of course, Rammstein. Many have spoken about a renaissance in German film-making with internationally acclaimed productions such as *Nowhere in Africa*

(2001), *Downfall* (2004), *The Life of Others* (2006) and *The White Ribbon* (2009). There are 102 German Nobel Prize winners (versus 113 in the UK and 309 in the U.S.), including two literature laureates over the last decade or so (Herta Müller in 2009 and Günter Grass in 1999). The country is one of the top five in book production with about 100,000 new titles per year.[28] The German government has invested heavily in culture promotion, as the web of Goethe Instituts and the global reach of Deutsche Welle attest. Mention should also be made of the "German pope" Benedict XVI (in office since 2005), who is still positively regarded worldwide despite on-going abuse scandals involving clergy.[29]

We also should not underestimate the lingering good feelings that so many still have after the country's hosting of the 2006 World Cup. Indeed, Germany's successful tradition in international soccer: three world championships (with Italy having four and Brazil five), four times a finalist, which is two times more than any other country, and current fifth global ranking[30]–is a major reason for its positive reputation, even if many complain about the German style of play. More generally, the country has a substantial legacy of achievement in world sports with internationally recognized athletes such as Katarina Witt, Boris Becker, Steffi Graf, and Michael Schumacher. After the 2010 Winter Games, it has the third most Olympic medals and gold medals (behind only the U.S. and USSR/Russia).[31]

In terms of education (see Helga Welsh above), various reform efforts (all-day school, achieving better performance, addressing the gap between indigenous Germans and newcomers) are underway. In the OECD's PISA assessment program, the country is average or above average in many areas–sixteenth in math in 2003 (France, Japan and Canada do better); and eighth in science in 2006 (Japan and Canada are more highly ranked).[32] Although many think that the zenith of German higher education has passed and that the country's universities are no longer the Humboldtian model that they once were, major reforms (*Excellenzinitiativ*) are underway. The country is the third most popular destination for studying abroad with 190,000 students in 2006 (versus 318,000 in the UK and 590,000 in the U.S.).[33]

Internationalism and openness also manifest themselves in tourism. Worldwide, Germany is the ninth most visited country with 24.9 million entries in 2008 (although well below France with 79.3 million, the U.S. with 58 million and Spain with 57.3 million)[34] and "poor, but sexy" Berlin has become the third most visited city in Europe (behind Paris and London).[35] These visitors come to enjoy everything related to beer (Munich's Hofbräuhaus and Oktoberfest), Bavarian *Gemütlichkeit* for some, and for others, Berliner *Schnauze.* They cruise the Rhine, sunbathe on Sylt, ski the Zugspitze, visit Neuschwanstein castle (which almost made it on the list of the "New Seven Wonders of the World"),[36] visit some of the best art museums (such as the Alte Pinakothek in Munich or the Städel Museum in Frankfurt), visit churches like Dresden's Frauenkirche or Cologne's Dom, and partake in the nightlife of Munich, Hamburg, and especially Berlin (site of legendary clubs such as SO36, E-Werk, Tresor, and now Berghain, recently voted the top club in the world).[37] Perhaps more importantly, Germans are the worldwide tourism champs having spent US $91 billion in 2008 (versus $79.7 billion by Americans and $68.5 billion by Britons).[38] In any case, the millions of German tourists worldwide are a big factor behind knowledge of Germany and constitute an under-appreciated form of cultural diplomacy.

People also may think of more "official" achievements. Germany is one of the richest countries in the world with a fifteenth place in the 2008 World Bank per capita GDP list ($44, 471, compared to sixteenth UK with $43, 489; fourteenth France with $45,982, the U.S. with $46,716, and first place Luxembourg with $111, 240).[39] Moreover, Germany is one of the best performers in terms of minimizing income inequality–despite the rise of the knowledge economy and the attendant deterioration of equality measures–and, with France, is the only country with a sizable population near the top of the rankings. With a Gini Index score of 28 (2005) it is tied with France and Norway at the fourteenth spot–versus ninety-second place for the U.S. (between Uruguay and Côte d'Ivoire).[40] Despite the need for further improvement, the country is one of the best performers on the World Economic Forum's Gender Gap Index–twelfth in 2009 (with the Nordic countries, the Netherlands, South Africa and the Philippines doing better), albeit slipping from fifth in 2006.[41] And according to the World Health Organization in 2000, the country had the twenty-fifth best health-care system in the world (France was first and Italy second), and the twenty-third highest average life expectancy at birth (as well as one of the oldest populations, a more dubious distinction).[42] More recent studies have given the German healthcare system higher marks: a 2009 study ranks it sixth out of thirty-three European countries.[43]

Quality of life factors also may affect assessments. It scores in the "very high" category of the United Nations' human development index (in the twenty-second spot, but with many larger countries such as France, Canada, and the U.S. assessed more highly).[44] Three of the top ten cities on the annual *Forbes* report of best places to live are German (Frankfurt, Munich and Düsseldorf); four of the top twenty (Berlin sixteenth).[45] *International Liv-*

ing ranks the country fourth (behind France, Australia, and Switzerland) for expatriate quality of life in 2010.[46] To this should be added comprehensive public transportation (indeed infrastructure is a big reason for its high international rankings), recycling programs, and environmental policy more generally, where the country has been a policy leader and is now set to benefit immensely from the predicted boom in "green" jobs. It has been an innovator with renewable forms of energy (especially wind and, ironically, solar power) and is the third best country in terms of the percentage of waste recycled.[47] The annual Environmental Performance Index ranks it seventeenth worldwide (although seventh France and fourteenth Britain are big countries that do better)–a score that is brought down because of air pollution from the still vibrant industrial sector and a penchant for fast cars.[48]

This flows into respect for *Modell Deutschland* in the more classical, political sense. Germany's pioneering mixed electoral system (with the combination of single member plurality constituencies and closed list proportional representation) has been emulated in a diverse array of countries including New Zealand, Mexico, Japan, and Russia (for a while). Other practices like the 5 percent electoral threshold and the constructive vote of non-confidence likewise have been influential. Despite a host of complaints in recent years,[49] the German party system is admired for the (usually) seriousness of political debate, clear but moderate partisanship, and a rather fully occupied party system. Unlike virtually every other European country, the radical Right has been virtually non-existent–a weakness generated by good governance, constitutional protections (Bundesverfassungsschutz), and cultural changes produced by the comprehensive official and civil societal process of coming to terms with its Nazi past.[50]

The Bundesbank is a model of central bank independence, the governing institutions of which were copied by many postcommunist Eastern European countries, the reformed Bank of England in the late 1990s, and, most famously, by the European Central Bank (based not by coincidence in Frankfurt). German "cooperative" federalism is well-regarded and many have tried to emulate the Rheinish social market economy. All international governance and democracy ratings rank Germany highly. *The Economist's* Democracy Index ranks it thirteenth in 2008, among larger countries only behind Australia (tenth) and Canada (eleventh); the World Bank puts it in the highest percentiles on all of its six governance indicators; and Transparency International ranks it fourteenth on its Corruption Perception Index, ahead of France, Japan, the U.S., and the UK.[51] A 2008 *Jane's* country risk assessment put Germany at seventeenth, with only the UK (seventh) being a large country ranked better.[52]

In terms of foreign policy, despite periodic criticism (discussed by Beverly Crawford and Abraham Newman above) such as the unilateral recognition of Croatia and Slovenia in 1991 or the dithering over humanitarian interventions in the former Yugoslavia, there is much respect for postwar and postunification Germany's "civilian" ethos stressing conflict resolution, peace-building, and international development.[53] Institutionally, this "normative power" has been buttressed by "self-binding" (*Einbindungspolitik*), which has embedded the country in a dense network of international institutions. The Global Peace Index places it sixteenth with Canada and Japan once again ranking better.[54] In 2006, Germany was the fifth-highest contributor of what the OECD deems official development assistance with US $10.35 billion–although at 0.36 percent of GNI it was thirteenth behind all northern European countries, France (0.47 percent), and the UK (0.52 percent), but better than the U.S.(0.17 percent), Japan, and Canada.[55]

Table 1: Germany in Cross-National Comparison

Indicator	Ranking	Year
BBC/PIPA World Public Opinion	1	2009
Tourism Expenditures	1	2008
Global Exports	2	2009
Number of Olympic Medals	3	through 2010
Number of International Students	3	2006
Number of Nobel Prize Winners	3	through 2009
International Living Expatriate Ranking	4	2010
OECD Official Developmental Aid	5	2006
Book Publishing	5	2007
FIFA World Soccer Rankings	5	March 2010
Euro Health Consumer Index	6	2009
WEF Global Competitiveness Report	7	2009-2010
OECD PISA Science	8	2006
WEF Gender Gap Index	12	2009
Economist Democracy Index	13	2008
Gini Coefficient	14	2005
Transparency International CPI	14	2009
World Bank per capita GDP	15	2008
OECD PISA Math	16	2003
Global Peace Index	16	2009
Environmental Performance Index	17	2010
Jane's Country Risk	17	2008
UN Human Development Index	22	2009
Life expectancy at birth	23	2005-2010
Heritage Index of Economic Freedom	23	2010
Ease of Doing Business	25	2010
WHO Healthcare Rankings	25	2000

Sources: please see endnotes.

Germany's foundational role and continuing strong support for the movement towards European unity must also be highlighted. The fact that the continent is now an unprecedented zone of prosperity where the "democratic peace" is well-anchored is unthinkable without constant German support for the European Union, as well as the high quality of democracy domestically. Also crucial have been material sacrifices—Germany as paymaster—including unquestioned support for the EURO. Although such policies appear to violate traditional notions of self-interest,[56] some have argued that such a stance has been generated by eminently pragmatic motives such as the need for international rehabilitation after 1945, the EURO being the "price" paid for rapid unification in 1990, or an effort to secure a "captive" internal market that benefits its export-dependent economy—indeed about two-thirds of all German exports go to other EU countries.[57] Admittedly, over the Schröder and Merkel years, a novel stance towards "Europe" is evident with more hard-nosed negotiation, rational self interest, and a willingness to exert power—especially visible vis à vis Turkey's application to join the EU and the Greek debt crisis in early 2010. Nevertheless, Germany's willingness to pay—in the 2007-2013 budgetary cycle, it transfers EURO 164 billion to the EU, but receives only EURO 78 billion despite the persistent problems in eastern Germany[58]—continues to be instrumental in making the European project work.

Finally, many may look at Germany as a model of coming-to-terms with a difficult past. Restitution and compensation afforded to victims of the Nazi regime has amounted to EURO 66 billion by the end of 2008 (and is on-going).[59] A more general reconciliatory policy towards its previously victimized neighbors (especially France and more recently Poland) has been pursued, and a "special relationship" with Israel is constantly affirmed. Germany has constructed a culture of contrition after years of debates in the political and public realms that acknowledges and commemorates the crimes previous generations committed. An honest confrontation with this past also has permeated educational curricula at many levels, ensuring that rising generations are (re)socialized into this memory culture. Partially as a result of these efforts, Germany now has the third largest Jewish community in Europe behind the UK and France, and for many years after unification it had the fastest-growing Jewish community in the world, thanks primarily to immigration from the former Soviet Union. And instead of "sitting on packed suitcases" as many did after 1945, the community (now over 100,000 strong) is vibrant—and not just in the biggest cities like Berlin, Frankfurt, or Cologne. Symbols of this renaissance include the (re)construction of synagogues in Munich and Dresden and the establishment of Jewish museums in Berlin and Erfurt.[60]

Unfortunately, there may be a dark side to Germany's current global popularity. Perhaps some still associate Germany with traditional, authoritarian, "Prussian" virtues–discipline, obedience, *Ordnung* (in the bad sense)–and admire the country as a consequence. Worse, many may see positive associations between Germany and its Nazi past–more benignly along the lines of Susan Sontag's thesis ("fascinating fascism") regarding Leni Riefenstahl,[61] or because of an abiding fascination with the epic battles of World War II (Rommel, the Desert Fox)–but also more insidiously, locating the Holocaust at the center of a tapestry of contemporary anti-Israeli and antisemitic prejudices.

Daring More Patriotism?

All-in-all, Germany has posted a noteworthy record of achievement over the last twenty years, especially when we keep in mind the challenges that unification created. Of course, as the contributors to these two special issues of *German Politics and Society* have noted, the country cannot rest on its laurels and must continue to address the challenges at home and abroad–East Germany, an ageing and declining population, integration of immigrants, a volatile and less democratic world that will demand greater intervention, the short and long-term fallout from the post 2008 financial and economic crisis, climate change, and the composition of the economy.

In light of the various achievements outlined above, perhaps contemporary Germans finally can allow themselves to "dare more pride." Recent discussions on national identity and patriotism do reveal attitudinal changes. In 2000-2001, conservatives prompted a debate about whether a German *Leitkultur* (dominant culture) existed, whether immigrants should adjust to these norms, and whether Germans should be proud of their country. After much acrimony–one Green politician called the CDU stance a "skinhead mentality"–President Johannes Rau tried to resolve the dispute, yet epitomized the awkwardness that postwar Germans long felt: "One cannot be proud of something that one has not achieved oneself. One can be happy and thankful to be German. But one cannot be proud of it, I believe." Schröder weighed in by opining: "I am proud of the achievements of the people and of the democratic culture. In this sense I am a German patriot who is proud of his country."[62] But, just a few years later–and after disagreements over new citizenship tests–President

Horst Köhler proclaimed at his swearing-in ceremony: "I love our land,"[63] which was remarkably well received.

Mass attitudes similarly have evolved. A 2001 survey found only 30 percent expressing pride in being German (7 percent of the eighteen to twenty-four and 9 percent of the twenty-five to twenty-nine age groups), 35 percent agreeing that they are "happy to be German, but not proud" and 27 percent (57 percent of the youngest cohort) "not concerning themselves with this question."[64] Data from 2003-2004 ranked western Germany twenty-eighth and eastern Germany thirty-third out of thirty-three countries (the U.S. was first and Venezuela second) on national pride measures.[65] Today, however, a more "normal" level of patriotism is widespread:

Table 2: National Feeling in Germany (2009)

	Percent Agreeing
"I am proud to be German."	60
"If you had a free choice, would you want German citizenship?"	80
"Should you no longer feel ashamed for your German-ness?"	83.6
"Despite history, it is time to be proud again of Germany."	74.6
"Do you want a stronger national and cultural consciousness?" West	72.6
East	73.8
"It is acceptable to fly the national flag on certain occasions."	60.9
"I would personally fly the flag on these occasions."	31.2
"I pay taxes, that's enough."	39.2
"The typical German is dutiful (*pflichtbewusst*) and achievement-oriented (*leistungsorientiert*)."	90.8
"The typical German values rules and order (*Ordnung*)."	89.7
"The typical German loves the homeland (*Liebe zum Vaterland*)."	81.8

Source: Universität Hohenheim, Institut für Sozialwissenschaften, Lehrstuhl für Soziologie, "Pressemitteilung: Die Deutschen lieben ihr Land," 15 May 2009.

The inflection point seems to have been the summer of 2006–what some have called a fairy tale (*Sommermärchen*)[66]–when the country hosted the World Cup. Of course, the national team was defeated in a heartbreaking (for some) semifinal loss in extra time (just before penalty kicks that everyone knows Germany would have won) to eventual winner Italy, but the hosting of the event was universally acclaimed. Held at the height of the last economic boom during magnificent summer weather, the country welcomed over 20 million people from abroad, all of whom celebrated a peaceful sports competition (in the state-of-the-art stadiums or the *Fanmeilen*) of the highest caliber.[67] For the first time in decades, a spontaneous mass of black-red-gold flags expressed a deep satisfaction with the country. That year, 69 percent of westerners and 61 percent of easterners said that they were happy (22 and 23 percent not happy) when they saw that national emblem.[68]

Indeed, the festive atmosphere of the impeccably organized event (Germans are still very good at *Ordnung* in the good sense) had an authenticity that rarely occurs–certainly not on command because of whatever official anniversary happens to be looming. That summer was the perfect symbol for the unified "new" Germany, and perhaps we should linger on that moment as we reflect on the twentieth anniversary of unification.

Notes

1. The sample consisted of 13,575 respondents in Australia, Canada, Chile, China, Central America (Costa Rica, El Salvador, Guatemala, Honduras, Nicaragua, Panama), Egypt, France, Germany, Ghana, India, Indonesia, Italy, Japan, Mexico, Nigeria, Philippines, Russia, Spain, Turkey, the UK and the U.S.A. See http://www.worldpublicopinion.org/pipa/pdf/feb09/BBCEvals_Feb09_rpt.pdf; accessed 14 July 2009.
2. Andrei S. Markovits and Simon Reich, *The German Predicament: Memory and Power in the New Europe* (Ithaca, 1997), 105.
3. "Der Holocaust und Auschwitz, das ist eben Gegenwart," *Der Tagesspiegel*, 10 February 2000.
4. Rogers Brubaker, *Citizenship and Nationhood in France and Germany* (Cambridge, 1992).
5. http://www.dw-world.de/dw/article/0,,2032295,00.html, 25 May 2006; accessed 1 February 2010.
6. http://www.transatlantictrends.de; accessed on 31 January 2010.
7. http://www.timesonline.co.uk/tol/news/uk/article6954571.ece, 13 December 2009; accessed 1 February 2010.
8. http://www.spiegel.de/international/germany/0,1518,620452,00.html, 22 April 2009; accessed 1 February 2010.
9. "Musilme sind die besseren Patrioten," *Süddeutsche Zeitung*, 7 May 2009.
10. http://www.migration-info.de/mub_artikel.php?Id=060502; accessed 1 February 2010; Data are from the 2005 microcensus.
11. Marc Morjé Howard, *The Politics of Citizenship in Europe* (New York, 2009), 29.
12. "The sick man of the euro," *The Economist*, 5 June 1999.
13. Geoffrey Garrett, *Partisan politics in the global economy* (New York, 1998).
14. http://www.weforum.org/en/initiatives/gcp/Global%20Competitiveness%20Report/index.htm; accessed 9 February 2010.
15. http://www.doingbusiness.org/economyrankings/; accessed 01 February 2010; "OECD fordert Lockerung des Kündigungsschutzes," *Spiegel online*, 26 March 2010, available at http://www.spiegel.de/wirtschaft/unternehmen/0,1518,685782,00.html; accessed 27 March 2010. The Heritage Foundation's 2010 Index of Economic Freedom puts the country twenty-third. See http://www.heritage.org/Index/Ranking.aspx; accessed 2 February 2010.
16. *The Economist*, 30 January 2010, 105.
17. See "A special report on Germany," *The Economist*, 13 March 2010.
18. See Jacob Heilbrunn, "Germany's New Right," *Foreign Affairs* 75, no. 6 (1996): 80-98; Jürgen Elsässer and Andrei S. Markovits, Andrei S. 1999. *Die Fratze der eigene Geschichte: Von der Goldhagen-Debate zum Jugoslawien Krieg* (Berlin, 1999).

19. http://www.adl.org/Anti_semitism/anti-semitism_global_incidents_2009.asp#UK; accessed 1 February 2010.

20. Timothy Garton Ash. "Trials, purges and history lessons: treating a difficult past in post-communist Europe," in *Memory and Power in Post-War Europe: Studies in the Presence of the Past*, ed. Jan-Werner Müller (Cambridge, 2002).

21. "Patriotismus der Heimwerker," Der Spiegel 19/2009.

22. Volker Kronenberg, "Verfassungspatriotismus in vereinten Deutschland," *Aus Politik und Zeitgeschichte* 28 (2009).

23. http://www.gfds.de/index.php?id=11; accessed 2 February 2010.

24. http://en.wikipedia.org/wiki/Economy_of_Germany.

25. Weert Canzler, "Transport Infrastructure in Shrinking (East) Germany," *German Politics and Society* 26, no. 2 (2008): 76-92

26. Dan Hough and Michael Koß, "Populism Personified or Reinvigorated Reformers? The German Left Party in 2009 and Beyond," *German Politics and Society*, 27 no. 2 (2009).

27. http://www.essen-fuer-das-ruhrgebiet.ruhr2010.de/; accessed 1 February 2010.

28. http://en.wikipedia.org/wiki/Books_published_per_country_per_year#cite_ref-boersenverein_4-0; accessed 9 February 2010.

29. http://pewforum.org/surveys/religionviews07/; accessed 6 July 2009.

30. http://www.fifa.com/worldfootball/ranking/lastranking/gender=m/fullranking.html; accessed 22 March 2010.

31. http://www.olympic.it/english/medal; accessed 22 March 2010. This number includes the German team, the united team (1956, 1960, 1964), West Germany (1968-1988) and East Germany (1968-1988). The overall number of medals (1619) may be a little inflated because East and West German athletes tended to do well in the same sports. The USSR/Russia/Unified Team (1992) has a total of 1752, but this does not take account of the post-1992 successor states. In any case, the U.S. total of 2552 would still be first.

32. http://en.wikipedia.org/wiki/Programme_for_International_Student_Assessment; accessed 9 February 2010.

33. http://afp.google.com/article/ALeqM5gQ_xk936jOQTJ0UG5Zgw2IoGpBqQ; accessed 6 July 2009.

34. World Tourism Organization, "Tourism Highlights 2009 Edition; http://www.unwto.org/facts/menu.html; accessed 2 February 2010.

35. http://germany-travel.suite101.com/article.cfm/berlin_welcomes_140_million; accessed 12 July 2009.

36. http://www.new7wonders.com/; accessed 2 February 2010.

37. http://www.olddjmag.com/?op=top100club; accessed 31 January 2010.

38. World Tourism Organization, "Tourism Highlights 2009 Edition; http://www.unwto.org/facts/menu.html; accessed 2 February 2010.

39. http://en.wikipedia.org/wiki/List_of_countries_by_GDP_(nominal)_per_capita#cite_ref-1; accessed on 2 February 2010.

40. http://www.nationmaster.com/graph/eco_dis_of_fam_inc_gin_ind-distribution-family-income-gini-index; accessed 2 February 2010.

41. http://www.weforum.org/pdf/gendergap/rankings2009.pdf; accessed 9 Februrary 2010.

42. http://www.photius.com/rankings/healthranks.html; http://en.wikipedia.org/wiki/List_of_countries_by_life_expectancy; accessed 9 February 2010.

43. http://www.healthpowerhouse.com/files/Report-EHCI-2009-090925-final-with-cover.pdf; accessed 23 February 2010.

44. http://hdr.undp.org/en/statistics/; accessed 2 February 2010.

45. http://www.forbes.com/2009/04/27/cities-best-live-lifestyle-real-estate-best-places-to-live_slide_21.html?thisSpeed=15000; accessed 16 July 2009. All of the other cities are in Central or Northern Europe (Vienna first and Zürich second), Canada, Australia, or New Zealand.

46. http://www.internationalliving.com/Internal-Components/Further-Resources/quality-of-life-2010; accessed 9 February 2010.

47. http://www.aneki.com/recycling_countries.html; accessed on 2 February 2010.

48. http://epi.yale.edu/; accessed on 2 February 2010; See also Stefal Theil, "No Country is More 'Green by Design,'" *Newsweek*, 7-14 July 2008.

49. See Simon Green and William E. Paterson, eds., *Governance in Contemporary Germany; The Semisovereign State Revisited* (Cambridge, 2005); Alister Miskimmon, William E. Paterson and James Sloam, eds., *Germany's Gathering Crisis: The 2005 Election and the Grand Coalition* (New York, 2009).

50. David Art, *The Politics of the Nazi Past in Germany and Austria* (New York, 2006).

51. http://www.economist.com/markets/rankings/displayStory.cfm?story_id=12499352; http://siteresources.worldbank.org/NEWS/Resources/wbindicators2006-.pdf; http://www.transparency.org/policy_research/surveys_indices/cpi/2009/cpi_2009_tabl e; accessed 2 February 2010.

52. Top "countries" included the Vatican, Monaco, Liechtenstein, San Marino, and Andorra. See http://www.timesonline.co.uk/tol/news/uk/article3613926.ece; accessed 22 March 2010.

53. See Sebastian Harnisch and Hans Maull, eds., *Germany as a Civilian Power?: The Foreign Policy of the Berlin Republic* (Manchester, 2001).

54. http://www.visionofhumanity.org/gpi/results/rankings.php; accessed 9 February 2010.

55. http://www.oecd.org/department/0,2688,en_2649_33721_1_1_1_1_1,00.html; accessed 2 February 2010.

56. "Germany's euro test," *The Economist*, 12 June 2003.

57. http://www.euractiv.com/en/priorities/germany-benefits-eu-membership-study/article-152137; accessed 2 February 2010.

58. http://en.wikipedia.org/wiki/Budget_of_the_European_Union#cite_note-OE20071116-4; accessed 2 February 2010. The Netherlands, Denmark and Sweden have an even worse net benefit per capita.

59. Federal Ministry of Finance, *Compensation for National Socialist Injustice* (Berlin, 2009), 43.

60. Jeffrey Peck, *Being Jewish in the New Germany* (New Brunswick, 2006).

61. Sontag, Susan. "Fascinating Fascism," in *Movies and Methods*, ed. Bill Nichols (Berkeley, 1976), pp. 31-43

62. Toby Helm, "President in row over German patriotism," *The Telegraph*, 20 March 2001; http://www.telegraph.co.uk/news/worldnews/1327252/President-in-row-over-German-patriotism.htmlhttp://www.focus.de/politik/deutschland/geruehrter-koehler_aid_82791.html; accessed 9 February 2010.

63. http://www.spiegel.de/spiegel/print/d-18818018.html, 21 April 2006; accessed 21 January 2010.

64. Ibid.

65. Tom W. Smith and Seokho Kim, "National Pride in Cross-national and Temporal Perspective," *International Journal of Public Opinion Research*, 18 (2006): 127-136, here 2, 10

66. See the film *Deutschland, ein Sommermärchen* (2006).

67. "Germany's World Cup Report Hails Economic, Social Success," Deutsche Welle, 7 December 2006; http://www.dw-world.de/dw/article/0,2144,2263053,00.html; accessed 9 February 2010.

68. Although by 2008 the percentages expressing happiness had dropped to 53 (West) and 43 (East). Renate Köcher, ed., *Allensbacher Jahrbuch der Demoskopie, 2003-2009* (Berlin, 2009), 39.

CONTRIBUTORS

• • • • • • • • • • • • • • •

CHRISTOPHER S. ALLEN is the Josiah Meigs Distinguished Teaching Professor in the Department of International Affairs at the University of Georgia. He is co-author of *European Politics in Transition*, now in its 6th edition. He has published articles on comparative political economy and on democratic representation in numerous journals including: *Harvard Business Review, Comparative Politics, Journal of Public Policy, Policy Studies Review, Party Politics, German Politics, Economic and Industrial Democracy*, and *Journal of Policy Analysis and Management*. This article is part of a larger book manuscript in progress entitled: *Ideas, Institutions and Organized Capitalism: Germany, Europe and 21st Century Economic Policy Models*.

JEFFREY J. ANDERSON is Graf Goltz Professor and Director of the BMW Center for German and European Studies at the Edmund A. Walsh School of Foreign Service and Professor of Government, Georgetown University. He is an expert in European politics, with special emphasis on the European Union and postwar German politics and foreign policy. Recent publications include, edited with G. John Ikenberry and Thomas Risse, *The End of the West? Crisis and Change in the Atlantic Order* (Ithaca, 2008); and *German Unification and the Union of Europe: The Domestic Politics of Integration Policy* (New York, 1999).

BEVERLY CRAWFORD is Adjunct Professor of Political Science and Political Economy at the University of California, Berkeley. She has published extensively on topics such as ethnic conflict, European politics, German foreign policy, technology transfer policy, postcommunist transitions, the European Union, the Barcelona Process, and globalization. She is the author of *Economic Vulnerability in International Relations* (New York, 1993) and *Power and German Foreign Policy: Embedded Hegemony in Europe* (Houndmills, 2007).

RUSSELL J. DALTON is Professor of Political Science at the University of California, Irvine. His recent publications include *Citizens, Context and Choice* (Oxford, 2010), *Democratic Challenges, Democratic Choices* (Oxford, 2004), and *The Oxford Handbook of Political Behavior* (Oxford, 2007). His scholarly interests include comparative political behavior, political parties, German politics, and empirical democratic theory.

RICHARD DEEG is Professor of Political Science at Temple University. After receiving his PhD from MIT, he was a Postdoctoral Fellow and Visiting Scholar at the Max Planck Institute for the Study of Societies in Cologne, Germany. His publications include *Finance Capitalism Unveiled: Banks and the German Political Economy* (Ann Arbor, 1999) and numerous journal articles on German and European political economy. His current research focuses on causes and mechanisms of institutional change in financial systems.

ANKE HASSEL is professor of public policy at the Hertie School of Governance in Berlin, Germany. She specializes in European Union labor relations and has written a book about the effects of European Monetary Union on national labor relations institutions and the emergence of social pacts. Since then, she has worked on the transformation of the German political economy since unification, with a particular focus on welfare and labor market reforms. She is a member of the editorial board of the *European Industrial Relations Journal* and the public administration journal *der moderne Staat*, as well as a member of the executive council of the Society for the Advancement of Socio-Economics.

RUTH HATLAPA is working on her dissertation on "Obamamania and anti-Americanism in Europe" at the Faculty of Philology and History of the Universität Augsburg. She has studied Cultural Studies, Political Science and History at the Humboldt Universität and the Freie Universität Berlin. Besides her academic activities she is engaged in educational projects against antisemitism.

DAGMAR HERZOG is Professor of History at the Graduate Center, City University of New York, where she teaches European history, Holocaust studies, and the histories of sexuality and gender. She is the author of *Sex in Crisis: The New Sexual Revolution and the Future of American Politics* (New York, 2008), *Sex after Fascism: Memory and Morality in Twentieth-Century Germany* (Princeton, 2005), and *Intimacy and Exclusion: Religious Politics in Pre-*

Revolutionary Baden (Princeton, 1996; New Brunswick, 2007), and editor of *Brutality and Desire: War and Sexuality in Europe's Twentieth Century* (New York, 2009). She is currently writing on European Sexualities, 1900-2000 for Cambridge University Press.

KONRAD H. JARAUSCH is Lurcy Professor of European Civilization at the University of North Carolina at Chapel Hill and Senior Fellow of the Zentrum für Zeithistorische Forschung in Potsdam. He has written or edited more than three dozen books on German and European history, most recently: *After Hitler: Recivilizing Germans, 1945-1995* (New York, 2006); *'Das stille Sterben ...' Feldpostbriefe von Konrad Jarausch aus Polen und Russland 1939-1942* (Paderborn, 2008); and *Das Ende der Zuversicht? Die siebziger Jahre als Geschichte* (Göttingen, 2008).

WILLY JOU is a doctoral candidate in political science at the University of California, Irvine. His research interests include public opinion in new democracies and electoral systems. His articles have appeared in *Party Politics, Japanese Journal of Political Science,* and *Journal of Democracy.*

ERIC LANGENBACHER is a Visiting Assistant Professor and Director of the Honors Program in the Department of Government, Georgetown University where he received his PhD in 2002. Book projects include *Launching the Grand Coalition: The 2005 Bundestag Election and the Future of German Politics* (New York, 2006), *Power and the Past: Collective Memory and International Relations* (co-edited with Yossi Shain, Washington, 2010), *The Mastered Past? Memory Regimes in Contemporary Germany* (under review). He is also Managing Editor of *German Politics and Society.*

CHARLES S. MAIER served as Director of Harvard University's Center for European Studies from 1994 to 2001 and fall 2006, and as Chair of the undergraduate Social Studies Program from 1991 to 1995, and as acting Chair during 2007-2008. He published *Dissolution: The Crisis of Communism and the End of East Germany* (Princeton, 1997), and *Among Empires: American Ascendancy and its Predecessors* (Cambridge, 2007) and currently is collaborating with William Kirby and Sugata Bose on a world history of the twentieth century and is writing on the rise and decline of territoriality and on the history of the modern state. Maier teaches undergraduate courses on world history in the modern era, World War I and World War II, political trials, and, together with Niall Ferguson, a two-semester sequence on international history.

ANDREI S. MARKOVITS, founder of *German Politics and Society* and its editor from 1983 to 2003, is Arthur F. Thurnau Professor and the Karl W. Deutsch Collegiate Professor of Comparative Politics and German Studies at the University of Michigan in Ann Arbor. He would like to express his gratitude to the Center for Advanced Study in the Behavioral Sciences (CASBS) of Stanford University for the fellowship in 2008/2009 that accorded him the time and financial support for research and writing yielding, among others, this article.

MYRA MARX FERREE (www.ssc.wisc.edu/~mferree) is Martindale-Bascom Professor of Sociology at the University of Wisconsin-Madison and Director of its Center for German and European Studies. Her recent scholarship includes *German Feminism since 1968* (Palo Alto, forthcoming) and *Global Feminism: Transnational women's activism, organizing, and human rights,* co-edited with Aili Tripp (New York, 2006). Her interest in frames and feminist discourse also informs *Shaping Abortion Discourse: Democracy and the Public Sphere in Germany and the US,* (Cambridge, 2002). She has been a guest professor in Germany at the University of Frankfurt and the Ruhr University in Bochum and in Australia at Flinders University in Adelaide, and has been an affiliated scholar at the Wissenschaftszentrum Berlin für Sozialforschung (WZB) and the Free University in Berlin. She was most recently a fellow at the American Academy in Berlin and a deputy editor of the *American Sociological Review.*

A. JAMES MCADAMS is the William M. Scholl Professor of International Affairs and Director, Nanovic Institute for European Studies, at the University of Notre Dame. He is the author of *Judging the Past in Unified Germany* (New York, 2001) and editor of *The Crisis of Modern Times* (Notre Dame, 2008).

JOYCE MARIE MUSHABEN (Ph. D., Political Science, Indiana University 1981) is a Professor of Comparative Politics, a Research Fellow in the Center for International Studies, and former Director of the Institute for Women's and Gender Studies (2002-2005) at the University of Missouri-St. Louis. Mushaben's books and monographs include *From Post-War to Post-Wall Generations: Changing Attitudes towards the National Question and NATO in the Federal Republic of Germany, 1949-1995* (Boulder, 1998); *Identity without a Hinterland? Continuity and Change in National Consciousness in the German Democratic Republic, 1949-1989* (Washington, 1993); and *The Changing Faces of Citizenship: Integration and Mobilization among Ethnic Minorities in*

Germany (New York, 2008). Her articles have appeared in *World Politics, Polity, West European Politics, German Politics, German Politics and Society,* the *Journal of Peace Research, Democratization, Citizenship Studies,* and *Femina Politica.* She has been a (three-time) Alexander von Humboldt Fellow, based at the Universities of Stuttgart, Frankfurt/Main, and Berlin's Humboldt University; in 1999 she received a Governor's citation and a *Trailblazer Award* for advancing women's rights on campus; and in 2007 she received the UM-St. Louis Chancellor's Award for Excellence in Research Creativity.

ABRAHAM L NEWMAN is an assistant professor at the Edmund A. Walsh School of Foreign Service at Georgetown University. He is the author of *Protectors of Privacy: Regulating Personal Information in the Global Economy* (Ithaca, 2008) and the co-editor of *How Revolutionary was the Digital Revolution?* (Stanford, 2006). His research has appeared or is forthcoming in *Comparative Political Studies, European Journal of International Relations, Governance, International Organization, Journal of European Public Policy, New Political Economy,* and the *Review of International Political Economy.*

BRAD PRAGER is Associate Professor of German and a member of the Program in Film Studies at the University of Missouri. His areas of research include Film History, Contemporary German Cinema, Holocaust Studies, and German Romanticism. He is the author of *The Cinema of Werner Herzog: Aesthetic Ecstasy and Truth* (London, 2007) and *Aesthetic Vision and German Romanticism: Writing Images* (Rochester, 2007). He is the co-editor of a volume on Visual Studies and the Holocaust entitled *Visualizing the Holocaust: Documents, Aesthetics, Memory* (Rochester, 2008), and of a forthcoming volume on contemporary German cinema entitled *The Collapse of the Conventional: German Film and its Politics at the Turn of the Twenty-First Century* (Detroit, 2010).

HILARY SILVER is Associate Professor of Sociology and Urban Studies at Brown University and Editor of *City & Community,* the journal of the Community and Urban Sociology Section of the American Sociological Association. She is also an Affiliate of the Center for European Studies at Harvard University where she co-chairs a study group on "Social Exclusion and Inclusion in an Expanded Europe." Professor Silver is comparing immigrant integration in East and West Berlin neighborhoods.

STEPHEN J. SILVIA is Director of Doctoral Studies at American University's School of International Service in Washington, D.C. He teaches international economics, international trade relations, and comparative politics. His research focuses on comparative labor markets, comparative industrial relations and comparative social policy in Germany, the European Union and the United States.

HELGA A. WELSH is Professor of Political Science at Wake Forest University. Her publications have focused on the history and politics of the former East Germany, German unification, transitional justice, the reform of higher education in Germany, and democratization processes in Central and Eastern Europe. Her articles have appeared in journals such as *Comparative Politics*, *European Journal of Education*, *Europe-Asia Studies*, *German Politics*, and *West European Politics*. She is one of the editors of "German History in Documents and Images," a project administered by the German Historical Institute in Washington, DC.

HOLGER C WOLF received his PhD in Economics from the Massachusetts Institute of Technology and is currently Associate Professor in the BMW Center for German and European Studies, Edmund A. Walsh School of Foreign Service, Georgetown University. His research interests focus on European economic integration and the German economy. Recent publications include with Atish Ghosh, Helge Berger and Anne-Marie Gulde, *Currency Boards in Retrospect and Prospect* (Cambridge, 2008) and with Anne-Marie Gulde and Atish Ghosh *Exchange Rate Regime* (Cambridge, 2003).

$\mathscr{I}$NDEX

• • • • • • • • • • • • • • •

A

Adenauer, Konrad, 13, 15-16, 20, 23, 25, 27, 28, 29, 30, 44, 45, 70, 77, 80, 84, 177, 292, 348, 379, 382, 389

Afghanistan, 67, 84, 105, 109, 114, 210, 289, 294, 297, 301, 305

Agenda 2010, 22, 229, 339, 351, 354, 399

Alignment, Realignment, Dealignment, 41, 254, 260, 262, 265, 268, 289

Anti-Americanism, v, 90-98, 104, 106, 108, 111, 112, 415

Anti-Semitism, 67, 94-96, 412

Assimilation, 42, 186-188, 201, 203, 204

Auschwitz, 21, 30, 39, 64-68, 83, 86, 87, 210, 411

B

Banks, 9, 113, 193, 313-314, 318, 363-368, 370, 373, 374, 375, 379, 382-384, 386-387, 391, 395, 415

Basic Law , Grundgesetz, 13, 21, 23, 36, 58, 59, 161, 163, 165, 185, 189

Bavaria, 70, 74, 102, 161, 170, 340, 403-404

Berlin, iii, vi, 1, 3, 5-6, 8, 14, 26, 28, 29, 33, 39, 40, 43, 44, 46, 47, 51, 53, 56, 59-60, 63, 65, 67, 69, 72-76, 82-83, 85, 87, 88, 91, 118-120, 124-125, 128, 129, 139-140, 145, 151, 155, 159, 161, 166, 167, 169-174, 178, 180, 181, 192, 194-196, 199-201, 202, 205, 206, 207, 209, 213, 217-218, 220, 224-225, 236-239, 241-243, 253, 277, 289, 299-300, 304, 305, 326, 340, 342, 402-405, 408, 409, 413, 415

Berlin Wall, Fall of Berlin Wall, 1-3, 51, 76, 81, 92, 110, 115-116, 121, 157, 162, 183, 201, 236-237, 241, 299-300, 350, 353, 360, 394, 297, 401

Bindenagel, J.D., 60-61

Birthrates, 26, 137, 144, 147-150, 190

Bismarck, Otto von, 184, 294, 302, 304, 316, 379, 382-385, 387

blühende Landschaften, blossoming landsc-paes, 239, 249, 402

Bohley, Bärbel, 59-60

Bologna Process, 273-274, 279-281, 285, 286

Bosnia, 39, 60, 95, 169, 297, 305

Brandt, Willy, 17-18, 26-27, 29, 46, 72, 77, 163, 265

Bundesbank, 16, 19, 67, 195, 289, 313, 406

Bundestag, 3, 59, 64, 67, 69, 72, 74, 76, 85, 87, 88, 101, 173, 181, 236, 246, 251-253, 263-264, 267, 268, 312, 400, 416

Bush, George W., 91, 93, 108, 113

C

Capital Mobility, Capital Formation, 344-345, 366, 392-393

Center against Expulsions, Zentrum gegen Vertreibungen, 72, 82

Christian Democratic Union (CDU, 6, 13, 20, 22-23, 30, 25, 38, 42, 64, 69, 70-72, 114, 138, 141, 155, 162, 173-174, 177-178, 180, 182, 198-199, 220-222, 228, 229, 240, 246, 249, 250, 252-260, 265-266, 267, 268, 292, 348, 380, 397, 409

Christian Social Union (CSU, 30, 35, 42, 70-71, 74, 141, 155, 156, 173, 177-178, 180, 199-222, 227, 228, 229, 241, 247, 252-256, 258-260, 265-268, 282, 380, 397

Citizenship, vi, 6, 18, 31, 71, 73, 144, 160, 162-166, 170-172, 174-175, 178, 181, 186, 203, 208-213, 225, 226, 227, 228, 397-398, 409-410, 411, 417-418

Cold War, 1,8, 14, 24-25, 37, 46, 63-64, 67-68, 74-75, 77, 136, 140, 163, 197, 210, 212-213, 226, 249, 291, 294-295, 306, 309, 315, 317, 366, 386

Collective Memory, v, 5, 16, 63, 76, 82, 210, 400, 416

Communism, 26-28, 29, 68, 141, 202, 258, 272, 416

Constructivism, Constructivist, 290, 309, 316

Corporate Governance, 351, 365-366, 368-369, 373, 374, 375, 376, 394

Czech Republic, Czechs, 74, 314